Mathematics Encyclopedia

Mathematics Encyclopedia

Max S. Shapiro
Executive Editor

Contributors

William K. Benton   H. T. Hyslett, Jr.

Karen W. Davis   Vivian Makhmaltchi

William R. Gondin   Nancy A. Maurice

Michele M. Nota

MADE SIMPLE BOOKS
Doubleday & Company, Inc.
Garden City, New York

NOTE: All of the material in this book was originally published as a part of *The Cadillac Modern Encyclopedia,* Cadillac Publishing Co., Inc., St. Louis, Mo.

Library of Congress Cataloging in Publication Data
Main entry under title:

Mathematics encyclopedia.

1. Mathematics—Dictionaries.   I. Shapiro, Max S.
QA5.M374   510′.3

ISBN: 0–385–12427–9
Library of Congress Catalog Card Number: 76–23817

Contents

Introduction   vii
Pronunciation Guide   ix
Mathematics Encyclopedia A–Z   1
Special Reference Section   215

TABLE NO.

1. The Greek Alphabet   217
2. Mathematical Abbreviations and Symbols   217
3. A Review of Mathematical Formulas, Laws and Terms   218
4. Weights and Measures (arranged in alphabetical order)   225
5. Weights and Measures (arranged by quantity and in ascending order of size)   229
6. Conversion Factors   233
7. Fundamental Constants   234
8. Roman Numerals   234
9. Addition Table   235
10. Multiplication Table   235
11. Numbers Table   235
12. Decimal and Percent Equivalents of Common Fractions   235
13. Derivatives   236
14. Integral Tables   237
15. Simple Interest Table   237
16. Compound Interest Table   239
17. Random Numbers   241
18. Powers, Roots and Reciprocals   242
19. Common Logarithm Table   250
20. Natural Logarithms   269
21. Values and Common Logarithms of Exponential and Hyperbolic Functions   273
22. Natural Trigonometric Functions   280
23. Logarithms of Trigonometric Functions   285

Introduction

Intended for practical use in school, home and business, *Mathematics Encyclopedia* contains all the mathematical topics covered by academic curricula through the college level. Sections on Arithmetic, Algebra, Geometry, Trigonometry, Analytic Geometry, Calculus, the "New Mathematics," and Statistics, to name only a few of the major topics, aid both the student in his coursework and the layman interested in teaching himself this crucial science. The entries include lucid explanations, problems with step-by-step solutions as well as hundreds of clear, functional drawings that aid immeasurably in understanding the text and in solving the problems. All of which represents a real advance beyond ordinary encyclopedic method.

Another important feature of this encyclopedia is the Special Reference Section. Here you will find the important tables used in Mathematics plus a wealth of additional reference information: a complete review of mathematical formulas; an A to Z listing of Weights and Measures arranged both alphabetically and by quantity in ascending order of size; Conversion Factors; Simple and Compound Interest Tables; Logarithms; Powers, Roots and Reciprocals; and much more.

The authors and editors of *Mathematics Encyclopedia* have endeavored to create a useful tool for their readers, one that will satisfy their need for an easy-to-use, comprehensive and up-to-date mathematical reference work. To this end, this volume has been thoroughly cross-referenced. Words appearing in small capital letters indicate that there is an entry under that heading. In addition the reader is referred to other entries by a *see* or *see also* reference. And finally a Pronunciation Guide immediately follows this page.

Pronunciation Guide

Pronunciation keys appear within parentheses following the last element of the entry heading. Example: **DESCARTES, RENE** (day-kahrt′ ru-nay′) . . . Keys are provided for selected entries, and when two or more entries have the same pronunciation, a key is provided only for one heading. In order to avoid using intricate symbol systems which are less familiar, a system of phonetic keys was devised using only the standard letters of the alphabet. Only primary stress is given. Combinations of silent letters are used where necessary to make the pronunciation clear. Below are the phonetic keys used, accompanied by a brief indication of how they are intended to be pronounced.

Vowels	
ay	*pay*
a	*pat*
ahr	*ark*
ah	*father*, Mar*ia*, p*o*t, h*o*t
e	p*e*t
ehr	*care, air*
ee	b*e*, r*ea*l
i	*ih* p*i*t
ahy	*pie, buy*
o	(or) *oh* n*o*, t*oe*
aw	p*aw*, f*or*
oi	n*oi*se, b*oy*s
au	*out*, ab*ou*t
oo	b*oo*t, n*ew*
uh	t*oo*k, sh*ou*ld
u	c*u*t, *a*bout, it*e*m, nati*o*n
ur	*u*rge, s*er*ge, f*ir*m

Consonants	
s	*c*ellar
sh	*sh*ell (unvoiced)
k	*c*ome
ch	*ch*ur*ch*
g	*g*a*g*
j	*j*udge
zh	plea*s*ure (voiced)
th	*th*in, *th*en (both voiced and unvoiced)

Foreign Sounds	
ah	Fr. *a*mi
uh	Fr. f*eu*, Ger. sch*ö*n
Kh	Ger. i*ch*, Scot. lo*ch*
ur	Fr. s*oeu*r
n	Fr. bo*n*, Port. sao (sau*n*)
oo	Fr. t*u*, Ger. *ü*ber

Mathematics Encyclopedia

ABACUS (ab'-u-kus), an ancient device used for computation; predecessor of the modern calculating machine. The abacus is still widely used, especially in China and Japan. The Japanese abacus, called a *soroban*, has five beads on each of nine vertical place rods. One bead on each rod is isolated above a center bar on the abacus. Each rod has PLACE VALUE in the DECIMAL NUMBER SYSTEM. Each bead below the center bar counts as a single

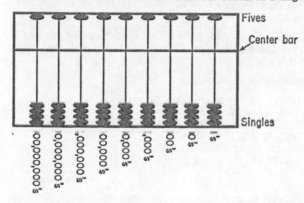

unit of the place, and each bead above the bar counts as five times the place value. Thus, one bead on the ten's rod below the bar is ten while the bead above on the same rod is 50. Beads "count" only as they are moved toward or away from the center bar.

The speed and accuracy of computation by abacus was effectively demonstrated in 1946, when a soroban was pitted against a modern electric desk calculator. The abacus won in addition subtraction, division, and in a combination of these, while the desk caluclator won only in multiplication.
Sample of addition on the abacus:

Add 62 to 126.
a. Set the 62 by moving up two singles on the 1's rod, one single on the 10's rod, and then move down the five on the 10's rod. Thus,

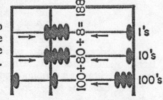

$$2 + 10 + 50 = 62.$$

b. Continue by setting the 126. Move down the five bead on the 1's rod, and move up one single on the same rod; then move up two singles on the 10's rod and one single on the 100's rod. Thus,

$$6 + 20 + 100 = 126.$$

c. Now to get total, read correct values on all rods from left to right at the center bar:

$$100 + 80 + 8 = 188$$

the sum of 62 and 126.

ABSCISSA (ab-sis'-sa), the horizontal or x-distance of any point from the y-axis in a system of rectangular coordinates (*see* COORDINATES, RECTANGULAR). Its sign is positive to the right of the y-axis and negative to the left of the y-axis. The coordinates of a point are given as an ORDERED PAIR (x, y). The first member of the ordered pair is the abscissa.

Ex. 1: The abscissa of the point $(1, 7)$ is 1.
Ex. 2: The abscissa of the point $(-3, 2)$ is -3.

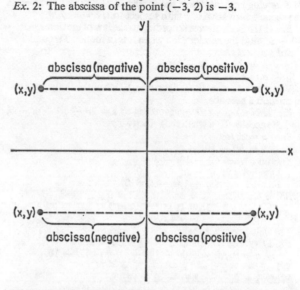

ABSOLUTE CONVERGENCE, a SERIES, $\Sigma|a_n|$, formed by taking the ABSOLUTE VALUES of terms of a series Σa_n may or may not converge even if Σa_n converges. When $\Sigma|a_n|$ does converge, the original series is said to converge absolutely. E.g., the series

$$1 - \frac{1}{2^2} + \frac{1}{3^3} - \frac{1}{4^4} + \frac{1}{5^4} \ldots \text{ is absolutely convergent, since}$$

the series $1 + \frac{1}{2^2} + \frac{1}{3^3} + \frac{1}{4^4} \ldots$ is convergent. A series which converges absolutely also converges in the ordinary sense. A series which converges but does not converge absolutely is said to converge conditionally (*see* CONDITIONAL CONVERGENCE).

ABSOLUTE VALUE, the value of a signed number without regard to its sign. For any number x the "absolute value of x" is denoted by the symbol $|x|$.

$$|x| = x, \text{ if } x \text{ is a positive number or zero and}$$
$$|x| = -x, \text{ if } x \text{ is a negative number.}$$

Ex. 1: a. $|2| = 2$ b. $|0| = 0$ c. $|-3| = 3$
Ex. 2: Graph the function $y = |x^3|$.

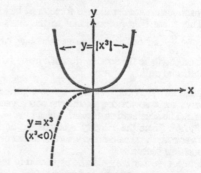

Note that where x^3 is positive or zero, the graph of $y = |x^3|$ is the same as the graph of $y = x^3$. However, $|x^3|$ is positive where x^3 is negative. Thus, the graph of $y = |x^3|$ is the mirror image of the graph of $y = x^3$ (dotted curve in the figure for $x < 0$. Since x^3 is negative when $x < 0$, the graph of $y = |x^3|$ is the solid curve shown in the figure.

ACCELERATION (ak-sel-er-ay'-shun), the derivative (*see* DE-RIVATIVE OF A FUNCTION), or the rate of change of the VELOCITY, v, of a body with respect to time, t. Acceleration is given by $a = dv/dt$. Since the velocity is the derivative of the position, s, of a moving body at time t, the acceleration may also be given as the second derivative of s with respect to t: $a = d^2s/dt^2$.

Ex. 1: If a body moves according to the law of motion $s = t^3 - 4t^2 - 3t$, find the acceleration when it is in motion 3 seconds.

Sol.: $a = d^2s/dt^2$

$a = d(3t^2 - 8t - 3)/dt$

$a = 6t - 8$.

When $t = 3$, $a = 18 - 8$, or $a = 10$ when the body has been in motion 3 seconds.

Ex. 2: If a body moves according to $s = 2t^3 - 5t^2 - 4t - 3$, find the acceleration when the velocity is zero.

Sol.: $v = dt/ds$

$v = 6t^2 - 10t - 4$.

Find t when $6t^2 - 10t - 4 = 0$.

Divide by 2: $3t^2 - 5t - 2 = 0$

Factor: $(3t + 1)(t - 2) = 0$

Solve for t: $3t + 1 = 0$; $t - 2 = 0$

$3t = 1$; $t = 2$

$t = -\frac{1}{3}$.

The velocity is zero when $t = -\frac{1}{3}$ and $t = 2$.

Find the acceleration at $t = -\frac{1}{3}$ and $t = 2$:

$a = dv/dt = d(6t^2 - 10t - 4)/dt = 12t - 10$.

When $t = -\frac{1}{3}$, $a = 12(-\frac{1}{3}) - 10 = -14$.

When $t = 2$, $a = 12(2) - 10 = 14$.

The acceleration is ± 14 when the velocity is zero.

Since velocity is a VECTOR quantity, acceleration is also a vector. Acceleration may change either the speed of an object, its direction, or both. Negative acceleration, that is, when the speed is decreased, is sometimes called deceleration. A body moving in a circle at constant speed is being acted on by a constant acceleration at right angles to the direction of its motion. For motion along a straight line, the change in velocity is equal to the acceleration a multiplied by the time t, so that the final velocity v is given by the original velocity v_0 plus the change in velocity, or

$$v = v_0 + at$$

For motion in a circle of radius r at a constant speed v, the acceleration is *centripetal*, that is directed toward the center, and is given by the equation

$$a_c = \frac{v^2}{r}$$

In order to produce an acceleration, a force must be exerted on an object. This force F is proportional to the mass m of the object, or $a = \dfrac{F}{M}$ according to the second law of motion. Acceleration of gravity is the acceleration of a freely falling body due to gravitational pull.

ACCELERATION VECTOR (ak-sel-er-ay'-shun), the derivative (*see* DERIVATIVE OF A FUNCTION) of the VELOCITY VECTOR with respect to time. The acceleration vector is given by $a = dv/dt = i\, d^2x/dt^2 + j\,d^2y/dt^2$. Since the velocity vector is the derivative of the POSITION VECTOR, the acceleration vector is the second derivative of the position vector.

The acceleration vector may also be expressed in terms of its tangential (*see* TANGENT VECTOR) and normal (*see* NORMAL VECTOR) components. Expressing v in terms of the tangent vector, T, $v = Tds/dt$. The derivative of this with respect to t gives

$a = dv/dt = Td^2s/dt^2 + \dfrac{ds}{dt}\dfrac{dT}{dt}$. By the chain rule, $\dfrac{dT}{dt} = \dfrac{dT}{ds}\dfrac{ds}{dt}$.

Since the normal vector $N_K = dT/ds$, $a = Td^2/dt^2 + \dfrac{ds}{dt}N_K\dfrac{ds}{dt} = Td^2s/dt^2 + N_K(ds/dt)^2$.

ACCUMULATION POINT (u-keum-eu-lay'-shun), a point x is an accumulation point of a SET A when every NEIGHBORHOOD of x contains at least one point of A distinct from x.

ACCUMULATOR (u-keum'-eu-lay-tor), an arithmetic part of a computing machine that adds to the stored number each new number that it receives. An accumulator is also called an *adder*.

ACRE, *see* TABLE NO. 4, 5.

ACUTE ANGLE, an ANGLE between 0° and 90° in ABSOLUTE VALUE.

ADDENDS, numbers to be added. E.g., the expression $8ab + 6ab + 2ab + ab$ consists of four addends, $8ab$, $6ab$, etc., whose sum is $17ab$.

ADDER, *see* ACCUMULATOR.

ADDITION, to add SIGNED NUMBERS: (1) if two numbers have like signs, find the sum of their ABSOLUTE VALUES and use the same sign; (2) if two numbers have opposite signs find the difference of their absolute values and use the sign of the number having the greater absolute value.

Ex. 1: Add $+5$ -2 -8 -2

            $+3$ -3 $+5$ $+6$

            $+8$ -5 -3 $+4$

When two or more signed numbers are to be added, it is simpler to first add all POSITIVE NUMBERS, next add all NEGATIVE NUMBERS, and then combine the two sums.

Ex. 1: Add $(-8) + (+5) + (-2) + (+6)$.

$(-8) + (+5) + (-2) + (+6) = +(5 + 6) -$

$(8 + 2)$

$= 11 - 10$

$= 1.$

To add POLYNOMIALS, it is convenient to place similar terms (*see* TERMS, SIMILAR) in columns and add their NUMERICAL CO-EFFICIENTS. Add each column independently of the other columns, observing rules for adding signed numbers.

Ex. 1: Add $4x^2 + 3xy + ab$ and $3x^2 + 7xy - 6ab$.

$4x^2 + 3xy + ab$

$3x^2 + 7xy + 6ab$

$7x^2 + 10xy - 5ab$

The numerical coefficients of like terms may also be added mentally and the sums of the unlike terms with their proper signs are then written as a simplified polynomial.

Ex. 2: Combine $6a^2 - 3ab - 2a^2 - b^2 - 2ab + b^2 + 3a^2 - 2b^2$.

Sol.: Add the like terms $6a^2 - 2a^2 + 3a^2$, the sum of which is $7a^2$. In like manner add the ab terms and the b^2 terms. Then write the three sums:

$$7a^2 - 5ab - 2b^2.$$

Columns of large numbers may be added by the following methods:

1. Partial Sums Method

2134	
4742	
7358	
+ 3972	
16	Sum of units
19	Sum of tens
20	Sum of hundreds
16	Sum of thousands
18206	

2. Carrying Method

2134	The sum of the unit's column is 16.
4742	Write 6 in the unit's place of the sum and carry the
7358	1 ten to the ten's column. Then the sum of the ten's
+ 3972	column is 20. Write 0 in the ten's column to serve as
18206	a place holder and carry the 2 hundreds to the hundred's column. The sum of the hundred's column is

22. Write 2 in the hundred's column and carry the 2 thousands to the thousand's column. Grouping numbers that equal 10 speeds any addition operation. Add from top to bottom, check by adding up.

The first method is helpful if long columns of large numbers are to be added because checking is simpler. *See also* PLACE VALUE.

ADDITION AXIOM, an AXIOM of EQUALITY (or INEQUALITY): If equal quantities are added to the same or equal quantities the sums are equal. E.g., if $a = b$ then $a + 2 = b + 2$. The axiom may be expressed symbolically as follows: If $a = b$ and $c = d$, then $a + c = b + d$.

ADDITIVE INVERSE. If, in a mathematical system, x and y are any two elements such that $x + y = 0$, then x is termed the additive inverse of y, and y is termed the additive inverse of x: e.g., in arithmetic 5 and -5 are additive inverses of each other because $5 + (-5) = 0$.

ADJACENT ANGLES (ad-jay'-sent), two angles that have a common vertex and a common side between them. In Fig. 1,

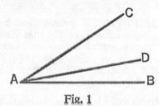

Fig. 1

$\angle BAD$ and $\angle DAC$ are adjacent angles; the common vertex is A, and AD is the common side between them.

If two adjacent angles are formed by PERPENDICULAR lines, the angles are equal, and each contains 90°. In Fig. 2, if $CD \perp AB$, then $\angle ADC = \angle CDB$.

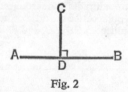

Fig. 2

AGE PROBLEM, in mathematics.

Ex.: A man is 7 times as old as his son. In two years the father will be only 5 times as old as his son. What is the age of each?

Sol.: Let

$$x = \text{son's age now}$$
$$7x = \text{father's age now}$$
$$x + 2 = \text{son's age in 2 years}$$
$$7x + 2 = \text{father's age in 2 years.}$$

Then
$$7x + 2 = 5(x + 2)$$
$$7x + 2 = 5x + 10$$
$$7x - 5x = 10 - 2$$
$$2x = 8$$
$$x = 4, \text{ years in son's age now}$$
$$7x = 28, \text{ years in father's age now.}$$

AHMES PAPYRUS (ahms pa'-pi-rus), also **Rhind Papyrus,** the oldest surviving work of ancient Egyptian mathematics from ab. 1600 B.C., and now in the British Museum. It was compiled by Ahmes, a scribe, from an earlier treatise dating ab. 2300 B.C.

ALGEBRA (al'-ji-brah), traditionally and still most commonly, the branch of mathematics in which operations of ARITHMETIC are generalized by the use of letters to represent quantities, as in FORMULAS and EQUATIONS.

The name "algebra" was taken from one of the works of Mohammed ibn-Musa al-Khowarizmi which was written in Bagdad ab. 825 A.D. The title was *Al-jabr w'al muqabalah*. The word *al-jabr* is Arabic while *muqabalah* is Persian and it is thought that each referred to an equation. This work was so important and had such influence upon European mathematicians that the name "algebra" was adopted, with various spellings.

The earliest known treatise which could be called algebraic is the AHMES PAPYRUS, now in the British museum and written ab. 1600 B.C. The only Greek to write extensively on algebra was Diophantus, who lived in about the mid-third century A.D. and was probably the first to use a symbol to represent an unknown quantity.

ALGEBRAIC CURVE (al-ji-bray -ik), the graph of an equation of the form

$$0 = P_0(x) + P_1(x)y + P_2(x)y^2 + Pn(x)y^{n'},$$

where $P_i(x)$ is a polynomial in x. E.g., $x^2 + xy^2 - 1 = 0$; $x^3 + xy + y^3 = 0; (x + 5)(y - 4) = 0$.
Other examples of algebraic curves are the CONIC SECTIONS. Curves which are not algebraic because they do not graph polynomial equations in x and y, are called TRANSCENDENTAL CURVES, e.g., TRIGONOMETRIC CURVES. For sample, *see* CURVE SKETCHING.

ALGEBRAIC EXPRESSION, a quantity made up of letters, NUMERALS, and other ALGEBRAIC SYMBOLS. The parts of an expression that are connected by plus and minus signs are the *terms* of an expression. The sign immediately preceding the term is the sign of that term. Thus, $3x^2yz^2$, $2a$, and x/y are expressions of one term each. The expression $3x - 2y$ has two terms, $3x$ and $-2y$. In the expression $2a^2b - 3ab/2c + 2a(b + c)$, the three terms are $2a^2b$, $-3ab/2c$, and $2a(b + c)$. If there is no sign preceding the term it is understood to be plus.

If an algebraic expression has one term, it is called a *monomial;* if it has two terms, it is called a *binomial;* if it has three terms, it is called a *trinomial.* An algebraic expression of more than one term is called a POLYNOMIAL.

ALGEBRAIC FUNCTION, any FUNCTION whose dependent value (*see* VARIABLE) is an ALGEBRAIC EXPRESSION. If y is a function of x such that values of y corresponding to every x can be found from $f_0(x)y^n + f_1(x)y^{n-1} + \ldots + f_{n-1}(x)y + f_n(x) = 0$, where $f_0(x), f_1(x), \ldots, f_n(x)$ are polynomials in x, then y is an

algebraic function of x. E.g., $y = \sqrt{\dfrac{x^2 + 1}{x^2 - 1}}$ is an algebraic function of x since $y^2 = \dfrac{x^2 + 1}{x^2 - 1}$,

$$y^2(x^2 - 1) = x^2 + 1,$$
$$(x^2 - 1)y^2 - (x^2 + 1) = 0, \text{ and}$$
$$(x^2 - 1)y^2 + (-x^2 - 1) = 0.$$

Here, $f_0(x) = x^2 - 1$, $f_1(x) = 0$, and $f_2(x) = -x^2 - 1$.

ALGEBRAIC NUMBER, a NUMBER that satisfies a polynomial equation with integral coefficients. Since a RATIONAL NUMBER is defined by $x = p/q$ where p and q are integers, x satisfies the equation $qx - p = 0$ which has integral coefficients. Therefore, every rational number is an algebraic number, and every non-algebraic number (TRANSCENDENTAL NUMBER) must be irrational. However, there are IRRATIONAL NUMBERS that are algebraic numbers: $\sqrt{2}$ satisfies $x^2 - 2 = 0$, a polynomial equation with integral coefficients. Not all numbers have been classified as either algebraic or transcendental. E.g., it is not yet known whether π^π is algebraic or transcendental.

ALGEBRAIC SYMBOLS, as in TABLE NO. 2, conventional signs which enable us to abbreviate mathematical expressions which otherwise would have to be made at length in words.

Ex. 1: If *n* represents a certain number, express the following algebraically:

1. The PRODUCT of 5 and the number. $5n$
2. The number divided by 3. $n/3$
3. 7 divided by 2 times the number. $7/2n$
4. 5 times the sum of the number and 6. $5(n + 6)$
5. The SQUARE ROOT of 2 less than the number. $\sqrt{n - 2}$
6. The number increased by 3. $n + 3$

Ex. 2: Represent the following:

1. The difference of *x* and *y*. $x - y$
2. The sum of 8 and *b* subtracted from *a*. $a - (8 + b)$
3. The product of 2, *a*, and *b*. $2ab$
4. The sum of *x* and *y* divided by the product of *x* and *y*. $(x + y)/xy$
5. The QUOTIENT when *b* divides *a*. a/b

ALGEBRA OF PROPOSITIONS, a two-valued BOOLEAN ALGE-BRA of logical relationships among PROPOSITIONS. Also called the **propositional calculus** or **symbolic logic,** it does for traditional logic what analytic geometry did for traditional geometry.

In this algebra the small letters, *p, q, r, . . .* generally stand for propositions. The algebra's unity and ZERO symbols, 1 and 0, stand for the truth values, true and false, respectively. Other standard symbols are:

$\sim$ for "not" or negation (*see* NEGATION, LOGICAL).

$\wedge$ or $\cdot$ (dot) for "and" or CONJUNCTION.

$\vee$ or $+$ for "or" or DISJUNCTION.

$\rightarrow$ for "if. . . , then . . ." or the conditional (*see* CONDI-TIONAL STATEMENT).

$\leftrightarrow$ for "if and only if . . ." or the bi-conditional (*see* BI-CONDITIONAL, LOGICAL).

Thus, $\sim p$ is read "not *p*;" $p \wedge q$, "*p* and *q*;" $p \vee q$, "*p* or *q*;" $p \rightarrow q$, "if *p*, then *q*;" $p \leftrightarrow q$, "*p* if and only if *q*."

ALGOL (al'-gol). In computer terminology, an acronym for **Algorithmic Language,** one of several major key automatic coding systems for computers. *ALGOL* is really a language, developed for the purpose of translating higher level instructions into the specific codes of the computer. *See* COMPUTER.

ALGORITHM (al'-guh-rith-um), any method that is used to perform a calculation. The term is applied more commonly to those methods of calculation that require repetition of some process, as in DIVISION, or finding the GREATEST COMMON DIVISOR by EUCLID'S ALGORITHM.

ALIQUOT PART (al-i-kwot'), any factor of an integer except the integer itself. For example, 2, 3, 5, 6, 15 are called aliquot parts of 30.

ALMAGEST (al'-muh-jest), title which the Arabians gave to a translation of *Megiste Syntaxis,* a treatise on astronomy by PTOLEMY ab 150 A.D. The word means "the greatest." This work formed a basis for the later development of trigonometry.

ALPHA (al-fah), the Greek letter symbolized by α. *See* TABLE NO. 1.

ALPHA ERROR, in STATISTICS, the error that results when a NULL HYPOTHESIS is erroneously rejected. The size of this error is usually denoted by α and chosen to be .005, .01, .05, or .10. An alpha error is also called a Type I error.

ALPHA LEVEL, in STATISTICS, the SIGNIFICANCE LEVEL of a test; the size of the ALPHA ERROR. If the alpha level of a test is .05, it means that 5 times out of 100, on the average, the NULL HYPOTHE-SIS would be rejected even though it is true.

ALTERNATE-INTERIOR ANGLES, when lines are cut by a TRANSVERSAL, the pairs of angles between the lines and on opposite sides of the transversal.

In the figure, alternate-interior angles are $\angle x$ and $\angle y$ and $\angle m$ and $\angle n$. If two PARALLEL LINES are cut by a transversal, the alternate-interior angles are equal. In terms of the figure, if $l \| l'$, then $\angle x = \angle y$ and $\angle m = \angle n$.

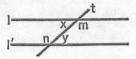

If two lines are cut by a transversal and the alternate-interior angles are equal, the lines are parallel. Thus, if $\angle x = \angle y$, or if $\angle m = \angle n$, then $l \| l'$.

ALTERNATING SERIES, a SERIES in which every other term is negative.

Ex.: $\sum_{n=1}^{\infty} (-1)^{n+1}/n = 1 - \tfrac{1}{2} + \tfrac{1}{3} - \tfrac{1}{4} + \cdots$ is an alternating series.

An alternating series is called a CONVERGENT SERIES if $a_n \rightarrow 0$ as $n \rightarrow \infty$ in such a way that $|a_{n+1}| \leq |a_n|$. *See also* CONDITIONAL CONVERGENCE.

ALTERNATION, the process by which a given PROPORTION is changed to another by interchanging the means, so that the first term is to the third term as the second is to the fourth.

Ex.: $a/b = c/d$, by alternation, $a/c = b/d$.

ALTERNATIVE HYPOTHESIS (hahy-pah-thuh-seez), in statistics, the hypothesis denoted H_1 or H_A, that is accepted if the NULL HYPOTHESIS is not accepted. A one-sided, or one-tailed, alternative contains either a "less than" symbol ($<$) or a "greater than" symbol ($>$). A two-sided, or two-tailed, alternative contains a "not equal to" symbol ($\neq$).

ALTITUDE OF A GEOMETRIC FIGURE, the PERPENDICULAR from any vertex to the opposite side, or to the opposite side extended. In PARALLELOGRAM *ABCD* (Fig. 1), *DE, GH,* and *CF* are altitudes to the base *AB*.

The altitude of a TRAPEZOID is the perpendicular from any point on one of the parallel sides to the other parallel side. In the trapezoid *ABCD* (Fig. 2), *DE* and *FG* are altitudes to base *AB*.

A TRIANGLE has three altitudes (one from each vertex) which are CONCURRENT at a point called the orthocenter. In OBTUSE TRI-ANGLE *LGF* (Fig. 3), altitudes *GQ, LD,* and *FJ* intersect at *S. S* is

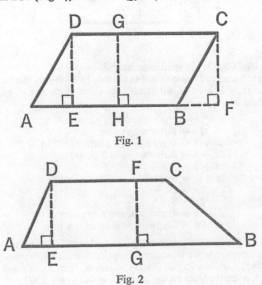

Fig. 1

Fig. 2

the orthocenter of triangle *LGF*. The altitude of an EQUILATERAL TRIANGLE may be found by the formula $h = \frac{s}{2}\sqrt{3}$, in which s represents any one of the equal sides and h represents the altitude to that side.

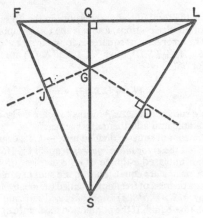

Fig. 3

In a RIGHT TRIANGLE, either leg is an altitude and the third side is the BASE. When an altitude is drawn to the base of a right triangle, (1) the two triangles formed are similar and each is similar to the original triangle; (2) the altitude is the MEAN PROPORTIONAL between the segments of the hypotenuse; and (3) either leg is the mean proportional between the hypotenuse and the segment of the hypotenuse adjacent to that leg. (See Fig. 4.)

1. $\triangle ACD \sim \triangle CDB$; $\triangle ACD \sim \triangle ACB$; $\triangle CDB \sim \triangle ACB$.

2. $\frac{r}{h} = \frac{h}{s}$.

3. $\frac{c}{b} = \frac{b}{r}$; $\frac{c}{a} = \frac{a}{s}$.

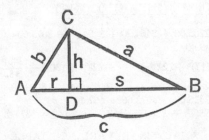

Fig. 4

AMBIGUOUS CASE (am-big'-eu-us), in the solution of triangles by TRIGONOMETRY, the case in which two sides and the angle opposite one of them are given. It is so called because one, two, or no triangles may be constructed depending on the relations of the given parts.

If the given parts are a, b, and A, the ALTITUDE h from C can be found from the equation $h/b = \sin A$; $h = b \sin A$. If A is acute and $a < b$ and if $a > b \sin A$, or if $a > h$, there will be two triangles, *ABC* and *AB'C*. (See Fig. 1.)

If A is acute, $a < b$, and $a = b \sin A$, or h, there is one triangle, a right triangle. (See Fig. 2.)

If A is acute, $a < b$, and $a = b \sin A$, or h, there can be no triangle and no solution. (See Fig. 3.)

If A is a right angle, there can be one solution if $a > b$, and no solution if $a = b$ or if $a < b$. If A is obtuse, there can be one solution if $a > b$, and no solution if $a = b$ or if $a < b$.

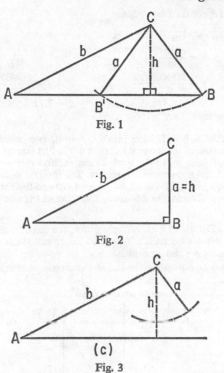

Fig. 1

Fig. 2

(c)

Fig. 3

Ex. 1: Solve triangle *ABC*, given $A = 54°$, $b = 16$, and $a = 9$.

$$h = b \sin A$$
$$h = 16 \times .8090 = 12.944.$$

Therefore, there can be no solution, because the altitude is greater than a.

Ex. 2: Solve triangle *ABC*, given $A = 37°$, $b = 15$, and $a = 10$.

$$h = b \sin A$$
$$h = 15 \times .6018 = 9.027.$$

Since $a > b \sin A$, two triangles may be constructed.

By the Law of Sines:

$$\frac{\sin B}{\sin A} = \frac{b}{a} \text{ and } \sin B = \frac{b \sin A}{a}.$$

Since angle B is determined by its sine, it may have two values which are supplementary; therefore either of the values may be taken. (See Fig. 4.)

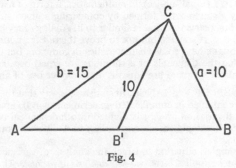

Fig. 4

$$\sin B = \frac{b \sin A}{a} = .9027$$

$B = 64° 30'$ or $115° 30'$ to the nearest minute.

$C = 180° + (A + B)$

$C = 78° 30'$ or $27° 30'$.

To find c, use the Law of Sines.

$$\frac{c}{\sin C} = \frac{a}{\sin A}$$

$$c = \frac{a \sin C}{\sin A}$$

$$c = \frac{10 \times .9799}{.6018} \qquad\qquad c = \frac{10 \times .4617}{.6018}$$

$$c = 16.3 \text{ in } \triangle ABC. \qquad c = 7.7 \text{ in } \triangle AB'C.$$

See also SINES, LAW OF.

AMICABLE NUMBERS (am'-i-kuh-bul), two numbers such that the sum of the integral FACTORS of the first (except the number itself) is equal to the second number, and vice versa. Thus, 220 and 284 are amicable numbers. The integral factors of 220 are 1, 2, 4, 5, 10, 11, 20, 22, 44, 55, and 110 and their sum is 284. The integral factors of 284 are 1, 2, 4, 71, and 142 and their sum is 220.

AMPLITUDE, of a COMPLEX NUMBER, the fixed positive angle which, when associated with a fixed length called the MODULUS, determines a point in a plane. E.g., the complex number $1 + \sqrt{3}i$, may be represented in an ARGAND DIAGRAM as in the figure.

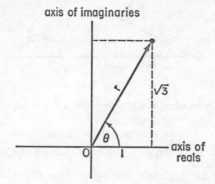

axis of imaginaries

Then θ is the angle whose TANGENT is $\sqrt{3}/1$ (arctan $\sqrt{3}/1$) or 30°. The amplitude of $1 + \sqrt{3}i$ is 30°. In general, the amplitude of the complex number $a + bi$ is arctan b/a.

Of a TRIGONOMETRIC CURVE, the greatest numerical ORDINATE of the curve of a graph of a TRIGONOMETRIC FUNCTION. In $y = \sin x$, the amplitude of the curve is 1; in $y = \frac{1}{2} \sin x$ it is $\frac{1}{2}$. In acoustics, intensity of a tone is determined by the amplitude and pitch is determined by the period.

ANALOG COMPUTER, *see* COMPUTER.

ANALOGY (u-nal'-uh-jee), in mathematics, a form of reasoning whereby a statement is formed by comparing a given structure with another structure that is similar to it. Analogy may be used to form new THEOREMS, but not to prove them. E.g., a RHOMBUS and a SQUARE have some characteristics in common, but to conclude that the diagonals of a rhombus are equal because the diagonals of a square are equal is an incorrect use of analogy.

ANALYSIS OF VARIANCE, in statistics, a way that the information contained in complicated experiments can be analyzed. The total variation present is divided into independent components, each component corresponding to a different source of variation.

The simplest situation to which the analysis of variance technique can be applied is the *one-way analysis of variance.* There are k independent samples of sizes $n_1, n_2, \ldots, n_k$ from k normal populations, each with variance σ^2. The NULL HYPOTHESIS is that the means of the k populations are equal, $H_0: \mu_1 = \mu_2 = \cdots = \mu_k$. The ALTERNATIVE HYPOTHESIS is that they are not all equal. The total variation present, called the *total sum of squares,* is composed of two separate pieces: the *among samples sum of*

squares, denoted by $SS(A)$; and the *within samples sum of squares* (or *error sum of squares*), denoted by $SS(E)$.

The formula for $SS(A)$ is

$$SS(A) = \left(\sum_{i=1}^{k} \frac{T_{i.}^2}{n_i} \right) - \frac{T_{..}^2}{n},$$

where $T_{i.}$ is the total of the observations in the ith sample, $T_{..}$ is the total of all observations, and n is the total number of observations. The error sum of squares is found from the relationship $SS(T) = SS(A) + SS(E)$, after $SS(A)$ and $SS(T)$ are found. The formula for $SS(T)$ is

$$SS(T) = (\Sigma\Sigma x_{ij}^2) - \frac{T_{..}^2}{n}.$$

The double summation $\Sigma\Sigma x_{ij}^2$ means "square every observation in every sample and add them all together."

The error sum of squares divided by $n - k$, its degrees of freedom, is called the *error mean square,* denoted by $MS(E)$. $MS(E)$ furnishes an unbiased estimate of σ^2, regardless of whether the population means are equal. The among sum of squares divided by $k - 1$, its degrees of freedom, is called the *among mean square,* denoted by $MS(A)$. $MS(A)$ is an unbiased estimate of σ^2 if the populations are equal. If the population means are not equal, the among mean square is expected to be larger than the error mean square. If it is significantly larger, the hypothesis of equal population means is rejected. The test-statistic is $F = \dfrac{MS(A)}{MS(E)}$. The null hypothesis of equal means is rejected if F is equal to or greater than the upper α-point of the F-distribution with $k - 1$ and $n - k$ degrees of freedom.

Ex.:

Sample 1	Sample 2	Sample 3
17	20	27
22	15	28
14	18	19
23	31	28
29	27	30
Totals 105 +	111 +	132 = 348

$$SS(A) = \frac{(105)^2}{5} + \frac{(111)^2}{5} + \frac{(132)^2}{5} - \frac{(348)^2}{15}$$

$$= 2205.00 + 2464.20 + 3484.80 - 8073.60$$

$$= 80.40$$

$$SS(T) = (17)^2 + (22)^2 + \cdots + (28)^2 + (30)^2 - \frac{(348)^2}{15}$$

$$= 289 + 484 + \cdots + 784 + 900 - 8073.60$$

$$= 8536.00 - 8073.60 = 462.40.$$

$$SS(E) = SS(T) - SS(A) = 462.40 - 80.40 = 382.00.$$

ANALYSIS OF VARIANCE TABLE

Source	Degrees of Freedom d.f.	Sample Sum of Squares S.S.	Mean Square M.S.	F
Among (A)	2	80.40	40.20	1.26 (not significant)
Within (E)	12	382.00	31.83	
Total	14	462.40	—	

ANALYSIS OF VARIANCE TABLE, a table that displays, for an analysis of variance, the sources of variation, along with the degrees of freedom, *d.f.,* and the sum of squares, *S.S.,* and the mean square, *M.S.,* for each source of variation. *See* ANALYSIS OF VARIANCE.

ANALYTIC FUNCTION, a complex-valued function of a complex variable which is differentiable. *See also* CAUCHY-RIEMANN EQUATIONS.

ANALYTIC GEOMETRY, *see* GEOMETRY, ANALYTIC.

ANCHOR RING, *see* TORUS.

ANGLE, a geometric figure formed by two RAYS (or half-lines) drawn from the same POINT. The symbol for angle is ∠. In Fig. 1, rays *BA* and *BC* meet in point *B* forming ∠*ABC*. The rays are called the sides of the angle and the point is its VERTEX. The size of an angle does not depend on the length of its sides.

There are three ways of naming an angle:
1. By the capital letter at the vertex, as ∠*B*.
2. By three capital letters, the vertex letter always in the middle, as ∠*ABC*.
3. By a small letter, or number, within the angle near the vertex, as ∠*x*.

If there are two or more angles at a vertex, they are never read by the single vertex letter. In Fig. 2, the two angles at *D* are read ∠*ADC* and ∠*BDC*. Small letters, or numbers, may be used, as ∠1 and ∠2 at *C*.

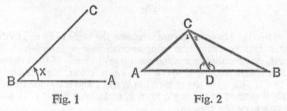

Fig. 1   Fig. 2

In a circle, the following theorems are used to measure angles:

A CENTRAL ANGLE is equal in degrees to its ARC. $\angle AOB \triangleq \overset{\frown}{AB}$. (See Fig. 3.)

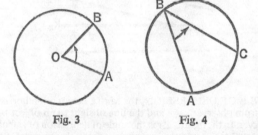

Fig. 3   Fig. 4

An INSCRIBED ANGLE is equal in degrees to one half its intercepted arc. $\angle ABC \triangleq \frac{1}{2}\overset{\frown}{AC}$. (See Fig. 4.)

An angle formed by two CHORDS intersecting in a circle is equal in degrees to one half the sum of its arc and the arc of its VERTICAL ANGLE. $\angle x \triangleq \frac{1}{2}(\overset{\frown}{AC} + \overset{\frown}{BD})$. (See Fig. 5.)

An angle formed by a TANGENT LINE and a chord drawn to the point of tangency is equal in degrees to one half the arc it intercepts. $\angle ABC \triangleq \frac{1}{2}\overset{\frown}{AB}$. (See Fig. 6.)

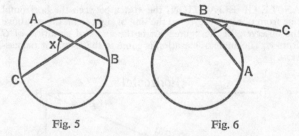

Fig. 5   Fig. 6

An angle formed by two secant lines, two tangent lines, or a SECANT LINE and a tangent line meeting outside the circle is equal in degrees to one half the difference of the intercepted arcs. $\angle A = \frac{1}{2}(\overset{\frown}{m} - \overset{\frown}{n})$. (See Fig. 7.)

One of the rays that form the angle is called the initial side of the angle. In trigonometry the initial side (*see* SIDE OF AN ANGLE)

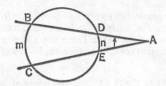

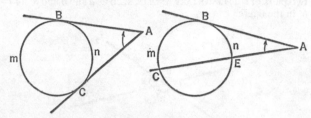

Fig. 7

is the side of the angle that coincides with the positive side of the *x*-axis. An angle is said to be a standard position angle if its vertex is the ORIGIN and its initial side coincides with the positive side of the *x*-axis. The other ray is called the terminal side (*see* SIDE OF AN ANGLE). In trigonometry, the terminal side of an angle is the final position of the rotating ray. (See Fig. 8.) The size of

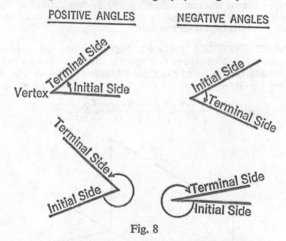

POSITIVE ANGLES   NEGATIVE ANGLES

Fig. 8

an angle is determined by its terminal side. An angle is considered to be of the QUADRANT in which its terminal side lies. The rotating ray may make more than one revolution. If the terminal side has been rotated counterclockwise from the initial side, the angle is said to be positive (See Fig. 9a.) If the terminal side has been rotated clockwise from the initial side, the angle is said to be negative. (See Fig. 9b.)

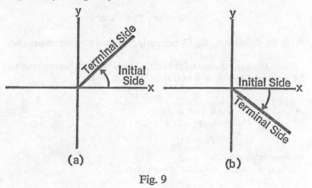

(a)   (b)

Fig. 9

Angles may be compared by assigning numbers to them which indicate their size. The units of angle measure most commonly used are DEGREES and RADIANS. There are 360 degrees, or two radians, in a complete rotation; other angles are given proportional numbers.

ANGLE BETWEEN TWO LINES, the angle of least measure (in ABSOLUTE VALUE) between two intersecting lines; also called the angle of intersection of the lines. Two intersecting lines form two pairs of SUPPLEMENTARY ANGLES, such as a and b and a' and b' in the figure.

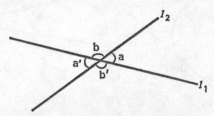

The angle between the two lines is a or a'. Since they are VERTICAL ANGLES, $a = a'$ (and $b = b'$).

If two lines in space do not intersect an angle between them may be defined by using another pair of lines which do intersect, one parallel (*see* PARALLEL LINES) to each of the original lines. The angle between the nonintersecting pair is then defined as the angle between the intersecting pair. *See also* ANGLE FROM ONE LINE TO ANOTHER; DIRECTION ANGLE·

ANGLE BETWEEN TWO PLANES, the DIHEDRAL ANGLE formed by the two planes. It is equal to the angle between their NORMALS. The cosine of the angle θ between the planes $A_1x + B_1y + C_1z + D_1 = 0$ and $A_2x + B_2y + C_2z + D_2 = 0$ is given by:

$$\cos \theta = \frac{\pm (A_1A_2 + B_1B_2 + C_1C_2)}{\sqrt{A_1^2 + B_1^2 + C_1^2}\ \sqrt{A_2^2 + B_2^2 + C_2^2}}$$

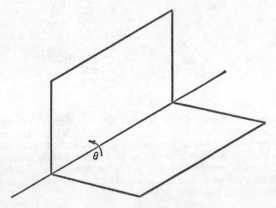

Angle Between Two Planes

If A_1, B_1, C_1 and A_2, B_2, C_2 are proportional, the phases are parallel.

Ex.: Find the cosine of the acute angle between the two planes $2x - 2y + 8z - 6 = 0$ and $x + 3y + 2z - 6 = 0$.

$$Sol.:\ \cos \theta = \frac{\pm (2 - 6 + 16)}{\sqrt{4 + 4 + 64}\ \sqrt{1 + 9 + 4}}$$

$$= \frac{\pm 12}{\sqrt{72}\ \sqrt{14}}$$

or approximately .9.
See also ANGLE BETWEEN TWO LINES.

ANGLE FROM ONE LINE TO ANOTHER, the angle of least positive measure from one line to the other. If a pair of lines l_1 and l_2 intersect at point P, then the angle from l_1 to l_2 is the smallest angle formed by rotating l_2 counterclockwise from l_1. There will be two such angles, such as a and a' in Fig. 1, but they are VERTICAL ANGLES and are therefore equal. In Fig. 1, the angle from l_1 to l_2 is a, while the angle from l_2, to l_1 is b.

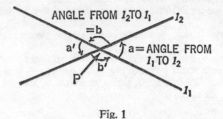

Fig. 1

If two lines in space do not intersect, the angle from one to the other may be defined by using another pair of lines which do meet, one parallel (*see* PARALLEL LINES) to each of the original lines. If $k_1 \| l_1$ and $k_2 \| l_2$, where k_1 and k_2 intersect, the angle from l_1 to l_2 is defined as the angle from k_1 to k_2, and the angle from l_2 to l_1 is defined as the angle from k_2 to k_1. (See Fig. 2.) *See also* ANGLE BETWEEN TWO LINES.

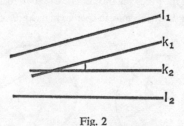

Fig. 2

ANGLE OF DEPRESSION, the ANGLE between the horizontal line from observer's eye and the line of sight to an object below observer. In the figure, $\angle y$ is the angle of depression of A from C, where AC represents the line of sight from observer at C to object A, and CD represents the horizontal.

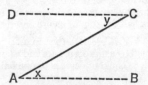

ANGLE OF ELEVATION, the ANGLE between the horizontal line from observer's eye and the line of sight to an object above the observer. In the figure, $\angle x$ is the angle of elevation of C from A. The angle of elevation is equal to the ANGLE OF DEPRESSION.

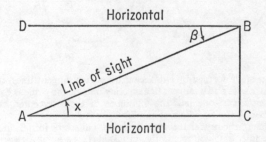

ANGLE OF INCLINATION, the positive angle between 0° and 180° that a line makes with the *x*-axis. (See figure.)

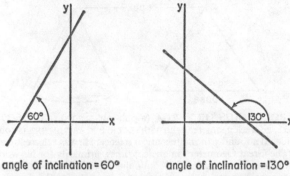

angle of inclination = 60°   angle of inclination = 130°

ANGLE OF INTERSECTION OF CURVES, the angle between the TANGENT LINES to the curves at the point of intersection (Fig. 1a). The angle of intersection of circles can be computed without using calculus, but most other curves require calculus. In the case of circles, use the fact that a tangent to a circle is perpendicular to the RADIUS to the point of contact.

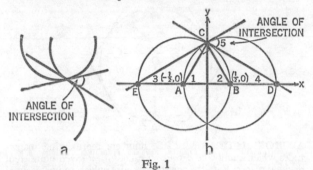

Fig. 1

Ex.: Circles of radius 1 are centered at $(-\frac{1}{2}, 0)$ and $(\frac{1}{2}, 0)$. Find their angle of intersection (See Fig. 1b.).
Sol.:
Method 1: Use the fact that the slopes of perpendicular lines (*see* SLOPE OF A LINE) are negative reciprocals; compute slopes and then find the angle in TABLE NO. 22.
Method 2: Observe that the cosine of angle 1 is $\frac{1}{2}$; therefore $\angle 1$ is 60°. Triangle *ACD* is a right triangle with $\angle 1$ in it, so $\angle 4$ is $90° - 60° = 30°$. Similarly, $\angle 3 = 60°$. Then $\angle ECD$ is 120°, and $\angle 5$ is 60°.
Method 3: $\triangle ABC$ is equilateral, so $\angle ACB = 60°$. $\angle ACB = \angle 5$. *See also* ANGLE BETWEEN TWO LINES.

ANGLES, EQUAL, in geometry:
1. All RIGHT ANGLES are equal.
2. All STRAIGHT ANGLES are equal.
3. BASE ANGLES of an ISOSCELES TRIANGLE and ISOSCELES TRAPEZOID are equal.
4. The angles of an EQUILATERAL TRIANGLE are equal.
5. ALTERNATE-INTERIOR ANGLES OF PARALLEL LINES are equal.
6. CORRESPONDING ANGLES of parallel lines are equal.
7. VERTICAL ANGLES are equal.
8. Complements of the same angle (*see* COMPLEMENTARY ANGLES), or of equal angles, are equal.
9. Supplements of the same angle, (*see* SUPPLEMENTARY ANGLES) or of equal angles, are equal.
10. Corr. angles of CONGRUENT POLYGONS are equal.
11. Corr. angles of SIMILAR POLYGONS are equal.
12. If two angles of one triangle are equal to two angles of another triangle, the third angles are equal.
13. Opp. angles of a PARALLELOGRAM are equal.

14. Equal ARCS of a CIRCLE have equal CENTRAL ANGLES.
15. INSCRIBED ANGLES which intercept the same or equal arcs are equal.
16. The DIAGONALS of a RHOMBUS bisect the angles through which they pass.
17. If two angles have their sides parallel, right side to right side and left side to left side, the angles are equal.

To construct an angle equal to a given $\angle ABC$ with given side *ED* (see figure), with any convenient radius and *B* as a center,

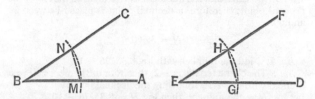

use a compass. Construct an arc that cuts *AB* at *M* and *BC* at *N*. With the same radius and *E* as a center, construct the arc that cuts *ED* at *G*. With a radius equal to the segment joining *M* and *N* and with *G* as the center, draw an arc that cuts the first arc at *H*. Draw *EF* passing through point *H*. $\angle DEF = \angle ABC$. Since radii of the same or of equal circles are equal, $BN = EH$, $BM = EG$, and $NM = HG$. $\triangle BMN \cong \triangle EGH$ (S.S.S.), and $\angle E = \angle B$.

ANGULAR DIAMETER, the diameter of an object from an observer's point of view, without reference to its distance. The angular diameter of the sun is about 32 min. of arc, the average angular diameter of the full moon, about 31 min. Of course, the actual diameters are much different, the sun's being about 865,000 mi. and the moon's only about 2,160 mi. The moon appears almost as large as the sun because it is much closer. As seen from the moon at the time of "full earth," U.S. astronauts evaluated the earth's angular area, the area of an object from an observer's point of view, about 13 times that of the full moon as seen from earth.

ANNULUS (an'-eu-lus), the region in the plane that is bounded by two CONCENTRIC circles. In the figure, where the radius of the larger circle is denoted by *R* and the radius of the smaller circle is denoted by *r*, the area of the annulus is $\pi R^2 - \pi r^2$ or $\pi(R^2 - r^2)$.

ANTECEDENT, the first term, or the NUMERATOR, of a RATIO. In the ratio x/y, x is the antecedent. *See also* CONSEQUENT.

ANTIDERIVATIVE OF A FUNCTION, the INDEFINITE INTEGRAL of that function, also called **Primitive Function**. For a function $f(x)$, the antiderivative is a function $g(x)$, such that $g'(x) = f(x)$. Hence, $g(x) = \int f(x)dx + c$.
Ex. 1: Find the antiderivative of $x^2 + 1$.
Sol.: Antiderivate $= g(x) = \int f(x)dx + c$
$$g(x) = \int f(x^2 + 1)dx + c$$
The antiderivative $= \frac{x^3}{3} + x + c$. (*See* TABLE NO. 14.)

Ex. 2: Find the antiderivative of $f(x) = 1/x^2 + x, x > 0$.
Sol.: $g(x) = \int (1/x^2 + x) + c$
$$g(x) = -1/x + x^2/2 + c.$$

ANTILOGARITHM, the number corresponding to a LOGA-RITHM. Finding an antilogarithm (abbreviated *antilog*) is the inverse of finding the logarithm of a number. If the mantissa is not in a Table of Logarithms, (TABLE NO. 22) the number is found by INTERPOLATION.

Ex. 1: Find the number whose logarithm is 1.59770.

Sol.: Let N = the number, then log N = 1.59770. The mantissa .59770 is found in the Table of Logarithms in the 0 column opposite 396 in the number column. The characteristic is 1 which indicates that the number has two digits to the left of the decimal point; therefore, a decimal point is placed between 39 and 60.

$$N = 39.60.$$

Ex. 2: Find the number with log 8.35296 − 10.

Sol.: The characteristic is −2, therefore the number will be a decimal with one zero following the decimal point. Let log N = the number, then log N = 8.35276 − 10.

$$N = .02253.$$

Ex. 3: Find the number whose logarithm is 4.87749.

Sol.: Let N = the number, then log N = 4.87749.

$$N = 75420.$$

Ex. 4: Find the number whose logarithm is 2.57464.

Sol.: The characteristic 2 indicates a number having three digits to the left of the decimal point. The mantissa .57464 is not in the table but lies between 57461 and 57473. We know the number is between 37550 and 37560. The last digit is determined by interpolation.

$$10\begin{bmatrix} \begin{array}{cc} Number & Mantissa \\ 37560 & 57473 \\ x\begin{bmatrix} 37550 + x \\ 37550 \end{bmatrix} & \begin{bmatrix} 57464 \\ 57461 \end{bmatrix}3 \end{array} \end{bmatrix}12$$

$$\frac{x}{10} = \frac{3}{12}; \quad 12x = 30; \quad x = 2\tfrac{6}{12} \text{ or approximately } 3.$$

$$37550 + x = 37553; \quad N = 375.53.$$

Ex. 5: Find the number whose logarithm is 9.893.46–10.

Sol.: The characteristic is −1, which indicates a decimal with no zeros following the decimal point. To simplify the interpolation, decimals are omitted and only the numbers and mantissas are used.

$$10\begin{bmatrix} \begin{array}{cc} Number & Mantissa \\ 78250 & 89348 \\ x\begin{bmatrix} 78240 + x \\ 78240 \end{bmatrix} & \begin{bmatrix} 89346 \\ 89343 \end{bmatrix}3 \end{array} \end{bmatrix}5$$

$$\frac{x}{10} = \frac{3}{5}; \quad 5x = 30; \quad x = 6.$$

$$78240 + x = 78246; \quad N = .78246.$$

See LOGARITHM, CHARACTERISTIC OF A; LOGARITHM, MANTISSA OF A.

ANY, in mathematics, the word used to indicate the most general case of a term or figure. "Any point on a line" means "whatever point one may choose to pick without exception" and hence "every point." If *any* point on the perpendicular bisector of a line segment is proved equidistant from the ends of the segment, then *every* point in the perpendicular bisector is also so proven. Since ISOSCELES, RIGHT and EQUILATERAL TRIANGLES have properties unique to each, "any" triangle should be represented by a SCALENE TRIANGLE so that conclusions reached will hold true for *all* triangles.

APEX, of a plane or solid geometric figure, the point that is the greatest distance from a given base line or plane. The apex of a triangle is the vertex opposite the side designated as the baes; of a cone, its vertex. (See figure.)

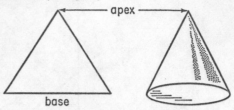

APOLLONIUS OF PERGA (a-puh-loh'-nee-us), ab. 255–170 B.C., a Greek geometer, who with EUCLID and ARCHIMEDES is considered a founder of mathematical science. He was referred to as "The Great Geometer" in ancient times, primarily for his work in CONIC SECTIONS. It was Apollonius who first used the terms PARABOLA, HYPERBOLA, and ELLIPSE to name the conics.

APOTHEM OF A REGULAR POLYGON (ap'-oh-them), the perpendicular from the center of the polygon to a side. The apothem is the RADIUS of the CIRCLE inscribed in the polygon. In the figure, OA is the apothem of the polygon and is also the radius of inscribed circle O.

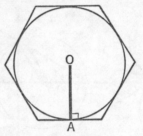

APPROXIMATE NUMBERS, numbers representing magnitudes which cannot be expressed exactly to a given number of decimal places. E.g., the square root of 2, which to five decimal places is 1.41421, is an approximate number. Before adding or subtracting approximate numbers round off the numbers to the same number of decimal places so that the sum, or difference, will have the same unit of measurement. E.g., given that $\sqrt{2} = 1.41421$ and $\sqrt{3} = 1.732$, to add $\sqrt{2}$ and $\sqrt{3}$, use $1.414 + 1.732$. Thus, the sum of $\sqrt{2} + \sqrt{3} = 3.146$.

The product of two approximate numbers should not have more SIGNIFICANT figures than either the multiplicand or the multiplier, nor should the quotient of two approximate numbers contain more significant figures than either the dividend or the divisor. Thus, to find the product of $\sqrt{2}$ and $\sqrt{3}$, multiply 1.414×1.732 which gives 2.449048, and round off the product to three decimal places. The product is 2.449. If computations involve both exact and approximate numbers, the result should have the same unit of measurement as the approximate number. *See also* ROUNDING OFF A NUMBER.

APPROXIMATION BY DIFFERENTIALS, *see* DIFFERENTIAL.

ARC (ahrk), the part of a CIRCLE between any two points on the

circle. The symbol for arc is ($\frown$). A *minor* arc is an arc less than a SEMICIRCLE and a *major* arc is an arc greater than a semicircle. Every CHORD of a circle has two arcs, but "a chord and its arc" usually means "a chord and its minor arc." In the figure, $\overarc{AB}$ is minor arc AB.

ARC COSECANT, abbreviated arc csc, one of the INVERSE TRIGONOMETRIC FUNCTIONS. Arc csc is the INVERSE FUNCTION of the direct cosecant function (*see* COSECANT OF AN ANGLE). The inverse function, $\theta = $ arc csc x, is read "theta is the angle whose cosecant is x." The symbol "csc^{-1}x" may be used for "arc csc x." *See also* ARC SINE.

ARC COSINE, abbreviated arc cos, one of the INVERSE TRIGONOMETRIC FUNCTIONS. Arc cos is the INVERSE FUNCTION of the direct cosine function (*see* COSINE OF AN ANGLE). The inverse function, $\theta = $ arc cos x, is read "theta is the angle whose cosine is x." The symbol "cos^{-1}x" may be used for "arc cos x." *See also* ARC SINE.

ARC COTANGENT, abbreviated arc cot, one of the INVERSE TRIGONOMETRIC FUNCTIONS. Arc cot is the INVERSE FUNCTION of the direct cotangent function (*see* COTANGENT OF AN ANGLE). The inverse function, $\theta = $ arc cot x, is read "theta is the angle whose cotangent is x." The symbol "cot ^{-1}x" may be used for "arc cot x." *See also* ARC SINE.

ARC DEGREE, a unit for measuring arcs of a circle. A CENTRAL ANGLE of one degree intercepts an arc whose measure is one degree. In Fig. 1, the central angle AOB of 50° intercepts arc AB. Therefore $\overarc{AB}$ contains 50°.

Since the sum of all the angle degrees around a point equals 360° and the sum of all the arc degrees of a circle equals 360°, then $\angle AOB \doteq \overarc{AB}$ and is read " $\angle AOB$ is equal in degrees to $\overarc{AB}$." We never say that $\angle AOB$ equals $\overarc{AB}$, because an angle does not equal an arc. In Fig. 2, $\overarc{AB} \doteq \overarc{CD}$ because they are intercepted by the same central angle. They are not equal in length.

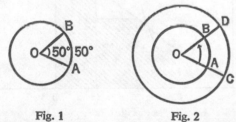

Fig. 1   Fig. 2

ARCHIMEDES (ahr-ki-mee'-deez), 287–212 B.C., Greek scientist. The greatest scientist of anc. times, he contributed to several branches of mathematics and physics, as well as to astronomy and technology. Archimedes was born in the Greek colony of Syracuse, on the I. of Sicily. He studied in Alexandria, where he invented the device now known as Archimedes' screw, a hollow helix wrapped around a cylinder and used to raise water. Returning to Syracuse, he investigated many different subjects. As a result of his studies of buoyancy, he published a treatise called *Floating Bodies*, which included the statement, now known as Archimedes' Principle, that an object immersed in a fluid is buoyed up by a force equal to the weight of the displaced fluid. Connected with these studies is the story of Archimedes' attempt to determine if a crown belonging to Hiero, king of Syracuse, was or was not made of pure gold. According to legend, Archimedes became aware of a means to solve the problem while taking a bath and was so excited that he rushed into the street, forgetting his clothes, crying *"Eureka, eureka!"* (I have found it.) Archimedes determined the specific gravity of the crown by submerging it in water, then compared this result to the specific gravity of pure gold, found by the same method. In addition to

his contributions to the field of hydrostatics, of which he may be considered the founder, Archimedes also founded the field of statics as applied to rigid bodies. He made important studies of EQUILIBRIUM and the CENTER OF MASS of an object and wrote on levers and other simple machines. He is reported to have once said to King Hiero, "Give me a place to stand and I will move the world," referring to the ability of a lever to overcome a large resistance with a small effort. In mathematics, Archimedes invented a system of numeration, known as the exponential system, which enabled him to indicate numbers as large as desired. He estimated the value of π to be between $3\frac{10}{70}$ and $3\frac{10}{71}$ by means of a geometric argument involving inscribed and circumscribed polygons. Named for him is the figure known as the *Archimedean spiral*, which has the equation $r = a\theta$ in polar coordinates. He also studied finite series and was particularly pleased with his discoveries regarding spheres and cylinders, which he asked to have inscribed on his tombstone. When Syracuse was beseiged by the Romans about 214 B.C., Archimedes designed several military devices, including a catapult and a grappling hook. When the Romans finally took the city, legend has it that Archimedes was intently studying some figures that he had drawn in the sand. As a soldier approached him, he exclaimed, "Don't step on my circles." The soldier was then reputed to have killed him.

Biblio.; Gardner, M., *Archimedes: Mathematician and Inventor* (1965); Jonas, A., *Archimedes and His Wonderful Discoveries* (1962).

ARC LENGTH, the length of an arc of a circle. If the arc is intercepted by a central angle of θ radians, the length is equal to the product of the RADIUS and the CENTRAL ANGLE in RADIANS. If s

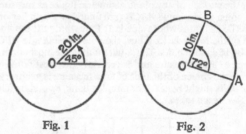

Fig. 1   Fig. 2

represents the length of the arc, r the radius of the circle, and θ the number of radians in the central angle, the formula is

$$s = r\theta.$$

Ex. 1: What is the length of the arc intercepted by a central angle of 45° if the radius of the circle is 20 in.? (See Fig. 1.)

Sol.:

$$1° = \frac{\pi}{180} \text{ radians}$$

$$45° = \frac{45\pi}{180} \text{ or } \frac{\pi}{4} \text{ radians}$$

$$s = 20 \times \frac{\pi}{4} = 5\pi \text{ in.}$$

The arc length has the same ratio to the circumference of the circle as the number of degrees in the arc has to 360°. Thus, if $n = $ the number of degrees in the arc,

$$\text{arc length } L = \frac{n}{360} \times 2\pi r.$$

Ex. 2: Find the length of $\overarc{AB}$ if it is intercepted by a central angle of 72° and if the radius of the circle is 10 in. (See Fig. 2.)

Sol.: A central angle is equal in degrees to its intercepted arc. Therefore, $n = 72°$.

$$L = \frac{72}{360} \times 2\pi \times 10$$

$$L = \frac{144}{36} \pi = 4\pi, \text{ or } 4 \times \frac{22}{7} = \frac{88}{7} = 12\frac{4}{7} \text{ in.}$$

ARC SECANT, abbreviated **arc sec,** one of the INVERSE TRIGONOMETRIC FUNCTIONS. Arc sec is the INVERSE FUNCTION of the direct secant function (*see* SECANT OF AN ANGLE). The INVERSE FUNCTION, $\theta =$ arc sec x, is read "theta is the angle whose secant is x." The symbol "$\sec^{-1}x$" may be used for "arc sec x." *See also* ARC SINE.

ARCS, EQUAL, in geometry:
   1. Equal CENTRAL ANGLES in a CIRCLE, or in EQUAL CIRCLES, have equal ARCS.
   2. Equal CHORDS in a circle, or in equal circles, have equal arcs.
   3. PARALLEL LINES in a circle intercept equal arcs.
   4. A line through the center of the circle PERPENDICULAR to a chord bisects the arcs of the chord.

ARC SINE, abbreviated **arc sin,** one of the INVERSE TRIGONOMETRIC FUNCTIONS. Arc sin is the INVERSE FUNCTION of the direct sine function (*see* SINE OF AN ANGLE). The inverse function, $\theta =$ arc sin x, is read "theta is the angle whose sine is x." The symbol "$\sin^{-1}x$" may be used for "arc sin x".
   Ex. 1: Find arc sin .50000.
   Sol.: $\theta =$ arc sin .50000. From the trigonometric tables (Table 22), the angle whose sine is .50000 is 30°. ∴ arc sin .50000 = 30°.

ARC TANGENT, abbreviated **arc tan,** one of the INVERSE TRIGONOMETRIC FUNCTIONS. Arc tan is the INVERSE FUNCTION of the direct tangent function (*see* TANGENT OF AN ANGLE). The inverse function, $\theta =$ arc tan x, is read "theta is the angle whose tangent is x." The symbol "$\tan^{-1}x$" may be used for "arc tan x." *See also* ARC SINE.

AREA, the surface of any plane geometric figure as measured in square units. In rectangle *ABCD* (see figure), the number of unit squares (i.e., squares whose side is 1) that would fill the interior surface of the figure is 15. Thus, the area of rectangle *ABCD* is said to be 15 square units. The square unit is the most commonly used unit of area measure and is certainly the most convenient. However, the choice of the unit of area measure is arbitrary: triangular units might be used, or circular units, as is shown in the figure. *See* TABLE NO. 4.

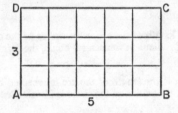

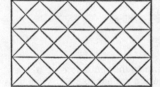

AREA BETWEEN TWO CURVES. If the curves $y = f(x)$ and $y = g(x)$ enclose a region like that shaded in the figure, then the area of this region may be found by integrating the height of the region, given by the difference in the values of the two functions, between the figure's left and right limits. These limits are usually found algebraically, by solving the equation $f(x) = g(x)$.
   Ex.: What is the area of the region enclosed by the curves $y = x^2$ and $y = x^3$?
   Sol.: These curves intersect where $x^2 = x^3$, or at $x = 0$ and at $x = 1$. Over this interval, x^2 is larger than x^3, so the height at x of the enclosed region is given by

$$h(x) = x^2 - x^3.$$

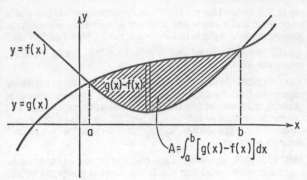

The area is then:

$$A = \int_{0}^{1} h(x)\, dx = \int_{0}^{1} [x^2 - x^3]dx = \frac{x^3}{3} - \frac{x^4}{4}\Big]_{0}^{1}$$
$$= \frac{1}{3} - \frac{1}{4} = \frac{1}{12}.$$

See also AREA; AREA UNDER CURVE; DEFINITE INTEGRAL.

AREA OF A GEOMETRIC SOLID, the sum of the AREA of its lateral faces and then the area of its BASE (or bases). This is called its total area. The area of the faces is called the lateral area.

AREA UNDER A CURVE. If $y = f(x)$ defines a continuous function of x on a CLOSED INTERVAL $[a, b]$, the AREA of the region bounded from above by the curve $y = f(x)$, from below by the x-axis, on the left by the vertical line $x = a$, and on the right by the vertical line $x = b$, may be approximated by dividing the region into strips which are rectangles. The area of the region is then approximately equal to the sum of the areas of the rectangles (Fig. 1). If the rectangles are made thinner, the approxi

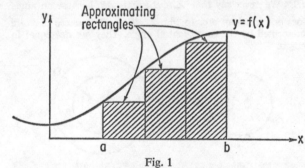

Fig. 1

mation to the area under the curve will be more accurate (Fig. 2). If the number of rectangles were allowed to increase without bound (the thinnest rectangles) the area under the curve would be exactly equal to the sum of the areas of the rectangles. Thus, the area under a curve is defined as the limit of the sums of inscribed rectangles as the number of rectangles increases without bound.
   By the MEAN VALUE THEOREM and the FUNDAMENTAL THEOREM OF CALCULUS, it can be shown that the limit of the areas of the inscribed rectangles is the DEFINITE INTEGRAL of $f(x)$ from a to b. Thus, the area under the curve $y = f(x)$ on a closed interval $[a, b]$ is given by

$$A = \int_{a}^{b} f(x)dx.$$

In calculating the area under a curve, let

$$A = \int_{a}^{b} f(x)dx = F(x)\Big]_{a}^{b} = F(b) - F(a).$$

Ex. 1: Find the area under the curve $y = x^2$ between 1 and 2. (See Fig. 3.)

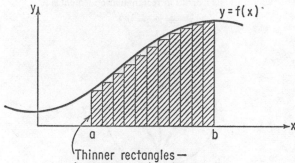

Thinner rectangles—
better approximation.

$$A = \int_a^b f(x)\,dx$$

Area = limit

Fig. 2

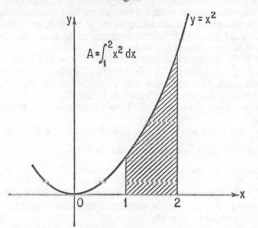

$$A = \int_1^2 x^2\,dx$$

$y = x^2$

Fig. 3

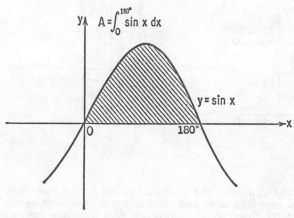

$$A = \int_0^{180°} \sin x\,dx$$

$y = \sin x$

Fig. 4

Sol.:

$$\int_1^2 x^2\,dx = \frac{x^3}{3}\bigg]_1^2$$

$$= \frac{2^3}{3} - \frac{1^3}{3} = \frac{7}{3}.$$

The area is 7/3 square units.

Ex. 2: Find the area under one arch of the sine curve. (See Fig. 4.)

Sol.: The left boundary of the first arch of the sine curve is $x = 0$. The right boundary is $x = 180°$.

$$A = \int_{.}^{180} \sin x\,dx$$

$$A = -\cos X\bigg]_0^{180}$$

$$A = -\cos 180° - (-\cos 0°)$$

$$A = -(-1) - (-1)$$

$$A = 1 + 1$$

$$A = 2 \text{ square units.}$$

ARGAND DIAGRAM (ahr′-gand dahy′-a-gram), a geometric representation of a COMPLEX NUMBER $z = x + iy$ as a point in the xy-plane, or as a VECTOR from the origin. In such a diagram, two axes are drawn perpendicular to each other (see Fig. 1), and the horizontal axis (x-axis) is called the real axis (or axis of reals) while the vertical axis (y-axis) is called the imaginary axis (or axis of imaginaries).

In Fig. 1, point A is located by moving 4 units in a positive direction along the real axis and then 3 units in a positive direction along the vertical line parallel to the imaginary axis.

A complex number represented as the vector $\overrightarrow{OA}$ from the origin to point A is shown in Fig. 2. *See also* COORDINATES, POLAR.

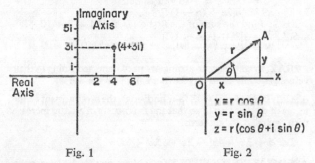

$x = r \cos \theta$
$y = r \sin \theta$
$z = r (\cos \theta + i \sin \theta)$

Fig. 1   Fig. 2

ARGUMENT, of a COMPLEX NUMBER is the AMPLITUDE of the complex number; of a FUNCTION, is the independent VARIABLE. The arguments in a table of values of a function are those elements in the DOMAIN of the function. Thus, in a table of TRIGONOMETRIC FUNCTIONS, the angles for which the functions are given are the arguments.

ARITHMETIC (u-rith′-muh-tik), the study of the positive REAL NUMBERS and ZERO. The term "arithmetic" usually refers to numerical computation involving the four fundamental operations: ADDITION, SUBTRACTION, MULTIPLICATION, and DIVISION that are performed in accordance with the AXIOMS for real numbers. This modern meaning of arithmetic is much more restrictive than that used before the 16th century, when arithmetic was called *arithmetica*, and included the study of POWERS and ROOTS, and investigations into such relationships among numbers as the PYTHAGOREAN THEOREM. Thus, classical *arithmetica* was the philosophical study of numbers and their properties that modern mathematicians call *Number Theory*.

The modern study of arithmetic, i.e., computation, was known by the Greeks and Romans as *logistics*, and was quite distinct from their *arithmetica*.

ARITHMETIC MEANS, all the terms between the first and the last terms of an ARITHMETIC PROGRESSION. The four arithmetic means in 1, 3, 5, 7, 9, 11, are 3, 5, 7, and 9. *See also* MEANS.

ARITHMETIC PROGRESSION, a number SERIES in which each term may be obtained from the preceding one by adding a CONSTANT. The constant is called the COMMON DIFFERENCE. In the series $1 + 4 + 7 + 10 + \cdots$ the common difference is 3. In the series $8 - 2 - 12 - \cdots$ the common difference is -10.

If a is the first term of an arithmetic progression, and d is the common difference, the sequence is $a, a + d, a + 2d, a + 3d$. So the nth, or general, term of any arithmetic progression is $a + (n - 1)d$. If l represents the nth, or last, term in an arithmetic progression the formula is

$$l = a + (n - 1)d.$$

With this formula, the value of any of the quantities l, a, n or d may be found if three are known.

Ex. 1: Find the 25th term of the arithmetic progression $4 + 7 + 10 + 13 + \cdots$.

Sol.: Since $a = 4$, $d = 3$, and $n = 25$, $l = 4 + (25 - 1)3 = 76$.

Ex. 2: Insert 5 arithmetic means between 12 and 30.

$$a = 12, l = 30, n = 7$$

using the formula $l = a + (n - 1)d$, solve for d.

Sol.: $30 = 12 + (7 - 1)d$
            $d = 3.$

The arithmetic means are 15, 18, 21, 24, 27.

The formula for finding the sum S of n terms of an arithmetic progression, if a is the first term and l is the last term, is:

$S = \frac{1}{2}n(a + l)$, or by substituting the formula,
$l = a + (n - 1)d$, then
$S = \frac{1}{2}n[a + a + (n - 1)d]$ or
$S = \frac{1}{2}n[2a + (n - 1)d]$.

Ex. 3: Find the sum of the first 6 terms of $4 + 7 + 10 +$.

Sol.: $S = \frac{6}{2}[2(4) + (6 - 1)3]$
      $S = 3(8 + 15) = 69.$

ARRAY, in statistics, an arrangement of items according to their value, generally from largest to smallest or vice versa.

ASCENDING POWERS (a-sehnd'-ing), the arrangement of the terms of a POLYNOMIAL so that the EXPONENTS of a letter increase with each succeeding term.

Ex.: $6 + 3x + 4x^2 - 2x^3 - 5x^4 + x^5.$

ASSOCIATIVE PROPERTY (u-soh'-see-ay-tiv). A binary operation, *, is said to be associative on the set, $S = \{a, b, c, \cdots\}$, if

$$(a * b) * c = a * (b * c);$$

i.e., if the operation may be performed on elements of S in any grouping. E.g., both addition and multiplication are associative on the real number system, since for any real numbers, a, b, c,

$(a + b) + c = a + (b + c)$ and $a \cdot (b \cdot c) = (a \cdot b) \cdot c.$
E.g., $(4 + 3) + 2 = 4 + (3 + 2)$ and $4(3 \times 2) = (4 \times 3)2$
       $7 + 2 = 4 + 5$ $4(6) = (12)2$
         $9 = 9.$ $24 = 24.$

However, neither subtraction nor division are associative on the set of real numbers, since in general

$(a - b) - c = a - b - c \neq a - (b - c) = a - b + c$
and $a/(b/c) = ac/b \neq (a/b)/c = a/bc.$
E.g., $(4 - 3) - 2 = 1 - 2 = -1 \neq 4 - (3 - 2) = 4 - 1 = 3$
and $4/(3/2) = 4(2/3) = 8/3 \neq (4/3)/2 = 4/(3 \times 2) = 2/3.$

ASSUMPTION (u-sump'-shun), a statement accepted without question for purposes of mathematical proof. A mathematical assumption is called an AXIOM or POSTULATE.

ASTROID (as'-troid), a HYPOCYCLOID of four cusps. The parametric equations of the astroid are:

$$x = a \cos^3 \theta$$
$$y = a \sin^3 \theta$$

The equation of the astroid in rectangular coordinates is

$$x^{2/3} + y^{2/3} = a^{2/3}$$

Astroid

ASYMPTOTE (as'-simp-toht), a straight line to which a curve approximates more and more closely (but never meets) as the distance from the ORIGIN increases. Some curves, e.g., CIRCLES, have no asymptotes; others have many: two TRIGONOMETRIC CURVES, the graphs of the TANGENT OF AN ANGLE, and the COTANGENT OF AN ANGLE behave asymptotically every 2π (360°) interval of the independent VARIABLE.

Ex. 1: Find the asymptotes of the curve $y = 1/x$ for $x > 0$.

Sol.: As x approaches 0, $1/x$ exceeds all limit. As x increases without limit, $1/x$ approaches 0. Hence, both the coordinate axes are asymptotes of this curve, as in Fig. 1.

If a curve is given as the ratio of two functions of x, as in $y = \dfrac{x_2 + 2}{x_2 - 1}$, the curve will have vertical asymptotes whenever the denominator is zero and the numerator is not.

Ex. 2: Locate the asymptotes of the curve $y = \dfrac{x_2 + 2}{x_2 - 1}$.

Sol.: The denominator is $x^2 - 1$, which is zero when $x = 1$ or $x = -1$. The vertical asymptotes are therefore the lines $x = 1$ and $x = -1$, as in Fig. 1b.

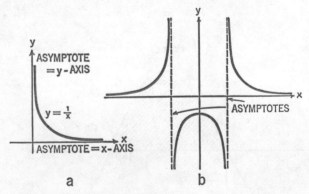

Fig. 1

The asymptotes of a HYPERBOLA are the straight lines which the hyperbola more and more closely approximates as the distance from the origin increases. Each hyperbola has two asymptotes. If the hyperbola is given in standard form $x^2/a^2 - y^2/b^2 = 1$, its asymptotes may be found as follows:

$$y^2/b^2 = x^2/a^2 - 1;$$
$$y^2 = x^2 b^2/a^2 - b^2;$$
$$y^2/x^2 = b^2/a^2 - b^2/x^2.$$

As x exceeds all limit, b^2/x^2 approaches 0, so y^2/x^2 approaches b^2/a^2. Hence the asymptotes are the lines $y = (b/a)x$ and $y = -(b/a)x$. See Fig. 2.

Ex.: Find the asymptotes of the hyperbola $x^2/4 - y^2/9 = 1$.
Sol.: Here, $a^2 = 4$, $b^2 = 9$. The asymptotes are therefore the lines:

$$y = (b/a)x = (3/2)x$$

and

$$y = (-b/a)x = (-3/2)x.$$

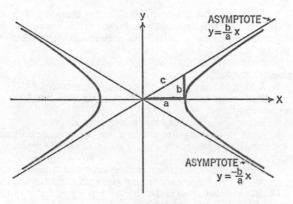

Fig. 2

ASYMPTOTIC CONE OF HYPERBOLOID OF TWO SHEETS (as-simp-toh'-tic hahy-pur'-boh-loid).

The standard HYPERBOLOID of two sheets (see Fig. 1a) has the equation:

$$x^2/a^2 + y^2/b^2 - z^2/c^2 = -1.$$

Its asymptotic cone (see Fig. 1b) separates the two halves of the hyperboloid, and it is the asymptotic surface of each half. The equation of the cone is:

$$x^2/a^2 + y^2/b^2 - z^2/c^2 = 0.$$

Any plane passed through the common axis of the hyperboloid and asymptotic cone will intersect the hyperboloid in a HYPERBOLA, and it will intersect the cone in a corresponding pair of ASYMPTOTES to this hyperbola. Hence the asymptotic cone can be generated by revolving such a pair of asymptotes about the common AXIS, just as the hyperboloid can be generated by revolving the corresponding hyperbola about the same axis.

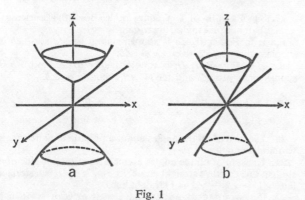

Fig. 1

AUTHORITY, for statements in proofs, *see* FORMAL PROOF.

AUXILIARY LINE (awg-zil'-yah-ree), a line that may be added to a geometric figure to simplify proof of a THEOREM or CONSTRUCTION. It is usually dotted to distinguish it from the given lines. E.g., to prove that the BASE ANGLES of an ISOSCELES TRIANGLE are equal, the BISECTOR OF AN ANGLE is constructed. If

$\triangle ABC$ (see figure) is isosceles, base AB (*see* BASE OF A GEOMETRIC FIGURE), VERTEX angle C is bisected. Line CD is an auxiliary line.

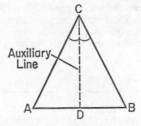

AVERAGE VALUE OF A FUNCTION. The average value V_a of a function $f(x)$ over the interval (a, b) is defined to be

$$V_a = \frac{\int_a^b f(x)dx}{b - a}.$$

Since $\int_a^b f(x)dx = A$, the AREA UNDER A CURVE $y = f(x)$, the average value V_a may be interpreted graphically as the altitude of a rectangle (the shaded rectangle in the figure) with base $= b - a$ and area $= A$.

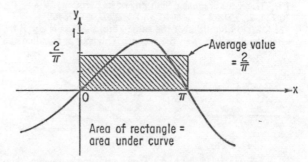

Ex.: What is the average value of the function $f(x) = \sin x$ over the first arch?
Sol.: The first arch extends from $x = 0$ to $x = \pi$.

Hence:

$$V_a = \frac{\int_0^\pi \sin x \, dx}{\pi - 0} = \frac{\left. -\cos x \right]_0^\pi}{\pi}$$

$$= \frac{-\cos\pi - (-\cos 0)}{\pi} = \frac{1 - (-1)}{\pi}$$

$$= \frac{2}{\pi}.$$

See also MEAN VALUE THEOREM FOR INTEGRALS.

AXIAL SYMMETRY, *see* SYMMETRY.

AXIOM (aks'-ee-um), a general mathematical statement accepted without proof to prove other, less obvious statements. It is impossible to "prove everything" without the fallacy of CIRCULAR REASONING. But mathematicians have always tried to make the least possible number of ASSUMPTIONS. The following are axioms of EQUALITY and of INEQUALITY:

1. If equals are added to equals, the SUMS are equal (ADDITION AXIOM).
If $x = 3$, and $y = 4$, then $x + y = 7$.
2. If equals are subtracted from equals, the DIFFERENCES are equal (SUBTRACTION AXIOM).
If $x = a$, and $y = b$, then $x - y = a - b$.

3. If equals are multiplied by equals, the PRODUCTS are equal (MULTIPLICATION AXIOM).

If $x = 3$, then $5x = 15$.

4. If equals are divided by equals, the QUOTIENTS are equal (DIVISION AXIOM). The DIVISOR may not be ZERO.

If $4x = 20$, then $x = 5$.

If the divisor is two the axiom may be stated, "Halves of equals are equal."

Ex.:

A———M———B   C———N———D

If $AB = CD$, and M and N are MIDPOINTS, then $AM = CN$.

5. A quantity may be substituted for its equal.

If $x + y = 8$, and $y = z$, then $x + z = 8$.

6. Quantities equal to the same quantity, or to equal quantities, are equal to each other.

Ex. 1: If $x = a$ and $y = a$, then $x = y$.

Ex. 2: If $x = m$, and $y = n$, and $m = n$, then $x = y$.

7. Like POWERS, or like ROOTS, of equals are equal.

Ex. 1: If $x = 4$, then $x^2 = 4^2$, or $x^2 = 16$.

Ex. 2: If $x^3 = 27$, then $\sqrt[3]{x^3} = \sqrt[3]{27}$, or $x = 3$.

8. A quantity equals itself. The word "identity" is used when this axiom is given as a reason for a statement. In $\triangle ACD$ and $\triangle CDB$ (Fig. 1), $CD = CD$.

9. The whole is equal to the sum of its parts.

In Fig. 2, $\angle BAC = \angle BAD + \angle DAC$.

10. The whole is greater than any of its parts.

In Fig. 2, $\angle BAC > \angle DAC$ and $\angle DAB < \angle BAC$.

11. Of two quantities of the same kind, the first is equal to, greater than, or less than the second. This axiom is called the

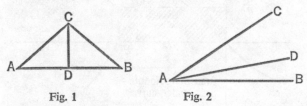

Fig. 1   Fig. 2

TRICHOTOMY LAW. If AB and CD are two line segments, then $AB = CD$, or $AB > CD$, or $AB < CD$.

12. If the first of three quantities is greater than the second (*see* INEQUALITY), and the second is greater than the third, then the first is greater than the third.

If $a > b$, and $b > c$, then $a > c$.

13. If equals are added to unequals, the sums are unequal in the same order.

Ex. 1: If $8 > 5$, and $3 = 3$, then $11 > 8$.

Ex. 2: If $2 < 7$, and $3 = 3$, then $5 < 10$.

14. If unequals are added to unequals in the same order, the sums are unequal in the same order.

If $8 > 5$, and $3 > 2$, then $11 > 7$.

15. If equals are subtracted from unequals, the differences are unequal in the same order.

Ex. 1: If $10 > 8$, and $4 = 4$, then $6 > 4$

Ex. 2: If $9 < 12$, and $6 = 6$, then $3 < 6$.

16. If unequals are subtracted from equals, the differences are unequal in the opposite order.

Ex. 1: If $10 = 10$, and $8 > 3$, then $2 < 7$.

Ex. 2: If $9 = 9$ and $3 < 5$, then $6 > 4$.

17. If unequals are multiplied by positive equals (*see* POSITIVE NUMBER), *the* products are unequal in the same order.

If $5 > 3$, then $15 > 9$.

18. If unequals are multiplied by negative equals (*see* NEGATIVE NUMBER), the products are unequal in the opposite order.

If $4 > 3$, then $-8 < -6$.

19. If unequals are divided by positive equals, the results are unequal in the same order.

If $12 > 9$, then $4 > 3$.

20. If unequals are divided by negative equals, the quotients are unequal in the opposite order.

If $20 > 16$, then $-5 < -4$.

The following are axioms in elementary geometry, having to do with points, lines, and geometric figures:

1. Any geometric figure can be moved without changing its size or shape.

2. Through two given POINTS only one straight LINE can be drawn.

3. A straight LINE SEGMENT is the shortest DISTANCE BETWEEN TWO POINTS. When applied to a TRIANGLE, this axiom may be stated: The sum of any two sides of a triangle is greater than the third side.

4. A straight line segment may be extended infinitely far in either direction.

5. A straight line segment has only one MIDPOINT.

6. Two straight lines in a plane are either PARALLEL LINES or intersecting lines.

7. Two straight lines may intersect at only one point.

8. Through a given point not on a line, there can be only one ine parallel to the given line. This is called the PARALLEL POSTULATE.

9. Only one PERPENDICULAR can be drawn to a straight line at a given point on the line, or from a given point not on the line.

10. The perpendicular is the shortest line segment that can be drawn from a given point to a given line.

11. In a PLANE, only one CIRCLE can be drawn with a given point as the center and a given segment as the RADIUS.

12. All radii of the same or of EQUAL CIRCLES are equal.

13. All DIAMETERS OF A CIRCLE, or of equal circles, are equal.

14. A straight line can intersect a circle at only two points.

15. An angle can be bisected by only one line (*see* BISECTOR OF AN ANGLE).

16. All RIGHT ANGLES are equal.

17. All STRAIGHT ANGLES are equal.

18. Complements of the same angle (*see* COMPLEMENTARY ANGLES), or of equal angles, are equal.

Ex. 1: In Fig. 3, if $\angle x$ is complementary to $\angle z$ and $\angle y$ is complementary to $\angle z$, then $\angle x = \angle y$.

Ex. 2: In Fig. 4, if $\angle x$ is complementary to $\angle m$ and $\angle y$ is complementary to $\angle n$ and $\angle m = \angle n$, then $\angle x = \angle y$.

Fig. 3   Fig. 4

19. Supplements of the same ıngle (*see* SUPPLEMENTARY ANGLES), or of equal angles, are equal.

Ex. 1: In Fig. 5, if $\angle a$ is supplementary to $\angle c$ and $\angle b$ is supplementary to $\angle c$, then $\angle a = \angle b$.

Ex. 2: In Fig. 6, if $\angle a$ is supplementary to $\angle c$ and $\angle b$ is supplementary to $\angle d$ and $\angle c = \angle d$, then $\angle a = \angle b$.

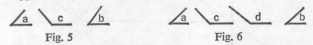

Fig. 5   Fig. 6

20. The sum of all the angles about a point in a plane equals two straight angles.

21. The sum of all the angles about a point on one side of a straight line equals a straight angle. In Fig. 7, if AB is a straight line, $\angle 1 + \angle 2 + \angle 3 = 1$ straight line.

22. If two ADJACENT ANGLES have their exterior sides in a straight line, they are supplementary. In Fig. 8, if AB is a straight line, then $\angle x$ is supplementary to $\angle y$.

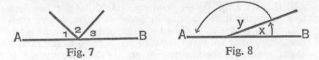

Fig. 7   Fig. 8

23. The exterior sides of two adjacent supplementary angles form a straight line. In Fig. 9, *AB* is a straight line.

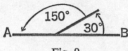

Fig. 9

AXIS (aks'-is), a straight line through the center of a plane or a solid figure, around which the parts are symmetrically arranged (see Fig. 1); also a line of reference, as in a GRAPH (see Fig. 2).

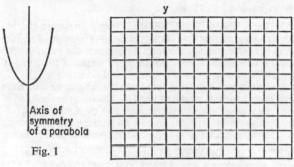

Axis of symmetry of a parabola

Fig. 1

x and y axes in the Rectangular coordinate system.

Fig. 2

AXIS, MAJOR, *see* MAJOR AXIS OF AN ELLIPSE.

AXIS, MINOR, *see* MINOR AXIS OF AN ELLIPSE.

AXIS OF SYMMETRY, if a figure possesses SYMMETRY, the line about which it is symmetric. Corresponding to any point on a symmetric figure there is another point called its symmetric image, at the same distance from the axis of symmetry but on the other side of it. The line segment through these two points is perpendicular to the axis and bisected by it. (See figure.)

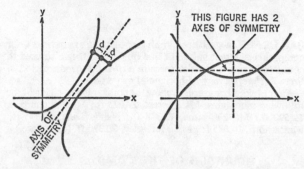

AXIS, POLAR, the fixed horizontal line directed to the right, or positively, from a point called the ORIGIN (see figure) in a system of polar coordinates (*see* COORDINATES, POLAR).

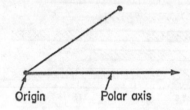

Origin   Polar axis

B

BAR GRAPH, a statistical graph (*see* GRAPHS, STATISTICAL), for comparing different values of like quantities. It is also used to compare increases and decreases in a quantity over a period of time. Bar graphs may be horizontal or vertical.

Ex.: Make a bar graph to show the comparative heights of the following mountains: Mt. Everest, 29,028 ft.; Mt. Kilimanjaro, 19,590 ft.; Mt. Fujiyama, 12,388 ft.; Nanda Devi, 25,645 ft.; Matterhorn, 14,685 ft.; Mt. McKinley, 20,320 ft. (See figure.)

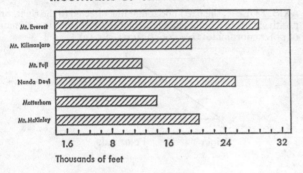

MOUNTAINS OF THE WORLD

Thousands of feet

BARYCENTER, *see* CENTER OF MASS.

BASE, in an exponential expression, the number that is used as a FACTOR a given number of times. In the expression, 3^4, where 3 is used as a factor 4 times, the 3 is the base. *See also* EXPONENTIAL NOTATION.

In PERCENTAGE, the base is the number of which the percent, or rate, is taken. In the example: Find 3% of 150; 150 is the base; 3% (or .03) is the rate; and the result, 4.5, is the percentage.

BASE ANGLES, of an ISOSCELES TRIANGLE, the two angles formed by the base (*see* BASE OF A GEOMETRIC FIGURE) and the equal sides of the triangle. In $\triangle ABC$ (Fig. 1), if $AB = BC$, angles A and C are the base angles. In an isosceles triangle the base angles are equal.

The base angles of a TRAPEZOID are the two angles formed by a base of the trapezoid and the legs of the trapezoid. Since a trapezoid has two bases, it has *two pairs* of base angles. In trapezoid $ABCD$ (Fig. 2) if BC // AD, one pair of base angles is $\angle B$ and $\angle C$, and the second pair is $\angle A$ and $\angle D$. In an isosceles trapezoid the base angles are equal. Thus, if $AB = CD$ in Fig. 2, $\angle B = \angle C$ and $\angle A = \angle D$.

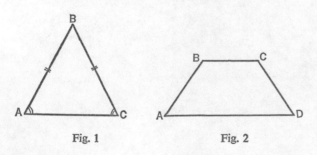

Fig. 1   Fig. 2

BASE e, the base used in the system of natural logarithms (*see* LOGARITHMS, NATURAL). Its value to 5 decimal places is 2.71828. The expression $\log_e 25$ may be written ln 25.

BASE OF A GEOMETRIC FIGURE, for a plane figure, the side to which an ALTITUDE OF A GEOMETRIC FIGURE is drawn. The base of an ISOSCELES TRIANGLE is the side opposite the vertex angle; it is the side included between the equal angles of the triangle. Bases of a TRAPEZOID are the two parallel sides.

In a GEOMETRIC SOLID, the base is the plane figure on which the solid is said to rest. PRISMS are named according to the kind of bases they have; rectangular, square, and triangular prisms. A rectangular prism having a square for a base is a CUBE. PYRAMIDS and CONES have one base; prisms and CYLINDERS have two bases.

BASE OF A LOGARITHM, the arbitrarily selected number which is raised to a power (the LOGARITHM) to obtain a given number. If 3 is the base, the logarithm of 81 is 4, since $3^4 = 81$. In logarithmic notation, this is written $\log_3 81 = 4$. In like manner, $\log_4 64 = 3$, $\log_2 8 = 3$, and $\log_5 25 = 2$. Any positive number except 1 can be used as a base in a system of logarithms.

"Log" is used to mean that the base is 10, and the system is known as *common logarithms;* "ln" is used to mean that the base is e, and the system is known as *natural logarithms* (*see* LOGARITHM, NATURAL). The base 2 is also becoming more common now in computer calculations.

BAYES' THEOREM, of CONDITIONAL PROBABILITY. If A_1, $A_2, \ldots, A_k$ denote k mutually exclusive events, none of which is impossible and exactly one of which must occur, and B denotes some event that can occur after any one of the k A-events has occurred, the probability that a particular one of the A-events, say A_j, preceded the occurrence of Event B, when Event B is known to have occurred, is given by

$$P(A_i|B) = \frac{P(A_j)P(B|A_j)}{P(A_1)P(B|A_1) + \cdots + P(A_k)P(B|A_k)}$$

The theorem is named for its originator, Thomas Bayes (1700–61), an English clergyman who was also an amateur mathematician.

Ex.: The maker of a small electrical gadget gets the components from three different suppliers. 500 parts per day from Supplier 1, 3 percent of which are defective; 1000 from Supplier 2, of which 2 percent are defective; 2000 from Supplier 3, of which $1\frac{1}{2}$ percent are defective. If, upon testing, a gadget is found to have a defective component, what is the probability that the component came from Supplier 2?

Define the following events: A_1, the component came from Supplier 1; A_2, the component came from Supplier 2; A_3, it came from Supplier 3; B, the component is defective.

$P(A_1) = 1/7.$	$P(B\|A_1) = 0.03.$
$P(A_2) = 2/7.$	$P(B\|A_2) = 0.02.$
$P(A_3) = 4/7.$	$P(B\|A_3) = 0.015$

By Bayes' Theorem,

$$P(A_2|B) = \frac{\frac{2}{7}(0.02)}{\frac{1}{7}(0.03) + \frac{2}{7}(0.02) + \frac{4}{7}(0.015)} = 0.31$$

BEARING, for indicating direction in air and sea navigation, the number of degrees in the angle whose initial SIDE is a line due north and whose terminal side is determined by a clockwise rotation. In the figure, the bearing of B from A is the number of degrees in θ.

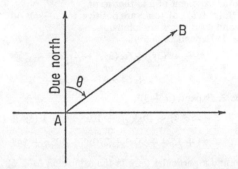

BERNOULLI TRIAL (bur-noo'-lee), in statistics, each of the trials in a BINOMIAL EXPERIMENT. A Bernoulli trial is also called a binomial trial.

BETA ERROR. In statistics, the type of error that is made when a NULL HYPOTHESIS is accepted although not true. The probability of making such an error is denoted by β. The beta error is also called the *Type II Error*. Although there is usually no specific relationship between the alpha and beta errors, as one is made smaller, the other becomes larger.

BIASED STATISTIC (bahy'-est), in statistics, when estimating the parameter of a random sample, if the expected value, E, of an estimator is not equal to the parameter it is supposed to estimate, the estimator is said to be biased.

BICONDITIONAL, LOGICAL, a PROPOSITION formed from two given propositions by using the connective "if and only if." If the two propositions are denoted by p and q, the biconditional "p if and only if q," may be written $p \leftrightarrow q$. It may also be expressed as "p is a necessary and sufficient condition for q." A biconditional statement is true if both propositions are true, or if both are false. An example of a logical biconditional in elementary geometry is "For all triangles t, t is isosceles if and only if its base angles are equal." The statement is true since any particular triangle is either isosceles and has equal base angles or it is not isosceles and has unequal base angles. A logical biconditional is also called an **equivalence**.

BIENAYME-CHEBYSHEV INEQUALITY, *see* CHEBYSHEV'S THEOREM.

BIJECTION, from set A to set B, a one-to-one correspondence between A and B. Hence, a bijection from A to B is a mapping from A into B that is an INJECTION and a SURJECTION.

BINAC, *see* COMPUTER.

BINARY DIGIT, *see* COMPUTER.

BINARY NUMBER SYSTEM (bahy'-nu-ree), a number system whose base is 2, and which uses two symbols, commonly 0 and 1. The place value of the digits in the binary system are powers of 2: 2^0, 2^1, 2^2, 2^3, 2^4, etc., or units, two, four, eight, 16, etc. Thus, the binary number 11011001 would be evaluated as follows:

2^7	2^6	2^5	2^4	2^3	2^2	2^1	2^0
128	64	32	16	8	4	2	1
1	1	0	1	1	0	0	1

Hence, the decimal equivalent of 11011001 is

$$1 \times 128 + 1 \times 64 + 0 \times 32 + 1 \times 16 + 1 \times 8 + 0 \times 4 + 0 \times 2 + 1 \times 1.$$
$$128 + 64 + 0 + 16 + 8 + 0 + 0 + 1 = 217.$$

Therefore, 11011001 in the binary system is equivalent to 217 in the decimal system.

Any number can be uniquely expressed as the sum of powers of 2. Thus, any number can be represented in the binary system. For example, the decimal number 437 can be expressed as powers of 2 as follows:

$$437 = 256 + 128 + 32 + 16 + 4 + 1$$
$$= 2^8 + 2^7 + 2^5 + 2^4 + 2^2 + 2^0.$$

In binary notation, placing zero in the position corresponding to the missing powers of 2, 437 would be written 11011011.

BINARY OPERATION, in modern algebra, a MAPPING, $*$, on a set, $\{a, b, c, \ldots\}$ which assigns to each ordered pair of elements, (a, b), a unique image, $a * b$; e.g., *see* ADDITION, MULTIPLICATION, SUBTRACTION, DIVISION. For the most common AXIOMS of binary operations also *see* CLOSURE; ASSOCIATIVE PROPERTY; COMMUTATIVE PROPERTY; DISTRIBUTIVE PROPERTY.

BINOMIAL (bahy-no'-mee-ul), an ALGEBRAIC EXPRESSION consisting of two terms.
Exs.: $a + b$; $4xy - 9$; and $3a + 2a/3b$.
Binomials whose terms have the same literal factors may be added by combining the SIMILAR TERMS. E.g., $(2x - 3y) + (6x + y) = (8x - 2y)$.
Any two binomials may be multiplied. Multiplication may be performed by applying the DISTRIBUTIVE PROPERTY and the ASSOCIATIVE PROPERTY.
Ex. 1: Multiply $(3x + y)$ by $(5x + 2y)$.
Sol.: Distribute $(3x + y)$:

$$(3x + y)5x + (3x + y)2y.$$

Distribute $5x$ and $2y$:

$$(3x)(5x) + (y)(5x) + (3x)(2y) + (y)(2y).$$

Associate and multiply:

$$15x^2 + 5xy + 6xy + 2y^2.$$

Associate and add:

$$15x^2 + 11xy + 2y^2.$$

The multiplication may also be performed as it is with numbers:

Ex. 2:
$$
\begin{array}{rl}
3x + y & \\
5x + 2y & \\
\hline
6xy + 2y^2 & \text{Multiplying by } 2y \\
15x^2 + 5xy & \text{Multiplying by } 5x \\
\hline
15x^2 + 11xy + 2y^2 & \text{Adding}
\end{array}
$$

The shortest method for multiplying two binomials is to form the products of the first term of each binomial, the last term of each, and the sum of the products of the first with the last and the last with the first.

Ex. 3:
$$+15x^2 \quad +2y^2$$
$$(3x + y)(5x + 2y)$$
$$+5xy$$
$$+6xy$$
$$\overline{+11xy}$$

The product is $15x^2 + 11xy + 2y^2$.
The following rules for special products of two binomials are often helpful:
   1. $(a + b)(a + b) = a^2 + 2ab + b^2$.
   Ex.: $(a + 3)(a + 3) = a^2 + 6a + 9$.
   2. $(a - b)(a - b) = a^2 - 2ab + b^2$.
   Ex.: $(a - 5)(a - 5) = a^2 - 10a + 25$.
   3. $(a + b)(a - b) = a^2 - b^2$.
   Ex.: $(a + 4)(a - 4) = a^2 - 16$.
   4. $(a + b)(a + c) = a^2 + a(b + c) + bc$.
   Ex.: $(a + 3)(a + 2) = a^2 + 5a + 6$.
   5. $(a - b)(a - c) = a^2 - a(b + c) + bc$.

Ex.: $(a - 5)(a - 3) = a^2 - 8a + 15$.
  6. $(ax + b)(cx + d) = acx^2 + x(ad + bc) + bd$.
  Ex.: $(3x + 2)(4x + 3) = 12x^2 + 17x + 6$.
See also, BINOMIAL, SQUARING A.

BINOMIAL DISTRIBUTION, in statistics, the probability function, $f(x)$, that gives the probability of x successes in the n trials.

$$f(x) = \frac{n!}{x!(n-x)}\pi^x(1 - \pi)^{n-x},$$

where x can take on any value from 0 to n.

The PARAMETERS of the binomial distribution are n and π: As soon as n and π are specified, the distribution is completely specified. The mean of the binomial distribution with parameters n and π is $n\pi$, and the variance is $n\pi(1 - \pi)$.

Ex.: The probability that a basketball player will make a foul shot is equal to .7 and is constant, and each foul shot attempt is independent of every other attempt. If he shoots 5 foul shots, what is the probability that he makes 4 of them? Here $m = 5$, $x = 4, \pi = .7$, and

$$P(4 \text{ out of } 5) = \frac{5!}{4!1!}(.7)^4(.3)^1 = \frac{120}{24}(.7)^4(.3)^1 = .360.$$

What is the probability that he makes at least 3?

$$\begin{aligned}P(\text{at least } 5) &= P(3 \text{ or } 4 \text{ or } 5) \\ &= P(3) + P(4) + P(5) \\ &= \frac{5!}{3!2!}(.7)^3(.3)^2 + \frac{5!}{4!1!}(.7)^4(.3)^1 + \frac{5!}{5!0!}(.7)^5 \\ &= .309 + .360 + .168 = .837.\end{aligned}$$

BINOMIAL, EXPANDING A, the process for finding the POLYNOMIAL obtained when the sum, or difference, of two numbers is raised to a power. While the expansions may be found by multiplication, the usual FORMULA is a set of rules called the BINOMIAL THEOREM.

BINOMIAL EXPERIMENT, in STATISTICS, a situation (either an experiment or a natural phenomenon) that satisfies the following conditions: (1) the situation consists of a fixed number, n, of trials; (2) every trial has only two outcomes, called "success" and "failure"; (3) every trial is independent of every other trial; and (4) the probability of success, π, is constant from trial to trial. Each of the trials is called a *binomial trial* or *Bernoulli trial*.

BINOMIAL, SQUARING A. The SQUARE of a BINOMIAL is always a TRINOMIAL.
  1. The first term of the trinomial is the square of the first term of the binomial.
  2. The middle term of the trinomial is twice the product of the two terms.
  3. The last term of the trinomial is the square of the second term of the binomial.
  4. The first and third terms are always positive. The middle term is positive, if the square is the sum of two numbers; and it is negative if the square is the difference of two numbers.
  Ex. 1: $(x + 3)^2 = x^2 + 6x + 9$.
  Ex. 2: $(2x - 3y)^2 = 4x^2 - 12xy + 9y^2$.
  Ex. 3: $(x - \frac{1}{2})^2 = x^2 - x + \frac{1}{4}$.
  Ex. 4: $(6 - a)^2 = 36 - 12a + a^2$.

BINOMIAL THEOREM, a set of rules for raising a BINOMIAL to any given POWER.
  If n is a power to which the binomial $(a + b)$ is raised, the following rules apply to the expansion of all binomials:
  1. The number of terms is $n + 1$.
  2. The first term is a^n and the last term is b^n.
  3. The EXPONENT of a decreases by 1 in each succeeding term and the exponent of b increases by 1 in each succeeding term.
  4. The sum of the exponents of a and b in any term is n.
  5. The COEFFICIENT of the first term is 1, of the second term n.

To find the coefficient of any term multiply the preceding term by the exponent of a in the preceding term and divide by 1 more than the exponent of b in that term.
  6. In $(a + b)^n$, all terms are positive; in $(a - b)^n$ odd terms are plus and even terms are minus.
  Ex. 1: Expand $(x - 3y)$:

$$x^4 - 4x^3(3y) + 6x^2(3y)^2 - 4x(3y)^3 + (3y)^4$$
or
$$x^4 - 12x^3y + 54x^2y^2 - 108xy^3 + 81y^4.$$

Ex. 2: Expand $(x + 3)^5$:

$$x^5 + 5x^4(3) + 10x^3(3)^2 + 10x^2(3)^3 + 5x(3)^4 + (3)^5$$
or
$$x^4 + 15x^4 + 90x^3 + 270x^2 + 405x + 243.$$

To find a particular term in the expansion $(a + b)^n$, without finding all of the preceding terms, the following rule may be used. To find the rth term:
  1. The EXPONENT of a is $n - (r - 1)$ or $(n - r + 1)$.
  2. The exponent of b is $(r - 1)$.
  3. The NUMERATOR of the COEFFICIENT has $(r - 1)$ FACTORS:

$$n(-1)(n - 2) \cdots (n - r + 2).$$

  4. The DENOMINATOR of the coefficient is $(r - 1)!$ *See* FACTORIAL NOTATION.
  5. In the expansion $(a + b)^n$, all terms are positive. In the expansion $(a - b)^n$, even numbered terms are negative, the others are positive.
  Ex.: Find the 6th term of $(x - y)^{11}$.
Since $n = 11$, $r = 6$, $(r - 1) = 5$, $(n - r + 1) = 6$, and $(n - r + 2) = 7$, the 6th term is

$$-\frac{11 \cdot 10 \cdot 9 \cdot 8 \cdot 7}{5 \cdot 4 \cdot 3 \cdot 2 \cdot 1} x^6y^5 = -462x^6y^5.$$

See also PASCAL'S TRIANGLE.

BINOMIAL TRIAL, *see* BERNOULLI TRIAL.

BISECTOR, a line, a POINT, or a plane that divides a figure into two equal parts. The point that divides a LINE SEGMENT into two equal parts is called a MIDPOINT.

BISECTOR OF AN ANGLE, the line that divides an ANGLE into two equal parts. An angle may have one and only one bisector.
  To construct the bisector of given $\angle ABC$ (see Fig. 1) using a compass, with a convenient RADIUS and with VERTEX B as a center, draw an arc cutting AB at D and BC at E. With E and D as centers, construct arcs intersecting at F. Draw BF the bisector of $\angle ABC$.
  Since radii of the same or of equal circles are equal, $BE = BD$ and $EF = FD$; $BF = BF$ by identity. Then $\triangle BEF \cong \triangle BDF$ (S.S.S.) and $\triangle EBF \cong \triangle FBD$ (corresponding parts of congruent triangles are equal).
  The BISECTOR of an EXTERIOR ANGLE of a triangle divides the opposite side externally into two segments that have the same ratio as the other two sides of the triangle. (*See* EXTERNAL DIVISION.) In $\triangle ABC$ (Fig. 2), if CE bisects exterior $\angle BCD$, then $AE/EB = AC/BC$.

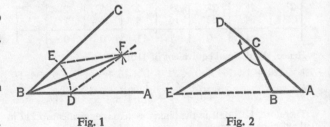

Fig. 1   Fig. 2

Ex.: If $AB = 6$, $BC = 9$, and $AC = 12$, find the segments made by the bisector of exterior angle at C. Substituting known values in the formula:

$$\frac{AE}{EB} = \frac{AC}{BC}$$
$$\frac{EB + 6}{EB} = \frac{12}{9}$$
$$9EB + 54 = 12EB$$
$$EB = 18$$
$$AE = 24.$$

If the equations of two intersecting lines are given, the equation of the bisector of the angle formed by the intersecting lines is found by using the fact that the distance of any point on the bisector of the angle is equidistant from the two lines. However, if DIRECTED DISTANCES are considered these distances will be opposite in sign. Thus, the locus of all points such that $d = -d'$ in Fig. 3 is the bisector of the angle between l_1 and l_2.

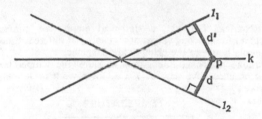

Fig. 3

Ex.: Find the line which bisects the smaller of the two angles between the lines $y = 2x$ and $y = 4x$.

Sol.: In standard first degree form, these equations are $2x - y = 0$ and $4x - y = 0$. To calculate the equation of points P for which $d = -d'$, use the formula for the DISTANCE FROM A POINT TO A LINE:

$$D = \frac{Ax + By + c}{\sqrt{A^2 + B^2}},$$ and substituting for d and d', gives,

$$\frac{2x - y}{\sqrt{4 + 1}} = -\frac{4x - y}{\sqrt{16 + 1}}$$
$$\sqrt{17}(2x - y) = (-4x + y)\sqrt{5}$$
$$2\sqrt{17}x - \sqrt{17}y = -4\sqrt{5}x + \sqrt{5}y$$
$$y = \left(\frac{2\sqrt{17} + 4\sqrt{5}}{\sqrt{17} + \sqrt{5}}\right)x.$$

Note that the slope of the bisector is $(2\sqrt{17} + 4\sqrt{5}/\sqrt{17} + \sqrt{5})$. This slope is not halfway between the slopes of l_1 and l_2; in general, the slope of the bisector of an angle is not midway between the slopes of the lines.

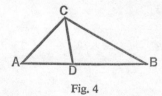

Fig. 4

The bisector of an interior angle of a triangle divides the side opposite the angle into segments proportional to the adjacent sides. In $\triangle ABC$, if CD bisects $\angle C$, then $AD/BD = AC/BC$. (See Fig. 4.)

Ex.: If $AB = 14$, $AC = 9$, and $BC = 12$, how long are the segments of AB formed by the BISECTOR of angle C?

$$\frac{AD}{14 - AD} = \frac{9}{12}, \text{ or } \frac{x}{14 - x} = \frac{3}{4}$$
$$4x = 42 - 3x$$
$$7x = 42$$
$$x = 6.$$

The two segments of AB are 6 and 8.

BISECTOR, PERPENDICULAR, see PERPENDICULAR BISECTOR OF A LINE SEGMENT.

BIT, a term coined from *binary digit*. It is the amount of information required to specify one of two alternatives, for example, to distinguish between 0 and 1 in binary notation, in information theory, and in computer terminology. The term bit is also used to define a unit of capacity in a storage device. The capacity in bits is the logarithm to the base two of the number of possible states of the device. A magnetic core, for example, has a flux flowing in one of two opposite directions and can therefore carry one bit of information. The presence or absence of a punched hole in a computer card can convey one bit of information. To represent four possible states (both cores magnetized in one direction, both in the other, the first one way and the second the other, and the reverse), two cores are necessary. Thus, to be able to indicate 16 states, it is necessary to have four indicating cores, and the capacity therefore will be four bits of information ($\log_2 16 = 4$). *See also* COMPUTER; BINARY NUMBER SYSTEM.

BLOCKS, in statistics, a simple method of experimental design used to obtain sample observations for ANALYSIS OF VARIANCE. An experimental unit is made up of blocks and treatments. E.g., an experimenter may wish to determine the results of 5 tests given to 5 different groups. The groups are the blocks and the tests are the treatments.

BOLYAI, JOHANN (bahl'-yoi), 1802–1860, Hungarian army officer who developed a system of geometry excluding EUCLID'S FIFTH POSTULATE. Bolyai's work was published in 1831 with the title *Absolute Science of Space*. His NONEUCLIDIAN GEOMETRY was based on the assumption that in a PLANE there are at least two lines parallel to a given line through a given POINT.

BOOLE GEORGE, 1815–1864, English mathematician; important in the history of LOGIC. Boole was entirely self-taught and became Professor of Mathematics at Queen's College, Cork, Ireland. His *Mathematical Analysis of Logic* (1847) went far towards the mathematical logic of today in its application of algebraic method to relationships in logic.

BOOLEAN ALGEBRA, the postulational structure of SETS; the algebra of subsets of a collection of subsets. In this algebra, the operations are $\cup$ cup and $\cap$ cap, which are defined by

$$A \cup B = (A + B) + (A \cdot B)$$
$$A \cap B = A \cdot B.$$

See UNION and INTERSECTION OF SETS.

The property of inclusion is defined by $A \subset B$ ("A is contained in B") if and only if $A \cap B = A$. The two-valued Boolean algebra whose elements are the empty set, $\varnothing$, and the set of one element, I, has the following properties:

1. $A \cup B = I$ if and only if A, B, or both, is I.

Thus,

$\cup$	$\varnothing$	I
$\varnothing$	$\varnothing$	I
I	I	$I.$

2. $A \cap B = \varnothing$ if and only if A, B, or both, is $\varnothing$.

Thus,

$\cap$	$\varnothing$	I
$\varnothing$	$\varnothing$	$\varnothing$
I	$\varnothing$	$I.$

The complement of A, denoted A', is defined as $I - A$ in Boolean algebra. Thus, for the two-valued Boolean algebra, $I' = \varnothing$, and $\varnothing' = I$.

BOUND, of a set of numbers, a number which is either less than or equal to, or greater than or equal to, every number in the set. If the number is less than or equal to every number in the set it is called a lower bound; if it is greater than or equal to every number, it is called an upper bound. For set $A = \{\frac{1}{2}, 1, 2, 4, 7\}$, $\frac{1}{2}$ is a lower bound of set A, and 7 is an upper bound.

The largest of a set's lower bounds is called the *greatest lower bound* (*GLB*); the smallest of its upper bounds is called the *least upper bound* (*LUB*).

BOURBAKI, NICHOLAS (buhr'-bah-kee), the collective pseudonym of a group of mathematicians, almost all French, who, since 1939, have been engaged in writing a comprehensive treatise on fundamental aspects of modern mathematics. It is commonly known that the membership of the group is a varying collection of mathematicians, none supposedly older than 50. The group is said to include, or have included, such major mathematicians as Henri Cartan, Claude Chevalley, Jean Dieudonné, André Weil, and Samuel Eilenberg. The work of the group appears in installments, up to 300 pages long, with the first appearing in 1939 and the 33rd in 1967. The approach to mathematics of the Bourbaki group is axiomatical. Much of it is written in a special notation, and chapters are followed by historical notes and exercises. In Bourbaki's technique, mathematics begins with set theory, which is followed by abstract algebra, general topology functions of a real variable, topological vector spaces, and the general theory of integration. The name appears to have come from Gen. Charles-Denis-Sauter Bourbaki, 1816–1897, a statue of whom stands in Nancy, where several members of the group once taught. The collective pseudonym was probably intended to obviate title pages with long lists of contributors. The series has become the standard reference of the fundamental aspects of modern mathematics.

BOWDITCH, NATHANIEL, 1773–1838, American sailing master, mathematician and astronomer. The son of a cooper, he left school at ten, went to sea at 22, and by the time he was 29 was master of his own ship. An omnivorous reader since boyhood, he taught himself mathematics and Latin, as well as several modern languages. In 1802, he published the first edition of *The New American Practical Navigator* which, after more than 60 editions, is still in print as *Bowditch's American Practical Navigator*. Offered a professorship of mathematics by Harvard, which he declined, Bowditch later translated, with an elaborate commentary, Pierre Simon de LAPLACE's *Méchanique céleste*.

Biblio.: Latham, J. L., *Carry on, Mr. Bowditch* (1955).

BRACES { }, one of the symbols for grouping two or more ALGEBRAIC EXPRESSIONS in order that they may be treated as a single unit. *See also* GROUPING SYMBOLS.

BRACKETS [ ], one of several pairs of GROUPING SYMBOLS, used to avoid confusion when working with ALGEBRAIC EXPRESSIONS to be treated as single units.

BRIGGS, HENRY, 1561–1630, English mathematician who devised the common, or base 10, system of LOGARITHMS, following the publication of a system of logarithms by his friend, John NAPIER. The word "characteristic" as used in logarithms first occurred in his *Arithmetica Logarithmica*, published in 1624.

BROKEN LINE, a line made up of straight LINE SEGMENTS, with no two consecutive segments lying in the same STRAIGHT LINE. In the figure, *ABCDE* is a broken line.

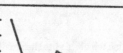

BROKEN-LINE GRAPH, a statistical graph (*see* GRAPHS, STATISTICAL) for showing values of a quantity at different times, used especially where the changes are irregular.

Ex.: Make a broken-line graph to show the temperature changes on successive days at 7 A.M. for a week in January. (See figure.)

TEMPERATURE

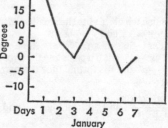

BUFFER, in a computer, the equivalent of "or" in the ALGEBRA OF PROPOSITIONS. Thus, the buffer in a computer transmits a signal when it receives any one of several signals.

C

CALCULUS (kal'-kyu-lus), the study of quantities that change or are in motion which are defined in terms of the LIMIT OF A FUNCTION. The basic problems of calculus are the determination of the TANGENT LINE to a curve, and of the AREA UNDER A CURVE. When defined exactly, these two quantities are related in a way that can be expressed as the FUNDAMENTAL THEOREM OF CALCULUS. Many other mathematical concepts are defined in terms of limits, including areas of irregular shapes, the instantaneous VELOCITY of a moving body whose speed is changing, the sums of INFINITE SERIES, and TRANSCENDENTAL NUMBERS like π.

Differential calculus is the branch of calculus which is used to solve problems in which the rate of change of a FUNCTION is found by a process called DIFFERENTIATION. Integral calculus deals with problems in which the function is unknown and is determined from the known rate of change by a process called INTEGRATION. Isaac NEWTON (1642–1727) developed calculus in order to solve problems connected with his work in physics and astronomy. Gottfried LEIBNITZ (1646–1716), at the same time, independent of Newton, developed this branch of mathematics along the same lines. It is Leibnitz's notation that is used today in calculus.

CANCEL (kan'-sel), in multiplication, to divide factors in a fraction such that their quotient is 1. Thus, $\frac{12}{3} = \frac{4 \cdot \cancel{3}}{\cancel{3}} = 4$. The 3 is said to have been "cancelled."

In addition, two numbers are said to cancel if their sum is 0. Thus, $+3 + (-3) = 0$, and the 3 is said to have been "cancelled."

CANTOR, GEORG (kan'-tor), 1845–1918, Russian mathematician b. in St. Petersburg (now Leningrad), although he is often considered a German since he studied and worked in Germany. He is best known for his work on the theory of numbers, particularly his work on transfinite numbers. It was Cantor who devised the method of forming a one–to–one correspondence between the elements of sets as a method of comparing the number of elements in a set. By making such a comparison it can be shown that the set of natural numbers (containing an infinite number of elements) has fewer elements than the set of points on a line segment (also containing an infinite number of elements). Cantor called the cardinal number of the set of natural numbers $\aleph_0$ (aleph-null), a transfinite number. This controversial approach to the concept of the infinite was revolutionary in that it challenged the process of deductive reasoning and led to critical investigations of the foundations of mathematics. His best known writing is *Contributions to the Founding of the Theory of Transfinite Numbers* (1915).

CAP, in mathematics, the symbol $\cap$ that is used to indicate intersection of SETS, Thus, $A \cap B$ may be read "A cap B" or "A intersection B."

CARDAN'S FORMULAS, for the solutions of the REDUCED CUBIC EQUATION,

$$z^3 + 3Hz + G = 0,$$

in which

$$H = \frac{3ac - b^2}{9a^2} \text{ and } G = \frac{2b^3 - 9abc + 27a^2d}{27a^3}.$$

The reduced equation is obtained from the general cubic equation

$$ax^3 + bx^2 + cx + d = 0$$

by means of the substitution $x = z - \frac{b^5}{3a}$.

Cardan's formulas for the solution of the reduced cubic are

$$z_1 = u + v, z_2 = \omega u + \omega^2 v, z_3 = \omega^2 u + \omega v,$$

where

$$\omega = -\frac{1}{2} + \frac{\sqrt{3}}{2} i \text{ and } \omega^2 = -\frac{1}{2} - \frac{\sqrt{3}}{2} i. \text{ (See OMEGA)},$$

$$u^3 = \frac{-G + \sqrt{G^2 + 4H^3}}{2} \text{ and } v = \frac{-H}{u}.$$

Ex.: Solve the equation $x^3 - 18x - 35 = 0$.
Sol.: The general form of the reduced cubic is $z^3 + 3Hz + G = 0$. Thus, $3H = -18$; $H = -6$; $G = -35$

$$u^3 = \frac{35 + \sqrt{361}}{2} = \frac{35 + 19}{2} = \frac{54}{2}$$

$$u^3 = 27$$

$$u = 3$$

$$v = \frac{-H}{u} = \frac{-(-6)}{3} = 2.$$

The roots of the given equation are

$$x_1 = u + v = 5,$$

$$x_2 = \omega u + \omega^2 v = \left(-\frac{1}{2} + \frac{\sqrt{3}}{2} i\right) 3 + \left(-\frac{1}{2} - \frac{\sqrt{3}}{2} i\right) 2 = \frac{-5}{2} + \frac{\sqrt{3}}{2} i,$$

and

$$x_3 = \omega^2 u + \omega v = \left(-\frac{1}{2} - \frac{\sqrt{3}}{2} i\right) 3 + \left(-\frac{1}{2} + \frac{\sqrt{3}}{2} i\right) 2 = \frac{-5}{2} - \frac{\sqrt{3}}{2} i.$$

CARDINAL NUMBER, a NUMBER that tells how many elements are contained in a SET of objects. ZERO and the NATURAL NUMBERS 1, 2, 3, . . . are cardinal numbers. *See also* ORDINAL NUMBERS.

CARDIOID (kar'-dee-oid), in a plane, the locus of a point, P, on a circle that rolls on an equal, fixed circle. Where the ORIGIN is on the fixed circle, and its diameter is the x-axis, if the diameter of the rolling circle and of the fixed circle is a and the angle between the positive x-axis and the line OP, is θ, the equation of the cardioid in polar coordinates (*see* COORDINATES, POLAR) is given by

$$OP = r = a(1 - \cos \theta).$$

In rectangular coordinates (*see* COORDINATES, RECTANGULAR), the equation of the cardioid is given by

$$x^2 + y^2 + ax = a\sqrt{x^2 + y^2}$$

A cardioid may be defined as an EPICYCLOID of one loop. It is a special case of the LIMACON. The curve is called a cardioid because of its heart shape.

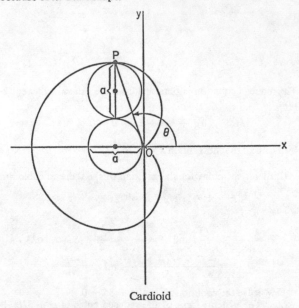

Cardioid

CARTESIAN COORDINATES (car-tee′-zhun), the system of rectangular coordinates (*see* COORDINATES, RECTANGULAR), so named in honor of René DESCARTES, the French philosopher and mathematician, who conceived many of the basic ideas of analytic geometry (*see* GEOMETRY, ANALYTIC) commonly termed coordinate geometry.

CARTESIAN PRODUCT, of two sets of objects, A and B, the set (written $A \times B$) of all ORDERED PAIRS in which the first component is an element of the first set, A, and the second component is an element of the second set, B. Thus, the Cartesian product of the set of even integers with the set of odd integers consists of the set of all pairs (E,O) where E is an even integer and O is an odd integer. This particular Cartesian product corresponds to a certain set of points in the COORDINATE PLANE.

    Ex.: Find the Cartesian product of the following sets:

$$A = \{p,q\}, B = \{s,t,u\}.$$

    Sol.: $A \times B = \{(p,s), (p,t), (p,u), (q,s), (q,t), (q,u)\}.$

CASH DISCOUNT, the practice of many business firms to allow buyers, especially commercial buyers, a lower price if they pay their bills promptly, frequently within ten days. Thus a buyer may receive a bill for $100.00 stating "2% or ninety days," meaning that he can pay $98.00 within ten days or $100.00 within ninety days. In effect, this gives the buyer ninety days credit at a cost of $2.00. Since ninety days is one-fourth of a year, that $2.00 payment represents an interest rate of approximately 8% on ninety days' credit. *See also* INTEREST.

CASTING OUT NINES, a method of checking an answer in a multiplication problem. The remainder found when the sum of the digits in the product is divided by 9 (the excess of nines) is equal to the excess of nines in the product of the excesses of nines in the two numbers being multiplied.

    Ex. 1: Multiply 345 by 274 and check by casting out nines.
    Sol.:

          345
          274
        1380
        2415
         690
       94530 Product.

The sum of the digits of the product is $9 + 4 + 5 + 3 + 0 = 21$. Since $\frac{21}{9} = 2\frac{3}{9}$, the excess of nines in the product is 3.

From the first factor:

$$3 + 4 + 5 = 12,$$
$$\frac{12}{9} = 1\frac{3}{9}, \text{Excess of Nines} = 3.$$

For the second factor:

$$2 + 7 + 4 = 13,$$
$$\frac{13}{9} = 1\frac{4}{9}, \text{Excess of Nines} = 4.$$

Multiply the excess of nines in the first factor by the excess of nines in the second factor:

$$4 \times 3 = 12,$$
$$\frac{12}{9} = 1\frac{3}{9}, \text{Excess of Nines} = 3.$$

This checks with the excess of nines in the product.
    Ex. 2: Check the following product by casting out nines.

$$341 \times 274 = 93434$$
$$9 + 3 + 4 + 3 + 4 = 23, 23/9 = 2\frac{5}{9}, \text{Excess of Nines} = 5.$$
$$3 + 4 + 1 = 8, \frac{8}{9} = \frac{8}{9}, \text{Excess of Nines} = 8.$$
$$2 + 7 + 4 = 13, \frac{13}{9} = 1\frac{4}{9}, \text{Excess of Nines} = 4.$$
$$4 \cdot 8 = 32, \frac{32}{9} = 3\frac{5}{9}, \text{Excess of Nines} = 5.$$

The answer is correct since the excess of nines in the product (5) is the same as the excess of nines in the product of the excesses of nines in each factor.

CATENARY (kat′-u-nehr-ee), the curve in which a uniform cord or cable hangs under its own weight. It is the graph of the hyperbolic cosine (*see* HYPERBOLIC FUNCTIONS). In the figure, $y = \cosh\frac{x}{a}$. The equation of the catenary in rectangular coordinates (*see* COORDINATES, RECTANGULAR) is given by $y = \frac{a}{2}(e^{az} + e^{-az})$ where a is the Y-INTERCEPT.

Catenary

CATENOID (kat'-u-noid), the SURFACE OF REVOLUTION that is generated by rotating a CATENARY about its axis.

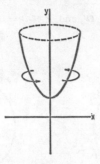

Catenoid

CAUCHY-RIEMANN EQUATIONS (koh-shee'-ree'-mahn), the pair of equations,

$$\partial u/\partial x = \partial v/\partial y$$
$$\partial u/\partial y = -\partial v/\partial x.$$

They express a necessary condition for the function $f(z) = u + iv$, to be differentiable at $z_0 = x_0 + iy_0$. *See also* COMPLEX NUMBER.

CELSIUS TEMPERATURE SCALE or centigrade temperature scale, a TEMPERATURE scale devised by Anders Celsius. (Abbreviation: C.). The reference points on the Celsius scale are 0°C. for the freezing point of water at normal pressure and 100°C. for the boiling point. The scale is often called *centigrade* because it is divided into 100 parts or degrees between the reference points. Since 5 centigrade degrees equals 9 fahrenheit degrees, Celsius temperatures may be converted to temperatures on the FAHRENHEIT TEMPERATURE SCALE by the formula:

$$F. = \frac{9}{5}C. + 32.$$

Ex.: Convert 30°C. to Fahrenheit.

Sol.: $F. = \frac{9}{5}(30) + 32.$

              $F. = 54 + 32.$

              $F. = 86.$

Thus, 30°C. = 86°F.

CENTER OF A CIRCLE. By definition, a CIRCLE is the LOCUS of points in the plane at a given distance from a given point. The

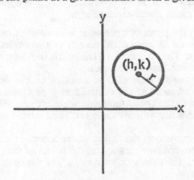

given point is called the center of the circle, and the given distance is the RADIUS. In the equation of the circle

$$(x - h)^2 + (y - k)^2 = r^2$$

the coordinates of the center are (h,k). (See figure.)

Ex. 1. Find the center of the circle given by the equation

$$(x - 2)^2 + (y + 1)^2 = 9.$$

Sol.: The center is at the point $(2,-1)$, since $h = 2$ and $k = -1$.

    Ex. 2: Locate the center of the circle given by the equation

$$x^2 + y^2 + 8x - 10y - 8 = 0.$$

Sol.: Using the method of COMPLETING SQUARES and simplifying,

$$(x + 4)^2 + (y - 5)^2 = 49.$$

The center is $(4,-5)$ since $h = -4$ and $k = 5$.

CENTER OF A HYPERBOLA (hahy-pur'-boh-lah), the midpoint of the segment between the foci of a HYPERBOLA. In the equation of the hyperbola,

$$\frac{(x - h)^2}{a^2} - \frac{(y - k)^2}{b^2} = 1,$$

(h,k) are the coordinates of the center.

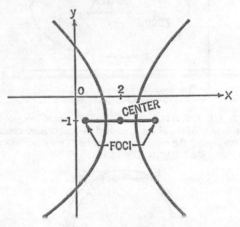

Center of a Hyperbola

Ex.: Find the center of the hyperbola given by the equation

$$\frac{(x - 2)^2}{3} - \frac{(y + 1)^2}{4} = 1.$$

Sol.: The center is $(2,-1)$, since $h = 2$ and $k = -1$.

CENTER OF AN ARC, the center of the CIRCLE of which the ARC is a part. In the figure, to find the center of $\overset{\frown}{AB}$, let C be any point on $\overset{\frown}{AB}$. Draw $\overline{AC}$, $\overline{AB}$, and $\overline{BC}$ to form $\triangle ABC$. Construct the CIRCUMCENTER of $\triangle ABC$. With O as a center and OA as a radius, draw circle O. The center of $\overset{\frown}{AB}$ is O.

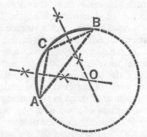

CENTER OF AN ELLIPSE, the midpoint of the segment joining the two foci of an ELLIPSE. If the segment joining the foci is parallel to a COORDINATE axis, the equation of the ellipse is

$$\frac{(x - h)^2}{a^2} + \frac{(y - k)^2}{b^2} = 1,$$

and the coordinates of the center are (h,k).

Ex. 1: Find the center

$$\frac{(x-2)^2}{9}\frac{(y+3)^2}{4} = 1$$

of the ellipse given by

Sol.: The center is at the point $(2, -3)$ since h is 2 and k is -3.

Ex. 2: Find the center of the ellipse given by $\frac{x^2}{2} + \frac{y^2}{4} = 1$.

Sol.: Since $x^2 = (x - h)^2 = (x - 0)^2$ and $y = (y - k)^2 = (y - 0)^2$, both h and k are zero. Thus, the center is at the point $(0,0)$, or the ORIGIN.

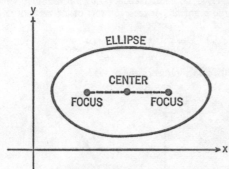

Center of an Ellipse

CENTER OF A REGULAR POLYGON (pah'-lee-gahn), the common center of the circle inscribed (*see* INSCRIBED CIRCLE) in the POLYGON and the circle circumscribed (*see* CIRCUMSCRIBED CIRCLE) about the polygon. (See figure.)

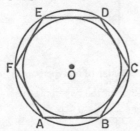

O is the center of Polygon — ABCDEF

CENTER OF GRAVITY, the CENTROID or point of concurrency of the MEDIANS of a triangle. *See* CENTER OF MASS.

CENTER OF MASS or **center of gravity,** the point at which all the mass of an object may be assumed, for mechanical purposes, to be concentrated. Although the mass of an object is actually distributed over the object's entire volume, there is always a single point at which the mass can be considered to be concentrated for purposes of dynamical analysis. Since the most important effect of a mass at the earth's surface is its WEIGHT, a measure of the force of gravity acting on it, the center of mass is often called the *center of gravity.* Forces acting through the center of mass cause no rotation, whereas unbalanced forces on any other point of the body will cause rotation. The center of mass of a regular solid of uniform composition is at its geometrical center. The center of mass is not necessarily within the object. For example, centers of mass of a ring, a spherical shell, and a horseshoe all lie outside the actual objects. Various practical as well as mathematical methods exist for locating the center of mass of an irregularly shaped object.

CENTIGRADE TEMPERATURE SCALE, *see* CELSIUS TEMPERATURE SCALE.

CENTRAL ANGLE OF A CIRCLE, an angle whose sides are radii of the CIRCLE and whose vertex is the center of the circle. In Fig. 1a, $\angle AOB$ is a central angle of $\odot O$.

A central angle is equal in degrees to the ARC it intercepts. In a circle, or in equal circles, equal central angles have equal arcs.

In Fig. 1, if $\odot O = \odot O'$, and $\angle AOB = \angle A'O'B'$, then $\widehat{AB} = \widehat{A'B'}$.

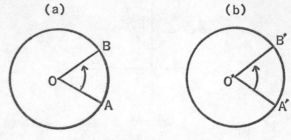

Fig. 1

CENTRAL ANGLE OF A REGULAR POLYGON, an angle whose vertex is the center of the CIRCUMSCRIBED CIRCLE and whose sides are radii drawn to the vertices of the POLYGON. In the figure, $\angle AOB$ is a central angle of REGULAR POLYGON *ABCDEF* (a regular hexagon). $\odot O$ is its circumscribed circle.

A central angle of a REGULAR POLYGON may be found by dividing $360°$ by the number of sides of the polygon. Each central angle in the figure equals $60°$.

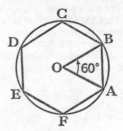

CENTRAL LIMIT THEOREM, the THEOREM in STATISTICS that states: If the random variable x has a distribution with mean μ and variance σ^2, then the random variable $(\bar{x} - \mu)/(\sigma/\sqrt{n})$ has a distribution that approaches the STANDARD NORMAL DISTRIBUTION as n increases without bound ($n =$ the size of the sample upon which $\bar{x}$ is based). Thus, if the sample size is large enough (usually at least 25 or 30 observations), then $\bar{x}$ is approximately normal with mean μ and variance σ^2/n.

CENTROID, the point of a region at which a physical model of the region would balance if the density of the model were perfectly uniform. The centroid of a triangle is the point of concurrency of the MEDIANS OF A TRIANGLE.

If a figure can be expressed as a region on the COORDINATE AXES, the coordinates of the centroid may be found. Each coordinate must usually be found separately, although if the figure possesses SYMMETRY around some line the centroid must be on that line.

If in two dimensions, the region whose centroid is to be found is the area between two curves, and the height of the region at x is $f(x) - g(x)$, then the y-coordinate, y^*, of the centroid of the region is:

$$y^* = \frac{\int_a^b \frac{1}{2}(f(x) + g(x))(f(x) - g(x))dx}{\int_a^b (f(x) - g(x))dx}.$$

The x-coordinate, x^*, may be found by expressing the width as a function of y, and using the following formula:

$$x^* = \frac{\int_a^b x(f(x) - g(x))dx}{\int_a^b (f(x) - g(x))dx}.$$

Ex.: What is the centroid of the quarter of the unit disk in the first quadrant?

Sol.: This quarter circle is symmetrical around the line $y = x$. Hence, we need only find one coordinate of the centroid, and set the other equal to it. It is simpler to find x^*:

$$x^* = \frac{\int_0^1 x(1 - x^2)^{1/2}dx}{\int_0^1 (1 - x^2)^{1/2}dx} = \frac{-\frac{1}{3}(1 - x)^{3/2}\Big]_0^1}{(\frac{1}{4})\pi} = \frac{1}{3}\cdot\frac{4}{\pi}.$$

The centroid, therefore, is $\left(\frac{4}{3\pi}, \frac{4}{3\pi}\right)$. A check will show that the calculation of y^* also gives this value. *See also* AREA UNDER A CURVE; INTEGRATION.

CGS SYSTEM, a system of units of measurement in the METRIC SYSTEM. The name is derived from the three basic units in this system—the centimeter, the gram, and the second. The CGS unit of force is the DYNE, equal to 1 gram-centimeter per square second. The unit of work, or energy, is the ERG, 1 dyne-centimeter. The CGS unit of heat energy is the calorie. There is no separate CGS unit for power. Two separate systems of CGS electrical and magnetic units exist. The *electrostatic* system of units defines the basic unit of charge, the *statcoulomb*, in such a way that the constant of proportionality in Coulomb's Law is equal to one. In the *electromagnetic* system of units, the definition of current rather than charge serves as the basis for the units. The *absolute electromagnetic unit of current*, or *abampere*, is defined as the current in a circular loop of wire of radius 1 centimeter that gives rise to a magnetic induction at the center of the circle of 2π gauss. Partly because of the much greater simplicity of the corresponding MKS units of electricity and magnetism, the MKS SYSTEM has generally replaced the CGS system in almost all applications, one exception being measurements of density. *See also* TABLE NO. 5.

CHAIN RULE, if $y = f(x)$ and $x = g(t)$ then $dy/dt = \frac{dy}{dx}\cdot\frac{dx}{dt}$. This socalled chain rule is used to differentiate a function of a function.

Ex. 1: If $y = x^3 - 3x^2 + 5x - 4$ and $x = t^2 + t$, find dy/dt.

$$Sol.: dy/dt = \frac{dy}{dx}\cdot\frac{dx}{dt}$$

$$dy/dx = 3x^2 - 6x + 5; dx/dt = 2t + 1.$$

Expressing dy/dx in terms of t, since $x = t^2 + t$, gives

$$dy/dx = 3(t^2 + t)^2 - 6(t^2 + t) + 5$$

and $\quad dy/dt = \frac{dy}{dx}\cdot\frac{dx}{dt}$

$$dy/dt = [3(t^2 + t)^2 - 6(t^2 + t) + 5](2t + 1).$$

If both sides of the expressing $dy/dt = \frac{dy}{dx}\cdot\frac{dx}{dt}$ are divided by dx/dt, an equivalent form of dy/dt is found to be

$$\frac{dy}{dx} = \frac{dy/dt}{dx/dt}.$$

This form is more useful when dealing with parametric equations.

Ex. 2: Given the PARAMETRIC EQUATIONS $x = 2t + 3$ and $y = t^2 + 1$, find dy/dx.

$$Sol.: dy/dx = \frac{dy/dt}{dx/dt}$$

$$dy/dt = 2t; dx/dt = 2$$

$$dy/dx = 2t/2 = t.$$

Expressing dy/dx in terms of x, use $x = 2t + 3$ to find $t = \frac{x-3}{2}$. Then $dy/dx = \frac{x-3}{2}$.

The chain rule is also applicable for PARTIAL DERIVATIVES. If $w = f(x,y,z)$ and the partial derivatives are continuous, and if C is the curve given by $x = x(t)$, $y = y(t)$, $z = z(t)$, the rate at which w varies along C as t changes may be found from:

$$\frac{dw}{dt} = \frac{\partial w}{\partial x}\frac{dx}{dt} + \frac{\partial w}{\partial y}\frac{dy}{dt} + \frac{\partial w}{\partial z}\frac{dz}{dt}.$$

Ex. 1: If $w = x^2 + y^2 + z^2$, find dw/dt along the curve $x = \sin t$, $y = \cos t$, $z = e^t$.

$$\begin{aligned}Sol.: dw/dt &= (2x)(\cos t) + (2y)(-\sin t) + (2z)(e^t)\\ &= (2\sin t)(\cos t) + (2\cos t)(-\sin t) + (2e^t)(e^t)\\ &= 2\sin t\cos t - 2\cos t\sin t + 2e^{2t} = 2e^{2t}.\end{aligned}$$

If x, y, and z depend on two variables r and s as in $x = x(r,s)$, $y = y(r,s)$, $z = a(r,s)$, partial derivatives of w with respect to r and s can be found by the following formula and the corresponding expression involving ∂s:

$$\partial w/\partial r = \frac{\partial w}{\partial x}\frac{\partial x}{\partial r} + \frac{\partial w}{\partial y}\frac{\partial y}{\partial r} + \frac{\partial w}{\partial z}\frac{\partial z}{\partial r}.$$

CHANCE VARIABLE, in statistics, another name for RANDOM VARIABLE or *stochastic variable*.

CHANGE OF VARIABLES, If $y = f(x)$ and $x = g(t)$, the substitution of $g(t)$ for x in $y = f(x)$ to produce $y = f[g(t)]$ is called a change of variables. In the new equation the first independent variable x does not appear, but the new independent variable t does.

Ex. 1: Perform a change of variables of t for x, if $y = x^2$ and $x = 2t$.

Sol.: $y = x^2 = (2t)^2 = 4t^2$.

Ex. 2: If $y = \sin x$ and $x = -3t + 3$, and x varies from 2 to 5, between what limits will t vary?

Sol.: Solve for t: $1 - x/3 = t$. When $x = 2$, $t = 1 - \frac{2}{3} = \frac{1}{3}$, and when $x = 5$, $t = 1 - \frac{5}{3} = -\frac{2}{3}$. Thus, t varies from $\frac{1}{3}$ to $-\frac{2}{3}$.

Ex. 3: If $x = 5y + 1$, $y = t^2$, and $t = \sqrt{s}$, perform two changes of variable.

Sol.: $x = 5y + 1 = 5(t^2) + 1 = 5(\sqrt{s})^2 + 1 = 5s + 1$.

CHARACTERISTIC OF A LOGARITHM, *see* LOGARITHM.

CHEBYSCHEV'S THEOREM (che-bih-shafs), the theorem in statistics that states if x is a random variable with mean μ and variance σ^2, then the probability that x takes on a value within k standard deviations of its mean is at least equal to $1 - \frac{1}{k^2}$. Symbolically, $P\{|x - \mu| < k\sigma\} \geq 1 - \frac{1}{k^2}$. This theorem is applicable to any distribution. Hence, although it has great generality, more precise results can be obtained when the particular distribution is known. For example, Chebyshev's Theorem implies that, no matter what distribution x has, the probability that x is within 3 standard deviations of its mean is at least $\frac{8}{9}$. However, if x is known to have a normal distribution, the probability that x takes on a value within 3 standard deviations of the mean is .9974.

CHI-SQUARED DISTRIBUTION, in statistics, a distribution $x^2_d = \sum_{i=1}^k x_i^2$, used to (1) test hypotheses about a population variance (*see* TESTS OF HYPOTHESES ABOUT A VARIANCE); (2) find confidence limits (*see* CONFIDENCE INTERVAL) for a population variance (*see* VARIANCE, POPULATION); (3) test the hypothesis that two criteria of classification are independent by means of a table known as a CONTINGENCY TABLE; and (4) test MULTI-NOMIAL HYPOTHESES. It is also used in the CHI-SQUARED GOODNESS-OF-FIT TEST.

CHI-SQUARED GOODNESS-OF-FIT TEST, a test of a statistical hypothesis that asserts that the population being sampled has a particular form. It is based on the quantity

$$x^2 = \sum_{i=1}^{k} \frac{(n - e_i)}{e_i}$$

For example, before proceeding to other tests for which normality must be assumed it might be desirable to test that a population is normal.

CHORD, the straight line segment from one point on a curve to another. The chord may or may not intersect the curve, or even lie upon it. (See Fig. 1.) Special chords are the diameters of a CIRCLE, the two axes (major and minor) of an ELLIPSE, the transverse axis of a HYPERBOLA, the latus rectum of a hyperbola, and the latus rectum of an ellipse.

CHORDS

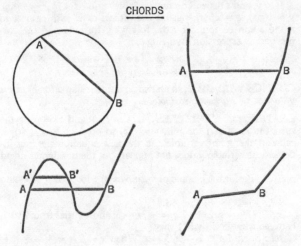

Fig. 1

In a circle, (1) equal chords have equal arcs, (2) equal chords are equidistant from the center of the circle, and conversely (Fig. 2), (3) the distance of a chord from the center of the circle is the PERPENDICULAR from the chord to the center; and (4) when two chords intersect in a circle, the product of the segments of one chord is equal to the product of the segments of the other chord.

Ex. 1: In circle O, chord AD = chord CB. The distance from chord AD to the center is 10, and the distance from CB to center is $3x - 5$. Find the value of x. (Fig. 3).

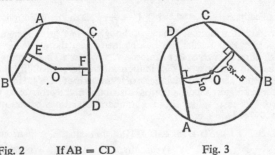

Fig. 2   If AB = CD
then OE = OF
If OE = OF
then AB = CD

Fig. 3

Sol.: Equal chords are equidistant from the center of the circle. Therefore,

$$3x - 5 = 10$$
$$3x \quad = 15$$
$$x \quad = 5.$$

Ex. 2: The segments of one of two intersecting chords are 6 in. and 10 in. The smaller segment of the second chord is 4 in. How long is the larger segment of the second chord? (Fig. 4.)

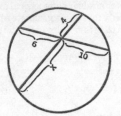

Fig. 4

Sol.: When two chords intersect in a circle, the product of the segments of one chord is equal to the product of the segments of the second chord. Therefore, if x is the length of the larger segment,

$$4x = 6 \times 10$$
$$4x = 60$$
$$x = 15.$$

CIRCLE (sur'-kul), a plane closed curve line all points of which are equidistant from a point within, called the CENTER OF A CIRCLE. The RADIUS (*plural*, radii) of a circle is the line segment from the center to any point on the circle. A DIAMETER OF A CIRCLE is the line segment through the center of the circle and having both end points on the circle. (See Fig. 1.) *See also* CONIC SECTIONS.

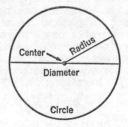

Fig. 1

The AREA of a circle is found by the FORMULA $A = \pi r^2$, where A represents the AREA and r the RADIUS.

Ex. 1: Find the area of a circle if the radius is 10 in.

Sol.: If $\pi = 3\frac{1}{7}$ and $r = 10$, then

$$A = \tfrac{22}{7} \times 10 \times 10 = \tfrac{2200}{7} = 314\tfrac{2}{7} \text{ sq. in.}$$

The circumference of a circle is the length of the CIRCLE. The RATIO of the circumference to the DIAMETER, or the QUOTIENT of the circumference divided by the diameter, is represented by the Greek letter π.

Then $\dfrac{C}{d} = \pi$ and $C = \pi d$.

Since $d = 2r$, the formula may also be $C = 2\pi r$. The approximate value of π commonly is $3\frac{1}{7}$ or 3.14. For greater accuracy 3.1416 is used.

Ex. 2: Find the area of a circle if the circumference is 44.

Sol.: Use the formula $C = 2\pi r$ to find the radius when the circumference is given. Then:

$$44 = 2 \times \tfrac{22}{7} r$$
$$44r = 308$$
$$r = 7$$

Substituting 7 for r in the area formula,

$$A = \frac{22}{7} \times 7 \times 7 = 154 \text{ sq. units.}$$

Given the COORDINATES of center and radius, the DISTANCE FORMULA may be used to write the equation of a circle. If the center is at a point (h,k), and the radius is r, then for (x,y) on the circle, by the PYTHAGOREAN THEOREM:

$$(x - h)^2 + (y - k)^2 = r^2. \text{ (See Fig. 2.)}$$

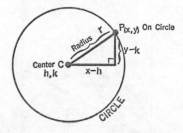

Fig. 2

Ex. 1: Write the equation of the circle with center (1,2) and radius 4.

Sol.: $(x - 1)^2 + (y - 2)^2 = 16.$

Ex. 2: Find the center and radius of the circle given by the following equation:

$$x^2 + y^2 - 4x + 6y - 3 = 0.$$

Sol.: COMPLETING SQUARES gives:

$$(x - 2)^2 + (y + 3)^2 = 16.$$

Therefore, the center is at $(2,-3)$ and $r = 4$.

Ex. 3: Graph: $x^2 + y^2 = 25.$ (See Fig. 3.)

Sol.: $y^2 = 25 - x^2$

and $y = \pm\sqrt{25 - x^2}.$

Substituting values for x gives the table:

x	y
0	± 5
± 3	± 4
± 4	± 3
± 5	0

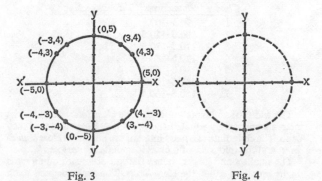

Fig. 3   Fig. 4

If $x^2 + y^2 = r^2$, the RADIUS of the circle is the SQUARE ROOT of r. In $x^2 + y^2 = 25$, the radius is 5 and its center is the origin. Therefore, the graph may be drawn without a table of values, by marking off a distance of 5 units from the origin on the axes, and sketching the circle. (See Fig. 4.)

CIRCLE GRAPH, a statistical GRAPH for showing the relation of parts of a quantity to the whole. The parts are expressed as percentages, or fractions, of the whole, which is illustrated as a circle, or 360°.

Ex.: Make a circle graph to show National Defense Education Act fellowships awarded from 1959 to 1962, inclusive. (See figure.)

Express the fellowships for each study as a fraction of the total number awarded and take that fractional part of 360°, ROUNDING OFF to the nearest degree. For example, $(422/5,538) \times 360° = 27°$.

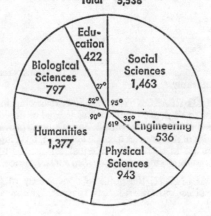

N.D.E.A. FELLOWSHIPS AWARDED
Total   5,538

CIRCLE OF CURVATURE, at a point P on the curve $y = f(x)$, the tangent circle whose radius is the RADIUS OF CURVATURE at P, and whose center is on the concave side of the curve. (See figure.) *See also* CURVATURE OF PLANE CURVE.

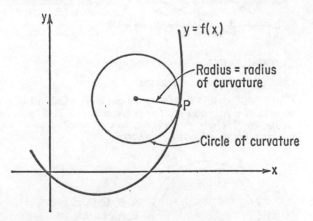

CIRCULAR FUNCTIONS, the TRIGONOMETRIC FUNCTIONS, defined in a CIRCLE whose center is the origin of a Cartesian coordinate system (*see* COORDINATES, RECTANGULAR). In the figure, θ is a POSITIVE ANGLE with terminal side OP of length r (always considered positive), the circular functions are defined as follows:

$$\sin \theta = \frac{y}{r}; \ \cos \theta = \frac{x}{r}; \ \tan \theta = \frac{y}{x} \ (x \neq 0); \ \csc \theta = \frac{r}{y} \ (y \neq 0);$$

$$\sec \theta = \frac{r}{x} \ (x \neq 0); \ \cot \theta = \frac{x}{y} \ (y \neq 0).$$

The sign of the function is determined by the sign of x and y, depending upon the quadrant in which P falls. The terms "cir-

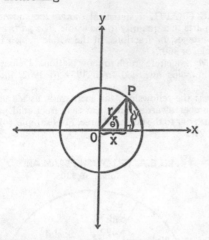

$$x = 2a \sin^2 \theta,$$
$$y = 2a \tan \theta \sin^2 \theta,$$

where θ is the angle between the positive x-axis and OP. The equation of the cissoid in polar coordinates (*see* COORDINATES, POLAR) is given by $OP = r = 2a \tan \theta \sin \theta$; in rectangular coordinates (*see* COORDINATES, RECTANGULAR), $y^2(2a - x) = x^3$.

The curve is often called the *cissoid of Diocles* (ab. 200 B.C.), who first studied and named it "cissoid," which means "ivy-like."

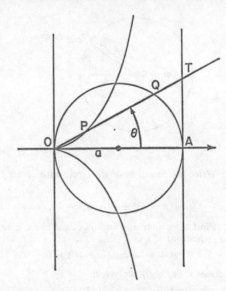

cular functions" and "trigonometric functions" may be used interchangeably.

CIRCULAR REASONING, fallacious reasoning in which the statement to be proved (conclusion) is used as an authority for one of the reasons in the proof. For example, proving that the base angles of an isosceles triangle are equal, by using the reason "if two sides of a triangle are equal, the angles opposite are equal" is using circular reasoning. *See* FORMAL PROOF.

CIRCUMCENTER, the point of concurrency of the PERPENDICULAR bisectors of the sides of a triangle. *See also* CONCURRENT LINES.

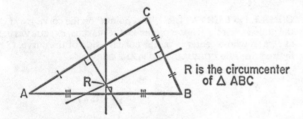

R is the circumcenter of △ ABC

CIRCUMCIRCLE, *see* CIRCUMSCRIBED CIRCLE.

CIRCUMFERENCE, *see* CIRCLE.

CIRCUMSCRIBED CIRCLE, the circle on which all of the vertices of a POLYGON lie. The polygon is then said to be inscribed in the circle. A circle can be circumscribed about any REGULAR POLYGON and all TRIANGLES.

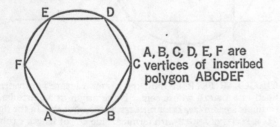

A, B, C, D, E, F are vertices of inscribed polygon ABCDEF

CIS, the abbreviation of $\cos \theta + i \sin \theta$. *See also* COMPLEX NUMBER.

CISSOID (si'-soid), in a plane, if a tangent is drawn to a fixed circle of radius a at one end (A) of its diameter OA, and OT is drawn intersecting the circle at Q and the tangent at T, the locus of point P on OT such that $OP = QT$ as OT is rotated about point O. (See figure.) The PARAMETRIC EQUATIONS of the cissoid are

CIVIL TIME, solar time measured from certain internationally agreed upon meridians. Each of these meridians defines a standard time zone approximately 15° of longitude wide. All clocks within the zone are set to the zone, or standard time. There is a difference of one hour between two adjacent standard time zones. In summer, clocks within a zone may be set ahead to keep daylight-saving, or summer, time.

CLASSIFIED DATA, in statistics, when a sample is composed of many observations, the numerical interval that contains them is frequently divided into subintervals called *classes*, and only the classes and the number of observations that each contains is displayed. The data are then said to have been classified, and the table that displays them is called a *frequency distribution*. A typical one is:

Class	Boundaries	Frequencies
1	90.5–100.5	5
2	100.5–110.5	11
3	110.5–120.5	7
4	120.5–130.5	10
5	130.5–140.5	16
6	140.5–150.5	9
7	150.5–160.5	3

The width of a class is known as the *class interval*. The class intervals are usually equal, although it is not essential that they be so. The endpoints of a class interval are known as *class boundaries*, and the midpoint of a class is called the *class mark*.

The smallest and largest values that an observation in a class might equal are called the *class limits*. The limits depend upon the accuracy with which measurements are given. For example, if measurements are taken to the nearest integer, and if the boundaries of a class are 100.5 and 110.5, the class limits are 101 and 110.

The classes may be specified either in terms of class boundaries or class limits. If classes are specified in terms of their limits (such as 91–100, 101–110, 111–120, ···), the boundaries of the classes are taken as being halfway between the upper limit of one class and the lower limit of the next class (90.5, 100.5, 110.5. ···), as in the example above.

The *class frequency* is the number of observations contained in a class.

CLOSED INTERVAL, a segment of a NUMBER LINE between two points A and B which includes its own end points. It consists of all x such that $A \leq x \leq B$ and is symbolized by $[A, B]$. If a given INTERVAL does not contain either end point, it is called an open interval and is symbolized by (A,B); if it includes only one end point it is called either half-open or half-closed, and is symbolized as either $(A,B]$ or $[A,B)$ with the bracket at the closed end.

CLOSED LINE, a broken line or a curved line that encloses a part of a PLANE. (See figure.)

CLOSED SET, a POINT SET which includes all of its LIMIT POINTS. This is a generalization of the idea of a CLOSED INTERVAL. Examples of closed sets are a single point (see Fig. 1), and the fractions of the form $1/n$ on a number line, together with zero (see Fig. 2).

Fig. 1   Fig. 2

A circular disk which includes its bounding circle is also a closed set (see Fig. 3), whereas the interior of the disk, excluding the bounding circle is not closed because each of the points of the bounding circle is a limit point of the set, but is not a member of the set (see Fig. 4). *See also* OPEN SET.

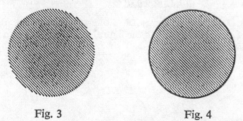

Fig. 3   Fig. 4

CLOSURE. A BINARY OPERATION, $*$, is said to be closed on the SET, $S = \{a, b, c, \cdots\}$, if for every pair of elements (a,b) of S, the image $a * b = c$ is also an element of S. E.g., the binary operations of ADDITION and MULTIPLICATION are both closed on the set of NATURAL NUMBERS, since all sums and products of natural numbers are also natural numbers. But the binary operation of SUBTRACTION is not closed on the set, since it may result in a negative number; and the binary operation of DIVISION is not closed on the set since it may result in a fraction. (Note: Neither negative numbers nor fractional numbers are members of the set of natural numbers.) Subtraction is closed, however, on the set of integers; and division is closed on the set of rational numbers.

CLUSTER SAMPLING, in statistics, a method of sampling in which the individual members of the sample are not taken randomly, one at a time, but in groups, called *clusters*, which are themselves taken at random. For example, to take a sample of a large dormitory complex for men at a large university, a number of suites of rooms (with four men to a suite) might be selected at random and every occupant of each of the suites included in the sample. Note that the members of the sample (the men) are not selected individually and at random, but the clusters (the suites) to which they belong are taken at random.

CODING, in statistics, a method which simplifies calculation of the sample MEAN, variance (*see* VARIANCE, SAMPLE) and MEAN ABSOLUTE DEVIATION. Primarily for CLASSIFIED DATA, and used only rarely when desk calculators are available, the usual procedure is: Assign integers to each of the class marks, with the zero somewhere near the "center" of the frequency distribution. Let u_i denote the integer assigned to the class mark x'_i. Then the mean is

$$\bar{x} = b + c\bar{u},$$

and the variance is

$$s_x{}^2 = c^2 s_u{}^2,$$

where b denotes the class mark to which zero is assigned, $\bar{u} = \dfrac{\sum_{i=1}^{k} u_i f_i}{n}$, and c denotes the width of the class INTERVAL.

Ex.: Find, by coding, the mean and variance of the following frequency distribution.

	Class Mark x_i	Freq f_i	u_i
	378.55	7	−3
$c = 20$	398.55	11	−2
	418.55	8	−1
	438.55	15	0
	458.55	13	1
	478.55	5	2

The center of this distribution seems to occur at about 438.55; so, assign the integer 0 to this class mark. The u-values assigned to the class marks larger than 438.55 are consecutive positive integers; those assigned to the class marks smaller than 438.55 are consecutive negative integers. These u-values are shown in the last column of the table.

The formula for the mean, $\bar{x}$, is $\bar{x} = b + c\bar{u}$. In our case, $\bar{x} = 438.55 + 20\,\bar{u}$.

Find $\bar{u}$: $\bar{u} = \dfrac{\sum_{i=1}^{k} u_i f_i}{n}$, $\quad n = 7 + 11 + 8 + 15 + 13 + 5$,

$\bar{u} = \dfrac{1}{59}[(-3)(7) + (-2)(11) + \cdots + (2)(5)] = \dfrac{-28}{59} = -.4746.$

Then $\qquad \bar{x} = 438.55 + 20(-.474576) = 429.058$

and $\qquad\qquad s_x{}^2 = c^2 s_u{}^2 = 400 s_u{}^2.$

Find $s_u{}^2$: $\qquad s_u{}^2 = \dfrac{1}{58}\left[\Sigma u_i{}^2 f_i - \dfrac{(\Sigma u_i f_i)^2}{59} \right],$

$\Sigma u^2 f_i = (-3)^2(7) + (-2)^2(11) + \cdots + (2)^2(5) = 148,$

$s_u{}^2 = \dfrac{1}{58}\left[148 - \dfrac{(-28)^2}{59} \right] = \dfrac{1}{58}[148 - 13.2881]$

$= \dfrac{134.7119}{58} = 2.3226,$

and $s_x{}^2 = 400(2.322618) = 929.04.$

COEFFICIENT, any letter or number used as a FACTOR of the remaining factors in a PRODUCT. In the expression $6ab$, 6 is the numerical coefficient of ab, a is the literal coefficient of $6b$, and b is the coefficient of $6a$. If no numerical coefficient is written before a letter, the coefficient is understood to be 1. Thus x means $1x$, and ab means $1ab$. *See also* ALGEBRAIC EXPRESSION; LITERAL NUMBER.

COEFFICIENTS IN A BINOMIAL EXPRESSION, *see* BINOMIAL, EXPANDING A.

COFACTOR, of an element in the rth row and hth column of a DETERMINANT, the value of the *minor* of that element if $r + h$ is even, or the negative of the value of the minor of the element if $r + h$ is odd.

COFUNCTIONS, functions of COMPLEMENTARY ANGLES. Three pairs of trigonometric cofunctions are: sine and cosine, tangent and cotangent, and secant and cosecant. Each function of an acute angle is equal to the cofunction of its complementary angle. E.g.,

$$\sin 30° = \cos 60°$$
$$\tan 50° = \cot 40°$$
$$\sec 72° = \csc 18°.$$

COIN PROBLEMS. *Ex.* 1: A boy has twice as many dimes as quarters and three more nickels than dimes. If the value of the coins is $2.90, how many coins of each kind has he?

Sol.: Let x = number of quarters.
Then $2x$ = number of dimes
and $2x + 3$ = number of nickels.
     $25x$ = number of cents in x quarters.
     $10(2x)$ = number of cents in $2x$ dimes.
     $5(2x + 3)$ = number of cents in $2x + 3$ nickels.
     290 = number of cents in $2.90
     $25x + 10(2x) + 5(2x + 3) = 290$
     $25x + 20x + 10x + 15 = 290$
     $55x = 275$
     $x = 5$ quarters
     $2x = 10$ dimes
     $2x + 3 = 13$ nickels.
Check: $1.25 + 1.00 + .65 = $2.90.

Ex. 2: A purse contains 16 coins consisting of nickels and dimes. Find the number of coins if their value is $1.15.

Sol.: Let x = number of dimes
then $16 - x$ = number of nickels.
     $10x$ = number of cents in x dimes.
     $5(16 - x)$ = number of cents in $(16 - x)$ nickels.
     115 = number of cents in $1.15
     $10x + 5(16 - x) = 115$
     $10x + 80 - 5x = 115.$
     $5x = 35$
     $x = 7$ dimes
     $16 - x = 9$ nickels.
Check: $.70 + .45 = $1.15.

COLLINEAR POINTS (ku-li'-nee-ur), POINTS lying in the same straight line.

COLOGARITHM, the logarithm of the reciprocal of a number:

$$\text{colog } N = \log \frac{1}{N} = \log 1 - \log N = 0 - \log N.$$

Cologarithms are used in computations with division. Instead of subtracting a logarithm from another, its cologarithm is added.

Ex. 1: Find the colog of 28.3.

Sol.: $\text{colog } 28.3 = \log \dfrac{1}{28.3}$.

        $\log 1 = 10.00000 - 10$
      $\log 28.3 = \underline{1.45179}$
    $\text{colog } 28.3 = \overline{8.54821 - 10.}$

Ex. 2: Find $\dfrac{1.24 \times 39.8}{.849}$.

Sol.: The logarithms of 1.24 and 39.8 are added, and from the sum, the log of 8.49 is subtracted. Computation can be done with only addition by using the colog of .849.

$$\log .849 = 9.92891 - 10, \text{ so colog } .849 = .07109.$$

       $\log 1.24 = .09342$
       $\log 39.8 = 1.59988$
   $\text{colog } .849 = \underline{.07109}$
        $\log N = \overline{1.76439.}$

Find the antilog of 1.76439.

$$10\begin{bmatrix} \begin{array}{cc} Number & Mantissa \\ 58130 & 76440 \\ x\begin{bmatrix} 58120 + x & 76439 \\ 58120 & 76433 \end{bmatrix} 6 \end{array} \end{bmatrix} 7$$

$$N = 58.129.$$
$$\frac{1.24 \times 39.8}{.849} = 58.129.$$

COMBINATION, as distinguished from a PERMUTATION, an unordered set of objects. The number of unordered sets of r objects that can be formed from n different objects is called the *number of combinations of n objects taken r at a time*, and is equal to $\dfrac{n!}{r!(n - r)!}$. Various symbols are used to denote this number, among them are $_nC_r$, $\binom{n}{r}$, and $C(n,r)$. The number $\binom{n}{r}$ is also called a *binomial coefficient.*

Ex.: Ten people want to attend a concert, but there are only 7 tickets remaining. How many different sets of 7 people can buy the available tickets? The answer is: $\binom{10}{7} = \dfrac{10!}{7!3!} = \dfrac{10 \cdot 9 \cdot 8}{1 \cdot 2 \cdot 3} = 120.$

COMMENSURABLE QUANTITIES, quantities in which the same unit of measure can be contained an integral number of times. Two segments $3\frac{1}{8}$ in. and $2\frac{1}{4}$ in. are commensurable because $\frac{1}{8}$ in. can be contained 25 times in $3\frac{1}{8}$ in. and 18 times in $2\frac{1}{4}$ in. Quantities that are not commensurable are called *incommensurable*, e.g., the numbers 2 and 3.

COMMON ANGLE, an ANGLE of one TRIANGLE that is also an angle of another triangle. In the figure, $\angle A$ is the common angle of $\triangle ABD$ and $\triangle AEC$.

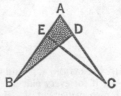

In proving that two overlapping triangles are congruent, the common angle may equal itself and the reason is "by identity." *See also* AXIOM (No. 8).

COMMON DENOMINATOR, *see* LOWEST COMMON DENOMINATOR.

COMMON DIFFERENCE, the CONSTANT by which each term in a number SERIES differs from the preceding term. In the series 35, 28, 21, 14, ... , the common difference is -7.

COMMON FACTOR, *see* FACTOR, COMMON MONOMIAL.

COMMON MULTIPLE, *see* LOWEST COMMON MULTIPLE.

COMMON RATIO, the number by which each term in a GEOMETRIC PROGRESSION is multiplied to obtain the term immediately following it. In the progression $3 + 9 + 27 + 81 \ldots$ the common ratio is 3. In the progression $2 - 4 + 8 - 16 + \cdots$ the common ratio is -2.

COMMON SIDE, a side of one TRIANGLE that is also a side of another triangle. In the figure, AB is a side of $\triangle ABC$ and also of $\triangle ABD$.

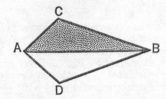

In proving that two overlapping triangles are congruent, the common side equals itself and the reason is "by identity."

COMMON TANGENT, *see* TANGENT, COMMON.

COMMUTATIVE GROUP, a GROUP in which the COMMUTATIVE PROPERTY holds for the defined operation. Thus, a group G with operation "O" is commutative if for a, b in G,

$$a \cdot b = b \cdot a.$$

A commutative group is also called an **abelian group**. The set of integers forms a commutative group.

COMMUTATIVE PROPERTY, a BINARY OPERATION, $*$, is said to be commutative on the set, $S = \{a, b, c, \ldots, \}$, if $a * b = b * a$ (read "a star b"). Both addition and multiplication are commutative on the REAL NUMBER system, since for any two real numbers, a and b, $a + b = b + a$, and $a \cdot b = b \cdot a$. E.g., $3 + 5 = 5 + 3 = 8$, and $3 \cdot 5 = 5 \cdot 3 = 15$. Neither division nor subtraction are commutative for the set of real numbers, since in general, $a - b \neq b - a$, and $a \div b \neq b \div a$. E.g., $6 - 3 = 3 \neq 3 - 6 = -3$, and $6 \div 3 = 2 \neq 3 \div 6 = \frac{1}{2}$.

SCALAR (dot) multiplication of VECTORS is commutative: $\mathbf{a} \cdot \mathbf{b} = \mathbf{b} \cdot \mathbf{a}$. But the VECTOR PRODUCT of vectors is not commutative, since $\mathbf{a} \times \mathbf{b} = -\mathbf{b} \times \mathbf{a}$.

COMPARISON TEST, for convergence of a SERIES. The series Σa_n, with all terms positive, converges if there is some CONVERGENT SERIES Σb_n such that for every n, $a_n < b_n$. Σa_n diverges if there is a DIVERGENT SERIES of positive terms Σc_n such that for every n, $a_n > c_n$. *See also* INTEGRAL TEST; RATIO TEST.

COMPASS, an instrument used to draw CIRCLES and ARCS of circles, to construct one line segment equal to another, and to compare lengths of line segments. (See figure.) A compass and a straight-edge are the only instruments permitted for a CONSTRUCTION in Euclidean GEOMETRY.

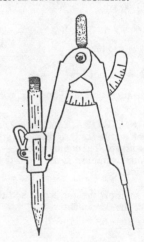

COMPLEMENTARY ANGLES, two angles whose sum equals a right angle (90°). The ACUTE ANGLES of a RIGHT TRIANGLE are complementary angles.

COMPLEMENT, LOGICAL, *see* NEGATION, LOGICAL.

COMPLETING SQUARES. A method of changing an expression of the form $x^2 + cx = 0$ into the alternate form $(x + a)^2 - b = 0$ by use of the fact that

$$x^2 + cx = \left(x + \frac{c}{2}\right)^2 - c',$$

where c' is a new constant.

Ex. 1: Put the following expression into the form

$$\left(x + \frac{c}{2}\right)^2 - c' = 0$$

by completing squares: $x^2 + 4x = 0$.

Sol.: Since

$$(x + 2)^2 = x^2 + 4x + 4, x^2 + 4x = (x + 2)^2 - 4.$$

Thus,

$$(x + 2)^2 - 4 = 0.$$

Completing squares is often useful in changing a QUADRATIC EQUATION into a standard form. This can be done only when the CROSS-PRODUCT TERM (the one involving xy) is zero, and ROTATION OF AXES may be needed to make the cross product term vanish.

Ex. 2: Use the fact that a circle of radius r and center at (h,k) has equation $(x - h)^2 + (y - k)^2 = r^2$ to find the center and radius of the following circle:

$$x^2 + y^2 + 4x - 6y = 3.$$

Sol.: Collect terms involving x and those involving y, and then complete the square:

$$x^2 + 4x = (x + 2)^2 - 4$$

and

$$y^2 - 6y = (y - 3)^2 - 9.$$

Therefore $(x + 2)^2 - 4 + (y - 3)^2 - 9 = 3$, or $(x + 2)^2 + (y - 3)^2 = 16$. The center is at $(-2,3)$, and the radius is 4.

COMPLEX FRACTION, a FRACTION that contains one or more fractions in its NUMERATOR, in its DENOMINATOR, or in both. To change a complex fraction to a simple fraction, divide the numerator by the denominator, or multiply both numerator and denominator by a common multiple of the denominators of the fractions.

Ex. 1: Simplify $\dfrac{1/2}{3/4}$.

Sol.: $1/2 \div 3/4 = 1/2 \times 4/3 = 2/3$.

Ex. 2: Simplify $\dfrac{3/4 - 2/3}{1/4 + 1/6}$.

Sol.:
$$(3/4 - 2/3) \div (1/4 + 1/6) = 1/12 \div 5/12 = 1/12 \times 12/5$$
$$= 1/5$$

or

$$\frac{(3/4 - 2/3)12}{(1/4 + 1/6)12} = \frac{9 - 8}{3 + 2} = \frac{1}{5}.$$

Ex. 3: Simplify $\dfrac{3/x + 4/y^2}{5x/2 - 2/x^2}$.

Sol.: $\dfrac{(3/x + 4/y^2)}{(5x/2 - 2/x^2)} \dfrac{2x^2y^2}{2x^2y^2} = \dfrac{6xy^2 + 8x^2}{5x^3y^2 - 4y^2}$

or

$$\frac{3/x + 4/y^2}{5x/2 - 2/x^2} = \frac{\dfrac{3y^2 + 4x}{xy^2}}{\dfrac{5x^3 - 4}{2x^2}} = \frac{3y^2 + 4x}{xy^2} \times \frac{2x^2}{5x^3 - 4} = \frac{6xy^2 + 8x^2}{5x^3y^2 - 4y^2}.$$

COMPLEX NUMBER, the sum of a REAL NUMBER and an IMAGI-NARY NUMBER. It is represented by the symbol $a + bi$ in which a and b are real numbers and $i = \sqrt{-1}$. If $b = 0$, the complex number becomes a real number; if $a = 0$, it becomes a pure imaginary. Any complex number should be changed to the $a + bi$ form before computations.

Ex. 1:   Add $5 + \sqrt{-3}$ and $2 - \sqrt{-12}$.
Sol.: $(5 + i\sqrt{3}) + (2 - 2i\sqrt{3}) = 7 - i\sqrt{3}$.
Ex. 2: $(\sqrt{-2} + \sqrt{-3})(\sqrt{-2} - \sqrt{-3})$.
Sol.: $(i\sqrt{2} + i\sqrt{3})(i\sqrt{2} - i\sqrt{3}) = 2i^2 - 3i^2$
$$= -2 + 3 = 1 \quad (i^2 = -1).$$
Ex. 3: $(3 - i\sqrt{2})^2$.
Sol.: $9 - 6i\sqrt{2} + 2i^2 = 7 - 6i\sqrt{2}$.

By using polar coordinates (*see* COORDINATES, POLAR), complex numbers may be written in polar form as $r(\cos\theta + i\sin\theta)$, abbreviated $r \operatorname{cis} \theta$, in which r is the MODULUS and θ is the AMPLITUDE. In Fig. 1,

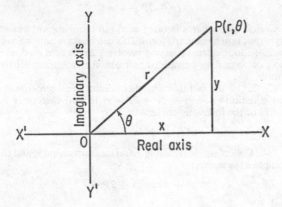

Fig. 1

$$\frac{x}{r} = \cos\theta \quad \text{and} \quad x = r\cos\theta$$
$$\frac{y}{r} = \sin\theta \quad \text{and} \quad y = r\sin\theta.$$

The complex number $x + yi = r\cos\theta + ri\sin\theta$
$$x + yi = r(\cos\theta + i\sin\theta)$$
$$x + yi = r\operatorname{cis}\theta.$$
Ex.: Express the complex number $-4 + 3i$ in polar form.

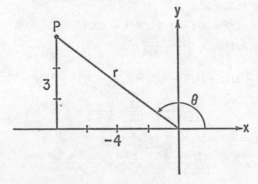

Fig. 2

Sol.: (See Fig. 2.) Let point P represent $-4 + 3i$.
$$x = -4, \quad y = 3$$

$r = \sqrt{x^2 + y^2} = \sqrt{16 + 9} = 5$, the modulus.
$$\theta = \text{ARC TAN}\, \frac{y}{x}$$
$$\theta = \arctan\left(\frac{3}{-4}\right) = 143°8', \text{ to nearest minute.}$$
$$P = 5 \operatorname{cis} 143°8'.$$

To represent a complex number on a system of rectangular coordinates (*see* COORDINATES, RECTANGULAR), points on the x-axis represent the real numbers and points on the y-axis represent the pure imaginary numbers. (See Fig. 3.) Every complex number $a + bi$ can be represented by a point on the plane, and every point in the plane can be represented by a complex number.

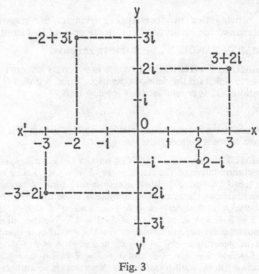

Fig. 3

To graph a complex number on a system of polar coordinates, et P be a point in the plane. Then OP is a line of definite length and makes the positive angle θ with the positive side of the x-axis. For every point in the plane there is a positive distance associated with a fixed positive angle, and for every fixed angle associated with a positive distance there is a unique point. This point is represented by an ORDERED PAIR (r, θ) in which r represents the directed line segment called the modulus, and θ represents the positive angle (rotated counterclockwise) called the amplitude. Then modulus $r = \sqrt{x^2 + y^2}$ and θ is the angle whose tangent is $\frac{y}{x}$.

If the point in the plane is $3 + 4i$,
$$\text{modulus } r = \sqrt{9 + 16} = 5,$$
$$\text{amplitude } \theta = \arctan\frac{y}{x}$$
$$\theta = \arctan\frac{4}{3}.$$

The amplitude is the angle whose tangent is $\frac{4}{3}$ and equals approximately $53°10'$.

COMPLEX NUMBER, CONJUGATE OF A, another complex number that differs from the given number only in the sign of the imaginary part (*see* IMAGINARY NUMBER). The conjugate of $a + bi$ is $a - bi$. The conjugate of a complex number is used to rationalize the denominator of a fraction.
Ex.: Divide $5 + 3i$ by $1 + 2i$.
Sol.: Write as a fraction and multiply the numerator and the denominator by the conjugate of the denominator.
$$\frac{5 + 3i}{1 + 2i} \cdot \frac{1 - 2i}{1 - 2i} = \frac{5 - 7i - 6i^2}{1 - 4i^2} = \frac{11 - 7i}{5}.$$

COMPLEX SERIES, a series of complex numbers such as Σz_n, where $z_n = a_n + b_n i$. It converges only if both Σa_n and Σb_n converge. *See also* COMPLEX NUMBER; SERIES.

COMPOSITE FUNCTION (kom-pah'-sit), a FUNCTION that can be written as the product of two or more functions, as $y^2 - 1$ which can be written as $(y - 1)(y + 1)$; hence a function that is factorable.

A function that represents a MAPPING that can be achieved by performing two simpler mappings in succession is said to be a composite function. E.g., if $g(x) = x^2$ and $h(x) = \sin x$, then $f(x) = \sin(x^2)$ can be written in the form $f(x) = h(g(x))$, read "f of x is equal to h of g of x" or, "f is the composition of h with g."

Ex.: $g(x) = \sqrt{1 - x}$, and $h(x) = \sqrt{x}$. Find $g(h(x))$, i.e., find the composition of g with h.

Sol.:
$$g(h(x)) = \sqrt{1 - h(x)}$$
$$= \sqrt{1 - \sqrt{x}}.$$

COMPOSITE NUMBER, a number that has two or more PRIME factors. Thus, 4, 6, and 10 are composite numbers since $4 = 1 \cdot 2 \cdot 2$, $6 = 1 \cdot 3 \cdot 2$, $10 = 1 \cdot 2 \cdot 5$. Numbers such as 3 or 5, which are PRIME NUMBERS, are not composite numbers. The expression "composite number" refers only to INTEGERS, not to RATIONAL NUMBERS or IRRATIONAL NUMBERS.

COMPOUND INTEREST, *see* INTEREST.

COMPOUND LOCUS, the set of POINTS that satisfies two or more sets of conditions. Each LOCUS is constructed and the point (or points) of intersection determines the compound locus.

Ex. 1: Find the locus of points a given distance from a given point and $\frac{1}{4}$ in. from a given line.

Sol.: In Fig. 1, given point O, distance r, and line through A and B, construct the following: (1) the locus of points a given distance r from given point O, which is a circle with O as the center and radius r and (2) the locus of points $\frac{1}{4}$ in. from the line through A and B, which is a pair of lines parallel to AB, each $\frac{1}{4}$ in. from AB. The required locus is a set of four points W, X, Y, and Z. With AB in different positions, the locus of points may be a set containing three points, two points, one point, or no points.

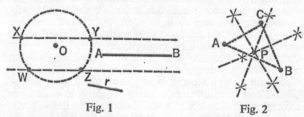

Fig. 1   Fig. 2

Ex. 2: Find the locus of points equidistant from three points.

Sol.: In Fig. 2, given points A, B, and C, construct the locus of points equidistant from two points, which is the perpendicular bisector of the segment joining the two points. Construct the perpendicular bisectors of the three segments joining the three points. The locus of points equidistant from three points A, B, and C is a set containing one point, P.

Ex. 3: Find all the points equidistant from the sides of a given angle and $\frac{1}{4}$ in. from a given line.

Sol.: In Fig. 3, given $\angle A$ and a line through B and C, con-

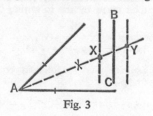

Fig. 3

struct the following: (1) the locus of points equidistant from the sides of an angle, which is the angle bisector and (2) the locus of points $\frac{1}{4}$ in. from line BC, which is a pair of lines parallel to BC and each $\frac{1}{4}$ in. from it. The required locus that satisfies both conditions is a set containing two points, X and Y.

COMPUTER, a device for performing logical operations, particularly mathematical computations, at speeds greater than are possible for a human being. The modern computer is a highly complex electronic machine capable of performing a million distinct operations a second. Contrary to some popular beliefs, computers are not superhuman. They are designed, built and operated by humans and are limited by the limits of their creators." Their great advantage is their speed, which enables them to perform in hours or even minutes what might take humans a lifetime. This ability to solve problems quickly saves not only time but also money and sometimes even lives. Today's most sophisticated computers can solve almost any possible problem that is presented to them, provided it is in a form they can manipulate. They can solve all types of mathematical problems as well as many problems in the physical and biological sciences; make business decisions for worldwide industries based on complicated economic, industrial and financial factors; operate an oil refinery or other complex establishments; direct a moon launching; or translate from one language to another.

History. The history of the computer dates back to efforts by the English mathematician Charles Babbage in the 1830's to design a calculating machine that would perform the basic mathematical operations automatically. His attempt failed, however, because the technology of the day was incapable of constructing his machine. It was not until 1944 that Howard H. Aiken of Harvard Univ. constructed the first, large-scale computer, built of both electrical and mechanical switches and relays. This computer was the forerunner of the *digital* type of computer, one that operates with digits, or numbers, and manipulates them to achieve the desired output information. The first electronic digital computer was completed in 1946 at the Univ. of Pennsylvania by John Mauchly and J. Presper Eckert. Their machine, called ENIAC (for Electronic Numerical Integrator and Calculator) had ab. 18,000 electron tubes and operated ab. 1,000 times faster than the Aiken machine. ENIAC was prewired and could perform its arithmetic and logical operations in just one way. The first computer with a memory, enabling the computer itself to make decisions and carry out a variety of operations, was BINAC, built in 1948. A variant of this computer was first built by Vannevar Bush, in 1930, at the Massachusetts Institute of Technology. It was then known as a *differential analyzer*, but now is called an analog computer and is able to solve problems involving continuously varying quantities rather than simply digits, as in the digital computer. The name *analog computer* comes from the fact that this type of computer operates by setting up electrical circuits whose voltages correspond, or are analogous to, the constants and variables in mathematical equations. The differential analyzer of Dr. Bush had shafts connected to each other through differential gears, similar to the gears mounted between the rear wheels of an automobile. Wheels on the ends of the shafts rested on rotating disks. The position of the wheels from the center of the disks and the amount that the disks rotated were analogous to the terms of a differential equation. The output of the differential analyzer was a curve drawn on graph paper. Today's analog computers use circuits instead of the wheels and disks of the differential analyzer.

Digital computer. A modern digital computer consists of three basic parts—a control unit, a memory or storage unit, and an arithmetic unit. The *control unit* supervises the operation of the computer in accordance with the instructions of a *program* inserted into the computer beforehand. *Programming* a computer involves preparing a complete sequence of instructions in a language that the computer can understand. There are various specialized *computer languages*, known by names such as FOR-

TRAN and ALGOL. The control unit reads the instructions of the program one by one and governs the operations of the computer circuits accordingly. The control unit contains an electronic clock that has a frequency of a million cycles per second, the computer performing one operation during each cycle. When the computer has completed all the operations required by the program, the control unit directs the completed information to auxiliary equipment attached to the computer.

The *memory unit* stores the data (information) and program entered into the computer. The memory is the most distinctive part of the computer; it was the invention of the memory that made possible the extremely high speeds and the adaptability of the computer, thus distinguishing it from calculating machines. Because of the memory, all of the data and instructions of the program, which are usually on punched paper tape or magnetic tape, can be read into the computer beforehand. Thus, once the computer is put in operation, it can function at the speed of its own electronic clock and is no longer dependent on the rate at which it can read a paper tape or magnetic tape feeding data to it.

Most computers have a *magnetic-core memory*, consisting of a large number of small rings, called *cores*, made of ferrite and strung together on a wire mesh. Each core has four wires running through it. Two of these wires, one running horizontally, the other vertically, determine the direction of magnetization. If the core is magnetized in one direction, it is said to be storing one *binary digit*, or *bit*, of information; if magnetized in the other direction, it is not storing information. The great simplicity of this system is made possible by using the BINARY NUMBER SYSTEM rather than the ordinary decimal system, which requires ten different digits. For the binary system, only two digits are necessary, 0 and 1. Thus, the two possible directions of magnetization of each core can be used to store either of these digits. This direction is in turn determined by the directions in which pulses of electricity pass through the horizontal and vertical wires. To change the magnetization of a particular core, pulses of electricity must pass through both wires simultaneously. A pulse of electricity through one wire alone is not sufficiently strong to change the magnetization of the core.

The other two wires passing through the core run diagonally. An *inhibit* wire prevents pulses of electricity from changing the magnetization of the core. A *sense* wire carries away a pulse of electricity induced in it by the changing magnetic field of a switched core. All four wires thus serve a function and together govern the storage and transferral of information in a specific core. In addition, the horizontal and vertical wires uniquely determine the position of each core. This position within the memory is called the *address* of the core, and the speed of the computer is determined primarily by the speed with which it can find a specific core and read out the bit of information stored at that address.

The *arithmetic unit* of the computer performs all the required logical and arithmetic operations. The arithmetic unit also contains *storage registers* in which information is kept temporarily while it is being worked on or while awaiting transfer into the memory unit. Ultimately, all mathematical operations, no matter how complex, can be reduced either to adding two numbers together or to subtracting one number from another. All that the arithmetic unit can do is add or subtract numbers. But its logic circuits enable the arithmetic unit to elaborate and combine the simple operations of addition and subtraction into the more complex operations necessary to perform calculus, matrix algebra, and various logic functions.

A computer by itself is incapable of accepting outside information or of delivering information. These functions are performed by auxiliary equipment attached to the computer. Information to be inserted into the computer is first placed on rolls of either punched paper tape or magnetic tape. The punched computer cards used by many banks and businesses are examples of the first type of input. For complex programs, however, magnetic tape is more common. The information is recorded in the form of magnetized spots on the tape. When the computer is ready to accept the information, the control unit starts the tape drive mechanism and ensures that the information is transferred into the storage unit of the computer. Likewise, information processed by the computer is read out into another roll of magnetic tape. The primary advantage of having rolls of magnetic tape is that the tape can transfer information at very high speeds, an important consideration if the computer is to be utilized with maximum efficiency. The output tape can then be fed into a printer or typewriter, which converts the information into printed lines. Alternatively, the tape can be fed to a cathode-ray tube where the information is converted into a diagram or words displayed on the face of the tube. A third alternative is to feed the tape into a machine that converts the information into a series of drawings or graphs on paper.

Analog computer. As mentioned, the analog computer differs from the digital computer in being able to analyze and solve problems involving continuously variable quantities. A modern analog computer has four main components—amplifiers, potentiometers, multipliers, and function generators. Together they are used to set up electrical circuits analogous to a wide variety of mathematical equations. The amplifiers magnify voltages in analogy to addition and decrease voltages in analogy to subtraction. Special integrating amplifying circuits integrate factors that change over a period of time. The potentiometers act as voltage dividers when they are connected to an amplifier circuit; they reduce the voltage by a constant factor. The multipliers are circuits which combine two or more voltages as if they were being multiplied together. Function generators are special circuits that perform certain functions, such as squaring a number or finding a square root, finding the sine or tangent of a number, finding a logarithm, and so on.

A complete analog computer consists of a large number of discrete components, including as many as a thousand amplifiers, all connected to a central *patchboard* similar in appearance and function to a telephone switchboard. To set up and solve a particular equation, the necessary components are connected together by electrical *patchcords* to simulate the mathematical equation being solved. The starting conditions and constants are inserted into the computer by turning the knobs connected to the appropriate components. When the computer is started, the voltages passing through the components are varied automatically in accordance with the terms of the equation. The output voltage represents the solution to the equation and can be converted into a curve drawn on graph paper.

Analog computers are used primarily to simulate complex events quickly. For example, an analog computer can simulate the performance of a supersonic jet aircraft under varying conditions. These conditions can be changed quickly to build up a family of curves that inform the designers almost immediately how the aircraft will perform in actual flight. Analog computers will also simulate the flight of a rocket, the trajectory of a bullet, and similar complex motions. Spacecraft contain computers to help astronauts make complicated decisions on adjustments to their flight paths. Special purpose analog computers are also used to direct antiaircraft batteries and to navigate ships.

CONCAVE POLYGON, *see* POLYGON.

CONCENTRIC (kahn-sen'-trik), a term used to describe two CIRCLES or SPHERES that have the same center. In the figure, O is the center of two concentric circles whose radii are OA and OB.

Ex.: Are the circles given by the following two equations concentric?

$$y^2 + x^2 - 2x - 4y - 4 = 0.$$
$$(x - 1)^2 + (y - 2)^2 = 25.$$

Sol.: Completing squares gives the following equation in standard form for the first circle:

$$(x - 1)^2 + (y - 2)^2 = 9.$$

By inspection of both formulas, the center of each circle is at (1,2). Therefore the circles are concentric.

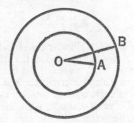

CONCHOID (kahn'-koid), the locus of points P and P' as line OQ rotates about O when P, P', Q and O are as follows: Given a line through the origin, O, intersecting the line $y = a$ at point Q, and points P and P' taken on line OQ such that QP and QP' are equal to some constant, b. The PARAMETRIC EQUATIONS of the conchoid are $x = a \tan \theta \pm b \sin \theta$, $y = a \pm b \cos \theta$, where θ is the angle from the positive x-axis to the line OP. In polar coordinates (*see* COORDINATES, POLAR), the equation of the conchoid is given by $OP = r = b + a \sec \theta$. In rectangular coordinates (*see* COORDINATES, RECTANGULAR), the equation is given by $(x - a)^2(x^2 + y^2) = b^2x^2$. The curve is also called the *Conchoid of Nicomedes*.

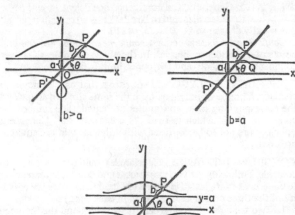

Chonchoid

CONCLUSION, in mathematics, the part of a THEOREM to be proved. *See also* CONDITIONAL STATEMENT.

CONCURRENT LINES (kahn-kur'-rent), three or more lines that pass through the same POINT.

The perpendicular BISECTORS of the sides of a triangle are concurrent at a point equidistant from the vertices. The point of concurrency is called the CIRCUMCENTER. In Fig. 1, the circumcenter of $\triangle ABC$ is O. It is the center of the circle with RADIUS AO that may be circumscribed about $\triangle ABC$.

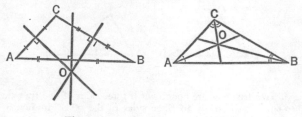

Fig. 1   Fig. 2

The bisectors of the angles of a triangle are concurrent at a point equidistant from the sides of the triangle. The point of concurrency is called the INCENTER. The incenter is the center of the circle inscribed in the triangle. In Fig. 2, the radius of the circle is the PERPENDICULAR from O, the incenter, to any side of the triangle.

The altitudes of a triangle are concurrent. The point of concurrency is called the ORTHOCENTER. In Fig. 3, O is the orthocenter.

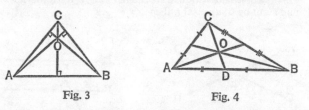

Fig. 3   Fig. 4

The MEDIANS OF A TRIANGLE are concurrent at a point two-thirds of the distance from each vertex to the midpoint of the opposite side. The point of concurrency of the medians of a triangle is called the CENTROID. It is the center of gravity of the triangle. In $\triangle ABC$ (see Fig. 4), $\overline{CO} = 2\overline{OD}$. If the median is 9 in., the centroid divides it into segments 3 in. and 6 in.

CONDITIONAL CONVERGENCE. A series Σa_n which includes some negative terms may converge even though the series $\Sigma |a_n|$ does not. It is then said to converge conditionally.

Ex.: $\sum_{n=1}^{\infty} (-1)^{n+1}/n = 1 - \frac{1}{2} + \frac{1}{3} - \frac{1}{4} \cdots$

converges. But $\Sigma |(-1)^{n+1}/n| = \Sigma 1/n$, which is the HARMONIC SERIES, is known to diverge. *See also* ABSOLUTE CONVERGENCE; ALTERNATING SERIES; SERIES.

CONDITIONAL EQUATION, as distinguished from an IDENTITY, an EQUATION which holds only for a definite number of values, if any. In the equation, $3x + 2 = 8$, the only value for x that satisfies the equation is 2. In the equation, $x^2 - 5x + 6 = 0$, the only values that satisfy the equation are 3 and 2. In the expression "$\sin x = 2$" and "$\log (-10) = x$," there are no values of x for which the statements of equality will make sense if the terms "sin" and "log" are taken as commonly defined.

Usually a conditional equation is referred to only as an equation.

CONDITIONAL PROBABILITY. The probability (*see* PROBABILITY OF AN EVENT) that an Event A occurs, given that an Event B has occurred or is certain to occur, is called "*the conditional probability of A, given B*" and is denoted $P(A \mid B)$. A formula in terms of initial probabilities is

$$P(A \mid B) = \frac{P(AB)}{P(B)}.$$

Since B is certain to occur, only those elements that correspond to the occurrence of B are in the SAMPLE SPACE. Hence, an alternative method of finding $P(A \mid B)$ is to reduce the sample space and find the probability that A will occur in the reduced sample space.

Ex.: Toss a coin 4 times and let B be the event of throwing at least 3 heads, and A be the event of throwing 4 heads.

$$P(A \mid B) = \frac{P(AB)}{P(B)} = \frac{1/16}{5/16} = \frac{1}{5}.$$

Alternatively, if Event B is certain to occur, then the reduced sample space would consist only of $HHHT, HHTH, HTHH, THHH, HHHH$. Each of these 5 events is equally likely, and only one of them is favorable to the outcome of Event A. Therefore, $P(A \mid B) = \frac{1}{5}$.

CONDITIONAL STATEMENT, a statement in which a specific conclusion follows a given condition or a set of conditions. The statement may be written in the if-then form. The if-clause states the given condition and the then-clause states the conclusion that follows. The condition stated in the if-clause is called the HYPOTHESIS.

Ex. 1: If two straight lines intersect, then the VERTICAL ANGLES are equal. In Fig. 1, if straight lines *AB* and *CD* intersect at *E*, then ∠1 = ∠2.

Ex. 2: If two PARALLEL LINES are cut by a TRANSVERSAL, the ALTERNATE-INTERIOR ANGLES are equal. In Fig. 2, if parallel lines *l* and *l'* cut by transversal *t*, then ∠x = ∠y.

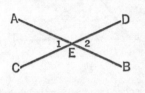

Fig. 1   Fig. 2

A declarative sentence such as, "An EQUILATERAL TRIANGLE is also equiangular" may be stated in the if-then form, "If a triangle is equilateral, then it is also equiangular."

CONE, the geometric figure formed by all the lines (called elements) which can be passed through a plane closed curve (called the base) and a fixed point (called the vertex) not in the plane of that curve. The name is applicable to either (1) the finite solid contained between the base and vertex (see Fig. 1) or (2) the compound sheet of two infinite nappes formed by all the elements extended indefinitely in both directions through the vertex (see Fig. 2). For the solid, if *B* is the area of the base and *h* is the altitude from the vertex to the plane of the base, the volume *V* is given by the formula:

$$V = \frac{Bh}{3}.$$

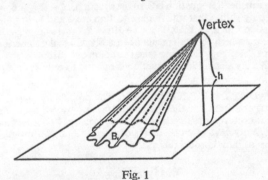

Fig. 1

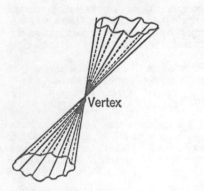

Fig. 2

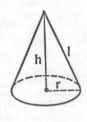

Fig. 3

A cone with a circular base is called a circular cone. If the radius of the base is *r*, then the formula for the volume, *V*, becomes:

$$V = \frac{\pi r^2 h}{3}.$$

A right circular cone is a circular cone in which the vertex lies directly over the center of the base so that the foot of the altitude, *h*, coincides with the center of the base (see Fig. 3). The altitude extended may also be termed the axis, since it is possible to generate a right circular cone by rotating any element through the vertex about this axis—altitude. Also, the segment, *l*, of any element between the vertex and the base may be termed the slant height. The formula for volume is as for other cones, but the formula for lateral area, *L*, is given by the special formula, $L = \pi r l$, in which *r* is the radius of the base.

CONFIDENCE INTERVAL, in statistics, an interval of numerical values within which a PARAMETER is said to lie with a certain degree of confidence (not probability). The interval might be given as a continued inequality, as $40 < \mu < 60$, or as an ordered pair, as (40,60).

The interpretation of the statement "$40 < \mu < 60$ is a 95 percent confidence interval for μ" is that, on the average, 95 out of 100 intervals found in the same manner (using different samples) will contain μ. Here the *confidence coefficient*, or *degree of confidence*, is .95. Generally, the confidence coefficient is said to be $1 - \alpha$, and the interval is said to be a $100(1 - \alpha)$ percent interval; α is usually chosen to be .01, .05, or .10.

Confidence limits, also called *confidence bounds*, are the end points of a confidence interval. In the above example, the lower confidence limit is 40, and the upper limit is 60.

CONGRUENT POLYGONS, POLYGONS that can be made to coincide. Congruent polygons have the same size and shape and the corresponding sides and angles are equal. The symbol for congruent is ≅, which is read "is congruent to." Congruent polygons are not to be confused with polygons that are equal in area only.

CONGRUENT TRIANGLES, triangles that can be made to coincide. Following are basic THEOREMS and COROLLARIES relating to congruent triangles: (Tic marks are used to indicate the equality of the three corresponding parts in each case.)

1. Two triangles are congruent if two sides and the included angle of one triangle are equal respectively to two sides and the included angle of the other. This assumption is abbreviated S.A.S. In Fig. 1, △*ABC* ≅ △*DEF* (S.A.S.). (Note: The angle must be included between the sides.)

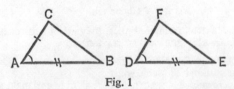

Fig. 1

2. Two triangles are congruent if two angles and the included side of one triangle are equal respectively to two angles and the included side of the other. In Fig. 2, △*ABC* ≅ △*DEF* (A.S.A.).

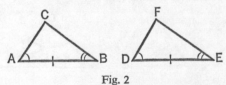

Fig. 2

3. Two triangles are congruent if three sides of one triangle are equal respectively to three sides of the other. In Fig. 3, △*ABC* ≅ △*DEF* (S.S.S.).

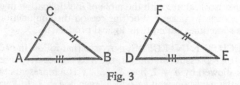

Fig. 3

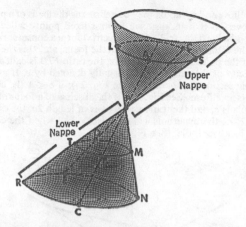

4. Two triangles are congruent if two angles and a side of one triangle are equal respectively to two angles and a side of the other. In Fig. 4, $\triangle ABC \cong \triangle DEF$ (S.A.A.).

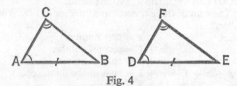

Fig. 4

5. Two RIGHT TRIANGLES are congruent if the two legs of one equal respectively the two legs of the other. In Fig. 5, $\triangle ABC \cong \triangle DEF$ (L.L.).

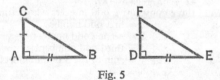

Fig. 5

6. Two right triangles are congruent if the HYPOTENUSE and one leg of one triangle are equal respectively to the hypotenuse and one leg of the other. In Fig. 6, $\triangle ABC \cong \triangle DEF$ (H.L.).

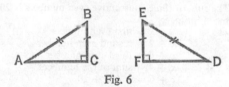

Fig. 6

7. Two right triangles are congruent if the hypotenuse and one ACUTE ANGLE of one triangle are equal respectively to the hypotenuse and acute angle of the other. In Fig. 7, $\triangle ABC \cong \triangle DEF$ (H.A.).

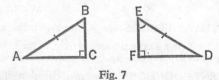

Fig. 7

8. CORRESPONDING PARTS OF CONGRUENT TRIANGLES are equal. In Fig. 1 above, since $\triangle ABC \cong \triangle DEF$ (S.A.S.); $BC = EF$, $\angle C = \angle F$, $\angle B = \angle E$. (Corr. parts of $\cong$ $\triangle$ are =.)

CONICAL SURFACE, a surface generated by a straight LINE moving so that it intersects a fixed curve and a point not in the plane of the curve. The moving line is called the *generatrix* of the surface, the fixed curve is the *directrix* of the surface, and the fixed point is the *vertex* of the surface. Each position of the generatrix is an *element* of the surface. Each of the two parts of the surface separated by the vertex is a *nappe* of the surface (upper nappe and lower nappe). In the figure, *RS* is the generatrix. Curve *TBM* is the directrix. *P* is the vertex. *APBC*, *LPMN* and *CPDE* are three of the elements. If the directrix of a conical surface is a circle, and its vertex is on a line PERPENDICULAR to the

plane of the circle that passes through the center of the circle, the surface is called a *circular conical surface.*

CONIC SECTIONS, the curves that are formed by the intersection of a plane and a right circular CONE. See Fig. 1.

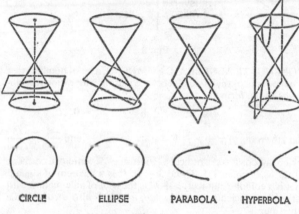

Fig. 1

When the plane is PERPENDICULAR to the AXIS of the cone, the figure is a CIRCLE. If a plane intersects all the ELEMENTS OF THE CONE but is not perpendicular to the axis, the section is an ELLIPSE. If the plane is parallel to an element, the slant height, the curve is a PARABOLA. If the plane intersects both parts of the conic surface, and is parallel to the axis, the curve is a HYPERBOLA. If the plane passes through the vertex, special cases result such as a single point (the vertex), a single straight line of indefinite length, (an element), or two such intersecting lines (a pair of elements). All conic sections are graphs of QUADRATIC EQUATIONS.

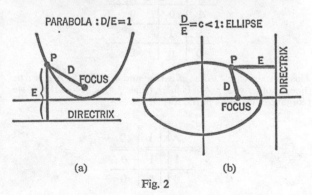

Fig. 2

The ellipse and parabola may be defined as the locus of a point that moves so that its distance from a fixed point (called the focus) and a fixed line (called the directrix) form a constant ratio. If F is the distance of the point from the focus, and D is the distance of the point from the directrix, the ratio F/D is called the eccentricity of the conic section, usually denoted by e. If $e = 1$ the conic section is a parabola (see Fig. 2a); if $e < 1$ the conic section is an ellipse. (See Fig. 2b.) If the abscissa of a focus of the hyperbola is c, and the transverse axis is of length $2a$, the essentricity, e, of the hyperbola is c/a. Also, $e > 1$ when the conic section is a hyperbola. (See Fig. 3.)

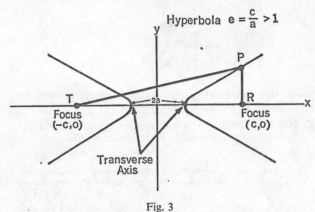

Fig. 3

CONJUGATE ALGEBRAIC NUMBERS, a set of numbers that are the roots of the same algebraic equation with rational coefficients in the form

$$a_0x^n + a_1x^{n-1} + \cdots + a_n = 0.$$

E.g., the roots of $x^2 + x - 1 = 0$ are $\dfrac{-1 + \sqrt{5}}{2}$ and $\dfrac{-1 - \sqrt{5}}{2}$, which are CONJUGATE radicals. Roots may be conjugate COMPLEX NUMBERS, such as $3 + 2i$ and $3 - 2i$. It is a theorem of algebra that if a complex number, $a + bi$ is the root of an equation with rational coefficients, its conjugate, $a - bi$ is also a root of the equation.

CONJUGATE OF A BINOMIAL, a second binomial that differs from the given binomial by only one sign. The conjugate of $(a + b)$ is $(a - b)$.

CONJUNCTION, ($\land$), in mathematics, in the ALGEBRA OF PROPOSITIONS, the assertion that two propositions are both true. E.g., $p \land q$, sometimes written $p \cdot q$, is read: "p is true and q is true," or "p and q" for short. The TRUTH TABLE for $p \land q$ is:

p	q	$p \land q$
1	1	1
1	0	0
0	1	0
0	0	0

This can be read: "When p is true and q is true, $p \land q$ is true (line 2); otherwise, $p \land q$ is false, (lines 3,4,5)." Note that if we reorganize this table in the format,

	q	
$\land$	1	0
---	---	---
p	1	1	0
	0	0	0

it becomes ISOMORPHIC with the table of multiplication in a two-valued BOOLEAN ALGEBRA. For this reason the conjunction of p and q is sometimes called their logical product.

CONSECUTIVE INTEGERS, INTEGERS that follow in order, as 7, 8, 9. If n represents an integer, the next consecutive integer is $n + 1$, followed by $n + 2, n + 3, \ldots$. If n represents an odd integer, the next consecutive odd integer is $n + 2$, followed by $n + 4, n + 6, \ldots$. If n represents an even integer, the next consecutive even integer is $n + 2$, followed by $n + 4$, $n + 6, \ldots$.

CONSECUTIVE NUMBER PROBLEMS.

Ex. 1: The sum of three consecutive integers in 129. What are the numbers?

Sol.: Let

$$x = \text{first number}$$

then

$$x + 1 = \text{second number}$$

and

$$x + 2 = \text{third number.}$$

$$x + x + 1 + x + 2 = \text{sum of the 3 integers.}$$

Therefore

$$3x + 3 = 129$$
$$3x = 126$$
$$x = 42, \text{ the first number.}$$
$$x + 1 = 43, \text{ the second number.}$$
$$x + 2 = 44, \text{ the third number.}$$

Check: $42 + 43 + 44 = 129$.

Ex. 2: Find three consecutive odd integers whose sum is 39.

Sol.: Let

$$x = \text{first odd number}$$

then

$$x + 2 = \text{second odd number}$$

and

$$x + 4 = \text{third odd number.}$$

$$x + x + 2 + x + 4 = \text{sum of the 3 odd numbers.}$$

Therefore

$$3x + 6 = 39$$
$$3x = 33$$
$$x = 11, \text{ the first odd number.}$$
$$x + 2 = 13, \text{ the second odd number.}$$
$$x + 4 = 15, \text{ the third odd number.}$$

Check: $11 + 13 + 15 = 39$.

Ex. 3: The sum of three consecutive even numbers is 20 more than the second integer.

Sol.: Let

$$x = \text{first even number}$$

then

$$x + 2 = \text{second even number}$$

and

$$x + 4 = \text{third even number}$$

$$x + x + 2 + x + 4 = \text{sum of the numbers.}$$

$$3x + 6 = x + 2 + 20$$
$$2x + 6 = 22$$
$$2x = 16$$
$$x = 8, \text{ the first even number.}$$
$$x + 2 = 10, \text{ the second even number.}$$
$$x + 4 = 12, \text{ the third even number.}$$

Check: $8 + 10 + 12 = 10 + 20$
$$30 = 30.$$

CONSECUTIVE NUMBERS, *see* CONSECUTIVE INTEGERS.

CONSEQUENT, in a RATIO, the second term, or the DENOMINATOR. In the ratio x/y, the consequent is y. *See also* ANTECEDENT.

CONSISTENT EQUATIONS, a system of equations that have at least one solution in common. Thus, $3x - y = 5$ and $4x + y = 9$ are equations with only one solution in common, and are said to be consistent and independent. Also, $2x + 4y = 10$ and $3x + 6y = 15$ have an infinite number of common solutions and, are said to be consistent and dependent. *See also* EQUATIONS, SYSTEMS OF LINEAR.

CONSTANT, in mathematics, as distinguished from a VARIABLE, a quantity which has a fixed value. E.g., 5 and π are constants; the sum of the interior angles of a POLYGON increases as the number of sides increases, but the sum of the exterior angles is constant since it remains 360° as the number of sides increases.

CONSTRUCTION, a geometric proposition in which a figure is drawn with straightedge and COMPASS only. Two axioms are necessary for all constructions:

1. One, and only one, straight line may be drawn between two points.

2. With any given point as the center and any given distance as the RADIUS a CIRCLE may be drawn.

It is necessary, as with theorems, to prove constructions. Constructions are included under the following entries: ANGLES, EQUAL; BISECTOR OF AN ANGLE; EXTREME AND MEAN RATIO; FOURTH PROPORTIONAL TANGENT LINE; PARALLEL LINES; PERPENDICULAR; PERPENDICULAR BISECTOR OF A LINE SEGMENT; THIRTY-SIXTY RIGHT TRIANGLE; TRIANGLE; TRISECTION OF A LINE SEGMENT.

CONTINGENCY TABLE. In some statistical situations, each member of a sample can be classified by two criteria. For example, if the members are people, each might be classified by hair color into k types (blonde, brown, black, etc.) and his eye color into r types (blue, brown, etc.). There are then kr combinations altogether, and the number of individuals in each of these categories may be conveniently shown by means of a table, which is known as a *contingency table*.

CRITERION 2

		1	2	$\cdots$	k	Totals
	1	O_{11}	O_{12}	$\cdots$	O_{1k}	R_1
Criterion 1	2	O_{21}	O_{22}	$\cdots$	O_{2k}	R_2
	$\cdot$	$\cdot$	$\cdot$		$\cdot$	$\cdot$
	$\cdot$	$\cdot$	$\cdot$		$\cdot$	$\cdot$
	$\cdot$	$\cdot$	$\cdot$		$\cdot$	$\cdot$
	r	O_{r1}	O_{r2}	$\cdots$	O_{rk}	R_r
Totals		C_1	C_2	$\cdots$	C_k	n

The NULL HYPOTHESIS that the two criteria of classification are independent can be tested by means of the CHI-SQUARED DISTRIBUTION. The ALTERNATIVE HYPOTHESIS is that the two criteria are not independent. In order to perform the test, calculate $x^2 = \Sigma \dfrac{(O_{ij} - E_{ij})^2}{E_{ij}}$, where O_{ij} denotes the observed number in the ith row and jth column of the contingency table and E_{ij} denotes the expected number (the number that we would expect if the criteria are, in fact, independent) in the ith row and jth column, and the summation is taken over all values of i and j (all rows and columns of the contingency table). The EXPECTED VALUES are found from the formula

$$E_{ij} = \frac{R_i C_j}{n},$$

where R_i denotes the total number of observations in the ith row, C_j denotes the total number of observations in the jth column, and n denotes the total number of observations in the entire sample.

In general, for a contingency table with r rows and k columns, x^2 has $(r-1)(k-1)$ DEGREES OF FREEDOM. The null hypothesis is rejected if the x^2 calculated from the data exceeds the upper α-point of the x^2-distribution with $(r-1)(k-1)$ degrees of freedom.

CONTINUOUS FUNCTION. A FUNCTION, $f(x)$, is said to be continuous at a point where $x = a$ if

$$\lim_{x \to a} f(x) = f(a).$$

Interpreted informally, this means that the function is continuous at any point where it does not "skip" from one value to a distant value, but instead "changes smoothly." Graphically, a continuous function has an unbroken line as its graph.

A function is said to be continuous throughout an INTERVAL if it is continuous at each point of the interval.

Ex.: Let $f(x)$ and $g(x)$ have the graphs sketched in the figure. Is either of them discontinuous? If so, at which point(s)?

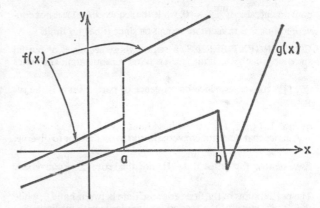

Sol.: The function $f(x)$ is discontinuous at $x = a$, while $g(x)$ is continuous at all points.

CONTINUOUS RANDOM VARIABLE, in statistics, a RANDOM VARIABLE that can (theoretically) take on any value in an interval of values. In general, any variable that is *measured* rather than *counted;* e.g., time, heights, weights, temperature, agricultural yields, are continuous.

CONTINUUM (kun-tin'-yoo-um), a compact connected SET. If a set contains at least two points, it contains an infinite number of points, since between any two points there is a third point. The set of real numbers is called the continuum of reals.

CONTRADICTION, LAW OF, in the ALGEBRA OF PROPOSITIONS, the principle that a proposition and its negation (*see* NEGATION, LOGICAL) cannot both be true at the same time. Thus $x = 8$ and $x \neq 8$ cannot be satisfied by the same replacement for x. It is the basis of the principle of dichotomy (*see* DICHOTOMY, LAW OF) which states that a proposition is either true or false, but not both, and it is a principle that is used in *proof* by *contradiction* (*reductio ad absurdum*).

CONTRAPOSITIVE OF A STATEMENT, a second statement in which the contradictory of the HYPOTHESIS of the given statement is interchanged with the contradictory of the CONCLUSION of the given statement. Thus, the contrapositive of the statement "h implies c" is "not c implies not h." If a statement that has one conclusion is true, its contrapositive is true; if the statement is false, its contrapositive is also false.

Statement: If two lines are cut by a TRANSVERSAL so that a pair of ALTERNATE-INTERIOR ANGLES are equal, the lines are parallel.

Contrapositive: If two nonparallel lines are cut by a transversal, the alternate-interior angles are not equal.

CONTROL CHART, in statistics, a GRAPH constructed by plotting the results of samples from some production process. A control chart is usually constructed with a horizontal line (the central line), that indicates the expected mean value (*see* EXPECTED VALUE) of some characteristic of the sample, and two lines on either side of the central line, that indicate the upper and lower control limits. (See figure.) A process is assumed to be under control so long as the sample proportions, where plotted, remain between the upper and lower control limits.

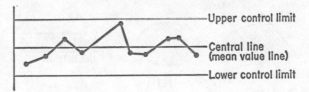

CONVERGENT SEQUENCE, a SEQUENCE that has a limit (*see* LIMIT OF A SEQUENCE). The sequence $1/n$; $n = 1, 2, 3, \ldots$ is convergent, since $\lim\limits_{n \to \infty} \dfrac{1}{n} = 0$, while the sequence $(-1)^n$ is not convergent, or is a DIVERGENT SEQUENCE since it has no limit.

CONVERGENT SERIES, a SERIES whose sequence of partial sums approaches a limit (*see* LIMIT OF A SEQUENCE). The series $\sum\limits_{n=0}^{\infty} (\tfrac{1}{2})^n$ converges, since its sequence of partial sums is the sequence $1, 1\tfrac{1}{2}, 1\tfrac{3}{4}, 1\tfrac{7}{8}, \ldots$, whose limit is 2.

A series that does not converge is said to oscillate or to diverge.

E.g., neither the series $\sum\limits_{n=0}^{\infty} (-1)^n$ nor the series $\sum\limits_{n=1}^{\infty} \dfrac{1}{n}$ converges.

The partial sums of the first series oscillate between 1 and 0, while the partial sums of the second become large without limit. *See also* COMPARISON TEST; INTEGRAL TEST; RATIO TEST.

CONVERSE of a theorem having one conclusion, the STATEMENT obtained by interchanging the CONCLUSION with one HYPOTHESIS.

Theorem: If two sides of a TRIANGLE are equal, the ANGLES opposite these sides are equal.

Converse: If two angles of a triangle are equal, the sides opposite these angles are equal.

Not all converses of true statements are true, as:

Statement: RIGHT ANGLES are equal angles.

Converse: Equal angles are right angles.

Some theorems have more than one converse. If a theorem has two hypotheses and two conclusions, five converses are possible. Both hypotheses may be interchanged with both conclusions, or each hypothesis may be interchanged with each conclusion.

Statement: If a line bisects the vertex angle of an ISOSCELES TRIANGLE, then it bisects the base and is PERPENDICULAR to the base.

Converses:

1. The perpendicular bisector of the base of a triangle bisects the vertex angle and the triangle is isosceles.

2. If a line bisects the vertex angle and the base of a triangle, it is perpendicular to the base and the triangle is isosceles.

3. If a line bisects a vertex angle of a triangle and is perpendicular to the base, it bisects the base and the triangle is isosceles.

4. If a line bisects the base of an isosceles triangle, it bisects the vertex angle and is perpendicular to the base.

5. If a line is perpendicular to the base of an isosceles triangle, it bisects the vertex angle and the base.

CONVEX POLYGON, *see* POLYGON.

CONVEX SET, a set of points in the plane (or in space) such that the line segment joining any two points lies entirely within the set. Thus a convex set is one which has no holes in it and which is not indented. Sometimes the definition is strengthened to include CLOSURE: All LIMIT POINTS of a convex set must be members of it (*see* CLOSED SET).

Ex. 1: Any straight line segment is convex.
Ex. 2: Any plane in three dimensions is convex.
Ex. 3: The figures shown in Fig. 1 are convex:

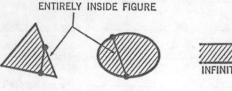

Fig. 1

Note that the intersection of any two convex sets (*see* INTERSECTION OF SETS) is also convex, while the UNION of two convex sets need not be, as Fig. 2 shows.

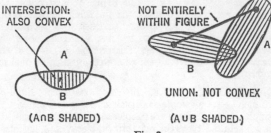

Fig. 2

COORDINATE (koh-or'-din-et), a number, or one of a set of numbers used to locate a point. To locate a point on a line, one coordinate must be given; in the PLANE, two coordinates are needed; and in space, three coordinates are necessary to locate a point. See NUMBER LINE; COORDINATES, CYLINDRICAL; COORDINATES, POLAR; COORDINATES, RECTANGULAR; COORDINATES, SPHERICAL.

COORDINATE GEOMETRY, *see* GEOMETRY, ANALYTIC.

COORDINATE LINE, *see* NUMBER LINE.

COORDINATE PLANE, a PLANE together with a set of COORDINATES in it. Since in this case every POINT corresponds to a pair of numbers, i.e., its coordinates, the coordinate plane is sometimes thought of as the SET of all pairs of numbers. (See figure.) These pairs are the CARTESIAN PRODUCT of the REAL NUMBERS with themselves.

See also, NUMBER LINE; COORDINATES, RECTANGULAR; VECTOR SPACE.

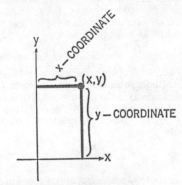

COORDINATES, CYLINDRICAL, a COORDINATE SYSTEM in which a point in space is located with reference to its height, z, above the xy-plane together with the polar coordinates (*see* COORDINATES, POLAR), (r,θ), of its projection on the xy-plane. The cylindrical coordinates of a point are given by an ordered triple, (r,θ,z).

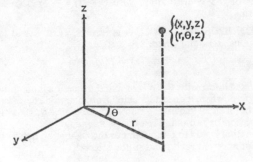

The relations between the rectangular coordinates (*see* COORDI-NATES, RECTANGULAR) of a point in space, (x,y,z) and its cylin-drical coordinates, (r,θ,z) are:

$$x = r \cos \theta$$
$$y = r \sin \theta$$
$$z = z.$$

See also COORDINATES, SPHERICAL.

COORDINATES, POLAR, a COORDINATE SYSTEM in which a point is located with reference to a fixed half line, or RAY, and the endpoint of the ray. The ray is called the polar axis (*see* AXIS, POLAR), and the end-point is called the POLE, or ORIGIN. The segment joining the point to the pole is the RADIUS VECTOR, de-noted by **r**. The directed angle with the polar axis as its terminal side (*see* SIDE OF AN ANGLE) is denoted by θ. The distance r is called the radial distance, and the angle θ is called the angle of the point. θ is always the POSITIVE ANGLE from the polar axis to the line through the point, and r is always a DIRECTED DISTANCE. Then r and θ are the polar coordinates of a point, P, which may be given by the ordered pair (r,θ). Any ordered pair (r,θ) deter-mines a unique point, P, but a point P has many sets of polar co-ordinates, e.g., (r,θ), $(r,\theta + n \cdot 360°)$, where n is an integer. (See Fig. 1a.)

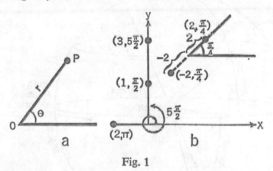

Fig. 1

Ex. 1: Plot the points $(1, \pi/2)$, $(2,\pi)$, $(3,5\pi/2)$ (*see* RADIAN) on a system of polar coordinates.
Sol.: See Fig. 1b.
Ex. 2: Plot the points $(2,\pi/4)$ and $(-2,\pi/4)$ on a set of polar coordinates.
Sol.: See Fig. 1b.

COORDINATES, RECTANGULAR, a COORDINATE SYSTEM used to locate a point with reference to two or three PERPENDICU-LAR lines. In the PLANE, a point is located in terms of its distance from each of two perpendicular lines, called axes. The horizontal axis is called the x-axis, and the vertical axis is called the y-axis. The point of intersection of the axes is called the origin. The coordinates of a point in such a system is an ordered pair, (x,y). The first component, x, is called the ABSCISSA and represents the distance of the point from the x-axis. The second component, y, is called the ORDINATE and represents the distance of the point from the y-axis. The abscissa is positive to the right of the origin and negative to the left of it. The ordinate is positive above the origin and negative below it.

The intersecting axes separate the plane into four parts called quadrants I, II, III, and IV. (See Fig. 1.) Rectangular Coordi-nates are also called Cartesian Coordinates after DESCARTES.

Ex. 1: Locate the point $A(4,5)$.
Sol.: From the origin, count four units to the right along the x-axis, and from there, count five units up along a line parallel to the y-axis.

Ex. 2: Locate (or plot) the points whose coordinates are $B(-3,4)$, $C(-2,-5)$, $D(4,-3)$.
Sol.: See Fig. 1.

In space, a point is located in terms of its distance from each of three intersecting planes, called the xy, xz, and yz-planes. The

three intersections of these planes are called the x, y, and z-axes. The coordinates of a point in space are given by an ordered triple, (x,y,z), in which the first component represents the dis-tance from the x-axis, the second represents the distance from the y-axis, and the third represents the distance from the z-axis.

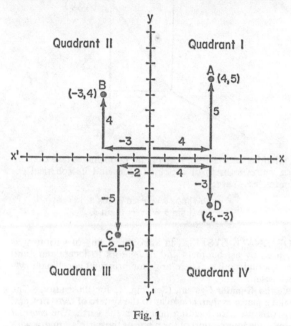

Fig. 1

Ex. 3: Plot the point $E(6,5,9)$.
Sol.: Beginning at the origin count six units to the right along the x-axis. (See Fig. 2.) From there, count five units along a line parallel to the y-axis; then count nine units along a line parallel to the z-axis.

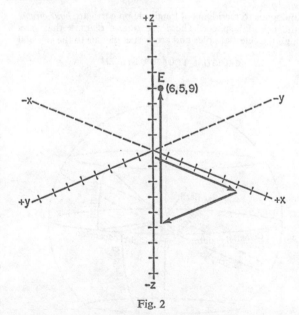

Fig. 2

COORDINATES, SPHERICAL (koh-or'-din-ayts sfir'-i-kal), a COORDINATE SYSTEM in which a point P in space is located with reference to its distance r from the origin, the angle ϕ from the positive z-axis to the line OP, and the angle θ from the positive x-axis to the line through the origin and the projection M of P

on the *xy*-plane. The spherical coordinates of *P* are given by the ordered triple (r,θ,ϕ). (See figure.)

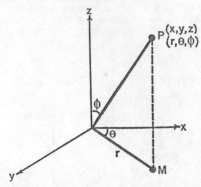

The relations between the rectangular coordinates (*see* COORDINATES, RECTANGULAR) of a point (x,y,z) and its spherical coordinates (r,θ,ϕ) are:

$$x = |\theta M| \cos\theta = r\sin\phi\cos\theta.$$
$$y = |\theta M| \sin\theta = r\sin\phi\sin\theta.$$
$$z = r\cos\phi.$$

COORDINATE SYSTEM, in astronomy, any of various systems used by astronomers and navigators to locate stars and other celestial bodies. There are four principal coordinate systems in use.

Celestial Equator System. (See Fig. 1, for illustration.) The celestial equator system is similar to the system of LATITUDE and LONGITUDE used for locating points on the earth. The *celestial equator* is the intersection of the plane of the earth's equator with the celestial sphere (Fig. 1). The angular distance of a body above or below the celestial equator is its *declination*. North and south declinations are indicated by N and S by + and −, respectively. Parallels of declination are like parallels of latitude on earth and range from 0° at the celestial equator to 90° at the N and S *celestial poles*.

Analogous to meridians of longitude on earth are *hour circles* on the celestial sphere. These are GREAT CIRCLES that pass through the celestial poles and are perpendicular to the celestial equator. The hour circle that passes through an observer's *zenith* (the point directly over his head) is his *celestial meridian*. The hour circle through the vernal EQUINOX is usually taken as the analogue of the PRIME MERIDIAN on earth. Instead of degrees of longitude E and W, two other kinds of units are used. Astronomers measure eastward from the vernal equinox along the celestial equator in units of time through 24 hours. This distance is the *right ascension* (RA) of a celestial body. Navigators measure westward from the vernal equinox through 360° to find the *sidereal hour angle* (SHA) of a body. Other kinds of hour angle may be used, depending upon the hour circle chosen as a reference. Local hour angle (LHA) is measured from the observer's celestial meridian. Greenwich hour angle (GHA) is measured from the hour circle above the prime meridian through Greenwich.

Horizon System. The horizon system of coordinates is used in cases where the description of a celestial body relative to the observer is desired. The *horizon* is the fundamental great circle analogous to the equator (see Fig. 2). The *zenith*, directly above

HORIZON SYSTEM

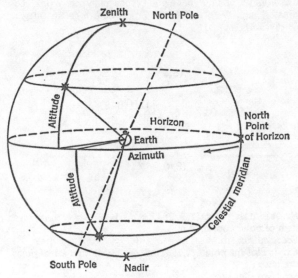

Fig. 2

the observer, and the *nadir*, directly below him, are analogous to the celestial poles. The angular distance of a celestial body above the horizon is its *altitude*. A body on the horizon has altitude 0°, one at the zenith has altitude 90°, and one below the horizon has a negative altitude. *Vertical circles*, which are great circles passing through the zenith and nadir and are perpendicular to the horizon, are the analogue of hour circles. The celestial meridian is both an hour circle and a vertical circle and is called the principal vertical circle. The direction of a body from the celestial meridian is measured from the N point along the horizon clockwise through 360°. This angular distance, the *azimuth* of the body, is analogous to right ascension or hour angle.

Ecliptic System. The ecliptic system is quite similar to the celestial equator system, except that the *ecliptic* is the fundamental great circle. The two points 90° distant from the ecliptic are the N and S ecliptic poles. Circles of latitude and longitude are used for locating celestial bodies. Longitude is measured eastward along the ecliptic from the vernal equinox. The ecliptic system is used mainly by astronomers.

Galactic System. The galactic system is still another system similar to the celestial equator system of coordinates and chiefly of interest to astronomers. Its fundamental great circle is the galactic equator, which is the intersection of the plane of the Milky Way with the celestial sphere.

CELESTIAL EQUATOR SYSTEM

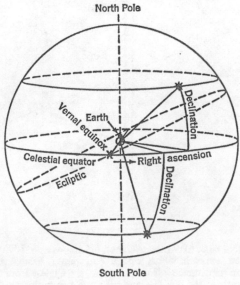

Fig. 1

COORDINATE SYSTEM, a method of locating and describing positions or points by assigning a number to them. The assigning numbers are called the COORDINATES of the point. A coordinate system may be one-, two-, or three-dimensional.

A one-dimensional coordinate system has one AXIS; it is a simple NUMBER LINE.

A two-dimensional coordinate system has two axes, and is used to locate a point in a PLANE. The Cartesian or rectangular coordinate system (*see* COORDINATES, RECTANGULAR), the polar coordinate system (*see* COORDINATES, POLAR), and the method of locating a point on the earth's surface by LONGITUDE and LATITUDE are examples of a two-dimensional coordinate system.

A three-dimensional coordinate system has three axes and is used to locate a point in space. The rectangular coordinate system may be extended to a three-dimensional system.

COPLANAR (koh-play′-nur), lying in a common plane. Any three points are always coplanar since there is at least one plane which can be passed through all three. Four (or more) points need not be coplanar. Two straight lines are coplanar only if they are PARALLEL LINES or if they intersect; otherwise they are SKEW lines.

Ex.: Are the following four points in space coplanar: (1,1,1), (2,2,2), (1,0,0), (2,2,3)?

Sol.: If they are, then the equation of some PLANE is satisfied for each of them. Substituting the COORDINATES of each point in the general equation of a plane gives the following four simultaneous equations:

$$A + B + C + D = 0$$
$$2A + 2B + 2C + D = 0$$
$$A + D = 0$$
$$2A + 2B + 3C + D = 0$$

If these are solvable, then the points are coplanar, otherwise not. But these equations have no common solution, so the points are not coplanar.

COROLLARY (kawr′-u-lehr-ee), a THEOREM derived from another theorem and one which follows the given theorem so obviously that little or no proof is necessary.

Theorem: If two sides and the included ANGLE of one TRIANGLE equal respectively two sides and the included angle of another triangle, the two triangles are CONGRUENT TRIANGLES.

Corollary: Two RIGHT TRIANGLES are congruent if two legs of one equal two legs of the other.

CORRELATION COEFFICIENT, a number between −1 and +1 which expresses the degree of the linear relationship between two or more sets of numbers. The correlation coefficient is usually designated by r and is given by

$$r = \frac{\sum\limits_{t=1}^{n}(x_t - x)(y_t - y)}{\sqrt{\sum\limits_{t=1}^{n}(x_t - x)^2 \cdot \sum\limits_{t=1}^{n}(y_t - y)^2}}$$

where x and y are the MEANS.

If $r = +1$, the two sets of numbers are in perfect positive relationship to each other. If $r = -1$, the numbers are in perfect negative relationship. If $r = 0$, the numbers are in no way related. E.g., if tests were given in two subjects, the scores correlated, and r found to be −1, it would indicate that those who scored highest on one test scored lower on the other; if $r = +1$ it would indicate that the highest scorers on one test were highest on the other; $r = 0$ would indicate no relationship at all between the scores on the tests.

$$r = \frac{n\Sigma x_t y_t - (\Sigma x_t)(\Sigma y_t)}{\sqrt{n\Sigma x_t^2 - (\Sigma x_t)^2}\sqrt{n\Sigma y_t^2 - (\Sigma y_t)^2}}$$

Ex.: Let x denote the score on the first quiz in a mathematics class and y denote the final average. A random sample of seven students had the following scores:

x	y	$x \cdot y$	x^2	y^2
74	76	5624	5476	5776
65	57	3705	4225	3249
98	98	9604	9604	9604
55	64	3520	3025	4096
74	73	5402	5476	5329
89	80	7120	7921	6400
64	76	4864	4096	5776
Total 519	524	39839	39823	40230

By the second formula,

$$r = \frac{n\Sigma x_t y_t - (\Sigma x_t)(\Sigma y_t)}{\sqrt{n\Sigma x_t^2 - (\Sigma x_t)^2}\sqrt{n\Sigma y_t^2 - (\Sigma y_t)^2}}, \quad n = 7.$$

$$r = \frac{(7)(39839) - (519)(524)}{\sqrt{(7)(39823) - (519)^2}\sqrt{(7)(40230) - (524)^2}}$$

$$= \frac{6917}{\sqrt{9400}\sqrt{7034}} = \frac{6917}{(96.95)(83.87)} = .85.$$

CORRESPONDING ANGLES, the pairs of angles in the same position with reference to the lines and to the TRANSVERSAL when two or more lines are cut by a transversal. When lines l and l' are cut by transversal t, as in the figure, the following pairs of corresponding angles are formed: $\angle x$ and $\angle y$; $\angle m$ and $\angle n$; $\angle r$ and $\angle s$; and $\angle w$ and $\angle z$.

If two PARALLEL LINES are cut by a transversal, the corresponding angles are equal. Thus, if $l \parallel l'$, then $\angle x = \angle y$; $\angle m = \angle n$; $\angle r = \angle s$; and $\angle w = \angle z$.

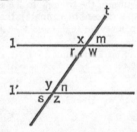

CORRESPONDING PARTS OF CONGRUENT TRIANGLES, the sides opp. the angles known to be equal and the angles opp. the sides known to be equal. Corresponding parts of CONGRUENT TRIANGLES are equal.

In Fig. 1, $\triangle ABC \cong \triangle DEF$ (S.A.S.),

$$BC(\text{opp. } \angle A) = EF(\text{opp. } \angle D),$$
$$\angle C(\text{opp. } AB) = \angle F(\text{opp. } DE),$$
$$\angle B(\text{opp. } AC) = \angle E(\text{opp. } DF).$$

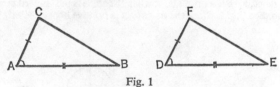

Fig. 1

In Fig. 2, $\triangle ABC \cong \triangle DEF$ (A.S.A.),

$$BC(\text{opp. } \angle A) = DF(\text{opp. } \angle E),$$
$$AC(\text{opp. } \angle B) = EF(\text{opp. } \angle D),$$
$$\angle C(\text{opp. } AB) = \angle F(\text{opp. } DE).$$

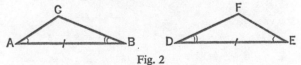

Fig. 2

In Fig. 3 $\triangle ABC \cong \triangle DEF$ (S.S.S.),

$$\angle A \, (\text{opp.} \, BC) = \angle D \, (\text{opp.} \, EF),$$
$$\angle B \, (\text{opp.} \, AC) = \angle E \, (\text{opp.} \, DF),$$
$$\angle C \, (\text{opp.} \, AB) = \angle F \, (\text{opp.} \, DE).$$

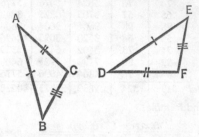

Fig. 3

CORRESPONDING SIDES OF SIMILAR TRIANGLES, the sides opposite the equal angles. Corresponding sides of similar triangles (*see* SIMILAR POLYGONS) are proportional.

In the figure, $\triangle ABC \sim \triangle DEF$ and

$$\frac{AC\,(\text{opp.}\,\angle B)}{DF\,(\text{opp.}\,\angle E)} = \frac{BC\,(\text{opp.}\,\angle A)}{EF\,(\text{opp.}\,\angle D)} = \frac{AB\,(\text{opp.}\,\angle C)}{DE\,(\text{opp.}\,\angle F)}$$

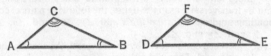

COSECANT OF AN ANGLE (koh-see′-kant), in geometry, the ratio of the hypotenuse of the triangle to the side opposite the angle. See Fig. 1. The cosecant of an angle is the reciprocal of its sine. The cosecant of an acute angle equals the secant of its complementary angle.

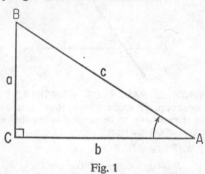

Fig. 1

In trigonometry, the cosecant of an angle is the ratio of the distance, r, to the ordinate, y, when the angle is in standard position. See Fig. 2. Since the ORDINATE is positive above the origin

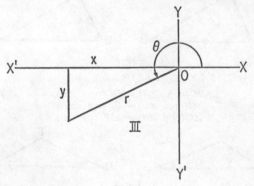

Fig. 2

and the distance is always considered positive, the cosecant is positive in quadrants I and II. The ordinate is negative below the origin, and hence the cosecant is negative in quadrants III and IV.

Ex. 1: Express csc 220° as a function of a positive acute angle.
Sol.: Csc 220° = csc (180° + 40°) = −csc 40°.

Fig. 3 shows the graph of cosecant x as x varies from

$$\frac{-3\pi}{2} \text{ to } \frac{5\pi}{2}.$$

The tables below show the changes in the cosecant as the angle is rotated through 360°. Note that the cosecant in quadrant III decreases in ABSOLUTE VALUE, and in quadrant IV, increases in absolute value.

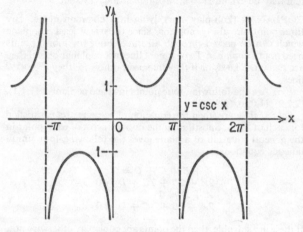

Fig. 3

The equation of the *derivative of cosecant* x is

$$\frac{d}{dx}(\csc x) = -\operatorname{ctn} x \csc x.$$

Notice that this derivative may be obtained from the derivative of sec x by replacing each function in this derivative by its COFUNCTION and adding a minus sign. The same process will produce the derivative of any trigonometric function from the derivative of its cofunction.

COSECANT OF THE QUADRANTAL ANGLES					
Angle	0°	90°	180°	270°	360°
	(0)	$\left(\frac{\pi}{2}\right)$	(π)	$\left(\frac{3\pi}{2}\right)$	(2π)
Cosecant	$\pm\infty$	1	$\pm\infty$	−1	$\pm\infty$

CHANGES IN COSECANT				
Quadrant	I	II	III	IV
Increases in Angle	0° − 90° $\left(0 - \frac{\pi}{2}\right)$	90° − 180° $\left(\frac{\pi}{2} - \pi\right)$	180° − 270° $\left(\pi - \frac{3\pi}{2}\right)$	270° − 360° $\left(\frac{3\pi}{2} - 2\pi\right)$
Changes in Cosecant	Decreases ∞ to 1	Increases 1 to ∞	Increases $-\infty$ to -1	Decreases -1 to $-\infty$
Sign	Positive	Positive	Negative	Negative

COSH X, the hyperbolic cosine of x, defined by:

$$\cosh x = \frac{e^x + e^{-x}}{2}.$$

The derivative of cosh. $\frac{d}{dx}(\cosh x) = \sinh x$. *See also* HYPERBOLIC FUNCTION; HYPERBOLIC RADIAN.

COSINE OF AN ANGLE (koh'-sahyn), in geometry, the ratio of the side adjacent to the angle to the HYPOTENUSE of a RIGHT TRIANGLE. See Fig. 1.

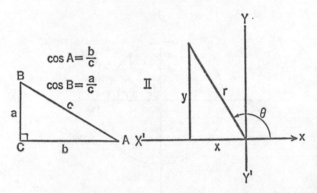

$$\cos A = \frac{b}{c}$$

$$\cos B = \frac{a}{c}$$

Fig. 1   Fig. 2 $\cos \theta = \dfrac{\text{abscissa}}{\text{distance}} = \dfrac{x}{r}$

The cosine of an acute angle equals the sine (*see* SINE OF AN ANGLE) of its complementary angle.

In trigonometry, the cosine of an angle is the RATIO of the ABSCISSA, x, to the distance, r, when the angle is in STANDARD ANGLE POSITION. See Fig. 2.

Since the abscissa is positive to the right of the origin, and the distance is always considered positive, the cosine is positive in QUADRANTS I and IV and negative in quadrants II and III.

Ex. 1: Express cos 125° as a function of a positive acute angle.
Sol.: cos 125° = cos (180° − 55°) = −cos 55°.

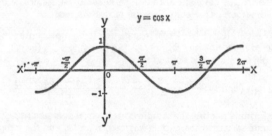

$y = \cos x$

Fig. 3

Fig. 3 shows the graph of cosine x as x varies from $-\pi$ to 2π. The following tables show the changes in the cosine as the angle is rotated through 360°. Note that in quadrant II the cosine increases in absolute value, and in quadrant III it decreases in absolute value.

CHANGES IN THE COSINE

Quadrant	I	II	III	IV
Changes in Angle	$0° - 90°$ $\left(0 - \dfrac{\pi}{2}\right)$	$90° - 180°$ $\left(\dfrac{\pi}{2} - \pi\right)$	$180° - 270°$ $\left(\pi - \dfrac{3\pi}{2}\right)$	$270° - 360°$ $\left(\dfrac{3\pi}{2} - 2\pi\right)$
Changes in Cosine	1 to 0	0 to −1	−1 to 0	0 to 1
Sign	Positive	Negative	Negative	Positive

COSINE OF THE QUADRANTAL ANGLES

Angle	0° (0)	90° $\left(\dfrac{\pi}{2}\right)$	180° (π)	270° $\left(\dfrac{3\pi}{2}\right)$	360° (2π)
Cosine	1	0	−1	0	1

The derivative of cos x, d/dx (cos x) = −sin x. This follows from the facts that (1) d/dx (sin x) = cos x and (2) cos x = sin $(\pi/2 - x)$. Differentiating line (2) gives

$$\frac{d}{dx}\cos x = \frac{d}{dx}\sin\left(\frac{\pi}{2} - x\right)$$

$$= \cos\left(\frac{\pi}{2} - x\right) \cdot \frac{d}{dx}\left(\frac{\pi}{2} - x\right) = \cos\left(\frac{\pi}{2} - x\right) \cdot (-1).$$

Since $\cos\left(\dfrac{\pi}{2} - x\right) = \sin x$,

$$d/dx\,(\cos x) = \sin x\,(-1) = -\sin x.$$

Ex.: What is the slope of the tangent to $y = \cos x$ at $x = \pi/4$ rdn?
Sol.: d/dx (cos x) = −sin x. Therefore the slope at $\pi/4$ is −sin $(\pi/4)$ = $-1/\sqrt{2}$, or approximately $-\frac{5}{7}$.

COSINES, LAW OF. For a plane triangle, *the square of any side of a triangle is equal to the sum of the squares of the other two sides minus twice the product of the two sides and the cosine of their included angle.* In formula form: $a^2 = b^2 + c^2 - 2bc \cos A$, where the sides are a, b, and c; and the angles are A, B, and C.

The law is used for solving triangles when given (1) two sides and the included angle, or (2) three sides.

Ex.: In $\triangle ABC$, $a = 12$, $b = 9$, and $C = 60°$. Find c. (See figure.)
Sol.: $c^2 = a^2 + b^2 - 2ab \cos c$,
$c^2 = 144 + 81 - (216 \cdot \frac{1}{2}) = 117$,
$c = \sqrt{117} = 10.8$.

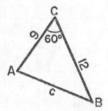

The formula is not adapted to logarithmic calculation. When two sides and the included angle are given it is usually preferable to use the Law of Tangents (*see* TANGENTS, LAW OF).

For a spherical triangle, where the sides are a, b, c, and the angles are A, B, C;
For angles:

$$\cos A = -\cos B \cos C + \sin B \sin C \cos a$$

For sides:

$$\cos a = \cos b \cos c + \sin b \sin c \cos A$$

COS^{-1} x, arc cos x. *See* ARC COSINE.

COTANGENT OF AN ANGLE (koh-tan'-jent), in geometry. In a RIGHT TRIANGLE, the ratio of the side adjacent to the angle to the side opposite the angle. The cotangent of an angle is the RECIPROCAL of the TANGENT OF AN ANGLE.

In trigonometry, the cotangent of an angle is the ratio of the ABSCISSA, x, to the ORDINATE, y, when the angle is in STANDARD ANGLE POSITION. See Fig. 1.

$$\cot \theta = \frac{\text{abscissa}}{\text{ordinate}} = \frac{x}{y}$$

Since the abscissa is positive to the right of the ORIGIN and negative to the left, and the ordinate is positive above the origin

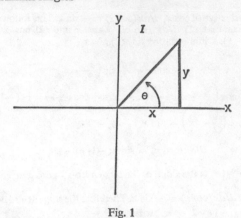

Fig. 1

and negative below it, the cotangent is positive in QUADRANTS I and II, and negative in quadrants II and IV.

Ex. 1: If $\theta = 300°$, $\cot 300° = \cot(360° - 60°) = -\cot 60° = -\tan 30°$.

Figure 2 shows the cotangent of x as x varies from $-\frac{3}{2}\pi$ to $\frac{2}{5}\pi$. The tables show the changes in the cotangent as the angle is rotated through 360°. Note that the cotangent increases in ABSOLUTE VALUE in quadrants II and IV.

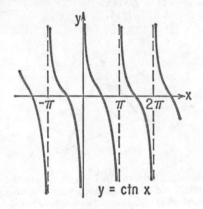

$y = \text{ctn } x$

Fig. 2

CHANGES IN THE COTANGENT

Quadrant	I	II	III	IV
Increases in Angle	$0° - 90°$ $\left(0 - \frac{\pi}{2}\right)$	$90° - 180°$ $\left(\frac{\pi}{2} - \pi\right)$	$180° - 270°$ $\left(\pi - \frac{3\pi}{2}\right)$	$270° - 360°$ $\left(\frac{3\pi}{2} - 2\pi\right)$
Changes in Cotangent	Decreases $+\infty$ to 0	Decreases 0 to $-\infty$	Decreases $+\infty$ to 0	Decreases 0 to $-\infty$
Sign	Positive	Negative	Positive	Negative

COTANGENT OF THE QUADRANTAL ANGLES

Angle	0° (0)	90° $\left(\frac{\pi}{2}\right)$	180° (π)	270° $\left(\frac{3\pi}{2}\right)$	360° (2π)
Cotangent	$\pm\infty$	0	$\pm\infty$	0	$\pm\infty$

The formula for the derivative of cotangent x, is $d/dx\,(\text{ctn } x) = -\csc^2 x$, from the fact that $d/dx\,(\tan x) = \sec^2 x$ and the fact that $\text{ctn } x = \tan(\pi/2 - x)$.

COTERMINAL ANGLES (koh-tur'-min-ul), two or more angles whose terminal sides coincide when the angles are in STAND-

ARD ANGLE POSITION. Two coterminal angles have the same trigonometric functions. E.g., 30° and 390° are coterminal angles. (See figure.)

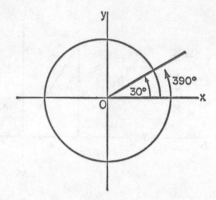

COTH x, the HYPERBOLIC FUNCTION, termed the hyperbolic cotangent of x, and defined by $\coth x = \dfrac{\cosh x}{\sinh x} = \dfrac{e^x + e^{-x}}{e^x - e^{-x}}$. The DERIVATIVE formula is $\dfrac{d}{dx}(\coth x) = -\operatorname{csch}^2 x$.

COT⁻¹ x, arc cot x. *See* ARC COTANGENT.

COUNTER, in a computer, an *adder* that receives addends of amount one; a unit adder.

COUNTING NUMBERS, *see* NATURAL NUMBERS.

COURSE, in navigation, the angle between the MERIDIAN line and the track of the ship. *See also* PLANE SAILING.

COVARIANCE, SAMPLE. In statistics, if a sample consists of n ordered pairs of observations, $(x_1,y_1), (x_2,y_2), \ldots, (x_n,y_n)$, the sample covariance is defined as

$$\operatorname{cov}(x,y) = \frac{\Sigma(x_i - \bar{x})(y_i - \bar{y})}{n-1} = \frac{n\Sigma x_i y_i - (\Sigma x_i)(\Sigma y_i)}{n-1}.$$

The formula relating the sample CORRELATION COEFFICIENT, r, the separate SAMPLE STANDARD DEVIATIONS, s_x and s_y and the sample covariance, $\operatorname{cov}(x,y)$, is

$$r = \frac{\operatorname{cov}(x,y)}{s_x s_y}.$$

COVERSED SINE OF θ, equals $1 - \sin\theta$, and is written cvs θ.

CRAMER'S RULE, for solving systems of linear equations in two or more unknowns, states that each unknown can be expressed as the ratio of two DETERMINANTS.

Ex. 1: Solve $\begin{cases} 2x + 3y = 12. \\ 3x - 4y = 1. \end{cases}$

The determinant of the denominator is the same for x and y and is the determinant of the COEFFICIENTS of x and y in the two equations: $\begin{vmatrix} 2 & 3 \\ 3 & -4 \end{vmatrix}$. The determinant of the numerator of x is obtained by replacing the coefficients of x in both equations by the constant terms: $\begin{vmatrix} 12 & 3 \\ 1 & -4 \end{vmatrix}$. The determinant of the numerator of y is $\begin{vmatrix} 2 & 12 \\ 3 & 1 \end{vmatrix}$. Therefore,

$$x = \frac{\begin{vmatrix} 12 & 3 \\ 1 & -4 \end{vmatrix}}{\begin{vmatrix} 2 & 3 \\ 3 & -4 \end{vmatrix}}; \quad y = \frac{\begin{vmatrix} 2 & 12 \\ 3 & 1 \end{vmatrix}}{\begin{vmatrix} 2 & 3 \\ 3 & -4 \end{vmatrix}}$$

$$x = \frac{(12)(-4) - (3)(1)}{(2)(-4) - (3)(3)} = \frac{-48 - 3}{-8 - 9} = \frac{-51}{-17} = 3.$$

$$y = \frac{(2)(1) - (3)(12)}{-17} = \frac{2 - 36}{-17} = \frac{-34}{-17} = 2.$$

Check: $\quad 2x + 3y = 12 \qquad\qquad 3x - 4y = 1$
$\qquad\qquad 2(3) + 3(2) = 12 \qquad (3)(3) - 4(2) = 1$
$\qquad\qquad\quad 6 + 6 = 12. \qquad\qquad\quad 9 - 8 = 1.$

Ex. 2: Solve $\begin{cases} 3x - 2y + 2z = 7 \\ x + y + z = 6 \\ 2x - y - 2z = 2. \end{cases}$

Let D = denominator, $\begin{vmatrix} 3 & -2 & 2 \\ 1 & 1 & 1 \\ 2 & -1 & -2 \end{vmatrix}$

Expanding by minors,

$$3\begin{vmatrix} 1 & 1 \\ -1 & -2 \end{vmatrix} - 1\begin{vmatrix} -2 & 2 \\ -1 & -2 \end{vmatrix} + 2\begin{vmatrix} -2 & 2 \\ 1 & 1 \end{vmatrix} =$$
$$3(-2 + 1) - 1(4 + 2) + 2(-2 - 2) =$$
$$-3 - 6 - 8 = -17.$$

$$x = \frac{\begin{vmatrix} 7 & -2 & 2 \\ 6 & 1 & 1 \\ 2 & -1 & -2 \end{vmatrix}}{D}; \quad y = \frac{\begin{vmatrix} 3 & 7 & 2 \\ 1 & 6 & 1 \\ 2 & 2 & -2 \end{vmatrix}}{D}; \quad z = \frac{\begin{vmatrix} 3 & -2 & 7 \\ 1 & 1 & 6 \\ 2 & -1 & 2 \end{vmatrix}}{D}.$$

$$x = \frac{7\begin{vmatrix} 1 & 1 \\ -1 & -2 \end{vmatrix} - 6\begin{vmatrix} -2 & 2 \\ -1 & -2 \end{vmatrix} + 2\begin{vmatrix} -2 & 2 \\ 1 & 1 \end{vmatrix}}{-17}$$

$$x = \frac{-7 - 36 - 8}{-17} = \frac{-51}{-17} = 3.$$

$$y = \frac{3\begin{vmatrix} 6 & 1 \\ 2 & -2 \end{vmatrix} - 1\begin{vmatrix} 1 & 2 \\ 2 & -2 \end{vmatrix} + 2\begin{vmatrix} 7 & 2 \\ 6 & 1 \end{vmatrix}}{-17}$$

$$y = \frac{-42 + 18 - 10}{-17} = \frac{-34}{-17} = 2.$$

$$z = \frac{3\begin{vmatrix} 1 & 6 \\ -1 & 2 \end{vmatrix} - 1\begin{vmatrix} -2 & 7 \\ -1 & 2 \end{vmatrix} + 2\begin{vmatrix} -2 & 7 \\ 1 & 6 \end{vmatrix}}{-17}$$

$$z = \frac{24 - 3 - 38}{-17} = \frac{-17}{-17} = 1.$$

Check: $3x - 2y + 2z = 7 \qquad x + y + z = 6$
$\qquad\quad 3(3) - 2(2) + 2(1) = 7 \qquad 3 + 2 + 1 = 6$
$\qquad\qquad 9 - 4 + 2 = 7 \qquad\qquad\quad 6 = 6.$
$\qquad\qquad\qquad\qquad 7 = 7.$
$\qquad\quad 2x - y - 2z = 2$
$\qquad\quad 2(3) - 2 - 2(1) = 2$
$\qquad\qquad 6 - 2 - 2 = 2$
$\qquad\qquad\qquad\qquad 2 = 2.$

See also DETERMINANT; EQUATIONS, SYSTEMS OF LINEAR.

CRITICAL REGION, in statistics, the REJECTION REGION for a test.

CRITICAL VALUES, in statistics, the numerical values that mark the beginning of the REJECTION REGION for a test. For one-sided ALTERNATIVE HYPOTHESES there is one critical value; for two-sided alternative hypotheses, there are two critical values.

CROSS PRODUCT, *see* VECTOR PRODUCT.

CROSS-PRODUCT TERM, the term Bxy in the general QUADRATIC EQUATION,

$$Ax^2 + Bxy + Cy^2 + Dx + Ey + F = 0.$$

If the cross-product term is zero (that is, if $B = 0$), the equation can be put into the standard form for a straight LINE, CIRCLE, or other CONIC SECTION (ELLIPSE, PARABOLA, HYPERBOLA) by COMPLETING SQUARES. If the cross-product term is not zero, a ROTATION OF AXES by the appropriate angle will make the cross-product term vanish. *See also* INVARIANT; SECOND DEGREE CURVE.

CRUCIFORM (kroo′-si-form), the graph of the equation $x^2y^2 - a^2x^2 - a^2y^2 = 0$. It is symmetric about the origin and coordinate axes; it has four branches, one in each quadrant asymptotic to the lines $x = \pm a$ and $y = \pm a$. (See figure.)

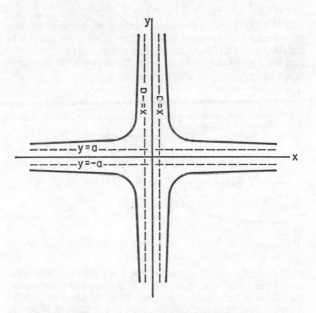

CRUNODE (kroo′-nohd), a point on a curve at which two branches of the curve have distinct tangents. (See figure.)

$CSC^{-1} x$, arc csc x. *See* ARC COSECANT.

CSCH X, the HYPERBOLIC FUNCTION, termed the hyperbolic cosecant of x, and defined by $\operatorname{csch} x = \dfrac{1}{\sinh x} = \dfrac{2}{e^x - e^{-x}}$. The derivative is $\dfrac{d}{dx}(\operatorname{csch} x) = -\operatorname{csch} x \coth x$. *See also* COSECANT OF AN ANGLE; DERIVATIVE OF A FUNCTION.

CUBE, a geometric solid whose 6 faces are squares. The formula for the volume of a cube with edge e is $V = e^3$. The formula for the area of all six faces is $A = 6e^2$. (See figure.)

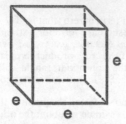

CUBE or cube power, the third POWER OF A NUMBER; e.g., the cube, or cube power, of 2 is 2^3 or 8; of x is x^3.

CUBE ROOT, one of three equal factors of a number. Finding the cube root of a number is the inverse of raising a number to the third power. If p is any number and $q^3 = q \cdot q \cdot q = p$, the number q is called a cube root of p. Symbolically we write $q = \sqrt[3]{p}$. The graph of $y = \sqrt[3]{x}$ is shown in the figure.

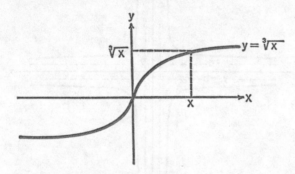

Finding a cube root of a number, p, is finding the solution to the cubic equation $x^3 = p$, or $x^3 - p = 0$. Since there are three roots for a third degree equation, for every REAL NUMBER (except zero) there are three cube roots, one real and two imaginary. When we seek a cube root of a number, we usually seek the real root.

   Ex. 1: Find the cube root of: a. 8; b. -8; c. 1; d. -1.
   Sol.: a. 2, because $2^3 = 2 \cdot 2 \cdot 2 = 8$; b. -2; c. 1; d. -1.
   Ex. 2: Find the cube root of 2.
   Sol.: The cube root is an infinite decimal number 1.71 . . .
See TABLE NO. 18 for cube roots of real numbers.
   The three cube roots of a real number may be found by solving the cubic equation $x^3 - p = 0$ for x. If $x^3 - p$ is the difference of cubes, the roots may be found by factoring.
   Ex. 3: Find the three cube roots of 1.
   Sol.: Solve $x^3 - 1 = 0$ for x.
$$(x - 1)(x^2 + x + 1) = 0.$$

When $x - 1 = 0$, $x = 1$, and when $x^2 + x + 1 = 0$, by the QUADRADIC FORMULA,

$$x = \frac{-1 \pm i\sqrt{3}}{2}.$$

The three cube roots of 1 are 1, $\dfrac{-1 + \sqrt{3}}{2}$ and $\dfrac{-1 - \sqrt{3}}{2}$.

When the equation does not contain the difference of cubes, the three cube roots of a real number may be found by using DE MOIVRE'S THEOREM. *See also* EQUATION, ROOT OF; ROOT; SQUARE ROOT.

CUBIC EQUATION, an equation of the third degree, such as $x^3 - x^2 - 9x + 9 = 0$. Many such equations can be solved by graphing, by factoring, or by a combination of these methods.

Ex.: Solve $x^3 - x^2 - 9x + 9 = 0$.
   1. By graphing:
   Let $f(x) = x^3 - x^2 - 9x + 9$, and make a table by assigning different values to x.

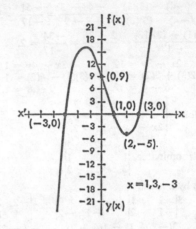

x	$f(x)$
0	9
1	0
2	-5
3	0
4	21
-1	16
-2	15
-3	0
-4	-35

If $x^3 - x^2 - 9x + 9 = 0$, the values of x are the 3 points where the graph crosses the x-axis.

$$x = 1, -3, +3.$$

   2. By factoring:
Group the terms:

$$(x^3 - x^2) - (9x - 9) = 0.$$

Factor:

$$x^2(x^2 - 1) - 9(x - 1) = 0,$$
$$(x - 1)(x^2 - 9) = 0,$$
$$(x - 1)(x - 3)(x + 3) = 0.$$
$$x - 1 = 0 \quad x - 3 = 0 \quad x + 3 = 0.$$
$$x = 1 \quad\quad x = 3 \quad\quad x = -3.$$

Cubic equations may also be solved by CARDAN'S FORMULA.

CUP, in mathematics, the symbol, $\cup$, used to indicate UNION of SETS. Thus, if set $A = \{3, 4, 5\}$ and $B = \{1, 2, 7, 8\}$, $A \cup B = \{1, 2, 3, 4, 5, 7, 8\}$. $A \cup B$ is read "A cup B" or "A union B."

CURVATURE OF PLANE CURVE, at any point on the curve $y = f(x)$, the rate, k, at which the direction of the curve angle, θ, changes with respect to its ARC LENGTH, s. The formula is

$$k = \frac{d\theta}{ds} = \frac{d\theta/dx}{ds/dx} = \frac{\frac{d}{dx}(\tan^{-1} f'(x))}{ds/dx} = \frac{\pm d^2y/dx^2}{[1 + (dy/dx)^2]^{3/2}}.$$

The sign of the curvature is that of ds/dx. (See figure.) The curvature of a straight line is zero.

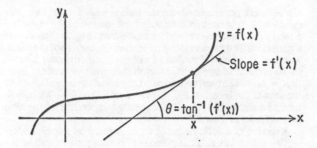

Ex. 1: What is the curvature of $y = x^2$ at $x = 2$?
Sol.:

$$k = \frac{\pm d^2y/dx^2}{[1 + (dy/dx)^2]^{3/2}} = \frac{\pm 2}{[1 + (2x)^2]^{3/2}} = \frac{\pm 2}{17^{3/2}} = +\frac{2}{17^{3/2}}$$

since $ds/dx > 0$ at $x = 2$. *See also* INVERSE TRIGONOMETRIC FUNCTIONS; DERIVATIVE OF A FUNCTION; RADIUS OF CURVATURE.

CURVE, *see* LINE.

CURVED LINE GRAPH, a statistical graph (*see* GRAPH, STATISTICAL) for showing gradual changes in a quantity.

Ex.: Make a graph to show the temperature changes from 6 A.M. to 6 P.M. on a day in June.

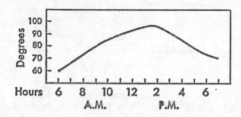

CURVED SURFACE, a surface which is not a PLANE.

CURVE SKETCHING, graphing a curve by using only the critical points, i.e., maximum (*see* MAXIMUM OF A FUNCTION), minimum (*see* MINIMUM OF A FUNCTION), and INFLECTION POINT. To sketch the graph of a function $y = f(x)$:

1. Differentiate the function, and solve the equation, $f'(x) = 0$.
2. Determine which of the points having zero derivatives (*see* DERIVATIVE OF A FUNCTION) are maxima and which are minima. Does the derivative reverse sign? If there is no sign change there is no EXTREMUM.
3. Use the SECOND DERIVATIVE TEST. Compute $f''(x)$, and evaluate it at each of the possible extrema. If $f''(x)$ is less than zero at a point, the function has a maximum at that point. If $f''(x)$ is greater than zero at a point, there is a minimum at that point.
4. Solve the equation $f''(x) = 0$. A solution is a point of inflection if $f''(x)$ changes sign.
5. Plot these points and join them by a smooth curve.

Ex. 1: Sketch the graph of $f(x) = x^3 - x$.

Sol.: $f'(x) = 3x^2 - 1$. Setting this equal to zero, $x = \pm\sqrt{1/3}$. The derivative changes sign at each of these points.
$f''(x) = 6x; f''(1/\sqrt{3}) = 6/\sqrt{3} > 0; f''(-1/\sqrt{3})$
$$= -6/\sqrt{3} < 0.$$
Thus, $f(x)$ has a maximum at $-1/\sqrt{3}$ and a minimum at $1/\sqrt{3}$. The points on the curve corresponding to these are

$$\left(-1/\sqrt{3}, \frac{2}{3\sqrt{3}}\right) \text{ and } \left(1/\sqrt{3}, \frac{-2}{3\sqrt{3}}\right).$$

The second derivative is zero at $x = 0$; $f''(x)$ changes sign at zero, so there is a point of inflection at (0,0).

Plotting these points and connecting them with a smooth curve gives the sketch shown in the figure.

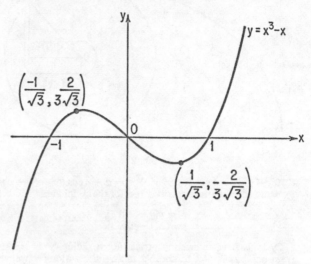

CUSP (kusp), a double point at which two tangents to a curve are coincident. A cusp of the first kind is one in which a branch

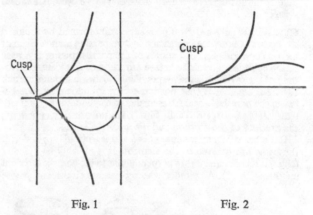

Fig. 1   Fig. 2

of the curve lies on both sides of the double tangent, as in the CISSOID in Fig. 1. A cusp of the second kind is one in which two branches of the curve lie on the same side of the double tangent, as in Fig. 2.

CYCLOID (sahy'-kloid), the path traced by a point on a CIRCLE when the circle rolls along a line. (See Fig. 1.) The equations for the cycloid may be found by using the fact that both COORDINATES of the moving point depend on the angle, θ (as in Fig. 2), from OP to the vertical.

The coordinates (x', y') of the center of the circle may be expressed as functions of θ: $x' = SA = AP$ (the distance the circle has rolled), and $y' = a$, (the radius of the circle). If θ is measured in RADIANS, $AP = a\theta$. Since $h = a\cos(270° - \theta) = -a\sin\theta$, $x = x' + h = a\theta - a\sin\theta = a(\theta - \sin\theta)$. Since $k = a\sin$

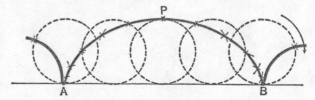

Fig. 1

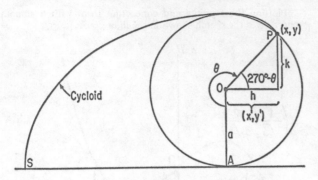

Fig. 2

$(270° - \theta) = -a\cos\theta$, $y = y' + k = a - a\cos\theta = a(1 - \cos\theta)$. Thus, the PARAMETRIC EQUATIONS for the cycloid are

$$x = a(\theta - \sin\theta),$$
$$y = a(1 - \cos\theta).$$

Cycloids have interesting properties: a sliding body travels from one fixed point to another more quickly along a cycloid than along any other path; the time taken to slide from any point on an inverted arch to the bottom is the same for all starting points; the strongest arch for a stone bridge is a cycloid. *See also* EPICYCLOID; HYPOCYCLOID.

CYLINDER (sil'-in-der), a geometric solid formed by a closed CYLINDRICAL SURFACE intersected by two parallel planes. Each of the two congruent closed curves of the parallel planes is a BASE of the cylinder. The altitude (*see* ALTITUDE OF A GEOMETRIC FIGURE) of the cylinder is the perpendicular between a point in each base. An element is that portion of the cylindrical surface between the parallel bases. All elements of a cylinder are equal and parallel. E.g., *AD*, *FE*, *BC* in Fig. 1. The volume of a cylinder is the product of the altitude and the area of a base.

If the bases of a cylinder are circles, it is a circular cylinder; if the bases are oblique to the elements it is an oblique cylinder (Fig. 2); if the elements are perpendicular to the bases it is a right cylinder (Fig. 1). A cylinder whose bases are circles and whose

elements are perpendicular to the base is called a right circular cylinder. A right circular cylinder may be generated by revolving a rectangle about one of its sides as the AXIS (Fig. 3). The axis of a right circular cylinder is the line joining the centers of the bases. The area of the lateral surface of a right circular cylinder is equal to the product of the altitude and the circumference of the base, or $S = 2\pi rh$. The total area equals the sum of the lateral area and the area of the bases, or $T = 2\pi rh + 2\pi r^2 = 2\pi r(h + r)$. The volume of a right circular cylinder equals the product of the base and altitude, or $V = \pi r^2 h$.

A section of a cylinder is the figure formed by a PLANE intersecting the cylinder. If the plane is PERPENDICULAR to all of the elements, it is a right section. Every section of a cylinder made by such a plane is both parallel and congruent to the base.

CYLINDRICAL COORDINATE SYSTEM (si-lin'-dri-kal), *see* COORDINATE SYSTEM; COORDINATES, CYLINDRICAL.

CYLINDRICAL SURFACE, the surface composed of all points on all lines (or line segments of equal length) that intersect a plane curve and are parallel to a fixed line not in the plane of the curve. Each line is an *element* or *generatrix*, and the curve is the *directrix*. (The curve need not be closed.) In Fig. 1, the directrix

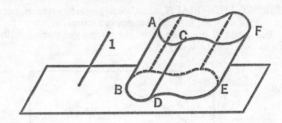

Fig. 1

is the curve (closed) *BDE*. Elements are *AB*, *CD*, and *EF*, each parallel to the fixed line *l*. Cylinders may be classified according to their directrices as in Fig. 2.

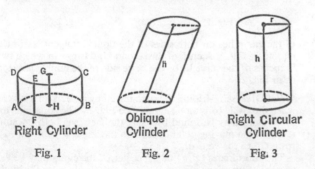

Right Cylinder   Oblique Cylinder   Right Circular Cylinder

Fig. 1   Fig. 2   Fig. 3

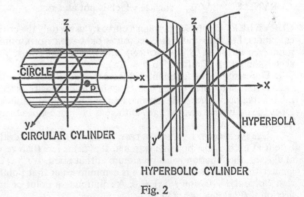

CIRCULAR CYLINDER   HYPERBOLIC CYLINDER

Fig. 2

D

DEAD RECKONING, procedure by which the geographical position of a ship or airplane at any instant is approximated from the known direction and estimated amount of progress since the last determined position. One way of estimating the distance is by logging the number of engine revolutions. Allowance must also be made for the probable drift effects of wind and current.

DECAGON (dek'-ah-gahn), a POLYGON having ten sides. To inscribe a regular decagon in a CIRCLE:

In $\odot O$ construct diameter (*see* DIAMETER OF A CIRCLE) CD PERPENDICULAR to diameter AB. Construct MIDPOINT M of RADIUS AO. With M as a center and a radius equal to MD draw an ARC cutting OB at N. Segment ON is the side of a decagon inscribed in a circle equal to $\odot O$. To inscribe a regular PENTAGON in a circle equal to $\odot O$, use segment DN as a side of the pentagon. (See figure.)

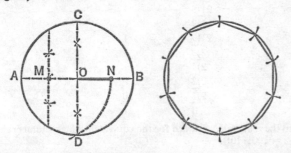

DECILE (de'-sahyl), in statistics, any of the nine numbers that separate a frequency distribution (*see* CLASSIFIED DATA) into ten equal parts. These deciles are equal to the 10th, 20th, ···, 90th PERCENTILES, and are called the first, second, ···, ninth deciles, respectively.

DECIMAL FRACTION, any proper FRACTION in which the DENOMINATOR is some power (*see* POWER OF A NUMBER) of 10. The denominators are not usually written but are indicated by the use of a dot, called the decimal point.

$$\frac{1}{10} = .1 \qquad \frac{1}{5} = \frac{2}{10} = .2$$
$$\frac{1}{10^2} = \frac{1}{100} = .01 \qquad \frac{1}{4} = \frac{25}{100} = .25$$
$$\frac{1}{10^3} = \frac{1}{1000} = .001 \qquad \frac{3}{8} = \frac{375}{1000} = .375$$
$$\frac{1}{10^3} = \frac{1}{10000} = .0001 \qquad \frac{3}{20} = \frac{15}{100} = .15$$

By the use of the decimal point, PLACE VALUE can be used to denote decimal fractions as well as whole numbers.

thousands	hundreds	tens	units		tenths	hundredths	thousandths
1	3	8	7	.	3	7	5

One thousand three hundred eighty-seven *and* three hundred seventy-five thousandths.

To add decimal fractions:

1. Write the ADDENDS so that the decimal points will be in a column.
2. Add zeros to decimals, if necessary, to have the same number of decimals in each addend.
3. Add digits.
4. Place decimal point in the SUM.

Ex. 1: Add 236.146 + 42.8 + 125.46 + 1284.9.

Sol.:
```
  236.146
   42.800
  125.460
 1284.900
 ————————
 1689.306
```

Ex. 2: Add $37\frac{1}{4} + 28\frac{1}{2} + 156\frac{5}{8} + 15\frac{7}{8}$.
Sol.: Change fractions to equivalent decimals.

$$37.25 + 28.5 + 156.625 + 15.875$$

```
  37.250
  28.500
 156.625
  15.875
 ———————
 238.250
```

To subtract decimal fractions:
1. The decimal point of the SUBTRAHEND must be immediately below the decimal point of the MINUEND.
2. Subtract as with whole numbers.
3. Place the decimal point in the DIFFERENCE.

Ex. 1: Subtract 39.48 from 76.54.

Sol.:
```
  76.54        Check:   37.06
 -39.48                +39.48
 ——————                ——————
  37.06                 76.54
```

Ex. 2: Find the difference of 156.5 and 38.875.

Sol.:
```
  156.500      Check:   117.625
 - 38.875              + 38.875
 ————————              ————————
  117.625               156.500
```

Ex. 3: From 185 subtract 109.48.

Sol.:
```
  185.00       Check:    75.52
 -109.48               +109.48
 ———————               ———————
   75.52                185.00
```

To multiply decimal fractions:
1. Multiply as for whole numbers.
2. Place a decimal point in the PRODUCT, so that it will have the same number of decimal places as there are in the sum of decimal places in the two numbers being multiplied.

Ex. 1: Find the product: 45.87 × 3.25.

Sol.:
```
   45.87
 × 3.25
 ———————
  2 2935
  9 174
 137 61
 ————————
 149.0775
```

Ex. 2: Multiply .254 by .301

Sol.:
```
      .254
    ×.301
      254
    7620
    .076454
```
(Note: A ZERO must be added to make the required 6 places.)

To divide decimal fractions:

1. Change the DIVISOR to a WHOLE NUMBER by moving its decimal point, if any, as many places to the right as necessary.
2. Move the decimal point of the DIVIDEND the same number of places to the right, adding zeros, if necessary.
3. Divide as with whole numbers.
4. Place a decimal point in the QUOTIENT. It should have as many decimal places as the changed dividend.

Rule 2 is derived by changing a divisor to its equivalent fraction.

(a) $378 \div .6 = 378 \div \frac{6}{10} = 378 \times \frac{10}{6} = \frac{3780}{6}$

and $\frac{3780}{6} = 3780 \div 6.$

Then, $378 \div .6 = 3780 \div 6.$

(b) $.378 \div .06 = .378 \div \frac{6}{100} = .378 \times \frac{100}{6} = \frac{37.800}{6}.$

Therefore, $.378 \div .06 = 37.8 \div 6.$

Ex. 1: Divide 34.944 by .24.

Sol.: Move both decimal points two places to the right.

$3494.4 \div 24$

```
        145.6        Check:   145.6
   24)3494.4                ×   .24
      24                      5 824
      109                    29 12
       96                    34.944
      134
      120
       144
       144
```

The required quotient is 145.6.

Ex. 2: Divide and carry the quotient to the nearest thousandth: $8.53 \div .136.$

Sol.: Move both decimal points three places; then divide 8530 by 136. The quotient must have three decimal places, therefore the division must be carried to 4 places. If the number in the 4th place is 5 or more, the thousandth place is increased by 1.

```
       62.7205         Check:   63.7205
  136)8530.0000              ×    .136
     816                        3763230
     370                       1 881615
     272                       6 27205
     980                       8 4299880
     952                       +  120   Remainder
     280                       8.5300000
     272
     800
     680
     120  Remainder
```

Therefore, the quotient to the nearest thousandth is 62.721.

To change a decimal to a PERCENT, move the decimal point two places to the right and add the percent symbol. E.g., $.25 = 25\%$; $.3 = 30\%$; $.125 = 12.5\%$ or $12\frac{1}{2}\%$.

DECIMAL NUMBER SYSTEM, a system of numeration for real numbers using the BASE ten. In this system a number is written according to PLACE VALUES for powers of ten using the digits 0 through 9. Thus, the number five hundred seventy-three in the base ten means $5 \times 10^2 + 7 \times 10^1 + 3 \times 10^0 = 5 \times 100 + 7 \times 10 + 3 \times 1 = 573$. A decimal point is used to separate the integral part of the number from the decimal part. The numerals to the left of the decimal point indicate the INTEGERS, and those to the right of the decimal point indicate the fractions. In the numeral 27.4, 27 is the integral part and 4 is the fractional part. Decimal numbers may be changed to numbers in another base. Thus, we may convert a decimal number to a number in the BINARY NUMBER SYSTEM.

Ex. 1: Convert 53_{10} to base two.

Sol.: The highest power of 2 contained in 53 is $2^5(32)$. $53 - 32 = 21$. The highest power of 2 contained in 21 is 2^4 (16). $21 - 16 = 5$. The highest power of 2 contained in 5 is 2^2 (4) with a remainder of 1. Now, 53 may be expressed as the sum of powers of 2: $1 \times 2^5 + 1 \times 2^4 + 0 \times 2^3 + 1 \times 2^2 + 0 \times 2^1 + 1$. Therefore, $53_{10} \cong 110101_2$.

Ex. 2: Convert 157_{10} to a binary number.

Sol.: The following ALOGARITHM is more commonly used to convert a number in base 10 to its equivalent number in base 2.

```
                    Remainders
   2)157
   2)78          1
   2)39          0
   2)19          1
   2)9           1
   2)4           1
   2)2           0
   2)1           0
     0           1
```

Read the remainders upward for the equivalent binary number: $157_{10} = 10011101_2$.

DECIMAL, REPEATING, a DECIMAL FRACTION which yields a remainder other than zero when the NUMERATOR of its EQUIVALENT FRACTION is divided by the DENOMINATOR. E.g., $1/3 = .3\ 1/3$ or $.3333\ldots$ $7/6 = 1.1\ 4/6$ or $1.166\ldots$ $1/9 = .1\ 1/9$ or $.111\ldots$

Any decimal fraction that is equivalent to a common fraction must either terminate or repeat. Every RATIONAL NUMBER is a repeating decimal: $5 = 5.000\ldots$ (where 0 repeats); $2/5 = .4000\ldots$ (0 repeats); $1/3 = .333\ldots$ (3 repeats). So called "decimal equivalents" of IRRATIONAL NUMBERS neither repeat nor terminate, and are, therefore, only approximations.

DECIMAL, TERMINATING, a DECIMAL FRACTION which yields a zero remainder at some point when the NUMERATOR of a FRACTION is divided by its DENOMINATOR. E.g., $2/5$ yields exactly .4 when 2 is divided by 5. Thus .4 is a terminating decimal. $1/8$ yields exactly .125 when 1 is divided by 8, so .125 is a terminating decimal.

DEDEKIND CUT (day'-de-kind), a partition of the set of RATIONAL NUMBERS into two-empty, disjoint sets, C_1 and C_2, with the property that every number in C_1 is less than every number of C_2, and one of the following: (1) there may be a greatest number in C_1; (2) there may be a least number in C_2; (3) there may be neither a greatest number in C_1 nor a least number in C_2.

If C_1 and C_2 have Property 1 or 2, the Dedekind cut defines the set of rational numbers. If C_1 and C_2 have Property 3, the cut defines the set of IRRATIONAL NUMBERS. Thus, the real number system may be constructed by means of Dedekind cuts, since it permits a precise definition of rational and irrational numbers.

DEDUCTIVE REASONING, a system of reasoning which proceeds from the general to the specific. Any deductive proof can be arranged in a pattern, called a *syllogism*, in which there are three steps:

1. A general statement.
2. A specific statement satisfying the HYPOTHESIS of the general statement.
3. A CONCLUSION based on the general and specific statements.

The general statement is the *major premise* and the specific statement is the *minor premise*. In geometry, the general statement, as the AUTHORITY for the truth of the conclusion, usually follows both the specific statement and the conclusion.

Ex. 1:
General statement: Complements of the same angle are equal.
Specific statement: $\angle x$ comp. $\angle z$ and $\angle y$ comp. $\angle z$.
Conclusion: $\angle x = \angle y$.

Note that the general statement is the authority for the conclusion.

Ex. 2:
General statement: If equals are subtracted from equals, the remainders are equal.
Specific statement: $x + y = 7$ and $y = 3$.
Conclusion: $x = 4$.

A geometric proof may consist of one or more syllogisms.

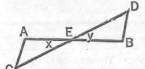

Ex. 3: Given segments AB and CD intersecting in E, $AE = BE$, and $CE = DE$; then $\triangle ACE \cong \triangle BDE$.

First syllogism:
General statement: VERTICAL ANGLES are equal.
Specific statement: $\angle x$ and $\angle y$ are vertical angles.
Conclusion: $\angle x = \angle y$.

Second syllogism:
General statement: Two triangles are congruent if two sides and the included angle of one triangle are equal respectively to two sides and the included angle of the other.
Specific statement: $AE = BE$; $CE = DE$; and $\angle x = \angle y$.
Conclusion: $\triangle ACE \cong \triangle BDE$.

The conclusion of the first syllogism is part of the specific statement in the second syllogism. *See also* FORMAL PROOF; INDUCTIVE REASONING.

DEFINITE INTEGRAL, for a function $f(x)$ in the INTERVAL from $x = a$ to $x = b$, the number which represents the area under the curve $y = f(x)$ within this interval. It is written: $\int_a^b f(x)\, dx$. Corresponding to any PARTITION, P, of the interval $[a,b]$ there are two sets of approximating rectangles, one of area A enclosing the region under the curve, the other of area A' enclosed by the region. (See figure.)

The height of a typical rectangle, r_i, in the first set is the maximum value of the function over its base, the subinterval (a_{i-1}, a_i), which occurs at some point x_i. The height of a typical rectangle r'_i in the second set is the minimum value of the function over (a_{i-1}, a_i), which occurs at x'_i. These heights are $f(x_i)$ and $f(x'_i)$ respectively, so that:

$$A = \sum_{i=1}^{n} f(x_i)(a_i - a_{i-1}) > \int_a^b f(x)\, dx,$$

$$A' = \sum_{i=1}^{n} f(x'_i)(a_i - a_{i-1}) < \int_a^b f(x)\, dx.$$

The width of the widest approximating rectangle in a given set is known as the MESH OF PARTITION, and approximations are made by taking the limit of each of the above expressions as the mesh approaches zero. If each of these limits exists and they are equal, this common limit is defined to be the integral. In symbols,

$$\int_a^b f(x)\, dx = \lim_{\text{mesh}\to 0} A = \lim_{\text{mesh}\to 0} A'.$$

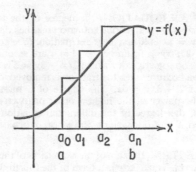

Approximation A

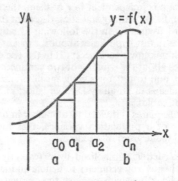

Approximation A'

For most common functions the integral exists, but functions are known in which the two sums do not have the same limit or do not exist. For the method of computing definite integrals, *see* FUNDAMENTAL THEOREM OF CALCULUS. *See also* AREA; AREA UNDER CURVE.

DEFINITION, CHARACTERISTICS OF A MATHEMATICAL. A good definition in mathematics has the following characteristics: (1) it names the term that is being defined; (2) it places the term in its smallest category or class; (3) it distinguishes the term from other elements in the category, without giving all of its properties; (4) it is reversible.

For example, the following definition of a parallelogram has the four characteristics of a good definition:

"A *parallelogram* is a *quadrilateral* whose opposite sides are parallel." The definition names the term that is being defined: a parallelogram; it places the term in its smallest category: quadrilateral (note that a parallelogram is also a POLYGON, but polygon is not the smallest, or most limiting, category in which it can be placed); it distinguishes a parallelogram from other quadrilaterals: its opposite sides are parallel (note that all of the properties of a parallelogram are not given, just the one that distinguishes it from any other quadrilateral); it is reversible: "a quadrilateral whose opposite sides are parallel is a parallelogram" is a true statement.

The following definitions also have the four characteristics of a good definition:

1. PERPENDICULAR lines are two lines that meet to form equal adjacent angles.
2. A RECTANGLE is a parallelogram that has one right angle.

DEGREE (°), in mathematics, the unit for measuring ANGLES. An angle of 1° equals 1/360 of a complete rotation. A degree may be further divided into 60 minutes, and a minute into 60 seconds. Forty two degrees, sixteen minutes, and thirty seconds is written 42°16′30″. *See also* ARC DEGREE.

DEGREE OF AN EQUATION, the degree of the term (*see* DEGREE OF A TERM) in an algebraic EQUATION that has the highest power. $x + 3y = 12$ is a first degree equation. (*See* EQUATION, LINEAR.) $x^2 = 25$; $xy = 9$; and $x^2 - y^2 = 4$ are second degree equations. (*See* QUADRATIC EQUATION.) $2/x - 3y = 5$ is a second degree equation because when the fraction is removed, the equation is written $2 - 3xy = 5x$. The degree of a DIFFERENTIAL EQUATION is the power of the highest order DERIVATIVE which appears. Thus, the degree of the differential equation $(y'')^2 + (y')^3 = 0$ is two. *See also* POWER OF A NUMBER, ORDER OF DIFFERENTIAL EQUATION.

DEGREE OF A TERM, the sum of the EXPONENTS of the LITERAL FACTORS of a term. Thus, $3x^3y$ is a term of the fourth degree.

DEGREE OF FREEDOM, in statistics, the number of unrestricted and independent (free) variables in a statistic. If a sampling of q variables is independent in r of them, there are r degrees of freedom. In elementary statistics, degree of freedom are encountered most frequently in the following situations: (1) in the use of t-tables to test hypotheses about the means of normal populations with unknown variances; (2) in the use of F-tables to test hypotheses about the equality of two variances from normal populations, and to test for significant differences between the population means in an analysis of variance; and (3) when using chi-squared tables.

When a sum of squares is divided by a number in order to obtain an estimate of a population variance, that number (the divisor) is called the degrees of freedom.

DELTA, a Greek letter, symbolized by Δ (capital) or δ. Δ is commonly used in analytic geometry to denote an increment, as in Δx (read "delta x"), which signifies the amount of change along the x-axis. "Thus $\Delta x = x_2 - x$". (See figure.) δ is used to denote the value of a MATRIX, i.e., the DETERMINANT of a matrix. δA is called the determinant function of δ matrix A. δ is also commonly used in statistics, as in *delta distribution*.

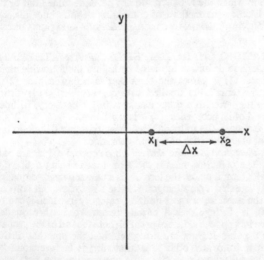

DEMOIVRE'S THEOREM (du-mwav'-ru). The theorem states: The nth power of a COMPLEX NUMBER is another complex number whose modulus is the nth power of the given modulus and whose amplitude is n times the given amplitude.

The trigonometric or polar form of the complex number $x + yi$ is $r(\cos \theta + i \sin \theta)$. (*See* COMPLEX NUMBER.) If the complex number is raised to any power n, when n is a positive integer, then

$$[r(\cos \theta + i \sin \theta)]^n = r^n(\cos n\theta + i \sin n\theta)$$
$$\text{or}$$
$$(r \operatorname{cis} \theta)^n = r^n \operatorname{cis} n\theta$$

Ex. 1: Find the third power of the complex number $1 + i$.

Sol.: In the figure, $\theta = $ arc tan 1 (*see* ARC TANGENT), $\theta = 45°$, or $\frac{\pi}{4}$; $r = \sqrt{1 + 1} = \sqrt{2}$,

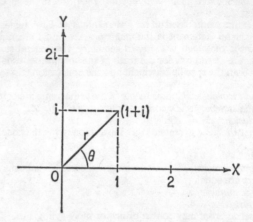

$$(1 + i)^3 = r^3(\cos 3\theta + i \sin 3\theta)$$
$$(1 + i)^3 = \sqrt{2}^3(\cos \tfrac{3}{4}\pi + i \sin \tfrac{3}{4}\pi)$$
$$(1 + i)^3 = 2\sqrt{2} \operatorname{cis} 135° = -2 + 2i.$$

If n is a fractional exponent, DeMoivre's Theorem may be used to obtain roots of a number. Every number has 2 square roots, 3 cube roots, 4 fourth roots, etc. Since the sine and cosine curves repeat every 360° or 2π radians, then

$$\sin \theta = \sin (\theta + 2\pi) \text{ and } \cos \theta = \cos (\theta + 2\pi).$$

Therefore the formula for n repetitions, when $n = 1, 2, 3$, etc. may be written

$$\sin \theta = \sin (\theta + 2n\pi) \text{ and } \cos \theta = \cos (\theta + 2n\pi).$$

Ex. 2: Find the three cube roots of 8.
Sol.: From DeMoivre's Theorem,

$$r^{1/3} \left(\cos \frac{\theta}{3} + i \sin \frac{\theta}{3} \right) \text{ or } r^{1/3} \cos \left(\frac{\theta + 2n\pi}{3} \right).$$

Since 8 may be written as the complex number $8 + i0$, then $r = 8$,

$$\theta = 0°, \quad \text{if } n = 0$$
$$\theta = 360°, \text{ if } n = 1$$
$$\theta = 720°, \text{ if } n = 2.$$

If $n = 3$, then $\frac{1080°}{3} = 360°$. Therefore, there are only 3 roots.

$$r^{1/3} \left(\cos \frac{0°}{3} + i \sin \frac{0°}{3} \right) = 8^{1/3} \operatorname{cis} 0° = 2(1 + 0i) = 2.$$

$$r^{1/3} \left(\cos \frac{360°}{3} + i \sin \frac{360°}{3} \right) = 8^{1/3} \operatorname{cis} 120° = 2\left(-\frac{1}{2} + i \frac{\sqrt{3}}{2} \right)$$
$$= -1 + i\sqrt{3}.$$

$$r^{1/3} \left(\cos \frac{720°}{3} + i \sin \frac{720°}{3} \right) = 8^{1/3} \operatorname{cis} 240° = 2\left(-\frac{1}{2} - i \frac{\sqrt{3}}{2} \right)$$
$$= -1 - i\sqrt{3}.$$

Therefore, the 3 cube roots of 8 are 2, $-1 + i\sqrt{3}$, and $-1 - i\sqrt{3}$.

DENOMINATE NUMBER (dee-nah'-min-et), a NUMBER that includes its unit of measure; e.g., 3 miles, 8 pounds, 2 quarts, etc.

A denominate number is said to be compound when expressed in two or more units, e.g., 3 yards 2 feet and 5 hours 30 minutes 45 seconds.

To change any denominate number to a corresponding denominate number of a larger unit, as inches to feet, pints to quarts, or ounces to pounds, *divide* the given number by the number of smaller units contained in one larger unit. See TABLE NO. 4, 5 (Weights and Measures).

Ex. 1: Change 57 inches to feet.
Sol.: 12 in. = 1 ft.

$$57 \text{ in.} = 57 \div 12 = 4\tfrac{3}{4} \text{ ft.}$$

Ex. 2: Change 32 quarts to pecks.
Sol.: 8 qt. = 1 peck.

$$32 \text{ qt.} = 32 \div 8 = 4 \text{ pecks.}$$

To change any denominate number to a corresponding denominate number of a smaller unit, as yards to feet, or gallons to quarts, *multiply* the given number by the number of smaller units contained in one larger unit.
Ex. 1: Change 3 miles to feet.
Sol.: 1 mi. = 5280 ft.

$$3 \text{ mi.} = 3 \times 5280 = 15{,}840 \text{ ft.}$$

Ex. 2: Change 2½ tons to pounds.
Sol.: 1 ton = 2000 lb.

$$2\tfrac{1}{2} \text{ tons} = 2\tfrac{1}{2} \times 2000 = 5000 \text{ lb.}$$

To add denominate numbers:
1. Add only like units of denominate numbers.
2. Change any unit in the sum to a higher unit, if possible.
Ex. 1: Add 12 ft. 6 in. and 8 ft. 9 in.

12 ft.	6 in.	
8 ft.	9 in.	
20 ft.	15 in.	15 in. = 1 ft. 3 in.

The sum is 21 ft. 3 in.
Ex. 2: Add 3 gal. 1 qt. 1 pt. + 2 gal. 3 qt. + 6 qt. 1 pt.

3 gal.	1 qt.	1 pt.	
2 gal.	3 qt.	0 pt.	
0 gal.	6 qt.	1 pt.	
5 gal.	10 qt.	2 pt.	10 qt. = 2 gal. 2 qt. and
			2 pt. = 1 qt.

The sum is 7 gal. 3 qt.
To subtract denominate numbers:
1. Subtract only like units.
2. If a unit in the MINUEND is smaller than the same unit in the SUBTRAHEND, exchange the next larger unit in the minuend for its equivalent in the smaller unit.
Ex. 1: Subtract 3 lb. 12 oz. from 8 lb. 10 oz.

$$\begin{array}{c} 7 \quad\; 26 \\ \text{Sol.:} \quad \cancel{8} \text{ lb.} \cancel{10} \text{ oz.} \\ -3 \text{ lb. } 12 \text{ oz.} \\ \hline 4 \text{ lb. } 14 \text{ oz.} \end{array}$$

Exchange 1 lb. for 16 oz. and add to 10 oz. Difference

Ex. 2: Subtract 50° 36′ 24″ from 180°.

Sol.:
180°	0′	0″		179°	59′	60″	
− 50°	36′	24″		− 50°	36′	24″	Difference
				129°	23′	36″	

To multiply denominate numbers:
1. If a DENOMINATE NUMBER is multiplied by some number, the resulting PRODUCT is a denominate number of the same kind.
2. If a linear measure is multiplied by a like linear measure, the product is a square measure; that is, feet times feet equal square feet. Also, if three linear measures are multiplied, the product is a cubic measure; as yards times yards times yards equal cubic yards.
Ex. 1: Multiply 3 hr. 15 min. 25 sec. by 6.

Sol.:
$$\begin{array}{c} 3 \text{ hr. } 15 \text{ min. } 25 \text{ sec.} \\ \times 6 \\ \hline 18 \text{ hr. } 90 \text{ min. } 150 \text{ sec.} \end{array}$$

150 sec. = 2 min. 30 sec. and 90 min. = 1 hr. 30 min.

Adjusted product is 19 hr. 32 min. 30 sec.
Ex. 2: Multiply 2 ft. 8 in. by 5 ft. 3 in.

Sol.: Change both numbers to feet.
$$2 \text{ ft. } 8 \text{ in.} \times 5 \text{ ft. } 3 \text{ in.} = 2\tfrac{2}{3} \text{ ft.} \times 5\tfrac{1}{4} \text{ ft.}$$

$$\frac{\cancel{8}^{2}}{\cancel{3}^{1}} \times \frac{\cancel{21}^{7}}{\cancel{4}} = 14 \text{ sq. ft.}$$

Change product to square yards.
$$14 \text{ sq. ft.} = 14 \div 9 = 1\tfrac{5}{9} \text{ sq. yd. or } 1 \text{ sq. yd. } 5 \text{ sq. ft.}$$

To divide denominate numbers:
1. Change a compound denominate number to its smallest unit before dividing.
2. Change the unit of the QUOTIENT to a larger unit, if possible.
3. If a denominate number is divided by a NUMERAL, the quotient is expressed in the same unit as the denominate number.
4. If a denominate number is divided by another denominate number of the same unit, the quotient is a nondenominate (or abstract) number.
Ex. 1: Divide 2 gal. 2 qt. 1 pt. into 3 equal measures.
Sol.: Change to pints and divide by 3.

$$2 \text{ gal. } 2 \text{ qt. } 1 \text{ pt.} = 21 \text{ pt.}$$
$$21 \text{ pt.} \div 3 = 7 \text{ pt. or } 3\tfrac{1}{2} \text{ qt.}$$

Ex. 2: How many times is 5 lb. 8 oz. contained in 67 lb. 6 oz.?
Sol.: 67 lb. 6 oz. = $67\tfrac{3}{8}$ lb. and 5 lb. 8 oz. = $5\tfrac{1}{2}$ lb.

$$67\tfrac{3}{8} \div 5\tfrac{1}{2} = \frac{539}{8} \div \frac{11}{2} = \frac{539}{\cancel{8}} \times \frac{\cancel{2}}{11} = \frac{539}{44} = 12\tfrac{1}{4}.$$

The answer is 12¼ times.

DENOMINATOR (dee-nah′-min-ay-tor), the DIVISOR in a FRACTION. In the fraction x/y, x is divided by y and y is the denominator. *See also* LOWEST COMMON DENOMINATOR.

DENSITY, in mathematics, a property of a SET. A set is said to be dense if every point in the set is an *accumulation point* of the set. That is, if each NEIGHBORHOOD of any point in the set contains another point in the set. The set of REAL NUMBERS is a dense set.

DEPARTURE, the linear measure in NAUTICAL MILES of the arc of a parallel of LATITUDE included between two MERIDIANS. *See* PLANE SAILING.

DEPENDENT EQUATIONS, two EQUATIONS whose GRAPHS coincide, because all numbers that satisfy one equation will satisfy the other.

$$\begin{cases} 2x - 3y = 4 \\ 4x - 6y = 8 \end{cases} \text{ are dependent equations}$$

since the second can be obtained by multiplying both members of the first by 2.

DEPENDENT VARIABLE, *see* VARIABLE.

DEPRESSION, ANGLE OF, *see* ANGLE OF DEPRESSION.

DERIVATIVE OF A FUNCTION (dee-riv′-u-tiv funk′-shun), the instantaneous rate of change of a FUNCTION with respect to a variable. The derivative of a function, $f(x)$ at a point a is the limit (*see* LIMIT OF A FUNCTION) of the DIFFERENCE QUOTIENT as x approaches a:

$$\lim_{x \to a} \frac{f(x) - f(a)}{x - a}. \text{ (See Fig. 1.)}$$

The derivative of $y = f(x)$ is usually denoted by y', $f(x)$, or dy/dx.

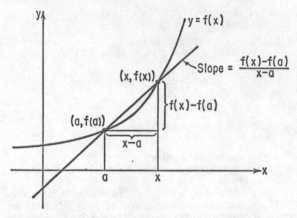

Fig. 1

The derivative of a function at a point may be interpreted as the slope (*see* SLOPE OF A LINE) of the TANGENT LINE to the curve at that point. Thus, for the curve given by $y = x^2 + 3x + 2$ (see Fig. 2), the derivative, $dy/dx = 2x + 3$, evaluated at any point on the curve, gives the slope of the tangent to the curve at that point. At $x = 1$, $2x + 3 = 5$. Therefore, the slope of the tangent line to the curve at (1,6) is 5, or $(\Delta y/\Delta x) = (5/1)$. (*See* DELTA.) At $x = -2$, $2x + 3 = -1$ and the slope of the tangent to the curve at $(-2,0)$ is $-1/1$.

The derivative may also be interpreted as the speed of a moving particle at a given instant: If $f(t)$ is the distance travelled by a particle in time t, the instantaneous rate at which the particle is moving at that moment is the derivative, $f'(t)$.

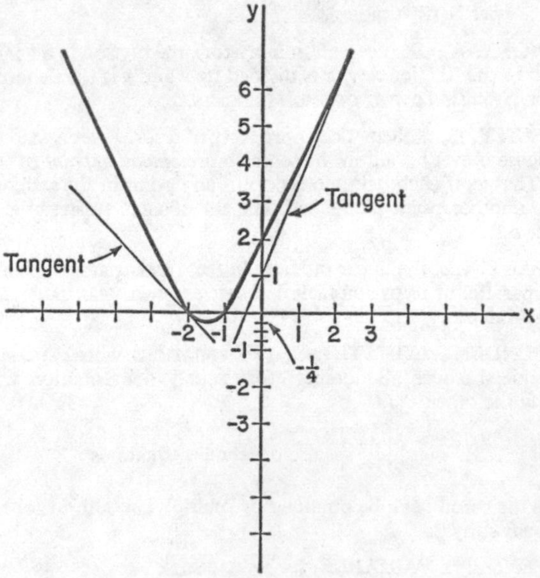

Fig. 2

The derivative of a POLYNOMIAL function, $y = x^n$ is found by the following rule, $\dfrac{dx^n}{dx} = nx^{n-1}$.

Ex.: a. $y = x^3$.
$dy/dx = 3x^2$.
b. $y = 6x^4$.
$dy/dx = 4 \cdot 6x^3 = 24x^3$.

The derivative of the sum of two functions is the sum of their derivatives:

$$\frac{d}{dx}\left(f(x) + g(x)\right) = \frac{d}{dx}f(x) + \frac{d}{dx}g(x).$$

Ex.: Differentiate: a. $2x^2 + 3x^5$.
b. $\sin x + \cos x$.
c. $\sin x + 1$.

Sol.: a. $\dfrac{d}{dx}(2x^2 + 3x^5) = \dfrac{d}{dx}(2x^2) + \dfrac{d}{dx}(3x^5) = 4x + 15x^4$.

b. $\dfrac{d}{dx}(\sin x + \cos x) = \cos x - \sin x$.

c. $\dfrac{d}{dx}(\sin x + 1) = \dfrac{d}{dx}(\sin x) + \dfrac{d}{dx}(1)$
$= \cos x + 0 = \cos x.$

The derivative of the product of two functions is given by the following rule:

$$\frac{d}{dx}(f(x)g(x)) = \left(\frac{d}{dx}f(x)\right)g(x) + f(x)\frac{d}{dx}g(x).$$

This is often abbreviated to
$$(uv)' = u'v + uv'.$$

Ex.: Differentiate a. $(\sin x)(\cos x)$.
b. $(x + 1)^2(x - 1)^3$.
c. $(x)(x)$.

Sol.: a. $\dfrac{d}{dx}(\sin x \cos x) = \dfrac{d}{dx}(\sin x) \cdot \cos x + \sin x \cdot \dfrac{d}{dx}\cos x$
$= \cos x \cos x - \sin x \sin x$
$= \cos^2 x - \sin^2 x.$

b. $\dfrac{d}{dx}((x + 1)^2(x - 1)^3) = \left(\dfrac{d}{dx}(x + 1)^2\right)(x - 1)^3$
$+ (x + 1)^2\dfrac{d}{dx}(x - 1)^3$
$= 2(x + 1)(x - 1)^3$
$+ (x + 1)^2(3(x - 1)^2).$

c. $\dfrac{d}{dx}(x)(x) = \left(\dfrac{d}{dx}(x)\right)x + x\left(\dfrac{d}{dx}(x)\right)$
$= 1 \cdot x + x \cdot 1 = 2x.$

If one function is the RATIO of two others, where the denominator function never has the value zero, then the derivative is given by the following rule:

$$\frac{d}{dx}\left(\frac{f(x)}{g(x)}\right) = \frac{f'(x)g(x) - f(x)g'(x)}{g^2(x)}.$$

This is often abbreviated to
$$\left(\frac{u}{v}\right)' = \frac{u'v - uv'}{v^2}.$$

Ex.: Differentiate: a. $\dfrac{x + 1}{x - 1}$. b. $\tan x$.

Sol.: a.

$$\frac{d}{dx}\left(\frac{x + 1}{x - 1}\right) = \frac{\left(\frac{d}{dx}(x + 1)\right)(x - 1) - (x + 1)\frac{d}{dx}(x - 1)}{(x - 1)^2}$$

$$= \frac{(x - 1) - (x + 1)}{(x - 1)^2} = \frac{-2}{(x - 1)^2}.$$

b. $\dfrac{d}{dx}\tan x = \dfrac{d}{dx}\left(\dfrac{\sin x}{\cos x}\right) = \dfrac{\cos^2 x + \sin^2 x}{\cos^2 x}$

$$= \frac{1}{\cos^2 x} = \sec^2 x.$$

The derivative of a composite function (function of a function) is given by the following rule:

$$\frac{d}{dx}(f(g(x))) = f'(g(x)) \cdot (g'(x)).$$

Ex.: Differentiate: a. $(x^2 + 1)^2$.

b. $\sin (x^2)$.

c. $\sin^2 (\cos x)$.

Sol.: a. $\dfrac{d}{dx}(x^2 + 1)^2 = 2(x^2 + 1) \cdot \dfrac{d}{dx}(x^2 + 1) = 2(x^2 + 1)(2x)$

$= 4x(x^2 + 1)$.

b. $\dfrac{d}{dx} \sin (x^2) = \cos (x^2) \cdot \dfrac{d}{dx} x^2 = 2x \cos (x^2)$.

c. $\dfrac{d}{dx} \sin^3 (\cos x) = 3 \sin^2 (\cos x) \cdot \dfrac{d}{dx} \sin (\cos x)$

$= 3 \sin^2 [\cos x] \left[\cos (\cos x) \cdot \dfrac{d}{dx} \cos x \right]$

$= 3 \sin^2 [\cos x][\cos (\cos x)][- \sin x]$.

(*See* TABLE NO. 13.)

The derivative of the derivative of a function, $y = f(x)$ is called the *second derivative*. It is denoted by y'', $f''(x)$ or d^2y/dx^2. The second derivative gives the rate of change of the tangent to a curve. Thus, from the second derivative it is possible to determine whether the curve is rising, falling, or at an INFLECTION POINT (changing direction). If the second derivative is positive at point P, the curve is concave upward (cupped to "hold water") at that point. If the second derivative is negative at P, the curve is concave downward (cupped to "spill water") at that point. If the second derivative is zero at a point P, then P is a point of inflection.

Ex.: If $y = x^3 + 3x^2 + 6x + 4$, find the inflection point of its graph. Is the curve rising or falling at $x = 0$ and $x = -3$?

Sol.: $y = x^3 + 3x^2 + 6x + 4$

$dy/dx = 3x^2 + 6x + 6$

and $d^2y/dx^2 = 6x + 6$.

When $d^2y/dx^2 = 0$ there is an inflection point.

$$6x + 6 = 0$$
$$6x = -6$$
$$x = -1$$

The curve changes direction at $x = -1$. When $x = 0$, $d^2y/dx^2 = 6$ (positive) so the curve is concave upward, or rising. When $x = -3$, $d^2y/dx^2 = -12$ (negative) so the curve is concave downward, or falling.

The second derivative may also be used to find maximum (*see* MAXIMUM OF A FUNCTION) and minimum (*see* MINIMUM OF A FUNCTION) points. A maximum or minimum occurs at the point where the slope of the tangent is zero, i.e., when the derivative is zero. To determine whether there is a maximum or minimum value at the point, the SECOND DERIVATIVE TEST may be used: Evaluate the second derivative at that point; if the second derivative is *positive* at the point the function is a minimum; if the second derivative is *negative*, the function has a maximum at the point.

Ex. 1: Find the abscissa of the maximum and minimum points of the graph of $y = x^3 - 3x^2 - 9x + 5$.

Sol.: $dy/dx = 3x^2 - 6x - 9$

$3x^2 - 6x - 9 = 0$

$x^2 - 2x - 3 = 0$

$(x - 3)(x + 1) = 0$

$x - 3 = 0 \quad x + 1 = 0$

$x = 3 \quad x = -1$

$dy/dx = 3x^2 - 6x - 9$

$d^2y/dx^2 = 6x - 6$

When $x = 3$, $6x - 6 = +12$ ∴ the graph is a minimum when $x = 3$. When $x = -1$, $6x - 6 = -12$ ∴ the graph is a maximum when $x = -1$.

Successive derivatives may be found for a function. The third derivative is denoted y''', $f'''(x)$, or d^3y/dx^3. The fourth is y'''', $f''''(x)$, or d^4y/dx^4, etc.

DESCARTES, RENÉ (day-kahrt' ru-nay'), 1596–1650, French mathematician and philosopher; educated at the Jesuit College of Le Fleche and studied in Paris. After serving as a soldier, he settled in 1629 in Holland where he published most of his work. He invented the method of combining algebra with geometry, now called analytic geometry (*see* GEOMETRY, ANALYTIC), in order to "correct the faults of each with the virtues of the other." The system of rectangular coordinates (*see* COORDINATES, RECTANGULAR) by which he did this are sometimes called Cartesian coordinates.

Descartes' thought (called Cartesianism) marks a turning point in the history of philosophy. He is considered the founder of modern epistemology, and many of his metaphysical distinctions have influenced all subsequent philosophy. Dissatisfied with the persistent disagreement he found among philosophers, he set out to establish a new method in philosophy modeled on mathematics. He began in his *Le Discours de la Methode* ("Discourse on Method," 1637) by doubting everything which he could bring himself to doubt. What remained after this systematic doubt was the Self; even in the act of doubting one's own existence one established it (since the I is required to do the doubting). Hence, the famous expression "*I think; therefore I am.*" From this basis Descartes attempted to re-establish, on a firmer footing those beliefs which he had formerly rejected as doubtful. In *The Principle of Philosophy* he proposed a cosmology embodying his theory of vortices to account for planetary motion. This work was very speculative and was soon supplanted by the very exact theories of Issac Newton. Besides his contributions to philosophy and mathematics Descartes made important discoveries in optics, and music theory.

Biblio.: Smith, N. K., *Studies in Cartesian Philosophy* (1962) and *New Studies in the Philosophy of Descartes* (1963). Anscombe, G. E. M., and Geach, P. T. (eds.), *Descartes: Philosophical Writings* (1954).

DESCENDING POWERS (de-sen'-ding), the arrangement of terms in an expression so that the EXPONENTS of one letter decrease in each succeeding term, as in $x^4 - 3x^3 + 2x^2 + x - 6$. If there are two letters in the expression they are usually arranged in ASCENDING POWERS of one letter and in descending powers of the other, as in $x^4 + x^3y + x^2y^2 + xy^3 + y^4$. See also ALGEBRAIC EXPRESSION.

DESIGN OF EXPERIMENTS (dee-zahyn'). That part of the subject of STATISTICS that is concerned with determining the proper statistical design to use in any particular experiment, taking into account the number of observations possible, the accuracy desired, and many other special considerations for that experiment.

DETERMINANT (dee-tehr'-min-ent), a square array of numbers. If a determinant has two rows and two columns, it is called a determinant of second order:

$$\begin{vmatrix} a & b \\ c & d \end{vmatrix}.$$

The value of this determinant is the difference of the products of its diagonals: $ad - bc$.

Ex. 1: Evaluate the determinant $\begin{vmatrix} 6 & 8 \\ 7 & 10 \end{vmatrix}$.

Sol.: $6 \times 10 - 8 \times 7 = 60 - 56 = 4$.

Ex. 2: Evaluate the determinant $\begin{vmatrix} -3 & -5 \\ 4 & 7 \end{vmatrix}$.

Sol.: $-3 \times 7 - (-5) \times 4 = -21 - (-20) = -21 + 20 = -1$.

A third order determinant is an array of numbers that has three rows and three columns, such as

$$\begin{vmatrix} a_1 & b_1 & c_1 \\ a_2 & b_2 & c_2 \\ a_3 & b_3 & c_3 \end{vmatrix}.$$

To evaluate a third order determinant by finding the difference of the products of its diagonals, it is helpful to re-write the first and second columns after the third column:

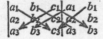

The value of this determinant is

$$a_1b_2c_3 + a_2b_3c_1 + a_3b_1c_2 - (a_3b_2c_1 + a_2b_1c_3 + a_1b_3c_2).$$

If the rows and column of any selected element are crossed out, the remaining elements form a lower order determinant called the MINOR of that element. Expansion of the third order determinant in terms of minors of the elements is somewhat easier:

$$a_1\begin{vmatrix}b_2 & c_2\\ b_3 & c_3\end{vmatrix} - a_2\begin{vmatrix}b_1 & c_1\\ b_3 & c_3\end{vmatrix} + a_3\begin{vmatrix}b_1 & c_1\\ b_2 & c_2\end{vmatrix}$$

Ex. 3: Evaluate $\begin{vmatrix}3 & 1 & 5\\ 1 & 2 & 3\\ 4 & 1 & 1\end{vmatrix}$.

Sol.: $3\begin{vmatrix}2 & 3\\ 1 & 1\end{vmatrix} - 1\begin{vmatrix}1 & 5\\ 1 & 1\end{vmatrix} + 4\begin{vmatrix}1 & 5\\ 2 & 3\end{vmatrix}$

$$3(2-3) - 1(1-5) + 4(3-10)$$
$$-3 + 4 - 28 = -27.$$

For solving systems of linear equations in two and three unknowns, using determinants, *see* CRAMER'S RULE; COFACTOR.

DIAGONAL, OF A POLYGON (dahy-ag'-un-al pah'-lee-gahn), a line segment joining any two nonconsecutive vertices of the polygon. In the figure, *EB, EC, DA, DB,* and *CA* are diagonals of PENTAGON *ABCDE. See also* PARALLELOGRAM.

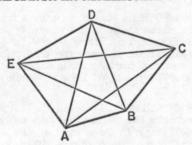

DIAMETER OF A CIRCLE, the line segment joining any two points on a circle and passing through the center. A diameter is the longest CHORD that can be drawn in a circle, and it bisects the circle.

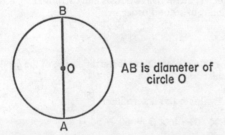

AB is diameter of circle O

DICHOTOMY, LAW OF (dahy-kah'-toh-mee), the principle that states that a PROPOSITION is either true or false, but not both. For two quantities *a* and *b*, exactly one statement is true: $a = b$, or $a \ne b$. Thus, $a = b$ implies $a \ne b$ is false, and vice versa. *See also* CONTRADICTION, LAW OF; TRICHOTOMY LAW.

DIDO'S PROBLEM (dahy'-dohz), the problem of finding the curve with a given perimeter that encloses the maximum area. The curve is a circle. It is called Dido's problem because Queen Dido of Carthage is said to have solved the problem when she was offered as much land as she could enclose with a cowhide. Cutting the hide into thin strips, she formed a semicircle along the coast of North Africa, thereby establishing the state of Carthage.

DIFFERENCE, the result, or answer, of a SUBTRACTION operation.

DIFFERENCE IN LATITUDE, *see* PLANE SAILING.

DIFFERENCE IN LONGITUDE, in minutes, along a parallel of LATITUDE equals the product of the DEPARTURE in NAUTICAL MILES and the secant of the latitude. In PARALLEL SAILING, the distance is the departure.

Ex.: A ship in latitude 42° 30′ N., longitude 58° 20′ W., sails due west 80 miles. What is the position of the point reached?

Sol.: Diff. longitude = departure $\times$ secant latitude.
Diff. long. = 80 $\times$ sec 42° 30′
= 80 $\times$ 1.356 = 108.5 miles.
Diff. longitude = 1° 48′ 30″.

The latitude remains that of the starting point, therefore the position is latitude 42° 30′ N., longitude 60° 8′ 30″ W.

DIFFERENCE OF TWO CUBES, a special case of FACTORING in which one factor is a BINOMIAL and one a TRINOMIAL:

Ex. 1: Factor $x^3 - y^3$.
Sol.: $x^3 - y^3 = (x - y)(x^2 + xy + y^2)$.
Ex. 2: Factor $8a^3 - 27b^3$.
Sol.: $8a^3 - 27b^3 = (2a - 3b)(4a^2 + 6ab + 9b^2)$. *See also* SUM OF TWO CUBES.

DIFFERENCE OF TWO SQUARES, a special case of FACTORING in which the FACTORS are the sum and the difference of the SQUARE ROOTS of the two squares: $x^2 - y^2 = (x + y)(x - y)$.

Ex.: Factor $16a^2 - 25y^2$.
Sol.: $16a^2 - 25y^2 = (4a + 5y)(4a - 5y)$.

DIFFERENCE QUOTIENT (kwoh'-shunt), the expression $\dfrac{f(x) - f(a)}{x - a}$ in the definition of the DERIVATIVE OF A FUNCTION $f(x)$ at $x = a$. For any x near a, this quotient is the slope of the SECANT LINE to the curve $y = f(x)$ through the points $(a, f(a))$ and $(x, f(x))$. (See figure.) Since this secant is an approximation to the tangent line where x is close to a, the difference quotient approaches the slope of the TANGENT LINE as the distance between x and a approaches zero.

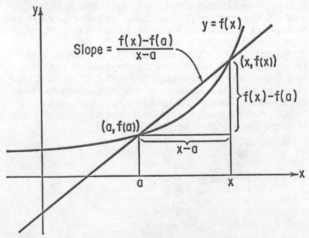

Other notations are sometimes used for this quotient. If the distance from a to x is denoted by Δx and the corresponding increment of $y = f(x)$ is denoted by Δy, the difference quotient can be written:

$$\frac{\Delta y}{\Delta x} = \frac{f(a + \Delta x) - f(a)}{\Delta x}$$

DIFFERENTIAL (dif-fur-en'-shal), in mathematics, if y is a FUNCTION of x, and a is a value of x for which $f(x)$ is defined, the differentials dx and dy are defined as

$$dx = x - a$$

and

$$dy = f'(a) \cdot dx.$$

Graphically, dy is the change in the height of the TANGENT LINE to the curve $y = f(x)$ at $x = a$ corresponding to a change of dx units along the x-axis. (See figure.) These changes may be positive or negative; i.e., increases or decreases.

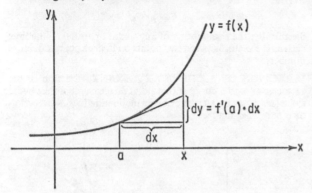

Ex. 1: What is the differential of $y = x^3$ for $dx = \frac{1}{2}$ at $a = 3$?

Sol.:
$$dy = f'(a) \cdot dx$$
$$= (2)(3)(\tfrac{1}{2}) = 3.$$

Differentials may be applied to find the approximate value of a function $y = f(x)$ at some point x, if its value and derivative (see DERIVATIVE OF A FUNCTION) for a nearby value of $x = a$ are known. The formula is:

$$f(x) \approx f(a) + f'(a) \cdot dx.$$

Ex. 2: Use differentials to find an approximation to $(2.32)^2$.

Sol.: Let $f(x) = x^2$. Since $2^2 = 4$, let $a = 2$, $dx = (2.32 - 2) = .32$. Then

$$f(x) = (2.32)^2 \approx f(2) + f'(2)(x - a)$$
$$= 4 + (4)(.32) = 5.28$$

Ex. 3: A cylinder 1 in. high of radius r has volume $V(r) = \pi r^2$. Use the fact that $V(1) = \pi$ to estimate $V(2)$ by differentials. Compare the approximation to the value of $V(2)$ given by the formula.

Sol.:
$$V(2) = V(1) + V'(1)(2 - 1)$$
$$= \pi + (2\pi)(1)$$
$$= \pi + 2\pi = 3\pi.$$

The value given by the formula is $\pi 2^2 = 4\pi$.

DIFFERENTIAL ANALYZER, see COMPUTER.

DIFFERENTIAL EQUATION, an equation that contains no more than two variables and DIFFERENTIALS or derivatives (see DERIVATIVE OF A FUNCTION) of one of the variables with respect to the other. An equation that contains partial derivatives is called a PARTIAL DIFFERENTIAL EQUATION; one containing total derivatives is called an ordinary differential equation. The order of an ordinary differential equation (see ORDER OF A DIFFERENTIAL EQUATION) is the order of the highest-ordered derivative that it contains. The degree of an ordinary differential equation (see DEGREE OF AN EQUATION) is its algebraic degree in the highest-ordered derivative in the equation. Thus, the ordinary differential equation $(y'') + 2b(y')^3 + y = 0$ is of order 2 and degree 1. Any relation free from derivatives, involving one or more of the variables, and consistent with the differential equation is called a solution of the equation. A solution of the equation $y'' + y' - 6y = 0$ is $y = e^{2x}$, since substituting e^{2x} and differentiating yields $4e^{2x} + 2e^{2x} - 6e^{2x}$ or 0. The equation $(4x^3 - y)dx + (2y - 3xy^2)dy = 0$ has as a solution the relation $x^4 - xy^3 + y^2 = c$, since differentiation of the relation yields the original differential equation. Note that the solution to an ordinary differential equation need not be unique: c can be any constant. See also LINEAR DIFFERENTIAL EQUATION OF FIRST ORDER; SEPARABLE DIFFERENTIAL EQUATION.

DIFFERENTIATION, the process of finding the DERIVATIVE OF A FUNCTION. See TABLE NO. 13.

DIGIT (dih'-jit), one of the symbols of a number system; for the DECIMAL NUMBER SYSTEM, any of the symbols 0, 1, 2, 3, 4, 5, 6, 7, 8, 9; for the BINARY NUMBER SYSTEM, the symbols 0, 1.

DIGITAL COMPUTER, see COMPUTER.

DIGIT PROBLEM. In solving a digit problem, if u is the units' digit, t the tens' digit and h the hundreds' digit, the three place number is $100h + 10t + u$. If the digits are reversed the new number is $100u + 10t + h$.

Ex.: The sum of the two digits of a number is 13. If the digits are interchanged, the number is increased by 27. Find the number.

Let	$u =$ units' digit,
	$t =$ tens' digit,
then	$10t + u =$ the number
and	$10u + t =$ the number reversed,
	$u + t =$ sum of the digits.
Therefore	$10u + t = 10t + u + 27,$
	$9u - 9t = 27.$ Divide by 9.

Then (1) $\quad \begin{cases} u - t = 3 \\ u + t = 13. \text{ Sum of digits is 13.} \end{cases}$
(2)

Add (1) and (2) $2u = 16,$
$$u = 8, t = 5.$$
The number is 58.

Check: $5 + 8 = 13$
$58 + 27 = 85$

See also EQUATIONS, SYSTEMS OF LINEAR.

DIHEDRAL ANGLE (dahy-hee'-dral), the figure formed by two intersecting planes. The planes are called the *faces* of the angle and the line of intersection is the EDGE. A dihedral angle is named by a point in one face, the edge, and then a point in the other face.

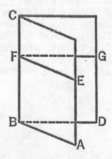

In the figure, planes AC and CD are the faces and BC is the edge. Therefore, the dihedral angle is $\angle A\text{-}BC\text{-}D$. It may also be named by the edge only, as $\angle BC$.

The angle formed by two lines, one in each plane and each perpendicular to the edge at the same point, is called the *plane angle of the dihedral angle*. In the dihedral angle shown in the figure, $\angle EFG$ is a plane angle. All plane angles of a dihedral angle are equal. If a plane angle is a right angle, the dihedral angle is a right angle and the planes are perpendicular.

DIMENSION (di-men'-shun), the property of length, width, or depth of an object. Geometrically, an object is said to have as many dimensions as there are axes (see AXIS) required to locate its position in space. Thus, the point $A(3)$, on a number line is said to be a point in one-dimension or one-space (see Fig. 1). The point $B(3,2)$ is a point in two-dimensions, or two-space (see

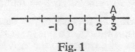

Fig. 1

Fig. 2). The point $C(5,2,0)$ is a point in three-dimensions, or three-space (see Fig. 3).

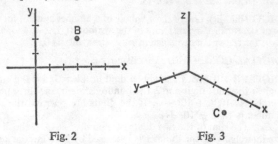

Fig. 2   Fig. 3

DIRECTED DISTANCE, the distance $b - a$ from point A to point B on a NUMBER LINE where a is the COORDINATE of point A and b is the coordinate of point B. If b is larger than a, the directed distance is positive; if a is larger than b, it is negative.

Ex. 1: Find the directed distance from the point -2 to the point -1.

Sol.: Since $a = -2$ and $b = -1$, the directed distance is $-1 - (-2) = +1$.

Ex. 2: Find the directed distance from the point -1 to the point -2.

Sol.: Since $a = -1$ and $b = -2$, the directed distance is $-2 - (-1) = -1$.

DIRECTED NUMBER, *see* SIGNED NUMBER.

DIRECTED SEGMENT, an INTERVAL on a NUMBER LINE of which one end point is called the starting, or initial, point, and the other is called the terminal point. The segment denoted by $\overrightarrow{AB}$ that starts at A and ends at B is then different from the segment denoted by $\overrightarrow{BA}$ that starts at B and ends at A. *See also* VECTOR.

DIRECTION ANGLE, for a LINE in the plane, the smallest positive angle between the line and the positive x-AXIS. For a line, p, in space, there is a line through the ORIGIN, parallel to p and divided into two HALF-LINES, h and h', by the origin. (See figure.) Corresponding to h there is a set of direction angles, designated α, β, and γ. Each of these angles is the smallest positive angle between h and the positive direction of one of the three axes. Similarly, the complements (*see* COMPLEMENTARY ANGLES) of these

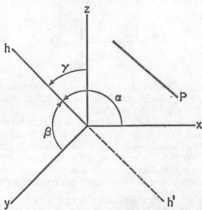

angles, α', β', γ', are three direction angles for h'. Either set is considered a set of direction angles for the original line p.

Ex.: What are the direction angles of a line parallel to the x-axis?

Sol.: $\alpha = 0°, \beta = 90°, \gamma = 90°$; or $\alpha = 180°, \beta = 90°, \gamma = 90°$.

DIRECTION COSINES, the cosines (*see* COSINE OF AN ANGLE) of the three DIRECTION ANGLES of a line in space. If α, β, and γ are the direction angles with respect to the x, y, and z-axes respec-

tively, l, m, and n denote the direction cosines, where l-cosine α, $m =$ cosine β, and $n =$ cosine γ.

DIRECTION NUMBERS, any set of three numbers proportional to the DIRECTION COSINES of a line in space. If the direction cosines are l, m, and n, then any three numbers a, b, and c are direction numbers if there is a constant of proportionality p so that:

$$a = pl, \, b = pm, \, c = pn.$$

Specifically, the components of any VECTOR parallel to the line, such as the vector between two points on it, are a set of direction numbers.

DIRECTION OF A CURVE AT A POINT, direction of the TANGENT LINE to a curve at that point as measured either by its slope (*see* SLOPE OF A LINE) or by its inclination (*see* INCLINATION OF A LINE). See figure.

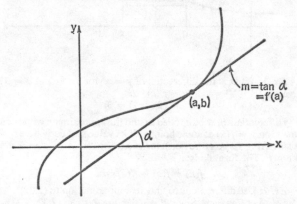

The slope of the tangent line to the curve $y = f(x)$ at the point (a,b) on the curve is the derivative (*see* DERIVATIVE OF A FUNCTION), $f'(a)$. The inclination of the tangent at that point is $\tan^{-1}(f'(a))$; i.e., the angle whose tangent is $f'(a)$ (*see* INVERSE TRIGONOMETRIC FUNCTIONS).

Ex.: What is the direction of $y = f(x) = x^2$ at $x = \frac{1}{2}$?

Sol.: $f'(x) = 2x$; for $x = \frac{1}{2}, f'(x) = 2(\frac{1}{2}) = 1$.

$$\tan^{-1}(1) = \pi/4 \text{ radians} = 45°.$$

DIRECTOR CIRCLE, of an ellipse or of a hyperbola, the CIRCLE that is the LOCUS of the intersection of two tangents to the ELLIPSE (see figure) or HYPERBOLA.

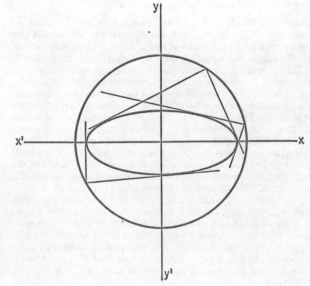

DIRECTRIX, *see* CONIC SECTIONS.

DISCOUNT, in finance, the sale of a promissory note or of a bill of exchange at less than its maturity value. The difference between the sale price and the maturity value is the interest paid the buyer for assuming the risk and waiting until the note or bill matures. The term also has a more general business meaning of selling a good or obligation to pay for less than its list price of par value.

DISCOUNT, in pricing, a reduction in the list price of an article. The *rate of discount* is the PERCENT off the list price. The price after the discount has been deducted, is the sales price, or the *net price*. The following formulas are used in problems involving discounts:

> Discount = Rate of Discount × List Price.
> Net Price = List Price — Discount.
> Rate of Discount = $\dfrac{\text{Discount}}{\text{List Price}}$.

If an article is discounted more than once, the first discount is deducted from the list price, then the second discount is taken on the new list price and deducted from it, etc. Although the two discounts must be taken separately, by the COMMUTATIVE PROPERTY of multiplication, they may be taken in any order.

Ex.: If an article is marked at $300 and successive discounts of 25% and 10% are allowed, what is the net price?

Sol.:
> 25% of $300 = $\frac{1}{4}$ × $300 = $75
> $300 — $75 = $225
>
> 10% of $225 = $\frac{1}{10}$ × $225 = $22.50
>
> $225.00
> —22.50
> ————
> $202.50 Net Price

DISCOUNT RATE, the loss to the seller from discounting a safe promissory note or bill of exchange figured as a percentage for one year. If, e.g., a promissory note worth $102.00 and due in six months is sold for $100.00, the discount rate is approximately 4%, i.e., the buyer gets an extra $2.00 for his $100.00 purchase after six months, or 4% a year. The buyer would pay less if there is any risk that the note would not be repaid.

DISCRIMINANT (dis-krim'-in-ant), of a QUADRATIC EQUATION, the expression, $b^2 - 4ac$, which is used to determine the nature of the roots. The discriminant is the RADICAND of the QUADRATIC FORMULA,

$$x = \frac{-b \pm \sqrt{b^2 - 4ac}}{2a}$$

in which a is the COEFFICIENT of x^2, b the coefficient of the x term, and c is the CONSTANT.

1. If $b^2 - 4ac = 0$, the roots are real (*see* REAL NUMBERS), rational (*see* RATIONAL NUMBERS), and equal.
Ex. 1: $x^2 + 2x + 1 = 0$
then $b^2 - 4ac = (2)^2 - 4(1)(1) = 4 - 4 = 0$.
2. If $b^2 - 4ac$ is positive and a PERFECT SQUARE, the roots are real, rational, and unequal.
Ex. 2: $3x^2 + 2x - 1 = 0$
then $b^2 - 4ac = (2)^2 - (4)(3)(-1) = 4 + 12 = 16$.
3. If $b^2 - 4ac$ is positive and not a perfect square, the roots are real, irrational, and unequal.
Ex. 3: $x^2 - 6x - 8 = 0$
then $b^2 - 4ac = (-6)^2 - (4)(1)(-8) = 36 + 32 = 68$.
4. If $b^2 - 4ac$ is negative, the roots are COMPLEX NUMBERS.
Ex. 4: $x^2 + 3x + 5 = 0$
then $b^2 - 4ac = (3)^2 - (4)(1)(5) = 9 - 20 = -11$.
The discriminant of $Ax^2 + Bxy + Cy^2 + Dx + Ey + F = 0$, is the expression $B^2 - 4AC$ which is INVARIANT under ROTATION; i.e., if the same curve is given by two different equations, one in terms of one pair of axes and the other in terms of a second pair

of axes which are tilted with respect to the first but have the same origin, the values of $B^2 - 4AC$ and $B'^2 - 4A'C'$ will be equal. (See figure.)

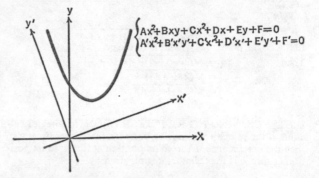

$$\begin{cases} Ax^2 + Bxy + Cx^2 + Dx + Ey + F = 0 \\ A'x^2 + B'x'y' + C'x'^2 + D'x' + E'y' + F' = 0 \end{cases}$$

The discriminant may be used to decide which CONIC SECTION is the graph of a given second degree equation by the following rule: If A and C are not both zero, then the curve is:

> a PARABOLA if $B^2 - 4AC = 0$,
> an ELLIPSE if $B^2 - 4AC < 0$,
> a HYPERBOLA if $B^2 - 4AC > 0$.

DISJUNCTION, ($\vee$), in the ALGEBRA OF PROPOSITIONS, the assertion that either, or both, of two propositions is, or are, true. E.g., $p \vee q$, sometimes written $p + q$, is read "p is true or q is true" or "p or q" for short. The truth table for $p \vee q$ is

	p	q	$p \vee q$
1.	1	1	1
2.	1	0	1
3.	0	1	1
4.	0	0	0

This can be read: "When p and q are both true (line 1), or when either p is true and q is false (line 2) or p is false and q is true (line 3), then $p \vee q$ is true; but when p and q are both false, then $p \vee q$ is also false (line 4)." Note that when this table is reorganized in the alternative format,

		q	q
	$\vee$	1	0
p	1	1	1
p	0	1	0

it becomes ISOMORPHIC with the table of addition in a two valued BOOLEAN ALGEBRA. For this reason the disjunction of p and q is sometimes called their logical sum.

DISPERSION, MEASURES OF, also called the *measures of variation*. In STATISTICS, any of several numerical indices of how scattered (i.e., dispersed or varied), the sample data are. The RANGE, MEAN ABSOLUTE DEVIATION, variance (*see* VARIANCE, SAMPLE; VARIANCE, POPULATION), and STANDARD DEVIATION are examples of such measures.

DISTANCE BETWEEN TWO PARALLEL LINES, the length of the PERPENDICULAR from a POINT on one line to the other line. PARALLEL LINES are everywhere equidistant.

DISTANCE BETWEEN TWO POINTS, the length of the LINE SEGMENT joining two points. A straight line segment is the shortest distance between two points. The distance between two points on a NUMBER LINE, $A(x_1)$ and $B(x_2)$, is the ABSOLUTE VALUE of the difference between their COORDINATES: $d = |x_2 - x_1|$.
Ex. 1: Find the distance between the points $A(3)$ and $B(-5)$.

Sol.: $D = |(-5) - (3)| = |-5 - 3| = |-8| = 8$.
or $D = |3 - (-5)| = |3 + 5| = |8| = 8$.

The distance between two points, (x_1, y_1) and (x_2, y_2) on a line in the plane is found by the DISTANCE FORMULA.

Ex. 1: Find the distance between the points $A(-1, 5)$ and $B(2, 1)$.

Sol.:

$$d = \sqrt{(x_2 - x_1)^2 + (y_2 - y_1)^2}.$$

Let A be the points (x_1, y_1) and B be the points (x_2, y_2).

Then
$$\begin{aligned} d &= \sqrt{[2 - (-1)]^2 + (1 - 5)^2} \\ &= \sqrt{(2 + 1)^2 + (-4)^2} \\ &= \sqrt{(3)^2 + (-4)^2} \\ &= \sqrt{9 + 16} = \sqrt{25} = 5. \end{aligned}$$

DISTANCE, FINDING BY INTEGRATION, in integral calculus, if the velocity of a moving body is a function of time, $v(t)$, then the net distance, N, from its position at time a to its position at time b is the definite integral, given by

$$N = \int_a^b v(t)\, dt.$$

If the integral is a negative number it indicates that the body has moved in a negative direction. Hence, if the point has doubled back on its path, the net distance travelled is less than the total distance. To find the total distance, T, which a body has travelled we can use the absolute value form of the definite integral. Then the total distance is given by

$$T = \int_a^b |v(t)|\, dt.$$

Alternatively, to find T we may split the time interval from a to b into periods when $v(t)$ is negative and periods when it is positive; then integrate separately over these intervals, and add the absolute values of the results.

Ex.: The velocity of a body is given by $v(t) = t^2 - 1$. Find the net distance (N) and the total distance (T) covered between $t = 0$ and $t = 3$.

Sol.:
$$\begin{aligned} N &= \int_0^3 t^2 - 1\, dt = \left(\frac{t^3}{3} - t\right)\Big]_0^3 \\ &= 27/3 - 3 = 6. \end{aligned}$$
$$\begin{aligned} T &= \left|\int_0^1 t^2 - 1\, dt\right| + \left|\int_1^3 t^2 - 1\, dt\right| \\ &= \left|\left(\frac{t^3}{3} - t\right)\Big]_0^1\right| + \left|\left(\frac{t^3}{3} - t\right)\Big]_1^3\right| \\ &= |-\tfrac{2}{3}| + |6\tfrac{2}{3}| = \tfrac{2}{3} + 6\tfrac{2}{3} = 7\tfrac{1}{3}. \end{aligned}$$

DISTANCE FORMULA, used to compute the distance between two points whose COORDINATES are known. If the coordinates of two points in the plane are (x_1, y_1) and (x_2, y_2), a right triangle may be constructed whose legs are of length $y_2 - y_1$ and $x_2 - x_1$. (See Fig. 1.) Then using the PYTHAGOREAN THEOREM, the distance is found to be:

$$d = \sqrt{(x_2 - x_1)^2 + (y_2 - y_1)^2}.$$

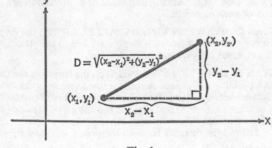

Fig. 1

Similarly, if the coordinates of two points in three dimensional space are (x_1, y_1, z_1) and (x_2, y_2, z_2), the distance is given by:

$$d = \sqrt{(x_2 - x_1)^2 + (y_2 - y_1)^2 + (z_2 - z_1)^2}.$$

Ex. 1: Find the distance between the points $(2, 1)$ and $(5, 5)$.
Sol.: Use the first formula above.

$$\begin{aligned} d &= \sqrt{(5 - 2)^2 + (5 - 1)^2} \\ &= \sqrt{3^2 + 4^2} \\ &= \sqrt{9 + 16} = \sqrt{25} = 5. \end{aligned}$$

Ex. 2: Find the length of the diagonal (*see* DIAGONAL OF A POLYGON) AC in PARALLELOGRAM $ABCD$, when the coordinates of A are $(0, 2)$, of B $(8, 2)$, of C $(12, 7)$, and of D $(4, 7)$. (See Fig. 2.)

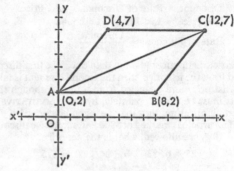

Fig. 2

Sol.:
$$\begin{aligned} d &= \sqrt{(x_2 - x_1)^2 + (y_2 - y_1)^2} \\ \overline{AC} &= \sqrt{(12 - 0)^2 + (7 - 2)^2} \\ \overline{AC} &= \sqrt{144 + 25} = \sqrt{169} \\ \overline{AC} &= 13 \text{ units.} \end{aligned}$$

Ex. 3: Find the distance between the points $(1, 1, 2)$ and $(-1, 2, 3)$ in three dimensions.
Sol.: Use the second formula above.

$$\begin{aligned} d &= \sqrt{(-1 - 1)^2 + (2 - 1)^2 + (3 - 2)^2} \\ &= \sqrt{(-2)^2 + 1^2 + 1^2} \\ &= \sqrt{6}. \end{aligned}$$

The distance between two points in polar coordinates, (r_1, θ_1) and (r_2, θ_2), is given by: $d = \sqrt{r_1^2 + r_2^2 - 2r_1 r_2 \cos(\theta_2 - \theta_1)}$ (See Fig. 3.)

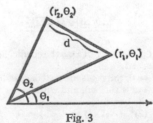

Fig. 3

Ex. 4: Find the distance between the following pairs of points:

     a. $(1, 0)$, $(1, \pi/2)$,
     b. $(2, \pi/4)$, $(3, \pi)$.

Sol.: a. Since $\theta_2 - \theta_1 = \pi/2$, $\sqrt{r_1^2 + r_2^2 - 2r_1 r_2 \cos(\theta_2 - \theta_1)}$
$$\begin{aligned} &= \sqrt{1 + 1 - 2\cos \pi/2} \\ &= \sqrt{1 + 1 - 2 \cdot 0} \\ &= \sqrt{2}. \end{aligned}$$

b. $\sqrt{r_1^2 + r_2^2 - 2r_1 r_2 \cos(\theta_2 - \theta_1)}$

$$= \sqrt{4 + 9 - 2(2)(3)\cos\left(\frac{3\pi}{4}\right)} = \sqrt{13 - 12\left(\frac{1}{\sqrt{2}}\right)}.$$

DISTANCE FROM A POINT TO A CIRCLE, the segment between the POINT and the CIRCLE, measured on the line joining the point to the center of the circle. In the figure, the distance from A to $\odot O$ is AB. The distance from C to $\odot O$ is BC.

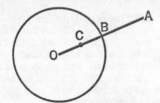

DISTANCE FROM A POINT TO A LINE, the length of the PERPENDICULAR from the point to the line. The distance from a point with COORDINATES (x',y') to a line whose equation is $Ax + By + C = 0$ is given by:

$$d = \frac{|Ax' + By' + C|}{\sqrt{A^2 + B^2}}.$$

Ex.: Find the distance from the point $(4,5)$ to the line $y = 2x + 3$.

Sol.: The equation of the line may be written in the form $Ax + By + C = 0$ as $2x - y + 3 = 0$.

$$d = \frac{|Ax' + By' + C|}{\sqrt{A^2 + B^2}}$$
$$= \frac{|2 \cdot 4 + (-1)5 + 3|}{\sqrt{2^2 + (-1)^2}}$$
$$= \frac{6}{\sqrt{5}}, \text{ or approximately } 2.7.$$

DISTANCE FROM A POINT TO A PLANE, the length of the PERPENDICULAR from the point to the plane. The distance from the point with COORDINATES (x',y',z') to the plane $Ax + By + Cz + D = 0$ is given by:

$$d = \frac{|Ax' + By' + Cz' + D|}{\sqrt{A^2 + B^2 + C^2}}.$$

Ex.: Find the distance from the point $(6,4,3)$ to the plane $x + 2y + 5z + 2 = 0$.

Sol.:

$$d = \frac{1 \cdot 6 + 2 \cdot 4 + 5 \cdot 3 + 2}{\sqrt{1^2 + 2^2 + 5^2}} = \frac{31}{\sqrt{30}}, \text{ or approximately } \pm 5.6.$$

See also NORMAL.

DISTANCE ON A SPHERE, *see* SPHERICAL DISTANCE.

DISTANCE ON THE EARTH'S SURFACE, the length in NAUTICAL MILES of the line which joins two points and which cuts all the MERIDIANS at the same angle. This should not be confused with the shortest distance between the two points, which is the arc of the GREAT CIRCLE passing through the two points. The advantage of the longer route is that it maintains a constant course direction. *See* LOXODROME.

DISTRIBUTION FUNCTION, in statistics, a function that gives the probability (*see* PROBABILITY OF AN EVENT) that a random variable will take on a value less than or equal to any specified value. Usually the distribution function is denoted $F(x)$, where $F(x) = P(x < x)$.

If x is a discrete random variable, then $F(x) = \sum_{t \leq x} f(t)$, where $f(t)$ is the probability function, and the summation is taken over all values of t less than or equal to x.

Ex.: If the probability function is

$x =$	0	1	2	3
$f(x) =$	$\frac{1}{8}$	$\frac{3}{8}$	$\frac{3}{8}$	$\frac{1}{8}$

the distribution function is

$$F(x) = \begin{cases} 0 & \text{for } x < 0. \\ \frac{1}{8} & \text{for } 0 \leq x < 1. \\ \frac{4}{8} & \text{for } 1 \leq x < 2. \\ \frac{7}{8} & \text{for } 2 \leq x < 3. \\ 1 & \text{for } x \geq 3. \end{cases}$$

If x is a CONTINUOUS RANDOM VARIABLE, then $F(x) = \int_{-\infty}^{x} f(t)dt$, where $f(t)$ is the probability density function.

Ex.: If the probability density function for a continuous random variable x is

$$f(x) = \begin{cases} x & \text{for } 0 \leq x \leq 1. \\ 2 - x & \text{for } 1 < x \leq 2. \\ 0 & \text{elsewhere.} \end{cases}$$

$$F(x) = \begin{cases} 0 & \text{for } x < 0. \\ \frac{x^2}{2} & \text{for } 0 \leq x \leq 1. \\ 2x - \frac{x}{2} - 1 & \text{for } 1 \leq x \leq 2. \\ 1 & \text{for } x > 2. \end{cases}$$

DISTRIBUTIVE PROPERTY (dih-strih'-byoo-tiv), a BINARY OPERATION, *, is said to be distributive over an operation, o, on a set, $S = \{a, b, c, \ldots, \}$, if $a * (b \circ c) = a * b \circ a * c$. Both MULTIPLICATION and DIVISION are distributive over ADDITION and SUBTRACTION on the REAL NUMBER system. E.g., $2(3 \pm 4) = 2 \cdot 3 \pm 2 \cdot 4 = 6 \pm 8 = 14$ or -2; and $\frac{8 + 50}{2} = 4 + 25 = 29$; and $\frac{30 - 10}{5} = 6 - 2 = 4$. ‡Note that addition is not distributive with respect to multiplication, i.e., $a + (bc) = (a + b)(a + c)$.

Other algebraic systems may be distributive. For example, if $\cap$ represents SET INTERSECTION, $\cup$ represents set UNION, and A, B, and C are sets, then:

$$A \cap (B \cup C) = (A \cap B) \cup (A \cap C)$$
$$A \cup (B \cap C) = (A \cup B) \cap (A \cup C)$$

That is, set union and set intersection are distributive with respect to each other. *See also* BOOLEAN ALGEBRA; DIVISION; GROUP; VECTOR ADDITION; VECTOR PRODUCT.

DIVERGENT SEQUENCE, a SEQUENCE that does not approach a limit (i.e., does not converge). *See also* CONVERGENT SEQUENCE, LIMIT OF A SEQUENCE.

DIVERGENT SERIES, a SERIES whose partial sums do not approach any limit. E.g., the series $1 + \frac{1}{2} + \frac{1}{3} + \frac{1}{4} + \cdots$ is a divergent series.

DIVIDEND, in banking and finance, payment to stockholders by a corporation from its earnings. In this form it is usually denoted as *dividend yield* or *return*. It is expressed as a percentage of the current price or the price paid for stock.

A *cumulative dividend* is the right of some preferred stockholders to be paid all their accumulated unpaid dividends before common stockholders can receive any dividends. If, e.g., a preferred stock has unpaid dividends of $1.00 a year for five years its owners must be paid $5.00 before common stockholders can be paid anything.

DIVIDEND, in DIVISION, the number that is to be divided. In a FRACTION, the NUMERATOR is the dividend.

DIVISION (dih-vih'-zhun), the process of determining the number of times a given number contains another number. In arithmetic the symbol for division is $\div$. Twelve divided by four is written $12 \div 4$. The number 12 is called the DIVIDEND and 4 is called the DIVISOR. Because 4 is contained in 12 three times, the answer, called the QUOTIENT, is 3. In multiplication, the example may be written $4 \times ? = 12$. Therefore, division is the INVERSE OPERATION OF MULTIPLICATION and the basic multiplication facts may be used for finding a quotient.

If a number does not contain another number an integral number of times, there will be a remainder. In the example, $27 \div 4$, the quotient is 6 with a remainder 3. $(6 \times 4) + 3 = 27$. *The dividend is always equal to the divisor times the quotient plus the remainder.*

The COMMUTATIVE PROPERTY does not apply to division. For example, $6 \div 3$ does not equal $3 \div 6$. Nor does the ASSOCIATIVE PROPERTY apply to division. For example,

$$(24 \div 6) \div 2 \neq 24 \div (6 \div 2)$$
$$4 \div 2 \neq 24 \div 3$$
$$2 \neq 8.$$

However, $24 \div 6 \div 2$ will have the same result, if 24 is divided by 6 and that quotient divided by 2, as it will if 24 is divided by 2 and then by 6. The answer is 2 for both operations, but this is not a case of the associative property. The DISTRIBUTIVE PROPERTY with respect to addition applies to division since the sum of two numbers divided by a third number is equal to the sum of the two quotients if each number is divided by the third. For example,

$$(8 + 4) \div 2 = (8 \div 2) + (4 \div 2)$$
$$12 \div 2 = 4 + 2$$
$$6 = 6.$$

If a two-place number is divided by a single digit number, the multiplication facts are used. Determine what number multiplied by the divisor equals the dividend.

Ex. 1: $56 \div 8$ or $8 \times ? = 56$. The quotient is 7. If the divisor is not a factor of the dividend, the quotient will contain a remainder.

Ex. 2: $47 \div 6$. Determine the number smaller than 47 and closest to it, for which 6 is a factor. $6 \times 7 = 42$, therefore, the quotient is 7 with a remainder of 5. The quotient may also be written as a fraction. The remainder is placed over the divisor 6 and added to 7. The quotient, then is written $7\frac{5}{6}$.

If the divisor is a single digit number and the dividend has more than two digits, it may be advisable to use a method called *short division.*

Ex. 3: Divide 656 by 4.

4)656
164

4 is contained in 6 one time with a remainder of 2. The remainder 2 represents 2 hundreds or 20 tens and must be added to the 5 tens. Then 25 contains 4 six times with a remainder of 1. Place the 6 under 5 and add 1 ten or 10 units to 6. Then 16 divided by 4 equals 4. Place the 4 in the quotient to make it complete.

Check: $164 \times 4 = 656$.

If the first digit of the dividend is smaller than the divisor, find the number of times the divisor is contained in the first two digits.

Ex. 4: Divide 7625 by 8.

42
8)7625
953 R 1

The number 72 is the largest number less than 76 that contains 8 an integral number of times. $76 \div 8 = 9$ with a remainder of 4. Proceed as in Ex. 3. The small numbers as shown may be helpful in remembering to add each remainder to the next digit.

Check: $953 \times 8 + 1 = 7625$.

If the divisor has two or more digits, "long division" is used.

Ex. 5: Divide 912 by 24.

38
24)912
72
192
192

Determine the number of times 24 is contained in 91. Trial and error may be necessary. We know that 2 is contained in 9 more than 4 times but $24 \times 4 = 96$. Therefore, the partial quotient must be 3. Write 3 above 1 and multiply 3 by the di-

visor; $3 \times 24 = 72$. Write 72 under 91 and subtract. Bring down the next digit. Now 192 becomes the dividend and it contains 24 eight times. Write 8 above 2 and multiply 8 by 24. There is no remainder. Check by multiplying 38 by 24 to obtain 912.

Ex. 6: Divide 21, 888 by 36

608
36)21888
216
288
288

Find the partial quotient when 218 is divided by 36. $36 \times 6 = 216$. Place 6 in the quotient and write 216, subtract from 218. When the next digit 8 is brought down, 28 becomes the new dividend. Because 28 will not contain 36, a zero must be placed in the quotient and the next digit brought down. 288 contains 36 exactly 8 times. Write 8 in the quotient and multiply 36 by 8.

Check:
608
×36
3648
1824
21888

Note: Always remember to place the zero in the quotient to serve as a place holder.)

Ex. 7: Divide 89,151 by 29.

3074 R 5
29)89151
87
215
203
121
116
5

Check: 3074
×29
27666
6148
89146
+5
89151

To divide by 10, move the decimal point one place to the left. To divide by 100, move the decimal point two places to the left. To divide by 1000, move the decimal point three places to the left.

$278 \div$	$10 = 27.8$.		$5.2 \div$	$10 = .52$.
$278 \div$	$100 = 2.78$.		$5.2 \div$	$100 = .052$.
$278 \div$	$1000 = .278$.		$5.2 \div$	$1000 = .0052$.

DIVISION AXIOM. An AXIOM of EQUALITY: If equal quantities are divided by the same or equal quantities, the QUOTIENTS are equal. E.g., if $a = b$ then $a \div 4 = b \div 4$. This axiom may be expressed symbolically as follows: If $a = b$ and $c = d$, then $a \div c = b \div d$. A special case of this axiom occurs when the equal quantities are divided by two; the axiom may then be stated "Halves of equal quantities are equal." *See also* INEQUALITY.

DIVISION BY LOGARITHMS, *see* LOGARITHMS, LAWS OF.

DIVISION BY ZERO, an undefined operation. It is not defined because it cannot be done in a manner consistent with the basic definitions and principles of mathematics. For any given DIVIDEND, a QUOTIENT can be made as large as we like by taking a divisor sufficiently small. Hence, a quotient with zero as its divisor would exceed any preassigned quantity. Thus, the limit (*see* LIMIT OF A FUNCTION) of the quotient $1/x$ as x approaches 0 is "infinity" (∞). This may be written

$$\lim_{x \to 0} \frac{1}{x} = \infty.$$

DIVISION, INVERSE OF, is MULTIPLICATION. $\frac{27}{3}$ can be thought of as meaning "that number, which multiplied by 3, equals 27."

DIVISION, LAW OF EXPONENTS FOR. The EXPONENT of any letter of the QUOTIENT is found by subtracting the exponent of that letter in the DIVISOR from the exponent of that letter in the DIVIDEND.

Exs.: $x^3 \div x^2 = x$; $\frac{x^7}{x^3} = x^4$; $\frac{x^4}{x^4} = 1$; $4^5 \div 4^3 = 4^2$; $\frac{x^5 y^3}{x^2 y} = x^3 y^2$.

DIVISION, LAW OF SIGNS FOR.

If the DIVIDEND and the DIVISOR have like signs, the QUOTIENT is positive. If the dividend and the divisor have unlike signs, the quotient is negative.

$$Exs.: \frac{-8}{-4} = 2; \frac{8}{4} = 2; \frac{-8}{4} = -2; \frac{8}{-4} = -2.$$

DIVISION OF A POLYNOMIAL BY A BINOMIAL.

1. Arrange the terms of the DIVIDEND and the DIVISOR in DESCENDING POWERS (or ASCENDING POWERS) of one letter.

2. Divide the first term of the dividend by the first term of the divisor to obtain the first term of the QUOTIENT.

3. Multiply the divisor by this term and subtract the PRODUCT from the dividend.

4. Continue this process until the first term of the remaining dividend cannot be divided exactly by the first term of the divisor.

5. Check by multiplying the quotient by the divisor and adding the remainder to the product to obtain the dividend.

Ex.: Divide $2x^3 - 3 + 8x - 7x^2$ by $2x - 3$.

$$
\begin{array}{r}
x^2 - 2x + 1 \\
2x - 3) \overline{2x^3 - 7x^2 + 8x - 3} \\
\underline{2x^3 - 3x^2} \\
-4x^2 + 8x \\
\underline{-4x^2 + 6x} \\
+2x - 3 \\
\underline{+2x - 3}
\end{array}
$$

Check: $(x^2 - 2x + 1)(2x - 3) = 2x^3 - 7x^2 + 8x - 3.$

DIVISION OF A POLYNOMIAL BY A MONOMIAL.

Divide each term of the POLYNOMIAL by the MONOMIAL.

Ex. 1: $(8x^3 - 12x^2 - 4x) \div 4x = 2x^2 - 3x - 1.$

Ex. 2: $(ab - ac + ad) \div a = b - c + d.$

Ex. 3: $\dfrac{15x^2y^3 + 10x^3y^4 - 5x^2y^2}{-5xy} = -3xy^2 - 2x^2y^3 + xy.$

DIVISION OF FRACTIONS,

in algebra, is the same as in arithmetic: Invert the divisor and multiply.

$$Ex.: \frac{-4a^3}{9b} \div \frac{-2a}{3b}$$

$$\frac{-4a^3}{9b} \times \frac{3b}{-2a} = \frac{2a^2}{3}.$$

DIVISION, SYNTHETIC,

in ALGEBRA, a short form of long division. Synthetic division simplifies the FACTORING of POLYNOMIALS. If a polynomial in x is divided by a BINOMIAL, $x - a$, and the remainder is zero, the binomial is a factor of the polynomial. Arrange the polynomial in DESCENDING POWERS and use only the numerical COEFFICIENTS for the DIVIDEND. If a power is missing, replace it with a zero. In Example 1, long division is included for comparison.

Ex. 1: Divide $x^3 - 3x - 4x + 12$ by $x + 2$.

Long Division	Synthetic Division

$$
\begin{array}{r}
x^2 - 5x + 6 \\
x + 2)\overline{x^3 - 3x^2 - 4x + 12} \\
\underline{x^3 + 2x^2} \\
-5x^2 - 4x \\
\underline{-5x^2 - 10x} \\
+6x + 12 \\
\underline{+6x + 12}
\end{array}
$$

$$
\begin{array}{r}
+2) \, 1 - 3 - 4 + 12 \\
+2 - 10 + 12 \\
\hline
1 - 5 + 6 \parallel 0
\end{array}
$$

The quotient is $x - 5x + 6$ with a remainder of zero.

The coefficient of x in the DIVISOR is 1 and the coefficient of x in the dividend is 1. 1 divided by 1 is 1, so bring down the 1 for the first term of the quotient. Multiply the 1 by the 2 in the divisor and place under the -3, subtract. Multiply -5 by 2 and place the -10 under -4. Subtract. Multiply 6 by 2 and place under 12.

There is no remainder. *The sign of the constant term in the divisor is usually changed in order that we may add rather than subtract.*

Ex. 2: Divide $3x^3 - 5x - 10$ by $x - 2$

Change -2 to $+2$ for the divisor. Remember to add each time.

$$
\begin{array}{r}
+2)3 + 0 - 5 - 10 \\
+6 + 12 + 14 \\
\hline
3 + 6 + 7 \parallel +4
\end{array}
$$

The quotient is $3x^2 + 6x + 7$ with a remainder of 4. Therefore, $x - 2$ is not a factor of $3x^3 - 5x - 10$. *See also* FACTOR THEOREM.

DIVISOR, in DIVISION, the number by which a given number is divided. In a FRACTION, the DENOMINATOR is the divisor.

DODECAGON (doh-dek'-a-gon), a POLYGON having 12 sides. A regular dodecagon can be inscribed in a CIRCLE by bisecting each of the sides of a regular HEXAGON inscribed in the circle.

DODECAHEDRON (doh-dek'-a-hee-dron), a POLYHEDRON having 12 faces.

DOMAIN, the term used to represent the SET of all the numbers which can be assigned to x, the independent VARIABLE, in an equation with two variables, such as $y = 3x - 5$. *Range* is term used to represent the corresponding values of y, the dependent variable.

$$y = 3x - 5.$$

If x is	0	1	2	3	4	5	6	7
then y is	-5	-2	1	4	7	10	13	16

The domain is $\{\ 0, 1, 2, 3, 4, 5, 6, 7, \ldots\ \}$.
The range is $\{-5, -2, 1, 4, 7, 10, 13, 16, \ldots\}$.

DOT PRODUCT OF TWO VECTORS, for any A and B, the SCALAR quantity $A \cdot B = |A||B| \cos \theta$, where θ is the angle between the vectors. See figure.

If $A = a_1i + a_2j + a_3k$, etc., then $A \cdot B = a_1b_1 + a_2b_2 + a_3b_3$.

Ex. 1: If $A = (1,1)$ and $B = (3,0)$, find $A \cdot B$.

Sol.: Since the ANGLES OF INCLINATION are 45° and 0° respectively, $\theta = 45°$. $A \cdot B = \sqrt{2} \cdot 3 \cos 45° = \sqrt{2} \cdot 3 \cdot \frac{1}{2} = 3$ or, $A \cdot B = 1 \cdot 3 + 1 \cdot 0 = 3 + 0 = 3$.

Two theorems make the dot product important:

1. The dot product is zero only for PERPENDICULAR vectors.

2. The dot product is INVARIANT under ROTATION OF AXES.

Ex. 2: Find the angle θ between the vectors $(3,-3)$ and $(-2,-2)$.

Sol.: Their dot product is $-2 \cdot 3 + -3 \cdot -2 = -6 + 6 = 0$. Then θ is the angle whose cosine is 0; therefore, $\theta = 90°$.

Ex. 3: Are the following vectors perpendicular? $A = (5,4)$, $B = (-17,13)$.

Sol.: $A \cdot B = 5(-17) + 4(13) \neq 0$. A is not $\perp B$.

The dot product is known as the *scalar product* because it is a pure number, or scalar, in contrast to the vector. *See also* VECTOR PRODUCT.

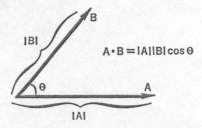

DOUBLE ANGLE FORMULAS, *see* TABLE NO. 3.

DOUBLE INTEGRAL, of a region A, of a function $F(x,y)$,

$$\int_A \int F(x,y)dA = \lim_{\Delta A \to 0} \sum_{R=1}^{n} F(x_k, y_k)\Delta A_k,$$

where $\triangle A = \triangle x \cdot \triangle y$. (See Fig. 1.) The double integral may be used to calculate the area or center of gravity of a region such as region A in Fig. 1. It may also be used to calculate the volume of a region, such as region B in Fig. 2, provided $F(x,y)$ is positive.

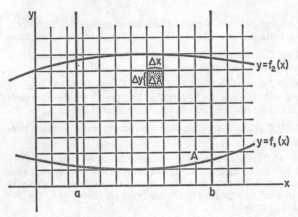

Fig. 1

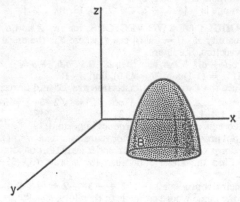

Fig. 2

In practice, the double integral is evaluated by calculating either one of the ITERATED INTEGRALS,

$$\int_A \int F(x,y)dx\,dy, \quad \int_A \int F(x,y)dy\,dx.$$

DUODECIMAL NUMBER SYSTEM, a system of numeration using a base of 12, instead of a base of 10 as in the DECIMAL NUMBER SYSTEM. Since the principle of position and of ciphered numeration are adaptable to any base, an early widespread and permanent use of the duodecimal number system might have occurred had it not been for the anatomical accident that human beings have ten fingers and ten toes. The duodecimal number system has several advantages that have been overlooked. E.g., in terms of divisibility of the base (when considering integers less than half the base), the 10 has two nondivisors (the integers 3 and 4), whereas in the duodecimal number system the 12 has only one nondivisor, 5. Expressed positively, the advantage of 12 is that it has the factors 2,3,4 and 6, while the 10 base has only the factors 2 and 5. Since it has more factors the duodecimal number system is obviously better adapted for DIVISION and for the representation of FRACTIONS than is the decimal number system.

In the duodecimal number system the Arabic numerals 0 through 9 are used, but instead of the numbers 10 and 11, two new ciphers are needed. The Duodecimal Society of America recommends the symbols X (*dek*) and Σ (*el*) for the two new ciphers.

The Romans used the duodecimal number system in dividing the foot and pound into twelfths and the year into 12 months. The words *inch* and *ounce* are derived from the Latin *uncia*, meaning a "twelfth." Similarly, *dozen* and *gross* are from the Roman duodecimal number system (the word dozen comes from the Latin *duodecim*, meaning "twelve").

Conversion to the duodecimal number system presents enormous difficulties. E.g., a complete revision of the tables for addition and multiplication would be needed and, of course, the system requires working with two new ciphers.

DUPLICATION OF THE CUBE, one of the three *classical problems* of antiquity, finding the edge of a CUBE with VOLUME equal to twice that of a given cube. Suppose the length of the edge of the given cube is a. To construct an edge of length b such that a cube of edge b has exactly twice the volume of a cube of edge a means that $b^3 = 2a^3$, or $b/a = \sqrt[3]{2}$. The problem cannot be solved using the tools of classical construction, i.e., the unmarked straight edge and compass, since it requires the geometric evaluation of $\sqrt[3]{2}$. Cube roots cannot be evaluated by means of a straight edge and compass alone.

E

e, the base in a system of natural logarithms (*see* LOGARITHMS, NATURAL). It is a transcendental (*see* TRANSCENDENTAL NUMBER), IRRATIONAL NUMBER and, therefore, it has a nonrepeating infinite decimal representation. To six decimal places, $e = 2.718284$. . . . *See also* BASE e.

E, spherical excess. *See* SPHERICAL TRIANGLE.

EARTH COORDINATE SYSTEM, a system of measurement in degrees of circles of LATITUDE and LONGITUDE on the globe. The system was devised by the Greeks 2,200 years ago for use in locating any point on the earth in relation to any other point and it is still used for that purpose by navigators. *See* COORDINATE SYSTEMS.

The system assumes that the earth is a perfect globe (which it is not, in reality). The *North Pole* and *South Pole* are used as starting points. Equidistant between the poles, an imaginary circle called the EQUATOR is drawn around the earth's surface. Parallel to the equator evenly spaced imaginary lines are drawn east to west. Another series of evenly spaced lines run north to south, perpendicular to the equator, gradually converging at the poles. This forms a grid system of intersecting lines. Those lines which are parallel to the equator are called parallels of latitude. Those which are perpendicular to the equator are called meridians of longitude.

All lines, if drawn as described above, form circles of 360° in circumference. Each degree (°) is divided into sixty minutes ('); each minute is divided into 60 seconds ("). The equator is designated 0° latitude and all other parallels are numbered away from the equator toward the poles. The poles are designated 90° North or South, since the distance from the equator to either pole is one-fourth of a circle or 90°. The meridians of longitude are numbered east and west from that meridian which runs through Greenwich Observatory, near London. This meridian was adopted by general agreement among nations in 1884.

All parallels of latitude north of the equator are designated North latitude and parallels south of the equator are South latitude. All meridians west of the 0°, or Greenwich meridian, are West longitude and all meridians east of Greenwich meridian are East longitude.

To locate any place on earth one has only to find the parallel of latitude and meridian of longitude which are nearest to the place. For example, New York City is located at latitude 40° 42' North and longitude 74° West. Moscow is at 55° 45' North and longitude 37° 34' East. These coordinates give the exact location of the two cities in reference to each other by means of the grid system.

ECCENTRICITY OF A HYPERBOLA (ek-sen-tri'-si-tee, hahy-pur'-boh-lah), a measure of the curvature of a HYPERBOLA. In the

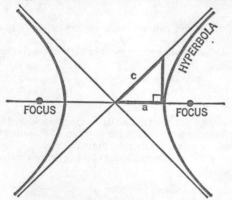

figure, the eccentricity, *e*, is defined as $e = c/a$. It is always greater than one. The larger it is, the more sharply curved is the hyperbola. *See also* ASYMPTOTE, CONIC SECTIONS.

ECCENTRICITY OF AN ELLIPSE (ek-sen-tri'-si-tee e-lips'), a measure of the elongation of an ELLIPSE. In the figure, the eccentricity, *e*, is defined as $e = c/a$.

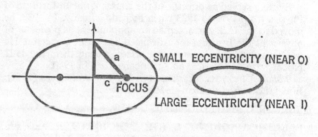

The eccentricity of any ellipse is always between zero and one. The extreme value zero corresponds to the degenerate ellipse, the CIRCLE. If the eccentricity is small, the ellipse is nearly circular, while if it is near one, the ellipse is decidedly elongated. *See also* CONIC SECTIONS.

EDGE (edj), an intersection of planes in a GEOMETRIC SOLID. E.g., in the figure, *AH*, *HE*, *DE*, *AD*, and *EF* are five of the 12 edges.

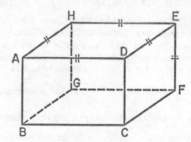

EFFICIENCY (ee-fi'-shin-see). In statistics, the efficiency of an ESTIMATOR, say $\hat{\theta}_1$, relative to a second estimator, say $\hat{\theta}_2$, is given by the ratio $\dfrac{\text{variance of } \hat{\theta}_1}{\text{variance of } \hat{\theta}_2}$.

Ex.: A sample of size 3 from a population with variance σ^2 is available to estimate μ. The efficiency of $\hat{\theta}_1 = \dfrac{x_1 + 2x_2 + 2x_3}{5}$ relative to $\hat{\theta}_2 = \dfrac{x_1 + x_2 + x_3}{3}$ is $\dfrac{\sigma^2/3}{9\sigma^2/25} = \dfrac{25}{27}$. This means that a sample of size 25 gives the same precision in the estimation of μ if $\hat{\theta}_2$ is used, as a sample of 27 does when $\hat{\theta}_1$ is used.

EINSTEIN, ALBERT (ahyn'-stahyn), 1879–1955, German physicist. Born in Ulm, he moved, as a child, first to Munich and finally to Zurich, where he graduated from the Swiss Federal Polytechnic School (1900). He continued his studies at the Univ. of Zurich and received a Ph.D. from that institution in 1905. It was during 1905 that he published three theories any one of which would have established his reputation as a major scientist of the times. The three in conjunction, together with his later work, establish him as one of the great intellects in the history of Western thought. His theory of Brownian motion was a convincing and final proof of the molecular theory of matter and put an end to one of the great scientific controversies of the 19th cent. His theory of the photoelectric effect ushered physics into the 20th cent. and the new era of quantum mechanics. His celebrated special theory of relativity entirely revamped all the laws of physics and established a new understanding of space and time. All of this work was published in 1905.

He made important contributions to the theory of radiation and in the interpretation of quantum mechanics. Most importantly, he extended his work on relativity and developed the general theory and consequent theory of gravitation. He then applied the general theory, published in 1916, to the universe as a whole, working on various cosmological models. From the mid 1920's until his death, he worked on many unsuccessful attempts to create a unified theory of gravitational and electromagnetic fields.

Einstein served as director of the Kaiser Wilhelm Institute of Physics from 1915 to 1933 when he fled Germany. In 1933, he moved to the U.S. and accepted an appointment as professor of physics at the Institute for Advanced Studies at Princeton. He was awarded many honors and prizes, among them the 1921 Nobel Prize. He became an American citizen in 1940.

Biblio.: Clark, R. W., *Einstein: The Life and Times* (1971); Infeld, L., *Albert Einstein* (1950).

ELECTRIC AND MAGNETIC UNITS, *see* TABLE NO. 5.

ELECTROMAGNETIC SYSTEM OF UNITS, *see* CGS SYSTEM; TABLE NO. 5.

ELECTROSTATIC SYSTEM OF UNITS, *see* CGS SYSTEM; TABLE NO. 5.

ELEMENTS OF A CONE, all the lines that represent the cone's slant height. *See also* CONE.

ELEMENTS OF A SET, *see* SET.

ELEVATION, ANGLE OF, *see* ANGLE OF ELEVATION.

ELIMINATING THE PARAMETER, a method of eliminating a superfluous VARIABLE. If two functions of a single PARAMETER are given and one can be solved for a variable, the resulting expression can be substituted for that variable, thus eliminating it. E.g., if $y = t^2$ and $x = 3t$, the second equation can be solved for t: $\frac{x}{3} = t$. Substituting $\frac{x}{3}$ for t in the equation for y gives:

$$y = \left(\frac{x}{3}\right)^2 = \frac{x^2}{9}$$ and the parameter t has been eliminated.

Ex. 1: Eliminate the parameter in the following equations:

a. $x = 4t$, $y = \sin t$.
b. $y = \sqrt{t}$, $x = t^4$.

Sol.:

a. $t = \frac{x}{4}$; $y = \sin\left(\frac{x}{4}\right)$.
b. $t = y^2$; $x = (y^2)^4 = y^8$.

It is not always possible to eliminate the parameter without complicating the procedure. E.g., the parametric equations, $y = t^2$, $x = t^4$, can be solved for t, but only by introducing extraneous roots, because two different numbers give y when squared; e.g., $2^2 = 4 = (-2)^2$. *See also* CHANGE OF VARIABLES.

ELIMINATION, in Algebra, a method for solving a pair of linear equations (*see* EQUATION, LINEAR) in two unknowns by combining them in a way to form a third equation with only one unknown.

Elimination of one of the variables may be achieved by addition or subtraction of the two linear equations. To eliminate a variable by addition or subtraction:

1. Multiply, if necessary, each term of one or both equations so that the NUMERICAL COEFFICIENTS of one of the variables are equal.

2. Add or subtract the two equations to eliminate the variable with like coefficients.

3. Solve the resulting equation in one variable.

4. Solve for the other variable by substituting the value found in Step 3 in one of the original equations.

5. Check by substituting values of both variables in each of the original equations.

Ex. 1: Solve for x and y: $3x - y = 5$ and $x + 2y = 11$.

Sol.: Multiply each term of the first equation by 2:

$$2(3x) - 2(y) = 2(5) \text{ or } 6x - 2y = 10$$

Add the resulting equation to the second of the original equations:

$$
\begin{array}{r}
6x - 2y = 10 \\
\underline{x + 2y = 11} \\
7x \quad\quad = 21
\end{array}
$$

Divide by 7: $x = 3$.

Substitute this value of x in one of the original equations and solve for y: $x + 2y = 11$

$$
\begin{aligned}
3 + 2y &= 11 \\
2y &= 8 \\
y &= 4.
\end{aligned}
$$

The solution to the pair of linear equations:

$$3x - y = 5 \text{ and } x + 2y = 11 \text{ is } x = 3 \text{ and } y = 4.$$

Check: Substitute these roots in each of the given equations:

$$
\begin{array}{ll}
3x - y = 5 & x + 2y = 11 \\
3(3) - 4 = 5 & 3 + 2(4) = 11 \\
9 - 4 = 5 & 3 + 8 = 11 \\
5 = 5. & 11 = 11.
\end{array}
$$

It is often necessary to multiply both of the two equations to get equal coefficients for one variable.

Ex. 2: Solve for x and y: $3x - 2y = 6$ and $4x - 3y = 7$.

Sol.: The coefficient of y can be made 6 in each equation by multiplying each term of the first equation by 3 and each term of the second by 2.

Multiplying each term of the first equation by 3:

$$3(3x) - 3(2y) = 3(6) \text{ or } 9x - 6y = 18.$$

Multiplying each term of the second equation by 2:

$$2(4x) - 2(3y) = 2(7) \text{ or } 8x - 6y = 14.$$

Subtract the two resulting equations:

$$
\begin{array}{r}
9x - 6y = 18 \\
\underline{8x - 6y = 14} \\
x \quad\quad = 4.
\end{array}
$$

Substitute this value of x in one of the original equations and solve for y:

$$
\begin{aligned}
3x - 2y &= 6 \\
3(4) - 2y &= 6 \\
12 - 2y &= 6 \\
-2y &= -6 \\
y &= 3.
\end{aligned}
$$

The roots of the pair of linear equations $3x - 2y = 6$ and $4x - 3y = 7$ are $x = 4$ and $y = 3$.

Check: Substituting these roots in both original equations:

$$
\begin{array}{ll}
3x - 2y = 6 & 4x - 3y = 7 \\
3(4) - 2(3) = 6 & 4(4) - 3(3) = 7 \\
12 - 6 = 6 & 16 - 9 = 7 \\
6 = 6. & 7 = 7.
\end{array}
$$

Elimination of one of the variables may be achieved by substituting for one variable its value in terms of the other variable. To eliminate a variable by substitution:

1. Solve for one variable in one of the equations in terms of the other variable.

2. Substitute this value of the variable in the second equation.
3. Solve the resulting equation in one variable.
4. Solve for the second variable by substituting the value found in Step 3 in one of the original equations.
5. Check by substituting the values of both variables in each of the original equations.

Ex. 2: Solve for x and y by the method of substitution: $x - y = 1$ and $3x - 2y = 1$.
Solve the first equation for x in terms of y.

Add y to each side: $x - y = 1$
$$x = 1 + y.$$

Substitute this value for x in the second original equation:

$$3x - 2y = 1$$
$$3(1 + y) - 2y = 1.$$

Solve for y: $3 + 3y - 2y = 1$
$$3 + y = 1$$
$$y = -2.$$

Substitute this value of y in $x = 1 + y$ to find the value of x:

$$x = 1 + (-2)$$
$$x = -1$$

The roots of the pair of linear equations $x - y = 1$ and $3x - 2y = 1$ are $x = -1$ and $y = -2$.

Check: Substituting these roots in both original equations:

$x - y = 1$	$3x - 2y = 1$
$-1 - (-2) = 1$	$3(-1) - 2(-2) = 1$
$-1 + 2 = 1$	$-3 + 4 = 1$
$1 = 1.$	$1 = 1.$

ELLIPSE (e-lips′), the CONIC SECTION that is formed when a PLANE intersects all of the elements of a CONE but is not PERPENDICULAR to the AXIS. An ellipse may be defined as the LOCUS of a point which moves so that the sum of its distances from two fixed points, called foci, is constant. It may be proved that the ellipse is also the locus of all points such that the ratio of the distance from one FOCUS to its distance from a straight line is equal to the eccentricity of the ellipse. The straight line is called the directrix of the ellipse. For an ellipse centered at the ORIGIN with both foci on the x-axis, there are two choices of directrix, one corresponding to each focus. If the ECCENTRICITY OF AN ELLIPSE is e, corresponding to the focus $(ae, 0)$ the directrix is the line $x = a/e$; and corresponding to the focus $(-ae, 0)$ the directrix is the line $x = -a/e$. See Fig. 1.

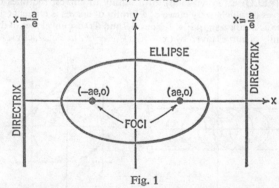

Fig. 1

If coordinate axes are drawn with the x-axis through the foci and the y-axis halfway between them, the algebraic conditions which must be satisfied by the ellipse can be calculated. If the sum of the distances from a point on the ellipse is $2a$, the equation of the ellipse is

$$x^2/a^2 + y^2/b^2 = 1, \text{ where } b^2 = a^2 - c^2.$$

If the foci are very close together, the ellipse is almost circular; and if they are far apart relative to the constant, the ellipse is almost a straight line. The CIRCLE is a degenerate case of the ellipse in which the foci are identical. If the foci are on the y-axis, the equation is $y^2/c^2 + x^2/b^2 = 1$, and if the center of the ellipse (the point halfway between the foci) is the point (h, k) rather than at the origin, the equation of the ellipse is $(x - h)^2/a^2 + (y - k)^2/b^2 = 1$.

To sketch the graph of an ellipse, plot the x and y-intercepts and draw the curve. To graph the equation of an ellipse we set up a table of values and plot each point.

Ex. 1: Sketch the ellipse $x^2/4 + y^2/9 = 1$.
Sol.: x-intercepts are at 2 and -2, y-intercepts at 3 and -3. See Fig. 2.

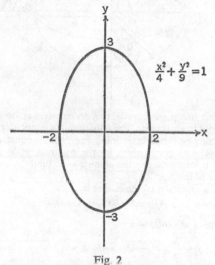

Fig. 2

Ex. 2: Graph $4x^2 + 9y^2 = 36$.
Sol.: Change the equation to the form $y = \pm \frac{2}{3}\sqrt{9 - x^2}$, and set up a table of values for x and y. Note that y is imaginary (*see* IMAGINARY NUMBER) when the ABSOLUTE VALUE of x is greater than 3. When the absolute value of y is more than 2, x is imaginary.

$$y = \pm \tfrac{2}{3}\sqrt{9 - x^2}$$

x	y
0	± 2
± 1	± 1.9
± 2	± 1.5
± 3	0

In the graph (Fig. 3), AB is the major axis (*see* MAJOR AXIS OF AN ELLIPSE) and is 6 units. CD, the minor axis (*see* MINOR AXIS OF AN ELLIPSE), is 4 units. *See also* ELLIPSE, MAJOR AXIS OF AN; ELLIPSE, MINOR AXIS OF AN.

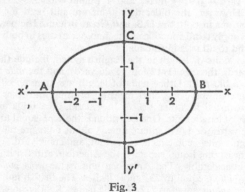

Fig. 3

ELLIPSOID (e-lip'-soid), a QUADRIC SURFACE, the graph of an equation of the form

$$x^2/a^2 + y^2/b^2 + z^2/c^2 = 1.$$

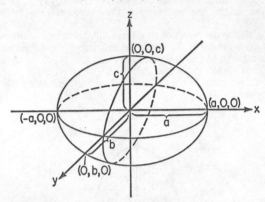

(See figure.) Any plane parallel to a COORDINATE PLANE intersects the ellipsoid in an ELLIPSE. The equation of a particular elliptical intersert may be found by holding one variable constant.

Ex. 1: The ellipsoid given by the equation $y^2/b^2 + z^2/c^2 = 1 - x^2/a^2$ is intersected by the plane $x = k$. Find the semiaxes of the ellipse of intersection.

Sol.: The equation of the ellipse is

$$y^2/b^2 + z^2/c^2 = 1 - k^2/a^2.$$

The semiaxes are therefore

$$y = \frac{b}{a}\sqrt{a^2 - k^2} \quad \text{and} \quad z = \frac{c}{a}\sqrt{a^2 - k^2}.$$

ELLIPTIC PARABOLOID, *see* PARABOLOID OF REVOLUTION.

EMPTY SET, in mathematics, the SET containing no elements; also called the **null set.** The empty set is symbolized by $\varnothing$ or $\{\}$. It is considered a subset of every set. Thus, the subsets of $A = \{1, 2, 3\}$ are $\{1\}$, $\{2\}$, $\{3\}$, $\{1, 2\}$, $\{1, 3\}$, $\{2, 3\}$, $\{1, 2, 3\}$, and $\{\}$.

ENGLISH SYSTEM, a system of weights and measures used in English-speaking countries throughout the world. It is based on the yard of length and the pound of weight or mass. In the U.S., these standards were based on the British standards until 1893. At that time, the American standards were redefined in terms of the standards of the METRIC SYSTEM, with the yard being defined as 3600/3937 meter and the pound as 10,000/22,046 kilogram. The British standards, however, remain independently defined. Thus, there are slight differences between the American and British units used in commerce. In 1959, all English-speaking countries agreed to redefine the yard and pound so that the same definitions would hold in all the countries. These new definitions are 1 yard = 0.9144 meter and 1 pound = 0.45359237 kilogram. However, the older definitions are still used for many applications in both the U.S. and Great Britain. The new definitions apply to all scientific and technological uses in both countries and to all uses in Canada.

Other units of length in the English system include the *foot* (1/3 yard), the *inch* (1/12 foot; 1/36 yard), and the *mile* (1,760 yards; 5,280 feet). Other units of length are more specialized, being used in surveying, cloth measure, printing, and other fields, and are listed in TABLE NO. 5. In general, area units are the squares of length units. One exception is the *acre*, equal to 4,840 square yards, or 1/640 square mile. Volume units are the cubes of length units—cubic inch, cubic foot, and cubic yard.

In measuring liquid capacity, the American and British units differ considerably. The American unit is the *wine gallon*, or simply *gallon*, equal to 231 cubic inches. The British unit is the *imperial gallon*, equal to 277.42 cubic inches. Subdivisions of the gallon in either system are the *quart* (1/4 gallon), the *pint* (1/2 quart), and the *gill* (1/4 pint). The British units are each ab. 20 percent larger than the American unit of the same name. The basic unit of dry capacity in the English system is the *bushel*, equal to 2150.42 cubic inches. It is divided into the *peck* (1/4 bushel), the *dry quart* (1/8 peck), and the *dry pint* (1/2 dry quart). The *imperial bushel*, used in Great Britain, is ab. 3 percent smaller than the American bushel and is also divided into pecks, dry quarts, and dry pints.

Three different systems of mass units are used in the English system. The *avoirdupois system* is used for most mass measurements. Its basic unit is the pound, sometimes called the avoirdupois pound. Subdivisions of the pound are the *ounce* (1/16 pound), the *dram* (1/16 ounce), and the *grain* (1/7000 pound). Multiples are the *short hundredweight* (100 pounds) and the *short ton* (2,000 pounds; 20 short hundredweights), used in the U.S., Canada, and S. Africa, and the *long hundredweight* (112 pounds) and the *long ton* (2,240 pounds; 20 long hundredweights), used in Great Britain. The *troy system* of mass units is based on the *troy pound*, a unit used in Great Britain until 1855 but since abandoned. It is used in the U.S. for coinage measurements. The only unit common to the troy and avoirdupois systems is the *grain*. The troy pound is 5,760 grains and is thus equal to 5760/7000 avoirdupois pound. Other troy units are the *troy ounce* (1/12 troy pound) and the *pennyweight* (1/20 troy ounce). The *apothecaries system* of units is related to the troy system, the *apothecaries pound* being equal to the troy pound and the *apothecaries ounce* being equal to the troy ounce. The *grain* is also common to the apothecaries system. Other apothecaries units are the *apothecaries dram* (1/8 apothecaries or troy ounce) and the *scruple* (1/3 apothecaries dram). As the name implies, apothecaries units are used in the preparation of medicines, although they are gradually being replaced by metric units.

In common language, the terms *mass* and *weight* are often used interchangeably, so that the pound of weight is often used when the pound of mass is what is meant. Strictly speaking, however, WEIGHT is a measure of the force of gravity, and the pound of weight is thus a force unit distinct from the pound of mass. Used in this sense, the pound of force equals the pound of mass multiplied by the acceleration of gravity, 32.174 feet per square second.

ENIAC, *see* COMPUTER.

ENVELOPE (en'-vu-lohp), of a family of curves, the lines or curves to which every curve of a family of curves is tangent (*see* TANGENT CURVES). In Fig. 1, lines *AB* and *CD* are envelopes of the family of curves given by $(x - \alpha)^2 + y^2 = r^2$. In Fig. 2, circle *O*,

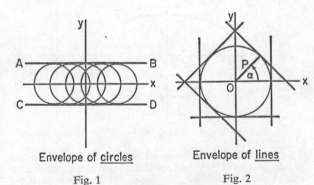

Envelope of <u>circles</u>   Envelope of <u>lines</u>

Fig. 1   Fig. 2

given by $x^2 + y^2 = p^2$ is the envelope of the family of straight lines $x \cos \alpha + y \sin \alpha = p$. In Fig. 3, the envelope of the family of ellipses $x^2/a^2 + y^2/b^2 = 1$, whose axes coincide and whose area is constant, is a pair of hyperbolas, $xy = \pm\dfrac{k}{2\pi}$.

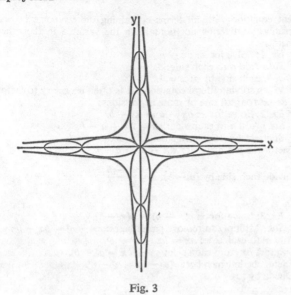

Fig. 3

To find the PARAMETRIC EQUATIONS of the envelope, write the equation of the family of curves in the form $f(x,y,\alpha) = 0$ and derive the equation $f_\alpha(x,y,\alpha) = 0$, the partial derivative of $f(x,y,\alpha)$ with respect to α. Then solve the two equations for x and y in terms of α.

Ex.: Find the equations of the envelope of the family of circles $(x - \alpha)^2 + y^2 = r^2$.

Sol.: $f(x,y,\alpha) = (x - \alpha)^2 + y^2 - r^2 = 0$. The partial derivative with respect to α (i.e., holding x, y, and r constant) is $f_\alpha(x,y,\alpha) = (x - \alpha) = 0$. Squaring both sides of the equation and subtracting $(x - \alpha)^2 = 0$ from $(x - \alpha)^2 + y^2 - r^2 = 0$ to eliminate α, gives $y^2 - r^2 = 0$, and $y = \pm r$, the equations of AB and CD in Fig. 1.

EPICYCLOID (ep-i-sahy'-kloid), the path traced by a point P on a circle which rolls along another circle on the outside. (See figure.)

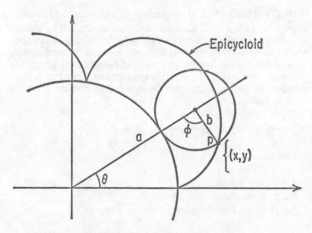

Epicycloid

If the fixed circle is centered at the origin and has radius a, while the moving circle has radius b and P starts out at the point $(a,0)$, then the PARAMETRIC EQUATIONS for the epicycloid are:

$$x = (a + b) \cos \theta - b \cos (\theta + \phi),$$
$$y = (a + b) \sin \theta - b \sin (\theta + \phi).$$

Since $a\theta = \phi b$ or $\phi = \dfrac{a\theta}{b}$ this can also be written as

$$x = (a + b) \cos \theta - b \cos \left(\frac{a + b}{b} \theta \right),$$
$$y = (a + b) \sin \theta - b \sin \left(\frac{a + b}{b} \theta \right).$$

See also CYCLOID; HYPOCYCLOID.

EQUAL ANGLES, *see* ANGLES, EQUAL.

EQUAL CIRCLES, circles with equal radii, or circles that can be made to coincide.

EQUALITY, in mathematics, a statement that two expressions represent or name the same thing. Thus, $25 + 7 = 32$ is an equality: the symbols $25 + 7$ represent the same quantity as the symbol 32. The following AXIOMS and rules of logic are the basic laws of the equality relation:

1. Reflexive property. Any quantity is equal to itself ($a = a$).
2. Symmetric property. If one quantity is equal to a second quantity, the second quantity is equal to the first (If $a = b$, then $b = a$).
3. Transitive property. If one quantity is equal to a second, and the second is equal to a third, the first quantity is equal to the third (If $a = b$ and $b = c$, then $a = c$).
4. Addition axiom. If $a + c = b + c$, then $a = b$; and if $a = b$ then $a + c = b + c$. (Note that c can be a NEGATIVE NUMBER. Thus, this statement includes the SUBTRACTION AXIOM.)
5. Multiplication axiom. If $c \neq 0$ and $ac = bc$ then $a = b$; and if $c \neq 0$ and $a = b$ then $ac = bc$. (Note c can be a FRACTION. Thus, this statement includes the DIVISION AXIOM.)

EQUAL LINE SEGMENTS, segments that can be made to coincide, or segments that have the same measure. *See also* LINE SEGMENTS, EQUAL.

EQUATION (ee-kway'-zhun), statement that two quantities are equal. An equation that contains variables may be true for some values of its variables, or for none. Sets of values that make the equation true are called *solutions* or *roots of the equation.* Examples of equations which have no solutions are: $\sin \theta = 2$ and $x = \log (-10)$. An equation which is not an identity is sometimes called a CONDITIONAL EQUATION. *See also* FUNCTION; QUADRATIC EQUATION; QUADRATIC FORMULA; ROOT; VARIABLE.

EQUATION, FIRST DEGREE, *see* DEGREE OF AN EQUATION; EQUATION, LINEAR.

EQUATION, FRACTIONAL, an equation in which the VARIABLE appears in the denominator, as $2/x - 1/x = 3$. The equation $x/2 + x/3 = 4$ is an equation with fractions, but is not a fractional equation. Both are solved in the same manner: first clear the equation of fractions by multiplying both members by the LOWEST COMMON DENOMINATOR. Then treat the resulting equation according to its degree in nonfractional form.

EQUATION, HOMOGENEOUS, *see* HOMOGENEOUS EQUATION.

EQUATION, LINEAR, an EQUATION in which no term is higher than the first degree (*see* DEGREE OF AN EQUATION); for example, $x + y = 8$. Such an equation is called linear because its GRAPH is always a straight line (*see* GRAPHS, LINEAR).

A linear equation in one variable is solved by changing the equation to one or more other equations that are simpler, but which have the same root or roots. These are called *equivalent equations.*

Rules for solving linear equations in one VARIABLE:
1. Remove PARENTHESES and clear FRACTIONS.
2. Simplify both members of the equation by combining LIKE TERMS.
3. Use the ADDITION AXIOM or SUBTRACTION AXIOM to transform the equation to one in which the variable appears alone in one member of the equation and all other terms appear in the other member of the equation.

4. Use the DIVISION AXIOM or the MULTIPLICATION AXIOM to make the coefficient of the variable equal 1.

5. By SUBSTITUTION, check the root in the original equation.

Ex. 1: Solve for x: $\dfrac{2x}{3} - \dfrac{1}{2} = 5 - \dfrac{x}{4}$.

Sol.: To clear fractions, multiply each term by the LOWEST COMMON DENOMINATOR, 12:

$$12\left(\dfrac{2x}{3}\right) - 12\left(\dfrac{1}{2}\right) = 12(5) - 12\left(\dfrac{x}{4}\right)$$
$$8x - 6 = 60 - 3x.$$

Add $3x$ to each side of the equation: $11x - 6 = 60$.
Add 6 to each member: $11x = 66$.
Divide each side by 11: $x = 6$.

Check: Substitute 6 for x in the original equation:

$$\dfrac{2x}{3} - \dfrac{1}{2} = 5 - \dfrac{x}{4}$$
$$\dfrac{2(6)}{3} - \dfrac{1}{2} = 5 - \dfrac{6}{4}$$
$$\dfrac{12}{3} - \dfrac{1}{2} = 5 - 1\tfrac{1}{2}$$
$$4 - \tfrac{1}{2} = 5 - 1\tfrac{1}{2}$$
$$3\tfrac{1}{2} = 3\tfrac{1}{2}.$$

Ex. 2: Solve for x: $2(x - 3) = 5(x - 2) - 8$.
Sol.: Multiply to remove parentheses: $2x - 6 = 5x - 18$.
Combine similar terms on each side: $2x - 6 = 5x - 18$.
Add 18 to each side: $2x + 12 = 5x$.
Subtract $2x$ from each side: $12 = 3x$.
Divide each side by 3: $4 = x$.

Check: Substitute 4 for x in the original equation:

$$2(x - 3) = 5(x - 2) - 8$$
$$2(4 - 3) = 5(4 - 2) - 8$$
$$2(1) = 5(2) - 8$$
$$2 = 10 - 8$$
$$2 = 2.$$

Ex. 3: Solve for y: $\dfrac{3y - 2}{5(y - 2)} = \dfrac{2}{5}$.

Sol.: Clear fractions by multiplying each term by the L.C.D., $5(y - 2)$:

$$\dfrac{5(y - 2)(3y - 2)}{5(y - 2)} = \dfrac{2}{5} \cdot 5(y - 2).$$

Simplify each side: $3y - 2 = 2(y - 2)$.
Remove parentheses: $3y - 2 = 2y - 4$.
Add 2 to each side: $3y = 2y - 2$.
Subtract $2y$ from each side: $y = -2$.

Check: Substitute -2 for y in the original equation:

$$\dfrac{3y - 2}{5(y - 2)} = \dfrac{2}{5}$$
$$\dfrac{3(-2) - 2}{5(-2 - 2)} = \dfrac{2}{5}$$
$$\dfrac{-6 - 2}{5(-4)} = \dfrac{2}{5}$$
$$\dfrac{-8}{-20} = \dfrac{2}{5}$$
$$\dfrac{2}{5} = \dfrac{2}{5}.$$

See also SYSTEMS OF EQUATIONS.

EQUATION, LITERAL, an equation in which one or more of the constant COEFFICIENTS are letters. Literal equations are solved as other equations (*see* EQUATION, LINEAR). By using the AXIOMS of EQUALITY, the equation should first be changed to an equiva-

lent equation with all terms containing the VARIABLE in one member and terms not containing the variable in the other member.

Ex. 1: Solve for x: $ax - a = 0$.
Sol.: Add a to each side: $ax = a$.
Divide each side by a: $x = 1$.
When solving literal equations, it is often necessary to factor (*see* FACTORING) one or more expressions:

Ex. 2: Solve for x: $ax - a = bx - b$.
Sol.: Add a to each side: $ax = bx + a - b$.
Subtract bx from each side: $ax - bx = a - b$.
Factor the left member: $x(a - b) = a - b$.

Divide each side by $(a - b)$: $x = \dfrac{a - b}{a - b}$
$$x = 1.$$

Ex. 3: Solve for x: $a(x - a) = b(x - b)$.
Sol.: Multiply to remove parentheses: $ax - a^2 = bx - b^2$.
Add a^2 to each side: $ax = bx + a^2 - b^2$.
Subtract bx from each side: $ax - bx = a^2 - b^2$.
Factor the left member: $x(a - b) = a^2 - b^2$.
Divide by $(a - b)$:

$$x = \dfrac{a^2 - b^2}{a - b}.$$

Simplify the right member by factoring and cancelling:

$$x = \dfrac{(a - b)(a + b)}{(a - b)}.$$
$$x = a + b.$$

Ex. 4: Solve the formula $1 = a + d(n - 1)$ for d:

$$a + d(n - 1) = 1.$$

Sol.: Subtract a from each side: $d(n - 1) = 1 - a$.

Divide each side by $(n - 1)$: $d = \dfrac{1 - a}{n - 1}$.

EQUATION, QUADRATIC, *see* QUADRATIC EQUATION.

EQUATION, SECOND DEGREE, a QUADRATIC EQUATION. *See also* DEGREE OF AN EQUATION.

EQUATIONS, RADICAL, equations in which the VARIABLE is a RADICAND, as $\sqrt{x} = 6$. Radical equations are solved by changing them to equations without a RADICAL by raising both members to an appropriate POWER. Since raising to the second power, or squaring, is the inverse (*see* INVERSE OPERATIONS) of finding the square root, when the variable appears as a square root, both members of the equation may be squared to give an equation without radicals.

Ex. 1: Solve for x: $\sqrt{x} = 6$.
Sol.: Square both members: $(\sqrt{x})^2 = (6)^2$
$$x = 36$$

Check: $\sqrt{x} = 6$
$$\sqrt{36} = 6$$
$$6 = 6.$$

Ex. 2: Solve for x: $\sqrt{4x + 9} = 5$.
Sol.: Square both numbers: $(\sqrt{4x + 9})^2 = (5)^2$
$$4x + 9 = 25$$
$$4x = 16$$
$$x = 4.$$

Check: $\sqrt{4x + 9} = 5$
Check: $\sqrt{4(4) + 9} = 5$
$$\sqrt{16 + 9} = 5$$
$$\sqrt{25} = 5$$
$$5 = 5.$$

If the variable appears as a cube root, the equation may be changed to an equivalent equation without radicals by raising each member to the third power (cubing).

Ex. 3: Solve for x: $\sqrt[3]{x} + 2 = 5$.

Sol.: Isolate the term containing the radical: $\sqrt[3]{x} = 3$.

Cube both members: $(\sqrt[3]{x})^3 = (3)^3$

$$x = 27.$$

Check: $\sqrt[3]{x} + 2 = 5$

$$\sqrt[3]{27} + 2 = 5$$
$$3 + 2 = 5$$
$$5 = 5.$$

If an equation has more than one term that contains a radical, it is necessary to raise both members to a power more than once.

Ex. 4: Solve for x: $\sqrt{x + 5} = \sqrt{x - 3} + 2$.

Sol.: Square both members: $(\sqrt{x + 5})^2 = (\sqrt{x - 3} + 2)^2$

$$x + 5 = x - 3$$
$$+ 4\sqrt{x - 3} + 4.$$

Combine terms: $4 = 4\sqrt{x - 3}$.

Since the equation still contains a radical, square both members:

$$(4)^2 = (4\sqrt{x - 3})^2$$
$$16 = 16(x - 3)$$
$$16 = 16x - 48$$
$$64 = 16x$$
$$4 = x.$$

Check: $\sqrt{x + 5} - \sqrt{x - 3} = 2$

$$\sqrt{4 + 5} - \sqrt{4 - 3} = 2$$
$$\sqrt{9} - \sqrt{1} = 2$$
$$3 - 1 = 2$$
$$2 = 2.$$

See also BINOMIAL, SQUARING A.

EQUATIONS, ROOTS OF, values of the VARIABLES which satisfy the condition of the equation. In the equation $4x = 20$, $x = 5$ is the root of the equation because 4 times 5 is 20. An equation may have more than one root; e.g., in $x^2 = 25$, $+5$ and -5 satisfy the equation, so both are roots. In the equation $x^2 - 5x + 6 = 0$, the roots are 3 and 2.

EQUATIONS, SYSTEMS OF LINEAR, two or more SIMULTANEOUS EQUATIONS of the first degree (*see* DEGREE OF AN EQUATION). If two equations in two unknowns are consistent and independent, their line graphs will intersect at a point, the coordinates of which are the values of x and y which satisfy the system.

If all the values of one equation satisfy the other equation, then the two consistent equations are called *dependent* equations and the lines of their graphs will coincide. $2x - 3y = 5$ and $4x - 6y = 10$ are dependent equations. The second equation is obtained by multiplying the first equation by 2. If there is no set of values that will satisfy both equations they are called *inconsistent* equations and the lines of their graphs will be parallel. Thus $x + y = 8$ and $x + y = 6$ are inconsistent equations, since it is obvious that no set of values can satisfy both equations.

There are three methods for solving INDEPENDENT EQUATIONS, or SIMULTANEOUS EQUATIONS.

1. Graphing (*see* GRAPHS, LINEAR)
2. Addition or SUBTRACTION
3. Substitution

Ex.: $\begin{cases} x + 2y = 8 \\ 2x - y = 6. \end{cases}$

Sol.: 1. By Graph:

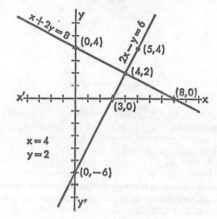

$x + 2y = 8$		
x	0	8	4
y	4	0	2

$2x - y = 6$

x	0	3	5
y	-6	0	4

The graphs intersect at (4,2). Both equations have the common solution

$$x = 4, y = 2.$$

2. By Addition or Subtraction:

$\begin{array}{ll} (1) & \{\ x + 2y = 8 \\ (2) & \{2x - \ y = 6 \\ (3) & \{\ x + 2y = 8 \\ (4) & \{4x - 2y = 12 \end{array}$

Add (3) and (4)
$$5x = 20$$
$$x = 4.$$
$$y = 2.$$

Substitute in (1)

Check: $x + 2y = 8$ $2x - y = 6$
$4 + 2(2) = 8$ $2(4) - 2 = 6$
$4 + 4 = 8.$ $8 - 2 = 6.$

3. By Substitution:

$\begin{array}{ll} (1) & \{x + 2y = 8 \\ (2) & \{2x - y = 6 \end{array}$

In (1) $x = 8 - 2y$

Substitute in (2) $2(8 - 2y) - y = 6$

Remove parentheses $16 - 4y - y = 6$
$$-4y - y = -16 + 6$$

Combine $-5y = -10$
$$y = 2.$$

Note: "If like signs are divided the quotient is plus."

Substitute in $x = 8 - 2y$ $x = 8 - 2(2)$
$$x = 4.$$

See also ELIMINATION.

EQUATOR, the fundamental great circle around the earth whose plane is perpendicular to the earth's axis of rotation; also, any similar great circle serving as a basis of a spherical COORDINATE SYSTEM, such as the celestial equator or the galactic equator.

EQUIANGULAR TRIANGLE, a TRIANGLE with all of its angles equal. Hence, each angle is 60°. An equiangular triangle is also an EQUILATERAL TRIANGLE.

EQUILATERAL TRIANGLE (ee-kwi-lat'-ur-al), a TRIANGLE in which all three legs are equal. An equilateral triangle is equiangular (*see* EQUIANGULAR TRIANGLE). Hence, each angle of an equilateral triangle is 60°. If each side has length s, the area is given by: $A = \dfrac{s^2 \sin 60°}{2}$ or $A = \dfrac{s^2\sqrt{3}}{4}$.

EQUILATERAL TRIANGLE

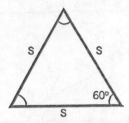

EQUIVALENCE RELATION, a relation "∗", defined on a SET A is an equivalence relation if it has the following properties, where a, b, and c are elements of set A:

1. $a * a$ (reflexive property).
2. If $a * b$, then $b * a$ (symmetric property).
3. If $a * b$ and $b * c$, then $a * c$ (transitive property).

The EQUALITY relation is an equivalence relation. In geometry, for triangles, congruence (*see* CONGRUENT POLYGONS) is an equivalence relation, as is similarity (*see* SIMILAR POLYGONS).

EQUIVALENT FRACTIONS, fractions that have the same value. An equivalent fraction may be formed from a given fraction by multiplying or dividing the NUMERATOR and DENOMINATOR of the given fraction by the same quantity. E.g., fractions that are equivalent to 4/6 are $\dfrac{4 \cdot 2}{6 \cdot 2}$ or $\dfrac{8}{12}$; $\dfrac{2(-5)}{3(-5)}$ or $\dfrac{-10}{-15}$; $\dfrac{4 \div 2}{6 \div 2}$ or $\dfrac{2}{3}$; $\dfrac{4(x^2y)}{6(x^2y)}$ or $\dfrac{4x^2y}{6x^2y}$: If an equivalent fraction is formed by multiplication, it is called an equivalent fraction in *higher terms;* if it is formed by division it is called an equivalent fraction in *lower terms.*

EQUIVALENT STATEMENTS, statements that have the same truth value.

1. If a THEOREM with one CONCLUSION is true, its contrapositive (*see* CONTRAPOSITIVE OF A PROPOSITION) is true. If the theorem is false, the contrapositive is false. Therefore, a theorem and its contrapositive are equivalent statements.

2. If a CONVERSE of a theorem with one conclusion is true, the nverse (*see* INVERSE OF A PROPOSITION) of the theorem is also true. If the converse is false, the inverse is also false. Therefore, a converse of a theorem and the inverse of the theorem are equivalent statements.

ERATOSTHENES OF ALEXANDRIA (er-u-tahs'-thu-neez), ab. 276–194 B.C., Greek mathematician, geographer, and literary critic. He calculated the circumference of the earth and its distance from the sun by comparing its altitude at Alexandria and Syene (near modern Aswan, Egypt) at the same time. He estimated a circumference of the earth of 26,600 mi., which is fairly close to the modern estimate of 24,894 mi. at the equator. Eratosthenes wrote on many subjects, including religion and drama. His 12-volume work *On Ancient Comedy* was a survey of Greek comedy. His *Geographia* was a description of the world of the Hellenes. Eratosthenes also invented a method of separating the PRIME NUMBERS by eliminating the multiples of each successive prime. The method is called the sieve of Eratosthenes.

ERATOSTHENES' METHOD, a method used by the Greek astronomer Eratosthenes in the 2nd cent. B.C. to determine the circumference of the earth. He used the fact that the sun was directly overhead—and therefore cast no shadow—at the Egyptian city of Syene on June 21. He then measured the shadow cast at Alexandria, a known distance from Syene, at noon on the same day and found the angle of the sun to be 7.2°. Since the rays of the sun are almost parallel as they reached the earth and since a vertical ray is directed at the center of the earth, the problem is solved by simple geometry, as shown in the figure. The distance between Syene and Alexandria, ab. 500 mi., must be 7.2°/360° of the earth's circumference, or Circumference = 500 mi. x $\dfrac{360°}{7.2°}$ = 25,000 mi. However, Eratosthenes computed the distance figure to be a little more than 500 mi., so that his circumference fig. came to 26,600 mi.

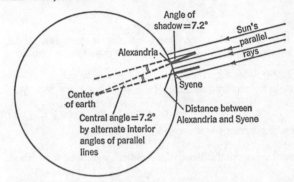

ERROR, the difference between a number and the approximation of that number. If A is an approximation of Q, the error, $E = A - Q$. *See also* ALPHA ERROR; PERCENT ERROR; RELATIVE ERROR.

ESTIMATE, *see* ESTIMATOR.

ESTIMATOR, in statistics, a random variable that is used to provide estimates of a PARAMETER. An *estimate* is a particular numerical value of an estimator. For instance, the random variable $\bar{x}$ is an estimator of the parameter μ. A particular value of $\bar{x}$, say $\bar{x} = 51.3$, is an estimate of μ.

EUCLID (yoo-klid), ab. 300 B.C., Greek mathematician known as the "Father of Geometry." He was a teacher of mathematics at the University of Alexandria at the time of Ptolemy I. Euclid summarized all the mathematical knowledge of his time in a systematic and logical textbook called the "Elements." This textbook remained in use, practically unchanged, for more than 2000 years. *See also* NONEUCLIDIAN GEOMETRY.

EUCLIDEAN GEOMETRY, the geometry that is based on Euclid's *Elements*, a treatise comprising 13 books, in which EUCLID summarized and organized the mathematical knowledge of his time (ab. 300 B.C.). *The Elements* is the earliest comprehensive Greek mathematical text, and the books on geometry covered almost all the ideas considered in a 20th century high-school course in geometry. Euclid presented the mathematical knowledge as a POSTULATIONAL SYSTEM made up of UNDEFINED TERMS, defined terms, AXIOMS, and THEOREMS.

EUCLID'S FIFTH POSTULATE seemed to have caused him some uneasiness. He avoided using it to prove at least two theorems. Other early geometers seemed to have shared his feeling, and many of them tried, unsuccessfully, to prove it. Early in the 18th century, the Italian mathematician Girolamo Saccheri (1667–1733) attempted to prove it. Although he was unsuccessful his work was used by BOYLAI and LOBACHEVSKY in the 19th century to develop (independently) a NONEUCLIDEAN GEOMETRY, later called hyperbolic geometry. In the same century, RIEMANN also developed a geometry (elliptic) based on Saccheri's work.

For centuries it was believed that Euclidean geometry was *the* description of the space in which we live. However, 20th century mathematicians, scientists, and philosophers have become more and more aware that the nonEuclidean geometries may provide a better description of our space.

EUCLID'S ALGORITHM, a method of finding the GREATEST COMMON DIVISOR (GCD) of two numbers by a process of repeated division. The larger of the two numbers is divided by the smaller. Then the remainder is divided into the smaller, and the new remainder divided into the previous remainder. This process is continued until a remainder of 0 is obtained. The last nonzero remainder is the GCD. To find the GCD of 4,284 and 14,586, divide 14,586 by 4,284:

$$14586 = 4284 \times 3 + 1734.$$

Next divide 4284 by the remainder, 1734:

$$4284 = 1734 \times 2 + 816.$$

Divide 1734 by the remainder, 816:

$$1734 = 816 \times 2 + 102.$$

Divide 816 by the remainder, 102:

$$816 = 102 \times 8 + 0.$$

Since $816 \div 102$ leaves remainder 0, the last nonzero remainder was 102, and 102 is the GCD.

   Ex. 1: Find the GCD of 108,966 and 76,219.

   Sol.:
$$108966 = 76219 \times 1 + 32747$$
$$76219 = 32747 \times 2 + 10725$$
$$32747 = 10725 \times 3 + 572$$
$$10725 = 572 \times 18 + 429$$
$$572 = 429 \times 1 + 143$$
$$429 = 143 \times 3 + 0.$$

The last nonzero remainder, 143, is the GCD.

EUCLID'S FIFTH POSTULATE, the last of the five postulates (*see* AXIOM) set down by EUCLID in his mathematical work, *The Elements*. The statement of the postulate in *The Elements* was, "If a line m intersects two lines p,q such that the sum of the interior angles on the same side of m is less than two right angles, then the lines p and q intersect on the side of m on which the sum of the interior angles is less than two right angles." This postulate is sometimes called *Euclid's Parallel Postulate*, and is often stated (particularly in the study of elementary geometry) as: "Through a given point not on a given line, one and only one line may be drawn parallel to the given line."

Euclid's Fifth Postulate has been called the most famous assumption in the history of mathematics. For centuries mathematicians tried to prove it as a THEOREM of Euclidean geometry, and instead discovered that denying it led to the development of NONEUCLIDEAN GEOMETRY.

EUDOXUS (yoo-dahk'-sus), ab. 370 B.C., a pupil of PLATO, defined PROPORTION to cover both incommensurable and COMMENSURABLE QUANTITIES. He investigated the area of a CIRCLE as a quantity lying between the areas of its inscribed and circumscribed POLYGONS.

EULER, LEONHARD (oi'-lehr), 1707–83, Swiss mathematician who introduced the abbreviations now used for TRIGONOMETRIC FUNCTIONS. Euler was the first to use the symbol e to denote the BASE of natural logarithms (*see* LOGARITHMS, NATURAL). Besides his vast and varied work in pure mathematics, he made many contributions to astronomy. His *Scientia Navalis*, containing his lunar theory, was a great aid to navigation.

EVALUATION, the process of finding the value of an ALGEBRAIC EXPRESSION.

   Ex.: If $a = 4$, $b = 3$, and $c = 2$, evaluate $2a^2b - 3c^3$.
$$2(4)(4)(3) - 3(2)(2)(2) = 96 - 24 = 72.$$

See also ORDER OF OPERATIONS.

EVEN FUNCTION, a FUNCTION $y = f(x)$ whose graph has SYMMETRY about the y-axis. If $f(x) = xf(-x)$, the function is symmetric about the y-axis, and is therefore an even function.

   Ex.: Which of the functions x^n are even?

   Sol.: Those for which n is even; e.g., x^2. *See also* ODD FUNCTION.

EVEN NUMBER, any number exactly divisible by two. An even number may be represented by $2n$, where n is an INTEGER other than zero.

EVENTS, EQUALLY LIKELY, in statistics, a set of events for which it is assumed that no one event is more likely to occur than any other, and hence that their probabilities (*see* PROBABILITY OF AN EVENT), P, are equal. E.g., let A be the event that a tossed coin will fall "heads," and B be the event that the coin will fall "tails." To say that "the coin is honest" is to assume that A and B are equally likely events, and hence that $P(A) = P(B)$.

EVENTS, INDEPENDENT, in statistics, two or more events are independent if the probability of their joint occurrence equals the product of their separate probabilities. E.g., if A and B are two events, and their probabilities are $P(A)$ and $P(B)$, A and B are independent if and only if $P(A \text{ and } B) = P(A) \mid (B)$. If two events are not independent, they are said to be dependent.

EVENTS, MUTUALLY EXCLUSIVE, in statistics, two or more events for which the occurrence of any one excludes the possibility of the occurrence of any other. E.g., on any given toss of a coin, the event, A, that it falls heads excludes the possibility of the event, B, that it falls tails. *See also* PROBABILITY OF AN EVENT.

EXPANSIONS BY SERIES, evaluations of functions by equivalent series; e.g.,

$$e^x = \sum_{n=0}^{\infty} \frac{x^n}{n!} = 1 + x + \frac{x^2}{2!} + \frac{x^3}{3!} + \cdots;$$

$$\ln(1 + x) = \sum_{n=1}^{\infty}(-1)^{n+1}\frac{x^n}{n} = x - x^2/2$$
$$+ x^3/3 - \cdots, -1 < x \le 1.$$

$$\sin x = \sum_{n=1}^{\infty}\frac{(-1)^{n+1}x^{2n-1}}{(2n-1)!} = x - \frac{x^3}{3!} + \frac{x^5}{5!} - \cdots.$$

$$\cos x = \sum_{n=0}^{\infty}\frac{(-1)^n x^{2n}}{(2n)!} = 1 - \frac{x^2}{2!} + \frac{x^4}{4!} + \cdots;$$

$$\tan^{-1}x = x - x^3/3 + x^5/5 - \cdots, -1 < x < 1.$$

$$\frac{1}{1-x} = 1 + 1/x + 1/x^2 + \cdots, -1 < x < 1.$$

See also TAYLOR SERIES.

EXPECTED VALUE, in statistics, the theoretical, or population, mean. The expected value of a random variable x is denoted $E(x)$ or μ_x. If x is a discrete random variable (*see* RANDOM VARIABLE, DISCRETE), $E(x) = \Sigma\, x_i f(x_i)$.

   Ex.: Let x have the following probability function.

$x_i =$	0	1	2	3
$f(x_i) =$	$\frac{1}{10}$	$\frac{5}{10}$	$\frac{2}{10}$	$\frac{2}{10}$

$$E(x) = \Sigma\, x_i f(x_i) = (0 \times \tfrac{1}{10}) + (1 \times \tfrac{5}{10})$$
$$+ (2 \times \tfrac{2}{10}) + (3 \times \tfrac{2}{10}) = \tfrac{3}{2}$$

If x is a CONTINUOUS RANDOM VARIABLE, $E(x) = \int_{-\infty}^{\infty} xf(x)dx$

   Ex.: Let x have the following probability density function:
$$f(x) = \begin{cases} \frac{2}{9}x(x-1) & \text{for } 0 < x < 3 \\ 0 & \text{elsewhere.} \end{cases}$$

$$E(x) = \int_0^3 x \cdot \tfrac{2}{9}x(x-1)dx = \frac{x^4}{18} - \frac{2x^3}{27}\Big]_0^3 = \frac{5}{2}.$$

The expected value of a function, say $g(x)$, of a discrete random variable is $E[g(x)] = \Sigma g(x_i)f(x_i)$. If x is continuous,

$$E[g(x)] = \int_{-\infty}^{\infty} g(x)f(x)dx.$$

EXPONENT, the number (or letter) written to the right and a little above the BASE to indicate how many times the base is to be used as a factor. In the expression a^2, 2 is the exponent, and indicates that the base a is used as a factor twice: $a \times a$. a^2 is read "a squared" or "a raised to the second power." a^3 is read "a cubed" and means $a \times a \times a$. If no exponent is written, as in the expression $3a$, or x, the exponent is understood to be 1. In expressions containing exponents, the operations of multiplication, division, raising to a power, and extracting a root are performed according to the following rules:

$$a^m \times a^n = a^{m+n}; \quad \text{e.g., } x^3 \times x^2 = x^5.$$
$$a^m \div a^n = a^{m-n}; \quad \text{e.g., } x^3 \div x^2 = x^1 \text{ or } x.$$
$$(a^m)^n = a^{m \cdot n}; \quad \text{e.g., } (x^3)^2 = x^6.$$
$$\sqrt[n]{a^m} = a^{m/n}; \quad \text{e.g., } \sqrt[2]{x^6} = x^3.$$

A fractional exponent indicates a root of an expression. For example, $x^{3/2}$ means $\sqrt[2]{x^3}$. A negative exponent indicates the reciprocal of the expression; x^{-1} means $1/x$; x^{-2} means $1/x^2$. An expression in which the exponent is zero is defined as the number one. Thus, $x^0 = 1$; $3^0 = 1$; $(x - 3y)^0 = 1$.

EXPONENTIAL DISTRIBUTION, in statistics, a probability density function for continuous random variables:

$$f(x) = \frac{1}{\theta} e^{-x/\theta}, \quad \text{where } x > 0.$$

The mean of the distribution is θ, and its variance is θ^2.

Probably the most important application of the exponential distribution is in calculating probabilities connected with the operating lifetimes of various pieces of equipment (e.g., electrical components).

EXPONENTIAL EQUATION, an equation in which the unknown is an exponent, as in $4^x = 64$. An exponential equation may be solved by expressing both members of the equation as powers of the same base, equating the exponents, and then solving the resulting equation. For example, $4^x = 64$ can be written $4^x = 4^3$. Then $x = 3$. If both members of the equation cannot be expressed as a power of the same base, the equation may be solved by logarithms. For example, $3^x = 7$ may be solved by logarithms as follows:

$$x \log 3 = \log 7$$
$$x = \frac{\log 7}{\log 3}$$
$$x = \frac{.84510}{.47712}$$
$$x = 1.771.$$

See also LOGARITHMS, SOLVING EXPONENTIAL EQUATIONS BY.

EXPONENTIAL FUNCTION (eks-poh-nen'-shal), a FUNCTION of the form a^x, in which a is a fixed positive number other than 1 and x varies. The graph of an exponential function is called an *exponential curve*.

Ex. 1: Sketch the exponential function $y = 2^x$.

Sol.: We may plot some of the points on the curve as follows:

x	-3	-2	-1	0	1	2	3	4
$y = 2^x$	$1/8$	$1/4$	$1/2$	1	2	4	8	16

Plotting these points and drawing the curve through them yields the following figure.

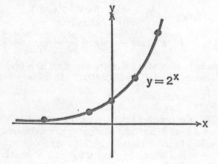

$y = 2^x$

Since exponential functions and LOGARITHMIC FUNCTIONS are INVERSE FUNCTIONS with respect to each other, logarithm tables may be used to find points on an exponential curve.

To plot the points on the curve $y = 5^x$, take the logarithm of both sides of the equation: $\log y = x \log 5$. To find the value of y corresponding to a given value of x, find the log of 5, multiply by x, and use the antilog of the result as y.

To differentiate the exponential function $y = a^x$, we use the relation

$$a^x = e^{x \ln a}.$$

Thus, $\dfrac{d}{dx} a^x = \dfrac{d}{dx} e^{x \ln a} = e^{x \ln a} \dfrac{d}{dx} x \ln a = a^x \ln a.$

Ex.: What is the slope of the tangent to the function $y = 2^x$ at $x = 3$?

Sol.: $y' = 2^x \ln 2 = 2^3 \ln 2 = 8 \ln 2$, or approximately 7.

EXPONENTIAL NOTATION, a number expressed as the POWER of some BASE. Thus, 4 to the third power is 64, written in exponential notation, is $4^3 = 64$. See also LOGARITHMIC NOTATION.

EXTERIOR ANGLE OF A POLYGON, an ANGLE formed by one side of the POLYGON and an adjacent side extended. The sum of the exterior angles of a polygon is always 360°, regardless of the number of sides of the polygon. Thus, each exterior angle of a REGULAR POLYGON of n sides is $360°/n$. Each exterior angle of a polygon is the supplement (see SUPPLEMENTARY ANGLES) of the interior angle (see INTERIOR ANGLES OF A POLYGON) at that VERTEX. Thus, in a regular polygon of n sides, each interior angle is

$$180° - 360°/n \text{ or } \frac{180(n - 2)}{n}.$$

An exterior angle of a TRIANGLE is equal to the sum of the two nonadjacent interior angles and greater than either one.

In the figure, $\angle DAC$ is an exterior angle. Another exterior angle may be formed at A by extending AC through A. A triangle has six exterior angles.

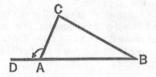

EXTERNAL DIVISION, the division of a LINE SEGMENT by a POINT on the line extended.

P ⊢- - -+- - -+- - -+- - - - + - - - - + - - - - ⊣ B
                              A

Point P divides segment AB externally into two segments AP and PB, such that $AP/PB = 3/7$. See also HARMONIC DIVISION.

EXTRANEOUS ROOTS, supposed "roots" that do not check in the original equation. When fractional equations are multiplied by a common denominator or when radical equations (see EQUATIONS, RADICAL) are squared, extraneous roots often are introduced because the resulting equation is not equivalent to the original equation. Solutions must therefore be checked to determine whether the root found is the solution of the original equation.

Ex. 1: Solve for x: $\dfrac{x}{x - 1} = \dfrac{1}{x(x - 1)} - \dfrac{2}{x}.$

Multiply through by the LOWEST COMMON DENOMINATOR, $x(x - 1)$

$$\frac{x^2(x-1)}{x-1} = \frac{x(x-1)}{x(x-1)} - \frac{2x(x-1)}{x}$$
$$x^2 = 1 - 2x + 2$$
$$x^2 + 2x - 3 = 0$$
$$(x+3)(x-1) = 0$$
$$x = -3, +1.$$

Check: $\dfrac{-3}{-3-1} = \dfrac{1}{-3(-3-1)} - \dfrac{2}{-3}$

$$\frac{3}{4} = \frac{1}{12} + \frac{2}{3}.$$

When the root, 1, is substituted in the original equation, the denominator is zero and division by zero is undefined. Therefore 1 is an extraneous root.

Ex. 2: Solve for x: $x - 3 = \sqrt{x+3}$.
Square both sides of the equation, then

$$x^2 - 6x + 9 = x + 3 \quad (\textit{See } \text{BINOMIAL},$$
$$x^2 - 7x + 6 = 0 \quad\quad\quad \text{SQUARING A})$$
$$(x-6)(x-1) = 0$$
$$x = 6, 1.$$

Check: $6 - 3 = \sqrt{6+3}$ or $3 = 3$
$1 - 3 = \sqrt{1+3}$ or $-2 \neq 2$.

Therefore 1 is an extraneous root. *See also* FACTORING; QUADRATIC EQUATIONS.

EXTREME AND MEAN RATIO, the division of a line into two segments, in which the longer segment is the MEAN PROPORTIONAL between the shorter segment and the whole segment.

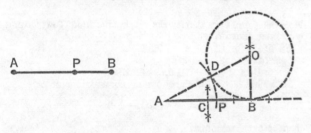

Fig. 1   Fig. 2

$$AB : AP = AP : PB.$$

A line 21 in. long is divided approximately in extreme and mean ratio if the two segments are 8 in. and 13 in. $8 : 13 = 13 : 21$.

Ex.: By construction divide a given line segment in extreme and mean ratio.

Sol.: Given segment AB, divide AB in extreme and mean ratio. Construct C the MIDPOINT of AB. Construct PERPENDICULAR to AB at B. On the perpendicular let $OB = AC = \frac{1}{2}AB$. With O as a center and a RADIUS equal to OB draw a CIRCLE. Draw AO cutting the circle at D. On AB mark off a segment AP equal to AD. P is the required point that divides AB in extreme and mean ratio. See Fig. 2.

$$AB : AP = AP : PB \text{ or } \overline{AP^2} = AB \times PB.$$

This construction can be proved as follows: AB is represented by a, AP by x, and PB by $(a - x)$, the proportion becomes $a : x = x : (a - x)$, or $x^2 = a(a - x)$. Since $OB = OD = \frac{1}{2}AB = \frac{1}{2}a$ and $AD = AP = x$, the construction can be proved by the PYTHAGOREAN THEOREM.

$$(x + \tfrac{1}{2}a)^2 = (\tfrac{1}{2}a)^2 + a^2$$
$$x^2 + ax + \tfrac{1}{4}a^2 = \tfrac{1}{4}a^2 + a^2$$
$$x^2 - a^2 = ax \text{ or } x^2 = a(a - x) \text{ or } \overline{AP^2} = (AB)(PB).$$

EXTREMES, the first and last terms of a PROPORTION. In the proportion, $a : b = c : d$, a and d are the extremes.

EXTREMUM (ek-stree'-mum), a minimum (*see* MINIMUM OF A FUNCTION) or a MAXIMUM OF A FUNCTION. (See figure.) The derivative (*see* DERIVATIVE OF A FUNCTION) at any extremum, when it exists, is always zero. *See also* EXTREMUM, DERIVATIVE AT; SECOND DERIVATIVE TEST.

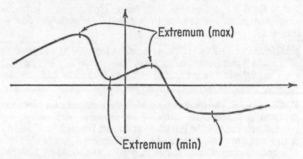

EXTREMUM, DERIVATIVE AT. At any EXTREMUM, if a derivative (*see* DERIVATIVE OF A FUNCTION) exists and is unique, it must be zero. This reflects the fact that, when it exists, the TANGENT LINE at an extremum is horizontal. Fig. 1 shows the graph of a function which does not have a unique derivative at an extremum, although the function may be so defined as to have both of what are termed a "left-handed derivative" and a "right-handed derivative." The graph in Fig. 2 has derivatives at all extrema.

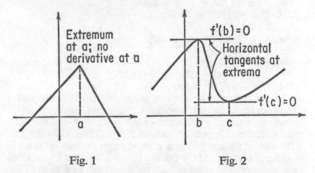

Fig. 1   Fig. 2

The derivative may be zero at points which are not extrema. E.g., the function $y = x^3$ has a derivative equal to 0 at $x = 0$, but it does not have an extremum there.

F

FACTOR, in mathematics, each of the numbers or letters multiplied together to obtain a given PRODUCT. Thus, 3 and 5 are the factors of 15; 2, a, and b are the factors of $2ab$.

FACTOR, COMMON MONOMIAL, a MONOMIAL that is a FACTOR of each term of an ALGEBRAIC EXPRESSION. In the expression $12a^4b^3c^2 - 9a^2b^2c + 3a^2b^2$, $3a^2b^2$ is a common monomial factor since it is a factor of each term. Thus, we may write the original algebraic expression in factored form as $3a^2b^2(4a^2bc^2 - 3ac + 1)$.

FACTORIAL NOTATION, $n!$ (read "n factorial"), the product of n and all the factors less than n. Thus, $n! = n(n-1)(n-2) \cdots$ until the last factor is 1; $5! = 5 \cdot 4 \cdot 3 \cdot 2 \cdot 1 = 120$. $0!$ is defined to be 1. *See also* TAYLOR SERIES.

FACTORING, the process by which the FACTORS of a given expression are found. In factoring an algebraic expression, the prime factors should be found. 18 is factored to be $3 \cdot 3 \cdot 2$. 6 and 3, or 9 and 2 are also factors of 18, but they are not PRIME factors. If a common monomial factor is present it should be factored out first and the second factor should be factored further if possible. There are several ways to factor an algebraic expression.

   1. Perfect-Square Trinomial,
$$x^2 + 2xy + y^2 = (x+y)(x+y) = (x+y)^2.$$

   2. The Difference of Two Cubes, $a^3 - b^3 = (a-b)(a^2 + ab + b^2)$.

   3. The Difference of Two Squares, $a^2 - b^2 = (a-b)(a+b)$.

   4. The Sum of Two Cubes, $a^3 + b^3 = (a+b)(a^2 - ab + b^2)$.

Ex. 1: Factor $4x^2 - 20xy + 25y^2$.

Sol.: $(2x - 5y)(2x - 5y)$, or $(2x - 5y)^2$.

Ex. 2: Factor $x^3 - 8y^3$.

Sol.: $(x - 2y)(x^2 + 2xy + 4y^2)$.

Ex. 3: Factor $16x^2 - 9y^2$.

Sol.: $(4x + 3y)(4x - 3y)$.

Ex. 4: Factor $8x^3 + 27y^3$.

Sol.: $(2x + 3y)(4x^2 - 6xy + 9y^2)$.

The two binomial factors of a trinomial that is not a perfect square are found by "trial and error." However, there are certain procedures that eliminate some of the guesswork. If a common monomial factor is present, remove it first. Then note the signs. If the sign of the third term is plus, the sign of both factors will be the same as that of the middle term. If the sign of the third term is minus, the signs will be unlike. If the first term of the trinomial has a coefficient of 1, the process is simplified.

Ex. 1: Factor $x^2 + 8x + 12$

Sol.: The first term of each binomial is x since $x \cdot x = x^2$. $(x + ?)(x + ?)$. The factors of 12 may be 3 and 4, 6 and 2, or 12 and 1. But the algebraic sum of the product of the two inner terms and the product of the two outer terms must be the same as the middle term of the trinomial. Then the factors are

$$\underbrace{(x + 2)\overbrace{(x + 6)}^{6x}}_{2x}$$

since $6x + 2x = 8x$.

Ex. 2: Factor $x^2 - 11x + 18$.

Sol.: $(x - 9)(x - 2)$.

Note: $-9x$ and $-2x = -11x$ and $(-9)(-2) = 18$.

Ex. 3: Factor $x^2 - x - 6$.

Sol.: $(x - ?)(x + ?)$.

Since the signs will be unlike in the factors, the algebraic sum of the products of the inner term and of the outer terms will be the difference of their ABSOLUTE VALUES, with the larger having the sign of the middle term. Therefore $-3x$ and $+2x = -x$. The factors are

$$(x - 3)(x + 2).$$

If the x^2 term has a coefficient other than 1, there are usually several possibilities. With practice and attention to the signs much of the trial and error can be dispensed with.

Ex. 4: Factor $6x^2 + 19x + 10$.

Sol.: $(3x + ?)(2x + ?)$.

Place the factors of 10, 5 and 2, so that the products of the outer and the inner terms are $15x$ and $4x$. Then the factors are

$$\underbrace{(3x + 2)\overbrace{(2x + 5)}^{15x}}_{4x}.$$

Note that 6 and 1 are also factors of 6, but it is found (by trial and error) that they do not work.

Ex. 5: Factor $12x^2 - xy - 20y^2$.

Sol.: $(4x + 5y)(3x - 4y)$.

Ex. 6: Factor $4a^2x - 10abx - 6b^2x$.

Sol.: First factor out the common monomial factor $2x$

$$2x(2a^2 - 5ab - 3b^2),$$

then factor the trinomial

$$2x(2a + b)(a - 3b).$$

See also BINOMIALS.

   To factor completely, it may be necessary to use more than one method.

Ex.: Factor completely: $4ax^4 - 4ay^4$.

Sol.: Factor the common monomial: $4a(x^4 - y^4)$ and factor the difference of squares two times:

$$4a(x^2 + y^2)(x^2 - y^2) = 4a(x^2 + y^2)(x + y)(x - y).$$

FACTOR, PRIME, a number or expression that has no FACTORS other than itself and 1. Thus 5, 7, 13, and x are prime factors.

FACTOR THEOREM, the rule that if $f(x)$ is a polynomial and $f(a)$ is zero, then $x - a$ is a FACTOR of $f(x)$. The Factor Theorem is used in finding roots of equations of higher degree than second.

Ex.: Solve for x: $f(x) = x^3 + x^2 - 4x - 4$.

Sol.: By testing values of x, it is found that when $x = 2$, $f(2) = (2)^3 + (2)^2 - 4(2) - 4 = 0$. So, $(x - 2)$ is a factor. Divide $x^3 + x^2 - 4x - 4$ by $(x - 2)$ and the QUOTIENT is $x^2 + 3x + 2$. Therefore, the factors are $(x - 2)(x^2 + 3x + 2)$. The second factor may be factored by inspection. Then the 3 factors are $(x - 2)(x + 2)(x + 1)$. This product becomes 0 when $x = 2$, $-2, -1$. Hence these are the three roots of $x^3 + x^2 - 4x - 4 = 0$. *See also* DIVISION, SYNTHETIC; QUADRATIC EQUATION; REMAINDER THEOREM.

FAHRENHEIT TEMPERATURE SCALE, a TEMPERATURE scale devised by G. D. Fahrenheit. Abbreviation: F. The reference points on the fahrenheit scale are 32°F. for the freezing point of water at normal pressure and 212°F. for the boiling point. Since 9 fahrenheit degrees equals 5 centigrade degrees, fahrenheit temperatures may be converted to temperatures on the CELSIUS TEMPERATURE SCALE by the formula:

$$C. = \tfrac{5}{9}(F. - 32).$$

Ex.: Convert 59°F. to centigrade.

Sol.: $C. = \tfrac{5}{9}(59 - 32)$
                $C. = \tfrac{5}{9}(27)$
                $C. = 15$

Thus, 59°F. = 15°C.

The fahrenheit scale is commonly used in the U.S. and other English-speaking countries. In scientific work the celsius scale is preferred.

FALLACIES IN GEOMETRIC REASONING (fal'-luh-seez):
(1) Unsound (or unwarranted) generalizations, (2) improper ANALOGY, (3) assumed CONVERSE, (4) assumed inverse (*see* IN-VERSE OF A PROPOSITION), (5) CIRCULAR REASONING, and (6) false ASSUMPTIONS.

F-DISTRIBUTION, in statistics, a continuous distribution that depends upon two parameters known as the DEGREES OF FREE-DOM. It is used when testing $H_0: \sigma_1^2 = \sigma_2^2$ by means of two independent random samples from two normal populations, and for finding confidence intervals for $\dfrac{\sigma_1^2}{\sigma_2^2}$. It is also used in testing hypotheses in an analysis of variance.

The numerical value to the right of which lies 100α percent of the area under the curve of the F-distribution with $n_1 - 1$ and $n_2 - 2$ degrees of freedom is denoted $F_\alpha(n_1 - 1, n_2 - 1)$. Tables of these values appear in most statistics books. The F-distribution has the property that $F_{1-\alpha}(n_2 - 1, n_1 - 1) = \dfrac{1}{F_\alpha(n_1 - 1, n_2 - 1)}$, so that the lower α-points, which are not tabulated, can be found from the upper α-points, which are tabulated.

FERMAT, PIERRE DE, 1601–1665, French amateur mathematician, founder of modern number theory. He invented many techniques of calculus, such as the use of the relation between horizontal tangents and extrema.

FIELD, an algebraic system, $\{F, +, \cdot\}$, made up of a set F and two operations on F, "$+$" (plus) and "$\cdot$" (times), with the following properties:
  1. $\{F, +, \cdot\}$ is an INTEGRAL DOMAIN.
  2. Each nonzero element, a, in F has an INVERSE ELEMENT, a^{-1}, in F, relative to the operation "$\cdot$".

These properties are summarized by $a \cdot a^{-1} = a^{-1} \cdot a = 1$. The system of RATIONAL NUMBERS and the system of REAL NUMBERS are examples of fields.

FIFTH POSTULATE, *see* EUCLID'S FIFTH POSTULATE.

FINITE SERIES (fahy-nahyt), a SERIES with a fixed number of terms. *See also* INFINITE SERIES.

FISHER, Sir RONALD, 1890–1962, a British statistician who made enormous and early contributions to many areas of statistics, especially in the area of the DESIGN OF EXPERIMENTS. His writings include *Statistical Methods for Research Workers* and *The Design of Experiments.*

FISHER'S Z TRANSFORMATION, in statistics, a transformation (named for Sir Ronald FISHER) performed upon the random variable r, the sample CORRELATION COEFFICIENT, to change it into a random variable that is approximately normal. The transformation is called the Fisher-z transformation, and is given by

$$z_F = \frac{1}{2}\log_e\left(\frac{1+r}{1-r}\right).$$

The random variable z_F is approximately normal (*see* NORMAL DISTRIBUTION) with MEAN $\dfrac{1}{2}\log_e\left(\dfrac{1+\rho}{1-\rho}\right)$ and variance $\dfrac{1}{n-3}$ (ρ is the population correlation coefficient and n is the size of the sample upon which r is based).

Statistical tables give the values of z_F that correspond to various values of r. Fisher's z transformation is used to test hypotheses about ρ and to find CONFIDENCE INTERVALS for ρ.

FITZGERALD-LORENTZ CONTRACTION, *see* LORENTZ TRANSFORMATION.

FOCI OF AN ELLIPSE, *see* ELLIPSE.

FOCUS, in mathematics, *see* CONIC SECTIONS.

FOLIUM OF DESCARTES (day-kahrt'), the curve which graphs the equation $x^3 + y^3 - 3axy = 0$. (See figure.)

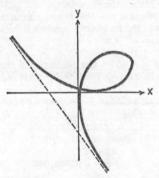

FOOT OF A PERPENDICULAR, the point at which a PERPENDICULAR intersects the line to which it is drawn. (See figure.) In $\triangle ABC$, E is the foot of perpendicular DE and G is the foot of perpendicular FG.

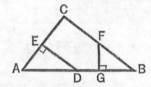

FORMAL PROOF, in geometry, a demonstration in the following five-step format:
  1. Statement of the THEOREM to be proved.
  2. A figure that illustrates the theorem.
  3. Restatement of the HYPOTHESIS in terms of the figure.
  4. Restatement of the CONCLUSION in terms of the figure.
  5. A logical series of statements with a reason (authority) for each statement. These statements begin with the hypothesis, are followed by deductions (*see* DEDUCTIVE REASONING) drawn from the facts stated in the hypothesis, and end with the conclusion. The reason for each statement in the proof must be one of the following: (1) the hypothesis, (2) a definition (*see* DEFINITION, CHARACTERISTICS OF A MATHEMATICAL), (3) an AXIOM, or (4) a previously proved theorem or COROLLARY.

If an AUXILIARY LINE is used, a statement (usually the first one) must tell the CONSTRUCTION that was used and the reason must give the authority for its construction. For examples of formal proofs, *see* THEOREM.

FORMULA, an algebraic EQUATION that expresses a rule in a concise form. The value of any letter in a formula is found by replacing the known letters with their values and solving for the remaining letter.

Ex. 1: The area of this trapezoid is 189 sq. in. The height is 9 in. and one of the bases is 15 in. How long is the other base? (See figure.)

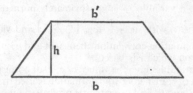

Sol.: The formula is $A = \frac{1}{2}h(b + b')$. Substituting the three known values, we have

$$189 = \frac{1}{2}(9)(15 + b)$$

Multiplying by 2, $378 = 9(15 + b)$

$$378 = 135 + 9b$$

Subtracting 135, $243 = 9b$

Dividing by 9,　$b = 27$ in., length of other base.

Ex. 2: A bomb dropped from a plane reaches the earth in 18 seconds. How high is the plane?

Sol.: The formula is $s = 16t^2$, where s is the number of feet the object falls and t the number of seconds it falls.

$$s = 16(18)^2$$
$$s = 16 \times 324$$
$$s = 5184 \text{ ft., the height of the plane.}$$

Ex. 3: If the interest on $600 for 2 years is $42, what is the rate of interest?

The interest formula is $i = prt$, where i represents the interest in dollars, r the rate per cent, and t the time in years.

$$i = prt$$
$$42 = 600 \times r \times 2$$
$$42 = 1200r$$
$$r = \tfrac{42}{1200} \text{ or } .035.$$

The rate of interest is $3\frac{1}{2}\%$.

Ex. 4: What is the volume of a SPHERE if its diameter is 7 in.?

The formula for finding the volume of a sphere is

$$V = \tfrac{4}{3}\pi r^3.$$

The radius is $3\frac{1}{2}$ in. Using $3\frac{1}{7}$ for π,

$$V = \frac{4}{3} \times \frac{22}{7} \times \frac{7}{2} \times \frac{7}{2} \times \frac{7}{2}$$

$$V = \frac{539}{3} = 179\tfrac{2}{3} \text{ cu. in.}$$

FORTRAN, *see* COMPUTER.

FOURIER, Baron **JEAN BAPTISTE JOSEPH** (foo-ryay′), 1768–1830, French mathematician and scientist, known mainly for his development of a mathematical analysis named after him, which is of the greatest importance in mathematical physics. He was largely self-educated, but his early work on numerical equations resulted in a professorship at the École Polytechnique, Paris. He accompanied Napoleon I to Egypt and, upon his return, became the prefect of Isère. He was made a baron in 1808. His later life was devoted to science. From his studies of heat conduction, published as *Théorie Analytic de la Chaleur,* he evolved the FOURIER SERIES, the expansion of a mathematical function or of an experimentally obtained curve in the form of a trigonometric series. Used as a method of determining the harmonic components of a complex periodic wave, it was a major contribution to that branch of mathematical physics known as harmonic analysis.

FOURIER INTEGRAL (foo-ryay′), the representation of a function $f(x)$ that has a finite number of infinite discontinuities, that is integral on any finite interval not containing any of these discontinuities and if

$$\int_{-\infty}^{\infty} \left| f(x) \right| dx$$

exists, then

$$f(x) = \tfrac{1}{2}\pi \int_{-\infty}^{\infty} \int_{-\infty}^{\infty} f(t) \cos\left[u(t - x)\right] dt \, du$$

See FOURIER SERIES.

FOURIER SERIES (foo-ryay′), a sum of an infinite number of trigonometric (sine and cosine) functions, used particularly in *Fourier analysis,* a method of determining the harmonic components of complex periodic waves found in a wide range of physical phenomena. It is mathematically indispensable in theories of heat, light, sound, electricity, and elsewhere in physics and applied mathematics. In general, the series has the form:

$$\tfrac{1}{2} a_0 + (a_1 \cos x + b_1 \sin x) +$$
$$(a_2 \cos 2x + b_2 \sin 2x) + \ldots$$

$$= \tfrac{1}{2}a_0 + \sum_{n=1}^{\infty} (a_n \cos nx + b_n \sin n x)$$

where the Fourier coefficients are:

$$a_n = \frac{1}{\pi}\int_{-\pi}^{\pi} f(x) \cos nx \, dx \quad (n = 0,1,2 \ldots)$$

$$b_n = \frac{1}{\pi}\int_{-\pi}^{\pi} f(x) \sin nx \, dx \quad (n = 1,2,3 \ldots)$$

A notable characteristic of a Fourier series is that it can be used to represent functions that are ordinarily represented by different parts of the interval. A change of variable is possible so that the interval extends from 0 to n, 0 to $2n$, L to $-L$, etc. If the function is defined on an infinite interval and is not periodic, it can be represented by the FOURIER INTEGRAL.

FOURTH DIMENSION, in mathematics, sometimes treated in a discipline called "four-dimensional geometry," although mathematicians may be considering many more than four dimensions. Solid GEOMETRY is based on three dimensions, *length, width* and *height.* This can be visualized easily, as, e.g., in the corner of a room, where it can be seen that three perpendicular lines can be drawn through a single point in space. *See* CARTESIAN COORDINATES; COORDINATES, POLAR. But some mathematical problems cannot be solved with only three dimensions. Mathematicians can use a space in which four perpendicular lines pass through a single point. We cannot visualize such a space but it can be dealt with mathematically. The fourth dimension in such cases is any variable quantity. E.g., space can be seen as four-dimensional if it is regarded as being made up of an infinite number of spheres instead of points, and then four references must be given in order to locate any one sphere. The fourth "reference" or dimension— is the length of the radius of a sphere. The other three are the three coordinates that locate the center of a sphere.

FOURTH PROPORTIONAL, to three given terms, the fourth term of the proportion in which the three terms are in the order given. In the proportion, $a : b = c : x$, x is the fourth proportional to a, b, and c. To find the fourth proportional to three numbers such as 6, 9, and 12, let x represent the fourth proportional. Then $6 : 9 = 12 : x$; $6x = 108$; $x = 18$, the fourth proportional.

If the quantities are LINE SEGMENTS, the fourth proportional to three line segments must be constructed.

Given segments a, b, and c (see figure), construct the fourth proportional x to a, b, and c.

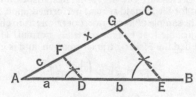

On AB of BAC, mark off segment $AD = a$ and $DE = b$. On AC mark off $AF = c$. Draw FD. Through E construct EG FD. (Construct $\angle DEG = \angle ADF$; corresponding angles of parallel lines are equal.) Then $FG = x$, and $a : b = c : x$, since a line parallel to one side of a triangle divides the other two sides proportionally.

FRACTION, a part of unit, or an indicated quotient of one number divided by another.

If a line is divided into four equal parts, one part is said to be one fourth of the line and is written 1/4. Three parts are three fourths, or 3/4, of the whole. If the same line is divided into eight equal parts, the equal parts are called eighths, and seven parts is written 7/8. The number of parts into which any unit is divided is called the DENOMINATOR of the fraction. The number of equal parts taken is called the NUMERATOR. Thus, 3/4 and 7/8, 4 and 8 are denominators and 3 and 7 are numerators. Proper fractions have a value less than one. In the figure, 2/4 of the first line represents 1/2 of the line, and 4/8 of the second line is 1/2 of that line. Thus, $2/4 = 4/8 = 1/2$. The fractions 2/4 and 4/8 are called EQUIVALENT FRACTIONS and both may be reduced to a lower term, 1/2. Fractions in computations should usually be reduced to the lowest terms, but in some operations it is necessary to change a fraction to an equivalent one in higher terms.

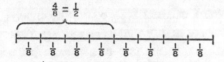

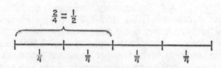

A fraction that has a value greater than one, such as $\frac{4}{3}$ and $\frac{9}{8}$ is called an *improper fraction*. Such a fraction may be changed to a mixed number (*see* MIXED EXPRESSION) by dividing the denominator into the numerator and carrying the remainder as a fractional part of the whole. E.g., $\frac{4}{3} = 1\frac{1}{3}$; $\frac{9}{8} = 1\frac{1}{8}$; $\frac{10}{3} = 3\frac{1}{3}$; $\frac{8}{3} = 2\frac{2}{3}$.

To reduce a fraction to lowest terms obtain an equivalent fraction by dividing the numerator and the denominator by the largest common FACTOR (*see* FACTOR, COMMON MONOMIAL). If the fraction contains a POLYNOMIAL, the polynomial should be factored. If every factor in the numerator is divided by a common factor, the numerator of the quotient is 1.

Ex. 1: Reduce $\frac{18}{27}$ to the lowest terms.
Divisors of 18 are 2, 3, 6, and 9.
Divisors of 27 are 3 and 9.
Therefore, 9 is the largest divisor and
$$\frac{18}{27} = \frac{2}{3}.$$

Ex. 2: Reduce $\frac{168}{192}$ to lowest terms.
Divisors of 168 are 2, 3, 4, 6, 8, 12, and 24.
24 is also a divisor of 192.
$$\frac{168}{192} = \frac{7}{8}.$$

Ex. 3: Reduce $6ab^2c/12ab^3c^2$ to lowest terms.
$$\frac{6ab^2c}{12ab^3c^2} = \frac{1}{2bc}.$$

Ex. 4: Reduce $(a^2 - ab)/(b - a)$ to lowest terms.
$$\frac{a^2 - ab}{b - a} = \frac{a(a - b)}{b - a}.$$

Change the sign of the fraction and the sign of the denominator to minus. If two signs are changed the value of the fraction re-

mains the same. To change the sign of a factor it is necessary to change the signs of each term of the factor.
$$-\frac{a(a - b)}{-(b - a)} = -\frac{a(a - b)}{(a - b)} = -a.$$

To change a fraction to a PERCENT divide the numerator of the fraction by the denominator. Move the decimal point two places to the right and add the percent symbol.
$$\tfrac{3}{8} = .375 = 37.5\% = 37\tfrac{1}{2}\%; \tfrac{1}{6} = .16\tfrac{2}{3} = 16\tfrac{2}{3}\%.$$
(*See* TABLE NO. 12.)

Ex. 5: Reduce $(x^2 - y^2)/(x - y)^2$ to lowest terms.
$$\frac{(x + y)(x - y)}{(x - y)(x - y)} = \frac{x + y}{x - y}.$$

Ex. 6: Reduce $(a + 2)/(a^2 + 5x + 6)$ to lowest terms.
$$\frac{(a + 2)}{(a + 2)(a + 3)} = \frac{1}{a + 3}.$$

Ex. 7: Reduce $(x^2 - y^2)/(ax - bx) + (ay - by)$ to lowest terms.
$$\frac{(x + y)(x - y)}{(ax - bx) + (ay - by)} = \frac{(x + y)(x - y)}{x(a - b) + y(a - b)}$$
$$= \frac{(x + y)(x - y)}{(a - b)(x + y)} = \frac{x - y}{a - b}.$$

The signs of a fraction are three in number: (1) the sign of the fraction; (2) the sign of the numerator; and (3) the sign of the denominator. If the sign is positive it is usually omitted. In the four fractions below, note that the value of each is the same.

$$+\frac{+6}{+3} = +(+2) = 2 \qquad -\frac{-6}{+3} = -(-2) = 2$$
$$+\frac{-6}{-3} = +(+2) = 2 \qquad -\frac{+6}{-3} = -(-2) = 2.$$

Therefore, the value of any fraction is not changed if any two of the three signs of a fraction are changed. Thus, a fraction may be written with only one sign, and it is usually written in front of the fraction; $-\frac{6}{3}$ represents $\frac{-6}{+3}$ or $\frac{+6}{-3}$.

To add or subtract fractions (1) change fractions to equivalent fractions with a common denominator; (2) add or subtract the numerators and place the result over the common denominator; and (3) reduce the resulting sum or difference to the lowest terms.

Ex. 8: $\tfrac{3}{4} + \tfrac{2}{3} + \tfrac{5}{6}$

Sol.: The LOWEST COMMON DENOMINATOR (L.C.D.) is 12. To change the three fractions to equivalent fractions with a common denominator of 12, multiply both numerator and denominator of the first fraction by 3, the second by 4, and the third by 2.

$$\frac{9 + 8 + 10}{12} = \frac{27}{12} = 2\tfrac{3}{12} \text{ or } 2\tfrac{1}{4}.$$

Ex. 9: $\tfrac{7}{8} - \tfrac{2}{3}$ L.C.D. = 24.

Sol.: $\dfrac{21 - 16}{24} = \dfrac{5}{24}.$

Ex. 10: $\dfrac{x - 3}{4} + \dfrac{2x + 1}{5}.$

Sol.: The lowest common denominator is 20. Since the denominator 4 must be multiplied by 5 to equal 20, the numerator must also be multiplied by 5. Therefore,

$$\frac{5(x - 3)}{5(4)} + \frac{4(2x + 1)}{4(5)} = \frac{5x - 15}{20} + \frac{8x + 4}{20}$$
$$= \frac{13x - 11}{20}.$$

Ex. 11: $\dfrac{x + 3}{x^2 - 7x + 12} - \dfrac{x - 3}{x^2 - 16}.$

Sol.: It is advisable to factor the denominators before finding the common denominator.

$$\frac{x+3}{(x-4)(x-3)} - \frac{x-3}{(x+4)(x-4)}.$$

The L.C.D. is $(x-4)(x-3)(x+4)$. Multiply the numerator and the denominator of each fraction by the factor missing in its denominator.

$$\frac{(x+4)(x+3)}{(x+4)(x-4)(x-3)} - \frac{(x-3)(x-3)}{(x-3)(x+4)(x-4)}$$

$$= \frac{x^2+7x+12}{(x+4)(x-4)(x-3)} - \frac{x^2-6x+9}{(x+4)(x-4)(x-3)}$$

$$= \frac{(x^2+7x+12) - (x^2-6x+9)}{(x+4)(x-4)(x-3)}$$

$$= \frac{x^2+7x+12-x^2+6x-9}{(x+4)(x-4)(x-3)}$$

$$= \frac{x^2+13x+3}{(x+4)(x-4)(x-3)}.$$

Note the change of signs when the second numerator is subtracted from the first. *See also* BINOMIAL.

Ex. 12: $1\frac{3}{4} + \frac{5}{12} + 2\frac{1}{8} + 2\frac{1}{3}$.

Sol.: Change the mixed numbers (*see* MIXED EXPRESSION) to improper fractions.

$$\frac{7}{4} + \frac{5}{12} + \frac{17}{8} + \frac{7}{3} \qquad \text{L.C.D.} = 24.$$

$$\frac{42+10+51+56}{24} = \frac{159}{24} = \frac{53}{8} = 6\frac{5}{8}.$$

If mixed numbers in a sum are large, it is simpler to add or subtract the fractions and the WHOLE NUMBERS separately. If the sum of the fractions is an improper fraction change to a mixed number and add the whole number to the sum of the whole addends.

Ex. 13: $129\frac{3}{4} + 87\frac{7}{8} + 104\frac{2}{3}$

$$129\frac{3}{4} = 129\frac{18}{24} \qquad \text{L.C.D.} = 24.$$
$$87\frac{7}{8} = 87\frac{21}{24}$$
$$104\frac{2}{3} = 104\frac{16}{24}$$
$$\overline{\qquad 322\frac{7}{24}.}$$

In the above, $\dfrac{18+21+16}{24} = \dfrac{55}{24} = 2\frac{7}{24}$, so the whole number 2 is added to the digit's column. The required sum is $322\frac{7}{24}$.

To multiply fractions (1) multiply the numerators of the fractions to obtain the numerator of the product; (2) multiply the denominators of the fractions to obtain the denominator of the product; and (3) reduce the resulting fraction to lowest terms. The operation is simplified by dividing a numerator and a denominator by the same factor before multiplying.

Ex. 14: Multiply $\frac{2}{3}$ by $\frac{4}{6}$.

Sol.: $\frac{2}{3} \times \frac{4}{6} = \frac{8}{18}.$

Ex. 15: Multiply $\frac{3}{4} \times \frac{4}{5}$.

Sol.: $\dfrac{3}{\cancel{4}} \times \dfrac{\cancel{4}}{5} = \dfrac{3}{5}.$

Ex. 16: Find $\frac{3}{4}$ of 48.

Sol.: A fractional part of a number implies multiplication.

$$\dfrac{3}{\cancel{4}} \times \dfrac{\overset{12}{\cancel{48}}}{1} = 36.$$

Ex. 17: $\dfrac{a^3b^2}{cd} \times \dfrac{cd^2}{ab^3} = \dfrac{a^2d}{b}.$

Ex. 18: $\dfrac{x^2-1}{x^2-2x-3} \cdot \dfrac{x^2-5x+6}{x^2-3x+2}$

Sol.: Factoring the numerators and denominators,

$$\frac{\cancel{(x+1)}\cancel{(x-1)}}{\cancel{(x-3)}\cancel{(x+1)}} \cdot \frac{\cancel{(x-3)}\cancel{(x-2)}}{\cancel{(x-2)}\cancel{(x-1)}},$$

then dividing out the factors common to the numerator and the denominator, the answer is 1.

To divide one fraction by another, invert the DIVISOR and multiply. The factoring and the inversion may be done in one step.

Ex. 19: Divide 3/8 by 1/2.

$$3/8 \div 1/2 = 3/8 \times 2/1 = 3/4.$$

Ex. 20: Divide 16 by 2/3.

$$16 \div 2/3 = 16/1 \times 3/2 = 24.$$

Ex. 21: Divide $6\frac{3}{4}$ by 3.

$$27/4 \div 3/1 = 27/4 \times 1/3 = 9/4 \times 1/1 = 9/4 \text{ or } 2\frac{1}{4}.$$

Ex. 22: $5\frac{5}{6} \div 5\frac{1}{4}$

$$35/6 \div 21/4 = 35/6 \times 4/21 = 5/3 \times 2/3 = 10/9 \text{ or } 1\frac{1}{9}.$$

Ex. 23: $\dfrac{a^2+a-12}{2a^2+8a} \div \dfrac{a^2-6a+9}{a^2-9}$

$$\frac{\cancel{(a+4)}\cancel{(a-3)}}{2a\cancel{(a+4)}} \cdot \frac{(a+3)\cancel{(a-3)}}{\cancel{(a-3)}\cancel{(a-3)}} = \frac{1 \cdot 1}{2a \cdot 1} \cdot \frac{(a+3) \cdot 1}{1 \cdot 1}$$

$$= \frac{a+3}{2a}.$$

FRACTION, COMPLEX, *see* COMPLEX FRACTION.

FRACTIONS, EQUIVALENT, *see* EQUIVALENT FRACTIONS.

FREGE, GOTTLOB, 1848–1925, German philosopher and mathematician, regarded along with BOOLE as the founder of modern mathematical logic. He established in his books, *Begriffsschrift* (1879) ("Explanatory Writings") and *Die Grundgesetze der Arithmetik* (1893 and 1903) ("The Foundations of Arithmetic"), such key notions in modern logic as quantifiers, rules of inference, hereditary property (which was later used in the logical analysis of the concept "number"), and many others. Russell pointed out an inconsistency in Frege's system by what is now known as Russell's paradox.

FREQUENCY DISTRIBUTION, *see* CLASSIFIED DATA.

FRUSTUM, *see* CONE.

FUNCTION, in mathematics, a rule which assigns to each element (the argument) of one SET, exactly one element (the value) of another set. For example, the rule might be, "Double the given number." This rule would be symbolized by the equation $y = 2x$, where x is the argument and y is the value. Since the value, y, depends upon the number that is chosen for x, y is said to be a function of x. Thus, the rule may be symbolized by $f(x) = 2x$ (read f of x equals two x). The set of numbers from which the argument may be chosen is called the DOMAIN of the function; the set of numbers which occur as values is called the *range of the function*. For the function $f(x) = 2x$, the domain may be defined as the set of REAL NUMBERS. Then the range of the function is the set of real numbers, since doubling a real number always yields a real number. If the domain of the function is limited to the set $\{1, 2, 3, 4\}$, then the range is the set $\{2, 4, 6, 8\}$, because if $x = 1$ and $f(x) = 2x$, then $f(1) = 2 \times 1 = 2$; $f(2) = 2 \times 2 = 4$; $f(3) = 2 \times 3 = 6$; and $f(4) = 2 \times 4 = 8$.

To be called a function, the rule must assign only one element of the range to each element of the domain. A rule that assigns more than one element of the range to each element of the domain is called a RELATION. E.g., if the rule is "Double the number and take the positive and negative value of the result," it would be symbolized $y = f(x) = \pm 2x$, and for each x chosen there would be two values for y. Thus, $f(x) = \pm 2x$ is not a function but a relation.

FUNCTIONS OF AN ANGLE OF 45°. In the figure, right triangle ABC is isosceles. $\angle A = \angle B = 45°$. If the two sides equal 1, by the PYTHAGOREAN THEOREM, the hypotenuse, AB equals $\sqrt{1^2 + 1^2} = \sqrt{2}$.

$$\sin A = \frac{1}{\sqrt{2}} = \frac{\sqrt{2}}{2}; \qquad \csc A = \sqrt{2};$$

$$\cos A = \frac{1}{\sqrt{2}} = \frac{\sqrt{2}}{2}, \qquad \sec A = \sqrt{2};$$

$$\tan A = \frac{1}{1} = 1, \qquad \cot A = 1.$$

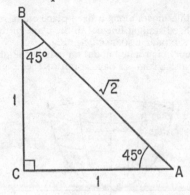

FUNDAMENTAL THEOREM OF CALCULUS, the theorem that, given the INDEFINITE INTEGRAL, or antiderivative,

$$\int f(x)dx = F(x) + C,$$

and the DEFINITE INTEGRAL,

$$\int_a^b f(x)dx = \lim_{\substack{mesh \to 0 \\ n \to \alpha}} \sum_{k=1}^{n} f(x_k)\Delta x_k,$$

then

$$\int_a^b f(x)dx = F(b) - F(a)$$

provided $g = f(x)$ is integrable over the INTERVAL from $x = a$ to $x = b$ and the required limit (*see* LIMIT OF A FUNCTION) exists.

The basic importance of this theorem is that it enables us to apply the formula techniques of formal integration to evaluate definite integral summations arrived at by the methods of differential approximation.

G

GALILEO GALILEI (gal-u-lee'-oh), 1564–1642, Italian philosopher, astronomer and physicist. This many-sided, extremely gifted man first studied medicine at the Univ. of Pisa but he soon renounced it for mathematics and dynamics.

He investigated the laws of motion, showing that Aristotle was wrong when he said that heavy things fall faster than light things. He discovered the isochronous swing of the pendulum and that a shot moved in a parabola. He improved the telescope for astronomical use and made important observations with it. After spending some time in Florence, then going to Padua, where he was professor of mathematics, he acquired a life professorship in Florence and also became philosopher and mathematician extraordinary to the Grand Duke of Tuscany in that city. His defense of the Copernican theory of the solar system made him unpopular with the ecclesiastical authorities, and he lived in retirement for some years. He continued to work however until the end of his life, even after he had lost his sight.

Galileo (as he is commonly known) is important in the history of philosophy through the way he used experimental method in conjunction with mathematical calculation. His two most important works are the *Dialogue concerning the Two Greatest Systems of the World* (1632) and the *Dialogues concerning The New Sciences* (1636).

Biblio.: De Santillana, G., *Crime of Galileo* (1955); Fermi, L. and Bernardini, G., *Galileo and the Scientific Revolution* (1961).

GAMMA, a Greek letter, symbolized by γ or Γ (cap). *See* TABLE NO. 1.

GAUSS, CARL FRIEDRICH (gohs), 1777–1855, German astronomer and mathematician. He pioneered the study of the fields of electromagnetism, developed the principle of arithmetic congruence, and the technique of graphing COMPLEX NUMBERS, and was one of the first mathematicians to give a formal presentation of the nature of the complex numbers. Through his early attempts to prove EUCLID'S FIFTH POSTULATE, he was led to develop the first NON-EUCLIDEAN GEOMETRY. He did not publish his ideas, however, but later encouraged LOBACHEVSKI and BOYLAI in their investigations into noneuclidean Geometry.

GAUSSIAN CURVE, in statistics, a normal curve. *See* NORMAL DISTRIBUTION.

GCD, *see* GREATEST COMMON DIVISOR.

GENERATRIX (jen-u-ray'-triks), a straight line, or a plane curve, which moves according to some law to form a surface.

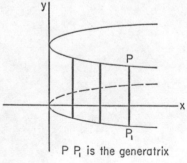

P P₁ is the generatrix

Fig. 1

If a straight line moves along a fixed plane curve so that it is parallel to a fixed straight line not in the plane of the curve, it generates a CYLINDRICAL SURFACE. See Fig. 1.

If a plane curve is rotated about an axis in the plane of the curve it generates a SURFACE OF REVOLUTION (See Fig. 2).

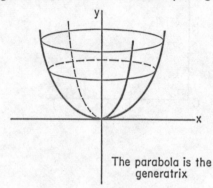

The parabola is the generatrix

Fig. 2

GEODESIC (jee-oh-de'-sik), on a surface, a curve that is the shortest distance between two points on the surface. On a SPHERE, a geodesic is an arc of a GREAT CIRCLE.

GEODESY, a branch of mathematics, dealing with the shape, size and curvature of the earth or substantial portions of it. The word itself means *earth-measurement*. Geodesy is also involved with the making of precise surveys and calculations to determine exact locations or positions on earth. It is also related to GEOMETRY.

Geodetic measurements form data for use in fixing exact control points for *triangulation* (the determination of distance), the basis for precise topographic surveys and production of maps (cartography). *Leveling* is a second important measurement obtained by geodetic means. The chief instruments used in geodesy include the *theodolite*, basically a powerful telescope attached to horizontal and vertical circles, mounted on a tripod, and used to measure horizontal and vertical ANGLES; *prismatic compass*, for quick-measuring of horizontal angles and BEARING and to get rough magnetic bearings in order to establish directions; *alidade*, a sighting rule for orienting plane tables; *clinometer*, for measuring height by reading ANGLES OF ELEVATION or ANGLES OF DEPRESSION in the field.

The more sophisticated and modern geodetic instruments include *tellurometer*, a device used to measure distance by recording the time it takes for electromagnetic waves to travel between two points, effective up to 50 mi.; the *geodimeter* makes the same distance recording as does the tellurometer, but uses light instead of electromagnetic waves. A major adjunct to modern geodesy is photogrammetry, the science of measuring and mapmaking by aerial photography.

Methods used to establish the weight and density of the earth and to map its surface include *leveling*, or the determination of elevation and TRIANGULATION. The U. S. Bureau of Coast and Geodetic Survey, a branch of the Department of Commerce, is charged with most of the nation's geodetic projects.

GEOID (jee'-oid), the figure of the earth considered as a spheroid of mean sea level surface continued through the continents. Such a concept reduces the earth to a spheroid of nearly uniform radius throughout. It is a useful concept in the study of *isostasy*, in earth measurement, and in *geophysics*. One of the most popular spheroid models devised is that by A. R. Clarke, called Clarke's spheroid of 1866.

GEOMETRIC DISTRIBUTION, in statistics, a function that gives the probability that the first success of a sequence of trials will occur on the *x*th trial of the sequence:

$$f(x) = (1 - \pi)^{x-1}\pi,$$

where π is the probability of success on a single trial. The trials must be independent, have only two outcomes (usually called "success" and "failure"), and the probability of success must be constant from trial to trial.

GEOMETRIC LOCUS, *see* LOCUS.

GEOMETRIC MEAN, of *n* positive numbers, the positive *n*th root of their product. E.g., the geometric mean of 9 and 4 is $\sqrt{36}$ or 6. The geometric mean of 2, 4, and 8 is $\sqrt[3]{64}$ or 4.

GEOMETRIC PROGRESSION, the sum of the terms of a geometric sequence, in which each term after the first is found by multiplying the preceding term by a fixed number, called the ratio. For example,

$$3 + 9 + 27 + 81 + \cdots$$

is a geometric progression in which the ratio is 3.

The last term of a geometric progression is obtained by using the FORMULA, $l = ar^{n-1}$, where *l* is the last term, *a* the first term, *r* the ratio, and *n* the number of terms.

Ex. 1: Find the 8th term of the geometric progression, if the first term is 3 and the ratio is 2.

Sol.:
$$l = ar^{n-1}$$
$$l = 3 \cdot 2^7$$
$$l = 3 \cdot 128 = 384.$$

Ex. 2: Find the 6th term of 81, 27, 9 . . . .

Sol.:
$$a = 81, \quad r = \tfrac{1}{3}, \quad n = 6.$$
$$l = ar^{n-1}$$
$$l = 81(\tfrac{1}{3})^5$$
$$l = 81 \times \tfrac{1}{243} = \tfrac{1}{3}.$$

The means of a geometric progression are the terms between the first and the last terms of the progression.

Ex.: Insert three geometric means between 5 and 80. $a = 5$, $l = 80$, $n = 5$; find *r* in the formula

Sol.:
$$l = ar^{n-1}$$
$$80 = 5r^4$$
$$r^4 = 16$$
$$r = 2.$$

The geometric means are 10, 20, and 40.

The sum of a geometric progression is expressed by the formula

$$s = \frac{ar^n - a}{r - 1}$$

Ex.: Find the sum of 5 terms of 2, 6, 18 . . . .

Sol.:
$$a = 2, \quad n = 5, \quad r = 3.$$
$$s = \frac{2(3)^5 - 2}{3 - 1}$$
$$s = \frac{2(243) - 2}{2}$$
$$s = \frac{484}{2} = 242.$$

The sum of the progression is 242, which may be verified by adding the terms 2, 6, 18, 54, and 162.

GEOMETRIC SERIES, an INFINITE SERIES of the form

$$\sum_{n=0}^{\infty} ar^n = a + ar + ar^2 + \cdots$$

It is a CONVERGENT SERIES (has a sum) if $|r| < 1$, and not otherwise. The sum, when the series converges, is

$$s = \frac{a}{1 - r}.$$

Ex.: In each of the following tell if the series converges. If so, find its sum.

$$\text{a.} \quad \sum_{n=0}^{\infty} \tfrac{1}{10}(2^n)$$

$$\text{b.} \quad \sum_{n=0}^{\infty} 3(\tfrac{1}{3})^n$$

Sol.: a. The series does not converge, since $|2| > 1$.
　　b. The series does converge, since $|\tfrac{1}{3}| < 1$;

the sum of the series is given by

$$s = \frac{3}{1 - \tfrac{1}{3}} = \frac{3}{\tfrac{2}{3}} = \frac{9}{2}.$$

GEOMETRIC SOLID, a three-dimensional figure formed by PLANE and CURVED SURFACES and enclosing a portion of space. In the figure, five geometric solids are shown.

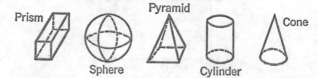

GEOMETRY (jee-om'-uh-tree). The branch of mathematics that considers the size and shape of figures. The word "geometry" is derived from the Greek words meaning "earth-measure." It was originally developed as an aid to land surveying in the ancient Near East. It was particularly important in Egypt, where the annual flooding of the Nile washed away all landmarks and necessitated yearly redistribution of farmlands. Egypt's empirical knowledge was transmitted to Greece, where it was developed into a formal science, i.e., a body of THEOREMS deductible from a set of AXIOMS.

Since the earth was assumed to be flat, ancient geometers considered such things as LINE SEGMENTS and angles in the plane. Gradually, geometry came to include lines and planes in the space of solids, and then space that was based on systems of coordinates, as in analytic geometry (*see* GEOMETRY, ANALYTIC). In the last century, geometry has been extended to include abstract spaces. *See also* EUCLID; NON-EUCLIDEAN GEOMETRY; TOPOLOGY.

GEOMETRY, ANALYTIC, geometry in which position is expressed by COORDINATES and the method of reasoning is primarily algebraic. Thus, in analytic geometry a circle, of radius *r* whose center is at the ORIGIN, is described by the equation $x^2 + y^2 = r^2$.

G.L.B., *see* GREATEST LOWER BOUND.

GLOBE, a model of the earth, or of the heavens as seen from the earth. Globes, which represent the earth, are called terrestrial globes, and those representing the heavens are called celestial globes. Globes are usually made by stretching printed gores over spheres, which are mounted to rotate around a rod serving as the earth's axis of rotation. Terrestrial globes are usually tilted 23.5° off the vertical to represent the earth's inclination in its orbit around the sun. The world's largest globe, located at the Babson Institute in Wellesley, Mass., is 28 ft. in diameter.

GÖDEL'S THEOREM, a theorem proved in 1931 by the mathematician Kurt Gödel which is often said to have far-reaching implications for philosophy, especially epistemology. In effect he proved that for any formal system adequate to number theory, there exists a true formula expressible in the system which cannot be proved within the system. Hence, at least for mathematics, no formal deductive system (axiomatic system, *see* AXIOM) can hope to encompass all the true statements of mathematics. The implication seems to be that we can never hope to systematize the whole of human knowledge within an axiomatic system—the paradigm or perfect systematization of knowledge according to many philosophers.

GOLDEN RECTANGLE, the rectangle thought by the ancient Greeks to have the most pleasing proportions. It is a rectangle whose length is the MEAN PROPORTIONAL between the width and the sum of the length and the width. If the width of the rectangle is represented by one unit, the length is represented by $\frac{\sqrt{5}+1}{2}$, or approximately 1.618 units. Therefore, the ratio of the width to the length of a golden rectangle is approximately 5/8. If the width is 5 units, the length is 1.618×5, or 8.09 units.

In the figure,

$$BC : AB = AB : (AB + BC)$$
$$(AB)^2 = BC(AB + BC)$$
$$(8)^2 = 5(13), \text{ approximately.}$$

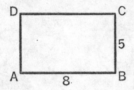

GOLDEN SECTION [from Latin *sectio aurea*], a term referring to a supposedly ideal or harmonious geometric relationship between two parts of a line, so divided that the shorter part of the line is to the longer part as the longer part is to the whole. The relationship may be mathematically expressed as $a:b = b:a + b$, and approximates the arithmetic ratio of 5:8. Cited in antiquity by the Roman architectural historian Vitruvius as a basis for the beautiful proportions of Greek structures, it was revived in the theorization of high Renaissance mathematicians, such as Luca Pacioli, who in his *Divine Proportion* (1509) professed to see in it a revelation of certain universal laws of nature. It has since been extensively employed by aestheticians to probe the compositional "secrets" not only of anc. masterpieces, such as the Parthenon, but of modern works, such as the paintings of Cezanne. *See* E. Loran, *Cezanne's Composition: Analysis of His Form* (1963). There are, however, many skeptics of such mathematical approaches to aesthetic relationships, not only among modern critics, but even among scholars of antiquity. Thus, the classical archaeologist William B. Dinsmoor warns against "the validity of numerous attempts to derive the plans of Greek temples from more or less intricate geometrical designs such as interrelated concentric circles . . . whirling squares, or the golden section." (*The Architecture of Ancient Greece*, 1954.)

GRADE or grad, in mathematics, 1/100 part of a RIGHT ANGLE when it is divided into 100 equal parts in the centesimal system of measuring angles.

GRADIENT in mathematics, for a function $w = F(x,y,z)$ the VECTOR, grad w or ∇w (read "del w"), whose components along the $x,y,$ and z axes are the partial derivatives of w:

$$\text{grad } w = \nabla w = \mathbf{i}\frac{\partial w}{\partial x} + \mathbf{j}\frac{\partial w}{\partial y} + \mathbf{k}\frac{\partial w}{\partial z}.$$

GRAM, *see* CGS SYSTEM; METRIC SYSTEM; MKS SYSTEM; TABLE NO. 5.

GRAPH, a diagram or chart showing the changes in any given quantity or changes in related quantities. Two major kinds are: (1) statistical graphs; and (2) graphs of FUNCTIONS expressed by EQUATIONS OF FORMULAS. *See also* GRAPH OF A FUNCTION; GRAPHS, STATISTICAL.

GRAPH OF A FUNCTION. If $f(x)$ is a function of x, then the set of points in the plane of the form $(x, f(x))$ is called the graph of $f(x)$. Since the y-coordinate of each of these points is the value of $f(x)$ at its x-coordinate, the graph is often symbolized by $y = f(x)$. To graph a function, it is usually more convenient to rewrite its equation in the form $y = f(x)$, choose values of x and calculate the values of y.

Ex.: Graph the function given by $x + y = 6$.

Sol.: Selecting convenient values of x, and calculating y gives:

x	$y = 6 - x$	y
-1	$y = 6 - (-1)$	7
0	$y = 6 - 0$	6
1	$y = 6 - 1$	5
2	$y = 6 - 2$	4

Plotting the points $(-1,7)$, $(0,6)$, $(1,5)$, $(2,4)$ gives the graph of the function. (See figure.) *See also* SLOPE OF A LINE.

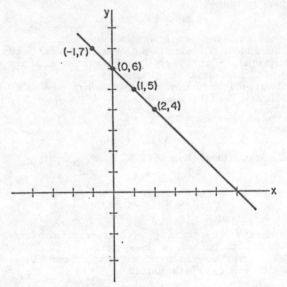

GRAPHS, LINEAR, the straight line graphs of first degree equations in two variables. *See* GRAPH OF A FUNCTION.

GRAPHS, STATISTICAL, BAR GRAPHS, BROKEN-LINE GRAPHS, CURVED LINE GRAPHS, and CIRCLE GRAPHS. Different graphs are suitable for different purposes, but all are extensively used because they give clear pictures of statistical facts and are more easily read than tables of facts.

GRAPH, x-INTERCEPTS OF, the points where the GRAPH crosses the X-AXIS. They represent the values of x when $y = 0$.

GRAPH, y-INTERCEPTS OF, the points where the GRAPH crosses the Y-AXIS. They represent the values of y when $x = 0$. In the formula, $y = mx + b$, the y-intercept is b.

GRAVITATION (grav-u-tay'-shun), an attractive force that exists between any two particles of matter. Because it applies to all objects in the universe, it is often referred to as *universal gravitation*. The physical law describing this force was formulated by Sir Isaac NEWTON and governs phenomena ranging from falling objects on the earth's surface to planets and stars moving through space. *Newton's law of gravitation* states that the gravitational force F between two objects whose masses are m_1 and m_2

is directly proportional to the product of their masses and inversely proportional to the square of the distance r between them, or:

$$F = G \frac{m_1 m_2}{r^2}$$

where G is a constant of proportionality called the *constant of gravitation*. Its value in the CGS SYSTEM is $6.673 \pm 0.003 \times 10^{-8}$ dyne-cm²/gm². Newton was able to show that *Kepler's Laws of Planetary Motion*, which were based on empirical observation, could be derived from the law of gravitation. Although it is often said that an object of small mass revolves around one of large mass—for example, that the moon revolves around the earth—actually the two objects both revolve around their common CENTER OF MASS. For a large difference in mass, the center of mass is very near the center of the large mass, so for practical purposes the small mass can be considered as revolving around the large mass. However, when precise astronomical measurements are involved, the mutual gravitational attraction of both bodies must be taken into account. In fact, the situation is quite complicated, because other bodies, such as the sun and other planets, cause variations, or perturbations, in the orbits of the earth and moon, while the earth and moon, in turn, exert forces on other bodies. The gravitational attraction of the earth for terrestrial objects is called *Gravity*. Gravity is responsible for the WEIGHT of objects on the earth's surface. The terms *gravity* and *gravitation* are often, but erroneously, used interchangeably. Gravitation is a universal phenomenon, while gravity is the gravitational effect due to the earth's mass. If the weight of an object mg, where m is its mass and g the acceleration of gravity, is set equal to the gravitational force at the earth's surface, one obtains:

$$g = GM/R^2$$

where M is the earth's mass and R is the earth's radius. If g, G, and R are known from independent experiments, the earth's mass can be estimated from this equation.

Gravitation is the weakest of the four known forces in nature. The others, in order of increasing strength, are the weak nuclear force (associated with nuclear and particle decay processes), the electromagnetic force, and the strong nuclear force (associated with nuclear binding force and strong particle interactions). A new insight into the nature of gravitation came with the publication of the general theory of relativity by Albert EINSTEIN (1916). Einstein showed that the inertial and gravitational masses of an object are equivalent, the effect of a gravitational field being the same as uniform ACCELERATION of the object. He went on to demonstrate that gravitational effects could be viewed as being a consequence of the geometry of space-time, which is altered in the neighborhood of a gravitating object.

GREAT CIRCLE, the circle in which a sphere is intersected by a plane that passes through the center of the sphere. All great circles of a sphere are equal. Other planes intersecting the sphere form *small circles*. The poles of either type of circle are the end points of the diameter that is perpendicular to the plane of the circle.

In the figure, circle O is a great circle and circle A is a small circle in a plane parallel to that of circle O. P and P' are poles of both circles. P may be the pole of other small circles whose planes are parallel to m, but it is the pole of only one great circle.

On a sphere, the shortest distance between two points is the minor ARC of the great circle joining these points. These great circle routes are used for air travel. *See also* GREAT CIRCLE NAVIGATION; GEODESIC; LOXODROME.

GREAT CIRCLE NAVIGATION, navigation in which the path of an airplane (or ship) is the minor arc of the GREAT CIRCLE through the point of departure and the point of arrival. The two points may be considered vertices of a SPHERICAL TRIANGLE of which the third *vertex* is one of the poles. If both points are in the same hemisphere, the pole of that hemisphere is taken. If the two points are in different hemispheres, either pole may be taken and either of the two spherical triangles may be used.

If A and B in the figure are both in the same hemisphere,

$b = 90°$ − latitude of A
$a = 90°$ − latitude of B
$c =$ great circle arc from A to B
$A =$ initial course
$B = 180°$ − course on arrival
$C =$ difference in longitude between A and B.

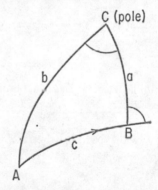

GREATEST COMMON DIVISOR, the largest number that is a divisor of each member of a SET of numbers. E.g., for the set containing the numbers 36 and 48, the greatest common divisor is 12. The greatest common divisor is sometimes written GCD. It may be found by EUCLID'S ALGORITHM.

GREATEST COMMON FACTOR, *see* GREATEST COMMON DIVISOR.

GREATEST LOWER BOUND, G.L.B., the largest number which is smaller than, or equal to, every member of a SET S. The greatest lower bound may or may not belong to the set.
Ex. 1: The G.L.B. of the set of numbers $\{1, \frac{1}{2}, \frac{1}{3}, \frac{1}{4}, \ldots\}$ is 0. Note that 0 is not a member of this set.
Ex. 2: The G.L.B. of the set of numbers $\{1, 2, 3, 4, 5, \ldots\}$ is 1. Note that 1 is a member of this set.
See also LEAST UPPER BOUND.

GROUP, an algebraic system, made up of a SET G and an operation, "$\circ$", on G with all of the following properties:
1. There exists an IDENTITY ELEMENT, e, in G relative to $\circ$. I.e., for a in G, $a \circ e = e \circ a = a$.
2. The operation is associative (*see* ASSOCIATIVE PROPERTY). I.e., for a, b, c in G, $a \circ (b \circ c) = (a \circ b) \circ c$.
3. Every a in G has an INVERSE ELEMENT a^{-1} relative to $\circ$. I.e., $a \circ a^{-1} = a^{-1} \circ a = e$.

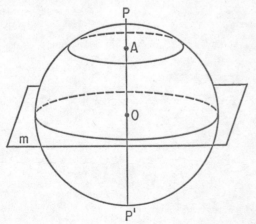

The set of integers forms a group under addition; the identity element is 0; and the inverse of any integer, x, is $-x$.

The integers do not form a group under multiplication. The identity element is 1, but 2, for example, has no inverse which is an integer.

The integers do not form a group under subtraction, since they are not associative. E.g., this equation is false:
$$1 - (2 - 3) = (1 - 2) - 3.$$

GROUPING SYMBOLS, devices for segregating two or more numbers to show that some operation is to be performed on all of them. Thus $10 - (3 + 2)$ means that the sum of 3 and 2 is to be subtracted from 10. And $(10 - 3) + 2$ means that 2 is to be added to the difference of 10 and 3.

Common grouping symbols are

	parentheses	$(a + b + c)$,
	brackets	$[a + b + c]$,
	braces	$\{a + b + c\}$,
and	vinculum	$\overline{a + b + c}$.

Rules for use of these symbols are:

1. Perform first any operations enclosed by parentheses or other grouping symbols.

2. Any sign before the symbol applies to the whole expression within it. If there is no sign as in $4(x + 2)$, multiplication is indicated.

3. When removing grouping symbols, if the sign immediately preceding the enclosed expression is positive, the symbols are removed with no change of signs. If the sign is negative, change all signs of the enclosed expression and remove the symbols.

4. If more than one form of symbols is used, remove the innermost symbols first. Then continue until all are removed.

Ex. 1: $8 - (5 + 3)$
$\qquad 8 - 2 = 6.$

Ex. 2: $10 + 3(4 - 1) - (4 + 5)$
$\qquad 10 + 9 - 9 = 10.$

Ex. 3: $a + (b - c)$
$\qquad a + b - c.$

Ex. 4: $a - (b - c)$
$\qquad a - b + c.$

Ex. 5: $4a - 3(b - c) + \overline{3a - b - c}$
$\qquad 4a - 3b + 3c + 3a - b - c$
$\qquad 7a - 4b + 2c.$

Ex. 6: $3\{2x - [-x + 2(y - z)] - 2y\}$
$\qquad 3\{2x - [-x + 2y - 2z] - 2y\}$
$\qquad 3\{2x + x - 2y + 2z - 2y\}$
$\qquad 6x + 3x - 6y + 6z - 6y$
$\qquad 9x - 12y + 6z.$

GROUP OF VECTORS. The VECTORS of any fixed dimension form a GROUP in which the operation is VECTOR ADDITION. The identity ELEMENT is the null vector. The INVERSE ELEMENT of any vector V is the oppositely oriented vector $-V$.

H

HALF LINE, the part of a straight line to one side of a point on it. It extends infinitely in one direction. (See figure.)

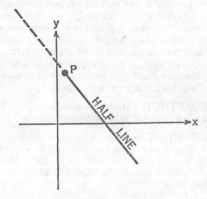

HALF PLANE, that part of any plane to one side of a straight line. E.g., the part of the coordinate plane which lies above the x-axis is a half plane, as is the part which lies above the line $y = x$.(See figure.)

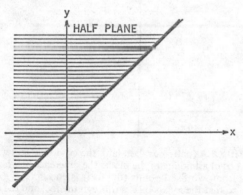

HARMONIC DIVISION, the division of a LINE SEGMENT externally and internally into segments that have the same RATIO.

$$\frac{AP}{PB} = \frac{AP'}{P'B} = \frac{3}{1}$$

Segment AB is divided internally by point P and externally by point P'. *See also* EXTERNAL DIVISION; INTERNAL DIVISION.

A├────┼────┼────┼──┤──┼──┤P'
            P   B

HARMONIC SERIES, the SERIES

$$\sum_{n=1}^{\infty} \frac{1}{n} = 1 + \frac{1}{2} + \frac{1}{3} + \frac{1}{4} + \cdots.$$

This series is DIVERGENT. *See also* GEOMETRIC SERIES, INFINITE; INTEGRAL TEST.

HAVERSINE OF AN ANGLE θ (ha'-vehr-sahyn), (abbreviated hav θ), equals $\frac{1}{2}(1 - \cos \theta)$.

In the formula for the sine of half an angle (*see* TABLE NO. 3 Half-Angle Formulas.)

$$\sin \tfrac{1}{2}\theta = \pm \sqrt{\frac{1 - \cos \theta}{2}}.$$

Therefore, $\qquad \pm\sqrt{\text{hav } \theta} = \sin \tfrac{1}{2}\theta.$

In Case IV of OBLIQUE TRIANGLES,

$$\sin \tfrac{1}{2} A = \sqrt{\frac{(s - b)(s - c)}{bc}}.$$

Therefore, $\qquad \text{hav } A = \dfrac{(s - b)(s - c)}{bc}.$

Similarly, $\qquad \text{hav } B = \dfrac{(s - a)(s - c)}{ac},$

and $\qquad \text{hav } C = \dfrac{(s - a)(s - b)}{ab}.$

HELIX (hee'-liks), (*plural*, helices), the path followed by a point moving on the surface of a circular CYLINDER at a constant angle to its elements. The position of the point at time t is given by the PARAMETRIC EQUATIONS:

$$\begin{aligned} z &= at, \\ x &= b \cos t, \\ y &= b \sin t. \end{aligned}$$

Two typical helices are shown in the figure.

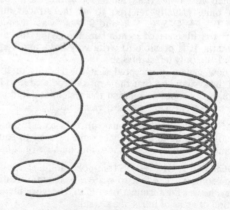

Ex.: By how much does the z-coordinate of the following helix increase in one turn around it?

$$\begin{aligned} z &= 2t, \\ x &= 3 \cos t, \\ y &= 3 \sin t. \end{aligned}$$

Sol.: The parameter t increases by 2π in one turn; therefore, z increases by $2(t + 2\pi) - 2t$, or 4π units.

HEPTAGON, a POLYGON having seven sides.

HERO'S FORMULA, named after Hero of Alexandria (3rd cent. A.D.) used to find the area of a triangle when three sides, a, b, and c are given:

$$A = \sqrt{s(s - a)(s - b)(s - c)}$$

where $s = \frac{1}{2}(a + b + c)$, called the semiperimeter

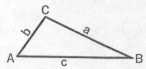

Ex.: Find the area of a triangle with sides 8 in., 15 in., and 17 in.

$Sol.: s = \frac{1}{2}(8 + 15 + 17) = 20.$

$A = \sqrt{20(20 - 8)(20 - 15)(20 - 17)}$
$= \sqrt{20(12)(5)(3)}$
$= \sqrt{4(5)(4)(3)(5)(3)} = 4(5)(3) = 60$ sq. in.

HEXAGON, a POLYGON having six sides. A side of a regular hexagon inscribed in a CIRCLE is equal to the RADIUS of the circle. If radii are drawn to two successive vertices of the hexagon, an EQUILATERAL TRIANGLE is formed. In the figure, radius r of circle O equals side s of the hexagon.

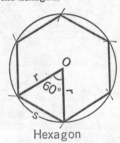

Hexagon

Radius r of $\odot O$ = side s of the hexagon.

HEXAHEDRON (hek'-sah-hee-dron), a POLYHEDRON having six faces.

HINDU-ARABIC NUMERAL SYSTEM, the NUMERAL system from which we adopted the symbols for writing the numbers one through nine. Usually referred to as the Arabic numerals, they are 1, 2, 3, 4, 5, 6, 7, 8, and 9. ZERO was introduced to represent the absence of a number. By giving the numerals PLACE VALUE, it is possible to write very large and very many numbers from only ten symbols.

It is now generally accepted that the Hindus in India developed the system and that the Arabs introduced it to Europe, therefore, it is proper to refer to the system as Hindu-Arabic. *See also* ROMAN NUMERAL SYSTEM; TABLE NO. 8.

HIPPIAS, OF ELIS (hip'-ee-us), ab. 425 B.C., inventor of a curve, called the quadratrix, that could be used to square the CIRCLE and to divide an ANGLE into any number of equal parts.

HIPPOCRATES, OF CHIOS (hih-pok'-rah-teez), ab. 460 B.C., a Greek geometer. The first to write a systematic treatment of geometry, he was a forerunner of EUCLID. His work included the calculation of areas of lunes of a SPHERE.

HISTOGRAM, a BAR GRAPH with no space between bars. It is used in STATISTICS to picture the frequency distribution of CLASSIFIED DATA. The area of each rectangle is proportional to the number of observations which that class contains. (See figure.)

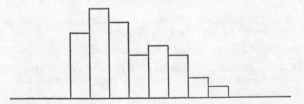

HOMOGENEITY OF VARIANCES (hoh-muh-juh-neh'-uh-tee), in statistics, equality of variances, sometimes assumed for statistical tests. Homogeneity of variances must be assumed in order to (1) use the independent samples T-TEST to test hypotheses about the differences of the means of two normal populations with unknown (but equal) variances and (2) perform an analysis of variance.

HOMOGENEOUS EQUATION (hoh-mah'-jee-nee-us), an EQUATION in which each term is of the same DEGREE. Thus $x^2 - xy + y^2 = 0$ and $x^2 - y^2 = 12xy$ are homogeneous equations. A homogeneous QUADRATIC EQUATION may be solved by FACTORING, or by the QUADRATIC FORMULA. This will give the value of one unknown in terms of the other.

HOMOLOGOUS (hoh-mal'-uh-gus), in mathematics, having the same relative position or value. Homologous elements of figures are corresponding elements of figures. These elements may be points, lines, or angles. For example, the sides of a polygon and the projection of the sides onto a plane are homologous elements. *See also* CORRESPONDING PARTS OF CONGRUENT TRIANGLES.

Homologous terms in a function are terms that serve a similar purpose in different functions. For example, the numerators of two equal fractions are homologous terms.

HOMOSCEDASTICITY (hoh-moh-sih-das-tis'-ih-tee), equality of variances; *see* HOMOGENEITY OF VARIANCES.

HORIZONTAL LINE, a line parallel to the x-axis in a COORDINATE PLANE. The ANGLE OF INCLINATION of any horizontal line is zero degrees, and its slope (*see* SLOPE OF A LINE) is therefore also zero. Any horizontal line can be expressed as a function of x in the following form:

$$af(x) = b \text{ or } f(x) = c,$$

where c is the y-intercept of the line. (See figure.)

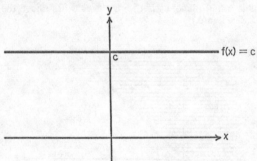

HYPERBOLA (hahy-pur'-boh-lah), the CONIC SECTION which is the LOCUS of all points in the plane, the difference of whose distances from two fixed points (the foci) is constant. If axes are drawn so that the x-axis passes through the foci and the ORIGIN lies halfway between them, the equation of the hyperbola is

$$\frac{x^2}{a^2} - \frac{y^2}{b^2} = 1$$

where $b = PQ$ in Fig. 1a and $2a$ is the constant difference between the distances.

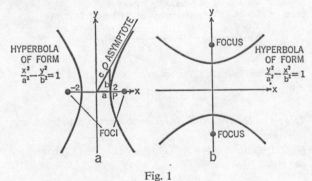

Fig. 1

If the foci are on a line parallel to the x-axis, but with the midpoint of the segment joining them located at the point (h,k) rather than at the origin, the equation is

$$\frac{(x-h)^2}{a^2} - \frac{(y-k)^2}{b^2} = 1.$$

If the foci are on the y-axis or on a line parallel to it, as in Fig. 1b, these equations become

$$\frac{y^2}{a^2} - \frac{x^2}{b^2} = 1 \quad \text{and} \quad \frac{(y-k)^2}{a^2} - \frac{(x-h)^2}{b^2} = 1$$

respectively. *See* ROTATION OF AXES.

Ex. 1: Sketch the following hyperbolas.

a. $\frac{x^2}{4} - \frac{y^2}{9} = 1.$

b. $\frac{y^2}{4} - \frac{x^2}{9} = 1.$

Sol.: a. x-intercepts are 2 and −2; there are no y-intercepts (i.e., the curve does not cross the y-axis). The graph looks like Fig. 1a.

b. y-intercepts are 2 and −2; there are no x-intercepts. The graph looks like Fig. 1b.

Ex. 2: Graph $xy = 6$.

Sol.: x and y must have like signs if their PRODUCT is +6. All points on the graph are $(+,+)$ or $(-,-)$. Therefore, the graph lies in the first and third QUADRANTS. The graph of $xy = -6$ would lie in the second and fourth quadrants since all points would be $(-,+)$ and $(+,-)$. There are no INTERCEPTS. If $x = 0$, then $y = 6/0$, and if $y = 0$, then $x = 6/0$, and division by zero is undefined. Therefore the axes are the asymptotes. The graph looks like Fig. 2.

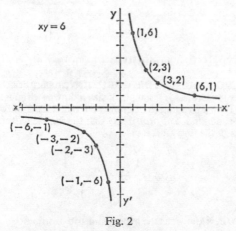

Fig. 2

Ex. 3: Graph $x^2 - y^2 = 9$.

Sol.: First graph the ASYMPTOTES. Let $x^2 - y^2 = 0$. By FACTORING, $(x+y)(x-y) = 0$, then $y = +x$ and $y = -x$. A table of values for these VARIABLES is as follows:

x	0	2	4	−2	−4
y	0	±2	±4	±2	±4

$$x^2 - y^2 = 9$$
$$y = \pm\sqrt{x^2 - 9}$$

x	y
0	$\pm\sqrt{-9} = \pm 3i$ (*see* IMAGINARY NUMBER)
±1	$\pm\sqrt{-8} = \pm 2i\sqrt{2}$ (*see* RADICAL)
±3	0
±5	±4

The two branches cross the X-AXIS at +3 and −3. There are no real values for y when the values of x are less than 3. The graph looks like Fig. 3.

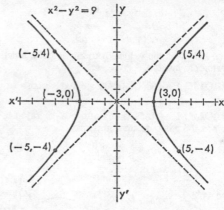

Fig. 3

The hyperbola may also be defined as the locus of points such that the RATIO of the distance from one of the foci to its distance from a particular straight line (the directrix) is constant. This constant is always greater than one, and is called the ECCENTRICITY OF A HYPERBOLA. There is a different directrix for each of the two foci.

The eccentricity of a hyperbola may also be defined independently as the ratio c/a. If this is done, and the foci of the hyperbola are at the points $(ae,0)$ and $(-ea,0)$, then the *directrices* of the hyperbola are:

1. Corresponding to the focus $(ae,0)$, the line $x = a/e$.
2. Corresponding to the focus $(-ae,0)$, the line $x = -a/e$. (See Fig. 4.)

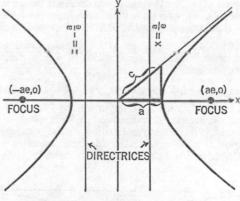

Fig. 4

HYPERBOLIC FUNCTION, a function that arises in the study of complex variables and has properties similar to those of a TRIGONOMETRIC FUNCTION. The hyperbolic functions are sinh x, cosh x, tanh x, etc. The first two are defined:

$$\sinh x = \frac{e^x - e^{-x}}{2}$$

and

$$\cosh x = \frac{e^x - e^{-x}}{2},$$

in which e is the BASE of the natural logarithms (*see* LOGARITHMS, NATURAL). The others are defined, as are the trigonometric functions, in terms of these two:

$$\tanh x = \frac{\sinh x}{\cosh x}; \qquad \coth x = \frac{\cosh x}{\sinh x};$$

$$\operatorname{sech} x = \frac{1}{\cosh x}; \qquad \operatorname{csch} x = \frac{1}{\sinh x}.$$

Their similarity to the trigonometric functions is shown in the formulas,

$$\cosh^2 x - \sinh^2 x = 1$$

and $$\frac{d}{dx}(\sinh x) = \cosh x.$$

TABLE NO. 223 gives the values of the hyperbolic functions. *See also* HYPERBOLIC RADIAN.

HYPERBOLIC PARABOLOID, *see* PARABOLOID OF REVOLUTION.

HYPERBOLIC RADIAN (hahy-pur-bah'-lic ray'-dee-an), the measure t in the PARAMETRIC EQUATIONS

and $$x = \cosh t$$
$$y = \sinh t.$$

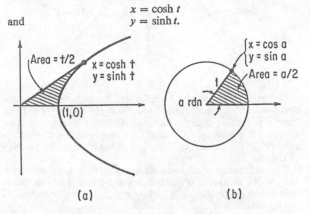

(a)   (b)

Fig. 1

The graph of the equations is a hyperbola as shown in Fig. 1a. The area of the shaded region can be shown to be $t/2$; this is analogous to the fact that the region shaded in the circle in Fig. 1b, has area $a/2$, where a is the RADIAN measure of the central angle. Thus, t may be considered to be a hyperbolic radian.

HYPERBOLIC SPIRAL, the graph, in polar coordinates (*see* COORDINATES, POLAR), of the equation $r\theta = a$, in which a is a positive constant.

Since $y = r \sin \theta$ and $r = {}^a\!/\theta$, $y = \dfrac{a \sin \theta}{\theta}$. When θ is very small, but positive, $\sin \theta/\theta$ is approximately 1, and so y is close to a. As θ increases, r decreases, and the point spirals in toward the ORIGIN. If r and θ are replaced by $-r$ and $-\theta$ respectively, the equation is not made false. The curve, therefore, has two symmetrical (*see* SYMMETRY) branches as shown in the figure.

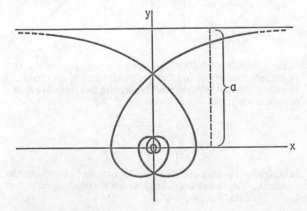

The term "hyperbolic spiral" is used because of the similarity of $r\theta = a$ to $xy = a$, which is the formula for a HYPERBOLA in rectangular coordinates (*see* COORDINATES, RECTANGULAR).

HYPERBOLOID (hahy-pur'-buh-loid), the graph of either of the following equations:

or
$$\frac{x^2}{a^2} + \frac{y^2}{b^2} - \frac{z^2}{c^2} = 1$$
$$\frac{x^2}{a^2} + \frac{y^2}{b^2} - \frac{z^2}{c^2} = -1.$$

The first hyperboloid is the SURFACE OF REVOLUTION generated by revolving the hyperbola $\dfrac{x^2}{a^2} - \dfrac{z^2}{c^2} = 1$ in the xz-plane about the z-axis (see Fig. 1a). The second (see Fig. 1b) is called the *hyperboloid of two sheets.* Sections parallel to the xy-plane are either ELLIPSES or CIRCLES, depending on whether $a = b$ or $a \neq b$, and sections cut by planes which include the z-axis are HYPERBOLAS.

The similar equation $\dfrac{x^2}{a^2} + \dfrac{y^2}{b^2} - \dfrac{z^2}{c^2} = 0$ has a CONE as its graph.

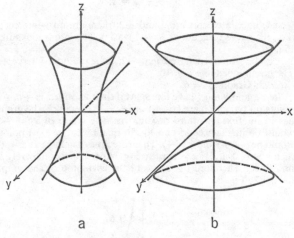

a   b

Fig. 1

HYPERGEOMETRIC DISTRIBUTION, in statistics, the PROBABILITY FUNCTION for a sample of size n drawn (without replacement) from a population of r objects of a first kind and s objects of a second kind. The probability that the sample will contain x objects of the first kind is given by

$$f(x) = \frac{\dbinom{r}{x} \cdot \dbinom{s}{n-x}}{\dbinom{r+s}{n}}.$$

Thus, $f(x)$ is known as the hypergeometric distribution. Its mean is $\dfrac{nr}{r+s}$ and its variance is $\dfrac{nrs(r+s-n)}{(r+s)^2(r+s-1)}$.

Ex.: There are 5 red and 4 blue marbles in a container. If 3 marbles are drawn from the container, without replacement, what is the probability that there will be two red and one blue?

$$P(2 \text{ red and 1 blue}) = \frac{\dbinom{5}{2}\dbinom{4}{1}}{\dbinom{9}{3}} = \frac{10.4}{84}$$

$$= .476 \text{ (approximately)}$$

HYPOCYCLOID (hahy-poh-sahy'-kloid), in a plane, the locus of a point, P, on a circle rolling on the inside of a fixed circle. If a is the radius of the fixed circle, b the radius of the rolling circle, and θ is the angle between the positive x-axis and the line of centers of the fixed circle and the rolling circle (see Fig. 1), the PARAMETRIC EQUATIONS of the hypocycloid are given by

$$x = (a - b) \cos \theta + b \cos \left(\frac{a - b}{b} \right) \theta$$

and

$$y = (a - b) \sin \theta - b \sin \left(\frac{a - b}{b} \right) \theta.$$

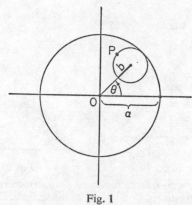

Fig. 1

In particular, if $b = \frac{a}{4}$, $x = a \cos^3 \theta$ and $y = a \sin^3 \theta$, then the hypocycloid is one of four cusps as in Fig. 2. A hypocycloid of four cusps is called an ASTROID. In rectangular coordinates (*see* COORDINATES, RECTANGULAR), the equation of the astroid is $x^{2/3} + y^{2/3} = a^{2/3}$.

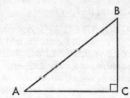

Fig. 2

HYPOTENUSE (hahy-paht'-u-noos), the side opposite the RIGHT ANGLE in a right TRIANGLE. (See figure.) *AB* is the hypotenuse of triangle *ABC*. *See also* PYTHAGOREAN THEOREM.

I

i, the abbreviation for the IMAGINARY NUMBER symbol, $\sqrt{-1}$.

ICOSAHEDRON (ahy-koh-sah-hee′-drun), a POLYHEDRON having twenty faces.

IDEAL POINT, in projective geometry, with the origin and unit point, one of the three reference points of the COORDINATE SYSTEM. The coordinate of the ideal point is the symbol ∞. The ideal point is a point at infinity.

IDEMPOTENT (ahy-dem′-poh-tent), a quantity that remains unchanged when multiplied by itself, one and zero are idempotents since $1 \cdot 1 = 1$ and $0 \cdot 0 = 0$.

IDENTITIES, TRIGONOMETRIC, equations that express relations between trigonometric functions and are true for all values of the variables for which the functions involved are defined. To prove that an equation is an identity, apply basic formulas to change either member of the equation into the exact form of the other, or transform both sides into an identical form. (*See* TABLE 3.)

Ex. 1: $\tan^2 \alpha \sin^2 \alpha = \tan^2 \alpha - \sin^2 \alpha$

$$= \frac{\sin^2 \alpha}{\cos^2 \alpha} - \sin^2 \alpha$$

$$= \frac{\sin^2 \alpha - \sin^2 \alpha \cos^2 \alpha}{\cos^2 \alpha}$$

$$= \frac{\sin^2 \alpha (1 - \cos^2 \alpha)}{\cos^2 \alpha}$$

$$= \frac{\sin^2 \alpha \sin^2 \alpha}{\cos^2 \alpha}$$

$\tan^2 \alpha \sin^2 \alpha = \tan^2 \alpha \sin^2 \alpha$

Ex. 2: $\tan \phi = \dfrac{1 - \cos 2\phi}{\sin 2\phi}$

$$= \frac{1 - (\cos^2 \phi - \sin^2 \phi)}{2 \sin \phi \cos \phi}$$

$$= \frac{1 - (1 - \sin^2 \phi - \sin^2 \phi)}{2 \sin \phi \cos \phi}$$

$$= \frac{2 \sin^2 \phi}{2 \sin \phi \cos \phi}$$

$$= \frac{\sin \phi}{\cos \phi}$$

$\tan \phi = \tan \phi$

Ex. 3: $\csc \beta = \cot \beta + \tan \dfrac{\beta}{2}$

$$= \frac{\cos \beta}{\sin \beta} + \frac{\sin \beta}{1 + \cos \beta}$$

$$= \frac{\cos \beta + \cos^2 \beta + \sin^2 \beta}{\sin \beta (1 + \cos \beta)}$$

$$= \frac{\cos \beta + 1}{\sin \beta (1 + \cos \beta)}$$

$$= \frac{1}{\sin \beta}$$

$\csc \beta = \csc \beta$

IDENTITY (ahy-den′-ti-tee).

1. The reason given in a FORMAL PROOF for a quantity which is equal to itself. In $\triangle ACD$ and BCD (see Fig. 1), $CD = CD$ by identity. In $\triangle ACE$ and BCD (see Fig. 2), $\angle C = \angle C$ by identity.

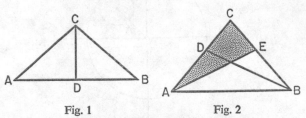

Fig. 1   Fig. 2

2. An EQUATION, as distinguished from a CONDITIONAL EQUATION, that is satisfied by all values of the variable. E.g.,

$$a + 2a = 3a$$

or $\qquad 2(3x + 4) + 2x + 1 = 8x + 9.$

IDENTITY ELEMENT. A member e of a collection S is called an identity element of the collection S relative to a BINARY OPERATION $*$ on S if for any member a in S it is true that $a * e = a$. For example, since for any REAL NUMBER a, it is true that $a + 0 = a$, the real number 0 is the identity element of the collection of real numbers relative to the binary operation of addition. However, since for any real number a it is true that $a \times 1 = a$, the real number 1 is the identity element of the collection of real numbers relative to the binary operation of multiplication. *See also* GROUP.

IFF, abbreviation for "if and only if." *See* BICONDITIONAL, LOGICAL.

IF-THEN STATEMENT, *see* CONDITIONAL STATEMENT.

IMAGE, in mathematics, for a MAPPING of each of the elements, a, of SET A INTO (or ONTO) the elements, b, of set B, each b that corresponds to an a is called the *image* of that a. Thus, for the mapping of $A = \{1, 2, 3, 4\}$ into $T = \{a, b, c\}$ where the correspondences are $1 \rightarrow a$, $2 \rightarrow b$, $3 \rightarrow c$, $4 \rightarrow b$, a is the image of 1, b is the image of 2 and 4, and c is the image of 3.

IMAGINARY NUMBER, a NUMBER of the form ci, where c is a REAL NUMBER and $i^2 = -1$. These are the COMPLEX NUMBERS whose real part is ZERO. The values of their powers are as follows: $i = \sqrt{-1} = i$, $i^2 = (\sqrt{-1})^2 = -1$, $i^3 = i^2 \cdot i = -i$, $i^4 = i^2 \cdot i^2 = 1$, $i^5 = i^2 \cdot i^3 = i$. The values repeat every four terms.

Methods for operating with imaginary numbers follow from those for operating with complex numbers, of which they are the nonreal components.

IMPLICATION, a proposition that is stated in the *if–then* form. In the ALGEBRA OF PROPOSITIONS, the implication "if p, then q" is written $p \rightarrow q$, read "p implies q." $p \rightarrow q$ is equivalent to "p is a sufficient condition for q" and "q is a necessary condition for p."

IMPLICIT DIFFERENTIATION, given an IMPLICIT RELATION between two variables, x and y, the derivative dy/dx can be found by treating each occurrence of y as its implied function of x as the entire equation is differentiated. The resulting formula for dy/dx is then found.

Ex. 1: Differentiate implicitly to find dy/dx in the equation $x^2 + y^2 = 1$.
Sol.: $2x + 2y \, dy/dx = 0$; $dy/dx = -2x/2y = -x/y$.
Ex. 2: Find dy/dx in $xy = 1$.
Sol.: $x \, dy/dx + y = 0$; $dy/dx = -y/x$.
Ex. 3: Find dx/dy in $x^2 + 2y = 1$.
Sol.: $2x \, dx/dy + 2 = 0$; $dx/dy = -1/x$.

IMPLICIT FUNCTION, *see* IMPLICIT RELATION.

IMPLICIT RELATION. In an equation such as $x^2 + y^2 = 1$ the possible values of each VARIABLE depend upon those assigned to the other, even though neither is stated explicitly as a function of the other; e.g., in $x^2 + y^2 = 1$, $y^2 = 1 - x^2$, and, explicitly, $y = \sqrt{1 - x^2}$. In such a case, the equation is said to express an implicit relation between the variables. In most mathematical literature until quite recently, however, such an equation was said to relate the variables as "implicit functions" of each other; they must be so treated in such basic operations as IMPLICIT DIF-FERENTIATION.

IMPROPER FRACTION, a FRACTION that has a NUMERATOR greater than the DENOMINATOR and, therefore, has a value greater than one; e.g., 9/8, 6/5, and 8/3.

IMPROPER INTEGRAL, a DEFINITE INTEGRAL $\int_a^b f(x)dx$ if either a or b is INFINITE, or if the function $f(x)$ is an UNBOUNDED FUNCTION on the CLOSED INTERVAL $[a, b]$. The definition of the definite integral is modified in the following cases.

$$\int_a^\infty f(x)dx = \lim_{u \to \infty} \int_a^u f(x)\,dx.$$

$\int_{-\infty}^b f(x)dx$ is defined analogously. Also, if $\lim\limits_{a \to b} f(x) = \infty$ or $-\infty$ then we define

$$\int_a^b f(x)\,dx = \lim_{r \to b} \int_b^r f(x)dx.$$

Ex.: Find a, $\int_1^\infty \dfrac{1}{x^2}\,dx$,   b, $\int_0^1 \dfrac{1}{x}\,dx$.

Sol.:

a. $\int_1^\infty \dfrac{1}{x^2}\,dx = \lim\limits_{u \to \infty} \int_1^u \dfrac{1}{x^2}\,dx = \lim\limits_{u \to \infty} \left[\dfrac{-1}{u} - \left(\dfrac{-1}{1} \right) \right] = 1.$

b. $\int_0^1 \dfrac{1}{x}\,dx = \lim\limits_{a \to 0} \int_a^1 \dfrac{1}{x}\,dx = \lim\limits_{a \to 0} [\ln 1 - \ln a] = -\infty;$ this integral diverges.

INCENTER, the point of concurrency of the BISECTORS of the ANGLES of a TRIANGLE. The incenter of a triangle is the center of the circle inscribed in the triangle. (See figure.) *See also* CONCUR-RENT LINES.

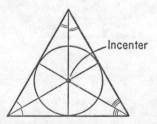
Incenter

INCLINATION OF A LINE, ANGLE OF INCLINATION of a line.

INCOMPLETE QUADRATIC EQUATION, a second degree equation (*see* DEGREE OF AN EQUATION) that does not contain the first power of the unknown letter, as $x^2 - 25 = 0$. *See also* POWER OF A NUMBER; QUADRATIC EQUATION.

INCONSISTENT EQUATIONS, a SYSTEM OF EQUATIONS that has no solution in common. Thus $x + y = 10$ and $x + y = 5$ are a pair of inconsistent equations. Their GRAPHS are parallel.

INDEFINITE INTEGRAL, for a function $f(x)$, another function $F(x)$ such that $F'(x) = f(x)$. Other terms for an indefinite integral are *antiderivative* and *primitive function*. The mathematical symbol for the expression "$F(x)$ is an indefinite integral of $f(x)$" is $F(x) = \int f(x)\,dx$.

If $F(x)$ is an indefinite integral of $f(x)$, then $F(x) + c$ is another indefinite integral. Hence, an arbitrary "$+c$" is usually added to indefinite integrals.

The process by which indefinite integrals are found is called INTEGRATION. *See also* DEFINITE INTEGRAL; FUNDAMENTAL THEO-REM OF CALCULUS; TABLE NO. 14.

INDEPENDENT EQUATIONS, a SYSTEM OF EQUATIONS that has only one solution in common. E.g., $x + y = 8$ and $x - y = 2$ are a pair of independent equations. The COORDINATES of the point of intersection of their GRAPHS are the values that satisfy both equations.

INDEPENDENT VARIABLE, *see* VARIABLE.

INDETERMINATE FORM, any one of the expressions: $0/0$, ∞/∞, $\infty \cdot 0$, $\infty - \infty$, 0^0, 1^∞, ∞^0. None of these can be assigned a definite meaning. However, functions which assume these forms for particular values of the independent VARIABLE may ac-tually approach a definite value as the independent variable ap-proaches a crucial argument; e.g., it may be proven that $\lim\limits_{\theta \to 0} \dfrac{\theta}{\sin \theta} = 1$. *See* ZERO; L'HÔPITAL'S RULE.

INDEX, in mathematics, the small number above a radical sign to indicate the root to be found. In $\sqrt[3]{27}$, 3 is the index and indi-cates that the CUBE ROOT is to be found. In $\sqrt{16}$, 2 is the index, but it is usually omitted in SQUARE ROOT.

Also, an index is a subscript or superscript, such as i and j in the expressions a_i and x^j, which serves to distinguish objects.

INDEX NUMBER, in statistics, a number that represents any percentage change in value or quantity relative to a base period. The base period is usually given the figure 100. E.g., in the con-sumer price index table, price indices are given on three major items in the U.S. economy for a seven-year period (1965–1971). The base period, 1967 was given the figure 100. Any change above or below 100 is expressed in percentages. These percent-ages are the index numbers. Thus, for *rent* the index number in 1961 was 102 and in 1970 it was 122.5, relative to the period 1957–1959. Thus rent is shown to have increased 20.5% over the period 1957–1959.

INDIRECT PROOF, a method for proving a statement when the known facts are insufficient to arrive at the CONCLUSION di-rectly. It is the method generally used in everyday reasoning when all but one of several possible conclusions are eliminated. In geometry, two variations of indirect proof are (1) by exclu-sion, and, (2) by coincidence.

There are three steps in an indirect proof by exclusion: (1) as-sume the possible conclusions other than the one desired; (2) show that each of these assumptions leads to a statement that contradicts a known fact or hypothesis; (3) then the desired con-clusion is true. This method is called *reductio ad absurdum*.

Ex. 1: If two angles of a triangle are unequal, the sides opposite these angles are unequal, the side opposite the greater angle being the greater side.

(See Fig. 1.) Given $\triangle ABC$ with $\angle A > \angle B$, prove $BC > AC$. Proof: (1) Assume $BC = AC$ or $BC < AC$. [Two quantities of the same kind are either equal or unequal; if unequal the first is either more than the second or less than the second.] (2) If $BC =$

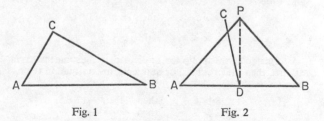

Fig. 1   Fig. 2

AC, then $\angle A = \angle B$. [If two sides of a triangle are equal, the angles opposite these sides are equal.] (3) If $BC < AC$, then $\angle A < \angle B$. [If one side of a triangle is less than a second side, the angle opposite the first side is less than the angle opposite the second side.] (4) But $\angle A > \angle B$. [Hypothesis] (5) Steps 2 and 3 are false. [They contradict the hypothesis.] (6) Therefore, $BC > AC$. [If the contradictory of a statement leads to a contradiction of a known fact, the statement is true.] An indirect proof by coincidence consists of drawing an auxiliary line and proving that it coincides with the given line.

Ex. 2: Any point equidistant from the end points of a line segment lies on the perpendicular bisector of the segment. (See Fig. 2.) Given *CD* is a perpendicular bisector of *AB*, *P* is a point equidistant from *A* and *B*, *AP = PB*, prove *P* lies on *CD*. *Proof:* (1) Draw *PD* from *P* to midpoint *D*. [A segment has only one midpoint and only one straight line may be drawn between two points.] (2) *AD = BD*. [The midpoint divides a segment into two equal parts.] (3) *AP = PB*. [Hypothesis.] (4) *PD = PD*. [Identity.] (5) $\triangle PDA \cong \triangle PDB$. [S.S.S.] (6) $\angle PDA = \angle PDB$. [Corresponding parts of congruent triangles are equal.] (7) Therefore, $PD \perp AB$. [If two lines form equal adjacent angles, the lines are perpendicular.] (8) But $CD \perp AB$. [Hypothesis.] (9) *PD* coincides with *CD;* therefore, *P* lies on *CD*. [There can be only one perpendicular to a point on a line.]

INDUCTIVE REASONING, reasoning in which generalizations are made from many specific cases. Conclusions arrived at inductively are never completely certain because observation and measurement are not absolutely accurate and because all possible cases may not have been studied. Anticipations of mathematical principles may be inductive as when, through many observations of ISOSCELES TRIANGLES, it is hypothesized that the BASE ANGLES of an isosceles triangle are equal. A FORMAL PROOF of this HYPOTHESIS must be deductive, however. *See also* DEDUCTIVE REASONING.

INEQUALITY, a statement that one quantity is larger or smaller than another. The statement that quantity *A* is less than quantity *B* is called a *strict inequality*, and is written $A < B$. The statement that *A* is either less than or equal to *B*, is called a *weak inequality* and is written $A \leq B$. These statements may also be written in reverse order as $B > A$, and $B \geq A$.

The following five axioms are used to solve an inequality.

1. If the same number is added to unequals, the sums are unequal in the same order.

If $a > b$,   then $a + c > b + c$.
If $a < b$,   then $a + c < b + c$.

2. If the same number is subtracted from unequals, the differences are unequal in the same order.

If $a > b$,   then $a - c > b - c$.

3. If unequals are subtracted from equals, the differences are unequal in the reverse order.

If $10 = 10$
and $7 > 3$
then $3 < 7$.

4. If unequals are multiplied, or divided, by the same POSITIVE NUMBER, then the PRODUCTS, or QUOTIENTS, are unequal in the same order.

If $x > y$,   then $3x > 3y$.

If $x < y$,   then $\frac{x}{2} < \frac{y}{2}$.

5. If unequals are multiplied, or divided, by the same NEGATIVE NUMBER, then the products, or quotients, are unequal in the reverse order.

If $8 > 6$,   then $-16 < -12$.
If $12 > 9$,   then $-4 < -3$.

A region in the plane may be defined by stating inequalities as conditions for membership in the region. E.g., the graph of all points whose *x*-coordinate is larger than 2 but less than 3 (written $\{x: 2 < x < 3\}$ is an infinite vertical strip. (See Fig. 1.)

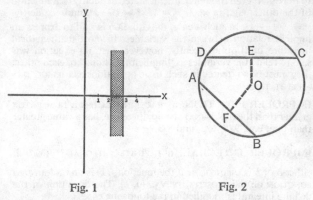

Fig. 1   Fig. 2

Inequalities of the type $Ax' + By' + C > 0$, or $Ax' + By' + C < 0$ are called *first degree inequalities*. If *L* is the line given by $Ax + By + C = 0$, where $B \neq 0$, any point (x',y') which is in the half-plane above *L* satisfies the first inequality, and any point (x',y') which is below the line satisfies the second.

Ex.: Are the following points above or below the line $5x - 3y + 2 = 0$? a. (2,3); b. (1,5); c. (−3,−4).

Sol.: a. $Ax' + By' + C = (5)(2) + (-3)(3) + 2 = +1 > 0$; the point is above the line. b. Below. c. Below.

The following are inequalities in a CIRCLE:

1. In a circle, or in EQUAL CIRCLES, the greater of two unequal central angles (*see* CENTRAL ANGLE OF A CIRCLE) has the greater ARC, and conversely.

2. In a circle, or in equal circles, the greater of two unequal CHORDS has the greater arc, and conversely.

3. In a circle, or in equal circles, the greater of two unequal chords is nearer the center.

In Fig. 2, if $DC > AB$, then $\overarc{DC} > \overarc{AB}$ and $OE < OF$.

The following are inequalities in triangles:

1. The sum of any two sides of a triangle is greater than the third side. In Fig. 3, $AC + BC > AB$.

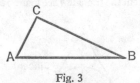

Fig. 3

Therefore, it is impossible to construct a triangle of sides 3, 5, and 8.

2. Any side of a triangle is greater than the difference of the other two sides. In Fig. 3, if $AB > BC$, then $AC > AB - BC$.

3. If one side of a triangle is greater than a second side the angle opposite the first side is greater than the angle opposite the second side. In Fig. 3, if $AB > BC$, then $\angle C > \angle A$.

4. If one angle of a triangle is greater than a second angle, then the side opposite the first angle is greater than the side opposite the second angle. In Fig. 3, if $\angle A > \angle B$, then $BC > AC$.

5. The hypotenuse of a right triangle is greater than either leg. In Fig. 4, $BC > AB$ and $BC > AC$.

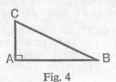

Fig. 4

6. An exterior angle of a triangle is greater than either non-adjacent interior angle. In Fig. 5, $\angle x > \angle A$ and $\angle x > C$.

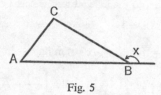

Fig. 5

INFINITE SERIES, a SEQUENCE with an unlimited number of terms. It is obvious there can be no sum of an infinite number of terms. We can, however, find the limit of the sum as the number of terms becomes infinite. In the series

$$1 + \tfrac{1}{2} + \tfrac{1}{4} + \tfrac{1}{8} + \tfrac{1}{16} + \cdots$$

the fraction becomes smaller and smaller. The sum of two terms is $1\tfrac{1}{2}$; of three terms, $1\tfrac{3}{4}$; of four terms, $1\tfrac{7}{8}$; of 5 terms, $1\tfrac{15}{16}$. It is clear the sum approaches 2 as a limit, but it never quite equals 2. The FORMULA for the sum of an infinite series, where $a = $ 1st term and $r = $ ratio, is

$$S = \frac{a}{1 - r}$$

Ex.: Find the sum of the infinite series

$$1 + \tfrac{1}{3} + \tfrac{1}{9} + \tfrac{1}{27} + \tfrac{1}{81} + \cdots$$
$$a = 1, \quad r = \tfrac{1}{3}$$
$$S = \frac{1}{1 - \tfrac{1}{3}}$$
$$S = \tfrac{3}{2}$$

The sum approaches the limit $1\tfrac{1}{2}$.

Not all series have sums; i.e., not all sequences of partial sums approach limits (see Ex. 1). An example of a series whose sum does exist is given in Ex. 2. When the sum does exist, we say the series converges; otherwise, that it diverges.

Ex. 1: The series $n = 1 + 2 + 3 + \cdots$ does not converge. The first few partial sums are 1, 3, 6, 10, . . . ; this sequence does not approach any limit.

Ex. 2: The series $\sum_{n=1}^{\infty} \tfrac{1}{2}n = \tfrac{1}{2} + \tfrac{1}{4} + \tfrac{1}{8} + \cdots$ does converge.

Its sum is 1. The first few partial sums of this series are $\tfrac{1}{2}, \tfrac{3}{4}, \tfrac{7}{8},$ $\tfrac{15}{16}, \ldots$; this sequence approaches 1 as limit.

See also CONVERGENT SEQUENCE; CONVERGENT SERIES; LIMIT OF A SEQUENCE.

INFINITY, a VARIABLE that becomes and remains larger (positively infinite) than any preassigned positive number, no matter how large; or becomes and remains less (negatively infinite) than any preassigned number. The symbol ∞ is used to indicate infinity.

INFLECTION POINT, a point at which the direction of curvature of a curve changes. (See figure.)

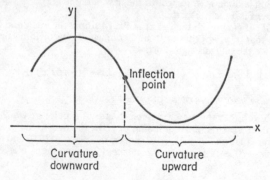

If a curve is the graph of a function, its inflection points may be located by using the derivatives of the function (*see* DERIVATIVE OF A FUNCTION). The second derivative at a point of inflection is always zero (*see* SECOND DERIVATIVE TEST). However, even when $f''(a) = 0$, there may not be an inflection point at a (see Ex. 2). The crucial factor is that the sign of the second derivative must change from positive or negative or vice versa, passing through zero at the inflection point. This is because the sign of the second derivative reflects the direction of curvature of the graph. $f''(x) > 0$ indicates curvature upward, while $f''(x) < 0$ indicates curvature downward.

Ex. 1: Locate the inflection points of the curve

$$y = x^3 - 3x^2 + 2x.$$

Sol.: $f''(x) = 6x - 6$; $6x - 6 = 0$ when $x = 1$. If $x < 1$, $f''(x) < 0$, while if $x > 1, f''(x) > 0$. Thus $f''(x)$ changes sign at $x = 1$, and $f(x)$ has an inflection point at $x = 1$.

Ex. 2: Let $y = x^4$. Calculate $f''(0)$. Does $f(x)$ have an inflection point at $x = 0$?

Sol.: $f''(x) = \dfrac{d}{dx} 4x^3 = 12x^2$; $f''(0) = 12(0)^2 = 0$. To decide whether $f''(x)$ changes signs, notice that $12x^2$ is positive for all x. Thus $f''(x)$ cannot change signs, and $y = x^4$ does not have a point of inflection at $x = 0$. Nevertheless, $f''(0) = 0$.

INITIAL RAY, *see* COORDINATES, POLAR.

INITIAL SIDE, *see* SIDE OF AN ANGLE.

INJECTION, in mathematics, from set A to set B, a one-to-one FUNCTION whose DOMAIN is A, and whose RANGE is contained in B.

INSCRIBED ANGLE, an ANGLE whose sides are CHORDS of the CIRCLE and whose vertex is on the circle. In Fig. 1, $\angle ABC$ is an inscribed angle.

An inscribed angle is equal in degrees to one-half of its intercepted ARC. In Fig. 2, $\angle B \triangleq \tfrac{1}{2}\overset{\frown}{AC}$.

Inscribed angles which intercept the same arc are equal. In Fig. 3, $\angle A = \angle B$ because they intercept $\overset{\frown}{CD}$.

An angle inscribed in a semicircle is a RIGHT ANGLE. In Fig. 2, $\overline{AB}$ is a diameter of circle O. Therefore, $\angle C$ is a right angle, because $\angle C$ intercepts a semicircle (180°), and an inscribed angle is equal in degrees to one half of its intercepted arc.

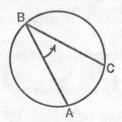

Fig. 1

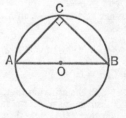

Fig. 2

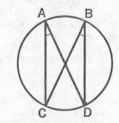

Fig. 3

INSCRIBED CIRCLE, a CIRCLE constructed inside a POLYGON such that the sides of the polygon are TANGENT LINES of the circle. A circle can be inscribed in any REGULAR POLYGON. (See figures.)

Circle O is inscribed in:

an EQUILATERAL TRIANGLE   a SQUARE   a regular HEXAGON

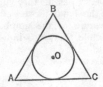

INTEGER (in'-tih-jur), any of the numbers . . . -2, -1, 0, $1, 2$, . . . , sometimes referred to as "whole numbers," or "counting numbers." However, they are not the same as the NATURAL NUMBERS which do not include NEGATIVE NUMBERS.

INTEGER PROBLEMS.

Ex. 1: Four times a certain number increased by 12 equals 48 decreased by twice the number. What is the number?

Sol.: x = the number.
$$4x + 12 = 48 - 2x$$
$$6x = 36$$
$$x = 6.$$

Check: $4(6) + 12 = 48 - 2(6)$
$$36 = 36.$$

Ex. 2: The sum of two numbers is 122 and one of the numbers is 46 more than the other. Find the numbers.

Sol.: Let x = the smaller number
and $x + 46$ = the larger number.
$$x + x + 46 = 122$$
$$2x + 46 = 122$$
$$2x = 76$$
$$x = 38, \text{ the smaller number.}$$
$$x + 46 = 84, \text{ the larger number.}$$

Check: $38 + 84 = 122.$

INTEGRAL, *see* ANTIDERIVATIVE OF A FUNCTION; DEFINITE INTEGRAL.

INTEGRAL DOMAIN, an algebraic system $\{S, +, \cdot\}$ made up of a SET S, and two operations on S "$+$" (plus), and "$\cdot$" (times), with the following properties:

1. Both operations are associative (*see* ASSOCIATIVE PROPERTY). I.e., for a, b, c in S,
$$a + (b + c) = (a + b) + c \text{ and } a \cdot (b \cdot c) = (a \cdot b) \cdot c.$$

2. Both operations are commutative (*see* COMMUTATIVE PROPERTY). I.e., for a, b in S,
$$a + b = b + a \text{ and } a \cdot b = b \cdot a.$$

3. The operation "$\cdot$" is distributive relative to "$+$". I.e., for a, b, c in S,
$$a \cdot (b + c) = a \cdot b + a \cdot c \text{ and } (b + c) \cdot a = b \cdot a + c \cdot a.$$

4. There exists an IDENTITY ELEMENT, 0, in S relative to "$+$", and an identity element, 1, in S relative to "$\cdot$". I.e.,
$$a + 0 = 0 + a = a \text{ and } a \cdot 1 = 1 \cdot a = a.$$

5. Each element, a in S has an INVERSE ELEMENT, $-a$, in S, relative to "$+$". I.e.,
$$a + (-a) = (-a) + a = 0.$$

6. The cancellation law holds relative to "$\cdot$". I.e., for a, b, c in S,
$$\text{if } a \cdot c = b \cdot c \text{ and } c \neq 0, a = b.$$

INTEGRAL TEST FOR CONVERGENCE, the criterion that, if Σa_n is a SERIES of positive terms which decrease as n increases, and if $f(x)$ is a decreasing function such that $f(n) = a_n$, then both the series and the IMPROPER INTEGRAL $\int_1^\infty f(x)dx$ converge, or both diverge.

Ex.: Prove that $\Sigma \frac{1}{n}$ diverges, while $\Sigma \frac{1}{n^2}$ converges.

Sol.: According to the integral test, we need only show that $\int_1^\infty \frac{1}{x} dx = \infty$, while $\int_1^\infty \frac{1}{x^2} dx = n < \infty.$

$$\int_1^\infty \frac{1}{x} dx = \lim_{a\to\infty} \int_1^a \frac{1}{x} dx = \lim_{a\to\infty}[\ln a - \ln 1] = \infty;$$

$$\int_1^\infty \frac{1}{x^2} dx = \lim_{a\to\infty}\int_1^a \frac{1}{x^2} dx = \lim_{a\to\infty}\left[\frac{-1}{a} - \frac{-1}{1}\right] = 1.$$

See also COMPARISON TEST; RATIO TEST.

INTEGRATION, in mathematics the process of finding the definite or INDEFINITE INTEGRAL in CALCULUS. The DEFINITE INTEGRAL is the limit of the areas of rectangles bound by a curve. If a function, f, is a non-negative and CONTINUOUS FUNCTION over the CLOSED INTERVAL $[a, b]$, the area under its graph is

$$A_a{}^b = \lim \Sigma f(c_k)\Delta x.$$

The indefinite integral is the function whose derivative is given. For example, given the DERIVATIVE OF A FUNCTION, $dy/dx = 2x$, the function, F, of x might be $F(x) = y = x^2$, $F(x) = y = x^2 + 2$, $F(x) = y = x^2 - 2$ or, in general, $F(x) = y = x^2 +$ constant c, or $F(x) = y = x^2 + c$.

The FUNDAMENTAL THEOREM OF CALCULUS relates the definite and indefinite integrals by proving that the limit of the AREA UNDER A CURVE can be evaluated by integration. Thus,

$$A_a{}^b = \lim \Sigma f(c_k)\Delta x = \int f(x)dx]_a{}^b$$
$$= F(x)_a{}^b$$
$$= F(b) - F(a).$$

See also AREA UNDER A CURVE, CALCULATION OF; TABLE NO. 14.

INTEGRATION BY PARTS. If u and v are both functions of x, then

$$\int uv'dx = uv - \int u'v \, dx$$

This follows from differentiating the formula for the derivative of a product of two functions.

Ex.: Find $\int x \sin x \, dx.$

Sol.: Let $x = u$, $\sin x = v'$. Then $v = -\cos x$ and
$$\int x \sin x \, dx = -x \cos x - \int -\cos x \, dx = \sin x - x \cos x + c.$$

See also ANTIDERIVATIVE OF A FUNCTION; DERIVATIVE OF A FUNCTION; TABLE NO. 14.

INTEGRATION BY SUBSTITUTION. Differentiating the chain rule for the derivative of a composite function shows that

$$\int f(g(x)) \cdot g'(x) \, dx = F(g(x)) + c,$$

where F is an ANTIDERIVATIVE OF A FUNCTION, f. In effect, integration is done with respect to the new variable $g(x)$.

Ex.: Find $\int \sin x^2 \, x \, dx.$

Sol.: If $g(x) = x^2$, then $g'(x) = 2x$. Multiply the integrand by 2 so that $g'(x)$ appears in it, and compensate by dividing by 2 outside the integral sign. Then

$$\int \sin x^2 \, x \, dx = \tfrac{1}{2} \int \sin x^2 \cdot 2x \, dx = \tfrac{1}{2}(-\cos x^2) + c.$$

See also DERIVATIVE OF A FUNCTION; TABLE NO. 14.

INTERCEPT, the x, y, or z-coordinate of a point at which a graph crosses the corresponding axis. In the figure, the graph of the equation $2x - 3y = 12$ crosses the x-axis at $(6,0)$ and the y-axis at $(0, -4)$. Hence, the x-intercept is 6, and the y-intercept is -4.

Ex.: Find the *y*-intercept of a. $y = 2x + 1$. b. $y = 2x^3 - 4$.
Sol.: Let $x = 0$ and solve for *y* in each case:

a. $y = (2)(0) + 1 = 1 = y$-intercept.
b. $y = 2(0^3) - 4 = -4 = y$-intercept.

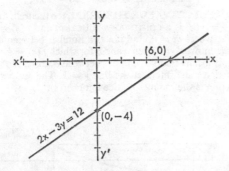

See also LINE, EQUATION OF.

INTERDECILE RANGE, in statistics, a measure of dispersion (*see* DISPERSION, MEASURES OF) that is equal to the ninth DECILE minus the first decile.

INTEREST, in finance, the price paid for the use of money over a period of time. Interest is usually expressed in terms of a percentage of the money involved, i.e., the *interest rate.* There are four main components of interest when considering the economic cost of borrowing money.

1. *Financial risk,* the percentage charged to offset the possibility that the debtor will repudiate all or part of his obligation to pay. The risks of debtor non-repayment differ, and this accounts for most of the difference between interest rates charged at the same moment of time to different borrowers.

2. *Purchasing power risk,* the percentage charged to offset the possibility that the money with which the obligation is repaid will not have the same purchasing power as the money which was lent. This component can add greatly to the coast of borrowing in inflationary conditions. It is a major cause of the high cost of capital in countries with chronic inflations.

3. *Interest rate risk,* the percentage charged to offset the possibility that a change in interest rates will change the market value of the obligation. If, e.g., a $100.00 annuity bond is sold with a 4% interest rate and interest rates for similar bonds later issued rise to 5%, the market value of the original $100.00 bond would fall to $80.00 since, earning $4.00 a year, it would be equivalent to an $80.00 bond earning 5%.

4. *Pure interest,* the percentage charged for the right to use the money. This component is what is meant by interest in economic theory. It is approximated by short-term government obligations in which the financial risk is zero and time too short for the purchasing power and interest rate risks to be very important.

Rate and kinds of interest.

The *nominal rate of interest* is the stated or official rate of interest on a security. A $100.00 bond e.g., might pay $5.00 a year interest and thus have a nominal rate of interest of 5%. But if it sold for $50.00, the $5.00 a year interest would give it, other factors aside, a 10% *real rate of interest.* The latter is the rate paid on a security based on its market price.

A *Negative rate of interest* is one which deducts from, rather than adds to the principal. In practice this can arise where a bank imposes a service charge for handling demand deposits or where money depreciates at a higher rate than it earns as interest, e.g., if money declines in value 8% a year and brings only 6% interest, there is a negative rate of interest of 2%.

Prime rate of interest is the interest rate charged business borrowers with an established credit rating.

Legal Interest is the rate charged and enforced by the courts, when the terms of a loan do not set specific interest. It is set in the U.S. by state law. It should not be confused with the maximum rate of interest allowable under state law.

A *simple interest* is one on the principal sum only, i.e., none on any accumulated interest.

Compound interest is one paid on both original capital and on the accumulated past interest. Compound interest permits capital to grow at a faster rate than would otherwise be possible, e.g., it takes a sum of money 20 years to double at 5% at simple interest (*see* above) but only about 14 years to double at compound interest.

Theories of interest.

1. **Loanable funds theory,** an explanation of the determination of the interest rate first developed by John Maynard Keynes and the Neoclassical economists. Interest is viewed as the price paid 1) for the use of borrowed (loanable) funds, and 2) in order to induce people to reduce their cash balance. The equilibrium interest rate is determined by the demand for and supply of loanable funds in the credit market. The over-all demand for loanable funds arises from demand by consumers, business, and govt. for investment purposes and for hoarding, the liquidity preference of the community. The over-all supply of loanable funds comes from saving and from new money created by the banking system.

2. **Marginal utility theory of interest,** an explanation of the rate of interest as equating the marginal utility derived from the last marginal unit of consumption with the marginal utility derived from the last marginal unit of investment. A 5% interest rate, e.g., would mean that savers' present consumption is worth 105% of equal future consumption to them, i.e., they are indifferent as to whether they save or spend their last unallocated dollar when it commands a 5% interest rate. A 6% interest rate would induce them to save more and a 4% interest rate would induce them to save less. Theory is basically similar to 3. below.

3. **Abstinence theory of interest,** an explanation of the rate of interest as a premium paid to savers to induce them to save. This premium is considered necessary because of the tendency to prefer present enjoyment to future enjoyment. It is paid by borrowers because of their expectations of profit from investing the savings or because of present necessity.

4. **Classical theory of interest,** an explanation of the determination of the interest rate. It held that the interest rate was determined by the supply of and demand for real capital (or real savings). Underlying the supply of real savings were such factors as the thrift habits of the people and their time preference for current over future consumption. Underlying the demand for real capital was the diminishing marginal productivity of capital. The theory did not admit to the role of monetary forces affecting the interest rate. It was based on assumptions of the existence of long-run full employment and a purely competitive economy. Sometimes called the "time preference" theory of the interest rate.

Biblio.: Conrad, J. W., *Introduction to the Theory of Interest* (1959); Keynes, J. M., *General Theory of Employment, Interest and Money* (1936); Lutz, F. A., *Theory of Interest* (1968).

INTEREST, in mathematics, money paid for the use of money. The money borrowed is called the principal. The amount of interest, or the PERCENTAGE, is determined by the length of time for which the money is borrowed, and a rate of interest, or PERCENT. The sum of the principal plus the interest for a specific time is called the *amount.*

Simple interest is paid only on the principal, and the annual interest is found by multiplying the principal by the rate. The time for which the money is borrowed is expressed in years, or a fraction of a year. Thus, Interest = Principal × Rate × Time in years or $i = Prt$. Amount = Principal + Interest. *See* TABLE NO. 15.

Ex. 1: Find the simple interest and the amount, if $1500 is borrowed for a period of 2 years at 4% interest.

Sol.: Principal = $1500; Annual rate = 4% or .04 or 4/100; Time = 2 years.

$1500 Principal
×.04 Rate
$60 Interest for 1 year, or
$120 Interest for 2 years.

$1500 Principal
+$ 120 Interest
$1620 Amount.

or $1500 × $\frac{1}{100}$ × 2 = $120, interest for 2 years.
$1500 + $120 = $1620, Amount.

Compound interest is paid on the sum of the principal and the accumulated interest. It is usually compounded twice a year.

Ex. 2: A man deposits $500 in a savings account. The bank pays 3% interest compounded semi-annually. How much money does he have at the end of the year?

Sol.:

$500 Principal
×.03 Rate
$15.00 Interest for 1 yr.
$\frac{1}{2}$ × $15.00 = $7.50 Interest for 6 mos.
$500 + $7.50 = $507.50 Amount at end of 6 mos.
$507.50 New principal
×.03
$15.2250 or $15.23 Interest for 1 yr.
$\frac{1}{2}$ × 15.23 = $7.62 Interest for 2nd 6-month period.
$507.50
+7.62
$515.12 Amount on deposit at end of the year.

The amount, A, of compound interest may be found by the formula $A = P(1 + r)^n$, where n = the number of years.

Ex. 3: Find the amount of $1,000 at 2% compounded annually for three years.

Sol.: From the formula,

$$A = 1000(1 + .02)^3$$

Expanding the binomial,

$$A = 1000[(1)^3 + 3(1)^2(.02) + 3(1)(.02)^2 + (.02)^3]$$
$$A = 1000(1 + .06 + .0012 + .000008)$$
$$A = 1000(1.061208)$$
$$A = 1061.208000 \text{ or } \$1,061.21.$$

Banks use a compound interest table, from which the interest can be quickly determined. *See also* BINOMIAL THEOREM; TABLE NO. 16.

INTERIOR ANGLES OF A POLYGON, the angles formed by two sides of a POLYGON. The sum of the interior angles of a polygon equals $(n - 2)$ STRAIGHT ANGLES. The formula is $S = (n - 2)180°$, in which n is the number of sides of the polygon.

Ex. 1: Find the sum of the interior angles of a polygon of 9 sides.

Substituting 9 for n in the formula, $S = 7(180)$ or $1260°$.

Ex. 2: Find the number of sides of a polygon if the sum of its angles is 2340°.

$$2340 = (n - 2)180$$
$$2340 = 180n - 360$$
$$180n = 2700$$
$$n = 15 \text{ sides.}$$

If a polygon of n sides is a REGULAR POLYGON (equilateral and equiangular) each interior angle equals $\frac{(n - 2)180°}{n}$.

Ex. 3: Find the number of degrees in each interior angle of a regular polygon of 12 sides.

$$\text{Each int. } \angle = \frac{(12 - 2)180}{12} = \frac{1800}{12} = 150°.$$

Since each interior angle is the supplement of its adjacent exterior angle, it is sometimes simpler to find the exterior angle first.

$$\text{Each ext. } \angle = \frac{360}{n} = \frac{360}{12} = 30°.$$
$$\text{Each int. } \angle = 180 - 30 = 150°.$$

INTERMEDIATE VALUE THEOREM, the theorem that states that if $y = f(x)$ is a CONTINUOUS FUNCTION and $f(a) = m$, and $f(b) = n$, where $m \neq n$, and if k is a number between m and n, there is a number c between a and b for which $f(c) = k$. Graphically, this means that somewhere between a and b the graph of the function must intersect the line $y = k$. The ABSCISSA of the intersection is the number c. (See figure.)

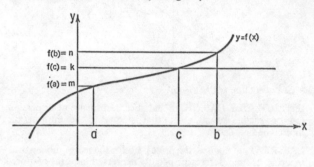

To prove the intermediate value theorem let c equal the LEAST UPPER BOUND of this set. Then using INDIRECT PROOF, show that $f(c)$ cannot be larger than k and that it cannot be smaller than k. Thus, we can conclude that $f(c) = k$.

INTERNAL DIVISION, the division of a LINE SEGMENT by a POINT on the line.

Point P divides AB internally into two segments AP and PB. $AP/PB = 3/4$. *See also* HARMONIC DIVISION.

INTERPOLATION (in-tur-poh-lay'-shun), in mathematics, the process by which LOGARITHMS or values of TRIGONOMETRIC FUNCTIONS may be found when they do not appear in the table.

When using 5-place logarithm tables (*see* TABLE NO. 19) the logarithm of a 4 digit number may be read directly from the table. The logarithm of a 5 digit number may be found by interpolating.

Ex. 1: Find the logarithm of 18327.

Sol.: The log of 18327 lies between the log of 1832 and 1833. Forming a proportion from the ratio of the differences between 18330 and 18320 and 18327 and 18320 and the ratio of the corresponding differences between their mantissas will give the difference between mantissa of 18327 and that of 18320. A tabular arrangement is used, and x represents the difference between the mantissas of 18327 and 18320.

Number	Mantissa
18330	26316
18327	26293 + x
18320	26293

$$7/10 = x/23$$
$$10x = 161$$
$$x = 16.1, \text{ or approximately 16.}$$

The required mantissa is .26293 + x, or .26293 + 16 = .26309. The logarithm of 18327 is 4.26309.

Similarly, when the mantissa of a logarithm is not in the table, the ANTILOGARITHM may be found by interpolating.

Ex. 2: Find the number whose logarithm is .83062.

Sol.: .83062 is not found in the table, but it is between the mantissas .83059 and .83065 which are in the table. Using a tabular arrangement, find the differences between the mantissas and the corresponding numbers and solve the proportion. x represents the difference between 6770 and the required number.

Number	Mantissa

$$10\left[\,_{x}\!\left[\begin{matrix} 67710 \\ 67700 + x \\ 67700 \end{matrix}\right.\right.\quad\left.\left.\begin{matrix} 83065 \\ 83062 \\ 83059 \end{matrix}\right]3\,\right]6$$

$$x/10 = 3/6$$
$$6x = 30$$
$$x = 5.$$

The required number is $67700 + x$, or $67700 + 5$ or 67705. Since the characteristic is 0, the decimal is placed between the first two digits. 6.7705 is the required number. (*See also* LOGARITHM, CHARACTERISTIC OF A.)

When using a table of trigonometric functions given in ten-minute intervals (*see* TABLE NO. 22), a function of an angle between these intervals may be found by interpolation.

Ex. 3: Find the sine of 15°16′.

Sol.: The table gives the sine of 15°10′ and 15°20′; the given angle lies between them. Using a tabular arrangement, find the differences between the angles and the corresponding values of the sine functions. x represents the difference between the sine of 15°16′ and 15°10′.

Angle	Sine Function

$$10\left[\,_{6}\!\left[\begin{matrix} 15°\,20' \\ 15°\,16' \\ 15°\,10' \end{matrix}\right.\right.\quad\left.\left.\begin{matrix} 2644 \\ 2616 + x \\ 2616 \end{matrix}\right]x\,\right]28$$

$$6/10 = x/28$$
$$10x = 168$$
$$x = 16.8, \text{ or approximately 17.}$$

The required sine is $.2616 + x$, or $.2616 + 17 = .2633$.

INTERQUARTILE RANGE (in tur kwawr′-tahyl raynj), in statistics, a measure of dispersion that is equal to the distance between the first and third QUARTILES in a distribution. The interquartile range includes the middle half of the values in a frequency distribution.

INTERSECTING CHORDS IN A CIRCLE. In GEOMETRY:

1. If two CHORDS intersect in a CIRCLE, the product of the segments of one chord equals the product of the segments of the other chord.

2. An angle formed by two intersecting chords in a circle is equal in degrees to one half the sum of its intercepted arc and the arc of its VERTICAL ANGLE.

Ex. 1: In Fig. 1, find the length of *CD*.

Sol.: $3 \cdot 4 = 2x$; $6 = x$; $CD = 2 + 6 = 8$.

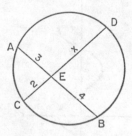

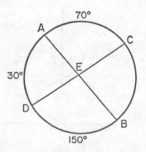

Fig. 1   Fig. 2

Ex. 2: In Fig. 2, find the number of degrees in $\angle AEC$.

Sol.: $\angle AEC \doteq \frac{1}{2}(70 + 150) \doteq \frac{1}{2}(220) \doteq 110°$.

INTERSECTION OF LINES. Two nonparallel lines in a plane intersect in exactly one point. If a pair of lines is specified by a pair of equations, the COORDINATES of their point of intersection give the common solution of the two equations.

Ex.: Find the point of intersection of the lines:

$$y = 2x + 3$$
$$y = 3x - 2.$$

Sol.: Subtract the second equation from the first, to get:

$$0 = -x + 5.$$

Thus, $x = 5$. Either equation then yields y. E.g.,

$$y = 2x + 3 = (2)(5) + 3 = 13$$

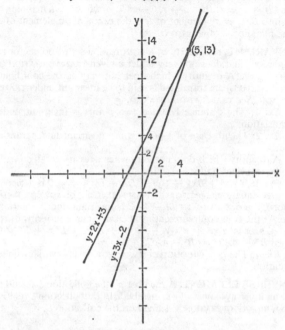

Thus, when the graphs of the two equations are drawn, their intersection is the point (5,13). (See figure.)

Two nonparallel lines in space may fail to intersect; in this case, they are called SKEW LINES. If two lines in space do intersect, their common point may be found by the same method.

INTERSECTION OF LOCI, *see* COMPOUND LOCUS.

INTERSECTION OF SETS, for two sets, A and B, the third set consisting of all elements which are in both sets. Symbolically, using the standard sign $\cap$ for "intersection" and $\in$ for "is an element of": $A \cap B =$ all elements p such that $p \in A$ and $p \in B$. The figure shows the representation of $A \cap B$ using a Venn diagram.

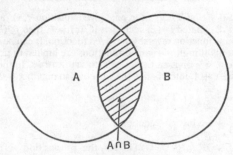

The following equations are useful:

$$A \cap (B \cap C) = (A \cap B) \cap C.$$
$$A \cap A = A.$$

Ex.: If $A = \{1, 3, 4, 7\}$ and $B = \{1, 2, 4, 6, 9\}$ find $A \cap B$.
Sol.: The elements that are in set A and set B are 1 and 4. Thus, $A \cap B = \{1, 4\}$.
See also UNION.

INTERVAL, in mathematics, the set of points bounded by two fixed end points on a NUMBER LINE; hence, also the numbers corresponding to these points. E.g., it is possible to say that two is in the interval with end points zero and five. *See also* CLOSED INTERVAL; OPEN INTERVAL.

INTO, a MAPPING of set A into set B that associates with each element, a, of set A a unique element, b, of set B. If $A = \{5, 6, 7, 8\}$ and $B = \{r, s, t\}$ then $5 \rightarrow r, 6 \rightarrow s, 7 \rightarrow s, 8 \rightarrow r$ is a mapping of A into B. If every element of B is the IMAGE of an element of A the mapping is of A ONTO B.

INVARIANT, a property of a FUNCTION, a set of points, or an equation, that does not vary under a given TRANSFORMATION OF THE PLANE. A quantity which does not vary as the coordinate axes (*see* AXIS) are translated is said to be invariant under TRANSLATION (*See* TRANSLATION OF AXES).
Ex. 1: The distance between two points is invariant under translation.
Ex. 2: The abscissa of a point is not invariant under translation.
A quantity which does not vary when axes are rotated is said to be invariant under ROTATION.
Ex. 3: If $Ax^2 + Bxy + Cy^2 + Dx + Ey + F = 0$ is a second degree equation (*see* DEGREE OF AN EQUATION; QUADRATIC EQUATION), the DISCRIMINANT $B^2 - 4AC$ is invariant under rotation; i.e., if the equation representing the same curve in terms of rotated axes is $A'x_1^2 + B'x_1y_1 + C'y_1^2 + D'x_1 + E'y_1 + F' = 0$, then $B'^2 - 4A'C' = B^2 - 4AC$.
Ex. 4: The DOT PRODUCT OF TWO VECTORS is invariant under rotation.

INVERSE ELEMENT. A member a' of a collection S is said to be an inverse element of the member a of the collection S relative to a BINARY OPERATION * defined on the collection S, if

$$a' * a = e,$$

where e is an IDENTITY ELEMENT of the collection S relative to the binary operation *. For example, since $5 + (-5) = 0$ and 0 is the identity element of the collection of REAL NUMBERS relative to the binary operation of addition the real number (-5) is called the "inverse element" of the real number 5 relative to the binary operation of addition of real numbers; 5 is called the inverse element of (-5) relative to addition. Note, since $5(1/5) = 1$ and 1 is the identity element of the collection of real numbers relative to the binary operation of multiplication, the real number 1/5 is called the inverse element of the real number 5 relative to the binary operation of multiplication of real numbers; 5 is called the inverse element of 1/5 relative to multiplication.

INVERSE FUNCTION, for any given function $f(x)$, another function designated $f^{-1}(x)$ such that if $f(a) = b$, then $f^{-1}(b) = a$. The inverse function reverses the given function. It can be strictly defined only if multiple valued functions are limited to principal values; e.g., *see* INVERSE TRIGONOMETRIC FUNCTIONS. In the equation $y = 3x + 1$, interchange the variables to obtain $x = 3y + 1$, then $y = \dfrac{x - 1}{3}$. Therefore, the equations $y = 3x + 1$ and $y = \dfrac{x - 1}{3}$ are inverse functions.

INVERSE OF A PROPOSITION, the proposition formed by contradicting the HYPOTHESES and the conclusion. For the proposition $h \rightarrow c$, the inverse is $\sim h \rightarrow \sim c$.
E.g., *Statement:* If two sides of a triangle are equal, the angles opposite these sides are equal.

Inverse: If two sides of a triangle are unequal, the angles opposite these sides are unequal.
An inverse statement is not necessarily true if the statement is true.
E.g., *Statement:* If two angles are RIGHT ANGLES, they are equal.
Inverse: If two angles are not right angles, they are not equal.
The inverse and the CONVERSE of a theorem are EQUIVALENT STATEMENTS. If the converse of a theorem is true, the corresponding inverse is also true. If the converse of a theorem is false, the inverse is false.

INVERSE OPERATIONS, pairs of operations that reverse each other. When applied to the same element they nullify or cancel out each other; e.g., addition $(x + n)$ and subtraction $(x - n)$, since $x + n - n = x$; multiplication $(n \cdot x)$ and division (x/n), since $n \cdot x/n = x$; or raising to a power (x^n) and extracting a root $(\sqrt[n]{x})$, since $\sqrt[n]{x^n} = x$. *See also* ADDITIVE INVERSE; MULTIPLICATIVE INVERSE.

INVERSE SQUARES, LAW OF, a mathematical proportion, in which some quantity varies inversely as the square of a second quantity. Many physical laws are of this form, with a force or the intensity of some quantity varying inversely as the square of the distance. For example, forces due to GRAVITATION, electricity, and magnetism all follow the law of inverse squares. The intensity of electromagnetic radiation, including visible light and all other forms, varies inversely as the square of the distance from the source. Such a relationship makes distance the key factor in many situations. As an example, if the distance of an object from a given light source is doubled, the illumination of the object is only one-fourth its original value. Moving the object five times as far from the source results in a reduction of the illumination to 1/25 of the original value. On the other hand, a comparable increase is observed, if the object moves closer to the source; halving the distance increases the illumination by a factor of four.

INVERSE TRIGONOMETRIC FUNCTIONS, functions in which an angle θ is dependent on the value of $\sin \theta$ (or $\cos \theta$, $\tan \theta$, etc.), a direct TRIGONOMETRIC FUNCTION of θ. In the equation $y = \sin \theta$, if y is the independent VARIABLE, then θ is a function of y and is written

$$\theta = \text{arc sin } y, \text{ or } \theta = \sin^{-1} y.$$

This is read "θ is the inverse sine of y" or "θ is the angle whose sine is y." (The symbol "$\sin^{-1} y$" is not the same as "$(\sin \theta)^{-1}$," the reciprocal, $\dfrac{1}{\sin \theta}$.) The symbols "sin" and "arc sin" ("$\sin^{-1}$")

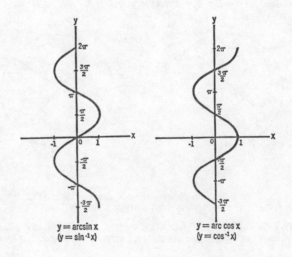

$y = \text{arcsin } x$
$(y = \sin^{-1} x)$

$y = \text{arc cos } x$
$(y = \cos^{-1} x)$

indicate INVERSE FUNCTIONS. The direct function $y = \sin \theta$ and its inverse function $\theta = \arc \sin y$ ($\sin^{-1} y$) are equivalent equations.

Each of the trigonometric functions has only one value' whereas the inverse functions have infinitely many values; e.g., the angle whose sine is 0.5000 may be 30, 150, 390, etc. The smallest of these is its principal value.

The equations $x = \sin y$ and $y = \sin x$ express the same relation between x and y; thus, the graphs of a trigonometric function and its inverse function are the same except that the x and y axes are interchanged with respect to the curve. (See figures.)

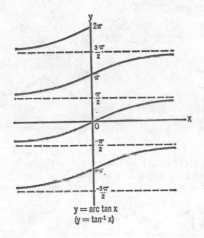

$y = \arc \tan x$
($y = \tan^{-1} x$)

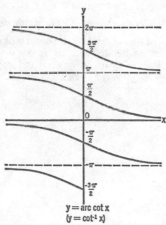

$y = \arc \cot x$
($y = \cot^{-1} x$)

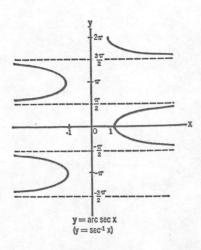

$y = \arc \sec x$
($y = \sec^{-1} x$)

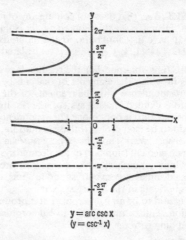

$y = \arc \csc x$
($y = \csc^{-1} x$)

INVERSE VARIATION, *see* VARIATION.

INVERSION, in mathematics, the process by which a given PROPORTION is changed to another by inverting the two RATIOS, so that the second term is to the first term as the fourth is to the third. If $a/b = c/d$, then $b/a = d/c$ by inversion.

INVOLUTE (in'-voh-loot), of a plane curve, the LOCUS of a fixed point on a string stretched along the curve, as it is held taut and unwound from the curve. Any point on the string will describe an involute. Thus, a given curve has an infinite number of involutes (see figure), which are called parallel curves since the distance between any two of them is constant. The TRACTRIX is the involute of the CATENARY.

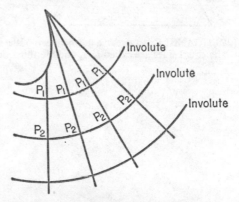

INVOLUTION, the process of raising to a power. Thus, the process of cubing 2 is involution.

A function which is its own inverse is called an *involution*. For example, $y = 1/y'$ is an involution.

IRRATIONAL EQUATIONS, *see* EQUATIONS, RADICAL.

IRRATIONAL NUMBER, a REAL NUMBER which cannot be expressed as the RATIO of two INTEGERS; i.e., a NUMBER that is not a RATIONAL NUMBER; e.g., PI (π), $\sqrt{2}$, $\sqrt{3}$, $-\sqrt{2}$, $\sqrt{2}/2$, $2^{\sqrt{2}}$, etc. In any INTERVAL of a NUMBER LINE, no matter how small, there are an infinite number of irrational numbers. This property of the irrational numbers is known as DENSITY. The distance between two points is always a real number, but it may be rational or irrational. E.g., the distance from the ORIGIN to the point in the plane whose COORDINATES are (1,1) is $\sqrt{2}$, which is irrational.

ISOCHRONOUS PROPERTY (ahy-sahk'-roh-nus), of a curve, the property that the time of descent of a particle sliding, without friction, to a lowest point is the same at every starting point on the curve. A CYCLOID (inverted) has this property.

ISOLATED SET, a *set* that does not contain any of its ACCUMULATION POINTS. Hence, a set that contains only isolated points, i.e., points that have a NEIGHBORHOOD that contains no other point in the set. $A = \{1, \frac{1}{2}, \frac{1}{3}, \frac{1}{4}, \ldots\}$ is an isolated set.

ISOMORPHIC (ahy-soh-mor'-fic), the relation between two (or more) systems in which the elements of one can be put into a one-to-one correspondence with the elements of the other, *and* for the operations defined on each system, the results of the operations can be put into a one-to-one correspondence. The two systems are said to be isomorphic if these conditions exist. E.g., the DECIMAL NUMBER SYSTEM and the BINARY NUMBER SYSTEM are isomorphic: each element (number) of the decimal system can be expressed as a binary number; sums, differences, products, and quotients in the decimal system correspond to sums, differences, products and quotients in the binary system.

A MAPPING is said to be an isomorphism if it produces an isomorphic relation. Thus a mapping is an isomorphism if it is a one-to-one mapping ONTO.

ISOMORPHISM, in mathematics, *see* ISOMORPHIC.

ISOSCELES SPHERICAL TRIANGLE, *see* SPHERICAL TRIANGLE.

ISOSCELES TRAPEZOID (ahy-sahs'-su-leez trap'-u-zoid), a TRAPEZOID in which the nonparallel sides are equal. In the figure, leg AD = leg CB in isosceles trapezoid $ABCD$. The base angles of an isosceles trapezoid are equal. Thus, in trapezoid $ABCD$, $\angle D = \angle C$ and $\angle A = \angle B$.

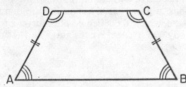

ISOSCELES TRIANGLE, a TRIANGLE in which two of the sides are equal. The equal sides are called *legs*, and the third side is called the *base*. (See figure.) The angle opposite the base is called the *vertex angle*, and each angle opposite the equal sides is called a *base angle*. The vertex of an isosceles triangle is the VERTEX of the vertex angle. Isosceles Triangles have the following properties:

1. Base angles of an isosceles triangle are equal.
2. A line parallel to the base of an isosceles triangle forms another triangle that is isosceles and similar to the given triangle.
3. The BISECTOR of the vertex angle of an isosceles triangle is the PERPENDICULAR bisector of the base.
4. The bisector of an exterior angle (*see* EXTERIOR ANGLE OF A POLYGON) at the vertex of an isosceles triangle is parallel to the base of the triangle.

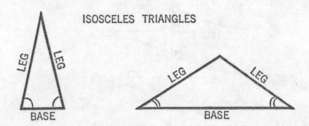

ISOSCELES TRIANGLES

ITERATED INTEGRAL (it'-uh-rayted in'-ti-gruhl), for a function $F(x,y)$ which is defined on a region in the plane bounded by the curves $y = g(x)$ and $y = h(x)$ and the lines $x = a$ and $x = b$, the integral:

$$\int_a^b \left(\int_{g(x)}^{h(x)} F(x,y)dy \right) dx, \text{ or } \int_a^b dx \int_{g(x)}^{h(x)} F(x,y)dy.$$

The iterated integral of a function $F(x,y,z)$ is

$$\int dx \int dx \int F(x,y,z)dy = \iiint F(x,y,z)dy\, dx\, dz.$$

By an extension of the FUNDAMENTAL THEOREM OF CALCULUS, it can be proved that an iterated integral is equal to the corresponding double integral or triple integral, and may be used to evaluate them. *See also* VOLUME UNDER A SURFACE.

J

JACOBIAN (jay-koh'-bee-an), for a TRANSFORMATION OF THE PLANE $x = f(u,v)$, $y = g(u,v)$ which may be interpreted as a MAPPING of a REGION A of the xy-plane into the region G of the uv-plane and given by

$$\int_A \int \theta(x,y)dxdy = \int_G \int \phi\,[f(u,v),g(u,v)]\,\frac{\partial(x,y)}{\partial(u,v)}\,dudv,$$

the *Jacobian* is the PARTIAL DERIVATIVE $\frac{\partial(x,y)}{\partial(u,v)}$ and is defined by the DETERMINANT:

$$\frac{\partial(x,y)}{\partial(u,v)} = \begin{vmatrix} \dfrac{\partial x}{\partial u} & \dfrac{\partial x}{\partial v} \\ \dfrac{\partial y}{\partial u} & \dfrac{\partial y}{\partial v} \end{vmatrix}.$$

For n functions $f_i(x_1,x_2,x_3, \ldots, x_n)$, $i = 1, 2, 3, \ldots n$, the Jacobian is:

$$\frac{\partial(f_1,f_2,f_3,\ldots f_n)}{\partial(x_1,x_2,x_3,\ldots x_n)} = \begin{vmatrix} \dfrac{\partial f_1}{\partial x_1} & \dfrac{\partial f_1}{\partial x_2} & \dfrac{\partial f_1}{\partial x_3} & \cdots & \dfrac{\partial f_1}{\partial x_n} \\ \dfrac{\partial f_2}{\partial x_1} & \dfrac{\partial f_2}{\partial x_2} & \dfrac{\partial f_2}{\partial x_3} & \cdots & \dfrac{\partial f_2}{\partial x_n} \\ \cdots & \cdots & \cdots & \cdots & \cdots \\ \dfrac{\partial f_n}{\partial x_1} & \dfrac{\partial f_n}{\partial x_2} & \dfrac{\partial f_n}{\partial x_3} & \cdots & \dfrac{\partial f_n}{\partial x_n} \end{vmatrix}.$$

JOINT PROBABILITY FUNCTION, in statistics, a function that gives the probability that each of two (or more) random variables takes on a particular value. The variables are usually denoted x, y, z, etc., or x_1, x_2, x_3, etc. The joint probability function might be given as a formula, such as

$$f(x,y) = \frac{\dbinom{4}{x}\dbinom{4}{y}\dbinom{44}{5-x-y}}{\dbinom{52}{5}},$$

or as a table:

y \ x	0	1	2	
0	$\frac{1}{10}$	$\frac{2}{10}$	$\frac{1}{10}$	$\frac{4}{10}$
1	0	$\frac{1}{20}$	$\frac{3}{20}$	$\frac{2}{10}$
2	$\frac{1}{10}$	$\frac{3}{20}$	$\frac{3}{20}$	$\frac{4}{10}$
	$\frac{2}{10}$	$\frac{4}{10}$	$\frac{4}{10}$	

The marginal probability function for x is obtained by adding, for each x-value, across all the y-values. It is

$x =$	0	1	2
$f(x) =$	$\frac{2}{10}$	$\frac{4}{10}$	$\frac{4}{10}$

The marginal probability function for y is obtained by adding the probabilities, for each y-value, across all the x-values. It is

$y =$	0	1	2
$g(y) =$	$\frac{4}{10}$	$\frac{2}{10}$	$\frac{4}{10}$

These individual probability functions are known as *marginal probability functions* because the probabilities appear in the margin of the joint probability function table.

For continuous random variables a joint probability density function is used.

K

KAPPA, the Greek letter symbolized by κ, or K (cap). *See* TABLE NO. 1.

KILOGRAM, *see* METRIC SYSTEM; MKS SYSTEM; TABLE NO. 5.

KITE, a QUADRILATERAL which has two pairs of adjacent sides equal. In the figure, *ABCD* is a kite. The longer diagonal *AC* divides the kite into two congruent triangles *ADC* and *CBA*. The shorter diagonal *BD* divides the kite into two isosceles triangles *ABD* and *DCB*.

Since *A* and *C* are each equidistant from the ends of *BD*, *AC* is the perpendicular bisector of *BD*. *See also* PERPENDICULAR BISECTOR OF A LINE SEGMENT.

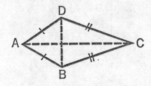

KLEIN BOTTLE (klahyn), a representation of a one-sided surface which is closed, and has no boundary. Hence, a surface in which all points are internal points. A Klein bottle (see figure) is formed by pulling the open end of a bottle through one side of the bottle and joining it to the closed end.

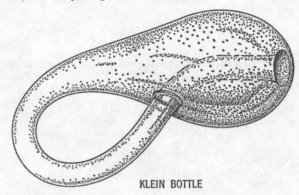

KLEIN BOTTLE

KNOT (naht), the unit of speed in navigation, equal to one NAUTICAL MILE (6080.27 ft.) per hour. E.g., if a ship sails 15 knots, it means that it sails at a speed of 15 nautical miles per hour. *See* TABLE NO. 4.

L

LAGRANGE, JOSEPH LOUIS (lah-graynzh), 1736–1813, a French mathematician, who headed the Committee on Weights and Measures, which adopted the METRIC SYSTEM. He worked in CALCULUS and laid the foundations for later work by LAPLACE He played a significant part in verifying Newton's theory of gravitation. Lagrange also wrote on mechanics and astronomy.

LAPLACE, Marquis **PIERRE SIMON DE**, 1749–1827, French astronomer and mathematician. He was appointed professor at the Ecole Militaire in Paris at the age of 18. His greatest work was his *Celestial Mechanics*, published in five volumes over a period of 26 years, whose purpose was to demonstrate the stability of the solar system by a rigorous application of Newtonian mechanics. He is also known for his nebular hypothesis of the origin of the solar system, which he put forward in a footnote of a popular work he had written on astronomy. His work in astronomy included devising methods of calculating the motions of the planets and of TIDES. In mathematics he is generally considered the founder of the theory of probability, evolved the method of LEAST SQUARES and adapted analysis to physics.

LAPLACE'S DIFFERENTIAL EQUATION (lah-plah′-sez), the PARTIAL DIFFERENTIAL EQUATION

$$\frac{\partial^2 u}{\partial x^2} + \frac{\partial^2 u}{\partial y^2} + \frac{\partial^2 u}{\partial z^2} = 0.$$

This equation is also symbolized by Δu, and called the Laplace operator. Gravitational, electrostatic, magnetic, electric and velocity potentials satisfy Laplace's equation under certain conditions.

LATIN SQUARE, in statistics, a square array of n symbols used to order the observations in a DESIGN OF EXPERIMENTS.

LATITUDE, the angular distance of a point on the earth from the equator, measured north or south (and labeled N or S) along the meridian through the point; also, any similar coordinate in various celestial COORDINATE SYSTEMS, such as celestial latitude in the ecliptic system and galactic latitude in the galactic system. The latitudes of the equator, north pole, and south pole are 0°, 90° North, and 90° South, respectively. *See also* EARTH COORDINATE SYSTEM.

LATTICE POINT, a POINT whose COORDINATES are both integers. The lattice points are the intersections of horizontal lines at

LATTICE POINTS

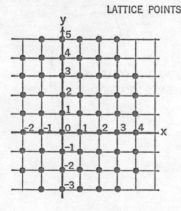

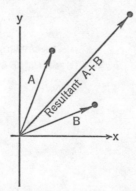

integral distances from the *x*-axis and vertical lines at integral distances from the *y*-axis.

If each lattice point is thought of as a VECTOR, with initial point at the original and terminal point at the lattice point, then the resultant of any two such vectors (*see* RESULTANT OF TWO VECTORS) is also a lattice-point vector. The lattice-point vectors form a vector space which is a subspace of the vector space of the plane. (See figure.)

LATUS RECTUM OF ELLIPSE (la′-tus rek′-tum e-lips′), (*plural*, latera recta), a CHORD of an ELLIPSE passing through one foci (*see* CONIC SECTION) and perpendicular to the MAJOR AXIS OF AN ELLIPSE. The two latera recta have equal lengths. If the equation of the ellipse is $\frac{x^2}{a^2} + \frac{y^2}{b^2} = 1$, then the length of a latus rectum is $\frac{2b^2}{a}$. (See figure.)

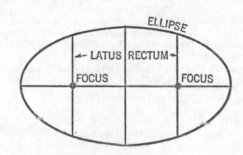

LAW OF COSINES, *see* COSINES, LAW OF.

LAW OF SINES, *see* SINES, LAW OF.

LAW OF TANGENTS, *see* TANGENTS, LAW OF.

LCM, *see* LEAST COMMON MULTIPLE.

LEAST COMMON MULTIPLE, the smallest number that is divisible by each member of a SET of numbers. E.g., for the set containing the numbers 10 and 4, the least common multiple is 20. The least common multiple is sometimes called the LCM. It may be found by computing multiples of each number in a set and determining which multiples are common to each number, and then selecting the smallest of the common multiples. However, it is usually faster to find the multiples of the largest number in the set and test them for divisibility with the other numbers in the set.

Ex. 1: Find the LCM of 3, 5, and 8.
Sol.: Find some multiples of 8:

$8 \times 1 = 8$	$8 \times 6 = 48$	$8 \times 11 = 88$
$8 \times 2 = 16$	$8 \times 7 = 56$	$8 \times 12 = 96$
$8 \times 3 = 24$	$8 \times 8 = 64$	$8 \times 13 = 104$
$8 \times 4 = 32$	$8 \times 9 = 72$	$8 \times 14 = 112$
$8 \times 5 = 40$	$8 \times 10 = 80$	$8 \times 15 = 120$

Testing for divisibility with the other numbers in the set, note that 24 is divisible by 3 but not by 5; 40 is divisible by 5 but not by 3; 120 is divisible by 3, 5, and 8. Therefore, the LCM is 120.

Another method of finding the LCM is to factor each number into its prime (*see* PRIME NUMBER) FACTORS, and form the LCM by calculating the products of the highest powers of the distinct factors.

Ex. 2: Find the LCM of 6, 15, and 16.

Sol.: Find the prime factors of each number.

$$6 = 2 \times 3, \qquad 15 = 3 \times 5, \qquad 16 = 2^4.$$

Forming the product of the distinct prime factors gives $2^4 \times 3 \times 5 = 16 \times 3 \times 5 = 16 \times 15 = 240$, the LCM.

LEAST SQUARES, in statistics, for a sample of n pairs of observations, $(x_1, y_1), (x_2, y_2), \ldots , (x_n, y_n)$, the method used to obtain an estimate of the relationship that gives y-values in terms of x-values.

Although the relationship between the x and y values might be assumed to be quadratic, cubic, exponential, or some other form, most frequently it is assumed to be linear. The straight line that best fits the n points, called a *least-squares line* or *regression line*, has the equation

$$y = m + b(x - \bar{x}),$$

where $\quad m = \dfrac{\sum\limits_{i=1}^{n} y_i}{n} \quad$ and $\quad b = \dfrac{\sum\limits_{i=1}^{n} (x_i - \bar{x}) y_i}{n}.$

The coefficients of the curve that best fits the data are called *regression coefficients*. In the equation $y = m + (x - \bar{x})$, m and b are regression coefficients. (Sometimes, in this linear case, only the b is called a regression coefficient.)

Ex.: A mathematics instructor wonders whether a student's score on the first quiz of a semester can be used to predict his final average for the semester. The scores that 7 students made on the first quiz (x) and their final average (y) are given. Find the regression line that predicts y-values (final averages) given x-values (scores on the first quiz).

Sol:

x:	74	65	98	55	74	89	64
y:	76	57	98	64	73	80	76

$$m = \frac{524}{7} = 74.86.$$

$$\bar{x} = \frac{519}{7} = 74.14.$$

The best formula to use when computing b is

$$b = \frac{n \Sigma xy - (\Sigma x)(\Sigma y)}{n \Sigma x^2 - (\Sigma x)^2}.$$

Using this formula,

$$b = \frac{7(39839) - (519)(524)}{7(39823) - (519)^2} = .736.$$

The regression line is

$$y = 74.86 + .736(x - 74.14)$$
$$y = .736x + 20.29.$$

LEAST UPPER BOUND (L.U.B.), the smallest number which is greater than or equal to every member of a given SET. It is usually accepted as an AXIOM that every set of real numbers which has an upper bound has a least upper bound, or L.U.B.

Ex. 1: The L.U.B. of the interval [0, 1] is 1. Note that 1 is a member of the set.

Ex. 2: The L.U.B. of the set $\{\frac{1}{2}, \frac{2}{3}, \frac{3}{4}, \frac{4}{5}, \ldots\}$ is 1, even though 1 is not a member of the set.

Ex. 3: The set of all positive integers, $\{1, 2, 3, 4, \ldots\}$, has no L.U.B.

See also GREATEST LOWER BOUND.

LEGS OF A RIGHT TRIANGLE, the two sides of the TRIANGLE that include the RIGHT ANGLE.

LEIBNITZ, GOTTFRIED WILHELM Baron von, (lahyp'-nits) or Leibniz, 1646–1716, German philosopher, mathematician and one of the outstanding thinkers of the 17th cent. He was an in-ventor (independently of, but at the same time as, NEWTON) of infinitesimal CALCULUS and a leading exponent of the systematization of all knowledge. His early interest in logic led him to the idea of a universal scientific language in which complex concepts would be built up out of their simpler components. Although his work in this area was not recognized until fairly recently, much of it is an anticipation of modern symbolic logic. A rationalist, he rejected Descartes' metaphysics and argued that there were a plurality of simple substances, MONADS, each of which mirrors the rest of the universe. These *monads* do not interact with each other; rather, God, the supreme *monad* and perfect being, instituted a pre-established harmony among them as they each developed in accordance with their own determinate nature and simultaneously reflected the development of others. God, in creating a world, necessarily chose the best of all possible worlds (a view which Voltaire parodied in *Candide*). His chief writings include *Théodicée* (1710), *Monadologie* (1714), and *Système nouveau de la nature* (1695).

Biblio.: Russell, Bertrand, *A Critical Exposition of the Philosophy of Leibnitz* (2nd ed. 1937).

LEMMA (lem'-mah), a THEOREM that is proved in order to use it in the proof of another theorem.

LEMNISCATE (lem-nis'-kayt), the LOCUS of a point P which moves such that the product of its distances from two fixed points is a constant. (See figure.) The equation of the curve in polar coordinates (*see* COORDINATES, POLAR) is given by

$$r^2 = a^2 \cos 2\theta.$$

In rectangular coordinates, its equation is given by

$$(x^2 + y^2)^2 = a^2(x^2 - y^2).$$

The curve is also called the *lemniscate of Bernoulli*, who first studied it.

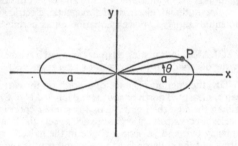

LENGTH, of a straight line segment, the distance between its end points; of a curved segment, the limit of the length of approximating POLYGONS as the polygons approach more and more closely to the curve. (See figure.)

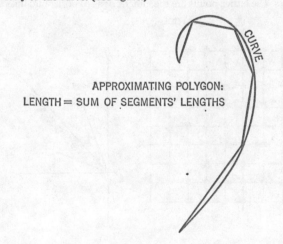

APPROXIMATING POLYGON:
LENGTH = SUM OF SEGMENTS' LENGTHS

The length of the plane curve $y = f(x)$ may be found by the INTEGRATION formula:

$$L = \int_{x1}^{x_2} \sqrt{1 + (f'(x))^2}\, dx.$$

The length of the curve given by two PARAMETRIC EQUATIONS $x = f(t)$, $y = g(t)$ may be found by the integration formula:

$$L = \int_{t1}^{t_2} \sqrt{(f'(t))^2 + (g'(t))^2}\, dt.$$

These formulas are based on approximations to the curve consisting of segments of TANGENT LINES whose length is found by using the PYTHAGOREAN THEOREM.

Ex.: What is the length of the curve $y = \sqrt{x^3}$ between $x = 0$ and $x = 1$?

Sol.:
$$L = \int_0^1 \sqrt{1 + \left(\frac{d}{dx} x^{3/2}\right)^2}\, dx$$
$$= \int_0^1 \sqrt{1 + (\tfrac{3}{2}x^{1/2})^2}\, dx = \int_0^1 \sqrt{1 + \tfrac{9}{4}x}\, dx$$
$$= \tfrac{4}{9}[(\tfrac{2}{3}(1 + \tfrac{9}{4}x)^{3/2})]_0^1] \approx 1.4.$$

LEONARDO DA PISA (lay-oh-nahr'-do dah pee'sah), 1170–1250, an Italian mathematician, also known as **Fibonacci**. One of the greatest mathematicians of his time, he wrote treatises on the application of algebra to geometry. In 1202, he published his *Liber Abaci* and brought about the introduction of Arabic notation into Europe.

LEVEL CURVE, for a surface $z = f(x,y)$, those points (x,y) for which z equals a constant c.
    Ex.: $z = x^2 + y^2$ is a paraboloid with vertex at $(0,0,0)$. Those points (x,y) for which $f(x,y) = x^2 + y^2 = 1$ form a circle of radius 1 and center $(0,0,1)$. This circle is the level curve for 1. *See also* GRADIENT.

LEVELING, a branch of GEODESY, concerned chiefly with finding horizontal lines and determining differences of elevation between any two points on the earth's surface. One of the problems of leveling is the bending of light rays by the earth's atmosphere, causing errors in the reading of surveying instruments. Since this error due to refraction is proportional to the square of the distance being measured, it can be lessened by breaking up the distance between two points whose relative altitudes are being sought, for example. The technique of leveling has been known since the time of the anc. Egyptians.
    A point between two points in question is used as a reference point. The horizontal is established by means of a liquid surface or a bubble in a vial (like a carpenter's level), and readings are made to each of the points. The difference in altitude is the difference between the two readings. In studies involving the earth's surface, geodetic surveyors measure altitude from the surface of a spheroid called the geoid, defined by average sea level, with the tides averaged out and extended under the land areas.

L'HÔPITAL or **L'Hospital, GUILLAUME FRANÇOIS ANTOINE,** Marquis **DE SAINTE-MESME,** 1661–1704, French mathematician. He was a student of the celebrated Johann Bernoulli and, after his studies with this master, wrote the first comprehensive treatise on the infinitesimal calculus, a subject then in its infancy. His main original contribution to mathematics was contained in this work. Known as L'HÔPITAL'S RULE, it permits one to calculate the limit of a quotient when both the numerator and the denominator approach zero.

L'HÔPITAL'S RULE (loh-pi-tal'), the principle that $\lim\limits_{t \to a} \dfrac{f(t)}{g(t)} =$
$\lim\limits_{t \to a} \dfrac{f'(t)}{g'(t)}$. It is used to evaluate $\lim\limits_{t \to a} \dfrac{f(t)}{g(t)}$ when $\lim\limits_{t \to a} f(t)$ and $\lim\limits_{t \to a} g(t)$ are both 0 or ∞, thus resulting in an INDETERMINATE FORM.

    Ex.: Evaluate $\lim\limits_{x \to 2} \dfrac{x^2 - 4}{x^2 + x - 6}$.

Sol.: Since $\lim\limits_{x \to 2} x^2 - 4 = \lim\limits_{x \to 2}(x^2 + x - 6) = 0$, apply L'Hôpital's Rule to find

$$\lim_{x \to 2} \frac{x^2 - 4}{x^2 + x - 6} = \lim_{x \to 2} \frac{2x}{2x + 1} = \frac{4}{5}.$$

LIKE TERMS, algebraic terms having identical literal factors, such as $8x^2y$ and $-7x^2y$. Like terms, or similar terms, may be combined: $5x + 3x = 8x$; $3x^2y - 7x^2y = -4x^2y$. *See also* ALGEBRAIC EXPRESSION.

LIMAÇON (lee-mah-sawn'), the polar coordinate (*see* COORDINATES, POLAR) graph of a function of the form,

$$r = a \cos \theta - 1.$$

The sketch of the graph of $r = 2 \cos \theta - 1$, where $a = 2$, is shown in the figure.

Point	A	B	C	D	E	F	G	H	I	J
θ.	0°	30°	60°	90°	120°	150°	180°	210°	240°	270°
r	1	.7	0	-1	-2	-2.7	-3			

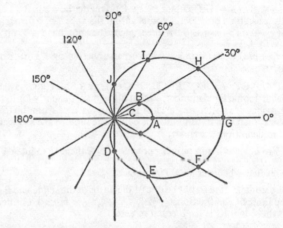

LIMIT OF A FUNCTION. For a function $y = f(x)$, A is the limit of $f(x)$ as x approaches a if for every value of x near the value a, $f(x)$ is near A. This statement applies only to numbers near a, not to a itself. The value of $f(a)$ need not be A, and in fact, f may not even be defined at a. To make the word "near" completely unambiguous, the following formal definition (termed a delta-epsilon definition) is used: A is the limit of $f(x)$ as x approaches a if, for every positive ϵ however small, there is a positive δ such that when $0 < |x - a| < \delta$ then $|f(x) - A| < \epsilon$. (See Fig. 1.) A is the limit of $f(x)$ as x approaches a is written $\lim\limits_{x \to a} f(x) = A$.

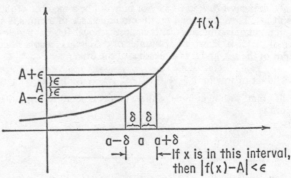

Fig. 1

Ex. 1: Find each of the following.

a. $\lim\limits_{x\to 2} 2x$ b. $\lim\limits_{x\to 3} x^2$ c. $\lim\limits_{x\to \frac{\pi}{2}} \sin x$

Sol.: a. 4 b. 9 c. 1.

Ex. 2: Does the function $g(x)$ in Fig. 2 have a limit at $x = 0$? Why?

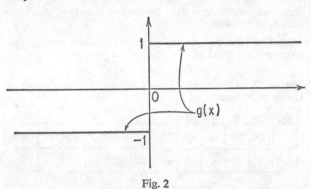

Fig. 2

Sol.: Let $\epsilon = \frac{1}{2}$. Then, for every A, no matter how small a δ one chooses, there are always points within distance δ of 0 for which $|g(x) - A| > \frac{1}{2} = \epsilon$. Therefore, $g(x)$ does not have a limit at $x = 0$.

See also CONTINUOUS FUNCTION; DERIVATIVE OF A FUNCTION; LIMIT OF A SEQUENCE.

LIMIT OF A SEQUENCE. If the terms of a SEQUENCE tend toward some fixed number, so that all terms sufficiently far in the sequence are within any arbitrarily small distance from the fixed point, then this fixed number is called the limit of the sequence. This definition is written;

$$\lim_{n\to\infty} a_n = A$$ if and only if, for every $\epsilon > 0$ there is an integer N

so that whenever $m > N$, $|a_m - A| < \epsilon$.

The limit itself need not be one of the terms of the sequence. E.g., the limit of the fractions $\frac{1}{2}, \frac{1}{3}, \frac{1}{4}, \ldots, \frac{1}{n}, \ldots$ is zero, but none of the fractions is itself equal to zero.

Ex. 1: What is the limit of the sequence $\left\{\dfrac{1}{n}\right\}$?

Sol.: $\lim\limits_{n\to\infty} \dfrac{1}{n} = 0$, as is apparent from the first few terms: $1, \frac{1}{2}$,

$\frac{1}{3}, \ldots$

Ex. 2: Does the sequence $\{(-1)^n\}$ approach any limit?

Sol.: It does not. Instead, it oscillates between -1 and $+1$; the first few terms are $-1, 1, -1, 1, \ldots$.

See also SERIES.

LIMIT POINT, a point P of a POINT SET if, no matter how small a distance is chosen, some point of the set other than P is within that distance of P. P itself may or may not be a member of the point set. Thus, any point on the circumference of a circle is a limit point of the interior disk it encloses, though it is not a member of the disk. However, the center of the circle is also a limit point of the set, and it is a member of the disk.

The set of fractions $\frac{1}{2}, \frac{1}{3}, \frac{1}{4}, \frac{1}{5}, \ldots, \dfrac{1}{n}, \ldots$ has zero as its limit point, although none of these points is equal to zero. (See figure.)

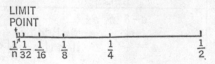

LINE, in geometry, an undefined term which has only one dimension—length. Lines may be straight, curved or broken, but when unqualified, the term usually means a straight line, and is drawn with a straight edge as a guide. A straight line is the shortest distance between two points, a straight line may extend infinitely far in both directions. A curve is a line no part of which is straight. A broken line is a succession of LINE SEGMENTS. If a line extends infinitely far from a point, in one direction only, it is called a ray. (See figure.)

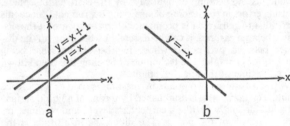

In the figure, line l contains points A and B. That part of the line between and including the two points is a line segment.

LINEAR DIFFERENTIAL EQUATION OF FIRST ORDER, a DIFFERENTIAL EQUATION that can be put into the form $y' + Ay = B$.

LINEAR EQUATION, *see* EQUATION, LINEAR.

LINEAR EQUATIONS, SYSTEMS OF, *see* EQUATIONS, SYSTEMS OF LINEAR.

LINEAR FUNCTION, a FUNCTION of the form $y = mx + b$. Its graph is a straight line.

LINE, EQUATION OF, an EQUATION whose graph is a LINE. The equation of a line may be put into various standard forms (also called normal forms). *See* NORMAL; SLOPE-INTERCEPT FORM OF AN EQUATION OF A LINE; SLOPE-POINT FORM OF AN EQUATION OF A LINE; TWO-POINT FORM OF AN EQUATION OF A LINE.

Ex. 1: The line parallel to the x-axis and one unit above it is the graph of the function $f(x) = 1$; its equation is $y = 1$.

Ex. 2: The line through the origin which bisects the first quadrant is the graph of the equation $y = x$ (see Fig. 1a). The line through the origin which bisects the second quadrant is given by $y = -x$ (see Fig. 1b).

Fig. 1

When a represents the X-INTERCEPT and b the Y-INTERCEPT of a line, the *intercept form of an equation of a line* is $\dfrac{x}{a} + \dfrac{y}{b} = 1$.

Ex. 3: The equation of a line with x-intercept 4 and y-intercept 3 is in the form

$$\frac{x}{a} + \frac{y}{b} = 1,$$

where

$$\frac{x}{4} + \frac{y}{3} = 1$$

or

$$3x + 4y = 12.$$

If the equation of a line is given in rectangular coordinates (*see* COORDINATES, RECTANGULAR) as $ax + by + c = 0$, it may be changed to polar coordinates (*see* COORDINATES, POLAR) by substituting for x and y in the parametric equations, $x = r \cos \theta$, $y = r \sin \theta$, to find

$$r = f(\theta) = \frac{-c}{a \cos \theta + b \sin \theta}.$$ (See Fig. 2.)

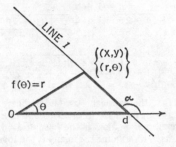

Fig. 2

Ex. 4: Find the polar equation of the line $y = 1 - x$.
Sol.: $a = 1$, $b = 1$, $c = -1$. The equation is

$$r = \frac{1}{\cos\theta + \sin\theta}.$$

If only the intercept d and inclination α of a line are given in polar coordinates, it can be shown that

$$r = f(\theta) = \frac{d\sin\alpha}{\cos\alpha(\sin\theta + \cos\theta\sin\alpha)}.$$

LINE INTEGRAL, for a directed curve (C) in space from A to B (see figure), and a scalar function $w = w(x,y,z)$, the integral

$$\int_C w\, ds = \lim \sum_{i=1}^{n} w(x_i, y_i, z_i)\Delta s_i$$

where Δs is the length of a subarc on the curve C.

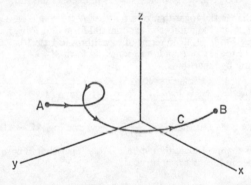

LINE SEGMENT, part of a straight line between two points on the line. The line itself extends infinitely in two directions, but the segment is finite. E.g., a TRIANGLE consists of three line segments rather than of three lines; each side is the line segment between two vertices. The segment between points A and B on a line may be denoted by $\overline{AB}$, with a bar over the letters to distinguish it from AB, the (infinite) line through A and B.

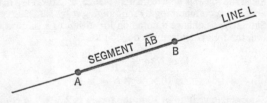

If the segment is considered to include the two points it is called a *closed segment;* if it includes neither, it is an *open segment;* if it includes only one of them, it is called a *half-open,* or *half-closed, segment. See also* CLOSED INTERVAL; DIRECTED SEGMENT; INTERVAL; OPEN INTERVAL.

LINE SEGMENTS, EQUAL, in geometry:
1. Radii of the same, or of equal, CIRCLES are equal.

2. Diameters (*see* DIAMETER OF A CIRCLE) of the same, or of equal, circles are equal.
3. If two ANGLES of a TRIANGLE are equal, the sides opposite these angles are equal.
4. Sides of an EQUILATERAL TRIANGLE are equal.
5. An EQUIANGULAR TRIANGLE is also equilateral.
6. Corresponding sides of CONGRUENT TRIANGLES are equal.
7. Lines from any point on the PERPENDICULAR BISECTOR OF A LINE SEGMENT to the ends of the segment are equal.
8. Perpendiculars from any point on the bisector of an angle to the sides of the angle are equal.
9. PARALLEL LINES are equidistant.
10. Segments of parallel lines between parallels are equal.
11. If parallel lines intercept equal segments on one TRANSVERSAL they intercept equal segments on any transversal.
12. Opposite sides of a PARALLELOGRAM are equal.
13. Diagonals of a parallelogram bisect each other.
14. Diagonals of a RECTANGLE are equal.
15. Diagonals of a square are equal.
16. In a circle, or in equal circles, CHORDS having equal ARCS are equal.
17. A line through the center of a circle perpendicular to a chord bisects the chord.
18. In a circle, or in equal circles, equal chords are equidistant from the center.
19. In a circle, or in equal circles, chords equidistant from the center are equal.
20. TANGENT LINES to a circle from a point are equal.
21. The midpoint of the HYPOTENUSE of a RIGHT TRIANGLE is equidistant from the vertices of the triangle.
22. In a $30° - 60°$ right triangle, the side opposite the $30°$ angle is equal to one half of the hypotenuse.
23. A line segment joining the midpoints of two sides of a triangle is equal to one half of the third side.

LITERAL EQUATION, *see* EQUATION, LITERAL.

LITERAL EXPRESSIONS, in mathematics, ALGEBRAIC EXPRESSIONS containing letters and other ALGEBRAIC SYMBOLS.

LITERAL NUMBER, a letter used as a symbol for a number, as n or x. *See also* ALGEBRAIC SYMBOLS.

LITUUS (lit'-yoo-us), the LOCUS of a point, P, such that the length of the RADIUS VECTOR OP varies inversely as the vectorial angle, θ. The curve has a trumpet shape (see figure) from which it gets its name. The equation of the lituus is given by $r^2\theta = a$.

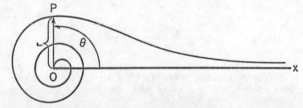

LOBACHEVSKI, NICOLAI IVANOVITCH, (lu-bu-chef'-skee), 1793–1856, Russian mathematician. The son of a peasant family, he showed remarkable genius at an early age. He entered the University of Kazan at 13, and became Professor of mathematics there when he was 21. Lobachevski was the first mathematician to make public (through his lectures) his NON-EUCLIDEAN GEOMETRY. BOLYAI also developed a non-Euclidean geometry at the same time, but the discoveries of the two men were made independently. Lobachevski published his theory in 1829. His name is transliterated from the Russian in several ways: Lobachevsky, Lobatschewsky, and Lobatcheffsky.

LOCATION, MEASURES OF, statistics that provide a measure of where the "center" of a sample is. The most familiar measures of location are the MEAN, MEDIAN, and MODE.

LOCUS (loh'-kus) (*plural*, loci), a geometric figure containing the set of all points that satisfy a given condition, or a set of conditions. E.g.:

1. The locus of points a given distance from a given point is a CIRCLE having the given point as the center and the given distance as the RADIUS. In Fig. 1, point O is the center and the distance is r.

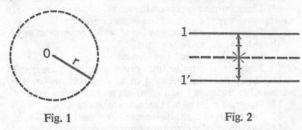

Fig. 1   Fig. 2

2. The locus of points equidistant from two parallel lines is a line parallel to each of the given lines and midway between them. In Fig. 2, $l \parallel l'$.

3. The locus of points a given distance from a given line is a pair of lines parallel to the given line and the given distance from it. In Fig. 3, the line is l and the distance d.

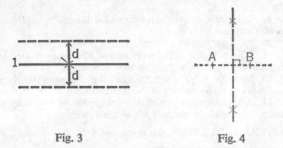

Fig. 3   Fig. 4

4. The locus of points equidistant from two points is the PERPENDICULAR BISECTOR OF A LINE SEGMENT joining the two points. In Fig. 4, the points are A and B.

5. The locus of points within an angle and equidistant from the sides of the angle is the bisector of the angle. In Fig. 5, the angle is $\angle A$.

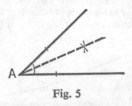

Fig. 5

6. The locus of the vertex of a right triangle with the HYPOTENUSE as the base is a circle with the given hypotenuse as a DIAMETER.

7. The locus of points the sum of whose distances from two fixed points is constant is an ELLIPSE.

8. The locus of points the difference of whose distances from two fixed points is constant is the HYPERBOLA.

9. The locus of points equidistant from a fixed line and a fixed point is a PARABOLA.

Ex. 1: The locus of all points (x,y) whose distance from a fixed point (h,k) is 1 is a circle of radius 1. The equation of this locus is

$$(x - h)^2 + (y - k)^2 = 1.$$

Ex. 2: Find the equation of the locus of all points P which have the property that the distance d from P to $(2,0)$ is 1 larger than the distance d' from P to $(-2,0)$.

Sol.: Write down the condition, substitute analytic (i.e., algebraic) equivalents, and simplify:

$$d = 1 + d'$$
$$\sqrt{x^2 + (y - 2)^2} = 1 + \sqrt{x^2 + (y + 2)^2}$$
$$x^2 + (y - 2)^2 = 1 + 2\sqrt{x^2 + (y + 2)^2} + x^2 + (y + 2)^2$$
$$-4y - 1 = 2\sqrt{x^2 + (y + 2)^2}$$
$$16y^2 + 1 - 8y = 4(x^2 + y^2 + 4 + 2y)$$
$$12y^2 - 4x^2 - 16y - 15 = 0, \text{ left hand branch only.}$$

LOGARITHM, the exponent used to indicate the POWER to which a BASE must be raised in order to obtain a given number. In the expression $3^4 = 81$, 3 is the base and 4 is the power to which 3 is raised to obtain 81. Thus, 4 is the logarithm of 81 to the base 3. In logarithmic notation, this is written $\log_3 81 = 4$, and is read "the log of 81 to the base 3 is 4." Similarly, $\log_2 32 = 5$ is read "the log of 32 to the base 2 is 5." If a is a positive number, it can be shown by calculus that $\log_a x$ exists for any positive number. However, since a positive number raised to any power, positive or negative, gives a positive number, negative numbers have no logarithms.

Any positive number other than 1 may be used as a base for logarithms. For example, $\frac{1}{2}$ may be used. Then, $\log_{1/2} 4 = -2$. The most common bases for logarithms are 2, 10, and from calculus, the number 2.718 . . . which is designated by e. When the base 10 is used, the logarithms are called COMMON LOGARITHMS; when the base e is used, they are called natural logarithms. See TABLE NO. 19. See also INTERPOLATION.

LOGARITHM, CHANGING BASE OF A. The logarithmic form of any number can be expressed as follows:

$$\text{Log}_B N = P, \text{ where } B^P = N \text{ in exponential form.}$$

To change the logarithm of a number N from one base to another, write the number in exponential form and solve for N.

Ex.: Find $\log_3 81$ in terms of logarithms in base 10.
Sol.: $\log_3 81 = P$ and in exponential form $3^P = 81$.
Solving by logarithms:

$$P\log_{10} 3 = \log_{10} 81$$
$$P = \frac{\log_{10} 81}{\log_{10} 3} \text{ and } \log_3 81 = \frac{\log_{10} 81}{\log_{10} 3}.$$

Going a step further, $P = \dfrac{1.90849}{.47712} = 4$ and $\log_3 81 = 4.00000$.

To change a logarithm in base a to a logarithm in base b, the following formula may be used:

$$\log_b N = \frac{\log_a N}{\log_a b}.$$

Thus to change a natural logarithm (base e) to a common logarithm (base 10) the formula is:

$$\log_e N = \frac{\log_{10} N}{\log_{10} e}$$

or $\log_{10} e \times \log_e N = \log_{10} N$.

Since the $\log_{10} e$ is approximately .43425, a natural log may be changed to a common log by multiplying it by .43425.

Similarly, to change a common logarithm to a natural logarithm, the following formula may be used:

$$\log_{10} N = \frac{\log_e N}{\log_e 10} = \frac{\ln N}{\ln 10}$$

or $\ln 10 \times \log_{10} N = \ln N$.

Since the logarithm of 10 in the base e is 2.30259, a common logarithm may be changed to a natural logarithm by multiplying it by 2.30259. *See also* LOGARITHMS, SOLVING EXPONENTIAL EQUATIONS BY; TABLE NO. 19; TABLE NO. 20.

LOGARITHM, CHARACTERISTIC OF A, the integral, or whole part of a logarithm. Consider the following table. Each exponent is the characteristic of the logarithm (base 10) of the number on the right.

$$10^5 = 100,000$$
$$10^4 = 10,000$$
$$10^3 = 1,000$$
$$10^2 = 100$$
$$10^1 = 10$$
$$10^0 = 1$$
$$10^{-1} = 0.1$$
$$10^{-2} = 0.01$$
$$10^{-3} = 0.001$$
$$10^{-4} = 0.0001$$
$$10^{-5} = 0.00001$$

Note that most numbers are not integral powers of 10; therefore, their logarithms contain decimals. For example, the power to which 10 is raised to obtain 84 must be between 1 and 2, since 84 is more than 10^1 and less than 10^2.

$$10^{1.92428} = 84 \text{ or } \log 84 = 1.92428.$$

The characteristic is 1 and the decimal .9243 is the mantissa.

To determine the characteristic of a logarithm:

1. If a number is greater than 1, the characteristic of its logarithm is positive and is one less than the number of figures to the left of the decimal point. The characteristic of 379.4 is 2; that of 1.32 is 0; and the characteristic of 5689 is 3.

2. If a number is less than 1, the characteristic of its logarithm is negative and is one less than the number of zeros immediately following the decimal. The characteristic of 0.324 is −1; and the characteristic of .0064 is −3.

3. If the characteristic is negative, a convenient notation is 9 + mantissa − 10 if the characteristic is −1; 8 + mantissa − 10 if the characteristic is −2; etc. The logarithm of 0.723 is 9.85914 − 10.

See also SCIENTIFIC NOTATION; POWER OF A NUMBER; TABLE NO. 19.

LOGARITHM, DERIVATIVE OF A. The derivative of the natural logarithm of x, $\ln x$, equals $1/x$; since the natural logarithm of a positive number is defined as the integral

$$\ln x = \int_i^x \frac{1}{t}\, dt,$$

and from integral calculus, if

$$F(x) = \int_a^x f(t)dt \text{ is differentiable,}$$

$F'(x) = f(x)$. Thus,

$$\frac{d}{dx}(\ln x) = \frac{1}{x}.$$

If u is a positive differentiable function of x, by the chain rule for derivatives,

$$\frac{d}{dx}(\ln u) = \frac{d}{du}\ln u \frac{du}{dx} = \frac{1}{u}\frac{du}{dx}.$$

Ex. 1: Differentiate $g(x) = \ln (x^2)$.

Sol.: $\quad \dfrac{d}{dx}[\ln (x^2)] = \dfrac{1}{x^2}\dfrac{d}{dx}x^2 = \dfrac{2x}{x^2} = \dfrac{2}{x}.$

Ex. 2: Differentiate $\ln (f(x))$.

Sol.: $\quad \dfrac{d}{dx}[\ln (f(x))] = \dfrac{1}{f(x)}\dfrac{d}{dx}f(x) = \dfrac{f'(x)}{f(x)}.$

To differentiate logarithms to bases other than e (any logarithm other than the natural logarithm), use the definition of $\log_a x$:

$$\log_a x = \frac{\ln x}{\ln a}.$$

Differentiate both sides:

$$\frac{d}{dx}\log_a x = \frac{1}{x \ln a}.$$

Ex. 3: Compare the slopes of the tangents to the curves $y = \ln x$ and $y = \log_{10} x$ at $x = 1$.

Sol.: $\dfrac{d}{dx}\ln x = \dfrac{1}{x}$; at $x = 1$, this has value 1. Thus, $\dfrac{d}{dx}\log_{10} x = \dfrac{1}{x \ln 10}$; at $x = 1$, this has the value $\dfrac{1}{\ln 10}$, or approximately .435.

LOGARITHMIC CURVE, the graph of a LOGARITHMIC FUNCTION. The graph of $y = \log_a x$ may be obtained by reflecting the graph of the corresponding EXPONENTIAL FUNCTION, $y = 2^x$, through the line $y = x$ (Fig. 1). Figures 2 and 3 show the natural logarithmic curve (*see* LOGARITHMS, NATURAL) and the common logarithmic curve (*see* LOGARITHM) respectively.

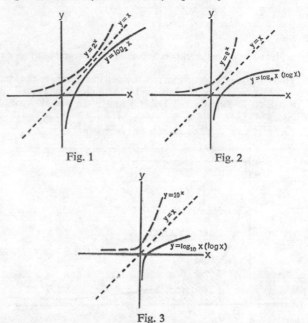

Fig. 1   Fig. 2

Fig. 3

LOGARITHMIC DIFFERENTIATION, when differentiating expressions involving products or powers of FUNCTIONS, the process taking the logarithm of the expression and differentiating the result.

Ex. 1: Differentiate logarithmically the function $y = \sin x \cos x$.

Sol.: $\quad \ln y = \ln (\sin x) + \ln (\cos x)$

$$\frac{d}{dx}(\ln y) = \frac{y'}{y} = \frac{\cos x}{\sin x} + \frac{-\sin x}{\cos x}$$

$$y' = \left(\frac{\cos x}{\sin x} - \frac{\sin x}{\cos x}\right)\sin x \cos x = \cos^2 x - \sin^2 x.$$

Ex. 2: Find dy/dx if $y = x^x$, where x is larger than 0.

Sol.: $\quad \ln y = x \ln x$

$$\frac{y'}{y} = x\left(\frac{1}{x}\right) + \ln x$$

$$y' = (1 + \ln x)x^x.$$

LOGARITHMIC FUNCTION, the INVERSE FUNCTION of the EXPONENTIAL FUNCTION. If the exponential function is expressed as $y = a^x$, its inverse function (found by interchanging x and y) is $x = a^y$. Solving for y would give the usual form of the inverse function: "y is the inverse exponential in the base a." This may be written $y = \log_a x$ and read "y is the logarithm of x in the base a." $y = a^x$ and $y = \log_a x$ are *not* equivalent; they express inverse relations. Their graphs (see figure) are the mirror images of each other. However, $y = \log_a x$ is equivalent to the exponential function $x = a^y$.

Ex. 1: Express $y = 2^x$ as an *equivalent* logarithmic function.

Sol.: $x = \log_2 y$.

Ex. 2: Find the *inverse* of $y = 2^x$.

Sol.: $y = \log_2 x$.

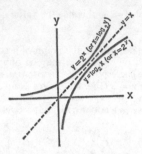

The natural LOGARITHM is defined by the integral in $t \int_1^t \frac{1}{x}\, dx$.

Thus, the natural logarithm of t is equal in measure to the area under the curve $y = 1/x$ between 1 and t, with a minus sign if t is less than 1. (See figure.) Natural logarithms are also called Napierian Logarithms in honor of John NAPIER. *See also* LOGARITHM, CHANGING BASE OF A; TABLE NO. 20.

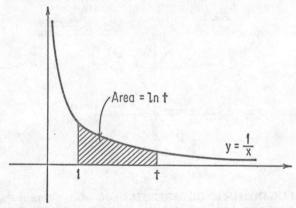

LOGARITHMIC NOTATION, the form in which a number is written if it is expressed as a LOGARITHM. Thus, $\log_4 64 = 3$ is expressed using logarithmic notation. *See also* EXPONENTIAL NOTATION.

LOGARITHM, INTEGRAL OF A.

$$\int \ln |x|\, dx = x \ln |x| - x + C.$$

See also LOGARITHMS, NATURAL.

LOGARITHM, MANTISSA OF A, the decimal part of the logarithm of a number. The mantissa of the logarithm of any two, three, or four digit number can be found directly in a Table of Logarithms (TABLE NO. 19). To find the mantissa of 63, find the number 630 in the N column. To the right of 630, in the column headed by 0, is its mantissa, .79934. Always place the decimal point before the mantissa. The mantissa of 3467 found to the right of the number 346 and in the column headed by 70, is .53995. The mantissa is always the same regardless of the position of the decimal point in the number. The mantissa for 7 is the same as the mantissa for 70 or 700. The characteristics, however, are different for each number. Thus, using the same mantissa for the three significant figures and determining the characteristic by the simplified rules:

$$\begin{aligned} \log 3.467 &= 0.53995 \\ \log 34.67 &= 1.53995 \end{aligned}$$

$$\begin{aligned} \log 346.7 &= 2.53995 \\ \log 3467 &= 3.53995 \\ \log .3467 &= 9.53995 - 10 \\ \log .03467 &= 8.53995 - 10 \\ \log .003467 &= 7.53995 - 10 \end{aligned}$$

See also LOGARITHM, CHARACTERISTIC OF A.

LOGARITHM, NUMBER CORRESPONDING TO A, *see* ANTILOGARITHM.

LOGARITHM OF THE RECIPROCAL, *see* COLOGARITHM.

LOGARITHMS, BASE 10, the base commonly used for a system of logarithms. All numbers are expressed either accurately or approximately as powers of 10. The logarithm of a number to the base 10 is called a common logarithm. Unless otherwise noted all logarithms are to the base 10 and the 10 is usually omitted. The expression $10^2 = 100$ may be written $\log 100 = 2$. *See* TABLE NO. 19.

LOGARITHMS, COMMON, a system of LOGARITHMS in which the base (*see* BASE OF A LOGARITHM) is 10. *See also* TABLE NO. 19.

LOGARITHMS, LAWS OF. Since a logarithm is an EXPONENT, the laws are the same as the Laws of Exponents:

$$\log xy = \log x + \log y,$$
$$\log \frac{x}{y} = \log x - \log y,$$
$$\log x^n = n \log x,$$
$$\log \sqrt[n]{x} = (1/n) \log x.$$

Ex. 1: Multiply 178 by 324.

Sol.: Let $N = 178 \times 324$.

$$\begin{aligned} \log N &= \log 178 + \log 324. \text{ (See TABLE NO. 19.)} \\ \log 178 &= 2.25042 \\ \log 324 &= 2.51055 \\ \log N &= \overline{4.76097.} \end{aligned}$$

Interpolate to find the number that corresponds to the logarithm with a characteristic 4 and a mantissa .76097.

	Number	Mantissa
	57680	76103
	57670 + x	76097
	57670	76095

$$\frac{x}{10} = \frac{2}{8}; \; 8x = 20; \; x = 2\tfrac{4}{8} \text{ or approximately 3,}$$

$57670 + x = 57673$; $N = 57,673$.

$178 \times 324 = 57,673$ approximately.

Note that mantissas of logarithms are approximate to five decimal places. Therefore, answers are approximate to five SIGNIFICANT FIGURES.

Ex. 2: Divide 5.34 by 78.2.

Sol.: Let $N = 5.34 \div 78.2$.

$$\begin{aligned} \log N &= \log 5.34 - \log 78.2. \\ \log 5.34 &= 10.72754 - 10 \\ \log 78.2 &= 1.89321 \\ \log N &= \overline{8.83433 - 10.} \end{aligned}$$

	Number	Mantissa
	68290	83436
	68280 + x	83433
	68280	83429

$$\frac{x}{10} = \frac{4}{7}; \; 7x = 40; \; x = 5\tfrac{5}{7} \text{ or approximately 6.}$$

$68280 + x = 68286$; $N = .068286$.

$5.34 \div 78.2 = .068286$ approximately.

Ex. 3: Find 18^4 by logarithms.

Sol.: Let $N = 18^4$.

$$\log 18^4 = 4 \log 18$$
$$\log 18 = 1.25527$$
$$\underline{\times\, 4}$$
$$\log 18^4 = 5.02108.$$
$$\log N = 5.02108.$$

Find the ANTILOG of 5.02108.

$$10\begin{bmatrix} x \begin{bmatrix} 10500 \\ 10490 + x \\ 10490 \end{bmatrix} \end{bmatrix} \quad \begin{matrix} Number \\ \end{matrix} \quad \begin{matrix} Mantissa \\ 02119 \\ 02108 \\ 02078 \end{matrix} \Big] 30 \Big] 41$$

$$\frac{x}{10} = \frac{30}{41}; \quad 41x = 300; \quad x = 7.3 \text{ or approximately } 7.$$

$10490 + x = 10497$. The antilog of .02118 is 1.0497. The characteristic of 5 indicates that the decimal points should be six digits to the right of the decimal point and $N = 104{,}970$.
$18^4 = 104{,}970$ approximately.

Ex. 4: Find $\sqrt[3]{84.2}$.

Sol.: Let $N = \sqrt[3]{84.2}$.

$$\log N = \tfrac{1}{3} \log 84.2$$
$$\log 84.2 = 1.92531.$$
$$\tfrac{1}{3} \log 84.2 = .64177.$$

The antilog of .64177 is 4.383, so $N = 4.383$.
$\sqrt[3]{84.2} = 4.383$ approximately.

See also LOGARITHM, CHARACTERISTIC OF A; LOGARITHM, MANTISSA OF A.

LOGARITHMS, NATURAL, logarithms to the base e, an irrational number $= 2.71828\,\ldots$, which is the limit of the sum of the series

$$1 + \frac{1}{1} + \frac{1}{2!} + \frac{1}{3!} + \frac{1}{4!} + \cdots$$

as the number of terms is indefinitely increased. This limit was chosen because it simplifies certain formulas of differential and integral calculus involving logarithmic functions. Another symbol for $\log_e x$ is $\ln x$.

LOGARITHMS OF TRIGONOMETRIC FUNCTIONS, *See* TABLE NO. 22.

LOGARITHMS, SOLVING EXPONENTIAL EQUATIONS BY. In an equation such as, $3^x = 81$, x may be found by changing 81 to the base 3, then $3^x = 3^4$ and $x = 4$. Exponential equations may be solved by assuming the logarithms of both members are equal. *See* TABLE NO. 19.

Ex. 1: Solve $5^x = 136$.

Sol.:
$$\log 5^x = \log 136$$
$$x \log 5 = \log 136$$
$$x = \frac{\log 136}{\log 5}$$
$$x = \frac{2.13354}{.69897}$$
$$x = 3.0524.$$
$$5^{3.0524} = 136.$$

Ex. 2: Solve $3^{x-1} = 8$.

Sol.:
$$\log 3^{x-1} = \log 8.$$
$$(x - 1) \log 3 = \log 8$$
$$x - 1 = \frac{\log 8}{\log 3}$$
$$x - 1 = \frac{.90309}{.47712} = 1.8928$$
$$x = 1 + 1.8928 = 2.8928.$$
$$3^{1.8928} = 8.$$

Ex. 3: Solve $\sqrt{3^x} = 13$.

Sol.:
$$3^{x/2} = 13$$
$$\log 3^{x/2} = \log 13$$
$$\frac{x}{2} \log 3 = \log 13$$
$$\frac{x}{2} = \frac{\log 13}{\log 3}$$
$$\frac{x}{2} = \frac{1.11394}{.47712}$$
$$x = \frac{2(1.11394)}{.47712}$$
$$x = \frac{2.22788}{.47712}$$
$$x = 4.6694.$$

See also EXPONENTIAL EQUATION.

LOGARITHMS, TABLE OF COMMON, *see* TABLE NO. 19.

LOGARITHMS, TABLE OF NATURAL, *see* TABLE NO. 20.

LOGIC, most generally the study of the principles which distinguish correct from incorrect reasoning (inference, argument) and the codification of such principles in systems of rules and axioms for the purpose of explicit validation of such reasoning. Logic should be distinguished from the study of reasoning or thought, which is more correctly a psychological study since such reasoning may, or may not, conform to the principles of logic. Aristotle, in his analysis of the SYLLOGISM, provided the first systematic treatment of logic. Logic may be broadly divided into the areas of inductive logic and deductive logic, the latter being further subdivided into such areas as combinatory logic, modal logic (study of arguments involving such terms as "possible," "necessary" etc.), deontic logic (study of the connections between statements about obligation—e.g., if X is obligatory, then it cannot be forbidden), and so on. Deductive logic is said to be a formal science (along with mathematics) since it abstracts from the content of statements and studies their form or structure with the intent of discovering the formal relations (of entailment, inconsistency, etc.) which obtain among such statements by virtue of their form. This interest has led to the introduction of special symbols to reflect the structure or form of a statement so that the mutual relations between such statements can more easily be discovered, codified, and embodied in formal proofs (*see* SYMBOLIC LOGIC). RUSSELL, WHITEHEAD, FREGE, BOOLE, and Gödel are among the chief contributors to logic in the last 100 years.

LOGICAL COMPLEMENT, *see* NEGATION, LOGICAL.

LONGITUDE, the angular distance of a point on the earth east or west of the PRIME MERIDIAN, measured through 180° and labeled E or W; also, any similar coordinate in various celestial COORDINATE SYSTEMS, such as celestial longitude in the ecliptic system. *See* MIDDLE LATITUDE SAILING; EARTH COORDINATE SYSTEM.

LOWEST COMMON DENOMINATOR (L.C.D.), the smallest number that is exactly divisible by each of the DENOMINATORS in a group of FRACTIONS. In $\dfrac{3}{4a} + \dfrac{2}{3a^2}$, the L.C.D. is $12a^2$.

LOWEST COMMON MULTIPLE (L.C.M.), of two or more ALGEBRAIC EXPRESSIONS, the expression of lowest degree that will exactly contain each of the expressions. To find the L.C.M. of two or more expressions, find the prime FACTORS of each expression. Take each factor the greatest number of times it occurs in any one of the expressions and find the product of the different prime factors.

Ex. 1: Find the L.C.M. of $2a^2x$, $4ax^2$, $6ax$.

Sol.:
$$2a^2x = 2 \cdot a \cdot a \cdot x$$
$$4ax^2 = 2 \cdot 2 \cdot a \cdot x \cdot x$$
$$6ax = 3 \cdot 2 \cdot a \cdot x$$

Then   L.C.M. $= 2 \cdot 2 \cdot 3 \cdot a \cdot a \cdot x \cdot x = 12a^2x^2$

Ex. 2: Find the L.C.M. of $x^2 - y^2$; $(x + y)^2$; $xy - y^2$.

Sol.:
$$x^2 - y^2 = (x + y)(x - y)$$
$$(x + y)^2 = (x + y)(x + y)$$
$$xy - y^2 = y(x - y)$$

Then   L.C.M. $= y(x + y)(x + y)(x - y)$

See also PRIME NUMBERS.

LOXODROME (lahx-oh-drohm), on a SPHERE, a curve that cuts all parallels under the same angle. The course of a ship that travels in the same direction is a loxodrome. A loxodrome is commonly called a *rhumb line* or *Mercator track*.

LUB, *see* LEAST UPPER BOUND.

LUNE, *see* SPHERE.

M

MACLAURIN SERIES (mac-law'-rin), a function $f(x)$ that can be expressed as a power series

$$\sum_{n=0}^{\infty} \frac{f^n(a)}{n!}(x-a)^n = f(a) + f'(a)(x-a)$$
$$+ \frac{f''(a)}{2}(x-a)^2 + \cdots,$$

also called a Taylor series at a. The Taylor series at $a = 0$ is the Maclaurin series of the function. Since $(x - 0)^n = x^n$, Maclaurin series are usually the simplest Taylor series. However, the Maclaurin series may fail to exist, and series at $a \neq 0$ may be the only ones available (see *Ex.* 2).

Ex. 1: Use the fact that $a_n = \dfrac{f^n(a)}{n!}$ (TAYLOR'S THEOREM) to find the Maclaurin series for the function e^x.

Sol.: All the derivatives of e^x are equal; evaluating them at zero shows that $f''(0) = e^0 = 1$. Thus, $a_n = \dfrac{1}{n!}$, and the Maclaurin series is

$$e^x = \frac{1}{0!} + \frac{1}{1!}x + \frac{1}{2!}x^2 + \frac{1}{3!}x^3 + \frac{1}{4!}x^4 + \frac{1}{5!}x^5 + \cdots$$
$$= \sum_{n=0}^{\infty} \frac{x^n}{n!}.$$

Ex. 2: Does the function $\ln x$ have a Maclaurin series?

Sol.: Since $f(0)$ is not defined, there is no Maclaurin series, although other Taylor series may be found.

MAGIC SQUARE, a square arrangement of numbers such that the sum of numbers in each row, column, and diagonal is the same, as, e.g., in the magic square shown in which the sum is 34.

16	3	2	13
5	10	11	8
9	6	7	12
4	15	14	1

MAJOR AXIS OF AN ELLIPSE, the CHORD through the foci of an ELLIPSE, extending from one side of the ellipse to the other,

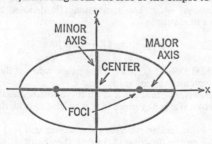

but not projecting outside it. It is the longest chord through the center of the ellipse, and the ellipse is symmetric about it. (See figure.) *See also* MINOR AXIS OF AN ELLIPSE.

MANN-WHITNEY U-TEST, in statistics, a test that is used to test the NULL HYPOTHESIS that two populations have equal MEDIANS versus a specified ALTERNATIVE HYPOTHESIS. The necessary assumptions are that the populations are continuous, have identical form, and that the samples are independent. The Mann-Whitney U-Test is equivalent to the RANK-SUM TEST, and except for the actual statistic used to make the test (and the tables to which it is referred), the procedure is identical to that for the rank-sum test.

The observations from the two independent samples are arranged together in order from smallest to largest. The smaller sample (of size n_1) is called Sample 1. If the samples are the same size, either may be denoted Sample 1. Sample 2 is of size n_2. Ranks are assigned to the observations (rank 1 for the smallest observation,), with equal observations being assigned the mean of the ranks that they occupy. Let R be the sum of the ranks of the observations from Sample 1. The statistic

$$U = n_1 n_2 + \frac{n_1(n_1 + 1)}{2} - R$$

(or $U' = n_1 n_2 - U$, if $U' < U$) is used to test the hypothesis. Tables of the significant values of U (or U') are available.

If both samples contain at least 9 or 10 observations, then U (or U') is a particular value of a random variable that is approximately normal, with mean $\dfrac{n_1 n_2}{2}$ and variance $\dfrac{n_1 n_2(n_1 + n_2 + 1)}{12}$.

MANTISSA, *see* LOGARITHM, MANTISSA OF A.

MAPPING, in mathematics, an operation which matches each element of a SET with another element, termed its image, in the same set, in a subset of that set, or in another set. A *many-to-one mapping* matches more than one element to each image; e.g., the equation $y = x^2$ matches each pair of real numbers, n and $-n$, with the same image, n^2. A *one-to-one mapping* matches each element with one and only one image; e.g., the mapping specified by the equation $y = -x$. A *one-to-many mapping* matches each element with more than one image; e.g., the mapping specified by the equation $y = \pm\sqrt{x}$, which maps n into both $+\sqrt{n}$ and $-\sqrt{n}$.

MARGINAL PROBABILITY FUNCTION, *see* JOINT PROBABILITY FUNCTION.

MATHEMATICAL MODEL, a mathematical construction (for instance, a formula) that is a description, in mathematical terms, of some natural phenomenon used to give information about that part of reality. For example, the BINOMIAL DISTRIBUTION,

$$f(x) = \binom{n}{x} \pi^x (1 - \pi)^{n-x},$$ might be selected as an appropriate

model for giving probabilities about families with four children. (The number of trials is fixed at four, each trial has two outcomes, the probability of having a boy is the same on each of the four trials, and the trials are independent. Thus, all the assumptions of the binomial distribution can be considered satisfied, and the choice of model is a realistic one.)

If the mathematical description of the natural phenomenon is valid, the model can be used to obtain new information about the phenomenon, just by mathematical manipulation. *See also* MULTINOMIAL DISTRIBUTION.

MATHEMATICS, the collective name applied to all those sciences in which operations in logic are used to study the relationship between quantity, space, time and magnitude. Traditionally, the mathematical sciences have been arranged into two general levels for study purposes, starting with **elementary mathematics,** the first level. The latter begins with *Arithmetic* which deals with numbers, followed by *Algebra*, which is an extension of arithmetic dealing with symbols and the solution of equations. *Geometry* follows algebra, traditionally. It is the science that treats of measurement, properties and relationships of line, point, angle, surface and solid. *Trigonometry* follows and is the last or highest of the elementary mathematics. It deals with the properties of triangles, trigonometric functions and their applications. Higher mathematics includes all the more advanced fields of study beyond trigonometry, such as *calculus, non-Euclidean geometry, projective geometry, set theory* and *topology*. Much of higher mathematics deals with extensions into abstract sciences of those systems first studied in elementary mathematics. Examples are *Boolean algebra* and *analytic geometry*.

The entire field of mathematics may be separated into **applied mathematics** and **pure** or **abstract mathematics.** Applied mathematics is the application of mathematics to practical problems, as when using geometry in architecture or mathematics as applied to navigation, STATISTICS, bookkeeping or accounting. Pure or abstract mathematics has the main purpose of advancing mathematical knowledge for its own sake. Much of higher mathematics is pure or abstract mathematics and a considerable portion of elementary mathematics is applied mathematics. Of course many of the abstract sciences have had, or may eventually be found to have, application to practical problems.

Mathematics employs a special kind of language using symbols, numerals and letters. Their use is determined by the rules of logic within each of the fields of study and serve as a means of short-cut, both in thinking and in visual representation. For mathematical symbols and abbreviations, *see* TABLE NO. 2. For a review of mathematical formulas, terms and laws, *see* TABLE NO. 3. TABLE NOS. 4 through 23 are additional mathematical tables.

Historically the first two branches of mathematics were arithmetic and geometry; both originated at about the same time in Egypt and Babylonia—as applied mathematics. These were transformed into systems of logic by the Greeks, starting in the 6th cent. B.C. E.g., *see* PYTHAGORAS; EUCLID; ARCHIMEDES; ERATOSTHENES OF ALEXANDRIA. Arithmetic was augmented during the Middle Ages by algebra, chiefly through the work of Arabic mathematicians, who built their system upon the foundations laid by the Greeks. Trigonometry, originally a branch of astronomy, became a separate science through the work of Arab mathematicians, chiefly Abul Wefa (fl. 10th cent. A.D.) and Nasir Eddin (fl. 13th cent.). In the 17th cent. arithmetic and algebra were combined in analytic geometry, principally through the work of DESCARTES. Analytic geometry opened the way toward several new disciplines in higher mathematics, starting with calculus. The latter was developed independently by LEIBNITZ and NEWTON. The theory of probability followed, formulated by PASCAL. Non-Euclidean geometry (mainly elliptic geometry and hyperbolic geometry) were developed by Johann BOLYAI (1802–1860) and N. I. LOBACHEVSKI (1793–1856). Projective geometry was first developed by Jean-Victor Poncelet in ab. 1822. A few years later wide advances were made in the theory of equations by Niels Abel (1802–1829) and Evariste Galois (1811–1832). The latter founded the theory of functions. Topology grew into a major science chiefly with the work of Jules Henri Poincaré in the theory of functions and in mathematical physics. The SET theory which now pervades all mathematics is primarily due to Georg CANTOR (1845–1918), who also introduced TRANSFINITE NUMBERS,

and Bertrand Russell, who also stimulated the development of symbolic logic.

All the mathematical subjects are extensively treated elsewhere in the text and tables; only a few of the major articles are cross-referenced below (for other mathematical subjects, see under individual entry heads): ALGEBRA; ARITHMETIC; BOOLEAN ALGEBRA; CALCULUS; GEOMETRY; GEOMETRY, ANALYTIC; NON-EUCLIDEAN GEOMETRY; PERMUTATION; PROBABILITY THEORY; PROJECTIVE GEOMETRY; RANDOM NUMBERS; SET; STATISTICS; SYMBOLIC LOGIC; TOPOLOGY; TRIGONOMETRY.

Biblio.: Boyer, C. B., *History of Mathematics* (1968); Person, Russell B., *Essentials of Mathematics* (1968).

MATRIX, a rectangular ARRAY of numbers. Consider matrices in which each row is formed by the COEFFICIENTS of the terms of an EQUATION. For example, a system of two equations (*see* SYSTEMS OF EQUATIONS) in two unknowns with its matrix in BRACKETS is

$$\begin{cases} x + y = 4 \\ 3x - y = 8 \end{cases} \qquad \begin{bmatrix} 1 & 1 & 4 \\ 3 & -1 & 8 \end{bmatrix}$$

The system can be solved by various operations on the matrix until it takes the form $\begin{vmatrix} 0 & 1 & b \\ 1 & 0 & a \end{vmatrix}$. Since the first column represents the coefficients of x and the second column the coefficients of y, it is obvious that $y = b$ (there is no x in the first row) and $x = a$ (there is no y in the second row). To solve the system apply the same operations as those applicable to a DETERMINANT, as follows:

$\begin{bmatrix} 1 & 1 & 4 \\ 3 & -1 & 8 \end{bmatrix}$ Write its matrix.

$\begin{bmatrix} 1 & 1 & 4 \\ 4 & 0 & 12 \end{bmatrix}$ Replace the 2nd row with the sum of the 2 rows.

$\begin{bmatrix} 1 & 1 & 4 \\ 1 & 0 & 3 \end{bmatrix}$ Divide the 2nd row by 4.

$\begin{bmatrix} 0 & 1 & 1 \\ 1 & 0 & 3 \end{bmatrix}$ Subtract 2nd row from the 1st and place the difference in the 1st row.

From the matrix the solution is $x = 3$ and $y = 1$.

Ex.: Solve the following system of equations by matrices:

Sol.: $\begin{cases} 3x - y = 1 \\ 4x - y = 3 \end{cases}$

$\begin{bmatrix} 3 & -1 & 1 \\ 4 & -1 & 3 \end{bmatrix}$ Write matrix from coefficients of equations and the constant terms.

$\begin{bmatrix} 3 & -1 & 1 \\ 1 & 0 & 2 \end{bmatrix}$ Subtract 1st row from 2nd and replace 2nd row with the difference.

$\begin{bmatrix} 3 & -1 & 1 \\ 3 & 0 & 6 \end{bmatrix}$ Multiply 2nd row by 3.

$\begin{bmatrix} 0 & 1 & 5 \\ 3 & 0 & 6 \end{bmatrix}$ Subtract 1st row from 2nd and place in 1st row.

$\begin{bmatrix} 0 & 1 & 5 \\ 1 & 0 & 2 \end{bmatrix}$ Divide 2nd row by 3.

From the matrix the solution is $x = 2$ and $y = 5$.

Note that a square array, such as the matrix $\begin{bmatrix} a & c \\ b & d \end{bmatrix}$, always written with brackets, has a corresponding number which is its determinant $ad - bc$. The determinant is denoted by vertical sidelines. For example,

$$\begin{vmatrix} 3 & 1 \\ 2 & 4 \end{vmatrix} = 12 - 2 = 10.$$

MAXIMUM OF A FUNCTION, greatest value of the function, if it has such an extreme value.

$f(x)$ has a *relative maximum* at a if there is some NEIGHBORHOOD of a such that if x is any point in this neighborhood, then $f(x) \leq f(a)$.

The function has an *absolute maximum* at a if $f(x) \leq f(a)$ for every x where the function is defined. (See figure.)

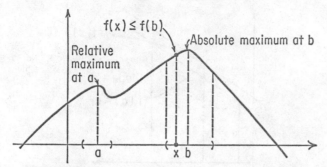

$f(x) \leq f(b)$

Relative maximum at a

Absolute maximum at b

Fig. 1

Ex.: Prove that the constant function $f(x) = 1$ has a relative maximum at every point.

Sol.: Let a be any value of x. Then $f(a) = 1$. Let $s = a - 1$, $r = a + 1$. For every x in the interval from s to r (this set is a neighborhood of a) $f(x) = 1$. Then, for every such x, certainly $f(x) \leq f(a)$. Therefore the definition is satisfied, and $f(x)$ has a relative maximum at a.

See also CURVE SKETCHING; EXTREMUM; EXTREMUM, DERIVATIVE AT; MINIMUM OF A FUNCTION.

MEAN, the average of two or more quantities. *See also* ARITHMETIC MEANS; GEOMETRIC MEAN.

MEAN ABSOLUTE DEVIATION, in statistics, a measure of dispersion (*see* DISPERSION, MEASURE OF) that gives the average distance of the sample observations from their mean. It is denoted M.A.D. and is defined by

$$\text{M.A.D.} = \frac{\sum_{i=1}^{n} |x_i - \bar{x}|}{n} .$$

If the observations are classified into k, classes, the mean absolute deviation is given by

$$\text{M.A.D.} = \frac{\sum_{i=1}^{k} |x'_i - \bar{x}| f_i}{n} ,$$

where x'_i denotes the midpoint of the ith class; f_i, the frequency of the ith class; n, the total number of observations; and k, the number of classes.

MEAN, POPULATION, *see* EXPECTED VALUE.

MEAN PROPORTION, a PROPORTION in which the means are the same. The mean value is called the MEAN PROPORTIONAL. Thus, $x : 3 = 3 : y$ is a mean proportion in which 3 is the mean

proportional between x and y. Thus, $\frac{2}{r} = \frac{r}{5}$ is a mean proportion

in which r is the mean proportional between 2 and 5.

The following THEOREMS in plane geometry involve mean proportions:

1. If an ALTITUDE is drawn to the HYPOTENUSE of a RIGHT TRIANGLE, (a) the altitude is the mean proportional between the segments of the hypotenuse (see Fig. 1), and (b) either leg is the mean proportional between the whole hypotenuse and the segment of the hypotenuse adjacent to that leg (see Fig. 2).

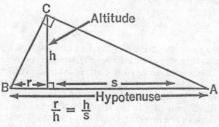

Altitude

Hypotenuse

$$\frac{r}{h} = \frac{h}{s}$$

Fig. 1

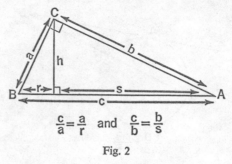

$$\frac{c}{a} = \frac{a}{r} \quad \text{and} \quad \frac{c}{b} = \frac{b}{s}$$

Fig. 2

2. If a TANGENT LINE and a SECANT LINE are drawn to a CIRCLE from the same external point, the tangent is the mean proportional between the whole secant and the external segment of the secant. (See Fig. 3.)

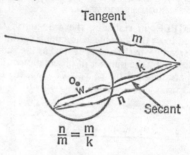

Tangent

Secant

$$\frac{n}{m} = \frac{m}{k}$$

Fig. 3

MEAN PROPORTIONAL, either mean between the first and fourth terms of a PROPORTION, when the two means are equal. If $a : b = b : c$, then b is the mean proportional between a and c, and $b^2 = ac$.

In a triangle:

1. The altitude to the HYPOTENUSE of a RIGHT TRIANGLE is the mean proportional between the segments of the hypotenuse. In Fig. 1, $AD/CD = CD/DB$.

2. Either leg of a right triangle is the mean proportional between the hypotenuse and its PROJECTION on the hypotenuse. In Fig. 1, $AD/AC = AC/AB$ and $DB/BC = BC/AB$.

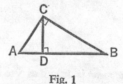

Fig. 1

In a circle:

1. The perpendicular from any point on a CIRCLE to a diameter (*see* DIAMETER OF A CIRCLE) is the mean proportional between the segments of the diameter. In Fig. 2, $AD/CD = CD/DB$.

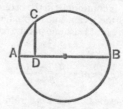

Fig. 2

2. If a TANGENT LINE and a SECANT LINE are drawn to a circle, the tangent is the mean proportional between the secant and its external segment. (See Fig. 3.)

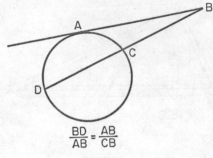

$$\frac{BD}{AB} = \frac{AB}{CB}$$

Fig. 3

MEANS, the second and third terms of a PROPORTION. In the proportion $a : b = c : d$, b and c are the means. *See also* ARITHMETIC MEANS; GEOMETRIC MEAN.

MEAN, SAMPLE, in statistics, the ARITHMETIC MEAN, commonly referred to as the average. The sample (arithmetic) mean is denoted $\bar{x}$ (read "x-bar") and is defined as the sum of the observations divided by the number of observations. If the sample observations are denoted by $x_1, x_2, \ldots, x_n$, the mean is defined by

$$\bar{x} = \frac{x_1 + x_2 + \cdots + x_n}{n} = \frac{\sum\limits_{i=1}^{n} x_i}{n}.$$

If the data are classified into k classes, then the mean is given by

$$\bar{x} = \frac{x'_1 f_1 + x'_2 f_2 + \cdots + x'_k f_k}{n} = \frac{\sum\limits_{i=1}^{k} x'_i f_i}{n}$$

where x'_i denotes the midpoint of the ith class, f_i denotes the FREQUENCY of the ith class, and n denotes the total number of observations.

The sample mean $\bar{x}$ is an estimate of the population mean μ, also called the EXPECTED VALUE of x, denoted $E(x)$.

The harmonic mean and the geometric mean are two other means, but are seldom used. The *sample harmonic mean* is defined as $\dfrac{1}{\sum\limits_{i=1}^{n} \dfrac{1}{x_i}/n}$.

The *sample geometric mean* is defined as $\sqrt[n]{x_1 x_2 \cdots x_n}$.

MEAN SQUARE, in statistics, a sum of squares divided by the DEGREES OF FREEDOM, used in the ANALYSIS OF VARIANCE.

MEAN SQUARED DEVIATION, *see* VARIANCE, SAMPLE.

MEAN VALUE THEOREM (M.V.T.). If $f(x)$ is a FUNCTION for which $f'(x)$ exists and is continuous in the CLOSED INTERVAL $[a, b]$, and m is the slope of the secant line through the points $(a, f(a))$ and $(b, f(b))$, then there is at least one point c between a and b for which

$$f'(c) = m = \frac{f(b) - f(a)}{b - a}.$$

Geometrically, this means that there is a point, c, where the tangent to the curve $y = f(x)$ is parallel to the mentioned secant. (See Fig. 1.)

An important special case, to which the general theorem can be reduced by algebraic manipulation, is ROLLE'S THEOREM, for which we take $f(b) = f(a) = m = 0$.

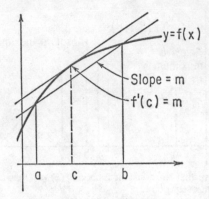

Fig. 1

Ex. 1: Let $f(x) = x^2 - x + 1$, $a = 1$, and $b = 3$. What is the point which M.V.T. asserts to exist?

Sol.: The M.V.T. asserts that a point c between 1 and 3 exists for which

$$f'(c) = m = \frac{(3^2 - 3 + 1) - (1^2 - 1 + 1)}{3 - 1} = 3.$$

This point c may be found by calculating $f'(x)$, setting this equal to m, and solving for x, as follows:

$$f'(x) = 2x - 1; \; 2x - 1 = 3; \; 2x = 4; \; x = 2.$$

Thus, $c = 2$. We may check by calculating $f'(2)$: $f'(2) = 2(2) - 1 = 4 - 1 = 3$.

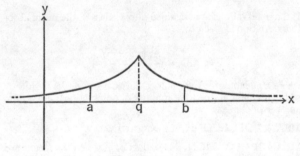

Fig. 2

Ex. 2: Does the M.V.T. apply to the function with the graph shown in Fig. 2 above? Why?

Sol.: It does not apply, since $f'(x)$ is not continuous at every point between a and b. Specifically, $f'(x)$ is discontinuous at $x = q$.

See also MEAN VALUE THEOREM EXTENSION; MEAN VALUE THEOREM FOR INTEGRALS.

MEAN VALUE THEOREM EXTENSION. If both $f'(x)$ and $g'(x)$ exist and are continuous on the interval $[a, b]$, then there is a point c, $a < c < b$, so that

$$\frac{f'(c)}{g'(c)} = \frac{f(b) - f(a)}{g(b) - g(a)}.$$

If these two functions are thought of as PARAMETRIC EQUATIONS of a curve, so that $y = f(t)$ and $x = g(t)$, then the above equation may be interpreted as saying that for some value c of t, $a < c < b$. The tangent to the curve has the same slope as the line joining the points corresponding to $t = a$ and $t = b$. The slope of the tangent at c is the left half of the above equation, while the slope of the line on $(g(a), f(a))$ and $(g(b), f(b))$ is the right half. *See also* MEAN VALUE THEOREM.

MEAN VALUE THEOREM FOR INTEGRALS. The Mean Value Theorem for Integrals states that if the function $f(x)$ meets the conditions of the basic MEAN VALUE THEOREM, then there is some point c between a and b for which

$$f(c)(b - a) = \int_a^b f(x)\,dx.$$

Geometrically, this means that the shaded rectangle in the figure has the same square measure as the area which lies under the curve within the same interval $[a, b]$.

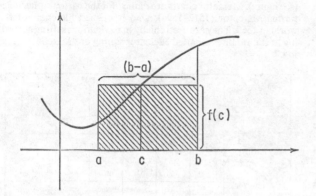

Since $\int_a^b f(x)\,dx = F(b) - F(a)$, where $F(x)$ is an integral of $f(x)$, we can write

$$f(c)(b - a) = F(b) - F(a).$$

This statement is equivalent to the statement of Mean Value Theorem for derivatives. The two Mean Value Theorems are really only two different interpretations of the same fact, one expressed in terms of slopes, the other in terms of areas.

Ex.: The M.V.T. for Integrals asserts that some point exists for the function $y = x^2$ between $a = 1$ and $b = 4$. What is this point?

Sol.: The point is at c so that $f(c)(4 - 1) = \int_1^4 x^2\,dx$ may be found by calculating the area A and then solving the equation $f(x)(4 - 1) = A$.

$$A = \int_1^4 x^2\,dx = \frac{x^3}{3}\Big]_1^4 = \frac{4^3 - 1^3}{3} = \frac{63}{3} = 21.$$

Then $f(x)(4 - 1) = 21$, or $(x^2)(3) = 21$; so $x = \sqrt{21/3} = \sqrt{7}$. Thus, $c = \sqrt{7} \approx 2.65$. *See also* AREA UNDER CURVE.

MEASUREMENT, the process of determining the extent, capacity, amount, or degree of some quantity; also, the result of such a determination. A measurement is expressed as a number and a *unit*, which is the basic amount of the quantity being measured. Thus, a measurement of 15.7 in. means that a given length was found to be 15 times the length of the basic unit, one inch, plus 7/10 of an inch. The different units used for various quantities are listed in TABLE NOS. 4, 5. The two basic systems of units in general use are the METRIC SYSTEM and the ENGLISH SYSTEM.

The physical embodiment of a unit is called a *standard*. Thus, a meter stick is a standard of length equal to 1 meter. The basic standards of measurement are kept in the national bureaus of standards of different countries. For most nations these are based on the basic metric standards kept at Sèvres, France, the headquarters of the International Bureau of Standards. Occasionally, a unit may be defined in terms of its standard, as the kilogram is defined as a unit of mass equal to the mass of the International Prototype Kilogram at Sèvres. In recent years, the trend has been to atomic standards, which are more reliable and are reproducible anywhere in the world. The meter and the second are now defined in this way. This is a far cry from anc. times, when units named for the finger, hand, or foot were defined simply by the size of these parts of the person making the measurement.

Since some quantities are considered fundamental and others are derived from them, it is not necessary to have standards for all basic units (*see also* DIMENSION). Thus, the standard meter, kilogram, and second also serve to define the square meter of area, cubic meter of volume, newton of force, joule of energy, and watt of power. When combined with the coulomb of charge, which is the fundamental unit of electricity, they define the other electric units, such as the ampere, ohm, and volt. In addition to the basic units for each quantity, there are also often other units, which usually are even multiples or fractions of the basic unit, that can be used for measuring the same quantity. For example, the yard is the basic unit of length in the English system, but the inch, foot, and mile are also used. Thus, one can usually choose a unit whose size is appropriate to the particular measurement. Also, special units have been defined for measurements of very large or very small quantities—the astronomical unit for distances within the solar system, the light-year and the PARSEC for stellar and galactic distances, the Angstrom unit for extremely small distances, as between atoms in a solid, and the atomic mass unit for the mass of individual atoms and molecules.

Many methods exist for making measurements, some direct, but most of them indirect. A direct method involves placing the quantity in question in direct contact with a standard of measurement, such as a meter stick, a yard stick, or a thermometer. Indirect measurements may involve using geometry or trigonometry, as in finding the height of a distant object by triangulation or the distance to a star by the PARALLAX method. The spectrum of light from an astronomical object is used for many indirect measurements. For example, it can be used to find the surface temperature. The shifting of lines from their usual position in the spectrum is often interpreted as due to the Doppler Effect and thus gives an estimate of the speed of an object toward or away from an observer. For very distant galaxies, this "red shift" not only gives their speed, but also their distance, according to Hubble's Law. Sometimes an object may be too small to measure directly by ordinary methods but is still measured easily by a simple indirect method. For example, the thickness of a single page of this book can not be measured easily with a ruler, but by measuring the thickness of 100 pages, then dividing the result by 100, one arrives at the desired value quite quickly.

All of the various methods of measurement are designed to provide a result that is both accurate and precise. *Accuracy* refers to the correctness of a measurement. *Precision* refers to the fineness of the measurement; a measurement of 3.74 meters is more precise than one of 4. meters, although both might be accurate. The precision of any measurement is limited by the measuring instrument used. A meter stick, for example, might have markings to the nearest millimeter, so that estimates can be made to the nearest tenth of a millimeter. Often there may be no need of great precision. A measurement of $8\frac{1}{2}$ mi. as the accurate distance between two towns is precise enough for most motorists. A measurement of 5.832 mi. for the same distance, although more precise, may be useless because it is inaccurate.

Various natural limitations arise when one attempts to make highly precise measurements. For example, the Brownian Motion and similar phenomena result in an uncertainty because they cause "noise" which interferes with the "signal" corresponding to the desired measurement. At the smallest level, the mere act itself of making a measurement leads to uncertainty. In order to measure a given quantity, one must interact with the object having this quantity. This interaction in turn disturbs the object, a fact that has considerable consequences for objects at the atomic level. Heisenberg's Uncertainty Principle is the expression of the absolute limitation on the precision with which certain related quantities can be measured at this level.

MEASURE OF VARIATION, in statistics, measure of dispersion (*see* DISPERSION, MEASURE OF).

MECHANICS RULE, a method of approximating the *square root* of a number. To find the square root of a number by the mechanics rule, an estimate of the square root is made and used as the divisor, with the original number as dividend. The approximate square root is the average of the quotient and the estimate.

Ex.: Find $\sqrt{2}$ by the mechanics rule.

Sol.: Estimate: 1.5

$$
\begin{array}{r}
1.333 \\
1.5\overline{)20.000}
\end{array}
$$

Divide 1.5 into 2:

Average of 1.5 and 1.33:

$$
\begin{array}{r}
1.5000 \\
1.3333 \\
\hline
2)2.8333 \\
\hline
1.4167
\end{array}
$$

Thus, $\sqrt{2} \approx 1.4167.$

MEDIAN (mee'-dee-an), in statistics, after the observations of a sample are ranked in order (usually from smallest to largest), the middle observation if the number of observations is odd, or the ARITHMETIC MEAN of the two middle observations if the number of observations is even.

If the data are classified, the class that contains the middle observation is known as the *median class*. The median of data that have been classified can be found from the formula

$$\text{median} = l_m + \frac{J_m}{c_m} \cdot \left(\frac{n}{2} - F_{m-1} \right),$$

where l_m denotes the lower boundary of the median class; f_m, the frequency of the median class; c_m, the width of the interval of the median class; and F_{m-1}, the cumulative frequency of the classes up to, but not including, the median class.

MEDIAN OF A TRAPEZOID, the LINE SEGMENT that joins the MIDPOINTS of the nonparallel sides of the TRAPEZOID. The median of a trapezoid is parallel to the bases and is equal to one half their sum. In the figure, segment EF is the median of trapezoid $ABCD$, $EF \parallel AB$ and CD, and $EF = \frac{1}{2}(AB + CD)$.

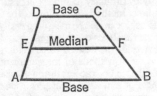

MEDIAN OF A TRIANGLE, the LINE SEGMENT joining a VERTEX of a triangle to the MIDPOINT of the opposite side. (See figure.) All three medians of a triangle meet at a point called the centroid. *See* CONCURRENT LINES.

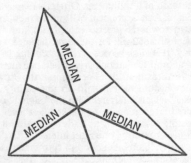

MEMORY UNIT, *see* COMPUTER.

MERCATOR CHART (mur-kay'-tor), a map made by means of a projection in which a correspondence is made between a point on the earth's surface and points on the *xy*-plane. In such a projection, a point with LATITUDE ϕ, LONGITUDE θ is represented by the point (x,y) such that $x = \theta$, $y = \ln (\sec \phi + \tan \phi)$. On a Mercator chart meridians are represented by lines parallel to the *y*-axis.

The mercator projection is conformal; i.e., the angle between a curve or the sphere and an intersecting parallel is unchanged by mapping. A straight line on the chart with slope $\tan \alpha$ corresponds to a curve on the sphere cutting all parallels under the same angle α. This curve is called a rhumb line or LOXODROME (see figure). Mercator charts are named for the cartographer, Gerardus Mercator (1512–1594), who published his chart of the world in 1569. They are used chiefly in navigation; sailing according to rhumb lines is called Mercator sailing or "Mercator tracking."

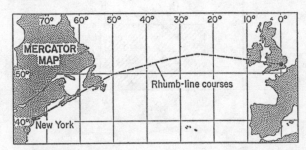

MERIDIAN, a GREAT CIRCLE passing through the geographic poles of the earth, perpendicular to the equator (see figure); also, any similar great circle, such as those used in various celestial COORDINATE SYSTEMS. The *celestial meridian* is the HOUR CIRCLE passing through an observer's ZENITH. The meridian which passes through Greenwich, England is (by international agreement) called the PRIME MERIDIAN. *See also* EARTH COORDINATE SYSTEM.

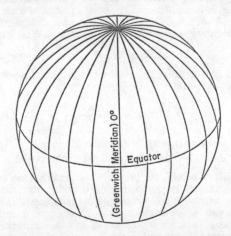

MESH OF PARTITION, largest of the distances between adjacent points of a PARTITION. The mesh of the partition (P) is sometimes called its size.

Ex. 1: What is the mesh of the following partition of the interval $[1, 4]$? $P = \{1, 2, 2\frac{1}{2}, 4\}$

Sol.: The distances between adjacent points are $2 - 1 = 1$; $2\frac{1}{2} - 2 = \frac{1}{2}$; $4 - 2\frac{1}{2} = 1\frac{1}{2}$. The largest of these is $1\frac{1}{2}$, which is the mesh. *See also* AREA UNDER CURVE; DEFINITE INTEGRAL.

METER, *see* METRIC SYSTEM; MKS SYSTEM; TABLE NO. 5.

METRIC SYSTEM, a decimal based system of WEIGHTS AND MEASURES, whose fundamental units are the *meter* of length and the *gram* of mass or weight. Fractions and multiples of the basic metric units all differ by powers of 10, so that converting from one unit to another merely involves moving the decimal point in a measurement. These fractions and multiples are indicated by the use of prefixes, as follows:

FRACTIONS			MULTIPLES		
Prefix	*Value*		*Prefix*	*Value*	
deci-	1/10	10^{-1}	deka-	10	10^1
centi-	1/100	10^{-2}	hecto-	100	10^2
milli-	1/1000	10^{-3}	kilo-	1000	10^3
micro-	1/1,000,000	10^{-6}	mega-	1,000,000	10^6
nano-	1/1,000,000,000	10^{-9}	giga-	1,000,000,000	10^9
pico-	1/1,000,000,000,000	10^{-12}	tera-	1,000,000,000,000	10^{12}

Thus, a millimeter is one-thousandths of a meter, while a megawatt is a million watts. The metric system was developed in France following the French Revolution. It was originally intended that the basic units be defined in a simple manner related to known physical properties of substances. For example, the meter was to be 1/10,000,000 of the distance from the N. Pole to the Equator, while the kilogram was to be the mass of 1,000 cubic centimeters of water at its temperature of maximum density (ab. 4°C.). The *liter* was to be the volume occupied by 1 kilogram of water and thus equal to 1,000 cubic centimeters. However, because of slight errors in surveying the basic distance, the values of the meter and kilogram do not actually correspond to their original definitions. (It is the kilogram, rather than the gram, that serves as the standard of mass because of the small size of the gram.) Thus, for many years the meter was defined by its international standard, a platinum-iridium bar of X-shaped cross section with two scratches on it marking the two ends of the standard meter when the bar is at 0°C. This standard, however, has since been replaced by an atomic standard, with the meter defined as 1,650,763.73 wavelengths of the red-orange light from an atom of krypton-86 under specified conditions. The kilogram is still defined by the International Prototype Kilogram, a platinum-iridium cylinder kept at the International Bureau of Weights and Measures at Sèvres, France. The liter retains its original definition as the volume of a kilogram of water and thus is not exactly equal to 1,000 cubic centimeters, or 1 cubic decimeter, but rather to 1.000028 cubic decimeters.

The metric system was officially adopted in France in 1799 and was made compulsory in 1837. It was also adopted by many other countries and is now the only system of weights and measures in continental Europe and is the legal system throughout Latin America and in much of Asia.

The English-speaking countries, however, including the U.S., still use the ENGLISH SYSTEM of weights and measures, which is much older than the metric system and based on less precise standards. The metric system was made legal in the U.S. in 1866 but it is only recently that concerted efforts have been made to adopt it for general use. Two different sets of derived units exist in the metric system. One of these, the MKS SYSTEM, is based on the meter of length, the kilogram of mass, and the second of time. Its derived units include the newton of force, the *joule* of work or energy, and the *watt* of power. The CGS SYSTEM is based on the centimeter, the gram, and the second. Its units, which are smaller than the MKS units, include the DYNE of force and the ERG of work or energy. The MKS system is generally preferred because of the more practical size of its units and because of the greater simplicity of the electric and magnetic units derived from its units (*see* TABLE NO. 4). For conversion factors relating the units of the metric system to those of the English system, *see* TABLE NO. 5.

MIDDLE LATITUDE SAILING, the method for finding a difference in LONGITUDE, *DL.* The DEPARTURE, *p,* between two places is measured on the parallel of LATITUDE halfway between the parallels of latitude of the starting point, L_1, and of the destination, L_2. Then the difference in longitude equals the product of the departure and the secant of one half the sum of the latitudes of starting point and destination. $DL = p \sec \frac{1}{2}(L_1 + L_2)$. *See also* PLANE SAILING; PARALLEL SAILING.

MIDPOINT, in mathematics the POINT that divides a LINE SEGMENT into two equal parts. If one point has coordinates (x_1, y_1), and the other has coordinates (x_2, y_2), the midpoint M has coordinates given by

$$M = \left(\frac{x_1 + x_2}{2}, \frac{y_1 + y_2}{2} \right).$$

Ex. 1: Find the coordinates of the midpoint M of the segment joining $A(-3,2)$ and $B(5,4)$. (See figure.)

$$x = \frac{-3 + 5}{2} = 1 \quad \text{and} \quad y = \frac{2 + 4}{2} = 3$$

The coordinates of midpoint M are (1,3).

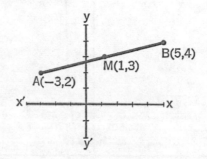

Ex. 2: Find the coordinates of the midpoints of the sides of the triangle whose vertices are

$$A(-3,0), \; B(5,-2), \text{ and } C(1,4).$$

Abscissa of midpoint of $AB = \frac{1}{2}(-3 + 5) = 1.$
Ordinate of midpoint of $AB = \frac{1}{2}(0 - 2) = -1.$
Coordinates of midpoint of AB are (1,−1).
Coordinates of midpoint of AC are (−1,2)
Coordinates of midpoint of BC are (3,1).

MIDRANGE, in statistics, a measure of location, equal to the ARITHMETIC MEAN of the smallest and largest observations in the sample:

$$\text{Midrange} = \frac{\text{Largest Observation} + \text{Smallest Observation}}{2}.$$

E.g., if the largest observation in a sample is 179 and the smallest is 118, the midrange is $\frac{179 + 118}{2} = \frac{297}{2} = 148.5.$

MIL, a unit of measure for angles. 1 mil is 1/6400 of a complete rotation (360°). 1 mil is .05625°, and approximately 1/1000 radian. (See figure.)

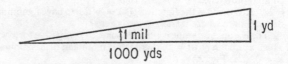

MINIMUM OF A FUNCTION, smallest value of the function, if it has such an extreme value.

A FUNCTION $f(x)$ is said to have a relative minimum at $x = a$ if there is some NEIGHBORHOOD of a such that, if x is any point in this neighborhood, then $f(x) \geq f(a)$.

The function is said to have an absolute minimum if $f(x) \geq f(a)$ for every x where the function is defined.

Minima can usually be located because if a function and its DERIVATIVE are both continuous (*see* CONTINUOUS FUNCTION), at a minimum its derivative is zero. Not all zero derivatives indicate minima, however (see Ex. 2).

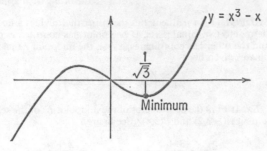

Fig. 1

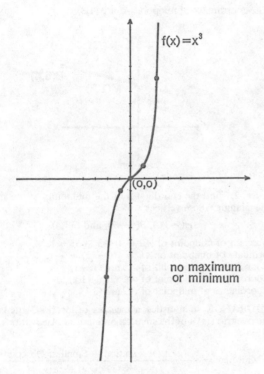

Fig. 2

Ex. 1: Sketch the function $x^3 - x$. At what point does it have a relative minimum? Does it have an absolute minimum?

Sol.: To find the minima, we set $f'(x) = 0$ and solve for x. The result is a minimum at $1/\sqrt{3}$. The function has no absolute minimum because as x approaches $-\infty$, $x^3 - x$ becomes arbitrarily small (approaches $-\infty$). (See Fig. 1.)

Ex. 2: Why does the function $f(x) = x^3$ fail to have a minimum or maximum where its derivative is zero?

Sol.: Because its value is positive for $x > 0$, negative for $x < 0$. Thus, although $f'(0) = 0$, there is no minimum or maximum at $x = 0$. (See Fig. 2.)

See also CURVE SKETCHING; EXTREMUM; EXTREMUM, DERIVATIVE AT; MAXIMUM OF A FUNCTION; SECOND DERIVATIVE TEST.

MINOR, in mathematics, of an element in a determinant, the DETERMINANT formed by striking out the row and column in which the element occurs. The minor of a, in $\begin{vmatrix} a & b & c \\ d & e & f \\ g & h & i \end{vmatrix}$ is $\begin{vmatrix} e & f \\ h & i \end{vmatrix}$.

MINOR AXIS OF AN ELLIPSE, the CHORD through the center of the ELLIPSE perpendicular to the MAJOR AXIS (*see* MAJOR AXIS OF AN ELLIPSE). It is the shortest chord through the center of the ellipse, and the ellipse is symmetric about it. (See figure.)

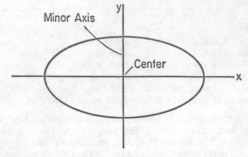

MINUEND (min'-yoo-end), the number from which another number is taken in a SUBTRACTION operation. If 24 is subtracted from 38, the minuend is 38; if $3a - 4$ is subtracted from $7a - 2$, the minuend is $7a - 2$.

MIXED EXPRESSION, the algebraic sum (or difference) of a POLYNOMIAL and an algebraic fraction or, in arithmetic, the sum of an INTEGER and a fraction with the plus sign omitted. To change the mixed number $2\frac{3}{4}$ to a fraction, the whole number 2 is changed to a fraction with DENOMINATOR 4, that is $\frac{8}{4}$, which is added to $\frac{3}{4}$ to obtain the simple fraction $\frac{11}{4}$. The method is shortened by multiplying the whole number 2 by the denominator 4 and adding the NUMERATOR 3 and placing over denominator 4 In like manner, a mixed expression can be changed to a fraction

$3x - 4 - \dfrac{2}{x}$ is changed to the fraction, $\dfrac{3x^2 - 4x - 2}{x}$, by multiplying the integral expression, $(3x - 4)$ by the denominator x and adding algebraically the numerator -2 and placing over denominator x. The resulting fraction should be simplified or reduced, if necessary.

Ex. 1: Change $a - b + b^2/(a + b)$ to a fraction.

$$\frac{(a - b)(a + b) + b^2}{a + b} = \frac{a^2 - b^2 + b^2}{a + b} = \frac{a^2}{a + b}.$$

To change any fraction to a mixed number, divide the numerator by the denominator and add algebraically the remainder over the denominator.

Ex. 2: Change $(12a^2 - 20a + 3)/4a$ to a mixed expression.

$$3a - 5 + \frac{3}{4a}.$$

MIXED NUMBER, a number made up of a whole number and a fraction. E.g., $3\frac{2}{5}$ is a mixed number. Although it is written in the same way that multiplication is indicated in mathematics, the mixed number indicates the *sum* of the whole number and fraction. Thus, $3\frac{2}{5}$ means $3 + \frac{2}{5}$. To operate with mixed numbers it is best to change them to IMPROPER FRACTIONS. This can be done by changing the whole number part to an EQUIVALENT FRACTION with the same DENOMINATOR as the fraction, and adding it to the fraction part.

Ex. 1: Change $3\frac{2}{5}$ to an improper fraction.

Sol.: Change 3 to an equivalent fraction whose denominator is 5:

$$3 = \tfrac{3}{1} = \tfrac{3}{1} \cdot \tfrac{5}{5} = 15/5.$$
$$\text{Add: } 15/5 + 2/5 = 17/5.$$
$$\therefore \ 3\tfrac{2}{5} = 17/5.$$

Another way to change a mixed number to an improper fraction is to multiply the whole number part by the denominator of the fraction part, add the numerator to that product, and use the sum as the numerator with the original denominator of the new equivalent improper fraction. This method is preferred since it is accomplished faster.

Ex. 2: Change $3\frac{2}{5}$ to an improper fraction.

Sol.: To determine the denominator:

$$3 \times 5 + 2 = 15 + 2 = 17$$
$$\therefore 3\frac{2}{5} = 17/5.$$

MIXTURE PROBLEMS.

Ex. 1: A grocer mixes two brands of tea, one of which he sells for 90¢ a pound and the other for 65¢ a pound. How many pounds of each can he mix, to have a blend of 40 pounds that sells for 75¢ a pound?

Sol.: Let $\quad x =$ pounds of 90¢ tea,
then $\qquad 40 - x =$ pounds of 65¢ tea.
$\qquad 90x =$ cents for x pounds at 90¢.
$\qquad 65(40 - x) =$ cents for $40 - x$ pounds at 65¢.
$\qquad 75(40) =$ cents for 40 pounds at 75¢.

$$90x + 65(40 - x) = 75(40)$$
$$90x + 2600 - 65x = 3000$$
$$90x - 65x = 3000 - 2600$$
$$25x = 400$$
$$x = 16 \text{ pounds at } 90¢.$$
$$40 - x = 24 \text{ pounds at } 65¢.$$

Check: $16(.90) + 24(.65) = 40(.75)$
$\qquad\quad \$14.40 + \$15.60 = \$30.00.$

Ex. 2: To a 3 gallon mixture of alcohol and water that is 60% alcohol, how much pure alcohol must be added to make a 70% mixture?

Sol: Let $\quad x =$ gallons of alcohol to be added.
$\qquad 3 =$ gallons of 60% mixture.
$\qquad x + 3 =$ gallons of new 70% mixture.
alcohol in 3 gal. + alcohol added = alcohol in new mix.

$$.60(3) + x = .70(x + 3)$$
$$1.8 + x = .7x + 2.1$$
$$x - .7x = 2.1 - 1.8$$
$$.3x = .3$$
$$x = 1 \text{ gallon of pure alcohol.}$$

Check: $\qquad (.60)3 + 1 = (.70)4$
$\qquad\qquad\quad 1.8 + 1 = 2.8$
$\qquad\qquad\qquad\quad 2.8 = 2.8.$

MKS SYSTEM, a system of units of measurement in the METRIC SYSTEM. The name is derived from the three basic units in this system—the *meter*, the *kilogram*, and the *second*. The MKS unit of force is the *newton*, equal to 1 kilogram-meter per square second. The unit of work or energy is the *joule*, 1 newton-meter. The MKS unit of heat energy is the *kilocalorie*, the heat required to raise 1 kilogram of water 1 degree Celsius (*see* CELSIUS TEMPERATURE SCALE). The unit of power is the *watt*, equal to 1 joule per second. The system of electric and magnetic units based on MKS units is called the *MKS-practical system*. Its basic unit is the *coulomb* of charge. See TABLE NOS. 5, 6. A second system of metric units also in use is the CGS SYSTEM. In recent years, however, the MKS system has been preferred for most uses and has largely replaced the CGS system, except in the measurement of density.

MODE, in statistics, the observation (or observations) that occurs most frequently. If two observations occur equally frequently and more frequently than any other, the sample is said to be *bimodal*. If three observations occur equally frequently and more frequently than any other, the sample is said to be *trimodal*. If all observations occur equally frequently, the sample is said to have no mode.

If the data are classified, the class which contains the most observations is said to be the *modal class*.

Exs.: The mode of the sample 72, 63, 69, 76, 81, 76 is 76. The sample 72, 63, 69, 76, 81, 63, 76, 90 is bimodal, 63 and 76 are both modes.

MODULUS (moj'-uh-lus), of a complex number, the fixed length which, together with a fixed positive angle, called the amplitude, determines a point in a plane. In the figure, P is a point in the plane and OP is a line of fixed length which connects the point with the ORIGIN and which makes a fixed positive angle θ with OX, the positive side of the x-axis. The number which the point represents is (r,θ). The modulus $r = \sqrt{x^2 + y^2}$.

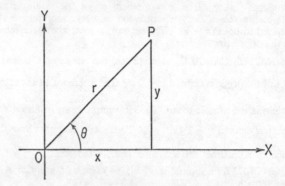

MOEBIUS STRIP (muh'-bee-us), a surface with only one side. A Moebius strip is made by making a half-twist in a strip of paper, and fastening the ends together (see parts a and b of the figure). Since the Moebius strip is a surface of one side, if a line is drawn down the middle of the strip, it will meet the starting point, after covering both sides of the original strip of paper, without the pencil having been lifted. (See c.) If the Moebius strip is then cut along the line, it will remain in one piece. (See d.) If cut again, two interlocking pieces will result. (See e.)

How to make a Moebius Strip

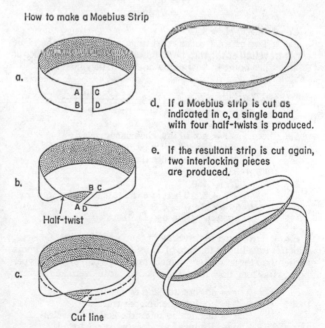

a.

b. Half-twist

c. Cut line

d. If a Moebius strip is cut as indicated in c, a single band with four half-twists is produced.

e. If the resultant strip is cut again, two interlocking pieces are produced.

MOMENT GENERATING FUNCTION, in statistics, a function that generates the theoretical moments, usually about the origin, for a distribution. The moment generating function of the probability distribution of a random variable is given by the expected value of e^{tx}.

$$M_x(t) = E(e^{tx}) = \sum_i e^{tx_i} f(x_i),$$

where the summation extends over all x_i within the range of the random variable x. The first moment is used to compute the MEAN value of a given set of data; the second moment to compute the variance (see VARIANCE, POPULATION; VARIANCE, SAMPLE) and STANDARD DEVIATION.

MOMENT, POPULATION. In statistics, the rth population moment about the origin is defined to be $E[x^r]$, (where E denotes EXPECTED VALUE). The first moment about the origin is the population mean. The rth population moment about the mean is defined to be $E[(x - \mu)^r]$. The second moment about the mean is the population variance.

MOMENT, SAMPLE. In statistics, the rth sample moment about the origin is defined as $\frac{1}{n} \sum_{i=1}^{n} x_i{}^r$. The first moment about the origin is the sample mean. The rth sample moment about the mean is defined as $\frac{1}{n} \sum_{i=1}^{n} (x_i - \bar{x})^r$. The second moment about the mean is sometimes defined as the sample variance.

MONOMIAL (moh-noh'-mee-ahl), an ALGEBRAIC EXPRESSION of one term, such as,

$$a; \ 3xy; \ \frac{a^2b}{3c}; \ \text{and} \ \frac{a + b}{c + d}.$$

MOTION PROBLEMS, solved by the FORMULA $d = rt$, or distance equals rate times time.

Ex. 1: How many hours will it take an automobile to travel 300 miles at an average rate of speed of 40 miles per hour?

$$d = rt$$
$$300 = 40t$$
$$t = 7\tfrac{1}{2} \text{ hours.}$$

Check: $40 \times 7\tfrac{1}{2} = 300$.

Ex. 2: Two cars 450 miles apart travel toward each other. One car is traveling at the rate of 40 miles per hour and the other at 35 miles per hour. In how many hours will they meet?

Sol.: Let $t =$ no. of hrs. each car travels
then $40t =$ no. of miles faster car travels.
    $35t =$ no. of miles the other car travels.
  $40t + 35t = 450$
    $75t = 450$
     $t = 6.$ Therefore the cars will meet in 6 hrs.
Check: $(40)(6) + (35)(6) = 450$
   $240 + 210 = 450.$

Ex. 3: Two cars are traveling in the same direction. One car, which is traveling at the rate of 35 miles per hour, leaves 2 hours earlier than the second car, which travels at a rate of 55 miles per hour. How long does it take the second car to overtake the first?

Sol.: Let $t =$ no. hrs. the 2nd or faster car travels,
then $t + 2 =$ no. hrs. the first car travels.
    $55t =$ distance in miles the 2nd car travels.
  $35(t + 2) =$ distance in miles the 1st car travels.

Since they will have traveled the same distance when the second car overtakes the first, then

$$55t = 35(t + 2)$$
$$55t = 35t + 70$$
$$20t = 70$$
$$t = 3\tfrac{1}{2} \text{ hours.}$$
Check: $(55)(3\tfrac{1}{2}) = (35)5\tfrac{1}{2}$
   $192\tfrac{1}{2} = 192\tfrac{1}{2}.$

Ex. 4: Two planes leave the same airport traveling in opposite directions. The first traveling at $\frac{3}{4}$ the speed of the second leaves at noon. Two hours later the second plane leaves. If they are 1,500 miles apart at 4 o'clock what is the rate of speed of each plane?

Sol.: Let $r =$ rate of the 2nd or faster plane,
then $\frac{3}{4}r =$ rate of the 1st plane.

If the slower plane travels from 12 o'clock until 4 o'clock, then it will have flown ($\frac{3}{4}r$ times 4 hrs) miles, or $3r$ miles. The faster plane will have flown $2r$ miles in 2 hrs. Together they will have flown 1500 miles.

$$2r + 3r = 1500$$
$$5r = 1500$$
$$r = 300 \text{ miles per hour, 2nd plane.}$$
$$\tfrac{3}{4}r = 225 \text{ miles per hour, 1st plane.}$$
Check: $(2)(300) + (4)(225) = 1500$
    $600 + 900 = 1500.$

MOTION PROBLEMS, INVOLVING WATER AND AIR CURRENTS.
Ex. 1: A man traveled downstream for 2 hours. The return trip took 5 hours. If the boat's rate in still water is 7 miles per hour, what is the rate of the stream? The distance, rate, time formula, $d = rt$, is used.

Sol.: Let $r =$ rate of stream,
     $7 + r =$ rate of boat downstream,
     $7 - r =$ rate of boat upstream,
      $2 =$ hours downstream,
$d = rt; \ (7 + r)2 =$ miles downstream in 2 hours,
      $5 =$ hours upstream,
   $5(7 - r) =$ miles upstream in 5 hours,
then $2(7 + r) = 5(7 - r)$ distance is same each way.
    $14 + 2r = 35 - 5r$
      $7r = 21$
      $r = 3$ miles per hour, rate of stream.
Check: $2(7 + r) = 5(7 - r)$
   $2(7 + 3) = 5(7 - 3)$
     $20 = 20.$

Ex. 2: A pilot flying with a tail wind made a trip of 240 miles in 1 hr. 12 min. The return trip took $1\frac{1}{2}$ hours. There was no change in the direction or speed of the wind. Find the speed of the wind.

Sol.: $x =$ speed of plane in still air
and $y =$ speed of wind,
then $x + y =$ speed of plane with wind
and $x - y =$ speed of plane against wind.
  $1\tfrac{1}{5}(x + y) =$ distance in 1 hr. 12 min.
  $1\tfrac{1}{2}(x - y) =$ distance in $1\tfrac{1}{2}$ hrs.
   $\tfrac{6}{5}(x + y) = 240$
   $\tfrac{3}{2}(x - y) = 240$
   $\begin{cases} x + y = 200 \\ x - y = 160 \end{cases}$
    $2x = 360$
    $x = 180$ miles per hour, speed of plane.
Substitute value of x in equation $x + y = 200$.
   $x + y = 200$
  $180 + y = 200$
    $y = 20$ miles per hour, speed of wind.

Check: If speed of plane is 180 miles per hour and speed of wind is 20 miles per hour, then the plane's speed with the wind is 200 miles per hour, and against it is 160 miles per hour.

$$1\tfrac{1}{5}(200) = 1\tfrac{1}{2}(160)$$
$$240 = 240.$$

Ex. 3: A stream flows 2 miles per hour. A man takes 4 hours longer to row 12 miles upstream than to row the same distance downstream. How fast can he row in still water?

Sol.: Let

r = rate in still water

and 2 = rate of stream,

then $r + 2$ = rate downstream

and $r - 2$ = rate upstream.

12 = distance.

$$\frac{12}{r + 2} = \text{hours downstream.}$$

$$\frac{12}{r - 2} = \text{hours upstream.}$$

$$\frac{12}{r + 2} + 4 = \frac{12}{r - 2} .$$

LOWEST COMMON DENOMINATOR $= (r + 2)(r - 2).$

$$\frac{12(r + 2)(r - 2)}{r + 2} + 4(r + 2)(r - 2) = \frac{12(r + 2)(r - 2)}{r - 2}$$

$$12(r - 2) + 4(r + 2)(r - 2) = 12(r + 2).$$

Divide by 4.

$$3(r - 2) + (r + 2)(r - 2) = 3(r + 2)$$

$$3r - 6 + r^2 - 4 = 3r + 6$$

$$r^2 = 16$$

$$r = 4 \text{ miles per hour.}$$

The negative square root is not used since -4 miles has no meaning.

Check: The rate upstream is 2 miles per hour and the rate downstream is 6 miles per hour. It takes 6 hours at 2 miles per hour to go 12 miles upstream and 2 hours to go 12 miles at 6 miles per hour. Therefore, it takes 4 hours longer to go upstream than it does to go the same distance downstream.

MULTINOMIAL DISTRIBUTION, in statistics, the PROBABILITY FUNCTION for an experiment that consists of n independent trials, each of which has k ($k > 2$) outcomes; where the probability that the ith outcome will occur is constant from trial to trial and equal to π_i; and where the probability that in the n trials there will be x_1 outcomes of the first kind, x_2 of the second kind, . . . , and x_k of the kth kind; denoted by

$$f(x_1, x_2, \ldots , x_k) = \frac{n!}{x_1! x_2! \ldots x_k!} .$$

Ex.: The probability that a baseball player gets a base hit in any time at bat is .3; that he gets a walk, .1; that he makes an out, .6. If he comes to bat 5 times in one game, what is the probability that he gets 2 hits, 1 walk, and strikes out 2 times?

$$f(2,1,2) = \frac{5!}{2! 1! 2!} (.3)^2 (.1)^1 (.6)^2 = .10.$$

(Note: It is assumed that the times at bat are independent, and that the probabilities of hits, walks, and outs are constant from trial to trial. This is an example of a MATHEMATICAL MODEL.)

MULTINOMIAL HYPOTHESIS, in statistics, a hypothesis about the parameters (theoretical probabilities) of a MULTINOMIAL DISTRIBUTION. The NULL HYPOTHESIS is

$$H_0: \pi_1 = (\pi_1)_0, \, \pi_2 = (\pi_2)_0, \, \ldots , \, \pi_k = (\pi_k)_0.$$

The ALTERNATIVE HYPOTHESIS is that not all of the inequalities in H_0 are true.

In order to test H_0 versus H_1 at the α SIGNIFICANCE LEVEL, calculate

$$x^2 = \sum_{i=1}^{k} \frac{(O_i - E_i)^2}{E_i}$$

where O_i denotes the number of the ith outcomes observed, E_i denotes the number of ith outcomes expected [$E_i = n(\pi_i)_0$, where n is the total number of trials]. If x^2 exceeds the upper α-point of the CHI-SQUARED DISTRIBUTION, reject H_0. The DEGREES OF FREEDOM is $k - 1$. (If any cell has an expected frequency of less than 5, combine it with other cells. Subtract one degree of freedom for every cell combined like this.)

MULTIPLE-DEGREE-OF-FREEDOM SYSTEM, a mechanical system for which two or more coordinates are required to define completely the position of the system at any instant. A satellite circling the earth, for example, is a three-degree-of-freedom system, since it is necessary to specify its distance from the center of the earth, its longitude, and its latitude, in order to indicate its position at any given instant. *See* COORDINATE SYSTEMS.

MULTIPLICATION, the process by which a number or quantity is added a given number of times. 4 times 2 means $2 + 2 + 2 + 2$; 3 times a means $a + a + a$. There are several symbols for multiplication:

1. $\times$ may be used in arithmetic, but is confusing when used with letters in algebra.

2. $\cdot$, a dot, placed above the line between two numbers, as $3 \cdot 4$, but generally used with letters, as $a \cdot b$.

3. No sign between letters, as abc.

4. Parentheses, or other symbols of grouping, as $x(x^2 + x + 1)$ or $x[(x - 1) - (x + 2)]$.

The number, or expression, that is being multiplied is called the *multiplicand.* If $3x^2 - x + 2$ is multiplied by $2x$, the multiplicand is $3x^2 - x + 2$.

The number by which the multiplicand is multiplied is called the *multiplier.* In 384×16, 16 is the multiplier. The multiplicand and multiplier are known as *factors.* The result obtained in multiplication is called the *product.*

Multiplication is commutative (*see* COMMUTATIVE PROPERTY), so numbers may be taken in any order: $3 \cdot 2 = 2 \cdot 3$; $ab = ba$; the ASSOCIATIVE PROPERTY holds, so numbers may be grouped (or associated) in any order: $abc = a(bc) = (ac)b$; the DISTRIBUTIVE PROPERTY holds over addition: $3(a + b) = 3a + 3b$.

In multiplication, EXPONENTS of like letters or numbers are added. Thus $x^3 \cdot x^2 = x^5$; $a^2 h^3 \cdot a h = a^3 h^4$; $3^4 \cdot 3^5 = 3^9$; and $(3a^3 bc)(2ab^2 c) = 6a^4 b^3 c^2$.

To multiply signed numbers:

1. If two positive numbers are multiplied, their product is positive, as $(+a)(+b) = +ab$.

2. If two negative numbers are multiplied, their product is positive as $(-a)(-b) = +ab$.

3. If a positive number is multiplied by a negative number, their product is negative, as $(+a)(-b) = -ab$ or $(-a)(+b) = -ab$.

To multiply monomials:

1. Determine the sign of the product.

2. Multiply the NUMERICAL COEFFICIENTS.

3. Write each of the letters in the product, adding the EXPONENTS of like letters.

Ex. 1: $(-3ab) 5 = -15ab$

Ex. 2: $(-4a^2 b)(-2abc) = 8a^3 b^2 c$

Ex. 3: $(-2xy)(-3x^2)(-4xy^3) = -24x^4 y^4.$

To multiply a polynomial by a monomial, multiply each term of the POLYNOMIAL by the MONOMIAL and add the PRODUCTS.

Ex. 1: Multiply $6x^2 - 3x + 4$ by 3.

$$3(6x^2 - 3x + 4) = 18x^2 - 9x + 12.$$

Ex. 2: Multiply $5x - 3y + 6z$ by $4a$.

$$4a(5x - 3y + 6z) = 20ax - 12ay + 24az$$

To multiply a polynomial by a binomial, or by another polynomial, the polynomial, as the multiplicand, is multiplied by each term of the binomial (or polynomial) as the MULTIPLIER, and the different products combined.

Ex.: Multiply $a^2 - 3a + 2$ by $a - 3$.

$$
\begin{array}{r}
a^2 - 3a + 2 \\
a - 3 \\
\hline
a^3 - 3a^2 + 2a \\
- 3a^2 + 9a - 6 \\
\hline
a^3 - 6a^2 + 11a - 6
\end{array}
$$

Notice that like terms are placed under like terms. If necessary arrange the multiplicand and the multiplier in either ASCENDING POWERS or DESCENDING POWERS of one letter.

Check: Divide the product by the multiplier.

$$
\begin{array}{r}
a^2 - 3a + 2 \\
a - 3\overline{)a^3 - 6a^2 + 11a - 6} \\
a^3 - 3a^2 \\
\hline
- 3a^2 + 11a \\
- 3a^2 + 9a \\
\hline
2a - 6 \\
2a - 6 \\
\hline
\end{array}
$$

Numbers of two or more digits may be multiplied by the following methods:

1. If the multiplier is a single-digit number.

$$
\begin{array}{r}
3279 \\
\times 8 \\
\hline
72 \\
56 \\
16 \\
24 \\
\hline
26232
\end{array}
$$

By this method, every digit of the multiplicand is multiplied by 8; each partial product is placed under the digit that is used, and the partial products are added. However the "carrying method" is much shorter. Multiply 8×9. The product is 72. Place the 2 in the unit's place of the product and remember to carry the 7 tens. Multiply 7 by 8 and add 7. $7 \times 8 = 56$; $56 + 7 = 63$. Place the 3 in the tens column and remember to carry 6. $8 \times 2 = 16$ and $16 + 6 = 22$. Place 2 in the hundreds column and carry 2. Finally $8 \times 3 = 24$ and $24 + 2 = 26$.

2. If the multiplier has two or more digits.

Proceed as above for the units' digit of the multiplier. Then multiply by the tens digit, but place the first partial product under the ten's digit.

$$
\begin{array}{r}
3487 \\
\times 28 \\
\hline
27896 \\
6974 \\
\hline
97,636
\end{array}
\qquad
\begin{array}{r}
8746 \\
\times 235 \\
\hline
43730 \\
26238 \\
17492 \\
\hline
2,055,310
\end{array}
$$

Check each multiplication to make certain the carried numbers are added. If large products are marked off with commas in groups of three from right to left, the reading of the product is facilitated. The first product above is read "ninety-seven thousand six hundred thirty-six." The second product is read "two million fifty-five thousand three hundred ten."

3. If there is a zero in the multiplicand.

$$
\begin{array}{r}
4208 \\
47 \\
\hline
29456 \\
16832 \\
\hline
197,776
\end{array}
$$

$7 \times 8 = 56$. Write 6, carry 5. $7 \times 0 = 0$ and $0 + 5 = 5$.

4. If there is a zero in the multiplier.

$$
\begin{array}{r}
3246 \\
306 \\
\hline
19476 \\
97380 \\
\hline
993,276
\end{array}
$$

Note that the single zero is placed in the second row instead of a row of zeros.

5. If a number is multiplied by 10, add one zero to that number. Add two zeros, if the number is multiplied by 100, etc.

$$24 \times 10 = 240.$$
$$24 \times 100 = 2,400.$$
$$24 \times 1000 = 24,000.$$

6. If a number is multiplied by .1, move the decimal point one place to the left. Move it two places to the left if it is multiplied by .01, three places when multiplying by .001, etc.

$$624 \times .1 = 62.4.$$
$$624 \times .01 = 6.24.$$
$$624 \times .001 = .624.$$

MULTIPLICATION AXIOM. An AXIOM OF EQUALITY: If equal quantities are multiplied by the same or equal quantities, the PRODUCTS are equal. E.g., if $a = b$ then $3a = 3b$. This axiom may be expressed symbolically as follows: If $a = b$ and $c = d$, then $ac = bd$. A special case of this axiom occurs when the equal quantities are multiplied by two; the axiom may then be stated "Doubles of equal quantities are equal." *See also* INEQUALITY.

MULTIPLICATIVE INVERSE (mul-tih-pli-kay'-tiv), of any number a, is $1/a$ when a is unequal to zero. The multiplicative inverse of 3 is $\frac{1}{3}$. *See also* INVERSE OPERATIONS.

MVT, *see* MEAN VALUE THEOREM.

N

N!, (N Factorial), *see* FACTORIAL NOTATION.

NAPIER, JOHN (nay'-pee-ehr), 1550–1617, Scottish mathematician, the inventor of LOGARITHMS. In 1617 shortly before his death, Napier published his *Rabdologia*, the name of the method for using certain numerating rods to simplify multiplication and division. These rods were commonly called "Napier's bones."

NAPIERIAN LOGARITHMS, *see* LOGARITHMS, NATURAL.

NAPIER'S RULES, two rules used to solve RIGHT SPHERICAL TRIANGLES. Either of the drawings in the figure may be used for applying Napier's Rules. C is omitted and A, B, and c have been replaced by co-A, co-B, and co-c to indicate COFUNCTIONS. Thus, $\sin(\text{co-}A) = \cos A$ and $\tan(\text{co-}c) = \cot c$.

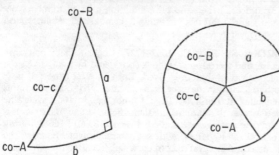

Napier's Rules are as follows:
1. The sine of any middle part is equal to the product of the tangents of the adjacent parts. E.g. $\sin a = \tan(\text{co-}B)\tan b$; then

$$\sin a = \cot B \tan b \text{ or } \tan b = \sin a \tan B.$$

Also, $\sin(\text{co-}B) = \tan a \tan(\text{co-}c)$ or $\cos B = \tan a \cot c$.
2. The sine of any middle part is equal to the product of the cosines of the opposite parts.

$$\sin a = \cos(\text{co-}c)\cos(\text{co-}A) \text{ or } \sin a = \sin c \sin A.$$

Also, $\sin(\text{co-}c) = \cos a \cos b$ or $\cos c = \cos a \cos b$.
Any of the five parts may be taken as the middle part.

NAPPE (nap), one of the two parts into which a CONICAL SURFACE is separated by the VERTEX. The part of the surface above the vertex is called the *upper nappe*, and that below it is called the *lower nappe*. (See figure.)

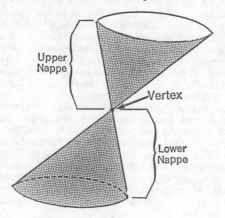

NATIONAL BUREAU OF STANDARDS, a U.S. federal agency within the Dept. of Commerce. It provides the research and data for the national measurement systems, technological services for industry and services to promote public safety. Its chief offices and divisions are: The **Institute for Basic Standards** which is in charge of all systems of physical measurement and furnishes data to keep uniformity in measurement; the **Institute For Materials Research** which conducts research on properties of materials used in industry and the **Institute For Applied Technology** which coordinates public and private research for new materials or innovation in industry. There is also a center for the computer sciences within the bureau. The National Bureau of Standards was established in 1901.

NATURAL LOGARITHMS, *see* LOGARITHMS, NATURAL.

NATURAL LOGARITHMS, TABLE OF, *see* TABLE NO. 20.

NATURAL NUMBER, a positive INTEGER (*see* POSITIVE NUMBER), e.g., 1, 2, 3, ... The SET of natural numbers is also known as the *counting numbers*. ZERO, NEGATIVE NUMBERS, FRACTIONS, IRRATIONAL NUMBERS, and DECIMAL FRACTIONS are *not* natural numbers. Thus, -1, $\frac{1}{2}$, π (pi), $-\frac{1}{3}$, and .5502 are not members of the set of natural numbers.

NATURAL TRIGONOMETRIC FUNCTIONS, for an acute angle, the ratios of the sides of a right triangle that contain the angle. In right triangle ABC, where $C = 90°$ and the sides are a, b, and c, for acute angle A, the trigonometric functions of A are defined as follows: (See Fig. 1.)

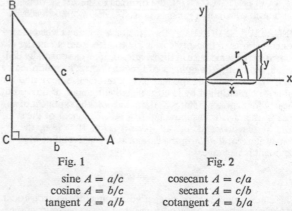

Fig. 1   Fig. 2

$$\text{sine } A = a/c \qquad \text{cosecant } A = c/a$$
$$\text{cosine } A = b/c \qquad \text{secant } A = c/b$$
$$\text{tangent } A = a/b \qquad \text{cotangent } A = b/a$$

These definitions are extended to include functions of any angle by considering angle A on the CARTESIAN COORDINATE system (see Fig. 2). Then for A in STANDARD ANGLE POSITION,

$$\text{sine } A = \frac{\text{ordinate}}{r} = \frac{y}{r} \cdot \qquad \text{cosecant } A = \frac{r}{\text{ordinate}} = \frac{r}{y} \cdot$$
$$\text{cosine } A = \frac{\text{abscissa}}{r} = \frac{x}{r} \cdot \qquad \text{secant } A = \frac{r}{\text{abscissa}} = \frac{r}{x} \cdot$$
$$\text{tangent } A = \frac{\text{ordinate}}{\text{abscissa}} = \frac{y}{x} \cdot \qquad \text{cotangent } A = \frac{\text{abscissa}}{\text{ordinate}} = \frac{x}{y} \cdot$$

The values of trigonometric functions are given in TABLE NO. 22.

NAUTICAL MILE, the unit of measure used to measure distance on water. The U.S. Hydrographic office uses 6080.27 feet as 1 nautical mile. British admiralty uses 6080 feet as 1 nautical mile. *See* TABLE NO. 4.

NEGATION, LOGICAL, ($\sim$), in the ALGEBRA OF PROPOSITIONS, denial that a proposition is true; or, equivalently, assertion that the proposition is false. E.g., $\sim p$, sometimes written p', is the negation of proposition p, and is read: "p is false," or "p is not true," or "not p" for short. Its meaning is specified completely by the TRUTH TABLE,

p	$\sim p$
1	0
0	1

This can be read: When p is true, $\sim p$ is false (line 2), but when p is false, $\sim p$ is true (line 3). Note that the table is ISOMORPHIC with that for complements in two-valued BOOLEAN ALGEBRA. For this reason the negation of p is sometimes called the logical complement of p.

NEGATIVE ANGLE, an ANGLE generated by a clockwise rotation of a RAY. In the figure θ is a negative angle. A negative angle can be expressed as the POSITIVE ANGLE which has the same initial and terminal sides (*see* SIDE OF AN ANGLE). In the figure θ is equivalent to α.

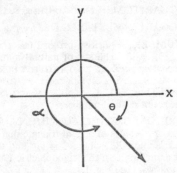

NEGATIVE DIRECTION, the distance to the left of, or below, the ORIGIN (zero) on a NUMBER LINE. *See also* SIGNED NUMBER.

NEGATIVE EXPONENT, the EXPONENT obtained when the exponent of a BASE in a DIVISOR is subtracted from a smaller exponent of the same base in the DIVIDEND. If an exponent, by definition, represents the number of times a FACTOR is multiplied by itself, then a negative exponent has no meaning, since a number cannot be multiplied by itself a negative number of times. But the law for exponents states that, in division, the exponent of any base in the divisor is subtracted from the exponent of the same base in the dividend, or, $a^m \div a^n = a^{m-n}$. If $m = n$, the exponent is zero; if $m > n$, the exponent is positive; if $m < n$, the exponent is negative.

$$\frac{a^5}{a^3} = a^2; \frac{a^3}{a^5} = a^{-2} \text{ or } \frac{1}{a^2}$$

Therefore, any base with a negative exponent is the RECIPROCAL of the same base with a positive exponent. The following examples show terms with negative exponents changed to terms with only positive exponents.

$$\frac{x^3}{y^{-2}} = x^3 y^2.$$

$$\frac{3^{-2}}{3^{-5}} = \frac{3^5}{3^2} = 3^3 = 27.$$

$$\frac{c^{-2}}{b^{-2}} = \frac{b^2}{c^2}$$

$$\frac{a^{-1}b^{-2}c^{-5}}{a^3b^2c} = \frac{1}{a^4b^4c^4}$$

NEGATIVE NUMBER, a SIGNED NUMBER, indicated by a minus ($-$) sign preceding it, that indicates a NUMBER less than ZERO, or a number to the left of zero on a NUMBER LINE. -4, $-2/3$, $-3x$, are negative numbers.

NEGATIVE SYMBOL, minus sign ($-$), to denote the difference of two numbers, as $a - b$, and to denote the ADDITIVE INVERSE of a number. The additive inverse of the number 5 is -5. SIGNED NUMBERS to the left of or below the ORIGIN on a NUMBER LINE or a GRAPH are also written with a minus sign.

NEIGHBORHOOD (nay'-bur-huhd), in mathematics, a SET of numbers that are close to a fixed number. A neighborhood of a point c is any OPEN INTERVAL that contains c, and may be given by the INTERVAL $(c - h, c + k)$ where h and k are any positive numbers. A symmetric (*see* SYMMETRY) neighborhood of c is the open interval $(c - h, c + h)$ where h is any positive number. A neighborhood of c from which c has been deleted is called a deleted neighborhood of c. E.g., the open interval $(-1,5)$ is a neighborhood of 1. It is also a neighborhood of 0, or of 4.9, or every REAL NUMBER between -1 and 5. $(-1,5)$ is a symmetric neighborhood of 2 and can be expressed as $(2 - 3, 2 + 3)$. If any one of the numbers between -1 and 5 is removed, the resulting set becomes a deleted neighborhood of that number. E.g., if 3 is removed from $(-1,5)$, the UNION of the open intervals $(-1,3)$ and $(3,5)$ (i.e., the set containing all real numbers between -1 and 5 but not including 3) is a deleted neighborhood of 3.

NEWTON, Sir ISAAC, 1642–1727, English mathematician, physicist, and astronomer, who is considered by many to be the greatest scientist that ever lived. Born at Woolsthorpe, near Grantham, Lincolnshire, he was educated at the local schools and enrolled at Trinity College, Cambridge, in 1661, where he studied under the famous mathematician Isaac Barrow. His greatest discoveries were made between 1665 and 1668. During this period, he invented, with contributions from Barrow, the differential and integral CALCULUS, which he called the direct and inverse method of fluxions. He also investigated infinite series and founded the calculus of finite differences. In physics, he formed the basic concepts of his work in mechanics, including the inverse-square law of gravitation but did not have sufficient data available yet to check it to his satisfaction. Also around this time, he discovered and named the spectrum of colors formed by passing white light through a glass prism. After observing that each color, or wavelength, had a different index of refraction, Newton concluded that no refracting telescope could be constructed that would be free of chromatic aberration. This conclusion was erroneous, as was shown by the invention of the achromatic lens by Dollond, but it led Newton to invent the reflecting telescope, using a lens rather than a mirror to focus the light. James Gregory had invented a reflecting telescope in 1663 but had never constructed one. The reflecting telescope has become perhaps the principal instrument of modern astronomy. Newton's system of optics viewed light as having a particle, or corpuscular, nature, rather than a wave nature. Nevertheless, he studied and explained most of the phenomena, such as diffraction and interference, that are usually associated with waves.

Newton was a shy person and disliked controversy. Because of this, he tended to withhold his work if it seemed likely to provoke a dispute. His *Optiks*, which was written between 1665 and 1675, was not published until 1704 because of disputes with Hooke and Huygens, who favored a wave theory of light. Differences with Hooke again arose in connection with his work on mechanics and gravitation, which Newton had completed in the 1680's. It was only because of Halley, who published the work at his own expense, that Newton did not remove critical parts of it in order to avoid controversy. This work, titled *Philosophiae naturalis principia mathematica* ("Mathematical Principles of Natural Philosophy") and known generally as the *Principia*, is Newton's greatest work. In it, he formulated three basic laws of motion:

(1) an object at rest or in motion tends to remain at rest, or in motion, in a straight line unless acted on by external forces; (2) a change in motion, or ACCELERATION, is directly proportional to the force exerted on an object and inversely proportional to its mass; (3) to every action there is an equal and opposite reaction. When he combined these laws with his law of universal gravitation, he was able to give a physical explanation for the elliptical orbits of planets and other astronomical bodies described by *Kepler's Laws of Planetary Motion.*

Modern physics can be said to begin with Newton's work. So great was his prestige in later generations that his particle theory of light held sway even in the face of considerable experimental evidence favoring the wave theory. In his own lifetime, however, Newton was the center of several disputes, with his part usually being defended by various supporters, who were less shy and sometimes less generous than Newton himself. One argument arose with the astronomer royal, Flamsteed, over some astronomical data that Flamsteed was hesitant to provide. Another, more serious dispute occurred between Newton and LEIBNITZ over priority in the invention of the calculus, which Leibnitz had independently discovered about the same time. Newton was at Cambridge from 1667, succeeding Barrow in the Lucasian chair of mathematics in 1669.

In 1687, the year the *Principia* was published, Newton began to take an interest in politics and other subjects outside science. In 1689 and again in 1701, he was elected a member of Parliament to represent Cambridge Univ. In 1696, he entered public service as warden of the mint and continued in various positions for several years. He also wrote on theology, history, chronology, and alchemy. He maintained his interest in science, however, and served as pres. of the Royal Society from 1703 until his death.

Biblio.: Koyre, Alexandre, *Newtonian Studies* (1965); Turnbull, H. W., and Scott, J. F. (eds.), *The Correspondence of Isaac Newton* (1959–1961); Brewster, David, *Memoirs of the Life, Writings, and Discoveries of Sir Isaac Newton* (1855).

NEWTON'S METHOD, to find a root of the equation $f(x) = 0$, the following technique for finding the corresponding point at which the curve $y = f(x)$ crosses the x-axis. Let x_1 be any point at which $f(x)$ is defined, and let:

$x_2 = $ the x-intercept of the tangent to $y = f(x)$ at x_1,

$$= x_1 - \frac{f(x_1)}{f'(x_1)} ;$$

$x_3 = $ the x-intercept of the tangent to $y = f(x)$ at x_2,

$$= x_2 - \frac{f(x_2)}{f'(x_2)} ;$$

The limit r of the sequence of points $x_1, x_2, x_3, \ldots$ is then a root of $f(x) = 0$. (See figure.)

See also DERIVATIVE OF A FUNCTION; LIMIT OF A SEQUENCE; TANGENT LINE.

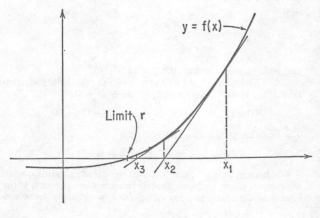

NICOMEDES (nik-oh-mee'-deez), ab. 180 B.C., inventor of a curve, called the CONCHOID, by which an angle can be trisected.

NILPOTENT (nil'-poh-tent), an element that equals zero when raised to some power. The element zero is a nilpotent, since 0 to any power is zero. The MATRIX $M = \begin{bmatrix} 2 & 0 & -4 \\ 3 & 0 & 0 \\ 1 & 0 & -2 \end{bmatrix}$ is nilpotent since $M = 0$.

NINE POINT CIRCLE, *see* EULER, LEONHARD.

NOMOGRAM (nom'-oh-gram), a graph with three lines (or curves) with scales constructed for three variables so that a straight line connecting two of the scaled lines gives the related values of the third variable at its intersection with the third line (see figure). A nomogram is also called a *nomograph.*

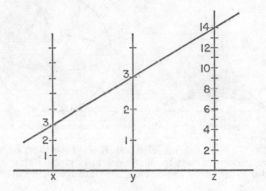

NON-EUCLIDEAN GEOMETRY (eu-klid'-ee-an), *elliptic* and *hyperbolic* geometry, created by denying EUCLID'S FIFTH POSTULATE. Many mathematicians shared Euclid's apparent discomfort about the Fifth Postulate (*see* AXIOM) of EUCLIDEAN GEOMETRY: "If a line m intersects two lines p, q such that the sum of the interior angles on the same side of m is less than two right angles, then the lines p and q intersect on the side of m on which the sum of the interior angles is less than two right angles." EUCLID had avoided using the postulate in the proofs of at least two THEOREMS, and for centuries mathematicians had tried to prove the postulate as a theorem. It was slowly realized that other assumptions must be made in order to prove it. This meant that the Fifth Postulate was independent of the first four.

In 1733, an Italian Jesuit priest and mathematician, Girolamo Saccheri (1667–1733) published *Euclidis ab Omni Naevo Vindicatos* in which he tried to clear Euclid of criticism of his Fifth Postulate by the method of *reductio ab absurdum* (*see* INDIRECT PROOF). Thus, he considered three cases which were equivalent to stating that the sum of the angles of a triangle is *equal* to 180°, *less* than 180°, and *greater* than 180°. Saccheri dismissed the less than and greater than cases. But these hypotheses are now recognized as the postulates that at *most one* and at *least one* line is parallel to a given line through a given point. Thus, what Saccheri unintentionally succeeded in doing was to illustrate that denying the Fifth Postulate can result in a POSTULATIONAL SYSTEM different from Euclid's that can be developed without self-contradiction.

It was not until the 19th cent. that BOLYAI and LOBACHEVSKI, working independently, developed the geometry based on Saccheri's less than hypothesis. It is now known as *hyperbolic geometry.* And in the same century, RIEMANN developed a geometry based on Saccheri's greater than hypothesis, now called *elliptic geometry.*

From letters written by GAUSS during the time Bolyai's work was published (1831–1832) we know that Gauss had also investigated hyperbolic geometry as early as 1798. Although he did not publish his work, in 1824 he wrote to a friend that he had developed his ideas to the point where he was able to solve all but a few problems in the new geometry.

Fig. 1

Hyperbolic geometry may be visualized on a surface known as a pseudosphere (see Fig. 1). A triangle in this geometry looks like that in Fig. 2. Elliptic geometry may be visualized on the surface of a sphere (Fig. 3). *ABC* is a triangle in this geometry.

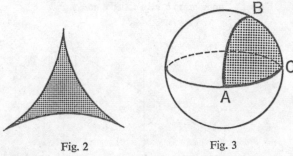

Fig. 2   Fig. 3

The German mathematician Felix Klein (1849–1929) made important contributions to elliptic geometry in the 19th century, and EINSTEIN, in the 20th century, used it to develop his theory of relativity.

NORMAL, in mathematics, the PERPENDICULAR from a point to a line, or to a TANGENT LINE to a curve.

The normal to a line is the perpendicular from the ORIGIN to the line. If the length of the segment along this perpendicular (i.e., the distance of the origin from the line) is p and the perpendicular has an ANGLE OF INCLINATION α, the original line has the equation: $x \cos \alpha + y \sin \alpha - p = 0$. (See Fig. 1.)

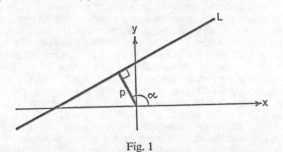

Fig. 1

Ex.: Find the normal form equation of the line whose equation is $y = x + 3$.

Sol.: The distance of this line from the origin is $3/\sqrt{2}$; its angle of inclination is 45°. Its normal form equation is therefore

$$x \cdot \frac{1}{\sqrt{2}} + y \cdot \frac{1}{\sqrt{2}} - \frac{3}{\sqrt{2}} = 0.$$

A linear equation (*see* EQUATION, LINEAR) can be put into normal form as follows: If the line is given by $Ax + By + C = 0$ the normal form is $\frac{Ax}{R} + \frac{By}{R} + \frac{c}{R} = 0$ where $R = \pm \sqrt{A^2 + B^2}$, + or − according to whether B is + or −.

The normal to a plane CURVE is the straight line perpendicular to the tangent to the curve at the point of tangency. The SLOPE (*see* SLOPE OF A LINE) of the normal line is the negative reciprocal of the slope of the tangent; i.e., if the slope of the tangent is m, the slope of the normal is $-1/m$ (see Fig. 2). Thus, if the slope of

the tangent is known, the equation of the normal line can be written.

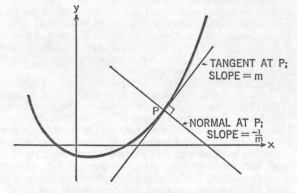

Fig. 2

Ex. 1: If the tangent to the curve $y = x^2$ at $x = 1$ has slope 2, write the equation of the normal to the point (1,1) on the curve.

Sol.: The slope of the normal is $-\frac{1}{2}$. The point-slope form of its equation (*see* LINE, EQUATION OF) is

$$(y - 1) = -\tfrac{1}{2}(x - 1).$$

Since the tangent line has slope $f'(a)$, the normal line has slope $-1/f'(a)$. Thus, the equation of the normal can be written

$$y = f(a) + \frac{-1}{f'(a)}(x - a).$$

The normal to a plane is any straight line perpendicular to the plane (i.e., perpendicular to every line in the plane through the point of intersection). If the plane is given by the equation:

$$Ax + By + Cz + D = 0,$$

then the direction numbers of any normal line are A, B, and C, and the normal line has the PARAMETRIC EQUATIONS:

$$x = At + x_1,$$
$$y = Bt + y_1,$$
$$z = Ct + z_1,$$

where (x_1, y_1, z_1) is any point on the normal.

Ex. 1: Does the normal to the plane $x - y - z - 1 = 0$ which passes through the origin also pass through the point (1,1,1)?

Sol.: The line has the following equations:

$$x = t,$$
$$y = -t,$$
$$z = -t.$$

(1,1,1) is not on this line.

Ex. 2: Find the equation of the plane which is normal to the line

$$x = t + 1,$$
$$y = 3t + 3,$$
$$z = 2t + 3,$$

and which passes through the point (2,2,5).

Sol.: This point is not on the normal, but it satisfies the equation of the plane. Thus $1x + 3y + 2z + D = 0$;

$$1 \cdot 2 + 3 \cdot 2 + 2 \cdot 5 + D = 0; \quad -18 = D.$$

The equation of the plane is:

$$x + 3y + 2z - 18 = 0.$$

The normal to a SURFACE is the straight line perpendicular to the tangent plane to the surface at the point of tangency. If the equation of the tangent plane at a point $P = (x', y', z')$ on the surface $z = f(x,y)$ is $A(x - x') + B(y - y') + C(z - z') = 0$, the normal to the surface at P has the equation

$$\frac{x - x'}{f_x(x',y')} = \frac{y - y'}{f_y(x',y')} + \frac{z - z'}{-1}.$$

The normal VECTOR is the unit vector that is perpendicular to the unit tangent vector at the point of tangency. The length of the unit tangent vector T is constant. dT/ds therefore represents the change in direction of T as it moves along the curve. It can be shown that $dT/ds = Nk$, where N is the unit normal vector obtained by rotating T through 90° in the counterclockwise direction, and k is the curvature of C.

NORMAL APPROXIMATION TO THE BINOMIAL, in statistics, whenever $n\pi \geq 5$ and $n(1 - \pi) \geq 5$, the normal distribution gives a convenient and satisfactory approximation to the binomial distribution. The normal curve that best fits the theoretical HISTOGRAM of the binomial distribution with parameters n and π should have the same mean and variance as that binomial distribution, namely, $n\pi$ and $n\pi(1 - \pi)$, respectively.

The probability that the binomial random variable equals a particular value, say r (the area of the shaded rectangle in the figure) is approximately equal to the probability that the normal random variable takes on a value between $r - \frac{1}{2}$ and $r + \frac{1}{2}$.

Ex.: A pair of dice is tossed 100 times. What is the approximate probability that a total of 7 will be tossed 15 times? What is the approximate probability that a total of 7 will be thrown at least 20 times?

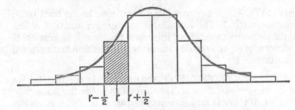

$n\pi = \dfrac{100}{6} = 16.67.$

$n\pi(1 - \pi) = 100\left(\dfrac{1}{6}\right)\left(\dfrac{5}{6}\right) = 13.89.$

$\sqrt{n\pi(1 - \pi)} = 3.73.$

$P(\text{exactly 15 sevens}) = P_N(14.5 < X < 15.5)$

$\qquad = P\left(\dfrac{14.5 - 16.67}{3.73} < Z < \dfrac{15.5 - 16.67}{3.73}\right)$

$\qquad = P(-.58 < Z < -.31) = .097.$

$P(\text{at least 20 sevens}) = P_N(X > 19.5) = P\left(Z > \dfrac{19.5 - 16.67}{3.73}\right).$

$\qquad = P(Z > .76) = .2236.$

NORMAL DISTRIBUTION, in statistics, a distribution given by

$$f(x) = \frac{1}{\sigma\sqrt{2\pi}} \exp\left[-\frac{1}{2}\left(\frac{x - \mu}{\sigma}\right)^2\right].$$

The graph of $f(x)$ is a bell-shaped curve. (See figure.) The maximum point occurs at the MEAN of the distribution. About 68 percent of the area under the curve lies within one STANDARD DEVIA-

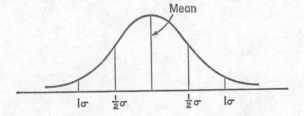

TION of the mean, and about 95 percent lies within two standard deviations of the mean.

Substituting $z = (x - \mu)/\sigma$, changes any normal distribution into the STANDARD NORMAL DISTRIBUTION, for which tables are widely available. The equation of the standard normal distribution is

$$f(z) = \frac{1}{\sqrt{2\pi}} e^{-z^2/2}.$$

Many natural phenomena (heights, weights, errors in measurement, etc.) have distributions that can be described satisfactorily by the normal distribution. Many statistics have distributions that are either normal or approximately so.

NORMAL RANDOM VARIABLE, in statistics, a variable that has a NORMAL DISTRIBUTION.

NORMAL VECTOR, to a curve, at a point P on the curve, is given by

$$N = -i \sin \phi + j \cos \phi$$

where ϕ is the slope of the TANGENT LINE at P. N is the unit normal vector obtained by rotating the unit TANGENT VECTOR, T, ($T = i \cos \phi + j \sin \phi$) through 90° in a counterclockwise direction. Since $dT/d\phi$ is the perpendicular to T, $dT/d\phi = N$. The normal vector may also be expressed as the derivative (see DERIVATIVE OF A FUNCTION) of the tangent vector with respect to the length of an arc, s, of the curve. If the curve is directed so that ϕ is an increasing function of s, then the curvature $\kappa = d\phi/ds$.

From the CHAIN RULE, $dT/ds = \dfrac{dT}{d\phi}\dfrac{d\phi}{ds}$ and $dT/ds = N\kappa$.

NOTATION, SCIENTIFIC, *see* SCIENTIFIC NOTATION.

NULL HYPOTHESIS, the statistical hypothesis being tested in any experimental situation. A null hypothesis is usually about one or more PARAMETERS of one or more populations. It is denoted by H_0. Frequently the null hypothesis is set up as a "straw man"—the experimenter hopes to be able to reject it and accept the ALTERNATIVE HYPOTHESIS, which is denoted H_1. For example, if the usual method of teaching a certain unit in mathematics results in an average score of 79, and an experimenter tries a new method, which he hopes is superior to the old, he would select $\mu = 79$ as the null hypothesis and $\mu > 79$ as the alternative hypothesis. He hopes to be able to reject H_0. The null hypothesis always contains an equal sign; the alternative hypothesis never does. Rejection of H_0 does not mean that it is certain that H_1 is true.

NULL SET, *see* EMPTY SET.

NUMBER, a concept of quantity, usually of a collection of units. The value of the quantity is given by a symbol, called a NUMERAL. The number of houses in the figure is five, symbolized by the numeral "5". Numbers may be classified, according to the kind of units in the collection. *See* COMPLEX NUMBER, IMAGINARY NUMBER; IRRATIONAL NUMBER; NATURAL NUMBERS; NEGATIVE NUMBER; POSITIVE NUMBER; RATIONAL NUMBER; REAL NUMBERS.

NUMBER LINE, a LINE each point of which is associated with the number that gives its distance from a fixed point (the ORIGIN) on the line. A number line is sometimes called a *coordinate line*. The number which is associated with a given point is called the COORDINATE of that point.

To find the distance between any two points on a number line, subtract one coordinate from the other and disregard the sign of the difference, because distance is an unsigned number. (To indicate DIRECTED DISTANCE, use the sign.) Thus, the distance is the ABSOLUTE VALUE of the differences. The distance from the origin to the point associated with the number one is called the UNIT DISTANCE (see figure).

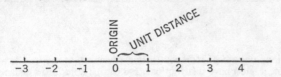

Ex.: Find the distance between the following pairs of points:

a. $p = 3, q = 2$.
b. $p = -2, q = 1$.
c. $p = 1, q = -3$.

Sol.: a. The distance is $3 - 2 = 1$.
b. The *difference* is $-2 - 1 = -3$; the *distance* is 3.
c. The *difference* is $1 - (-3) = 1 + 3 = 4$; the *distance* is 4.

The number line may be used to illustrate addition and subtraction of SIGNED NUMBERS. On any horizontal line select a point O and using any convenient unit, mark off equal distances to the right and to the left of O. The distances to the right of O are numbered 1, 2, 3, etc., and those to the left $-1, -2, -3$, etc. The starting point, O, represents ZERO. A number to the right of zero is a POSITIVE NUMBER, and a number to the left of zero is a NEGATIVE NUMBER. A is three units to the right of O and is represented by $+3$; B is three units to the left of O and is represented by -3. Because AO and BO are each three units in length, they have the same absolute value. (The signs represent directions.)

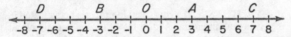

The sign of the number can also be interpreted as meaning motion: $+3$ would then mean move three units to the right from any point on the line; -4 would mean move four units to the left from any point. Then, to find the sum of $+3$ and $+4$, count three units to the right of zero, to point A. From A move four units to the right to C, which is seven units to the right of O. Thus, the sum $(+3) + (+4) = +7$. To add -3 and -4, move left from O three units to B, then left four units to D. The sum $(-3) + (-4) = -7$. To add $+7$ and -4, start at O and move to the right seven units to C, and then four units to the left to A. Thus, $(+7) + (-4) = +3$. To add $+6$ and -10, from O move six units to the right, and from there move ten units to the left: $(+6) + (-10) = -4$.

To subtract 3 from 7 means to find the number which when added to 3 gives 7. On the number line, A has coordinate 3 and C has coordinate 7. Counting to the right $(+)$ from A, there are four units from A to C. Thus, $(+7) - (+3) = +4$. To subtract -3 from -7, find a number which when added to -3 will give -7: count from -3 to the left $(-)$ four units to -7. $(-7) - (-3) = -4$. To subtract -3 from $+7$ count from -3 to the right $(+)$ to $+7$. There are ten units so $(+7) - (-3) = +10$. To subtract 6 from -2, count from 6, eight units to the left $(-)$ to -2: $(-2) - (6) = -8$.

NUMBERS, CONSECUTIVE, *see* CONSECUTIVE NUMBER PROBLEMS; CONSECUTIVE INTEGERS.

NUMERAL, a symbol for representing a NUMBER. E.g., the number five may be written with the Arabic numeral 5 or with the Roman numeral V. *See also* HINDU-ARABIC NUMERAL SYSTEM; ROMAN NUMERAL SYSTEM.

NUMERATOR, the DIVIDEND in a FRACTION. In the fraction $\frac{3}{4}$, the numerator is 3. The numerator in a proper fraction is less than the DENOMINATOR; in an improper fraction, it is greater. If the numerator equals the denominator, the fraction becomes the whole number 1.

NUMERICAL COEFFICIENT, the numerical FACTOR of an ALGEBRAIC EXPRESSION. In the expression $7x^3y^4$, 7 is the numerical coefficient. If there is no numerical factor, as in x^2y, it is understood to be 1.

O

OBLIQUE ANGLE (oh-bleek′), an angle that is either an ACUTE ANGLE or an OBTUSE ANGLE; hence, one that is neither a RIGHT ANGLE nor a STRAIGHT ANGLE. Thus, an angle that does not equal 90° or 180° is an oblique angle.

OBLIQUE TRIANGLE (oh-bleek′), a triangle in which there is no RIGHT ANGLE. To solve an oblique triangle, three parts, at least one of which is a side, must be given. The four possible cases are (I) a side and two angles, (II) two sides and the angle opposite one of them, (III) two sides and the included angle, and (IV) three sides.

Case I. If two angles are given, the third angle may be found easily, since $A + B + C = 180$. Use the Law of Sines (*see* SINES, LAW OF) to find the other two sides,

$$\frac{a}{c} = \frac{\sin A}{\sin C} \text{ and } \frac{b}{c} = \frac{\sin B}{\sin C}.$$

To check the solution, the equation above may be added to obtain $\dfrac{a + b}{c} = \dfrac{\sin A + \sin B}{\sin C}$.

Ex.: Given $A = 58°20′$, $B = 42°30′$, and $c = 18.61$. Find C, a, and b. (See Fig. 1.)

Sol.: 1. $C = 180 - (A + B)$
$C = 180 - 100°50′ = 79°10′$.

2. To find a: $a = \dfrac{c \sin A}{\sin C}$.

$\log a = \log c + \log \sin A - \log \sin C$.
$\log 18.61 = \quad 1.26975$
$\log \sin 58°20′ = \dfrac{9.92999 - 10}{11.19974 - 10}$
$\log \sin 79°10′ = \dfrac{9.99219 - 10}{}$
$\log a = \quad 1.20755$
$a = 16.13$.

3. $\log b = \log c + \log \sin B - \log \sin C$.
$\log 18.61 = \quad 1.26975$
$\log \sin 42°30′ = \dfrac{9.82968 - 10}{11.09943 - 10}$
$\log \sin 79°10′ = \dfrac{9.99219 - 10}{}$
$\log b = \quad 1.10724$
$b = 12.80$.

Check: $\dfrac{a + b}{c} = \dfrac{\sin A + \sin B}{\sin C}$.

$\dfrac{16.13 + 12.80}{18.61} = \dfrac{.8511 + .6756}{.9822}$
$\dfrac{28.93}{18.61} = \dfrac{1.5267}{.9822}$
$1.554 = 1.544$.

Check by logarithms:
$\log 28.93 = 1.46135$ $\log 1.5267 = 10.18375 - 10$
$\log 18.61 = 1.26975$ $\log .9822 = 9.99216 - 10$
$\log \text{quotient} = .19160.$ $\log \text{quotient} = .19159.$

Case II. See AMBIGUOUS CASE.

Case III. If two sides and the included angle are given, use the Law of Cosines to find the third side. The Law of Sines is used to find the other angles.

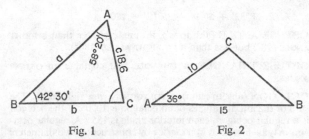

Fig. 1   Fig. 2

Ex.: Given $b = 10$, $c = 15$, and $A = 36°$. (See Fig. 2.) Find B, C, and a.

Sol.: $a^2 = b^2 + c^2 - 2bc \cos A$.
$a^2 = 100 + 225 - 300(.8090)$
$a^2 = 82.3$
$a = 9.07$.

$\sin B = \dfrac{b \sin A}{a}$ and $\log \sin B = (\log b + \log \sin A) - \log a$.

$\log 10 = \quad 1.00000$
$\log \sin 36° = \dfrac{9.76922 - 10}{10.76922 - 10}$
$\log 9.07 = \quad .95761$
$\log \sin B = \quad 9.81161 - 10$
$B = 40°24′$.
$C = 180 - (A + B) = 103°36′$.

Check: $\dfrac{a + b}{c} = \dfrac{\sin A + \sin B}{\sin C}$.

$\dfrac{10 + 9.07}{15} = \dfrac{.5878 + .6481}{.9720}$
$1.27 = 1.27$.

Case IV. If three sides of the triangle are given, use the LAW OF COSINES to find the angles.

Ex.: Given $a = 15$, $b = 20$, and $c = 24$. Find angles A, B, and C.

Sol.: 1. $a^2 = b^2 + c^2 - 2bc \cos A$.

$$\cos A = \frac{b^2 + c^2 - a^2}{2bc}$$

$$\cos A = \frac{751}{960}$$

$\log 751 = 12.87564 - 10$
$\log 960 = \quad 2.98227$
$\log \cos A = \dfrac{9.89337 - 10}{}$
$A = 38°32′$.

2. $\cos B = \dfrac{a^2 + c^2 - b^2}{2ac}$.

$$\cos B = \frac{225 + 576 - 400}{720} = \frac{401}{720}$$

$\log 401 = 12.60314 - 10$
$\log 720 = \quad 2.85733$
$\log \cos B = \dfrac{9.74581 - 10}{}$
$B = 56°9′$.

3. $\cos C = \dfrac{a^2 + b^2 - c^2}{2ab}$.

$$\cos C = \frac{225 + 400 - 576}{600} = \frac{49}{600}.$$

$$\begin{aligned} \log 49 &= 11.69020 - 10 \\ \log 600 &= \underline{2.77815} \\ \log \cos C &= 8.91205 - 10 \\ C &= 85°19'. \end{aligned}$$

Check: $38°32' + 56°9' + 85°19' = 180$.

OBTUSE ANGLE (ahb-toos'), an angle greater than a RIGHT ANGLE (90°) but less than a STRAIGHT ANGLE (180°).

OBTUSE TRIANGLE, a TRIANGLE that contains an OBTUSE ANGLE.

OCTAGON (ahk'tu-gahn), a POLYGON having eight sides. The sum of the interior angles of an octagon is 1080°. If the octagon is a regular octagon, each interior angle is 135°. A regular octagon may be inscribed in a CIRCLE by constructing two diameters (*see* DIAMETER OF A CIRCLE) PERPENDICULAR to each other and bisecting the lines joining the ends of the diameters. (See figure.) *See also* POLYGON, REGULAR.

OCTAHEDRON (ahk-tuh-hee'drun), a POLYHEDRON having eight faces.

OCTAL NUMBERS, a system of numeration having a BASE of 8 and the digits 0, 1, 2, 3, 4, 5, 6, and 7. To convert a decimal number to an octal number, divide the number by 8. The remainders, reading from last to first, are the digits of the octal number.

Ex. 1: Convert 157_{10} to an octal number.

Sol.:

$$\begin{array}{r|l} 8)157 & \text{Remainders} \\ 8)19 & 5 \\ 8)2 & 3 \\ 0 & 2 \end{array}$$

$$157_{10} = 235_8.$$

To convert from a binary number to an octal number,
1. Group the binary number in threes from the right.
2. The equivalents of the groups, in order, form an octal number.

Ex. 2: $1010100111_2 = \underset{1}{001}\ \underset{2}{010}\ \underset{4}{100}\ \underset{7}{111} = 1247_8.$

In like manner, an octal number may be converted to a binary number.

Ex. 3: $216_8 = \underset{2}{010}\ \underset{1}{001}\ \underset{6}{110} = 10001110_2.$

See also DECIMAL NUMBER SYSTEM; BINARY NUMBER SYSTEM.

ODD FUNCTION, a FUNCTION whose graph is symmetrical about the ORIGIN; hence, one for which $f(-x) = -f(x)$.

Ex.: Which of the functions x^n are odd functions?
Sol.: If n is odd, $f(-x) = -f(x)$, e.g., $f(x) = x^3$. (See figure).

Then

x	$f(x)$	$f(-x)$	$-f(x)$
0	0	$0 = 0$	$0 = 0$
1	1	$(-1)^3 = -1$	$-(1)^3 = -1$
2	8	$(-2)^3 = -8$	$-(2)^3 = -8$

and $f(-x^3) = -f(x^3)$.

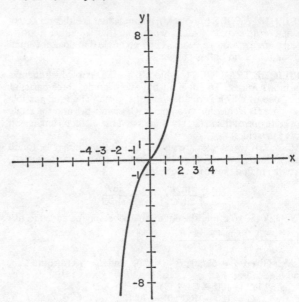

See also EVEN FUNCTION.

ODD NUMBERS, numbers which are not EVEN NUMBERS; i.e., those not divisable by 2; e.g., 1, -13, 129. In general, an odd number may be expressed as $2n + 1$, where n is any number.

OMEGA (oh-mee'-gah), the Greek letter, symbolized by ω. ω, ω^2 and 1 are the three cube roots of unity. Thus, $\sqrt[3]{1} = 1$, ω, ω^2.

$$\omega = \frac{-1}{2} + \frac{\sqrt{3}}{2}i; \omega^2 = \frac{-1}{2} - \frac{\sqrt{3}}{2}i.$$

In polar form (*see* COMPLEX NUMBER),

$$\omega = \cos 120° + i \sin 120°; \omega^2 = \cos 240° + i \sin 240°.$$

See also CUBIC EQUATION.

ONTO (on'-too), a MAPPING of a SET A is a mapping *onto* set B if each element of B is the IMAGE of at least one element of A. E.g., if set $A = \{1, 2, 3, 4\}$ and set $B = \{a, b, c\}$ and a mapping $A \rightarrow B$ is defined as $1 \rightarrow a$, $2 \rightarrow a$, $3 \rightarrow b$, $4 \rightarrow c$, the mapping is *onto* since each element of B is the image of at least one element of A. If the mapping $A \rightarrow B$ is defined as $1 \rightarrow a$, $2 \rightarrow y$, $3 \rightarrow a$, $4 \rightarrow y$, the mapping is *not onto* since an element of B, namely, b, is not the image of any element of A. *See also* INTO; SURJECTION.

OPEN INTERVAL, segment of a NUMBER LINE which does not include the end point. It is composed of all x between two numbers A and B, but not including either A or B. In symbols, $A < x < B$. The open interval is denoted (A,B). An interval which does include its end points is called a CLOSED INTERVAL, and is denoted $[A,B]$. An interval which includes only one of the end points is termed either half-open or half-closed. Symbols for the latter are $(A,B]$ if $A < x \le B$ and $[A,B)$ if $A \le x < B$. The intervals are said to be open on the left and on the right, respectively.

OPEN SET, a POINT SET, A, such that each point in A is in an interval in which all the points are points in A. The set of points in an OPEN INTERVAL is an open set. E.g., $A = \{x : -2 < x < 2\}$. Any point between -2 and 2 can be located in an interval such that the points in the interval are points in A. (See Fig. 1.)

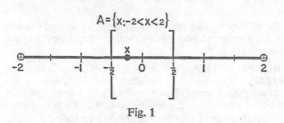

Fig. 1

x is a point in the interval. All the points in this interval are points in A

The set of interior points of a CIRCLE (excluding the points on the circle) is an open set. (See Fig. 2.) The complement of an open set is a CLOSED SET, and an open set may be defined as the complement of a closed set.

Fig. 2

x is a point in the set of interior points of circle O

ORDERED PAIR, two elements in a definite SEQUENCE. E.g., the number elements, 1 and 2, form two different ordered pairs, (1,2) and (2,1). The elements are the same but the order (sequence) is opposite. The coordinates (x,y) of all points in the plane are ordered pairs.

ORDER OF A DIFFERENTIAL EQUATION, that of the highest order DERIVATIVE OF A FUNCTION which appears in the equation; e.g., the order of the DIFFERENTIAL EQUATION $y'' + (y')^3 + y^5 = 0$ is 2 because the highest ordered derivative is y'', which is of the second order. *See also* DEGREE OF AN EQUATION.

ORDER OF OPERATIONS, in a series of algebraic operations.
1. MULTIPLICATIONS and DIVISIONS in the given order are always performed first.
2. Then ADDITIONS and SUBTRACTIONS are performed in any order.
3. If PARENTHESES, POWERS, or ROOTS are included in the series, these indicated operations are performed *before* multiplications and divisions.
In the expression $4 + 12 \div 2$, divide 12 by 2, then add 4. The result is 10. Note that 4 is the first term and $12 \div 2$ is the second term. However, the expression $(4 + 12)/2$ is only one term and is treated as any fraction. Add 4 and 12, then divide by 2 to obtain the quotient 8.
Simplify the following:
1. $6 \div 2 + 3 \times 2$
$3 + 6 = 9$
2. $\dfrac{8 - 3 \times 2}{4}$
$\dfrac{8 - 6}{4} = \dfrac{2}{4} = \dfrac{1}{2}$

3. $5 + 3(2 + 3) - 3^2 - 6 \div 2 + \sqrt{16}$
$5 + 3 \cdot 5 - 9 - 6 \div 2 + 4$
$5 + 15 - 9 - 3 + 4$
$24 - 12 = 12.$

See also POWER OF A NUMBER.

ORDINAL NUMBER, a NUMBER that denotes the order of an element in a SET; e.g., 1st, 2nd, and 3rd, 4th, 5th, 6th, . . .; read first, second, and third, fourth, fifth, sixth. *See also* CARDINAL NUMBER.

ORDINARY DIFFERENTIAL EQUATION, a DIFFERENTIAL EQUATION involving no PARTIAL DERIVATIVES.

ORDINATE, the vertical or y-distance from the x-axis of any point in a system of rectangular coordinates (*see* COORDINATES, RECTANGULAR). It is positive above the x-axis and negative below. E.g., if the coordinates of a point are (5,6), the ordinate is $+6$ and the point is located 6 units above the x-axis. *See also* ABSCISSA.

ORIGIN, the point at which the axes of a coordinate system intersect. Every coordinate of the origin is zero; in a plane, the origin is the point (0,0) (see Fig. 1a); in three-dimensions, the origin is the point (0,0,0) (see Fig. 1b).

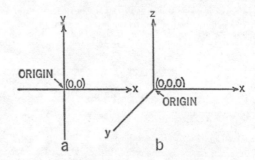

a　　　　b

ORTHOCENTER, the point of concurrency of the altitudes of a triangle. *See also* ALTITUDE OF A GEOMETRIC FIGURE; CONCURRENT LINES.

ORTHOGONAL (awr-thog'-uhn-uhl), PERPENDICULAR. Conventionally, two curves are said to be orthogonal at a common point if their TANGENT LINES at that point are perpendicular.
Ex. 1: Tell whether the following curves are orthogonal.

$$y = f(x) = (x - 1)^2, \text{ and } y = g(x) = x^2.$$

Sol.: They intersect at the point $(\frac{1}{2}, \frac{1}{4})$. Since $f'(\frac{1}{2}) = -1$, while $g'(\frac{1}{2}) = 1$, their tangents at the common point are perpendicular and the curves are orthogonal. (See Fig. 1.)

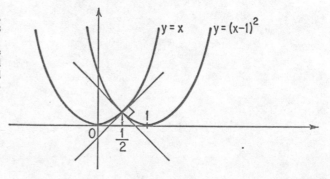

Fig. 1

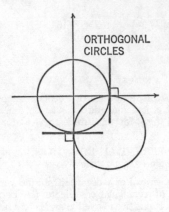

ORTHOGONAL
CIRCLES

Fig. 2

Ex. 2: Tell whether the following circles are orthogonal.

$$x^2 + y^2 - 1 = 0, \text{ and } (x - 1)^2 + (y + 1)^2 = 1.$$

Sol.: They intersect at the points (1,0) and (0,−1), and at each point one circle has a vertical tangent while one has a horizontal tangent; they are orthogonal. (See Fig. 2.) *See also* SLOPE OF A LINE.

OSCULATING PLANE (ahs′-kyu-lay-ting), for a curve at point P, the plane containing both the TANGENT VECTOR at P and the NORMAL VECTOR at P.

OUGHTRED, WILLIAM (aw′-tred), 1575–1660, an Englishman whose *Clavis Mathematicae*, published in 1631, included a section on ALGEBRA. Oughtred experimented with many ALGEBRAIC SYMBOLS and was responsible for the symbol $\times$ for MULTIPLICATION. He also adapted NAPIER's logarithms to a scale.

P

PAIRED *T*-TEST. In statistics, the paired *t*-test pairs observations from two normal populations (these are *not* two independent random samples). The hypothesis H_0: $\mu_1 - \mu_2 = \Delta_0$ can be tested against the appropriate ALTERNATIVE HYPOTHESIS as follows: The second member of each pair of observations is subtracted from the first; the resulting differences are then treated as observations from a single normal population, and the *t*-TEST for a single sample is applied as it ordinarily is.

The individual members within each pair should be as alike as possible in all aspects except the different treatments that they are given. A paired *t*-test is frequently used in "before-after" experiments.

PAPPUS' THEOREMS. 1. The first of these theorems is that if a region R is revolved around an axis A which does not pass through R, then the volume of the resulting solid equals the area of R multiplied by the length of the circle traced by its CENTROID. This theorem gives an easy way to find the volume of a solid of revolution. **2.** The second Theorem of Pappus is that the area of the SURFACE OF REVOLUTION generated by an arc C when revolved around an axis which does not intersect it is given by the length of C multiplied by the length of the circle traced by its centroid.

Ex.: What is the volume of the torus (doughnut) generated by the circle of radius 1 and center (2,0) when revolved about the *y* axis? (See figure.)

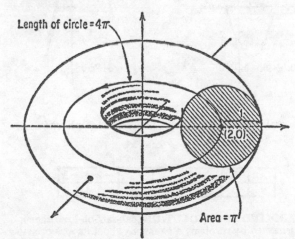

Length of circle = 4π

(2,0)

Area = π

Sol.: According to Pappus' first theorem, the volume is found by multiplying the area of the circle, which is π, by the length of the circle described by its centroid. Since the centroid of a circle is its center, in this case (2,0), this length is 4π. The volume V is therefore:

$$V = (4\pi)(\pi) = 4\pi^2, \text{ or approx. } 39.4.$$

See also DEFINITE INTEGRAL; SHELL METHOD.

PARABOLA (pah-rab'-oh-lah), a CONIC SECTION formed when a plane intersects a right circular CONE and is parallel to an element. The path of a thrown ball and that of a projectile fired from a gun approximate the path of a parabola. If light or sound waves emanate from the fixed point, or focus, they are reflected by the parabola in rays parallel to the axis and perpendicular to the fixed line. For this reason, the parabola is a good shape for automobile headlights, reflection telescopes, and radar screens.

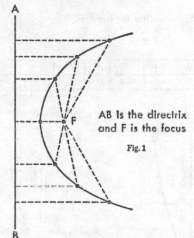

AB is the directrix and F is the focus

Fig. 1

Analytically, a parabola is the locus of points in the plane equidistant from a fixed point, called the focus, and a line, called the directrix. (See Fig. 1.) If COORDINATES are plotted with the *y*-axis parallel to the directrix and passing through the point halfway between the focus and the directrix (the vertex), the equation of a parabola is in the form, $y^2 = 4px$, where p is the distance of the focus from the origin. By interchanging x and y, and/or inserting a minus sign, the equations of parabolas opening in four directions are:

1. $y^2 = 4px$ opens to right (see Fig. 2a)
2. $y^2 = -4px$ opens to left
3. $x^2 = 4py$ opens upward (see Fig. 2b)
4. $x^2 = -4py$ opens downward

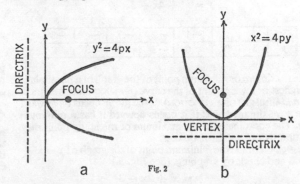

$y^2 = 4px$

DIRECTRIX

FOCUS

a

$x^2 = 4py$

FOCUS

VERTEX

DIRECTRIX

b

Fig. 2

Ex. 1.: What are the focus and directrix of the parabola whose equation is $y^2 = 12x$?

Sol.: The equation of a parabola has the form $y^2 = 4px$. Therefore $4p = 12$, and from this, $p = 3$. The focus is at the point (3,0), and the directrix is the line $x = -3$.

The equation of the parabola symmetric about the y-axis is the general QUADRATIC EQUATION with the ZERO replaced by y, or $y = ax^2 + bx + c$. The parabola of this equation opens upward if a is positive and downward if a is negative. The parabola of the equation $x = ay^2 + by + c$ opens to the right if a is positive and to the left if a is negative.

The line around which the GRAPH of a parabola is symmetric is called the axis of symmetry. The axis can be determined from the formula $x = -b/2a$, derived from the general quadratic equation $y = ax^2 + bx + c$.

Ex. 2: Graph $y = x^2 - 2x - 3$. (See Fig. 3.)

$$a = 1, \quad b = -2.$$
$$x = \frac{-b}{2a} = \frac{-(-2)}{2} = 1.$$

Then, $x = 1$ is the equation for the axis.

$$y = x^2 - 2x - 3.$$

x	0	1	2	3	4	−1	−2
y	−3	−4	−3	0	5	0	5

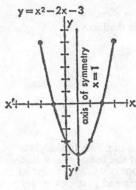

$y = x^2 - 2x - 3$

Fig. 3

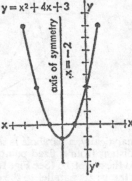

$y = x^2 + 4x + 3$

Fig. 4

Ex. 3: Graph $y = x^2 + 4x + 3$. (See Fig. 4.)

$$a = 1, \quad b = 4.$$
$$x = \frac{-b}{2a} = \frac{-4}{2} = -2.$$

The equation for the axis is $x = -2$.

$$y = x^2 + 4x + 3.$$

x	0	1	−1	−2	−3	−4	−5
y	3	8	0	−1	0	3	8

The maximum or minimum point of the graph of a parabola is the highest or lowest point of the curve (*see* MAXIMUM OF A FUNCTION *and* MINIMUM OF A FUNCTION). If the graph opens downward it has a maximum point; if it opens upward it has a minimum point. The coordinates of the maximum or minimum point may be found by COMPLETING SQUARES.

Ex. 4: Determine the minimum point of the graph of $y = x^2 + 2x - 3$ and check by graphing. (See Fig. 5.)

$$y = x^2 + 2x - 3$$
$$y + 3 = x^2 + 2x$$

Make the right member a PERFECT SQUARE by adding 1. Add 1 to both sides of the equation.

$$y + 3 + 1 = x^2 + 2x + 1$$
$$y + 4 = (x + 1)^2$$

Since $(x + 1)^2$ can never be negative, its minimum value must be 0; therefore, x must equal -1.

$$\text{When } x = -1, y = -4$$

The coordinates of the minimum point of the graph are $(-1, -4)$.

$$y = x^2 + 2x - 3.$$

x	0	1	2	−1	−2	−3	−4
y	−3	0	5	−4	−3	0	5

Ex. 5: Determine the maximum point of the graph of $y = 3 - 2x - x^2$. (See Fig. 6.)

$$y = 3 - 2x - x^2$$
$$y - 3 = -2x - x^2$$

Complete the square by adding -1 to both members of the equation.

$$y - 4 = -1 - 2x - x^2, \text{ or}$$
$$y - 4 = -(1 + 2x + x^2)$$
$$y - 4 = -(1 + x)^2$$

The right side of the equation has its maximum value of 0 when $x = -1$.

$$\text{When } x = -1, y = 4.$$

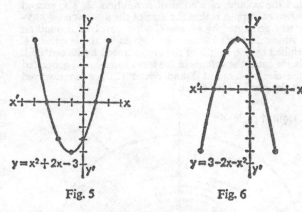

$y = x^2 + 2x - 3$

Fig. 5

$y = 3 - 2x - x^2$

Fig. 6

The coordinates of the maximum point of the graph are $(-1, 4)$

$$y = 3 - 2x - x^2.$$

x	0	1	2	−1	−2	−3
y	3	0	−5	4	3	0

PARABOLOID OF REVOLUTION (pah-rab'-oh-loid), the surface generated by revolving a PARABOLA about its AXIS OF SYMMETRY. Thus, sections formed by vertical planes are parabolas. A paraboloid of revolution is given by the equation: $\frac{x^2}{a^2} + \frac{y^2}{b^2} = z$; where $a = b$, a section formed by passing a horizontal plane through the surface at $z = k$ is a CIRCLE. (See Fig. 1.) If $a \ne b$, the section formed by $z = k$ is an ELLIPSE, and the surface is called an *elliptic paraboloid*. (See Fig. 2.) If $b < 0$, and $a \ne b$, the surface is called a *hyperbolic paraboloid*.

Planes parallel to the xz-plane intersect the hyperbolic paraboloid in parabolas opening upward, while planes parallel to the yz-plane intersect it in parabolas opening downward. Horizontal planes (parallel to the xy-plane) intersect it in hyperbolas, which open to right and left if $z > 0$, and open in the direction of the y-axis if $z < 0$. The xy-plane itself intersects the hyperbolic pa-

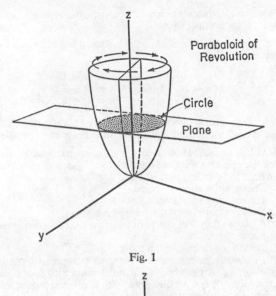

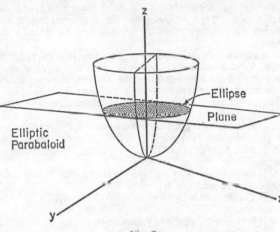

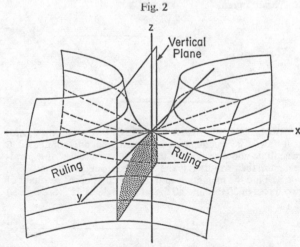

Fig. 1

Fig. 2

Fig. 3

raboloid in two straight lines which intersect at the origin; the lines are called rulings. (See Fig. 3.)

PARALLAX, the angular difference in the apparent positions of an object against a more distant background as viewed from two different places. It can be illustrated by holding a pencil at arm's length and looking at it first with one eye and then with the other.

Geocentric parallax is the difference in positions of an object viewed from the center of the earth and the surface of the earth, as shown in Fig. 1.

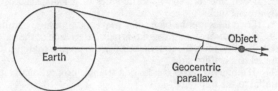

Fig. 1

By means of parallax, the distance to a celestial body can be estimated. Even the nearest stars, however, are too distant to have any geocentric parallax. The parallax of stars within ab. 100 light-years is measured from two opposite points in the earth's orbit. This is called *stellar, heliocentric,* or sometimes *trigonometric,* parallax, and is equal to half the actual angle measured, as shown in Fig. 2. More distant stars have smaller and smaller parallaxes increasingly difficult to measure, and their distances must be estimated by other methods.

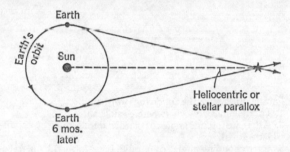

Fig. 2

PARALLELEPIPED (par-al-lel-u-pahy'-ped), a PRISM whose bases are enclosed by PARALLELOGRAMS. If the lateral edges are not perpendicular to the base, it is an oblique parallelepiped. If the lateral edges are PERPENDICULAR to the base, it is a right parallelepiped. If a right parallelepiped has rectangles for bases, it is called a *rectangular parallelepiped,* or a rectangular solid. If all of the faces of the parallelepiped are squares, the figure is a cube. (See figure.)

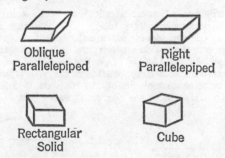

PARALLEL LINES, straight lines in the same plane that do not meet no matter how far they are extended. Following are classic theorems for proving two lines parallel.

1. If two lines lie in the same plane and do not intersect even when extended, the lines are parallel.
2. If two lines form equal ALTERNATE INTERIOR ANGLES with a TRANSVERSAL, they are parallel.
3. If two lines form equal CORRESPONDING ANGLES with a transversal, they are parallel.
4. If two lines form supplementary interior angles on the same side of a transversal, they are parallel.

5. If two lines are each parallel to a third line, they are parallel.

6. If two lines are each PERPENDICULAR to the same line, they are parallel.

7. If two lines are the opposite sides of a PARALLELOGRAM, they are parallel.

8. If two lines are the bases of a TRAPEZOID, they are parallel.

9. The MEDIAN OF A TRAPEZOID is parallel to each of the bases.

10. If a line joins the MIDPOINTS of two sides of a triangle, it is parallel to the third side.

11. If a line divides two sides of a triangle proportionally it is parallel to the third side.

To construct parallel lines, use the second theorem: To construct a line parallel to AB through point P not on AB (see Fig. 1), draw a line through P intersecting AB in Q. With P as a vertex and the line QP as a side, construct an angle equal to $\angle BQP$. Through P and the point of intersection of the two arcs at R, draw CD. (Two points determine a line.) $CD \parallel AB$, because two lines are parallel if they form a pair of equal alternate interior angles with a transversal.

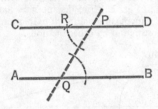

Fig. 1

Parallel lines have the following properties:

1. Parallel lines are everywhere equidistant.

2. Alternate interior angles of parallel lines formed by a transversal are equal.

3. Corresponding angles of parallel lines formed by a transversal are equal.

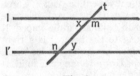　　　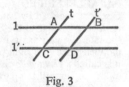

Fig. 2　　　　　　　Fig. 3

4. Interior angles between parallel lines on the same side of a transversal are supplementary. In Fig. 2, if $l \parallel l'$, then $\angle x$ is supplementary $\angle n$ and $\angle m$ is supplementary $\angle y$.

5. Segments of parallels between parallels are equal. In Fig. 3, if $l \parallel l'$ and $t \parallel t'$, then $AC = BD$, and $AB = CD$.

6. If parallel lines intercept equal segments on one transversal, they intercept equal segments on any transversal. In Fig. 4, if $l_1 \parallel l_2 \parallel l_3$ and if segment a = segment b, then $c = d$.

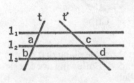　　　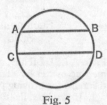

Fig. 4　　　　　　　Fig. 5

7. Parallel lines in a circle intercept equal arcs. In Fig. 5, if $AB \parallel CD$, then $\overset{\frown}{AC} = \overset{\frown}{BD}$.

In modern analytic geometry, the condition that two lines be parallel is that they have the same slope (*see* SLOPE OF A LINE) if they are in a plane, or that they have proportional sets of DIREC-

TION NUMBERS if they are in space. Two VECTORS are parallel only if their vector product equals 0.

Ex.: Are the lines specified by the following sets of parametric equations parallel?

$$l_1\begin{cases} y = t + 1 \\ x = 2t - 1 \\ z = 3t \end{cases} \qquad l_2\begin{cases} y = 2t - 1 \\ x = 6t + 3 \\ z = 9t + 5 \end{cases}$$

Sol.: Two sets of direction numbers are (1,2,3) and (2,6,9). These are not proportional; therefore the lines are not parallel.

PARALLELOGRAM (par-al-lel′-oh-gram), a QUADRILATERAL in which the opposite sides are parallel. (See figure.) A parallelogram has the following properties:

1. The opposite sides are equal.

2. The opposite angles are equal.

3. The consecutive angles are supplementary.

4. A diagonal divides the parallelogram into two congruent triangles.

5. The diagonals bisect each other.

The RHOMBUS, RECTANGLE, and SQUARE are special types of parallelograms. A rhombus is a parallelogram with four equal sides; a rectangle is a parallelogram with four equal angles; and a square is a parallelogram with four equal sides and four equal angles.

If a parallelogram has equal angles, i.e., is a rectangle or square, the diagonals are equal. If the parallelogram has equal sides, i.e., is a rhombus or square, the diagonals are perpendicular to each other and bisect the angles of the parallelogram.

To prove that a quadrilateral is a parallelogram, use one of the following theorems:

1. If both pairs of opposite sides are parallel, the quadrilateral is a parallelogram.

2. If both pairs of opposite sides are equal, the quadrilateral is a parallelogram.

3. If two opposite sides are both equal and parallel, the quadrilateral is a parallelogram.

4. If the diagonals bisect each other, the quadrilateral is a parallelogram.

5. If both pairs of opposite angles are equal, the quadrilateral is a parallelogram.

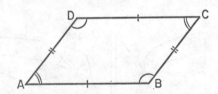

PARALLELOGRAM LAW OF FORCES, the law that states that if two forces acting on a body at a point are represented in magnitude and direction by the two adjacent sides of a parallelogram, their resultant is the diagonal from that point.

Ex.: Find the magnitude and the direction of the resultant of two forces of 30 lbs. and 40 lbs. at an angle of 45°. (See figure.)

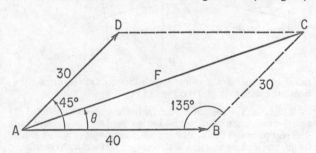

Sol.: By the Law of Cosines (*see* COSINES, LAW OF):

$$F^2 = AB^2 + BC^2 - 2(AB)(BC) \cos 135°$$
$$F^2 = (40)^2 + (30)^2 - 2 \cdot 40 \cdot 30 \cos 135°$$
$$F^2 = 1600 + 900 - 2400(-\tfrac{1}{2}\sqrt{2})$$
$$F^2 = 1600 + 900 + 1200\sqrt{2}$$
$$F = 64.8 \text{ lbs. to the nearest tenth.}$$

By the Law of Sines (SEE SINES, LAW OF):

$$\frac{\sin\theta}{30} = \frac{\sin 135°}{64.8}.$$

$$\log \sin\theta = \log 30 + \log \sin 135 - \log 64.8.$$

$$
\begin{array}{rl}
\log 30 = & 1.47712 \\
\log \sin 135° = & 9.84949 - 10 \\
\hline
& 11.32661 - 10 \\
\log 64.8 = & 1.81158 \\
\hline
\log \sin\theta = & 9.51503 - 10 \\
\theta = & 19°6'32''.
\end{array}
$$

PARALLEL POSTULATE, *see* EUCLID'S FIFTH POSTULATE.

PARALLEL SAILING, sailing on a course due east, or a course due west, along a parallel of LATITUDE. In parallel sailing, the distance sailed is the DEPARTURE.

PARALLELS OF LATITUDE, CIRCLES of the earth's surface whose PLANES are parallel to the plane of the equator. *See* LATITUDE.

PARAMETER (pah-ram'-e-tur), an independent VARIABLE other than one represented on a COORDINATE axis. The most common parameter is time, denoted by t; e.g., the distance of a moving point from a reference point may be given as a function of time, such as $D = t^2$, using the parameter t. Parameters also commonly occur when a curve is defined using PARAMETRIC EQUATIONS for the coordinates. *See also* CHANGE OF VARIABLES.

PARAMETRIC EQUATIONS (par-u-me'-trik), equations by which the COORDINATES of a curve in the plane may be described as two functions of a single VARIABLE. One equation gives the x-coordinate of the point on the curve corresponding to a value of the variable (parameter), while the other gives its y-coordinate:

$$x = f(t) \text{ and } y = g(t).$$

These two are called parametric equations, and the variable, t, is called the parameter. The parameter may be interpreted as time, and the curve as the path of a point whose position at time t is given by the parametric equations.

Ex. 1: Plot the points on the curve given by the parametric equations:

$$x = t^3 \text{ and } y = t^2,$$

which correspond to $t = 0$, $t = 1$, $t = -1$, $t = 2$. Sketch the curve through them.

Sol.: $t = 0$: $x = 0$, $y = 0$. $t = 1$: $x = 1$, $y = 1$. $t = -1$: $x = -1$, $y = 1$. $t = 2$: $x = 8$, $y = 4$. (See Fig. 1a.)

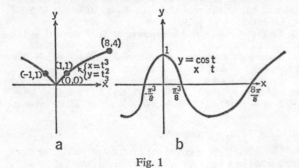

Fig. 1

Ex. 2: The position of a moving point at time t is given by the parametric equations:

$$y = \cos t \text{ and } x = t^3.$$

Sketch its path. How far from the origin is it at $t = 0$?

Sol.: (See Fig. 1b.) At $t = 0$, $y = \cos 0 = 1$, $x = 0^3 = 0$, so the point is at $(0,1)$. Its distance from the origin is 1.

Given two points A and B in the plane with coordinates (x_1, y_1) and (x_2, y_2) respectively, any point P on the LINE SEGMENT between them has coordinates of the form:

$$(x_1 + t(x_2 - x_1), y_1 + t(y_2 - y_1)),$$

where $0 \leq t \leq 1$. When $t = 0$, the point P is coincident with A, while when $t = 1$, $P = B$. This formula is a representation of the segment $\overline{AB}$ in terms of the parameter t.

This representation may be used to divide the line segment into any RATIO. If the segments AP and PB are to be in the ratio r (i.e., $AP/PB = r$), then the ratio of t to $1 - t$ is also r. In other words,

$$\frac{AP}{PB} = \frac{t}{(1 - t)}.$$

Ex. 3: What point P divides the line segment joining $(1,0)$ to $(3,1)$ into the ratio of 1 to 2?

Sol.: $\dfrac{AP}{PB} = \dfrac{1}{2} = \dfrac{t}{1 - t}$; therefore, $1 - t = 2t$, or $t = \tfrac{1}{3}$. When $t = \tfrac{1}{3}$, P has coordinates (x, y) given by:

$$x = x_1 + \tfrac{1}{3}(x_2 - x_1) = 1 + \tfrac{1}{3}(3 - 1) = 1\tfrac{2}{3}.$$
$$y = y_1 + \tfrac{1}{3}(y_2 - y_1) = 0 + \tfrac{1}{3}(1 - 0) = \tfrac{1}{3}.$$

Thus, $P = (1\tfrac{2}{3}, \tfrac{1}{3})$.

Given a CIRCLE of radius r and center, the ORIGIN, the definitions of the functions $\sin\theta$ and $\cos\theta$ (where θ is the angle marked in Fig. 2), can be used to express the coordinates of any point on the circle: $P = (r\cos\theta + r\sin\theta)$. The point P varies as x varies, but it remains on the circle. If x varies from 0 to 2π, the point P

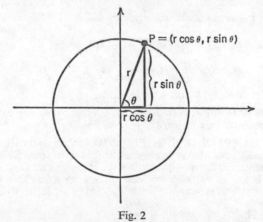

Fig. 2

traces the entire circle. The formula $P = (r\cos\theta + r\sin\theta)$ is called a parametric representation of the circle.

If the parameter t is used instead of θ, and t is thought of as representing time, the path followed by a point whose coordinates at time t are $(r\cos t, r\sin t)$ is a circle of radius r.

An ELLIPSE with center at the origin may be represented by the parametric equations:

$$x = a\cos t \text{ and } y = b\sin t.$$

If $a \geq b$, the foci of the ellipse will be on the x-axis, while if $b \geq a$, the foci will be on the y-axis. If $a = b$ (a special case included in both the first two conditions), the foci coincide and are located at the origin, which is on both axes. *See also* CHANGE OF VARIABLES; PARAMETER; TRIGONOMETRIC FUNCTIONS.

PARENTHESES, ( ), (pah-ren'-thah-sis), in mathematics, one of several pairs of GROUPING SYMBOLS.

The following are rules for removing parentheses:

1. If the expression (*see* ALGEBRAIC EXPRESSION) enclosed in PARENTHESES is preceded by a *plus* sign, remove the parentheses with no sign change. For example, $3a^2 + (b^2 - c^2) = 3a^2 + b^2 - c^2$ and $3a^2 + (-a^2 - b^2) = 3a^2 - a^2 - b^2$ or $2a^2 - b^2$.

2. If the expression in parentheses is preceded by a *minus* sign, change the signs of all the terms enclosed in the parentheses and combine if necessary. Examples are: $5x^2 + 3y^2 - (2x^2 - y^2) = 5x^2 + 3y^2 - 2x^2 + y^2$, or $3x^2 + 4y^2$; and $a - (-a + b - c) = a + a - b + c$, or $2a - b + c$.

PARSEC, a unit of distance used in astronomy. The word is derived from the first three letters of the words *parallax* and *second*. One parsec is the distance of a body from the sun whose heliocentric PARALLAX is 1 second of arc. It is equal to 3.26 light-years, or in common distance units, ab. 19.3 trillion mi. or 31 trillion kilometers. The distance of a body in parsecs can be computed easily if its parallax is known, since the distance in parsecs is the reciprocal of the parallax in seconds. *See* TABLE NO. 5.

PARTIAL DERIVATIVE (pahr'-shal), If $z = f(x,y)$, then by fixing x we can consider z as a function of the single variable y. Similarly, by fixing y we can consider z as a function of x. We can differentiate either of these with respect to the variable, resulting in a partial derivative. Thus, the partial derivative of $f(x,y)$ with respect to x at (a,b) is

$$\lim_{h \to 0} \frac{f(a + h, b) - f(a,b)}{h}.$$

This is denoted by "$f_x(a,b)$" or "$D_x(a,b)$" or "$\left(\dfrac{\delta f}{\delta x}\right)_{(a,b)}$"

Similarly, the partial derivative with respect to y is

$$\lim_{h \to 0} \frac{f(a, b + h) - f(a,b)}{h} = f_y(a,b) = D_y(a,b) = \left(\frac{\delta f}{\delta y}\right)_{(a,b)}.$$

Ex.: Let $f(x,y) = x^2 y$. Find D_x (1,2) and D_y (1,2).

Sol.: $D_x(1,2) = \dfrac{d}{dx}(f(x,2)) = \dfrac{d}{dx}(2x^2) = 4x = 4.$

$D_y(1,2) = \dfrac{d}{dy}(f(1,y)) = \dfrac{d}{dy} y = 1.$

See also DIFFERENTIATION; SADDLE POINT.

PARTIAL DIFFERENTIAL EQUATION, one involving PARTIAL DERIVATIVES, e.g., $(\partial z/\partial x)^2 = k(\partial z/\partial y)^2$.

PARTIAL FRACTIONS, INTEGRATION BY, the ratio of two polynomials can always be rewritten as the sum of terms whose denominator is linear or quadratic and whose numerator respectively is a constant or linear. Each of these terms may then be integrated. This process is called integration by partial fractions.

Ex.: Find $\displaystyle\int \frac{4x + 2}{3x^2 + 7x + 2} dx.$

Sol.: $\dfrac{4x + 2}{(3x + 1)(x + 2)} = \dfrac{A}{3x + 1} + \dfrac{B}{x + 2}$

$4x + 2 = A(x + 2) + B(3x + 1)$

$4x + 2 = Ax + 3Bx + 2A + B$

$4x + 2 = x(A + 3B)x + 2A + B.$

Thus, $A + 3B = 4$ and $2A + B = 2.$

Then, $A = 2/5$ and $B = 6/5.$

Thus, $\displaystyle\int \frac{4x + 2}{3x^2 + 7x + 2} dx = \frac{2}{15} \int \frac{3dx}{3x + 1} + \frac{6}{5} \int \frac{dx}{x + 2}$

$= \dfrac{2}{15} \ln(3x + 1) + \dfrac{6}{5} \ln(x + 2) + c.$

PARTITION, for an interval [a,b], an arbitrarily selected set of points, $P = \{x_0, x_1, x_2, \ldots, x_n\}$ which divide [a, b] into the

subintervals [a, x_1], [x_1, x_2], etc. For example, in defining the AREA UNDER A CURVE between $x = a$ and $x = b$, approximating rectangles are formed, and their bases are specified according to their end points. The first end point is a and the last is b, and the collection of the end points is called the partition of the interval [a, b]. (See figure.) *See also* DEFINITE INTEGRAL, MESH OF PARTITION.

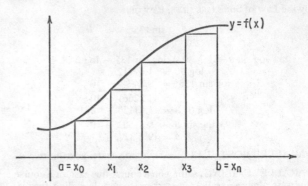

PASCAL, BLAISE, 1623–1662, French mathematician, physicist, and philosopher. He was one of the founders of the *Theory of Probability*. A religious mystic, he became associated with the Jansenists, a severe and austere, religious sect not unlike the Calvinists, with whom they shared the tenet of predestination. Pascal defended the Jansenists in his brilliant *Provincial Letters* (1656). His *Pensées* (1670), published posthumously, contain some of the basic ideas for an apologia of Christianity, notably his supposed proof that belief in God is no less rational than non-belief.

Pascal wrote *Traite du Triangle Arithmetique* which laid the foundation for the calculus of probabilities. The triangular arrangement of numbers which is now called PASCAL'S TRIANGLE was known before Pascal's time, but he studied it and discovered many of its properties. As a young man, he made important discoveries in physics, especially in the field of hydrostatics.

Biblio.: Mesnard, J., *Pascal* (1969); Steinmann, J., *Pascal* (1966).

PASCAL'S TRIANGLE, triangular arrangement of numbers which gives the NUMERICAL COEFFICIENTS of $(a + b)^n$ for any value of n.

$(a + b)^0$							1							
$(a + b)^1$						1		1						
$(a + b)^2$					1		2		1					
$(a + b)^3$				1		3		3		1				
$(a + b)^4$			1		4		6		4		1			
$(a + b)^5$		1		5		10		10		5		1		
$(a + b)^6$	1		6		15		20		15		6		1	
$(a + b)^7$	1	7		21		35		35		21		7		1

Notice the following patterns:

1. Each line begins with 1 and ends with 1.

2. Every other number is the sum of the two numbers to its right and left in the row above it. Thus, $10 = 6 + 4$; $21 = 6 + 15$; and $35 = 15 + 20$.

3. Each row read across is a power of 11. Thus, $121 = 11^2$; $1331 = 11^3$; etc.

4. The sum of each row is a power of 2, as $1 + 2 + 1 = 4$ or 2^2; $1 + 4 + 6 + 4 + 1 = 16$ or 2^4; etc.

5. Each row shows the coefficients for $(a + b)^n$. The coefficients of $(a + b)^5$ are 1, 5, 10, 10, 5, and 1. Then $(a + b)^5 = a^5 + 5a^4b + 10a^3b^2 + 10a^2b^3 + 5ab^4 + b^5$. *See also* BINOMIAL THEOREM.

PATCHBOARD, *see* COMPUTER.

PEDAL CURVE, the LOCUS of the foot of a perpendicular from a fixed point to a variable tangent to a fixed curve. If the fixed curve is a PARABOLA, and the fixed point is the vertex of the parabola, the pedal curve is a CISSOID (see figure).

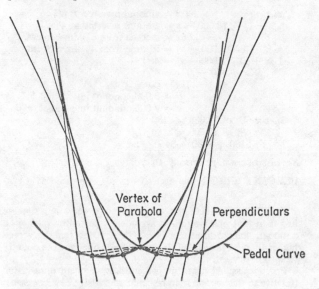

Vertex of Parabola

Perpendiculars

Pedal Curve

PEDAL TRIANGLE, a triangle formed by joining the feet of perpendiculars to the sides of a given triangle. Triangle *DEF* in the figure is the pedal triangle formed by joining the feet of altitudes *CF*, *AE*, and *BD*. In this pedal triangle, the altitudes bisect the angles.

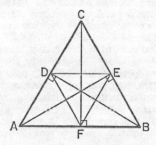

PENCIL, of circles, all circles that lie in the same plane and pass through two given points. The line joining these points is called the *radial axis*. (See Fig. 1.)

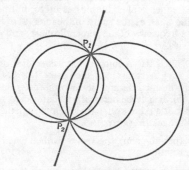

Pencil of circles
radial axis P₁ P₂

Fig. 1

A pencil of lines is the set of all lines in a given plane passing through a given point called the *vertex of the pencil* (See Fig. 2.)

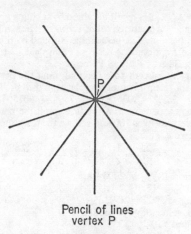

Pencil of lines
vertex P

Fig. 2

If the vertex is the IDEAL POINT, the pencil of lines is a *pencil of parallel lines*.

A pencil of planes is the set of all planes passing through a given line called the *axis of the pencil*. (See Fig. 3.)

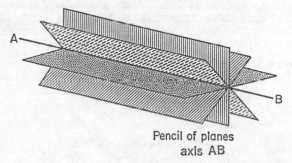

Pencil of planes
axis AB

Fig. 3

A pencil of spheres is the set of all spheres that pass through a fixed circle in a given plane, called the *radical plane of the pencil*. (See Fig. 4.)

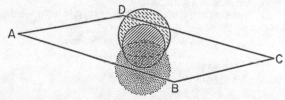

Fig. 4

PENTADECAGON, a POLYGON of 15 sides.

PENTAGON, a POLYGON with five sides. To inscribe a regular pentagon in a circle construct a DECAGON, and draw lines connecting every other VERTEX. Each interior angle of a regular pentagon measures 108°.

PERCENT, from the Latin *per centum*, meaning by the hundred, is the term for expressing a fraction having a denominator of 100. A percent may also be expressed in terms of an equivalent decimal. Three percent means "three out of every hundred" or three hundredths of any given number. Three percent is usually written with the numeral 3 followed by the symbol %.

$$3\% = \tfrac{3}{100} = .03; 25\% = \tfrac{25}{100} = \tfrac{1}{4} = .25.$$

In computations, percent is called the *rate*, as in the rate of INTEREST or the rate of DISCOUNT.

PERCENTAGE, the result obtained by taking a given PERCENT, or rate, of a given quantity, called the BASE. The symbol % is used to indicate percent. The percentage is found by multiplying the base by the fractional or decimal equivalent of the given percent. Thus, Base × Rate = Percentage.

To change a percent to a decimal, omit the percent symbol, and move the decimal point two places to the left. Thus, $80\% = .80$; $3\frac{1}{2}\% = 3.5\% = .035$; $\frac{3}{4}\% = .75\% = .0075$; $125\% = 1.25$.

To change a percent to a fraction, omit the percent symbol, place the percent over 100 and reduce the resulting FRACTION to its lowest terms. Thus,

$$25\% = \frac{25}{100} = \frac{1}{4}; \quad 12\frac{1}{2}\% = \frac{12\frac{1}{2}}{100} = \frac{125}{1000} = \frac{1}{8}.$$

Ex. 1: Find $12\frac{1}{2}\%$ of 2000 lbs.
Sol.: $12\frac{1}{2}\% = 12.5\% = .125$.
   $.125 \times 2000 = 250$.
   The percentage is 250 lbs.
Ex. 2: Find 75% of $356.00.
Sol.: $75\% = \frac{75}{100} = \frac{3}{4}$.
   $\frac{3}{4} \times 356 = 267$.
   The percentage is $267.00.

Computations involving percentages may involve three basic problems: finding the percentage, finding the base when the percentage and rate are given, or finding the percent when the percentage and base are given. Since Base × Rate = Percentage, Base = Percentage ÷ Rate, and Rate = Percentage ÷ Base.

Ex. 3: 32 is 40% of what amount?
Sol.: Find the base.

Percentage ÷ Rate = Base.
$32 \div .40 = 80$ or $32 \div \frac{2}{5} = 80$.

Ex. 4: What percent of 80 is 32?
Sol.: Find the rate.

Rate = Percentage ÷ Base.
$\frac{32}{80} = \frac{2}{5} = 40\%$ or $32 \div 80 = .40 = 40\%$.

Computations with percent are used extensively in business transactions, such as interest, discount, buying and selling, and commission.

The solution of percentage problems in algebra may also require computations with percent:

Ex. 5: A baseball team won 57 games and lost 38. What percent of its games did it win?
Sol.:   Let x = percent of games won.
              95 = games played.

$$\frac{x}{100} \times 95 = \text{games won}.$$

$$\frac{95x}{100} = 57$$

$$95x = 5700$$

$$x = 60, \text{percent of games won}.$$

Check: 60% of 95 = 57.
Ex. 6: A man sells a house for $20,000, realizing a profit of 25% on the cost. What was the original cost of the house?
Sol.:   Let x = cost of house.
              $.25x$ = profit on cost.
              $20,000$ = selling price.
              $x + .25x = 20,000$
              $1.25x = 20,000$
              $x = 16,000$, cost of house.

Check: 25% of $16,000 = $4,000
         $16,000 + $4,000 = $20,000.

Ex. 7: A man invested $10,000, part at 6% per year and the remainder at 4% per year. If his annual income from the two investments was $460, how much did he invest at each RATE OF INTEREST?

Sol.:   let x = amount invested at 6%.
      $10,000 - x$ = amount invested at 4%.
              $.06x$ = income from 6% investment.
      $.04(10,000 - x)$ = income from 4% investment.
      $.06x + .04(10,000 - x) = 460$
      $.06x + 400 - .04x = 460$
              $.02x = 60$
                 $x = 3,000$, amount invested at 6%.
                 $x = 7,000$, amount invested at 4%.

Check: 6% of $3,000 = $180
         4% of $7,000 = $280
         $180 + $280 = $460

See also DECIMAL FRACTIONS; MIXTURE PROBLEMS.

PERCENT ERROR, the RELATIVE ERROR expressed as a PERCENT.

PERCENTILE, in statistics, the percent of observations that are less than that observation. If a student's percentile rank on a national, standardized test is 84, this means that he scored higher than 84 percent of the students throughout the country who took the test.

For unclassified data, the percentile rank of an observation (relative to that sample) can be calculated easily. For CLASSIFIED DATA, the following formula can be used:

$$\text{Percentile rank of any observation, say } x = \frac{\left[F_{x-1} + \frac{(x - l_x)f_x}{c_x} \right] \cdot 100}{n}$$

where F_{x-1} denotes the cumulative frequency in all classes up to, but not including, the class containing x; l_x, the lower boundary of the class containing x; f_x, the frequency of the class containing x; c_x, the width of the interval of the class containing x; and n, the size of the sample.

The numerical value of the observation that corresponds to a given percentile rank, say p, is called the pth percentile. Some percentiles have special names. The 50th percentile is called the MEDIAN. The 25th, 50th, and 75th percentiles are called the first, second, and third QUARTILES. The 10th, 20th, etc., percentiles are known as DECILES.

The percentile that corresponds to any given percentile rank, p, is found by a formula similar to that for the median:

$$p\text{th percentile} = l_p + \left(\frac{pn}{100} - F_{p-1} \right) \cdot \frac{c_p}{f_p},$$

where l_p denotes the lower boundary of the class containing the pth percentile (hereafter called "the percentile class"); F_{p-1}, the cumulative frequency of all the classes up to, but not including, the percentile class; c_p, the width of the interval of the percentile class; f_p, the frequency of the percentile class; and n, the sample size.

PERFECT SQUARE, a number that has exact SQUARE ROOTS, as 16, x^2, and $25y^4$. A TRINOMIAL, such as $a^2 + 2ab + b^2$, is a perfect square trinomial because its two BINOMIAL factors are the same, $(a + b)$. It may be necessary to find the square root of a large number or a POLYNOMIAL to determine whether it has exact square roots. *See also* FACTORING.

PERIGON (per-ah-gahn), the ANGLE formed when a RAY makes a complete rotation.

PERIMETER (pur-rim'-u-tur), the sum of the lengths of the sides of a POLYGON. The perimeters of two similar polygons have the same RATIO as any two corresponding sides.

PERIOD, of a trigonometric function, the number of degrees within which a trigonometric function completes one cycle. E.g., for the function $y = \sin x$ (see Fig. 1), the period is 2π or 360°, since the graph begins at 0°, passes through its maximum and minimum value and returns to 0° in 2π radians or 360°. In general, for a function $y = \sin nx$ its period may be determined from the quotient $360/n$ or $2\pi/n$. Thus, the period of $y = \sin 2x$ is $360/2$ (or $2\pi/2$) or 180° (π radians). The curve completes a cycle in 180° (see Fig. 2).

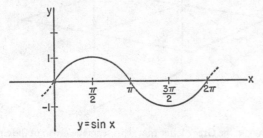

y = sin x

Fig. 1

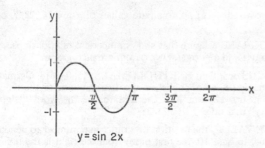

y = sin 2x

Fig. 2

PERIODIC FUNCTION, function which repeats the same sets of values at regular intervals; e.g., TRIGONOMETRIC FUNCTIONS.

PERMUTATION (pur-myoo-tay′-shun), an ordered arrangement of objects. E.g., the possible permutations of the letters a, b, and c are abc, acb, bac, bca, cab, and cba.

The number of ordered sets of r objects that can be formed from n distinct objects is called the number of permutations of n objects taken r at a time; it is denoted by $_nP_r$, ^nP_r, or $P(n,r)$; and is equal to $\dfrac{n!}{(n-r)!}$. If all n of the objects are arranged, there are $n!$ permutations.

The number of ways n distinct objects can be arranged in a circle is $(n - 1)!$

If the n objects consist of n_1 identical objects of a first kind, n_2 identical objects of a second kind, and so on, up to n_k objects of a kth kind, the number of distinct permutations is $\dfrac{n!}{n_1!n_2! \cdots n_k!}$.

Ex. 1: A student owns 8 books. There is room for only 4 books on his desk. How many arrangements of 4 books can be made from 8 books.

Sol.: $\qquad _8P_4 = \dfrac{8!}{(8-4)!} = 8\cdot7\cdot6\cdot5 = 1680.$

Ex. 2: How many distinguishable arrangements of 3 identical black marbles, 2 identical red marbles, and 3 identical white marbles can be made?

Sol.: $\qquad \dfrac{8!}{3!2!3!} = \dfrac{40320}{72} = 560.$

PERPENDICULAR (pur-pen-di′-kyoo-lar), either of two lines that form equal ADJACENT ANGLES, or RIGHT ANGLES, with each other. Only one perpendicular may be drawn from a point to a straight line, or through a point on the line. The distance from a point to a line is the length of a perpendicular to the line. The distance between two parallel lines is the perpendicular distance between them.

Two lines are perpendicular if any one of the following statements is true:

1. They form a right angle.
2. They form equal adjacent angles.
3. They are adjacent sides of a RECTANGLE.
4. They are adjacent sides of a SQUARE.
5. They are diagonals of a RHOMBUS.
6. They are diagonals of a square.
7. One line is a CHORD of a circle and the other passes through the center of the circle and bisects the chord.
8. They are lines drawn from a point on a circle to the ends of the DIAMETER OF A CIRCLE.
9. One is a TANGENT LINE to a circle and the other is a RADIUS drawn to the point of tangency.
10. The product of their slopes (*see* SLOPE OF A LINE) equals -1.

Two lines in space which do not intersect are not considered perpendicular even if two lines that are parallel to them and do intersect are perpendicular. (*See* SKEW LINES.) However, two vectors which are parallel to perpendicular lines are considered perpendicular even when they do not meet. The test is that their DOT PRODUCT equals 0.

If two lines are perpendicular (written $l_1 \perp l_2$), then the slope of the one line is the negative reciprocal of the slope of the other. Thus, if $l_1 \perp l_2$, the slope of l_1 is m_1 and the slope of l_2 is m_2, then $m_1 = -1/m_2$. (If one of the lines is vertical, and therefore has no slope, this relation does not hold; but then the perpendicular line would be horizontal and have slope 0.) To test two lines for perpendicularity, check their slopes to see if the relationship is satisfied.

Ex.: Which of the following pairs of lines are perpendicular?

a. The line through the points (1,1) and (2,4), and the line through the points (1,2) and $(-2,3)$.
b. The line $y = 3x + 5$ and the line $y = -\frac{1}{3}x$.
c. The line through the points (1,2) and (1,4) and the line through the points $(1,-2)$ and $(-1,-2)$.

Sol.: All three pairs are perpendicular.

a. The slopes are 3 and $-1/3$.
b. The slopes are 3 and $-1/3$.
c. The lines are vertical and horizontal.

To construct a perpendicular to line AB at point P on the line with P as a center and any convenient radius, construct arcs M and N intersecting AB. With M and N as centers and a radius greater than one half of MN, construct arcs intersecting in C. Draw CP. Therefore, $CP \perp AB$ at P. (See Fig. 1.) To prove that $CP \perp AB$, draw CM and CN. $CM = CN$ and $MP = PN$. (Radii of the same circle are equal.) C and P are each equidistant from M and N. Two points each equidistant from the end points of a line segment determine the perpendicular bisector of the segment.

To construct a perpendicular to line AB from point P, not on AB, with P as a center and any convenient radius construct an arc cutting AB at M and N. With M and N as centers and a radius greater than one half of MN construct a pair of arcs intersecting in C. Draw PC. Therefore, $PC \perp AB$ at D. (See Fig. 2.)

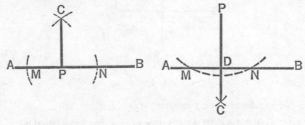

Fig. 1 Fig. 2

To prove $PC \perp AB$, draw $PM, PN, MC,$ and $NC. PM = PN$ and $MC = CN$. (Radii of the same circle are equal.) P and C are points equidistant from the ends of MN. Two points each equidistant from the ends of a line segment determine the perpendicular bisector of the segment.

PERPENDICULAR BISECTOR OF A LINE SEGMENT, the line through the MIDPOINT of a LINE SEGMENT and perpendicular to the segment. Any point on the perpendicular bisector of a line segment is equidistant from the end points of the segment. (See Fig. 1.) Hence, the perpendicular bisector of a line segment may be defined as the LOCUS of points in the plane which are equidistant from the end points of the segment. Since the slope (*see* SLOPE OF A LINE) of the perpendicular bisector is the negative reciprocal of the slope of the segment and the bisector passes through the midpoint of the segment (see Fig. 2), its equation may be written when the COORDINATES of the end points of the line segment are known.

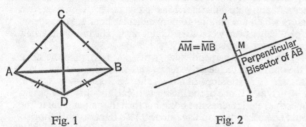

Fig. 1   Fig. 2

Ex.: What is the equation of the perpendicular bisector of the segment between the points (1,2) and (4,3)?

Sol.: The midpoint M of the segment is given by the midpoint formula.

$$M = \left(\frac{x_1 + x_2}{2}, \frac{y_1 + y_2}{2}\right) = \left(\frac{1 + 4}{2}, \frac{2 + 3}{2}\right) = \left(\frac{5}{2}, \frac{5}{2}\right)$$

The slope of the bisector is $-1/m$ where m is the slope of the segment.

$$m = \frac{\Delta y}{\Delta x} = \frac{y_2 - y_1}{x_2 - x_1} = \frac{3 - 2}{4 - 1} = \frac{1}{3}.$$

Thus, the equation of the bisector is

$$y = 5/2 + (-3)(x - 5/2),$$
$$y = 5/2 - 3x + 15/2,$$
$$y = -3x + 10.$$

To construct the perpendicular bisector of given line segment AB (see Fig. 3), with a radius greater than one half the length of AB and with points A and B as centers, use a compass to construct two pairs of arcs, intersecting at C and D. Draw line CD, the perpendicular bisector of AB. ($AC = BC$ and $AD = BD$ because radii of the same circle are equal. Therefore, CD is the perpendicular bisector of AB.)

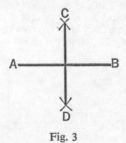

Fig. 3

See also CONSTRUCTION; INDIRECT PROOF.

PERPENDICULAR PLANES, two planes that form equal adjacent DIHEDRAL ANGLES. (See figure.)

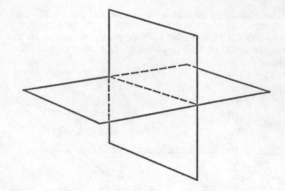

PI (pahy), π, the Greek letter that represents the RATIO of the circumference of a CIRCLE to DIAMETER of a CIRCLE. $\frac{C}{d} = \pi$. π is an IRRATIONAL NUMBER; approximate values of π are $3\frac{1}{7}$, 22/7, or 3.1416.

PICTOGRAM, a figure that shows numerical relationships. A BAR GRAPH and a BROKEN-LINE GRAPH are pictograms.

PITISCUS or Piticus **BARTHOLOMAUS,** 1560–1613, German mathematician, who published the first modern textbook of trigonometry. He was also the first to use the word "trigonometry" in a title.

PLACE VALUE, the position of a DIGIT in a number to denote its value. In base 10, the first place from the right is the unit's digit, the second place is the tens digit, the third place is the hundred's digit, and so on.

The number 364 means 3 hundreds + 6 tens + 4 units. Zero may be used as a place holder. The number 4 means 4 units. If it is followed by one zero, the number becomes 40, or forty. If it is followed by two zeros, the number becomes 400, or four hundred. The number three thousand sixty four, written 3064 means 3 thousands + no hundreds + 6 tens + 4 units.

billions	hundred millions	ten millions	millions	hundred thousands	ten thousands	thousands	hundreds	tens	units
2,	9	5	3,	6	4	1,	2	8	7

The number is read two billion, nine hundred fifty three million, six hundred forty one thousand, two hundred eighty-seven. Note that commas are used for groups of threes. Commas are only used for numbers of five or more digits.

PLANE, a surface in which a straight line joining any two of its points will lie wholly in the surface.

Planes have the following properties:

1. A plane is determined by three noncollinear points.
2. A plane is determined by a line and a point not on the line.
3. A plane is determined by two intersecting lines.
4. A plane is determined by two parallel lines.
5. The intersection of a plane and a straight line not in the plane is a point.
6. The intersection of two planes is a straight line.
7. An infinite number of planes can pass through one line or one point.

The equation of a plane is a linear equation (*see* EQUATION, LINEAR) in three variables:

$$Ax + By + Cz + D = 0. \quad \text{(See figure.)}$$

This equation may be solved for z, giving a formula for z as a function of the other two variables:

$$z = A'x + B'y + D'$$

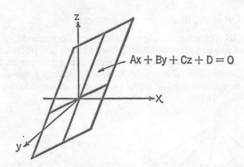

Ex. 1: What is the x-intercept of the plane $x + 2y + 3z + 2 = 0$?

Sol.: On the x-axis, both $y = 0$ and $z = 0$. Thus,

$$x + 2 = 0; \quad x = -2.$$

Ex. 2: Find the equation of the plane containing the points $(1,1,1)$, $(2,3,4)$, $(2,0,0)$.

Sol.: The general formula for the plane applies to each of the three points, giving us three simultaneous equations:

$$A + B + C + D = 0$$
$$2A + 3B + 4C + D = 0$$
$$2A + D = 0.$$

Solving for A, B, D in terms of C gives the plane's equation:

$$\frac{C}{4}x + \left(\frac{4}{3}C\right)y + Cz + \left(\frac{-C}{2}\right) = 0$$

or

$$\tfrac{1}{4}x + \tfrac{4}{3}y + z - \tfrac{1}{2} = 0.$$

PLANE SAILING, sailing on a LOXODROME or rhumb line. The course of the ship in plane sailing is the constant angle that the loxodrome makes with the MERIDIANS.

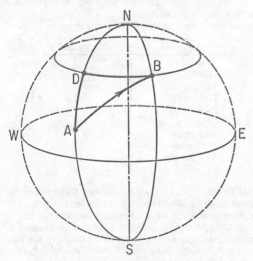

Fig. 1

In Fig. 1, arc AB is the distance a ship sails from A to B. Arc AD is a portion of the meridian that passes through A and is cut off by the parallel of latitude through B.

Representing spherical triangle ADB by a plane right triangle gives Fig. 2, in which AD represents a portion of the meridian NAS and the horizontal line DB represents a portion of the

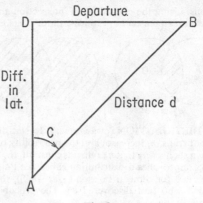

Fig. 2

parallel of latitude through B. Angle C is the COURSE angle and d is the distance travelled. Therefore,

$$\text{difference in latitude} = d \cos C,$$
$$\text{departure} = d \sin C.$$

The difference in latitude is North or South depending on the position of B with reference to A, and the DEPARTURE is East or West.

Ex.: Find the difference of latitude and the departure of a ship that travels N 30°, E 20 miles.

Sol.: departure $= 20 \sin 30° = 20 \times 0.5 = 10$ miles. diff. in lat. $= 20 \cos 30° = 20 \times 0.8660 = 17.32$ miles. Since a NAUTICAL MILE equals one minute, the difference in latitude is 17.32 minutes.

See also GREAT CIRCLE NAVIGATION.

PLATONIC SOLIDS, the name usually given to the five regular polyhedrons, not because PLATO discovered them but because he described them in his works. See also POLYHEDRON.

PLUS, in mathematics, the name given to the symbol $+$, used to indicate ADDITION and to indicate a POSITIVE NUMBER. The symbol also denotes "a little more" as in 3.27+ which means slightly more than 3.27.

POINT, in geometry, an undefined term described in Euclid's *Elements* as that which has no parts or the intersection of two lines. Points are named by capital letters and represented by dots. Analytically, each point in a plane is denoted by two COORDINATES (x,y), while each point in three dimensions is denoted by three coordinates (x,y,z). All figures in a plane, as well as the plane itself, may be thought of as a set of points.

POINT OF CONCURRENCY, the point in which CONCURRENT LINES intersect. The points of concurrency in a triangle are the following:

1. The CENTROID, or center of gravity, is the point where the medians (*see* MEDIAN OF A TRIANGLE) are concurrent.

2. The CIRCUMCENTER is the point where the perpendicular bisectors (*see* PERPENDICULAR BISECTOR OF A LINE SEGMENT) of the sides are concurrent.

3. The INCENTER is the point where the angle bisectors (*see* BISECTOR OF AN ANGLE) are concurrent.

4. The ORTHOCENTER is the point where the altitudes (*see* ALTITUDE OF A GEOMETRIC FIGURE) are concurrent.

POINT OF TANGENCY, the point where a TANGENT LINE touches a CIRCLE. If a RADIUS is drawn to this point, the tangent is PERPENDICULAR to the radius.

POINT SET, any collection of points. The collection may include isolated points, regions, or any combination. The LOCUS of any set of conditions is the point set whose elements satisfy the conditions. Using the operations of intersection and UNION, two point sets may be used to produce a third. (See figure.)

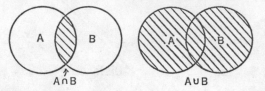

POISSON DISTRIBUTION (pwaw-sawn'). In statistics, when the number of trials, n, increases and the probability of success, π, decreases in such a way that $n\pi$ remains constant, the BINOMIAL DISTRIBUTION approaches a distribution called the Poisson Distribution (named for Simeon Poisson (1781–1840), the French mathematician who first discovered it). The probabilities are given by the formula

$$f(x) = \frac{e^{-n\pi}(n\pi)^x}{x!}.$$

The mean of the distribution is $n\pi$ and the variance is also $n\pi$.

POLAR COORDINATES, see COORDINATES, POLAR.

POLAR COORDINATE SYSTEM, see COORDINATE SYSTEM; COORDINATES, POLAR.

POLAR FORM, see COMPLEX NUMBER.

POLAR TRIANGLE, a SPHERICAL TRIANGLE in which the vertices are poles of the sides of another spherical triangle.

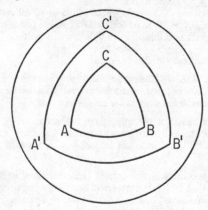

If A, B, and C in the figure are vertices of a spherical triangle, then A' would be the intersection of GREAT CIRCLES having B and C as poles. A' lies on the same side of BC as A and is a quadrant's distance (90°) from B and C. Great circles having A and C as poles intersect in B'. And in like manner, C' is a quadrant's distance from A and B as poles of great circles. Therefore, the spherical triangle $A'B'C'$ is a polar triangle of ABC.

If $A'B'C'$ is a polar triangle of ABC, then ABC is also a polar triangle of $A'B'C'$. Each angle of either polar triangle is the supplement of the opposite side of the other. E.g., A and $B'C'$ are supplementary, as are B' and AC.

POLE or ORIGIN, a fixed point, usually designated by O, on a directed line.

A point in the polar coordinate plane is specified by reference

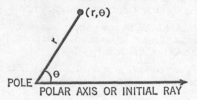

to a fixed RAY. The end point of the ray is called the pole of the system. A point is then given by its distance from the pole and the angle from the ray to the line through the point and the pole. (See figure.)

POLES OF A SPHERE, see GREAT CIRCLE.

POLYGON (pol'-ee-gon), a geometric plane figure made up of a number of straight LINE SEGMENTS joined at their end points. (See Fig. 1.) The line segments are called sides of the polygon and the point of intersection of two sides is called a VERTEX (plural, vertices). A line segment joining any two nonconsecutive vertices is called a diagonal.

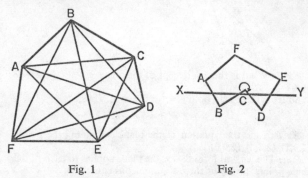

Fig. 1   Fig. 2

A concave polygon is a polygon in which at least one angle is greater than a STRAIGHT ANGLE. E.g., in Fig. 2, polygon $ABCDEF$ is concave. A line passing through a concave polygon may intersect it in four points.

A convex polygon is one in which each angle is less than a straight angle. Any line passing through a convex polygon intersects it in only two places. When the word "polygon" is used it usually means a closed, convex polygon.

A polygon is said to be equiangular if all of its angles are equal, and equilateral if all of its sides are equal. A polygon that is both equilateral and equiangular is called a REGULAR POLYGON. If polygons can be made to coincide, they are called CONGRUENT polygons. Similar polygons are polygons whose angles are equal and whose sides are proportional.

Polygons are named according to the number of sides:

Polygon	No. of Sides
Triangle	3
Quadrilateral	4
Pentagon	5
Hexagon	6
Heptagon	7
Octagon	8
Nonagon	9
Decagon	10
Dodecagon	12
n-gon	n

POLYHEDRAL ANGLE (pol-ee-hee'-dral), the figure formed when three or more planes intersect in a POINT. The point is the VERTEX. The intersecting planes are faces and the lines of t intersection are the edges of the polyhedral angle. Two adjacent faces of a polyhedral angle form a DIHEDRAL ANGLE. In the figure, if the vertex is P, and the edges are AP, BP, CP, and DP, the angle is named P-$ABCD$.

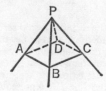

A polyhedral angle of three faces is a trihedral angle; of four faces, a tetrahedral angle.

POLYHEDRON (pol-ee-hee'-dron), a solid geometric figure formed by four or more PLANE surfaces enclosed by POLYGONS. The plane surfaces are called faces of the polyhedron. The intersections of the faces are the edges, and the points of intersection of the edges are the vertices. (See Fig. 1.) Polyhedrons are usually classified according to the number of faces.

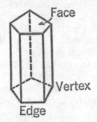

Face
Vertex
Edge

Fig. 1

A polyhedron with congruent (*see* CONGRUENT POLYGONS) faces and congruent POLYHEDRAL ANGLES is a regular polyhedron. There are only five regular polyhedrons. (See Fig. 2.)

Tetrahedron   Hexahedron   Octahedron

Dodecahedron   Icosahedron

Fig. 2

Regular Polyhedron	No. of Faces
Tetrahedron	4
Hexahedron	6
Octahedron	8
Dodecahedron	12
Icosahedron	20

POLYNOMIAL, an ALGEBRAIC EXPRESSION having more than one term. A polynomial with two terms is called a BINOMIAL; with three terms, a TRINOMIAL. The expression $4a^2 - 3a^3 + 5a^2 - a + 1$ is a polynomial having five terms. The derivative (*see* DERIVATIVE OF A FUNCTION) of the polynomial $P = a_0 + a_1x + a_2x^2 + \cdots + a_nx^n$ is

$$P' = a_1 + 2a_2x + 3a_3x^2 + \cdots + na_nx^{n-1}.$$

Ex. 1: Differentiate each of the following:
a. x^2 b. $x^3 - x + 1$ c. $7x^6 + 3x^4$
Sol.:

a. $\dfrac{d}{dx}x^2 = 2x.$ b. $P' = 3x^2 - 1.$ c. $P' = 42x^5 + 12x^3.$

Ex. 2: Find the first, second, and third derivatives of

$$P(x) = x^3 + 2x^2 + 3x + 4.$$

Sol.: $f'(x) = 3x^2 + 4x + 3.$
$f''(x) = 6x + 4.$
$f'''(x) = 6.$

The following formula is used to find the integral of polynomials:

$$\int (a_0 + a_1x + a_2x^2 + \cdots + a_nx^n)dx = a_0x + \frac{a_1x^2}{2} + \frac{a_2x^3}{3}$$
$$+ \cdots + \frac{a_nx^{n+1}}{n+1} + c.$$

Ex. 3: Integrate each of the following:

$$\text{a. } \int x^2\,dx \quad \text{b. } \int(3x^3 + x)\,dx$$

Sol.:   a. $x^3/3 + c$ b. $3x^4/4 + x^2/2 + c$

POLYNOMIAL CURVE (pol-ee-noh'-mee-al), the graph of a polynomial FUNCTION in one variable of the form

$$y = a_0 + a_1x + a_2x^2 + a_3x^3 + \cdots + a_nx^n,$$

where $a_0, a_1, \ldots a_n$ are constants and $a_n \neq 0$.

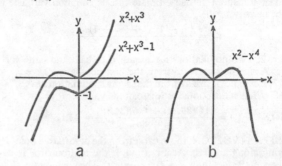

Fig. 1

The number n in the polynomial equation, the highest power of the variable, is called the degree of the polynomial $P(x)$, and it can be proved that the polynomial is equal to zero for no more than n values of x. Therefore, the graph of the polynomial will not touch the x-axis more than n times. It may, however, cross the x-axis fewer times than n, and may not even cross it at all. Examples of polynomials and their curves are shown in

a. $y = x^2 + x^3 - 1$ (see Fig. 1a).
b. $y = x^2 - x^4$ (see Fig. 1b).

POLYNOMIAL IN TWO VARIABLES, (in x and y), an expression of the form, $P_0 + P_1y + P_2y^2 + \cdots + P_ny^n$, in which the coefficients, $P_0, P_1, P_2 \cdots P_n$ are polynomials in the single variable x. This general expression can be rewritten in the following ways:

1. $(a_0 + a_1x + a_2x^2 + \cdots + a_nx^{m_1}) + (b_0 + b_1x + \cdots$
$+ b_mx^{m_2})y + (c_0 + c_1x + \cdots + c_kx^{m_3})y^2 + \cdots$
$+ (k_1 + k_2x + \cdots + k_{m_n}x^{m_n})y^n.$
2. $c_1 + c_2x + c_3y + c_4xy + c_5x^2 + c_6y^2 + c_7xy^2 + c_8x^2y$
$+ \cdots + c_kx^my^m.$

Examples of polynomials in two variables are:

$$x^2 + xy + y^2 - 1; \quad x + (x + x^2)y + (x + x^2 + x^3)y^2.$$

When a polynomial in two variables is set equal to zero it is called an algebraic equation; its graph is called an ALGEBRAIC CURVE. Curves which are not algebraic (and whose equations cannot be written as polynomials in two variables) are called TRANSCENDENTAL CURVES. The best known of them are the TRIGONOMETRIC CURVES and LOGARITHMIC CURVES.

POOLED ESTIMATE, in statistics, an estimate of a PARAMETER that is obtained by combining two or more independent estimates of the parameter. The pooled estimate is a weighted MEAN of the separate estimates.

A pooled estimate might be used in the test statistic used to test the hypothesis that two parameters from two different populations are equal. For example, when testing $H_0: \pi_1 = \pi_2$ for two binomial populations, a pooled estimate of the common value of π (by hypothesis) is used; namely,

$$p = \frac{n_1p_1 + n_2p_2}{n_1 + n_2}.$$

Ex. 1: In order to estimate π, the probability of throwing heads with a certain coin, one boy tossed it 65 times and a second tossed it 80 times. The first threw heads 55.3 percent of the time and the second 52.5 percent of the time. What is their pooled estimate of π?

Sol.: $\quad p = \dfrac{(65)(.553) + (80)(.525)}{65 + 80} = .537.$

One of the assumptions necessary to apply a test might be that certain parameters are equal. In testing a hypothesis about the difference of the means of two normal populations with unknown variances, it must be assumed that the variances are equal. In the test statistic a pooled estimate of this common variance is used; namely,

$$s_p^2 = \frac{(n_1 - 1)s_1^2 + (n_2 - 1)s_2^2}{n_1 + n_2 - 2}.$$

Ex. 2: Two populations are assumed to have the same variance. A sample of size 15 from the first population gave $s_1^2 = 39.72$; a sample of size 47 from the second population gave $s_2^2 = 31.18$. What is the pooled estimate of the variance?

Sol.: $\quad s_p^2 = \dfrac{(14)(39.72) + (46)(31.18)}{14 + 46} = 33.17.$

POSITION VECTOR, the VECTOR from the ORIGIN to a point P, moving along a curve. At any time, t, the motion of P is described by the functions $x = f(t)$, $y = g(t)$. The position vector is given by $\mathbf{R} = \mathbf{i}x + \mathbf{j}y$ or $\mathbf{R} = \mathbf{i}f(t) + \mathbf{j}g(t)$.

POSITIVE ANGLE, a rotation of a RAY in a counterclockwise direction. In the figure, θ is the positive angle formed by rotating OP. In such a rotation, the positive x-axis is the initial side (*see* SIDE OF AN ANGLE) and the final position of the ray is the terminal side. A positive angle is equivalent to the NEGATIVE ANGLE (α) with the same initial and terminal sides.

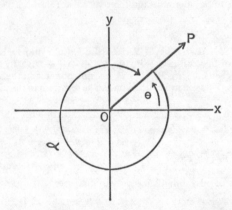

POSITIVE NUMBER, a SIGNED NUMBER, indicated by a plus sign ($+$) preceding it, that indicates a NUMBER greater than ZERO, or a number to the right of zero on a NUMBER LINE. $+5$, $+1/3$, $+2x$ are positive numbers. If a number has no sign before it, it is considered to be a positive number. Thus, in the ALGEBRAIC EXPRESSION $7 + 2x$, 7 is treated as $+7$.

POSTULATE, *see* AXIOM.

POSTULATIONAL SYSTEM (pahs-chu-lay'-shun-al), in mathematics, a structured body of knowledge that is based on a set of UNDEFINED TERMS and postulates (*see* AXIOM) that express relationships among the undefined terms. New elements in the system are defined in terms of the accepted undefined terms or in terms of elements previously defined. New statements or propositions are proven (*see* DEDUCTIVE REASONING) as THEOREMS of the system by using the postulates, definitions (*see* DEFINITION, CHARACTERISTICS OF), or previously proven theorems. The mathematical structure called "algebra" is an example of a postulated system. Its undefined terms are the literal symbols, e.g., x, y, z. Its postulates include such things as the ADDITION AXIOM, or the properties of EQUALITY. Defined terms include such symbols as

x^0, (*see* ZERO EXPONENT) defined as 1, and its theorems include such statements as $(a + b)^2 = a^2 + 2ab + b^2$ (*see* BINOMIAL, SQUARING A). Another example of a postulational system is EUCLIDEAN GEOMETRY. By a slight change in the postulates of that system a different postulational system—NON-EUCLIDEAN GEOMETRY—results.

POWER, of a test of a statistical hypothesis, the probability of rejecting that hypothesis. This probability depends upon the true (and unknown) value of the PARAMETER about which the hypothesis is being tested. In general, when the parameter equals the value that H_0 asserts that it does, the power will equal α (the SIGNIFICANCE LEVEL of the test). The larger the difference between the true and the hypothetical values of the parameter, the greater the power (the larger is the probability that H_0 will be rejected).

Ex.: Suppose that the hypothesis that a coin is honest is being tested against the hypothesis that the coin is not honest. Symbolically, $H_0 : \pi = .5$ vs. $H_1 : \pi \neq .5$, where π is the probability of tossing a head.

Sol.: The criterion for rejection of H_0 will be the obtaining of 5 heads or 5 tails in 5 tosses of the coin. Suppose that π is really .7. The POWER FUNCTION is $P(\theta) = \theta^5 + (1 - \theta)^5$. Then P(rejecting $H_0) = P(0$ or 5 heads$) = .1681 + .0024 = .1705$. For $\pi = .7$, the power of this test is .1705.

POWER FUNCTION, in statistics, $P(\theta)$, a function of the PARAMETER that gives (for any value of that parameter) the probability of rejecting H_0. Its graph is called the power curve. *See also* POWER.

POWER OF A NUMBER, the PRODUCT obtained when the number is used as a factor a given number of times. If the number 2 is raised to the second power, it means 2×2 and is written 2^2, which is read "2 squared." Thus, the second power of 2 is 4. Our number system, the DECIMAL NUMBER SYSTEM is based on powers of 10:

$$10^0 = 1, 10^1 = 10, 10^2 = 100, 10^3 = 1000, 10^4 = 10,000, \text{etc.}$$

The binary system of numeration is based on powers of 2:

$$2^0 = 1, 2^1 = 2, 2^2 = 4, 2^3 = 8, 2^4 = 16, \text{etc.}$$

POWER OF A POWER, the PRODUCT obtained when a number already raised to an indicated power is raised to another power, as $(x^4)^5$, which means x^4 used as a factor 5 times. In the example

$$(x^3)^2, x^3 \cdot x^3 = x^6; \text{ the exponent 3 is added 2 times.}$$

In the example

$$(x^3)^4, x^3 \cdot x^3 \cdot x^3 \cdot x^3 = x^{12}; \text{ the EXPONENT 3 is added 4 times.}$$

To raise a power to a power, multiply the exponent of the given power by the exponent of the power to which it is being raised. Therefore $(a^3)^9 = a^{27}$. Also, $(a^4)^{1/2} = a^2$; $(x^6)^{3/2} = x^9$; and $(x^a)^b = x^{ab}$.

POWERS AND ROOTS, TABLE OF, *see* TABLE NO. 18.

POWER SERIES, a SERIES of the form $\Sigma \, a_k x^k = a_0 + a_1 x + a_2 x^2 + \cdots$. *See also* TAYLOR SERIES.

POWERS OF A COMPLEX NUMBER, *see* DEMOIVRE'S THEOREM.

PRIME MERIDIAN, or LONGITUDE 0°, the MERIDIAN used as the origin in the measurement of longitude. It is the meridian that passes through the Royal Observatory in Greenwich, England.

PRIME NUMBER, a NATURAL NUMBER that has no integral (*see* INTEGER) FACTORS except itself and 1. Thus, 3, 7, 13, and 19 are prime numbers.

PRIMITIVE FUNCTION, the INDEFINITE INTEGRAL of a FUNCTION.

PRINCIPAL, a sum of money that is borrowed and for which a PERCENTAGE payment is required as INTEREST.

PRINCIPAL SQUARE ROOT, the positive SQUARE ROOT of a number. Every number has two square roots, e.g., the square root of 25 equals $+5$ and -5. The principal square root is $+5$. The radical symbol, $\sqrt{}$ indicates the principal root. Thus, $\sqrt{25} = +5$.

PRINCIPAL VALUE OF AN INVERSE FUNCTION, *see* INVERSE FUNCTION.

PRINCIPIA (prin-sip'-ee-u), the work, written by Isaac NEWTON, published in London in 1687 under the title *Philosophiae Naturalis Principia Mathematica*, in which he presented his theory of gravitation.

PRISM (prizm), a POLYHEDRON having two congruent faces in parallel planes and the other faces, PARALLELOGRAMS. The two polygons of the parallel planes are the bases. The parallelograms are the lateral faces, and the intersections of the lateral faces are the lateral edges. A prism has the following properties:
1. The lateral faces are enclosed by parallelograms.
2. The lateral edges are parallel and equal.
3. The bases are enclosed by congruent polygons.

A prism is named by the number of sides of the polygon that encloses the base. A prism is triangular, quadrangular, pentagonal, or hexagonal if its base has 3, 4, 5, or 6 sides, respectively.

A diagonal is a line segment that joins two vertices that do not lie in the same face or base. An altitude of a prism is the perpendicular from one base to the other base.

A prism in which the lateral edges are perpendicular to the bases is called a right prism. The lateral faces of a right prism are rectangles. The altitude of a right prism is equal to a lateral edge. (See Fig. 1.)

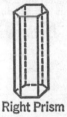 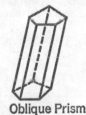

Right Prism   Oblique Prism

Fig. 1

A prism in which the lateral edges are not perpendicular to the bases is called an oblique prism. (See Fig. 1.)

The lateral AREA of a prism is the product of a lateral edge and the perimeter of a right section or $S = ep$. The lateral area of a right prism is the product of its altitude and the perimeter of the base.

The VOLUME of a prism is the product of the altitude and the area of the base, or $V = Bh$, when B is the area of the base and h is the altitude.

The figure formed when a plane intersects the lateral edges of a prism is called a section of a prism. If a plane intersects the lateral edges of a prism at right angles, the polygon is called a right section.

The part of a prism between a base and a section of the prism made by a plane not parallel to the base, is called a truncated prism. (See Fig. 2.)

A prism is inscribed in a cylinder when the lateral edges of the prism are elements of the cylinder. (See Fig. 3.)

Fig. 2   Fig. 3

PRISMATIC SURFACE, the surface generated by a line that always intersects a given POLYGON and is always parallel to a fixed line not in the same plane as the polygon. In the figure, *ABCDE* is the given polygon and *l* the fixed line. The polygon is the directrix (*see* CONIC SECTIONS) and the moving line the GENERATRIX. *AF* is an edge.

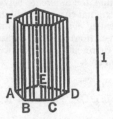

The surface of a PRISM is a closed surface made up of portions of intersecting planes.

PRISMATOID, a POLYHEDRON having two faces, called bases, in parallel planes, and all other faces, which are triangles or quadrilaterals, with their vertices in one or the other of the parallel planes. (See figure.) The altitude (*see* ALTITUDE OF A GEOMETRIC FIGURE) of a prismatoid is the distance (*see* DISTANCE BETWEEN TWO PARALLEL LINES) between its bases. The midsection is the section made by a plane parallel to the bases and midway between them. The VOLUME of a prismatoid is given by $V = \frac{1}{6}h(B_1 + 4B_m + B_0)$ where B_1 and B_0 are the areas of the bases, B_m is the area of the midsection, and h is the altitude.

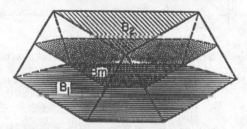

PROBABILITY FUNCTION, in statistics, a function, $f(x)$, which, upon substitution of a particular value of a discrete random variable (*see* RANDOM VARIABLE, DISCRETE), x, yields the probability that the variable will take on that value. The BINOMIAL DISTRIBUTION and POISSON DISTRIBUTION are examples of this type of probability function. Sometimes the probability function cannot be given as a formula, but must be given in a table, such as

$x =$	0	1	2
$f(x) =$	$\frac{1}{10}$	$\frac{2}{10}$	$\frac{7}{10}$

Occasionally a *probability density function*, for continuous random variables, is referred to as a probability function.

PROBABILITY OF AN EVENT. For an experiment that has n equally likely, mutually exclusive outcomes, r of which are favorable to the occurrence of Event A, then the probability of Event A, written $P(A)$, is defined to be r/n.

Ex. 1: A bag contains 3 blue, 7 white, and 5 red marbles. What is the probability of drawing a white marble?

Sol.: Drawing a marble can result in any one of 15 mutually exclusive, equally likely outcomes. Thus $n = 15$. A white marble may be drawn in 7 ways. Thus $r = 7$. $P(A) = 7/15$.

The probability of an event can also be defined as the limit of the ratio of favorable outcomes to total outcomes as the number of total outcomes increases without bound. *See also* CONDITIONAL PROBABILITY.

PROBABILITY THEORY, a branch of pure mathematics, the theoretical foundation of STATISTICS.

PRODUCT, the result, or answer, of a MULTIPLICATION operation. In algebra the product may be indicated. For example, $3ab$ is the product of 3 times a times b. The product may also be an ALGEBRAIC EXPRESSION of two or more terms.

PRODUCT, LOGICAL, *see* CONJUNCTION.

PROFIT, in accounting, the difference between the selling price and the sum of the original cost of an object and the selling expenses. This is also called *net profit*. If selling expenses (such as storage, labor, depreciation) are not considered, the profit is called *gross profit*. It represents the difference between the selling price and the original cost.

PROGRAM, *see* COMPUTER.

PROJECTILE, PATH OF, PARABOLA represented by PARAMETRIC EQUATIONS.

If a projectile is fired from the origin at an angle a with the horizontal, and the initial velocity of the projectile is V_0, then the x-component and y-component of the initial velocity are $x_0 = V_0 \cos a$ and $y_0 = V_0 \sin a$ respectively. (See figure.) The velocity in

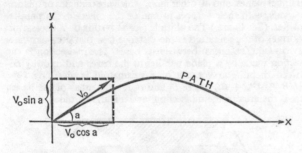

the x-direction remains unchanged, since gravity operates only in the y-direction. Therefore, the x-coordinate at time t is $x = tV_0 \cos a$. However, the y-coordinate of the projectile does not increase uniformly; it is given by the formula (from physics) $y = tV_0 \sin a - 16t^2$. Since this is a second degree, or quadratic, equation, its path is a parabola.

Ex.: Suppose a bullet is fired at an initial velocity of 64 ft./sec., at an angle of 30° from the horizontal. When will the bullet hit the ground? How far from the starting point will it be when it does?

Sol.: The bullet hits the ground when $y = 0$. This value of y may be represented by the equation $t \cdot 64 \cdot \frac{1}{2} - 16t^2 = 0$, and then $t = 2$ sec. At $t = 2$, x is found as follows:

$$x = 2 \cdot 64 \cdot \cos 30, \text{ which is approximately 111 ft.}$$

PROJECTION, of a point onto a line, the foot of the PERPENDICULAR from the point to the line. In Fig. 1, A' is the projection of A onto line l, and B' is the projection of B onto the line. $A'B'$ is the projection of segment AB on line l. In Fig. 2 ($\triangle ABC$), segment AD is the projection of AC segment onto AB, and segment BD is the projection of segment BC onto AB.

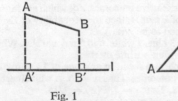

Fig. 1

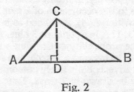

Fig. 2

The projection of a point in the plane onto one of the axes of a COORDINATE SYSTEM is the corresponding coordinate of that point; the projection onto the x-axis is the x-coordinate, and the projection onto the y-axis is the y-coordinate. (See Fig. 3a.)

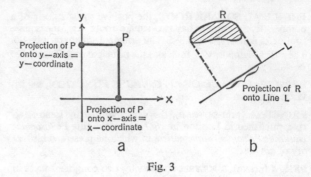

a   b

Fig. 3

The projection of a point onto a plane is the point in the plane at the foot of the perpendicular from the point to the plane. (See Fig. 4.)

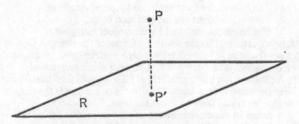

Fig. 4 Projection of P onto Plane R is P'

The projection of a region in the plane onto a line is the collection of the projections of all the points in the region (see Fig. 3b). The projection of a figure in space onto a plane is the shadow-like area made up of the projections of all the points in the figure (see Fig. 5).

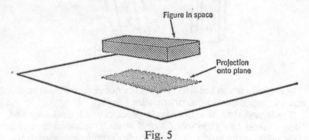

Fig. 5

PROJECTIVE GEOMETRY, a POSTULATIONAL SYSTEM which deals with the properties of geometric figures that remain unchanged when the figures are projected. Thus, projective geometry is not concerned with size, but with spatial relations.

PROOF, a logical argument, or sequence of statements, used to establish the truth of a statement. Once a proof of a statement is presented, the statement is called a THEOREM. *See also* INDIRECT PROOF.

PROPER FRACTION, a FRACTION in which the NUMERATOR is smaller than the DENOMINATOR. A proper fraction represents a part of a whole and, therefore, has a value less than one.

PROPORTION, a statement of equality between two ratios. A proportion may be written in two ways: $\frac{3}{4} = \frac{9}{12}$ or $3 : 4 = 9 : 12$; it is read "3 is to 4 as 9 is to 12." The four quantities are called the terms of the proportion. The first and fourth terms are called the *extremes* and the second and third terms are called the *means*.

A proportion, such as $\frac{a}{b} = \frac{b}{c}$, in which the means are the same is called a *mean proportion*. It can be proved that in a proportion, the product of the means is equal to the product of the extremes and conversely, if the product of the means is equal to the product of the extremes, two ratios form a proportion.

Ex. 1: Find x: $\dfrac{3}{7} = \dfrac{x}{63}$.

Sol.: $(3)(63) = (7)(x)$

$\qquad 189 = 7x$

$\qquad 27 = x$.

Ex. 2: Are $\dfrac{3}{50}$ and $\dfrac{2\frac{2}{5}}{40}$ equivalent fractions?

Sol.: If $(3)(40) = (2\frac{2}{5})(50)$, then $\dfrac{3}{50} = \dfrac{2\frac{2}{5}}{40}$.

$\qquad (3)(40) = 120$ and

$\qquad (2\frac{2}{5})(50) = 120$

$\qquad \therefore \dfrac{3}{50} = \dfrac{2\frac{2}{5}}{40}$

If the numerators of a proportion are equal, the denominators are equal:

$$\text{If } \frac{a}{b} = \frac{c}{d} \text{ and } a = c, \text{ then } b = d.$$

Ex. 3: Solve for x: $\dfrac{x^2}{4} = \dfrac{6-x}{4}$.

Sol.: The denominators are equal, so $x^2 = 6 - x$. Solving the quadratic equation,

$$x^2 + x - 6 = 0$$
$$(x+3)(x-2) = 0$$
$$x+3 = 0 \quad x-2 = 0$$
$$x = -3 \quad x = 2$$

In a series of equal ratios, the sum of the numerators is to the sum of the denominators as any numerator is to any denominator. Thus, if $\dfrac{2}{3} = \dfrac{4}{6} = \dfrac{8}{12}$, $\dfrac{14}{21} = \dfrac{2}{3}$.

If three terms of one proportion are equal to three terms of another proportion, then the fourth terms are equal:

If $\dfrac{a}{b} = \dfrac{c}{d}$ and $\dfrac{m}{n} = \dfrac{x}{y}$ and $a = m$; $c = x$, and $b = n$, then $d = y$.

If the product of two quantities equals the product of two other quantities, either pair may be the extremes in a proportion and the other pair the means.

Thus, if $ab = cd$ then $\dfrac{a}{c} = \dfrac{d}{b}$ or $\dfrac{c}{b} = \dfrac{a}{d}$ etc.

Five proportions may be derived from a given proportion:

$$\text{If } \frac{a}{b} = \frac{c}{d}, \text{ then}$$

1. $b/a = d/c$ is said to be derived by inversion;
2. $a/c = b/d$, by alternation;

3. $\dfrac{a+b}{b} = \dfrac{c+d}{d}$, by addition;

4. $\dfrac{a-b}{b} = \dfrac{c-d}{d}$, by subtraction; and

5. $\dfrac{a+b}{a-b} = \dfrac{c+d}{c-d}$, by addition and subtraction.

PROPORTIONAL, FOURTH, *see* FOURTH PROPORTIONAL.

PROPORTIONAL, MEAN, *see* MEAN PROPORTIONAL.

PROPORTIONAL, THIRD, *see* THIRD PROPORTIONAL.

PROPOSITION, a statement, usually a mathematical statement, which is either true or false. E.g., a THEOREM and the statement of a mathematical problem are propositions. *See also* IMPLICATION.

PROPOSITIONAL CALCULUS, *see* ALGEBRA OF PROPOSITIONS.

PROTRACTOR, an instrument for measuring ANGLES. A protractor has the shape of a semicircle. The 180 degrees in the semicircle are marked off along the curved part of the protractor, and the center of the CIRCLE of which it is part is marked on the straight edge. To measure an angle using a protractor, place the center at the VERTEX of the angle and a side of the angle along the straight edge of the protractor. Read the number of degrees at the point where the other side of the angle (or that side extended) intersects the curved part of the protractor. (See Figs. 1 and 2.)

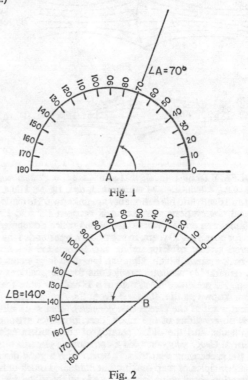

Fig. 1

Fig. 2

PSEUDOSPHERE (soo'-doh-sfir), the pseudospherical surface of PARABOLA type, a model of hyperbolic space. It is the surface of the NON-EUCLIDEAN GEOMETRY of LOBACHEVSKI and BOLYAI. On a pseudosphere, for a given line and a given external point, there is an infinite number of lines through the given point that will never intersect the given line. With this denial of EUCLID'S FIFTH POSTULATE, the sum of the angles of a triangle in hyperbolic space (see figure) is always less than 180.

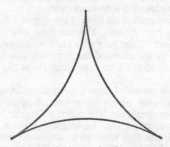

Triangle in hyperbolic space

PSEUDOSPHERICAL SURFACE, a surface whose total curvature has the same negative value at all of its points. A pseudospherical surface may be of elliptic type (see Fig. 1), hyperbolic type (see Fig. 2), or parabolic type (see Fig. 3). The parabolic type is called a PSEUDOSPHERE.

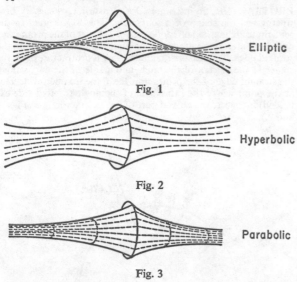

Fig. 1   Elliptic

Fig. 2   Hyperbolic

Fig. 3   Parabolic

PTOLEMY (tahl'-u-mee), in Latin Claudius Ptolemaeus, 2nd cent., A.D., astronomer of Alexandria, anc. Egypt. His dates of birth and death and his nationality are unknown. He made astronomical observations at Alexandria between 127 and 151 A.D. His fame rests on two works (*see below*) which dominated their fields for nearly 1,400 years. In astronomy, he extended the earth-centered system of Hipparchus and formulated the complex Ptolemaic system, which, although based on false assumptions, gave remarkably accurate predictions for the positions of the planets. He presented his system in a 13-volume work that later became known as the *Almagest* (from the Arabic article *al* and the first word of the Greek title *Megiste*). That work also contained observations of the moon, descriptions of astronomical instruments, and the oldest catalog of stars still in existence. Ptolemy's *Geography* occupied a comparable place in that field over the succeeding centuries. It began with a good discussion of the principles of map-making but contained much unreliable information about actual places, based mainly on the dead reckoning of sailors and stories brought back by travelers. Ptolemy also wrote on music and made important contributions to the development of TRIGONOMETRY. His great strength was not his originality so much as his ability to organize, improve on, and present in a clear fashion the work of his predecessors.

PYRAMID, the geometric solid formed by one NAPPE of a PYRAMIDAL SURFACE and a plane that intersects all the elements. It is a POLYHEDRON in which one face is a POLYGON and the other faces are triangles with a common vertex.

The polygon is called the base of the pyramid and the triangles are called the lateral faces. The common vertex of the lateral faces is the vertex of the pyramid. The intersections of the lateral faces are the lateral edges of the pyramid. The PERPENDICULAR from the vertex to the base is the altitude of the pyramid. (See Fig. 1.)

Pyramids are classified according to the polygon that encloses the base. Pyramids whose bases are triangles, quadrilaterals, pentagons, hexagons, etc. are called triangular, quadrangular, pentagonal, hexagonal, etc. A triangular pyramid is called a tetrahedron, and has four faces all of which are triangles.

A frustum of a pyramid is the part of the pyramid between its base and a section cut by a plane parallel to the base. (See Fig. 2.) Each lateral face of a frustum is a TRAPEZOID.

The total area of a pyramid is the sum of the areas of the lateral faces and the area of the base.

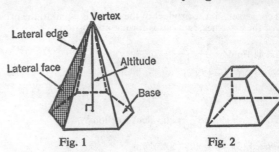

Fig. 1   Fig. 2

The volume of a pyramid equals 1/3 the product of the altitude and the area of the base, or $V = \frac{1}{3}Bh$, when B represents the area of the base, and h the altitude of the pyramid.

A pyramid whose base is a regular polygon is called a regular pyramid. The lateral faces of a regular pyramid are enclosed by congruent ISOSCELES TRIANGLES. The altitude of any of the lateral faces is called the slant height of a regular pyramid. The altitude of a regular pyramid passes through the center of the base. The lateral area of a regular pyramid is equal to one half the product of the slant height and the perimeter of the base, or $S = \frac{1}{2}lp$ when l is the slant height and p is the perimeter of the base.

PYRAMIDAL SURFACE, the surface generated by a line that intersects a fixed POLYGON and passes through a fixed point not in the same plane as the polygon. In the figure, the moving line AF is the GENERATRIX and the polygon $ABCDE$ is the directrix. (*See* CONIC SECTIONS.) The moving line in any of its positions is an element of the surface. The two parts of the surface separated by the fixed point O, or the vertex, are called nappes.

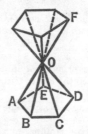

PYTHAGORAS (pi-thag'-oh-ras), 6th century B.C., Greek mathematician and philosopher, who with his students is credited with much of the important work in early Greek Mathematics, including the discovery of the PYTHAGOREAN THEOREM. He is known to have visited Egypt and Babylon where he may have found many of his ideas. Legend associates his interest in mathematics with alleged mystical qualities of numbers (odd numbers masculine, even numbers feminine; four the number of justice because it is the first perfect square, the product of equals, etc.). After his death, his school degenerated into a mystical sect, the PYTHAGOREANS.

PYTHAGOREAN RELATIONS (pith-u-gor'-ee-an), the three trigonometric relations derived from the PYTHAGOREAN THEOREM.

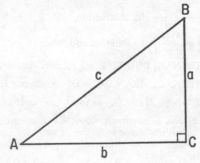

In the figure,

$$\frac{a}{c} = \sin A \quad \text{and} \quad \frac{b}{c} = \cos A.$$

By the Pythagorean Theorem,

$$a^2 + b^2 = c^2$$

Dividing by c^2,

$$\frac{a^2}{c^2} + \frac{b^2}{c^2} = \frac{c^2}{c^2}.$$

Substituting $\sin^2 A$ for $\left(\frac{a}{c}\right)^2$ and $\cos^2 A$ for $\left(\frac{b}{c}\right)^2$, then

$$\sin^2 A + \cos^2 A = 1.$$

In like manner, divide by b^2, then

$$\tan^2 A + 1 = \sec^2 A.$$

Divide by c^2 to obtain

$$\cot^2 A + 1 = \csc^2 A.$$

PYTHAGOREANS, a secret society founded by PYTHAGORAS in Crotona, a Greek city in Italy. They were chiefly interested in arithmetic, music, geometry, and astronomy, and their badge was a pentagram, a five-pointed star. They studied geometry for its own sake and were not interested in its practical applications as were the mathematicians at Alexandria. The influence of the group was so great it was finally dispersed for political reasons.

PYTHAGOREAN THEOREM. In any RIGHT TRIANGLE the square of the HYPOTENUSE is equal to the sum of the squares of the other two sides. (See Fig. 1.)

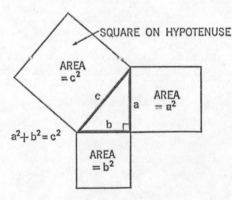

Fig. 1

Ex. 1: The hypotenuse of a right triangle is 25 ft. and one side is 15 ft. How long is the other side?

Sol.:
$$c^2 = a^2 + b^2$$
$$(25)^2 = (15)^2 + b^2$$
$$625 = 225 + b^2$$
$$b^2 = 625 - 225$$
$$b^2 = 400$$
$$b = \sqrt{400} = 20 \text{ ft.}$$

Ex. 2: Find the diagonal (*see* DIAGONAL OF A POLYGON) of a square if each side is 2 ft. (See Fig. 2.)

Sol.: The diagonal is the hypotenuse of the right triangle each side of which is 2 ft.

$$c^2 = a^2 + b^2$$
$$c^2 = (2)^2 + (2)^2$$
$$c^2 = 8$$
$$c = \sqrt{8} \text{ or } 2\sqrt{2} \text{ ft.}$$

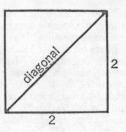

Fig. 2

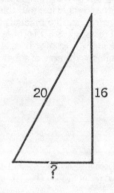

Fig. 3

In simplest RADICAL form the diagonal is $2\sqrt{2}$. The approximate length of the diagonal is found by multiplying the SQUARE ROOT of 2 by 2, or $1.414 \times 2 = 2.828$ ft.

Ex. 3: A ladder 20 ft. long just reaches a window that is 16 ft. from the ground. How far is the ladder from the foot of the building? (See Fig. 3.)

Sol.:
$$c^2 = a^2 + b^2$$
$$(20)^2 = (16)^2 + b^2$$
$$400 = 256 + b^2$$
$$b^2 = 144$$
$$b = 12 \text{ ft.}$$

PYTHAGOREAN THEOREM, ALGEBRAIC PROOF, a proof that the square of the hypotenuse of a RIGHT TRIANGLE is equal to the sum of the squares of the two legs.

Given right triangle ABC with right angle C, prove $c^2 = a^2 + b^2$. (See figure.) *Proof:* 1. Draw altitude h to the hypotenuse c, dividing c into segments x and y. [Only one perpendicular may be drawn to a line from a point. An altitude is the perpendicular from vertex to opposite side.] 2. $c/a = a/y$ and $c/b = b/x$. [If altitude is drawn to the hypotenuse of a right triangle, either leg is the mean proportional between the hypotenuse and the leg's projection on the hypotenuse.] 3. $a^2 = cy$ and $b^2 = cx$. [In a proportion, the product of the means equals the product of the extremes.] 4. $a^2 + b^2 = cx + cy$. [Equals added to equals are equal.] 5. $a^2 + b^2 = c(x + y)$. [Factor right-hand member.] 6. $a^2 + b^2 = c^2$. [Substitute c^2 for $c(x + y)$, since $c^2 = c(x + y)$.] (*See also* MEAN PROPORTIONAL.)

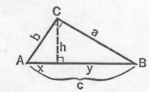

PYTHAGOREAN THEOREM, GEOMETRIC PROOF. In Euclid's proof of the PYTHAGOREAN THEOREM, the squares are geometric squares drawn on the sides of the triangle and the sum of the areas of the squares on the two legs is proved equal to the area of the square on the hypotenuse. Given triangle ABC (see figure) with right angle C and with squares on AC, BC, and AB, prove the area of square $ACGF$ + area of square $BKHC$ = the area of square $AMLB$. *Informal proof:* Draw CD perpendicular to ML. Draw BF and CM. $AEDM$ and $EBLD$ are rectangles (by definition). Triangle $FAB \cong$ triangle CAM (S.A.S.). Area of square $ACGF = bh$, or $(AF) \cdot (AC)$. Area of triangle $FAB = \frac{1}{2}bh$, or $\frac{1}{2}(AF) \cdot (BX)$. Then the area of triangle $FAB = \frac{1}{2}$ area square $ACGF$. If a parallelogram and a triangle have equal bases and altitudes, the area of the triangle is equal to one half the area of the parallelogram (square). In like manner, the area of triangle $CAM = \frac{1}{2}$ the area of rectangle $AEDM$ (base AM and equal altitudes AE and CY). Then the area of square $ACGF =$ the area of rectangle $AEDM$. Similarly, the area of square $BKHC =$ the area

of rectangle $EBLD$. Therefore, the area of square $ACGF$ + the area of square $BKHC =$ the area of square $AMLB$.

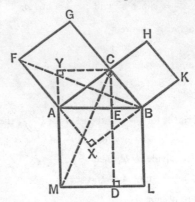

Q

QUADRANGLE, COMPLETE, the figure consisting of four COPLANAR points (vertices), no three of which are COLLINEAR POINTS, and six lines (sides) determined by them. (See Fig. 1.)

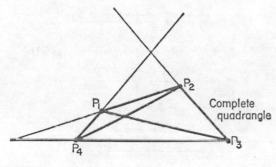

Fig. 1

The figure consisting of four points and four lines formed by taking the four vertices in order is called a *simple plane quadrangle*. (See Fig. 2.)

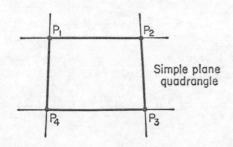

Fig. 2

QUADRANT, any one of the four parts of the plane formed by a system of rectangular coordinates (*see* COORDINATE SYSTEM). They are usually numbered by Roman numerals as shown in the figure. *See also* SPHERE.

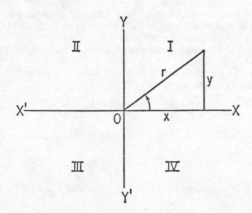

QUADRANTAL ANGLE, an ANGLE whose terminal side coincides with one of the axes. Angles of 90°, 180°, 270°, and 360° are quadrantal angles. (See figure.)

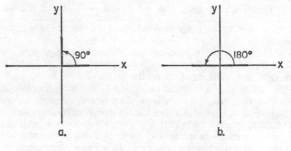

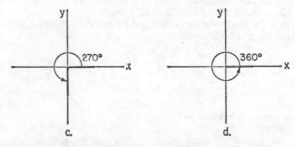

QUADRANTAL SPHERICAL TRIANGLE, a SPHERICAL TRIANGLE having one side equal to one fourth of a great circle (a QUADRANT), or 90°.

QUADRATIC EQUATION, an equation in one VARIABLE, of the form $ax^2 + bx + c = 0$, when $a \neq 0$. $x^2 - x - 2 = 0$ and $5x^2 + 2x - 7 = 0$ are quadratic equations.

A complete quadratic equation is an equation that contains both the first and second powers of the unknown letter and also the CONSTANT term, as $x^2 - x - 6 = 0$ and $3x^2 - 7x + 2 = 0$.

A quadratic equation in which the first power term or the constant term may be missing is called an incomplete quadratic as $x^2 - 9 = 0$ and $x^2 - 3x = 0$.

There are always two roots of a quadratic equation. However, the two roots may be equal. To find the roots of an incomplete quadratic equation, if the first power term is missing, place the constant term in the right member and take the SQUARE ROOT of both members.

Ex. 1: Solve $x^2 - 16 = 0$.

Sol.:
$$x^2 = 16$$
$$x = \pm 4.$$

The roots are 4 and −4.

Check:
$$x^2 - 16 = 0 \qquad\qquad x^2 - 16 = 0$$
$$(4)^2 - 16 = 0 \qquad\qquad (-4)^2 - 16 = 0$$
$$16 - 16 = 0 \qquad\qquad 16 - 16 = 0$$
$$0 = 0. \qquad\qquad 0 = 0.$$

Note that both positive and negative square roots are roots of the equation. If the constant term is missing, remove the common monomial factor and let each FACTOR equal zero.

Ex. 2: Solve $x^2 - 3x = 0$.

Sol.:
$$x(x - 3) = 0$$
$$x = 0$$
$$x - 3 = 0$$
$$x = 3.$$

The roots are 0 and 3.

There are four methods of solving a complete quadratic equation:

1. Factoring, only if the quadratic expression in the left member is factorable and the right member is zero.

2. Completing the Square, for any quadratic equation of the form $ax^2 + bx + c = 0$.

3. Quadratic Formula, $x = \dfrac{-b \pm \sqrt{b^2 - 4ac}}{2a}$ which is evaluated by substituting numerical values of a, b, and c in the equation.

4. Graphing. Not all roots can be determined by graphing. If roots are irrational, they can only be approximated. If roots are complex, they will not show on the graph.

The solution of a quadratic equation by factoring depends on the following principle: If the product of two or more factors equals zero, at least one of the factors equals zero. Therefore, it is possible to solve an equation if the right member is zero and if the left member is factorable. Each of the two binomial factors can be made to equal zero and solved as a linear equation (*see* EQUATION, LINEAR).

Ex. 3: Solve $x^2 + 7x + 12 = 0$.

Sol.: Factor the left member and let each factor equal zero. Solve for x in both equations.

$$(x + 3)(x + 4) = 0$$
$$x + 3 = 0$$
$$x = -3.$$
$$x + 4 = 0$$
$$x = -4.$$

The roots are -3 and -4.

Check:

$$x^2 + 7x + 12 = 0 \qquad x^2 + 7x + 12 = 0$$
$$(-3)^2 + 7(-3) + 12 = 0 \quad (-4)^2 + 7(-4) + 12 = 0$$
$$9 - 21 + 12 = 0 \qquad 16 - 28 + 12 = 0$$
$$0 = 0 \qquad\qquad 0 = 0$$

Ex. 4: Solve $x^2 - 4x + 4 = 0$.

Sol.:
$$(x - 2)(x - 2) = 0$$
$$x - 2 = 0$$
$$x = 2.$$
$$x - 2 = 0$$
$$x = 2.$$

The two roots are identical.

To solve a quadratic equation by completing the square:

1. Rearrange the equation so that the terms with the unknown letter are in the left member and the constant term in the right member.

2. If the coefficient of x is not 1, divide all terms of the equation by its coefficient.

3. Find the number that makes the left member a PERFECT SQUARE trinomial by taking $\frac{1}{2}$ of the coefficient of the x term and squaring it. Add to both members of the equation.

4. Take the square root of both members.

5. Solve the resulting LINEAR EQUATIONS.

Ex. 5: Solve $x^2 + 2x - 8 = 0$.

Sol.:
$$x^2 + 2x = 8$$
$$x^2 + 2x + 1 = 1 + 8$$
$$(x + 1)^2 = 9$$
$$x + 1 = \pm 3$$
$$x = -1 \pm 3$$
$$x = -1 + 3 \text{ or } 2.$$
$$x = -1 - 3 \text{ or } -4.$$

Check: $\quad x^2 + 2x - 8 = 0 \qquad\qquad x^2 + 2x - 8 = 0$
$$\quad (2)^2 + 2(2) - 8 = 0 \qquad (-4)^2 + 2(-4) - 8 = 0$$
$$\quad 4 + 4 - 8 = 0 \qquad\qquad 16 - 8 - 8 = 0$$
$$\quad 0 = 0. \qquad\qquad\qquad 0 = 0.$$

Ex. 6: Solve $4x^2 + 12x + 3 = 0$.

Sol.:
$$x^2 + 3x = -\tfrac{3}{4}$$
$$x^2 + 3x + (\tfrac{3}{2})^2 = (\tfrac{3}{2})^2 - \tfrac{3}{4}$$
$$x^2 + 3x + \tfrac{9}{4} = \tfrac{9}{4} - \tfrac{3}{4}$$
$$(x + \tfrac{3}{2})^2 = \tfrac{6}{4}$$
$$x + \tfrac{3}{2} = \pm \frac{\sqrt{6}}{2}$$
$$x = \frac{-3}{2} \pm \frac{\sqrt{6}}{2} \text{ or } \frac{-3 \pm \sqrt{6}}{2}.$$

A quadratic equation may be solved by QUADRATIC FORMULA:

$$x = \frac{-b \pm \sqrt{b^2 - 4ac}}{2a}.$$

Ex. 7: Solve $3x^2 + 2x - 5 = 0$.

$$a = 3, \ b = 2, \ c = -5.$$
$$x = \frac{-2 \pm \sqrt{(2)^2 - 4(3)(-5)}}{2(3)}$$
$$x = \frac{-2 \pm \sqrt{4 + 60}}{6}$$
$$x = \frac{-2 \pm 8}{6}$$
$$x = \frac{-2 + 8}{6} = \frac{6}{6} \text{ or } 1.$$
$$x = \frac{-2 - 8}{6} = \frac{-10}{6} \text{ or } \frac{-5}{3}.$$

Check:

$$3x^2 + 2x - 5 = 0 \qquad\qquad 3x^2 + 2x - 5 = 0$$
$$3(1)^2 + 2(1) - 5 = 0 \qquad 3\left(\frac{-5}{3}\right)^2 + 2\left(\frac{-5}{3}\right) - 5 = 0$$
$$3 + 2 - 5 = 0 \qquad\qquad 3\left(\frac{25}{9}\right) + \left(\frac{-10}{3}\right) - 5 = 0$$
$$0 = 0. \qquad\qquad\qquad \tfrac{25}{3} - \tfrac{10}{3} - \tfrac{15}{3} = 0$$
$$0 = 0.$$

If the general quadratic equation $ax^2 + bx + c = 0$ is written in the form $x^2 + bx/a - c/a = 0$, then

1. The sum of the roots is the coefficient of x with the opposite sign; or the roots $r_1 + r_2 = -b/a$.

2. The product of the roots is the constant term; or $r_1 r_2 = c/a$.

In the equation $x^2 + 7x + 10 = 0$, the sum of the two roots is -7 and their product is 10. These formulas may be used for finding an equation when the roots are given or for checking the roots of an equation after solving.

Ex. 8: Find the sum and the product of the roots of the equation $2x^2 - 5x = 12$.

Sol.: Change the equation to an equivalent equation with the right member equal to ZERO.

$$2x^2 - 5x - 12 = 0$$
$$a = 2, \quad b = -5, \quad \text{and} \quad c = -12$$

$r_1 + r_2 = -\dfrac{b}{a} = -\dfrac{-5}{2} = \dfrac{5}{2}$, the sum of the roots. $r_1 r_2 = \dfrac{c}{a} = \dfrac{-12}{2} = -6$, the product of the roots.

Ex. 9: Write an equation in x, the roots of which are 2 and $\frac{3}{2}$.

$$r_1 + r_2 = 2 + \frac{3}{2} = \frac{7}{2} = -\frac{b}{a}$$

$$r_1 r_2 = 2 \times \frac{3}{2} = 3 = c.$$

Substitute values for $-b/a$ and c in equation,

$$x^2 + \frac{bx}{a} + c = 0.$$

$$x^2 - \frac{7x}{2} + 3 = 0.$$

Clear of fractions by multiplying by 2,

$$2x^2 - 7x + 6 = 0.$$

Ex. 10: Find k in the equation $3x^2 - 5x + k = 0$, if one of the roots is 3.

$$3x^2 - 5x + k = 0$$

$$x^2 - \frac{5x}{3} + \frac{k}{3} = 0$$

Sum of roots $= -b/a = \frac{5}{3}$; if one root is 3, the other root is $\frac{5}{3} - 3 = -\frac{4}{3}$. Product of roots $= -\frac{4}{3} \times 3 = -4$, then

$$\frac{c}{a} = \frac{k}{3} = -4$$

$$k = -12.$$

Some quadratic equations of the form $ax^2 + bx + c = 0$, may be solved by graphing $y = ax^2 + bx + c$ and obtaining the values of x when $y = 0$. If the equation has irrational roots, they may be approximated from the graph. If the graph does not cross the X-AXIS there are no real values for x.

Ex. 11: Solve $x^2 - x - 6 = 0$ by graphing. (See Fig. 1.)

Sol.:

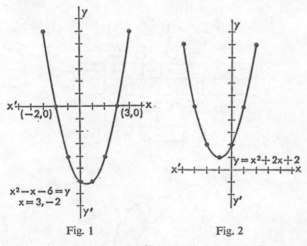

Fig. 1   Fig. 2

$$y = x^2 - x - 6$$

x	0	1	2	3	4	-1	-2	-3
y	-6	-6	-4	0	6	-4	0	6

$x = 3$ and -2, when $y = 0$.

Note the turning point of graph is between $(0, -6)$ and $(1, -6)$. If $x = \frac{1}{2}$, then $y = -6\frac{1}{4}$.

Ex. 12: Solve $x^2 + 2x + 2 = 0$. (See Fig. 2.)

$$y = x^2 + 2x + 2.$$

x	0	1	2	-1	-2	-3	-4
y	2	5	10	1	2	5	10

Roots are imaginary. Graph does not intersect the x-axis.

QUADRATIC EXPRESSION, in one VARIABLE, an expression of the form $ax^2 + bx + c$, in which a, b, and c are constants and $a \neq 0$.

QUADRATIC FORMULA, $x = \dfrac{-b \pm \sqrt{b^2 - 4ac}}{2a}$, derived from the QUADRATIC EQUATION $ax^2 + bx + c = 0$, by completing the SQUARE.

$$ax^2 + bx + c = 0$$
$$ax^2 + bx = -c.$$

Divide by coefficient of x^2

$$x^2 + \frac{bx}{a} = -\frac{c}{a}$$

Square $\frac{1}{2}$ of the COEFFICIENT of x and add to both members

$$x^2 + \frac{bx}{a} + \left(\frac{b}{2a}\right)^2 = \left(\frac{b}{2a}\right)^2 - \frac{c}{a}.$$

$$\left(x + \frac{b}{2a}\right)^2 = \frac{b^2 - 4ac}{4a^2}.$$

Take the square root of both members

$$x + \frac{b}{2a} = \frac{\pm\sqrt{b^2 - 4ac}}{2a}$$

$$x = -\frac{b}{2a} \pm \frac{\sqrt{b^2 - 4ac}}{2a}$$

$$x = \frac{-b \pm \sqrt{b^2 - 4ac}}{2a}.$$

See COMPLETING SQUARES.

QUADRATIC SYSTEMS, systems of two equations in two VARIABLES, at least one of which is a QUADRATIC EQUATION. Quadratic systems may be solved algebraically by substitution, by addition, by subtraction, or by graphing.

Ex. 1: Solve the quadratic system $x^2 - y^2 = 21$
$$x - 2y = 9.$$

Sol.: Solve the linear equation (*see* EQUATION, LINEAR) for one unknown in terms of the other, and substitute it in the quadratic equation. From the second equation, $x = 2y + 9$. Substitute the value of x in the first equation:

$$(2y + 9)^2 - y^2 = 21$$
$$4y^2 + 36y + 81 - y^2 = 21$$
$$3y^2 + 36y + 60 = 0$$
$$y^2 + 12y + 20 = 0$$
$$(y + 10)(y + 2) = 0$$
$$y + 10 = 0 \quad y + 2 = 0$$
$$y = -10 \qquad y = -2$$

Substitute both values of y in the second equation to find x:

$x = 2y + 9$	$x = 2y + 9$
$x = 2(-10) + 9$	$x = 2(-2) + 9$
$x = -20 + 9$	$x = -4 + 9$
$x = -11$ when $y = -10$.	$x = 5$ when $y = -2$.

The two sets of roots are: $x = -11, y = -10$; $x = 5, y = -2$. Check both sets of roots:

$x^2 - y^2 = 21$	$x^2 - y^2 = 21$
$(-11)^2 - (-10)^2 \overset{?}{=} 21$	$(5)^2 - (-2)^2 \overset{?}{=} 21$
$121 - 100 \overset{?}{=} 21$	$25 - 4 \overset{?}{=} 21$
$21 \overset{\surd}{=} 21.$	$21 \overset{\surd}{=} 21.$

Ex. 2: Solve the quadratic system $2x^2 + 3y^2 = 30$
$$4x^2 - 5y^2 = 16$$

Sol.: Multiply the first equation by 2 and subtract the two equations to eliminate the x^2 term. Solve for y.

Multiplying by 2: $4x^2 + 6y^2 = 60$
Subtracting $4x^2 - 5y^2 = 16$
$$11y^2 = 44$$
$$y^2 = 4$$
$$y = \pm 2.$$

Substitute the two values of y in the first equation:

when $y = +2$,   when $y = -2$,
$2x^2 + 3(2)^2 = 30;$ $2x^2 + 3(-2)^2 = 30.$
$2x^2 + 12 = 30$ $2x^2 + 12 = 30$
$2x^2 = 18$ $2x^2 = 18$
$x^2 = 9$ $x^2 = 9$
$x = \pm 3$ $x = \pm 3.$

The sets of roots are: $x = 3, y = 2;$ $x = -3, y = 2;$
$x = 3, y = -2; x = -3, y = -2.$

Ex. 3: Solve the quadratic system $3x^2 - 7xy + 2y^2 = 0$
$x^2 - 2xy + y^2 = 4$

Sol.: By FACTORING the first equation, find x in terms of y:

$$(3x - y)(x - 2y) = 0$$
$3x - y = 0 \quad x - 2y = 0$
$3x = y \quad\quad x = 2y.$
$x = y/3.$

Substitute the two sides of x in the second equation to find y:

$x = y/3, x^2 - 2xy + y^2 = 4.$ $x = 2y, x^2 - 2xy + y^2 = 4$
$(y/3)^2 - 2y(y/3) + y^2 = 4$ $(2y)^2 - 2y(2y) + y^2 = 4$
$y^2/9 - 2y^2/3 + y^2 = 4$ $4y^2 - 4y^2 + y^2 = 4$
$y^2 - 6y^2 + 9y^2 = 36$ $y^2 = 4$
$4y^2 = 36$ $y = \pm 2.$
$y^2 = 9$
$y = \pm 3.$

Substitute these values of y in the corresponding equation for x to find x:

$y = +3, x = y/3$ $y = -3, x = y/3$
$y = +2, x = 2y$ $y = -2, x = 2y$
$x = 3/3$ $x = -3/3$
$x = 1$ when $y = +3.$ $x = -1$ when $y = -3.$
$x = 4$ when $y = +2.$ $x = -4$ when $y = -2.$

The sets of roots are: $x = 1, y = 3; x = -1, y = 3;$
$x = 4, y = 2; x = -4, y = -2.$

Ex. 4: Solve the quadratic system $x^2 - xy + y^2 = 7$
$x^2 - y^2 = 8.$

Sol.: Change both equations to equivalent equations with the same constant term and subtract to form a quadratic equation equal to 0.

Multiply the first equation by 8: $8(x^2 - xy + y^2) = 8(7)$
Multiply the second equation by 7: $7(x^2 - y^2) = 7(8)$

Then $8x^2 - 8xy + 8y^2 = 56$
and $7x^2 \quad\quad - 7y^2 = 56.$
Subtracting $x^2 - 8xy + 15y^2 = 0.$
Factor: $(x - 3y)(x - 5y) = 0.$
Solve for x in terms of y:
$x - 3y = 0$ $x - 5y = 0$
$x = 3y$ $x = 5y$

Substitute both values of x in the second equation:

$x = 3y, x^2 - y^2 = 8$ $x = 5y, x^2 - y^2 = 8$
$(3y)^2 - y^2 = 8$ $(5y)^2 - y^2 = 8$
$9y^2 - y^2 = 8$ $25y^2 - y^2 = 8$
$8y^2 = 8$ $24y^2 = 8$
$y^2 = 1$ $y^2 = 8/24$
$y = \pm\sqrt{1}$ $y = \pm\sqrt{8/24}$
$y = \pm 1$ $y = \pm\sqrt{1/3}.$ By using the RATIONALIZING FACTOR, $\sqrt{3}$, $y = \pm\sqrt{3}/3.$

Substituting in the corresponding equation for x:

$x = 3y, y = +1$
$x = 3(1)$
$x = 3$ when $y = +1$
$x = 5y, y = +\sqrt{3}/3$
$x = 5(\sqrt{3}/3)$
$x = 5\sqrt{3}/3$ when $y = +\sqrt{3}/3$
$x = 3y, y = -1$
$x = 3(-1)$
$x = -3$ when $y = -1$
$x = 5y, y = -\sqrt{3}/3$
$x = 5(-\sqrt{3}/3)$
$x = -5\sqrt{3}/3$ when $y = -\sqrt{3}/3.$

The sets of roots are: $x = 3, y = 1; x = -3, y = -1;$

$x = 5\sqrt{3}/3, y = \sqrt{3}/3; x = -5\sqrt{3}/3, y = -\sqrt{3}/3.$

Ex. 5: Solve, by graphing, the quadratic system:
$$x^2 + y^2 = 17$$
$$x + y = 3.$$

(See Fig. 1.)

$x^2 + y^2 = 17$
$y^2 = 17 - x^2.$
$y = \pm\sqrt{17 - x^2}.$

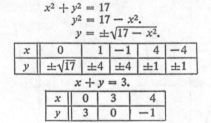

x	0	1	−1	4	−4
y	$\pm\sqrt{17}$	± 4	± 4	± 1	± 1

$x + y = 3.$

x	0	3	4
y	3	0	−1

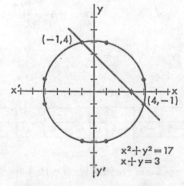

Fig. 1

The graph of $x^2 + y^2 = 17$ is a CIRCLE with the ORIGIN for its center and a RADIUS $= \sqrt{17}$ or 4.123. The GRAPH of $x + y = 3$ is a straight line. The two graphs intersect at points $(-1,4)$ and $(4,-1)$. Therefore, the solutions in common are $x = -1, y = 4$, and $x = 4, y = -1$

Ex. 6: Solve graphically

$$(x - 3)^2 + y^2 = 25$$
$$y = x^2 - 6x + 4.$$

(See Fig. 2.)

$$(x - 3)^2 + y^2 = 25$$

x	0	3	6	8	-2
y	±4	±5	±4	0	0

$$y = x^2 - 6x + 4$$

x	0	1	2	3	4	5	6
y	4	-1	-4	-5	-4	-1	4

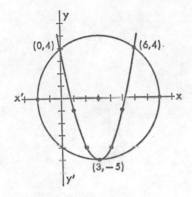

Fig. 2

The points of intersection that the circle and the PARABOLA have in common are (0,4), (6,4) and (3,−5). (3,−5) is a double root. The parabola is tangent to the circle.

The sets of roots are:

$$x = 0, y = 4; x = 6, y = 4; x = 3, y = -5.$$

(Note: Any equation of the form $x^2 + y^2 = r^2$ is a circle with radius r and its center at the origin. Any equation of the form $(x - a)^2 + (x - b)^2 = r^2$ is a circle with radius r and a center, with coordinates (a,b).)

Ex. 7: Solve graphically the system

$$x^2 + 4y^2 = 36$$
$$x^2 - y^2 = 16.$$

(See Fig. 3.)

$$x^2 + 4y^2 = 36$$

x	0	±6	±4	±4.5	±3	±5
y	±3	0	±2.2	±2	±2.6	±1.50

$$x^2 - y^2 = 16$$

x	4	-4	5	-5
y	0	0	±3	±3

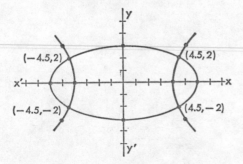

Fig. 3

The graph of $x^2 + 4y^2 = 36$ is an ELLIPSE whose major axis (*see* MAJOR AXIS OF AN ELLIPSE) is 12 units and minor axis (*see* MINOR AXIS OF AN ELLIPSE) is 6 units. The graph of $x^2 - y^2 = 16$ is a HYPERBOLA. The two graphs intersect in four points. The sets of roots are:

$$x = 4.5, \quad y = 2; x = 4.5, \quad y = -2;$$
$$x = -4.5, y = 2; x = -4.5, y = -2.$$

QUADRIC SURFACE, the graph of a SECOND DEGREE EQUATION in three variables. The intersection of a plane and any quadric section is always a CONIC SECTION. To explore the graph of a given second degree equation in three variables, set one VARIABLE equal to zero to find the conic section in which the graph intersects the plane of that coordinate.

The following second degree equation should have a quadric surface as its graph:

$$\frac{x^2}{a^2} + \frac{y^2}{b^2} + \frac{z^2}{c^2} = 1.$$

If either x, y, or z is set equal to zero, the result is an ELLIPSE. Therefore, the graph may be sketched as shown in the figure.

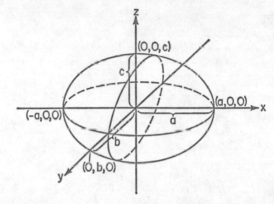

QUADRILATERAL (kwawd-ri-lat'-ur-al), a POLYGON having four sides. (See Fig. 1.) Special quadrilaterals and FORMULAS are illustrated in Fig. 2.

QUADRILATERALS

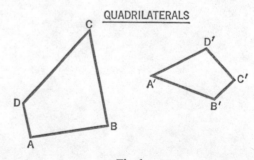

Fig. 1

SQUARE	RECTANGLE	PARALLELOGRAM	TRAPEZOID
$p = 4s$	$p = 2b + 2h$	$A = bh$	$A = \frac{1}{2}h(b + b')$
$A = s^2$	$A = bh$		
$d = s\sqrt{2}$			

Fig. 2

QUANTIFIER, in SYMBOLIC LOGIC, one of the two notational prefixes: (x) (the universal quantifier) which is read as "for all x . . . ;" and (∃x) (the existential quantifier) which is read as "there exists at least one x such that . . ." These two symbols are used to symbolize various propositions involving such terms as "some," "all," "none," "every," and so on. Either one may be defined in terms of the other; e.g. "all" (the universal quantifier) may be defined as "it is not the case that some (existential quantifier) are not."

QUARTIC, of degree four, or of order four. Thus, a quartic equation is a POLYNOMIAL equation of the fourth degree.

QUARTILE, in statistics, each of the three numbers that separate a frequency distribution (*see* CLASSIFIED DATA) into four equal parts. These quartiles are equal to the 25th, 50th, and 75th PERCENTILES, respectively.

QUOTIENT (kwoh′-shunt), the result when one number is divided by another. If 27 is divided by 3 the quotient is 9. In algebra the quotient of two algebraic terms (*see* ALGEBRAIC SYMBOLS) is written as a FRACTION or with the division symbol, as a/b or $a \div b$. The fraction is generally used.

R

RADIAN, a unit of measure of ANGLE and of ARC. A central angle of one radian intercepts an arc equal in length to the RADIUS of the circle. An arc of one radian is one intercepted by a central angle of one radian. (See Fig. 1.) Since the circumference of a circle equals $2\pi r$ and the central angle of the circumference equals 360°,

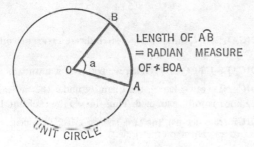

LENGTH OF $\widehat{AB}$
= RADIAN MEASURE
OF $\measuredangle$ BOA

Fig. 1

2π radians $= 360°$, or π radians $= 180°$.

1 radian $= \dfrac{180°}{\pi} = 57°17'45''$.

$1° = \dfrac{\pi}{180}$ radians or .01745 radians.

E.g.,

$90° = 90 \times \dfrac{\pi}{180}$ or $\dfrac{\pi}{2}$ radians.

$120° = 120 \times \dfrac{\pi}{180}$ or $\dfrac{2\pi}{3}$ radians.

$45° = 45 \times \dfrac{\pi}{180}$ or $\dfrac{\pi}{4}$ radians.

$\dfrac{3\pi}{2}$ radians $= \dfrac{3\pi}{2} \times \dfrac{180°}{\pi} = 270°$.

$\dfrac{4\pi}{3}$ radians $= \dfrac{4\pi}{3} \times \dfrac{180°}{\pi} = 240°$.

$\dfrac{\pi}{6}$ radians $= \dfrac{\pi}{6} \times \dfrac{180°}{\pi} = 30°$.

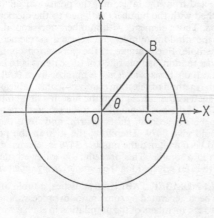

Fig. 2

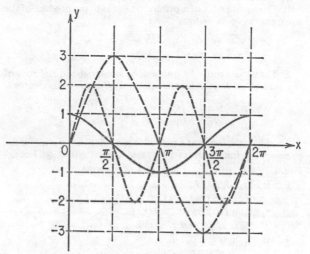

$y = \cos x$, amplitude = 1, period = 2π radians
$y = 3 \sin x$, amplitude = 3, period = 2π radians
$y = 2 \sin 2x$, amplitude = 2, period = π radians

Fig. 3

In graphing TRIGONOMETRIC FUNCTIONS, if the radius of the unit circle is used as the unit of length on the y-axis, then that same unit also represents a radian on the x-axis. This gives a truer relation between the angle and any of its functions. The unit circle in Fig. 2 may be used in graphing $y = \sin x$. Line BC represents $\sin \theta$, since $OB = OA = 1$, and θ is expressed in radians.

Ex.: On the same axes graph $y = \cos x$, $y = 3 \sin x$, and $y = 2 \sin 2x$.

Sol.: See Fig. 3.

RADICAL, an expression used to indicate the ROOT of a number. It consists of the number of which the root is to be taken, called the *radicand*, the symbol $\sqrt{}$ called the *radical sign*, and the indicated root called the *index*. The index is omitted in the square root. In the radical $\sqrt{3}$, 3 is the radicand, 2 is the omitted index. $\sqrt[3]{8}$ means the cube root of 8; $\sqrt[5]{32}$ means the fifth root of 32.

Powers and roots of radicals may be found according to the following laws:

1. The nth root of any number is equal to that number raised to the $1/n$ power, or $\sqrt[n]{a} = a^{1/n}$. This can be proved by showing that $\sqrt[3]{8} = 8^{1/3}$.

$$8^{1/3} = (2^3)^{1/3} = 2^{3/3} = 2,$$

which is the cube root of 8. And also

$$\sqrt{4} = 4^{1/2} = (2^2)^{1/2} = 2^{2/2} = 2.$$

The radical and the fractional EXPONENT may be used interchangeably.

2. The first law leads to the second, $(\sqrt[n]{a})^m = a^{m/n}$.

$$(\sqrt[3]{2})^2 \doteq 2^{2/3}.$$

3. If the index equals the exponent, $(\sqrt[n]{a})^n = (a^{1/n})^n = a$.
$$(\sqrt{7})^2 = 7 \text{ and } (\sqrt{39x^5y^9})^2 = 39x^5y^9.$$

4. A radical within a radical, $\sqrt[m]{\sqrt[n]{a}} = \sqrt[m]{a^{1/n}} = (a^{1/n})^{1/m} = a^{1/mn}$ or $\sqrt[m \cdot n]{a}$.
$$\sqrt[3]{\sqrt{64}} = \sqrt[3]{8} = 2 = \sqrt[6]{64} \text{ and}$$
$$\sqrt[5]{\sqrt[3]{a^{15}b^{30}}} = (a^{15}b^{30})^{1/15} = a^{15/15}b^{30/15} = ab^2.$$

The following are laws of square roots of radicals:

1. The square root of a product is equal to the product of the square roots of its factors.
$$\sqrt{ab} = \sqrt{a}\sqrt{b}; \quad \sqrt{36} = \sqrt{4}\sqrt{9} = 2 \cdot 3;$$
$$\sqrt{8} = \sqrt{4}\sqrt{2} = 2\sqrt{2}.$$

2. The square root of a quotient is equal to the square root of the numerator divided by the square root of the denominator.
$$\sqrt{\frac{a}{b}} = \frac{\sqrt{a}}{\sqrt{b}}; \quad \sqrt{\frac{4}{9}} = \frac{\sqrt{4}}{\sqrt{9}} = \frac{2}{3}; \quad \sqrt{\frac{5}{6}} = \frac{\sqrt{5}}{\sqrt{6}}.$$

To reduce the index of a radical, change it to an equivalent expression with fractional EXPONENT and reduce the fraction. For example, $\sqrt{x} = x^{1/2}$; $\sqrt[3]{x} = x^{1/3}$; and $\sqrt[3]{x^2} = x^{2/3}$.

Ex. 1: Simplify $\sqrt[6]{27}$.
$$\sqrt[6]{27} = (27)^{1/6} = (3^3)^{1/6} = 3^{3/6} = 3^{1/2} = \sqrt{3}.$$

Ex. 2: Simplify $\sqrt[8]{a^6b^2}$.
$$\sqrt[8]{a^6b^2} = (a^6b^2)^{1/8} = a^{6/8}b^{2/8} = a^{3/4}b^{1/4} = \sqrt[4]{a^3b}.$$

Ex. 3: Simplify $\sqrt[6]{a^2b^4c^2}$.
$$\sqrt[6]{a^2b^4c^2} = (a^2b^4c^2)^{1/6} = a^{2/6}b^{4/6}c^{2/6}$$
$$= a^{1/3}b^{2/3}c^{1/3} = \sqrt[3]{ab^2c}.$$

See also POWER OF A POWER.

Radicals having the same radicand and the same index are called similar radicals. In the expression $5\sqrt[3]{5} + 3\sqrt{2} + 4\sqrt{2}$, $3\sqrt{2}$ and $4\sqrt{2}$ are the similar radicals. Similar radicals may be added or subtracted in the same manner in which similar expressions are combined, as $3a + 4a = 7a$. Then, $3\sqrt{3} - 2\sqrt{3} + 4\sqrt{3} = 5\sqrt{3}$.

If the radicals are not similar, it is necessary to simplify them before combining. Radicals are simplified by separating the radicand into factors, one of which has an exact root. For example, $\sqrt{12} = \sqrt{4 \cdot 3}$ or $\sqrt{4}\sqrt{3} = 2\sqrt{3}$.

Exs.: Simplify and combine the following radicals:

1. $\sqrt{32} + \sqrt{2} - 2\sqrt{2} + \sqrt{18}$
$\sqrt{16 \cdot 2} + \sqrt{2} - 2\sqrt{2} + \sqrt{9 \cdot 2}$
$4\sqrt{2} + \sqrt{2} - 2\sqrt{2} + 3\sqrt{2} = 6\sqrt{2}$.

2. $\sqrt{3} - 2\sqrt{75} + 3\sqrt{48}$
$\sqrt{3} - 2\sqrt{25 \cdot 3} + 3\sqrt{16 \cdot 3}$
$\sqrt{3} - 10\sqrt{3} + 12\sqrt{3} = 3\sqrt{3}$.

3. $\sqrt{10} - \sqrt{50} + \sqrt{8} - 3\sqrt{2}$
$\sqrt{10} - \sqrt{25 \cdot 2} + \sqrt{4 \cdot 2} - 3\sqrt{2}$
$\sqrt{10} - 5\sqrt{2} + 2\sqrt{2} - 3\sqrt{2} = \sqrt{10} - 6\sqrt{2}$

4. $\sqrt{a^3b^3} + ab\sqrt{ab}$
$\sqrt{a^2 \cdot a \cdot b^2 \cdot b} + ab\sqrt{ab}$
$ab\sqrt{ab} + ab\sqrt{ab} = 2ab\sqrt{ab}$.

Reducing the index of a radical is also a process by which radicals are simplified.

The product of two radicals having the same index is a radical with that index and a radicand that is the product of the two radicands. For example, $\sqrt[3]{a} \cdot \sqrt[3]{b} = \sqrt[3]{ab}$ and $\sqrt{3} \cdot \sqrt{2} = \sqrt{6}$.

Exs.: Find the following products and simplify:

1. $\sqrt{12} \times \sqrt{3} = \sqrt{36} = 6$.
2. $2\sqrt{3} \times 3\sqrt{5} = 6\sqrt{15}$.
3. $\sqrt[3]{2} \times \sqrt[3]{4} = \sqrt[3]{8} = 2$.
4. $\sqrt{5x} \cdot \sqrt{10x^3} = \sqrt{50x^4} = \sqrt{25 \cdot 2x^4} = 5x^2\sqrt{2}$.

The quotient of two radicals, having the same index is a radical with that index and a radicand that is the quotient of the two radicands. Thus, $\frac{\sqrt{12}}{\sqrt{2}} = \sqrt{\frac{12}{2}} = \sqrt{6}$ and $\frac{\sqrt[3]{24}}{\sqrt[3]{3}} = \sqrt[3]{8} = 2$. If the DENOMINATOR will not divide the numerator exactly, both the numerator and the denominator are multiplied by a RATIONALIZING FACTOR to make the denominator rational. Thus,

$$\frac{\sqrt{10}}{\sqrt{3}} = \frac{\sqrt{3} \cdot \sqrt{10}}{\sqrt{3} \cdot \sqrt{3}} = \frac{\sqrt{30}}{3}$$

and
$$\frac{1}{\sqrt{5}} = \frac{\sqrt{5} \cdot 1}{\sqrt{5} \cdot \sqrt{5}} = \frac{\sqrt{5}}{5}.$$

RADICAL SIGN, the symbol $\sqrt{\ }$, to indicate a ROOT of a number is to be taken.

RADICALS IN EQUATIONS, *see* EQUATIONS, RADICAL.

RADICAND (rad'-i-kand), the quantity under the radical sign whose ROOT is to be extracted. Thus, in $\sqrt{5}$ the radicand is 5.

RADIUS (ray'-dee-us), the LINE SEGMENT from the center of a CIRCLE to any POINT on the circle.

RADIUS OF CURVATURE, at point P on the curve $y = f(x)$, the quantity $|1/k|$, where k is the curvature at P. *See also* CIRCLE OF CURVATURE.

RADIUS VECTOR, the rotating RAY that forms a positive or NEGATIVE ANGLE. The endpoint of the ray is the ORIGIN, and the final position of the radius vector is the terminal side of the angle (*see* SIDE OF AN ANGLE).

RADIX, the base number of a system of numeration. 10 is the radix in the DECIMAL NUMBER SYSTEM, 2 is the radix in the BINARY NUMBER SYSTEM. The base of a system of logarithms is also called the radix. Thus, 10 is the radix of the system of common logarithms (*see* TABLE NO. 19) and e is the radix of the system of natural logarithms (*see* TABLE NO. 20). The plural of radix is *radices* or *radixes*.

RANDOM NUMBERS, a set of numbers, arranged in tabular form, that are used to select a RANDOM SAMPLE of elements from a given population. Numbers are selected from the table according to some arbitrary procedure: E.g., choose the number from the first line first column, second line second column, etc. Each element in the population is numbered, and as a random number is selected from the table, and the positional digits chosen, it is matched with the numbers assigned to the elements of the population. Those elements with numbers corresponding to the digits in the random number are selected as elements of the random sample. For example, if the population contains 1000 items, and a random sample of 30 of these items is to be chosen, each of the 1000 items is assigned a number from 0001 to 1000. Using some method of selecting numbers from a table of random numbers such as the entries from the first line first column, etc., gives 53479. If the positional digits to be selected are arbitrarily chosen to be the second, third, fourth, and fifth, the number 53479 would give 3479. Therefore, the item in the population which had been assigned the number 3479 is selected as an item in the random sample. This procedure is followed until 30 elements have been selected for the sample. *See* TABLE NO. 17.

RANDOM NUMBER TABLE, in statistics, a table of numbers that have been generated by some random process. Numbers are assigned to the members of the population in such a way that the table of random numbers can be conveniently used. The sample will consist of the members of the population that correspond to the random numbers read from the table, and a RANDOM SAMPLE is assured. *See* TABLE NO. 17.

RANDOM SAMPLE, in statistics, a probability sample or simple random sample. For infinite populations, or for sampling with replacement from finite populations, a random sample is one for which every member of the population has an equal and independent probability (*see* PROBABILITY OF AN EVENT) of being in the sample.

When sampling without replacement from a finite population, a sample is random if the probability of obtaining it is the same as the probability of obtaining any other sample of the same size.

For statistical techniques to be correctly applied, and to make inferences about populations or their PARAMETERS, the sample must be random at some stage. A RANDOM NUMBER TABLE is usually used in selecting a random sample.

RANDOM VARIABLE, in statistics, for a SAMPLE SPACE with a probability measure, the real-valued function X, defined over the points of the sample space. X is also called the *chance variable*, and the *stochastic variable*.

RANDOM VARIABLE, DISCRETE, a RANDOM VARIABLE that can take on only isolated values. Any random variable that represents a CARDINAL NUMBER, e.g., accidents per month, children per family, etc., is a discrete random variable.

Some important PROBABILITY FUNCTIONS for discrete random variables are the BINOMIAL DISTRIBUTION, GEOMETRIC DISTRIBUTION, HYPERGEOMETRIC DISTRIBUTION, MULTINOMIAL DISTRIBUTION, and POISSON DISTRIBUTION.

RANGE, in statistics, a very simple measure of dispersion (*see* DISPERSION, MEASURES OF), the difference between the largest and the smallest observations in a sample. E.g., if scores on a test are 75, 85, 53, 92, and 98, the range is $98 - 53$ or 45.

RANGE, of a function, *see* DOMAIN.

RANK, of an observation, in statistics, the number of the position that it occupies in the sequence of ordered observations. The smallest is rank 1; the next smallest is rank 2; etc. The observations need not be numerical in order to assign ranks to them; ranks can be assigned on the basis of qualitative characteristics, such as "reliability" or "attractiveness" or "texture."

RANK CORRELATION COEFFICIENT, in statistics, a correlation coefficient that is calculated by using the ranks of the observations rather than the numerical observations themselves. If a random sample consists of n ordered pairs of observations, $(x_1,y_1), (x_2,y_2), \cdots , (x_n,y_n)$, the x-values may be ranked in order and the y-values ranked in order. If X_i denotes the rank occupied by x_i, and Y_i denotes the rank occupied by y_i, replacing the original observations by their ranks gives $(X_1,Y_1), (X_2,Y_2), \cdots , (X_n,Y_n)$. The rank correlation coefficient equals

$$\frac{\sum_{i=1}^{n} (x_i - \bar{x})(y_i - \bar{y})}{\sqrt{\sum_{i=1}^{n} (x_i - \bar{x})^2} \sqrt{\sum_{i=1}^{n} (y_i - \bar{y})^2}} .$$

This quantity can be shown to equal

$$1 - \frac{6 \cdot \sum_{i=1}^{n} (X_i - Y_i)^2}{n(n^2 - 1)} ,$$

which simplifies the computations. To use the rank correlation coefficient, no assumption of normality must be made.

RANK-SUM TEST, in statistics, to test the NULL HYPOTHESIS that two populations have equal medians against a specified ALTERNATIVE HYPOTHESIS. The necessary assumptions are that there are independent random samples from continuous populations that have identical form.

The observations from the two samples are combined and ranked in order, with the observations from the smaller sample distinguished in some way (by underlining them, say). The smaller sample is called Sample 1 and contains n_1 observations; the larger sample is called Sample 2 and contains n_2 observations. The observations are replaced by their ranks, with equal observations being replaced by the average of the ranks that they occupy. The ranks of the observations from Sample 1 are added and the sum denoted by R. Tables of CRITICAL VALUES for R are available. If tables are inadequate, use the fact that R is a particular value of a random variable that is approximately normal with mean

$$\mu_R = \frac{n_1(n_1 + n_2 + 1)}{2}$$

and variance $\qquad \sigma_R{}^2 = \frac{n_1 n_2(n_1 + n_2 + 1)}{12} .$

See also MANN-WHITNEY U-TEST.

RATE OF INTEREST, the PERCENT that is taken on a loan to pay for the use of the money. Rate is usually expressed in percent per year.

Rate(in hundredths) $\times$ Principal = Interest (for one year).

E.g., if \$200 is invested for one year at 4%, interest, the rate of interest is 4 percent. To find the amount of interest, multiply $.04 \times 200.00$. Thus, the amount of interest is \$8.00.

RATIO (ray'-shee-oh), the relationship between two quantities of the same kind, expressed as a FRACTION, or the *quotient* of one number divided by another number. The ratio of 5 to 8 may be written $5 : 8$ or $\frac{5}{8}$. Ratios should always be reduced to the lowest terms. The ratio of 6 inches to 18 inches $= \frac{6}{18}$ or $\frac{1}{3}$. Also, 4 ounces to 1 pound $= \frac{4}{16}$ or $\frac{1}{4}$ and 15 to 5 $= \frac{15}{5}$ or $\frac{3}{1}$.

A statement of equality between two ratios is a PROPORTION. E.g., $\frac{2}{4} = \frac{1}{2}$ is a proportion.

If either term of a ratio is a fraction, divide the numerator by the denominator to simplify the ratio.

$$\frac{4}{10\frac{2}{3}} = 4 \div 10\frac{2}{3} = 4 \div \frac{32}{3} = 4 \times \frac{3}{32} = \frac{3}{8} .$$

RATIO, EXTREME AND MEAN, *see* EXTREME AND MEAN RATIO.

RATIONAL CURVE, the graph of an equation of the form

$$y = \frac{N(x)}{D(x)} = \frac{a_0 + ax + a_2x^2 + \cdots + a_nx^n}{b_0 + bx + b_2x^2 + \cdots + b_mx^m} ,$$

in which both $N(x)$ and $D(x)$ are polynomials in x. Examples of rational curves are

$$y = \frac{1}{x} \text{ and } y = \frac{x + 5x + x^2}{x - x^3} .$$

When the denominator $D(x)$ of the fraction $N(x)/D(x)$ is small, the value of y is large; i.e., near the roots of $D(x)$ the value of y is large, though it may be either positive or negative. The fraction is not defined when $D(x) = 0$. These facts may be summarized by saying that the graph of a rational curve has a vertical ASYMPTOTE where the denominator $D(x)$ has a root (see figure).

Ex.: Find the asymptotes of the rational curve $y = \dfrac{x^2 + 1}{x^2 - 1}$.

Sol.: Vertical asymptotes occur at the roots of $D(x)$. In this case, $D(x) = x^2 - 1$. Therefore $D(x)$ has roots at $x = 1$ and $x = -1$. The lines $x = 1$ and $x = -1$ are the vertical asymp-

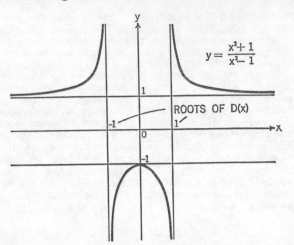

$$y = \frac{x^2 + 1}{x^2 - 1}$$

ROOTS OF D(x)

totes. As x becomes large, y approaches 1; the line $y = 1$ is the horizontal asymptote.

RATIONALIZING FACTOR (rash'-un-al-ahy-zing), the FACTOR by which the NUMERATOR and the DENOMINATOR of a radical fraction are multiplied to make the denominator rational. The PRODUCT of any number multiplied by itself will be a PERFECT SQUARE. If both the numerator and the denominator of the radical $\sqrt{\frac{3}{7}}$ are multiplied by $\sqrt{7}$, the denominator will be $\sqrt{49}$ which is rational.

$$\sqrt{\frac{3}{7}} = \sqrt{\frac{3 \times 7}{7 \times 7}} = \frac{\sqrt{21}}{\sqrt{49}} = \frac{\sqrt{21}}{7}.$$

If the fraction is $\frac{5}{8}$, it is simpler to multiply both terms by 2, as

$$\sqrt{\frac{5}{8}} = \sqrt{\frac{5}{8} \cdot \frac{2}{2}} = \frac{\sqrt{10}}{\sqrt{16}} = \frac{\sqrt{10}}{4}.$$

Exs.: Rationalize the following radicals and leave in the simplest radical form.

1. $\dfrac{\sqrt{8}}{\sqrt{3}} = \dfrac{\sqrt{8 \times 3}}{\sqrt{3 \times 3}} = \dfrac{\sqrt{24}}{3}.$ Simplify the numerator. $\dfrac{\sqrt{24}}{3} = \dfrac{\sqrt{4 \cdot 6}}{3} = \dfrac{2\sqrt{3}}{3}$ or $\dfrac{2}{3}\sqrt{3}.$

2. $\sqrt{\dfrac{9}{7}} = \dfrac{\sqrt{9 \cdot 7}}{\sqrt{7 \cdot 7}} = \dfrac{3}{\sqrt{7}} \times \dfrac{\sqrt{7}}{\sqrt{7}} = \dfrac{3\sqrt{7}}{7}.$

See also CONJUGATE ALGEBRAIC NUMBERS; RADICAL.

RATIONAL NUMBER, a NUMBER that can be expressed as the RATIO of two INTEGERS. E.g., 1 (1/1), 2 (2/1), 1/2, 1/4, 2/3, −1/4, etc.

If all the integers are marked off on a NUMBER LINE, each point that is midway between successive integers is also a rational number. (In fact, the MIDPOINT of the LINE SEGMENT between n and $(n + 1)$ is the number $\dfrac{2n + 1}{2}$.) The midpoint of every segment of length 1/2 is also a rational number, as is the midpoint of every segment of length 1/4, 1/8, etc. It follows that between any two points that represent a rational number there is *another* point that represents a rational number. This property of the rational numbers is known as DENSITY. Even though the rational numbers are dense, there *are* numbers on the number line that are *not* rational. E.g., $pi(\pi)$ and $\sqrt{2}$. In fact, between any two rational numbers there are infinitely many IRRATIONAL NUMBERS, and vice versa.

Since two or more numbers may be expressed as EQUIVALENT FRACTIONS, e.g., 1/2 and 2/4, equivalent fractions are considered as one rational number. Thus, each rational number corresponds to an infinite SET of fractions.

RATIONAL ROOT THEOREM, theorem stating that if a RATIONAL NUMBER p/q, is a root of a polynomial equation with integral coefficients,

$$a_0 x^n + a_1 x^{n-1} + \cdots + a_{n-1} x + a_n = 0,$$

then q is a FACTOR of a_n and p is a factor of a_n. Thus, for the equation $x^4 - 3x^3 - x^2 - 11x - 4 = 0$, a root, p/q, must have as its numerator some factor of 4, and as its denominator, some factor of 1. This indicates that a real root of this equation is an integer, since factors of 1 are 1. The factors of 4 are 1, 2, and 4, and by synthetic division (*see* DIVISION, SYNTHETIC), 4 is found to be a root.

RATIO OF SIMILITUDE (si-mil'-i-tood), the RATIO of any two corresponding sides of SIMILAR POLYGONS. In similar triangles, corresponding altitudes and perimeters have the same ratio of similitude as the corresponding sides.

RATIOS, TRIGONOMETRIC, *see* TRIGONOMETRIC FUNCTIONS.

RATIO TEST, for an infinite series, $u_1 + u_2 + u_3 + \cdots + u_n + u_{n+1} + \cdots$, the test for convergence or divergence. If $p = \lim\limits_{n \to \infty} \dfrac{u_{n+1}}{u_n}$, (1) the series converges if $p < 1$; (2) the series diverges if $p > 1$; (3) the series may converge or diverge if $p = 1$. Thus, the test fails if $p = 1$.

Ex.: Test for convergence or divergence:

$$1 + \frac{1}{2!} + \frac{1}{3!} + \cdots + \frac{1}{n!} + \cdots.$$

Sol.: $p = \lim\limits_{n \to \infty} \dfrac{\dfrac{1}{(n+1)!}}{\dfrac{1}{n!}} = \lim\limits_{n \to \infty} \dfrac{1}{n+1} = 0.$ Thus, the series converges. Its sum is e, the base of the system of natural logarithms (*see* LOGARITHMS, NATURAL).

RAY, a SET containing a point on a line and all points on one side of the given point. In the figure, the ray is called ray PA or $\overrightarrow{PA}$. (Note: The first point named is the endpoint of the ray.)

REAL NUMBER, a NUMBER that is the COORDINATE of a point on a NUMBER LINE. The SET of real numbers includes ZERO, the positive and negative RATIONAL NUMBERS, and the positive and negative IRRATIONAL NUMBERS. They are called *real numbers* to distinguish them from the IMAGINARY NUMBERS. The set of real numbers in UNION with the set of imaginary numbers constitutes the set of COMPLEX NUMBERS.

RECIPROCAL (ree-sip'-ruh-kal), of any number a, is $1/a$. The PRODUCT of any number and its reciprocal is 1. The reciprocal of 6 is $\frac{1}{6}$; of a/b is b/a; of $-\frac{2}{3}$ is $-\frac{3}{2}$. *See also* MULTIPLICATIVE INVERSE; TABLE NO. 18.

RECIPROCAL TRIGONOMETRIC FUNCTIONS,

$$\sin \theta = \frac{1}{\csc \theta}; \qquad \csc \theta = \frac{1}{\sin \theta};$$

$$\cos \theta = \frac{1}{\sec \theta}; \qquad \sec \theta = \frac{1}{\cos \theta};$$

$$\tan \theta = \frac{1}{\cot \theta}; \qquad \cot \theta = \frac{1}{\tan \theta}.$$

RECORDE, ROBERT (rek'-ahrd), 1510–1558, British mathematician, wrote *Whetstone of Witte* in 1557, the first English treatise on ALGEBRA.

RECTANGLE, a PARALLELOGRAM with one RIGHT ANGLE. (See figure.) Since a rectangle is a parallelogram it has all of the properties of a parallelogram. In addition, (1) all the angles of a rectangle are right angles and (2) the diagonals of a rectangle are equal.

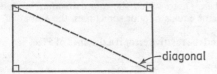

RECTANGULAR COORDINATE SYSTEM, *see* COORDINATE SYSTEM; COORDINATES, RECTANGULAR.

RECTANGULAR HYPERBOLA (hahy-pur'-buh-luh), a HYPERBOLA with perpendicular ASYMPTOTES. A standard form of the equation of the hyperbola is $\frac{x}{a^2} - \frac{y}{b^2} = 1$. A hyperbola written in this form is a rectangular hyperbola when $(b/a)(-b/a) = -1$.

Ex.: The hyperbola $x^2 - y^2 = 1$ is rectangular since $a - 1$, $b = 1$, and therefore $(a/b)(-a/b) = (1)(-1) = -1$.

RECTANGULAR SOLID, a PARALLELEPIPED having RECTANGLES for bases. Its volume, $V = lwh$, is the product of the altitude h and the width w and length l of the base.

REDUCED CUBIC EQUATION, the equation resulting when the second-degree term is removed from a CUBIC EQUATION in the form $ax^3 + bx^2 + cx + d = 0$. This transformation is accomplished by the substitution $x = z - \frac{b}{3a}$, which yields the reduced cubic

$$z^3 + 3Hz + G = 0,$$

where $H = \frac{3ac - b^2}{9a^2}$ and $G = \frac{2b^3 - 9abc + 27a^2d}{27a^3}$.

See also CARDAN'S FORMULAS.

REFERENCE ANGLE, for any given angle in standard position, the acute angle between the terminal side of the given angle and the horizontal axis.

In Fig. 1, α is the reference angle for angle θ in quadrant II. The functions of θ have the same ABSOLUTE VALUE as the functions of α. Thus, in Fig. 2, θ in quadrant III is 210°. $\angle AOB$, α, is 210° − 180° or 30°.

Sin 30° = $\frac{1}{2}$, cos 30° = $\sqrt{3}/2$, and tan 30° = $1/\sqrt{3}$ = $\sqrt{3}/3$.

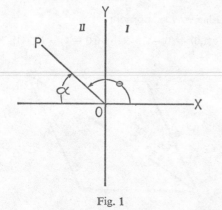

Fig. 1

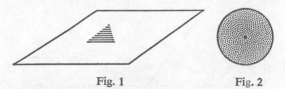

Fig. 2

In the third quadrant, AB is negative, and AO is negative. OB (the radius vector) is always considered positive. Thus,

sin 210° = $-\frac{1}{2}$, cos 210° = $-\sqrt{3}/2$, and tan 210° = $\sqrt{3}/3$.

See also TRIGONOMETRIC FUNCTIONS; RADICAL.

REFLEXIVE PROPERTY, *see* AXIOM; EQUALITY; EQUIVALENCE RELATION.

REGIOMONTANUS (reg'-ee-oh-mahn-tay'-nus), originally Johann Müller, 1436–1476, German mathematician and astronomer; b. in Königsberg (now Kaliningrad). The name "Regiomontanus" is the Latin rendition of the name Königsberg, meaning "King's mountain." Regiomontanus established an observatory and a printing press at Regensburg (Ratisbon) with the aid of friend and patron Bernhard Walther. In collaboration with Walther, he issued the *Ephemerides* (1475–1506), a large astronomical work used later by Columbus and other navigators. His *De Triangulis* (1464) is one of the first expositions of TRIGONOMETRY. He assisted in calendar reform under summons from Pope Sixtus IV, in 1472. During a subsequent visit to Rome, Regiomontanus was murdered. He had great mechanical ability, but he was primarily a mathematician. He was the first to discuss the algebra of the famous 4th cent. A.D. mathematician, Diophantus. Many of the instruments devised by Regiomontanus were described in his posthumous work, *Scripta*, published in 1544.

REGION, in the plane, the SET of points bound by the sides of a plane closed figure. The set is open if none of its boundary points are included and closed if all of the boundary points are included. The shaded portion of Fig. 1 is a closed triangular region. The set of interior points of a geometric figure is an open region, as the interior points (shaded) of circle O in Fig. 2.

Fig. 1   Fig. 2

REGRESSION COEFFICIENT, *see* LEAST SQUARES.

REGRESSION LINE, *see* LEAST SQUARES.

REGRESSION SUM OF SQUARES, in statistics, in a situation where a regression line is found that fits the pairs of observations, (x_1,y_1), (x_2,y_2), $\cdots$, (x_n,y_n), that part of the total sum of squares, $\sum_{i=1}^{n} (y_i - \bar{y})^2$, that is attributable to the relationship between y and x. It is also known as the *sum of squares due to regression*, and is equal to $b^2 \cdot \sum_{i=1}^{n} (x_i - \bar{x})^2$, where b is the *regression coefficient* (*see* LEAST SQUARES).

REGULAR POLYGON, a POLYGON that is both equilateral and equiangular. Four examples are given.

REGULAR POLYGONS

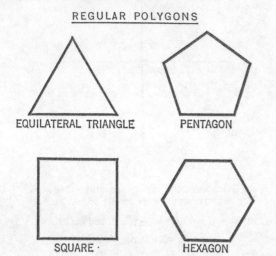

EQUILATERAL TRIANGLE   PENTAGON

SQUARE ·   HEXAGON

REJECTION RATE, in statistics, the proportion of the time that a TYPE I ERROR is made; the ALPHA LEVEL. Usually, the rejection rate is taken to be 0.01, 0.05, or 0.10, although it might be any other PROPORTION.

REJECTION REGION, in statistics, the RANGE of possible values of a test-statistic for which the NULL HYPOTHESIS is rejected.

RELATED RATES. If one physical quantity is related to another by a known equation, and information is given about the rate of change of one of them, the rate of change of the other can be found by differentiating the equation and using the known rate to simplify the result.

Ex.: Suppose a ladder 30 feet long leans against a wall, as in the figure. If the bottom end is pulled away from the wall at the constant rate of 5 feet per second, how fast will the top be moving down the wall when the bottom is eleven feet from the wall?

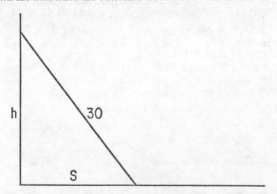

Sol.: We are given that $ds/dt = 5$, and want to find dh/dt. Since the ladder forms the hypotenuse of a right triangle, $h^2 + s^2 = 30^2 = 900$. Differentiating both sides with respect to time, since both h and s are functions of time, we have

$$2h\frac{dh}{dt} + 2s\frac{ds}{dt} = 0.$$

Then, $\frac{dh}{dt} = -\frac{2s}{2h}\frac{ds}{dt} = \frac{-s}{h}\frac{ds}{dt}$. The only unknown on the right is h, which may be found by using the original equation: $h^2 +$

$(11)^2 = 900$; $h = \sqrt{900 - 121} = \sqrt{779}$. Thus, $\frac{dh}{dt} = \frac{-11}{\sqrt{779}}(5) =$

$\frac{-55}{\sqrt{779}}$, which is approximately -2 feet per second. The negative sign indicates that distance h is decreasing.

See also DERIVATIVE OF A FUNCTION; IMPLICIT DIFFERENTIATION.

RELATION, in mathematics, a property such as EQUALITY, INEQUALITY, or congruence (*see* CONGRUENT POLYGONS) that is true for two objects in a particular order.

RELATIVE ERROR, the ratio of the amount of ERROR, E, to the number, Q, to which the approximation is made. Thus, relative error equals E/Q or sometimes, the ABSOLUTE VALUE of this ratio, $|E/Q|$.

Ex.: Find the relative error if a distance of 5 feet is measured as 5.23 feet.

Sol.: $Q = 5$; $E = 5.23 - 5$; $E = .23$.

$$\text{Relative error} = \frac{.23}{4} = .046.$$

RELIABILITY, in statistics, the sample variance (*see* VARIANCE, SAMPLE). The reliability of a test is the measure of the precision of the measurement. The CORRELATION COEFFICIENT between pairs of test scores on the same test (or a test essentially the same) by the same person is a measure of the reliability of the test.

REMAINDER THEOREM, for a polynomial $f(x)$, if $f(x)$ is divided by $x - a$ until there is a remainder that does not contain x, then the remainder is $f(a)$.

Ex.: Find the remainder when $x^3 - 4x^2 + 2x - 4$ is divided by $x - 2$.

Sol.: $f(2) = (2)^3 - 4(2)^2 + 2(2) - 4 = -8$.

If $f(x)$ is divided by $x - a$ and the remainder is 0, i.e., if $f(a) = 0$, then $x - a$ is a FACTOR of $f(x)$, and a is a ROOT of $f(x) = 0$.

REPEATING DECIMAL, *see* DECIMAL, REPEATING.

REPLICATION (rep-li-kay'-shun), in statistics, the repetition of an experiment under conditions that are identical with respect to at least one of the controllable conditions.

RESULTANT OF TWO VECTORS, for a chain of any two VECTORS **a** and **b**, the sum, vector **c** = **a** + **b** or **b** + **a**, from the initial point of the first to the terminal point of the second. Note that the resultant, or sum, is the same if the order of the two vectors is reversed; i.e., the resultant of **a** and **b** is the same as the resultant of **b** and **a**. (See figure.)

Ex. 1: What is the resultant of the following two vectors:
  a: length 1, angle of inclination with x-axis 45° and
  b: length 1, angle of inclination with x-axis 135°?
Sol.: Since they are of equal length and point in opposite directions, they cancel; their resultant is the null vector.

Ex. 2: What is the resultant of the following two vectors:

$$\mathbf{a} = (1,0) \quad \text{and} \quad \mathbf{b} = (0,-1)?$$

Sol.: Using VECTOR ADDITION:

$$(1,0) + (0,-1) = (1 + 0, 0 - 1) = (1,-1)$$

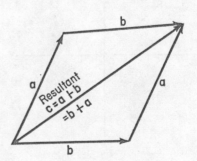

RHOMBOHEDRON (rahm-boh-hee'-drun), a six-sided PRISM whose faces are PARALLELOGRAMS.

RHOMBOID (rahm'-boid), a PARALLELOGRAM with no RIGHT ANGLES and adjacent sides not equal. (See figure.)

RHOMBUS (rahm'-bus), a PARALLELOGRAM in which a pair of adjacent sides are equal. (See figure.) Since a rhombus is a parallelogram it has all the properties of a parallelogram. In addition, (1) all sides of a rhombus are equal; (2) a diagonal bisects the angles through which it passes, (because a diagonal divides the rhombus into two ISOSCELES TRIANGLES); (3) the diagonals of a rhombus are PERPENDICULAR to each other.

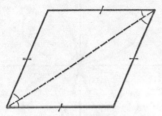

RHUMB LINE, *see* LOXODROME.

RIEMANN, BERNHARD (ree'-mahn), 1826–66, German mathematician who denied the postulate (*see* AXIOM) of Euclidean geometry that a line may be infinitely long. As a result he developed a NON-EUCLIDEAN GEOMETRY in which the following are true: All lines are of finite length; any pair of lines in the same plane intersect; the sum of the angles of a triangle is greater than a straight angle. Einstein's formulation of his theory of relativity makes use of Riemann's researches in geometry.

RIGHT ANGLE, any of the equal ADJACENT ANGLES formed by two PERPENDICULAR lines. A right angle contains 90° or $\frac{\pi}{2}$ radians.

It is one half of a STRAIGHT ANGLE. The symbol used to mark right angles is shown in the figure. All right angles are equal.

An angle is a right angle if **1.** It is formed by perpendicular lines; **2.** It is one of the angles of a RECTANGLE or of a SQUARE; **3.** It intercepts a semicircle; **4.** It is one of the angles formed by diagonals of a RHOMBUS or of a square; or **5.** It is formed by a tangent to a CIRCLE and a RADIUS drawn to the point of tangency.

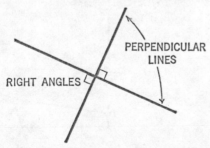

RIGHT CIRCULAR CONE, a circular CONE whose base is perpendicular to its axis. It is also called a *cone of revolution* and may be generated by revolving a RIGHT TRIANGLE about a leg or by revolving an ISOSCELES TRIANGLE about its altitude.

The slant height of a right circular cone is an ELEMENT OF A CONE.

The lateral area of a right circular cone is given by

$$A = \pi r h$$

where r is the radius of the base and h is the slant height.

The lateral area of a frustum of a right circular cone is given by

$$A = \pi h(r + r')$$

where h is the slant height and r and r' are the radii of the bases of the frustum.

RIGHT CIRCULAR CYLINDER, a circular CYLINDER whose bases are perpendicular to the axis. It is also called a *cylinder of revolution* and may be generated by revolving a RECTANGLE about one of its sides.

The VOLUME of a right circular cylinder is given by

$$V = \pi a^2 h$$

and its lateral area by

$$A = 2\pi a h$$

where a is the radius of the base and h is the altitude.

RIGHT SPHERICAL TRIANGLE, a SPHERICAL TRIANGLE having one RIGHT ANGLE. *See also* NAPIER'S RULES.

RIGHT TRIANGLE, a TRIANGLE having a RIGHT ANGLE. The side opposite the right angle is called the *hypotenuse*, and the other two sides are called *legs*. In right $\triangle ABC$ (see figure), $\angle C$ is a right angle; AB is the hypotenuse; and BC and CA are the legs. The following are properties of a right triangle:

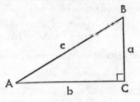

1. $c^2 = a^2 + b^2$, (PYTHAGOREAN THEOREM.)
2. $\angle A$ and $\angle B$ are complementary.
3. Area = $\frac{1}{2}ab$.
4. If $\angle A = 30°$, $a = \frac{1}{2}c$.
5. If $\angle B = 30°$, $b = \frac{1}{2}c$.
6. If D is midpoint of AB, then $AD = DB = CD$.
7. If $\angle A$ (or $\angle B$) = 45°, $\triangle ABC$ is an isosceles right triangle.

RIGID MOTIONS OF THE PLANE, any succession of ROTATIONS OF AXES and TRANSLATIONS OF AXES, which causes a change from one COORDINATE SYSTEM to another. Together, these rigid motions form a GROUP under the operation of successive application; e.g., if one rigid motion is followed by another, the result is still a rigid motion; the inverse of any rotation and translation is an equal rotation and translation in the opposite direction. Rigid motions of the plane are also called TRANSFORMATIONS OF THE PLANE. In plane geometry, superimposing one figure on another is a rigid motion.

RING, in mathematics, a SET with two BINARY OPERATIONS (called addition and multiplication) which have the following properties: **1.** the set is a COMMUTATIVE (or Abelian) GROUP under addition; **2.** for each pair of elements there is a unique product; **3.** multiplication is associative (*see* ASSOCIATIVE PROPERTY); **4.** multiplication is distributive (*see* DISTRIBUTIVE PROPERTY) over addition.

If multiplication is commutative (*see* COMMUTATIVE PROPERTY), the ring is called a *commutative ring;* if there is an IDENTITY ELEMENT for multiplication, it is called a *ring with unity* (or a ring with unit element).

ROLLE'S THEOREM (rohls thee'-u-rum), theorem stating that if a continuous function $f(x)$ crosses the x-axis at two points a and b, and $f'(x)$ exists and is continuous at every point in the interval, $[a,b]$ then there is at least one point c in this interval where $f'(c) = 0$. Geometrically, this special case of the MEAN VALUE THEOREM means that the graph has a horizontal tangent at least one point between a and b. (See figure.)

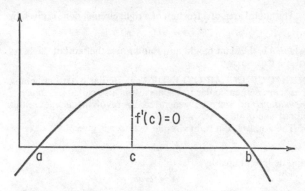

Ex.: Let $f(x) = x^2 - x$, $a = 0$, and $b = 1$. What point does Rolle's Theorem assert to exist?

Sol.: The theorem says there is a point c, $0 < c < 1$, so that $'(c) = 0$. To find it, set $f'(x) = 0$ and solve for x as follows:
$$f'(x) = 2x - 1.$$
$$2x - 1 = 0; \ 2x = 1; \ x = \tfrac{1}{2}.$$
Thus, $\qquad\qquad c = \tfrac{1}{2}.$

ROMAN NUMERAL SYSTEM, an ancient NUMERAL system still used for recording dates, for numbers on the faces of clocks, for chapter headings, and other places.

I	V	X	L	C	D	M
1	5	10	50	100	500	1000

If a letter is repeated, its value is repeated, as

$$II = 2, \ III = 3, \ XXX = 30, \text{ and } CC = 200.$$

However, only three successive equal symbols may be used, and one symbol may be used to the left of a greater symbol to denote a lesser value.

$$4 = 5 - 1 = V - I = IV;$$
$$9 = 10 - 1 = X - I = IX;$$
$$40 = 50 - 10 = L - X = XL;$$
$$90 = 100 - 10 = C - X = XC;$$
$$400 = 500 - 100 = D - C = CD;$$
$$900 = 1000 - 100 = M - C = CM;$$
$$6 = 5 + 1 = VI;$$
$$15 = 10 + 5 = XV;$$
$$70 = 50 + 20 = LXX;$$
$$80 = 50 + 30 = LXXX.$$

A bar over a Roman numeral indicates that its value is increased by 1000. For example, $\overline{V} = 5000$ and $\overline{IX}CC = 9200$. Two bars increase the value by a million, as $\overline{\overline{I}}$ denotes one million. One million may also be written $\overline{M}$. *See* TABLE NO. 8.

ROOT, in mathematics, **1.** contraction of "SQUARE ROOT," "CUBE ROOT," etc.; **2.** a given ARGUMENT (or value of the variable) that makes a function have value zero. In symbols, if $f(a) = 0$, then a is a root of the function $f(x)$. It is also called the root of the equation. If the function is graphed, its roots are the x-coordinates of the points at which the graph crosses the x-axis (the x-intercepts). The word "root" is often used for "solution"

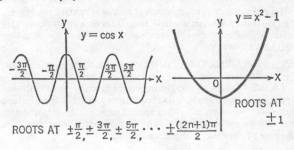

since the equation $f(x) = 0$ will have a solution where the function $y = f(x)$ has a root, and conversely.

Examples of roots of functions are indicated in the figure. Note that some functions have no roots; e.g., $f(x) = x^2 + 1$, $f(x) = |x| + 1$.

ROOTS OF A COMPLEX NUMBER, *see* DEMOIVRE'S THEOREM.

ROSE, the graph, in polar coordinates (*see* COORDINATES, POLAR) of the function, $r = \sin 2\theta$. Between 0° and 180°, sin varies from 0 to 1 and back to 0; between 180° and 360°, sin varies from 0 to -1 and back to 0. Since r is given by the sine of twice θ in the equation above, this cycle is repeated twice. The curve, called a four-leaved rose, is shown in the figure.

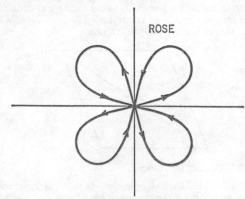

ROSE

To make more petals, graph $r = \sin 2n\theta$, where n is an integer. *See also* LIMACON; SINE FUNCTION OF AN ANGLE.

ROTATION, about a line or a point, rigid motion of a figure such that every point moves in a circular path about the line or point in a plane perpendicular to the line containing the point. Fig. 1 shows a rotation of triangle ABC about line rs. Fig. 2 shows a rotation of parallelogram $ABCD$ about point D.

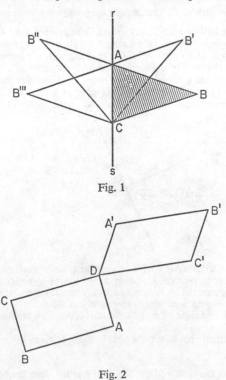

Fig. 1

Fig. 2

ROTATION OF AXES, a TRANSFORMATION OF THE PLANE in which there is an angle, called the angle of rotation, between the old axes and the new axes. If the angle of rotation is a, the coordinates (x',y') relative to the old COORDINATE SYSTEM may be calculated from the coordinates (x,y) relative to the new system, by the equations:

$$x = x' \cos a - y' \sin a;$$
$$y = x' \sin a + y' \cos a. \text{ (See figure.)}$$

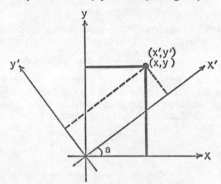

Ex. 1: What are the new coordinates of the point (1,2) after a rotation of 45°?

Sol.: Using the above formulas:

$$x = x' \frac{1}{\sqrt{2}} - y' \frac{1}{\sqrt{2}} = 1;$$
$$= x' y \frac{1}{\sqrt{2}} + y' \frac{1}{\sqrt{2}} = 2.$$

Solve simultaneously to find: $x' = \dfrac{3}{\sqrt{2}}$, $y' = \dfrac{1}{\sqrt{2}}$.

Ex. 2: Find the equation of the parabola $y = x^2$ after a rotation of the axes by 45°.

Sol.: Since $x = x' \cos 45° - y' \sin 45° = x'/\sqrt{2} - y'/\sqrt{2}$ and $y = x' \sin 45° + y' \cos 45° = x'/\sqrt{2} + y'/\sqrt{2}$, we may substitute for x and y and find the equation:

$$\frac{x'}{\sqrt{2}} + \frac{y'}{\sqrt{2}} = \left(\frac{x'}{\sqrt{2}} - \frac{y'}{\sqrt{2}} \right)^2.$$

ROUNDING OFF A NUMBER, perform the following steps:
1. Determine the number of places in the final answer.
2. Drop all DIGITS to the right of that place.
3. If the first digit to be dropped is less than 5, the last digit retained is not changed.
4. If the first digit dropped is more than 5, add 1 to the last digit retained.
5. If the only digit dropped is 5, make the last digit retained even.

Exs.: Round off the following numbers to the nearest hundredth:

$$4.323 \approx 4.32$$
$$68.047 \approx 68.05$$
$$12.235 \approx 12.24$$
$$5.685 \approx 5.68$$
$$26.3258 \approx 26.33$$

RUSSELL, BERTRAND ARTHUR WILLIAM, 3rd Earl Russell, 1872–1970, English philosopher and mathematician and one of the greatest voices for social reform of the 20th cent. He was elected Fellow of the Royal Society in 1908, received the Order of Merit in 1949, and the Nobel Prize for literature in 1950. He wrote more than 40 books on education, mathematics, philosophy and sex. He stood for Parliament on three occasions and was an active member of the House of Lords.

The main intention of Russell's work in mathematics and philosophy was to discover an objective truth, an incontrovertible certainty which could serve as the root upon which the structure of all knowledge might rest. At the International Congress of Philosophy in Paris in 1900, Russell discovered the work of Guiseppe Peano. He applied Peano's methods of logical symbolism when he wrote his *Principles of Mathematics* (1903). The *Principia Mathematica* (1910–1913), which he wrote with Alfred North WHITEHEAD, is one of the most important books of Western civilization. It is a molding of two previously distinct disciplines, mathematics and philosophy. The *Principia* demonstrated that all forms of mathematics and mathematical analysis could be expressed through the principles of symbolic logic. It re-established the Euclidian axiomatic method in modern mathematics by showing that, from but a few simple axioms, all of mathematics could be deduced. In reverse, logical analysis, applied to results, enabled the deduction of the most basic premises. In it Russell also proposed his theory of types to eliminate the paradox of the theory of aggregates. Russell treated philosophy as a science by applying to it the theory of logical analysis from the *Principia*. The *theory of descriptions* is one of Russell's most important contributions to logic. Russell can be considered a precursor of logical positivism and linguistic analysis. His logical atomism was an initiating factor in Wittgenstein's *Tractatus Logico-Philosophicus* (1921).

S

SADDLE POINT, a point in a surface at which the second directional DERIVATIVE OF A FUNCTION in one direction is positive, while in another direction it is negative.

SAMPLE, in statistics, a set of elements or observations that are obtained from a much larger set of elements, called a population, for the purpose of making inferences about the population.

SAMPLE SPACE, in statistics, the set of all the elements which are the possible outcomes of an experiment.

SATISFY AN EQUATION, a value of the VARIABLE which when substituted for the variable reduces the equation to an IDENTITY. The ROOT of an equation is said to satisfy the equation. E.g., 3 satisfies the equation $2x + 4 = 10$, since $2 \cdot 3 + 4 = 10$.

SCALAR (skay'-lahr), as contrasted with a VECTOR, a number that measures magnitude, positive or negative, as on a scale (hence the name), but not direction.

SCALAR PRODUCT, *see* DOT PRODUCT OF TWO VECTORS.

SCALENE TRIANGLE (skay-leen'), a TRIANGLE with no two sides equal. (See figure.)

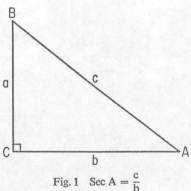

SCIENTIFIC NOTATION (sahy-un-tif'-ik), a notation for writing very large or very small numbers by using powers of 10. To write a number in scientific notation, write it as a product of a number between 1 and 10 and an integral power of 10. Thus 42,-000 may be written $4.2(10^4)$ and 836,000 as $8.36(10^5)$. In scientific notation .00018 is $1.8(10^{-4})$.

SECANT, *see* SECANT LINE; SECANT OF AN ANGLE.

SECANT FUNCTION OF AN ANGLE, in geometry, the ratio of the HYPOTENUSE of a RIGHT TRIANGLE to the side adjacent to the angle. (See Fig. 1.) The secant of an angle is the reciprocal of its cosine: Secant $\angle A = 1/\cos A$. The secant of an acute angle is equal to the cosecant of its complementary angle.

Fig. 1 $\text{Sec } A = \dfrac{c}{b}$

$\text{Sec } B = \dfrac{c}{a}$

The secant of any angle is defined as ratio of the distance to the ABSCISSA, when the angle is in STANDARD ANGLE POSITION.

In Fig. 2, $\sec \theta = \dfrac{\text{distance}}{\text{abscissa}} = \dfrac{r}{x}$. The graph of the function sec x as x varies from $-\frac{3}{2}\pi$ to $+\frac{3}{2}\pi$ is shown in Fig. 3. The tables show the changes in secant θ as θ is rotated through 2π radians. Note that the secant decreases in ABSOLUTE VALUE in quadrant II and increases in absolute value in quadrant III.

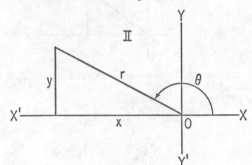

Fig. 2

Fig. 3

Use the fact that $\sec x = 1/\cos x$ together with the rule for differentiating quotients to find the derivative (*see* DERIVATIVE OF A FUNCTION) of the secant function:

$$\frac{d}{dx}(\sec x) = \frac{d}{dx}\left(\frac{1}{\cos x}\right) = \frac{\cos x \frac{d}{dx}1 - 1\frac{d}{dx}\cos x}{\cos^2 x}$$

$$= \frac{\sin x}{\cos^2 x} = \tan x \frac{1}{\cos x} = \tan x \sec x.$$

Ex.: At what point does the tangent to the curve $y = \sec x$ have slope 1?

Sol.: We must solve the equation, $\tan x \sec x = 1$. Use the definition of $\tan x$ to simplify:

$$1 = \tan x \sec x = \frac{\sin x}{\cos^2 x}; \sin x = \cos^2 x = 1 - \sin^2 x.$$

Thus $\sin^2 x + \sin x - 1 = 0$. This is a quadratic equation in $\sin x$: the QUADRATIC FORMULA gives:

$$\sin x = \frac{-b \pm \sqrt{b^2 - 4ac}}{2a} = \frac{-1 \pm \sqrt{1 - (-4)}}{2}$$

$$= \frac{-1 \pm \sqrt{5}}{2}.$$

We choose $\dfrac{1 + \sqrt{5}}{2}$ as $\sin x$; then $x = \sin^{-1}\left(\dfrac{1 + \sqrt{5}}{2}\right)$, which is approximately .66 radians (38°).

CHANGES IN THE SECANT

Quadrant	I	II	III	IV
Increases in angle	$0° - 90°$ $\left(0 - \dfrac{\pi}{2}\right)$	$90° - 180°$ $\left(\dfrac{\pi}{2} - \pi\right)$	$180° - 270°$ $\left(\pi - \dfrac{3\pi}{2}\right)$	$270° - 360°$ $\left(\dfrac{3\pi}{2} - 2\pi\right)$
Changes in secant	Increases $+1$ to $+\infty$	Increases $-\infty$ to -1	Decreases -1 to $-\infty$	Decreases $+\infty$ to $+1$
Sign	Positive	Negative	Negative	Positive

SECANT OF THE QUADRANTAL ANGLES

Angle	0° (0)	90° $\left(\dfrac{\pi}{2}\right)$	180° (π)	270° $\left(\dfrac{3\pi}{2}\right)$	360° 2π
Secant	1	$\pm \infty$	-1	$\pm \infty$	1

SECANT LINE, the line through two points on a curve. The segment of the secant which is between the two points is called a CHORD of the curve. The concept of secant is useful because, together with the concept of the LIMIT OF A FUNCTION, it enables us to define the TANGENT LINE to a curve in terms of the limit of the secant, and thus to define the direction and slope of a curved line at a point on it. (See Fig. 1.)

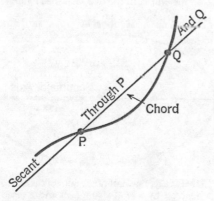

Fig. 1

Of a special interest in elementary geometry is the case of a secant which intersects a circle in two points. If two secants are drawn to a circle from the same point, the angle formed is equal in degrees to one-half the difference of the intercepted arcs. In Fig. 2, $\angle P \doteq (\tfrac{1}{2}\widehat{m} - \widehat{n})$.

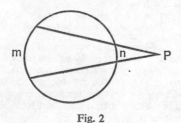

Fig. 2

If a tangent and a secant are drawn to a circle from the same point, the tangent segment is the MEAN PROPORTIONAL between the secant and its external segment.

SECH x, the hyperbolic secant of x, defined by

$$\operatorname{sech} x = \frac{1}{\cosh x} = \frac{2}{e^x + 1e^{-x}}.$$

The derivative of sech x is

$$\frac{d}{dx}(\operatorname{sech} x) = -\operatorname{sech} x \tanh x.$$

See also HYPERBOLIC FUNCTION.

SECONDARY PARTS OF A TRIANGLE, parts of a TRIANGLE other than its sides and interior angles. Thus, exterior angles, altitudes, medians, and angle bisectors are secondary parts of a triangle.

SECOND DEGREE CURVE, any curve whose equation is in the form

$$Ax^2 + Bxy + Cy^2 + Dx + Ey + F = 0.$$

where A, B, C, D, E, and F are constants of which A, B and C cannot all be 0. They are characterized by the fact that they never reverse their direction of curvature; each has only one "bend" in it. The CONIC SECTIONS (hyperbolas, parabolas, and ellipses) and the circle are all second degree curves and may be recognized from the equation by the following rules. The curve is **1.** a PARABOLA if either A or C is zero but not both; **2.** a CIRCLE if $A = C$ and B is 0; **3.** an ELLIPSE if A and C are unequal and have the same sign; **4.** a HYPERBOLA if A and C are unequal and have different signs.

If the coefficient B of the CROSS-PRODUCT TERM Bxy is zero, then the graph can be put in the standard form for the appropriate curve by completing squares. Also, in this case, the axis of symmetry of the graph will be parallel to one of the axes; if the cross-product term is not zero, the graph will be tilted.

Ex.: Determine which conic section is the graph of each of the following equations:

a. $2x^2 + xy + x + y = 0$.
b. $7x^2 + 7y^2 - 3x + 4y - 2 = 0$.
c. $5x^2 - 2xy + 3y^2 = 0$.

Sol.: a. Parabola; b. Circle; c. Hyperbola

SECOND DEGREE EQUATION, an equation of degree two (*see* DEGREE OF AN EQUATION). The most common second degree equations are QUADRATIC EQUATIONS of the form $y = ax^2 + bx + c$. However, equations of the form $ax^2 + by^2 = r^2$, $ax^2 + cxy + by^2 = r^2$, and $xy = k$ are also second degree equations.

SECOND DERIVATIVE, *see* DERIVATIVE OF A FUNCTION.

SECOND DERIVATIVE TEST, used to determine whether an EXTREMUM is a MAXIMUM OF A FUNCTION or a MINIMUM OF A FUNCTION, states that if $f(x)$ has an extremum at $x = a$, then $x = a$ is a maximum if $f''(a) < 0$, and $x = a$ is a minimum if $f''(a) > 0$. If $f''(a) = 0$, the extremum may be a maximum or a minimum. See Ex. 2.

To the left of the maximum in Fig. 1a, the derivative (*see* DERIVATIVE OF A FUNCTION) is positive, while to the right it is negative. Therefore, at a maximum, the derivative is decreasing and the SECOND DERIVATIVE is negative. A similar analysis indicates that the second derivative at a minimum is positive. (See Fig. 1b.)

Ex. 1: Prove that the function $y = \sin x$ has a maximum at $x = \pi/2$.

Sol.: $\dfrac{d}{dx}(\sin x) = \cos x$. Setting $\cos x = 0$, $x = \pi/2$. $\pi/2$ is an extremum of $y = \sin x$.

$$\frac{d}{dx}\left(\frac{d}{dx}(\sin x)\right) = \frac{d}{dx}(\cos x) = -\sin x;$$

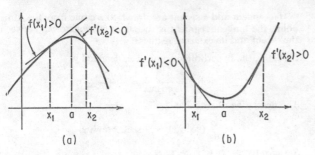

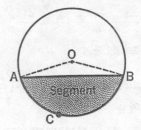

Fig. 1

$-\sin(\pi/2) = -1$; therefore, since $-1 < 0$, the extremum at $\pi/2$ is a maximum.

Ex. 2: Consider the functions $y = x^4$ and $y = -x^4$ to show that $f''(x) = 0$ may occur at either a minimum or a maximum, in addition to occurring at INFLECTION POINTS.

Sol.: $y = x^4$ has a minimum at $x = 0$, while $y = -x^4$ has a maximum at $x = 0$. However, the second derivative at zero of both functions is zero.

SECTION, PLANE, the plane geometric figure formed by intersecting a given geometric figure by a plane. If a plane intersects a conical surface, a straight line, two intersecting straight lines, CIRCLE, ELLIPSE, PARABOLA, or HYPERBOLA may be formed. These figures are called CONIC SECTIONS. The intersection is a circle if the plane is parallel to the plane of the base. (See figure.)

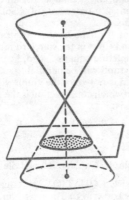

SECTOR OF A CIRCLE, the part of the interior of the CIRCLE formed by two radii and the ARC they intercept. (See figure.) The angle of the sector is the central angle formed by the radii. The area of a sector has the same ratio to the area of the circle as the angle of the sector has to 360°. Thus,

$$\frac{\text{Area Sector}}{\pi r^2} = \frac{\text{Angle of the Sector}}{360°}.$$

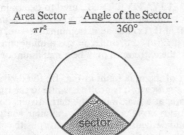

SEC^{-1} x, arc sec x. *See* ARC SECANT.

SEGMENT OF A CIRCLE, the part of the interior of the circle formed by a CHORD and its ARC. The area of a segment is found by subtracting the area of the triangle whose sides are two radii and the chord, from the area of the sector (*see* SECTOR OF A CIR-

CLE) that has the same arc as the segment. In the figure, Area of segment ACB = Area sector $OACB$ − Area $\triangle AOB$.

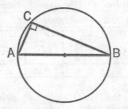

SEMICIRCLE, the ARC that is one-half of a CIRCLE. A DIAMETER OF A CIRCLE divides the circle into two semicircles. An angle inscribed (*see* INSCRIBED ANGLE) in a semicircle is a RIGHT ANGLE. In the figure, if segment AB is a diameter, $\angle ACB$ is a right angle, $\overset{\frown}{ACB}$ is one semicircle formed by the diameter, and $\overset{\frown}{AB}$ is the second semicircle.

SEMIMAJOR AXIS OF ELLIPSE, half the length of the MAJOR AXIS OF AN ELLIPSE. It is the segment from the center of the ellipse through one focus to a point P on the ellipse. Since its length is the average of the distances of the two foci from the point P, the length of the semimajor axis is half the sum of the distances of any point on the ellipse to the two foci. (See figure.)

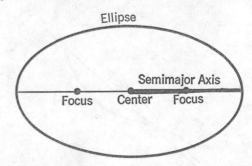

SEMIPERIMETER, one half of the sum of the sides of a TRIANGLE. It is denoted by $s = \frac{1}{2}(a + b + c)$ and is used in HERO'S FORMULA.

SEPARABLE DIFFERENTIAL EQUATION, a LINEAR DIFFERENTIAL EQUATION that can be written in the form $f(y)dy + g(x)dx = 0$. Its solutions are of the form $\int f(y)dy + \int g(x)dx = c$, where c is an arbitrary constant.

Ex.: Solve $dy/dx = e^{x-y}$.

Sol.: $e^{x-y} = e^x/e^y$, so the original equation is the same as
$$e^y dy - e^x dx = 0;$$
$$\int e^y dy - \int e^x dx = e^y - e^x = c.$$
Then $\quad e^y = e^x + c; y = \ln(e^x + c).$

SEQUENCE (*see'*-kwens), a SET of numbers in which each one is related in a definite way to the number that precedes it. An arithmetic sequence is one in which there is a constant difference between any two CONSECUTIVE INTEGERS, as 4, 6, 8, 10 . . . , in which the difference is 2. A sequence is geometric if each term after the first is multiplied by a CONSTANT term, as 3, 9, 27, 81. . . . The constant term, or RATIO, is 3.

A sequence may be given by specifying the value of the term x_n as a function of n. Thus the second sequence might be specified as the sequence of terms $(-1)^{n+1}n$. Using set notation, sequences are denoted by $\{x_n\}$; the second example given would be written $\{(-1)^{n+1}n\}$.

SEQUENTIAL TEST (see-kwen'-shal), in statistics, a type of hypothesis-testing in which the sample size is not fixed. After each member is taken from the population, the decision is made to accept the NULL HYPOTHESIS, to accept the ALTERNATIVE HYPOTHESIS, or to continue sampling. The criteria for acceptance of H_0 and for acceptance of H_1 depend upon the desired values of the ALPHA ERROR and BETA ERROR. A sequential test is also called a *sequential sampling* or a *sequential analysis*.

SERIES, the indicated sum of a SEQUENCE of terms, such as the series $1 + 3 + 5 + 7 + \cdots$ formed from the sequence 1, 3, 5, 7, ... *See also* ARITHMETIC PROGRESSION; GEOMETRIC PROGRESSION; DIVERGENT SERIES; CONVERGENT SERIES; RATIO TEST.

SERPENTINE (sur'-pen-tahyn), any curve with an equation of the form,

$$y = \frac{abx}{a^2 + x^2},$$

in which a and b are constants. (See figure.)

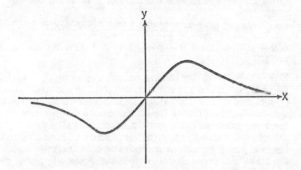

SET, any collection of objects or numbers. For example, a set of books, a set of the states of the United States, a set of the population of the United States, and a set of the PRIME NUMBERS between 1 and 50. A capital letter is used to denote a set and the members of the set are enclosed in braces, as, $P = \{2, 3, 5, 7, 11, 13\}$ which may be read "P is the set of prime numbers less than 15."

The members or individual parts that make up a set are called the *elements* of a set. The symbol $\in$ is used to designate an element. In the set $A = \{2, 3, 5, 7\}$ "2 is an element of set A" is written $2 \in A$. Then $4 \notin A$ means "4 is not an element of set A."

A set having no members or elements is called an *empty* set or *null* set. The symbol for a null set is ϕ or $\{\ \}$. The set $\{0\}$ should not be confused with the null set. It represents the set whose member is zero. The set of all the numbers between 10 and 15 having exact SQUARE ROOTS is an example of an empty or null set.

A *finite* set is a set with a definite number of elements. To designate a large set, such as the set of all the even numbers to and including 50, a series of three dots is used to show some members have been left out, as

$$\{2, 4, 6, 8, 10, \ldots, 50\}$$

An *infinite* set is a set in which there is no end to the number of members, as the set of all the even NATURAL NUMBERS,

$$\{2, 4, 6, 8, 10, \ldots\}$$

The three dots indicate the series goes on indefinitely.

Sets in which there is one-to-one correspondence between the members of each set are called *equivalent* sets. If $A = \{1, 2, 3, 4, 5\}$ and $B = \{5, 10, 15, 20, 25\}$, sets A and B each contain five elements. Thus, set A is equivalent to set B, written $A \leftrightarrow B$. All infinite sets are equivalent sets.

If two equivalent sets have identical elements, they are called *equal* sets. If $C = \{r, s, t, u\}$ and $D = \{s, r, u, t\}$, sets C and D each contain four elements. Thus, $C \leftrightarrow D$. The elements in C are the same as the elements in D. Thus the sets are equal, written $C = D$. Equal sets must be equivalent sets, but equivalent sets need not be equal.

If the members of any set A are also members of another set B, then set A is a subset of set B. If $A = \{a, b, c, d\}$ and $B = \{a, b, c, d, \ldots, z\}$ then A is a *proper subset* of B and is written

$$A \subset B.$$

The closed part of the symbol faces the smaller set. A is called a proper subset of B, because every element of A is an element of B, but there are elements of B that are not elements of A. If $C = \{d, c, b, a\}$ every element of A is an element of C, and every element of C is an element of A, then $A = C$. A is called an *improper subset* of C and is written $A \subset C$. Likewise, C is an improper subset of A.

The *intersection* of two sets is a set consisting of elements which are common to both sets. The symbol for intersection is $\cap$ (cap). Thus,

$$\{1, 2, 3\} \cap \{1, 4, 5\} = \{1\}.$$
$$\{1, 2, 3\} \cap \{4, 5, 6\} = \psi.$$
$$\{a, b, c\} \cap \{b, c, d\} = \{b, c\}.$$

The *union* of two sets is a set of all the elements in either of the two sets. The symbol for union is $\cup$ (cup). No element is counted more than once.

$$\{1, 2, 3\} \cup \{1, 3, 4, 5\} = \{1, 2, 3, 4, 5\}.$$
$$\text{If} \qquad A = \{a, b, c, d, e, f\}$$
$$\text{and} \qquad B = \{a, c, e, f\}$$
$$\text{and} \qquad C = \{a, b, c, d\}$$
$$\text{then } B \cup C = A.$$

The fixed set of which all the sets in any given discussion are its subsets is called the *universal set* or the DOMAIN. The universal set is designated by the capital letter U. A universal set may be all the students in a given school, the people in a particular room at a given time, or all the presidents of the United States. For example,

$$U = \{\text{all natural numbers}\}.$$
$$A = \{\text{all even numbers}\}.$$
$$B = \{\text{all prime numbers}\}.$$
$$C = \{\text{all numbers divisible by 5}\}.$$

In this case the universal set is infinite and the subsets $A, B,$ and C are infinite.

Although the real importance of sets is apparent only in the study of infinite numbers and other advanced subjects in mathematics, set theory provides a convenient and precise language for all branches of mathematics. For example, analytic geometry can be described more abstractly using sets. A point in the plane can be identified by its coordinates, and the plane may be considered as a set of points, or a set of ordered pairs, as (1,2) which identify the points in the plane. Any two sets of points, or point-sets, can be used to produce others by the following operations on the sets:

Set addition (union): The new set consists of all points that are in at least one of the sets.

Set multiplication (intersection): The new set consists of all points that are in both sets.

The rules for union and intersection are analogous to the operations of addition and multiplication of real numbers.

SEXAGESIMAL MEASURE (seks-ah-jes'-i-mal), the DEGREE system of measure in which a complete revolution is considered to be 360 degrees. Thus, the unit of measure, or 1 degree (°), is equal to 1/360 of a complete revolution. The degree is divided into 60 minutes (60′) and the minute into 60 seconds (60″). Twenty four degrees, thirty minutes, and forty-five seconds is written 24°30′45″.

SEXTANT, an instrument for measuring angles, using the principle of double reflection. It is usually used to determine the altitude of celestial bodies. The term was originally applied to instruments with arcs of 60°—one-sixth of a circle—but is now used for any instrument of this type regardless of the angle. The sextant was invented in 1730 by John Hadley in England and independently by Thomas Godfrey in the U.S. When using the sextant, the observer adjusts the instrument until the directly observed image of the horizon coincides with the doubly reflected image of the celestial body. The altitude of the celestial body is then twice the angle between the two mirrors and can be read from calibrations on the instrument. Because of the double reflection, instruments with an arc of 60° can measure angles up to 120°.

SEXTIC EQUATION, an equation of *degree* six.

SHEAF OF PLANES, all the planes that pass through a given point, called the center of the sheaf. (See figure.)

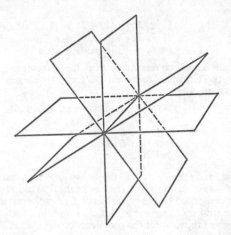

SHEET, of a surface, a part of a surface on which one can travel between any two points on the surface without leaving the surface. A MOEBIUS STRIP is a surface of one sheet.

SHELL METHOD, a method of finding the volume of a solid of revolution by using cyclindrical shells to approximate the solid. If the area under the curve $y = f(x)$ is revolved about the y-axis, then the volume of a shell of the type shown in the figure is $\Delta V \approx 2\pi x f(x)\Delta x$.
The sum of such elements' volumes approximates the solid's volume; the limit of the approximation as the shells' thicknesses

approach zero equals the volume exactly. This limit is an integral which may be evaluated by the fundamental theorem of calculus. If the solid's inner radius is a and its outer radius b, then its volume is

$$V = \int_a^b 2\pi x f(x).$$

Ex.: What is the volume of the solid with inner radius 1 and outer radius 3 generated by the region under the curve $y = 1 - (x - 2)^2$ when revolved about the y-axis?

$$Sol.: V = \int_1^3 2\pi x f(x)dx = \int_1^3 2\pi x(1 - (x - 2)^2)dx$$
$$= 2\pi \int_1^3 x dx - 2\pi \int_1^3 x(x - 2)^2 dx$$
$$= 2\pi\left(\frac{x^2}{2}\right)\Big]_1^3 - 2\pi\left(\frac{x^4}{4} - \frac{4x^3}{3} + \frac{4x^2}{2}\right)\Big]_1^3$$
$$= 2\pi(\tfrac{9}{2} - \tfrac{1}{2}) - 2\pi[(\tfrac{81}{4} - 36 + 18) - (\tfrac{1}{4} - \tfrac{4}{3} + 2)]$$
$$= 2\pi(\tfrac{8}{2}) - 2\pi(\tfrac{4}{3}) = 2\pi(4 - \tfrac{4}{3}) = \frac{16\pi}{3} \text{ cubic units.}$$

SIDE, of an ANGLE, either one of the RAYS that form the angle; of a POLYGON, any one of the LINE SEGMENTS that form the polygon.

SIGMA, the Greek letter symbolized by σ or Σ (cap). Σ is the symbol used to indicate a summation. $\sum_{k=}^5 4k$ means the sum of the product $4k$ for $k = 1, 2, 3, 4, 5$. Thus $\sum_{k=1}^5 4k = 4(1) + 4(2) + 4(3) + 4(4) + 4(5) = 4 + 8 + 12 + 16 + 20 = 60$. *See* TABLE NO. 1.

SIGNED NUMBER, a NUMBER preceded by a plus (+) or minus (−) sign, indicating a POSITIVE NUMBER (+) or NEGATIVE NUMBER (−). Signed numbers are also called directed numbers since the sign can indicate position (or direction) of a number, relative to ZERO on a NUMBER LINE. Positive numbers are to the right of zero and negative numbers are to the left of zero on a horizontal number line; positive numbers are above zero and negative numbers are below zero on a vertical number line. A signed number may be used to indicate such things as temperature above (+) or below (−) zero, or money lost (−) or gained (+).
The following are the laws of signs for operations with signed numbers:
1. ADDITION   To add numbers with the *same sign*, keep the sign and add the ABSOLUTE VALUES of the numbers. E.g., (+3) + (+4) = +7; (−5) + (−6) = −11.
To add numbers with *different signs*, keep the sign of the number with the larger absolute value and find the difference between the absolute values of the numbers. E.g., to add (−5) + (+3), keep the sign of 5 (−) and find the difference between 3 and 5 (2). The sum of −5 and +3 is −2.
2. SUBTRACTION   To subtract signed numbers, change the sign of the SUBTRAHEND (the number you are subtracting) and *follow the addition laws* for signed numbers. E.g., to subtract −8 from +3, change the sign of the subtrahend (−8) to plus; follow the laws for addition of +8 and +3, giving +11. Thus, (+3) − (−8) = +11. To subtract +7 from +2, change the sign of +7 to minus, follow the laws for addition of −7 and +2, giving −5. Thus (+2) − (+7) = −5.
3. MULTIPLICATION   In multiplication of numbers with the *same sign*, the PRODUCT is positive: (+3)(+4) = +12; (−2)(−5) = +10.
In multiplication of numbers with *different signs*, the product is negative: (+4)(−2) = −8; (−5)(+3) = −15.
4. DIVISION   In division of numbers with the *same sign*, the QUOTIENT is positive: (+30) ÷ (+5) = +6; (−20) ÷ (−2) = +10.
In division of numbers with *different signs*, the quotient is negative: (+45) ÷ (−5) = −9; (−21) ÷ (+3) = −7.
Notice that the laws of signs are the same for multiplication and division.

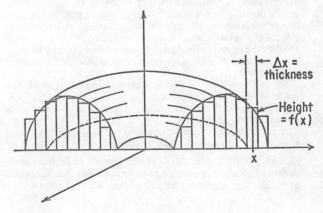

SIGNED-RANK TEST, in statistics, to test a NULL HYPOTHESIS about the median of a population. The assumptions are that the observations are from a continuous, symmetric population. The assumptions are more restrictive than those of the SIGN TEST, and allow more information to be used from the data than merely whether the observation is above or below the hypothetical median. In the signed-rank test the difference between the observation and the hypothetical median is considered. The hypothetical median is subtracted from each observation, the differences are arranged in order of their increasing absolute value, and ranks are assigned to them. Zero differences are discarded. Equal differences are assigned a rank that is the mean of the ranks that they occupy. The sum of the ranks occupied by the negative differences is found, and the sum of the ranks occupied by the positive differences is found. The theoretical distribution of the smaller of these two rank-sums (denoted by T) is known, and tables are available. If the sample size is large, T has a distribution that is approximately normal with mean $\mu_T = \dfrac{n(n+1)}{4}$ and variance $\sigma_{T^2} = \dfrac{n(n+1)(2n+1)}{24}$.

SIGNIFICANCE LEVEL, of a test, in statistics, the REJECTION RATE; the ALPHA LEVEL; the size of the type I error.

SIGNIFICANT, in statistics the value of a test statistic is said to be significant when it leads to rejection of the NULL HYPOTHESIS.

SIGNIFICANT FIGURES, numbers which are meaningful in terms of the degree of precision with which a measurement has been made. If a measurement is 6.0 inches, the zero is significant if it indicates the measurement has been made to the nearest tenth. In a number such as 2800, there are 4 significant figures if it has been computed to the nearest unit, 3 significant figures to the nearest ten, and 2 significant figures if it has been computed to the nearest hundred.

The PRODUCT of two approximate numbers should not contain more significant figures than either FACTOR. The QUOTIENT of two approximate numbers should not contain more significant figures than either the DIVIDEND or the DIVISOR.

SIGN TEST, in statistics, to test that the median of a population equals some specified value. The only assumptions are that the observations are from a continuous population that has a median. An observation greater than the hypothetical median is replaced by a plus sign, an observation less than the hypothetical median is replaced by a minus sign, and an observation equal to the hypothetical median is discarded.

If the NULL HYPOTHESIS is true, the number of plus signs (or, equivalently, of minus signs) is a binomial random variable, and this fact furnishes the basis for a test. Either binomial tables or, if the sample size is large, the NORMAL APPROXIMATION TO A BINOMIAL can be used.

If observations from two populations are paired, the sign test can be used to test the null hypothesis that the difference of the population medians equals any specified number. Then the second member of each pair is subtracted from the first, the hypothetical difference is subtracted from each observed difference, and the sign of the difference is recorded. If the null hypothesis is true, the number of plus signs is a binomial random variable.

SIGNUM FUNCTION (sig'-num), the FUNCTION denoted by sgn x (or sg x) defined by

$$\text{sgn } x = \begin{cases} -1 \text{ if } x < 0. \\ 0 \text{ if } x = 0. \\ +1 \text{ if } x > 0. \end{cases}$$

SIMILAR POLYGONS, POLYGONS having their corresponding angles equal and their corresponding sides proportional. The symbol for similar is $\sim$. Two TRIANGLES are similar if **1.** two angles of one are equal to two angles of the other; **2.** they are each similar to a third triangle; **3.** an angle of one triangle is equal to an angle of the other and the including sides propor-

tional; **4.** the corresponding sides of the two triangles are proportional.

To determine the corresponding sides of similar triangles determine the three pairs of equal angles. The pairs of corresponding angles are the sides opposite the equal angles.

In the figure, $\angle 1 = \angle 2$, $\angle A = \angle B$. Therefore, $\angle C = \angle D$. (If two angles of one triangle equal two angles of a second triangle, the third angles are equal.)

Equal Angles	Corresponding Sides
$\angle 1 = \angle 2$	AC and BD
$\angle A = \angle B$	CE and ED
$\angle C = \angle D$	AE and EB

Since the triangles are similar, the corresponding sides are in proportion: $AC/BD = CE/ED = AE/EB$. Note that the sides of one triangle are the numerators of the ratios and the sides of the other triangle are the denominators.

SIMILAR SOLIDS, solids bounded by similar surfaces. All SPHERES are similar solids and all CUBES are similar solids.

SIMPLE CLOSED CURVE, a curve that is closed and does not intersect itself. A CIRCLE, ELLIPSE, or a POLYGON are simple closed curves. *See also* LINE.

SIMPLE INTEREST, *see* INTEREST.

SIMPSON'S RULE, a method of approximating the area under a curve. Partition the interval $[a, b]$ (see figure) into an even number of equal intervals of length h, and approximate the area under each sub-arc of the curve $y = f(x)$ by a parabolic arc. A PARABOLA with a vertical axis may be drawn through any three points on a curve. A series of such arcs will fit the curve more closely than a broken line of chords. Summing the areas under each gives Simpson's Rule:

$$A \approx \frac{h}{3}(f(x_0) + 4f(x_1) + 2f(x_2) + 4f(x_3) + \cdots$$
$$+ 4f(x_{n-1}) + f(x_n)).$$

SIMULTANEOUS EQUATIONS (sahy-mul-tay'-nee-us), any set of equations to be considered as applying at the same time to the same variables in connection with the same problem. *See also* EQUATIONS, SYSTEMS OF LINEAR.

SINE OF AN ANGLE, in geometry, the ratio of the side of the triangle opposite the angle to the HYPOTENUSE. (See Fig. 1.) The sine of an angle is the reciprocal of the cosecant (*see* COSECANT OF AN ANGLE) of the angle: sine $\angle A = \dfrac{1}{\text{cosecant } \angle A}$. The sine of an acute angle is equal to the cosine (*see* COSINE OF AN ANGLE) of its complementary angle. The sine of $\angle A$ is abbreviated sin $\angle A$.

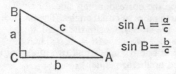

$$\sin A = \frac{a}{c}$$

$$\sin B = \frac{b}{c}$$

Fig. 1

The sine of any angle is defined in trigonometry as the ratio of the ORDINATE to the distance, r, when the angle is in STANDARD ANGLE POSITION. In Fig. 2, $\sin \theta = \frac{\text{ordinate}}{\text{distance}} = \frac{y}{r}$. The sine is positive in the first and second quadrants and negative in the third and fourth quadrants. Figure 3 shows the graphs of the sine x as x varies from $-\pi$ to 2π. The table shows the changes in the sine as θ is rotated through 360°. Note that the sine in Quadrant III increases in ABSOLUTE VALUE and decreases in absolute value in Quadrant IV. While the range of values is from $+1$ to -1, the absolute value varies from 0 to 1.

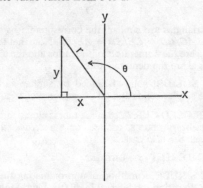

Fig. 2

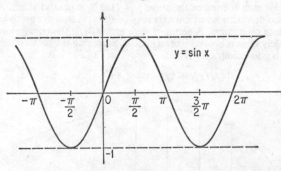

Fig. 3

The derivative of sin x, $\frac{d}{dx}(\sin x) = \cos x$. This formula is derived directly from the definition of the DERIVATIVE OF A FUNCTION by using the rules of trigonometry. The derivation is outlined below.

$$\frac{d}{dx}(\sin x) = \lim_{h \to 0} \frac{\sin(x+h) - \sin x}{h}$$

$$= \frac{\sin x \cos h + \sin h \cos x - \sin x}{h}$$

$$= \sin x \left(\frac{\cos h - 1}{h}\right) + \cos x \left(\frac{\sin h}{h}\right).$$

By geometry or algebra, it may be shown that $\lim_{h \to 0} \frac{\cos h - 1}{h} = 0$,

while $\lim_{h \to 0} \frac{\sin h}{h} = 1$. Thus, the limit of the last line above is simply cos x. That is, $\frac{d}{dx}(\sin x) = \cos x$.

Ex.: What is the slope of the tangent to $y = \sin x$ where $x = \pi/4$?

Sol.: The tangent's slope is the derivative; the derivative of sin x is cos x; therefore the slope of the tangent at $x = \pi/4$ is cos $\pi/4 = 1/\sqrt{2}$, which is approximately $1/1.41 \approx .707$.

See also TRIGONOMETRIC FUNCTIONS.

CHANGES IN THE SINE

Quadrant	I	II	III	IV
Increases in	0° — 90°	90° — 180°	180° — 270°	270° — 360°
Angle	$\left(0 - \frac{\pi}{2}\right)$	$(0 - \pi)$	$\left(\pi - \frac{3\pi}{2}\right)$	$\left(\frac{3\pi}{2} - 2\pi\right)$
Changes in *Sine*	Increases 0 to 1	Decreases 1 to 0	Decreases 0 to -1	Increases -1 to 0
Sign	Positive	Positive	Negative	Negative

SINE OF THE QUADRANTAL ANGLES

Angle	0°	90°	180°	270°	360°
Sine	0	1	0	-1	0

SINES, LAW OF. The law of sines states that in any triangle the ratio of a side to the sine of its opposite angle is equal to the ratio of any other side to the sine of its opposite angle. The formula is

$$\frac{a}{\sin A} = \frac{b}{\sin B} = \frac{c}{\sin C}.$$

The law is used for solving triangles when given (1) one side and two angles, or (2) two sides and an angle opposite one of the sides. *See* AMBIGUOUS CASE.

Ex.: Given $\triangle ABC$ with $A = 40°$, $B = 60°$, and $a = 10$. Find C, b, and c.

Sol.:

1. $C = 180° - (40° + 60°) = 80°$.

2. $\frac{b}{\sin B} = \frac{a}{\sin A}$ or $b = \frac{a \sin B}{\sin A}$.

   $$b = \frac{10 \sin 60°}{\sin 40°} = \frac{10 \times .8660}{.6428} = 13.5.$$

3. $\frac{a}{\sin C} = \frac{a}{\sin A}$ or $c = \frac{a \sin C}{\sin A}$.

   $$c = \frac{10 \times \sin 80°}{\sin 40°} = \frac{10 \times .9848}{.6428} = 15.3.$$

The law of sines for a SPHERICAL TRIANGLE ABC is

$$\frac{\sin a}{\sin A} = \frac{\sin b}{\sin B} = \frac{\sin c}{\sin C}.$$

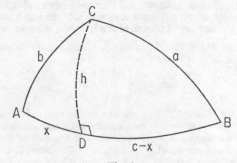

Fig. 1

In the oblique spherical triangle ABC shown in Fig. 1, a GREAT CIRCLE passes through C perpendicular to AB at D, forming right triangles ACD and BCD.

$$\text{Sin } h = \sin b \sin A \quad \text{and} \quad \sin h = \sin a \sin B.$$

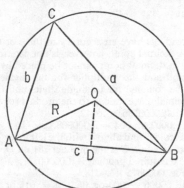

Fig. 2

(*See* NAPIER'S RULES.) Then, $\sin b \sin A = \sin a \sin B$. Divide both members of the equation by $\sin A \sin B$, then,

$$\frac{\sin b}{\sin B} = \frac{\sin a}{\sin A}.$$

In like manner, by passing a great circle through B and perpendicular to AC, $\dfrac{\sin a}{\sin A} = \dfrac{\sin c}{\sin C}$. Therefore, $\dfrac{\sin a}{\sin A} = \dfrac{\sin b}{\sin B} = \dfrac{\sin c}{\sin C}$.

The law of sines for an inscribed triangle states that the diameter of a circle circumscribed about a triangle is equal to the ratio of any side of the triangle to the sine of the opposite angle. If R in Fig. 2 denotes the radius,

$$2R = \frac{a}{\sin A} = \frac{b}{\sin B} = \frac{c}{\sin C}.$$

$\angle AOB = 2 \angle C$. (If, in a circle, an inscribed angle and a central angle intercept the same arc, the inscribed angle equals one half the central angle.) If OD is drawn perpendicular to AB, $\angle AOD = \angle C$ and $AD = DB$.

$$\sin AOD = \frac{AD}{R} = \sin C, \text{ and } AD = R \sin C.$$

$$AB \text{ (or } c) = 2R \sin C.$$

Similarly, $a = 2R \sin A$ and $b = 2R \sin B$. Therefore, $2R = \dfrac{a}{\sin A} = \dfrac{b}{\sin B} = \dfrac{c}{\sin C}$.

SINH x, the hyperbolic sine of x. By definition,

$$\sinh x = \frac{e^x - e^{-x}}{2}.$$

The derivative of the sinh x, $\dfrac{d}{dx}$ (sinh x) = cosh x. *See also* HYPERBOLIC FUNCTION; HYPERBOLIC RADIAN.

SIN⁻¹ x, arc sin x. *See* ARC SINE.

SKEW LINES (skyoo), lines in space which neither intersect nor are parallel.

Ex.: Are the following two lines skew? If not, where do they intersect?

$$\begin{array}{ll} x_1 = 3t + 1 & x_2 = 4t + 2 \\ y_1 = 2t & y_2 = 5t + 1 \\ z_1 = t & z_2 = 6t + 1. \end{array}$$

Sol.: If they intersect, then for one point $x_1 = x_2$, $y_1 = y_2$, and $z_1 = z_2$. To find the t corresponding to this point, take $x_1 = x_2$. Then, $3t + 1 = 4t + 2$; $t = -1$. When $t = -1$,

$$y_1 = 2(-1) = -2$$
and
$$y_2 = 5(-1) + 1 = -4.$$

These are unequal; therefore the lines do not intersect and so are skew, providing they are not parallel. By more complex methods, we can prove they are not parallel and hence are skew.

SLANT HEIGHT OF A CONE, *see* CONE.

SLIDE RULE, a mechanical device, consisting of logarithmic scales, with which certain mathematical operations can be performed easily and rapidly.

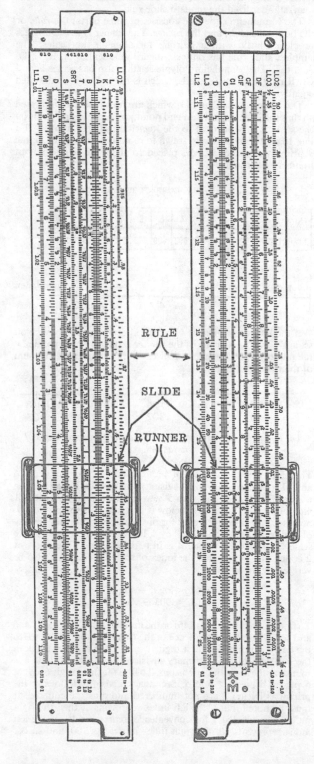

RULE

SLIDE

RUNNER

Logarithmic scales were used for mechanical computations as early as 1620. Edmund Gunter, an Englishman, claimed to have used a double scale; however, it is generally accepted that William OUGHTRED made such a device in 1621. Gunter invented a circular slide run in 1632. A straight slide rule from 1654 is now in the Science Museum at South Kensington, London. It is about two feet long and has a square cross section. Sir Isaac NEWTON suggested the use of a runner. Mannheim, a Frenchman, standardized the modern slide rule.

The Mannheim slide rule consists of three parts; the *rule*, or the body, the *slide*, and the *runner*. The runner is made of glass or clear plastic with a hairline for aligning the scales. The simplest slide rule has only six logarithmic scales; A, B, C, D, S, and T. The Mannheim Polyphase slide also has scales K and CI. It may also have scale L, which is the only scale calibrated equally.

The basic scales, C and D, which are identical, are calibrated so that the distance from an end point, or *index*, to any point on the scale is proportional to the logarithm of the number. If a line 10 centimeters long is drawn to represent scale C, or D, the 9 primary divisions can be placed to show the logarithms of numbers 1 through 10.

LOGARITHM TABLE, CORRECT TO THREE PLACES

Numbers	1	2	3	4	5	6	7	8	9	10
Logarithms	.000	.301	.477	.602	.699	.778	.845	.903	.954	1.000

If the left index of scale C on the slide is placed above 2 on scale D, and the hairline of the runner is placed on 4 in scale D, the number 8, on scale C in register with 4, represents the sum of the two logarithms.

$$\log 2 \ + \ \log 4 \ = \ \log 8$$
$$.301 \ + \ .602 \ = \ .903$$

The logarithm of a product equals the sum of the logarithms of its factors.

Therefore, 8 is the product of 4 and 2. To find the product of 6 and $1\frac{1}{2}$, place the left index register with 6 on the D scale. Place the hairline of the runner on 5 between the primary divisions 1 and 2 on scale C. Directly below it on scale D is the product 9. Scales C and D are also used for division. Division is the inverse of multiplication. To divide 8 by 4, locate 8 on the D scale, slide scale C so that the divisor 4 is in register with 8. The quotient 2 is on scale D opposite the index of scale C. This may also be verified by the log table.

$$\log 2 = \log 8 - \log 4$$
$$.301 = .903 - .602$$

To find a number such as 146 (or the numbers 1.46, 14.6, and .146 and so on) locate the sequence of the digits without reference to the decimal point. The first digit, 1, places the number between the first two of the 9 primary divisions. The second digit 4 is found on the secondary divisions. To find the third digit 6, count 6 places between 4 and 5. Secondary divisions following the primary division 2 are not numbered and must be counted. It must be noted that if the left index represents 1, then the right index, also labeled 1 for convenience, represents 10. If the left index represents 10, the right index represents 100, and so on.

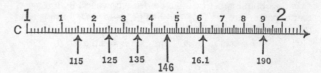

Slide rule readings have an accuracy to three or four significant figures. A decimal point, however, is not determined by the slide rule. If the decimal point cannot be placed by inspection, the multiplicand and the multiplier (or the dividend and the divisor) may be rounded off to single digits and the required number of decimal places added to the product (or quotient).

Ex. 1: Multiply .000186 × .0042.

Rounding off: .0002 × .004 = .0000008.

Locate 186 on scale D and align it with the left index of C. Opposite the multiplier 42 on C is the product 781 on D, to 3 significant digits. The required product is .000000781.

Ex. 2: Divide .0000575 ÷ .0038.

Rounding off: .00006 ÷ .004 or .06 ÷ 4 = $.01\frac{1}{2}$ or .015.

If 38 on scale C is in register with 575 on scale D, the dividend, 151, is read on D opposite the left index. The quotient to three decimal places is .015. The slide rule may be used for combinations of operations as well as for single computations.

Ex. 3: $$\frac{730 \times 656 \times 235}{490 \times 304}$$

Alternate the operations of multiplication and division. Ignore the answers for individual operations. Set hairline at 730 on scale D, move slide so that 490 on C is in register. Move hairline to 656 on C, then move slide so that 304 on C is in register. Move hairline to 235 on C and take the reading opposite it on scale D, which is 755. By rounding off each number to one significant digit,

$$\frac{700 \times 700 \times 200}{500 \times 300}$$ equals approximately 700, therefore,

there are 3 digits in the answer, 755.

Ex. 4: Solve for x in the proportion, $\frac{126}{49} = \frac{x}{287}$. $x =$ $\frac{126 \times 287}{49}$. Rounding off, $\frac{100 \times 300}{50}$, the value of x will be a 3 digit number. Place the hairline on 126 on scale D. Slide C so that 49 is in register. The right index will be opposite the quotient of this operation. Since 287 on C extends beyond the D scale, it will be necessary to interchange the indices. Place the hairline on the right index of C, then move the left index to the hairline. Move the hairline to 287 on C. In register on D is the required value of x. $x = 738$.

The A and B scales are identical. Their logarithmic scales are exactly half the lengths of those of the C and D scales. Scale A is used in combination with D for finding squares of numbers. Locate on scale D the number to be squared and set the hairline of the runner on this number. The square of the number will be in register on scale A. To find the square root of a number, locate the number on A, place the hairline of the runner on this number and its square root will be in register to scale D. If the number whose square root is to be found, has an odd number of digits, such as 9 and 144, use the left half of scale A. Use the right half for numbers with an even number of digits.

The D and K scales are used for finding cubes and cube roots. The cube of a number is found by locating the number on scale D. If the hairline of the runner is placed on this number, its cube will be in register on the K scale. To find the cube root of a number, locate the number on K, and if the runner is placed on this number, the cube root will be found in register on D. If the number has 1 digit, or 1 plus a multiple of 3 digits, as 8 or 1728, use the left third of the scale. For numbers of 2 digits, or 2 plus a multiple of 3 digits, as 27, use the middle third of K. If the number has an exact multiple of 3 digits, such as 125, use the right third of scale K.

Ex. 5: Find the cube root of .00000862.

$$\sqrt[3]{.000\ 008\ 620}$$

There is only 1 significant digit in the first group of 3's (not counting zeros), therefore, the left third of K is used. The cube root is approximately .0205.

The CI scale is the reciprocal scale and is used in combination with D. The reciprocal of any number on D can be found by placing the runner on that number and reading the number on CI in register. Conversely, the reciprocal of any number on CI may be found in like manner on D.

The L, or logarithm, scale is used in combination with scale D. If the indices are in exact register, the runner on D will give the reading of its logarithm on L.

Ex. 6: Find the logarithm of 362.
Set the hairline on 362 on D. The logarithm on L is 559. This represents the mantissa (*see* LOGARITHM, MANTISSA OF A). The characteristic (*see* LOGARITHM, CHARACTERISTIC OF A) is 2, therefore, log 362 = 2.559.

Ex. 7: Evaluate $(32.4)^{2/3}$.
Mantissa of 32.4 on L = 510, characteristic is 1.

$$\log (32.4)^{2/3} = \tfrac{2}{3} \times 1.510 = 1.007.$$

The number on D in register with .007 is 102. The antilog is 10.2.

Slide rules that have S and T scales are used for sine and tangent computations in combination with A and D respectively. If their indices are in register, the sine of an angle on scale S will be in register on scale A. For angles from 30′ to 5°45′ the sine will be on the left side of the scale and a zero is placed after the decimal in the sine reading. For angles from 5°45′ to 90°, the sines will be on the right side of the scale and no zero follows the decimal. For example, sin 3°30′ = .0610 and sin 50° = .7660.

The tangent of an angle is found in the same manner with a combination of the T and D scales. To find the tangent of an angle from 45° through 90° find the tangent of the complement of the angle and take its reciprocal reading on C1. For example, find the tangent of 50°. Locate its complement 40° on scale D and read the reciprocal in register on C1.

SLOPE-INTERCEPT FORM OF AN EQUATION OF A LINE,

the equation of a LINE in the form $y = mx + b$, in which m is the slope (*see* SLOPE OF A LINE) and b the Y-INTERCEPT. The equation $2x - 3y - 6 = 0$, changed to the slope-intercept form is $y = \tfrac{2}{3}x - 2$. The slope is 2/3 and the y-intercept is -2. If the slope of a line is known to be -5 and its y-intercept is 2/9 the equation of the line is $y = -5x + \tfrac{2}{9}$. *See also* LINE, EQUATION OF.

SLOPE OF A CURVE AT A POINT,

the slope of the TANGENT LINE to the curve at that point. When the tangent is vertical,

the slope of the line is not defined, so the curve has no slope at that point. (See figure.)

SLOPE OF A LINE,

the ratio of the change in y values (Δy) to the change in x values (Δx), of the coordinates of any two points on the line. The letter m is used to designate the slope of a line passing through points (x_1, y_1) and (x_2, y_2). $m = \dfrac{y_2 - y_1}{x_2 - x_1}$ or $\dfrac{\Delta y}{\Delta x}$ read "delta y over delta x."

The slope of a line is also the tangent (*see* TANGENT OF AN ANGLE) of the acute angle (ANGLE OF INCLINATION) that the line makes with the x-axis.

In $y = mx + b$, the SLOPE-INTERCEPT FORM OF AN EQUATION OF A LINE, the slope is the coefficient of x. If the equation is $3x + 2y = 8$, then $y = -\tfrac{3}{2}x + 4$ and the slope is $-3/2$.

The slope of a line parallel to the x axis is 0 since Δy is 0. A line parallel to the y axis has no slope since $\dfrac{\Delta y}{\Delta x}$ is undefined for $\Delta x = 0$.

If the line is not parallel to the x-axis or to the y-axis, its slope may be positive or negative, depending on the angle it forms with the x-axis. If the angle from the positive side of the x-axis is acute, the slope is positive; if the angle is obtuse, the slope is negative.

Ex. 1: In Fig. 1, line AB passes through points $(-3,-2)$ and $(1,4)$, and for those two points $\Delta x = 4$ and $\Delta y = 6$.

$$m = \frac{\Delta y}{\Delta x} = \frac{6}{4} = \frac{3}{2}$$

or

$$m = \frac{y_2 - y_1}{x_2 - x_1} = \frac{4 - (-2)}{1 - (-3)} = \frac{6}{4} = \frac{3}{2}.$$

The angle line AB makes with the x-axis is acute, therefore the slope of line AB is positive.

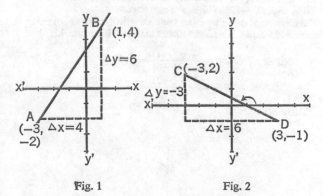

Fig. 1   Fig. 2

Ex. 2: In Fig. 2, line CD passes through points $(3,-1)$ and $(-3,2)$, and for those two points $\Delta x = 6$ and $\Delta y = 3$.

$$m = \frac{\Delta y}{\Delta x} = -\frac{3}{6} = -\frac{1}{2}$$

or

$$m = \frac{y_2 - y_1}{x_2 - x_1} = \frac{-1 - 2}{3 - (-3)} = \frac{-3}{6} = -\frac{1}{2}.$$

The angle line CD makes with the x-axis is obtuse, therefore the slope of line CD is negative.

If two lines are PARALLEL LINES their slopes are equal; conversely, if two lines have equal slopes the lines are parallel. If the slopes of opposite sides of a QUADRILATERAL are equal, the quadrilateral is a PARALLELOGRAM.

Ex. 3: Show that quadrilateral with vertices $A(-3,-3)$, $B(3,1)$, $C(5,5)$ and $D(-1,1)$ is a parallelogram. (See Fig. 3.)

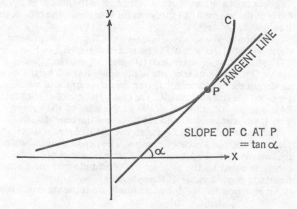

SLOPE OF C AT P
= tan α

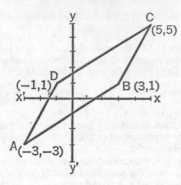

Fig. 3

Sol.: Slope of $AB = \dfrac{1-(-3)}{3-(-3)} = \dfrac{4}{6} = \dfrac{2}{3}$.

Slope of $CD = \dfrac{5-1}{5-(-1)} = \dfrac{4}{6} = \dfrac{2}{3}$.

Therefore, $AB \parallel CD$.

Slope of $BC = \dfrac{5-1}{5-3} = \dfrac{4}{2} = 2$.

Slope of $AD = \dfrac{1-(-3)}{-1-(-3)} = \dfrac{4}{2} = 2$.

Therefore $BC \parallel AD$.

It follows that $ABCD$ is a parallelogram.

If two lines are PERPENDICULAR the slope of one is the negative reciprocal of the slope of the other: $m_1 = -\dfrac{1}{m_2}$. The product of their slopes is -1. Conversely, if the product of the slopes of two lines equals -1, the lines are perpendicular.

Ex. 4: Show that the triangle with vertices $A(-5,-1)$, $B(6,-2)$, and $C(1,4)$ is a RIGHT TRIANGLE. (See Fig. 4.)

Sol.: Slope of $AC = \dfrac{4-(-1)}{1-(-5)} = \dfrac{5}{6}$.

Slope of $BC = \dfrac{4-(-2)}{1-6} = -\dfrac{6}{5}$.

Therefore, $AC \perp BC$.

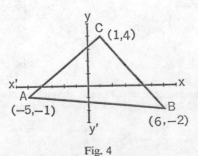

Fig. 4

It follows that $\angle C$ is a right angle and $\triangle ABC$ is a right triangle.

SLOPE-POINT FORM OF AN EQUATION OF A LINE, the equation of a line in the form $m = \dfrac{y_2 - y_1}{x_2 - x_1}$ in which m is the slope, (x_1,y_1) the coordinates of a given point, and (x_2,y_2) represent the coordinates of a second point on the line.

Ex.: Find the equation of a line if its slope is $\frac{3}{2}$ and the coordinates of a point on the line are $(-4,-9)$.

Sol.:

$$\frac{3}{2} = \frac{y-(-9)}{x-(-4)}$$

$$\frac{3}{2} = \frac{y+9}{x+4},$$

then $3x + 12 = 2y + 18$

or $3x - 2y = 6$.

SOLUTION OF AN EQUATION, the ROOT of the EQUATION.

SOROBAN, *see* ABACUS.

SPHERE, a closed surface all points of which are equidistant from a point within called the center. A LINE SEGMENT from the center to any point on the sphere is a RADIUS. A line segment through the center and joining two points on the sphere is a diameter. A sphere may be generated by revolving a SEMICIRCLE through 360° about its diameter as the axis.

A circle formed by the intersection of a sphere and a plane that passes through the center of the sphere is a great circle of the sphere. A circle formed by the intersection of a sphere and a plane is called a small circle of a sphere.

The SPHERICAL DISTANCE equal to one fourth of a great circle, is called a quadrant of a great circle on a sphere. If a point is at the distance of a quadrant from two points on the great circle (not the end points of a DIAMETER), it is the pole of the great circle. In sphere O (see Fig. 1), circle ABC is a great circle and P is the pole of circle ABC. PB and PC are quadrants.

The line through the center of the sphere PERPENDICULAR to the PLANE of a circle is called an *axis of a circle of a sphere.* In sphere O (see Fig. 2), if AB is perpendicular to the plane of circle C, it is the AXIS of the circle. The end points of the axis AB are the poles of the circle.

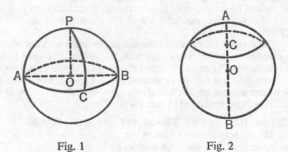

Fig. 1   Fig. 2

The polar distance of a circle of a sphere is the spherical distance from any point on the circle to the nearest pole. In Fig. 3, if PP' is the axis of small circle ABC, then $\overset{\frown}{PA}$ is the polar distance of the circle. $\overset{\frown}{PB}$ and $\overset{\frown}{PC}$ are also polar distances. If the circle is a great circle, the polar distance is a quadrant.

The area of a sphere is equal to four times the area of any great circle of the sphere. If S represents the area and r, the radius, the formula is $S = 4\pi r^2$.

The volume of a sphere is equal to one third of the product of the RADIUS and the area of the surface of the sphere, or $V = \frac{4}{3}\pi r^3$.

The part of a sphere between two great semicircles is a *lune of a sphere.* The angle of the lune is the angle formed by the intersection of the SEMICIRCLES. The area of the surface of a lune depends on the size of its angle. The area of a lune of $n°$ is equal to $2n$ SPHERICAL DEGREES or $n/360$ of the area of the sphere. In Fig. 4, semicircles ABC and ADC enclose the lune $ABCD$.

The surface of a sphere between two parallel planes that intersect the sphere is a *zone of a sphere.* The perpendicular between the two planes is the altitude of the zone. The area of a zone of a sphere is equal to the product of its altitude and the circumference of a great circle of the sphere or $S = 2\pi rh$.

An equation for the sphere is found from the DISTANCE FOR-

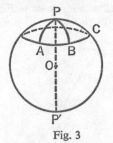

Fig. 3

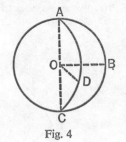

Fig. 4

MULA. If the center of the sphere is at the point (h,k,l) and the radius is r, the equation of the sphere is:

$$(x - h)^2 + (y - k)^2 + (z - l)^2 = r^2. \text{ See Fig. 5.}$$

Ex. 1: Give the equation of the sphere with center (1,3,2) and radius 2.

Sol.: $(x - 1)^2 + (y - 3)^2 + (z - 2)^2 = 4.$

Ex. 2: Find the center and radius of the sphere given by the equation below. Use the method of COMPLETING SQUARES to put it into the standard form given above.

$$x^2 + y^2 + z^2 + 4x - 6y + 10z + 1 = 0.$$

Sol.: Completing squares gives:

$$(x + 2)^2 - 4 + (y - 3)^2 - 9 + (z + 5)^2 - 25 + 1 = 0.$$

When constants are transposed we have:

$$(x + 2)^2 + (y - 3)^2 + (z + 5)^2 = 37$$

The center is at $(-2,3,-5)$ and the radius is $\sqrt{37}$.

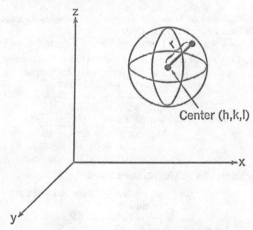

Center (h,k,l)

Fig. 5

SPHERICAL ANGLE, the angle on a sphere formed by two intersecting arcs of GREAT CIRCLES. The arcs are the sides of the

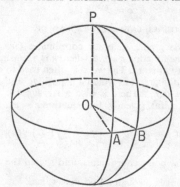

angle and the point of intersection is its vertex. A spherical angle is equal in degrees to the dihedral angle formed by the planes of the great circles.

In the figure, APB is a spherical angle, and AB is an arc of the great circle having as its pole vertex P. Dihedral angle A-PO-B is equal in degrees to its plane angle AOB, which is measured by $\overarc{AB}$. Therefore,

$$\angle APB \doteq \overarc{AB}.$$

SPHERICAL COORDINATE SYSTEM, see COORDINATE SYSTEM; COORDINATES, SPHERICAL.

SPHERICAL DEGREE, the unit for measuring a spherical surface. It is 1/90 of the surface of a TRIRECTANGULAR SPHERICAL TRIANGLE and the area of a trirectangular spherical triangle equals 1/8 the area of the sphere. Therefore, each of the 720° equal parts of a sphere is a spherical degree. In the figure, AB and AC are quadrants and $\overarc{BC} = 1°$, therefore the area of $\triangle ABC$ is one spherical degree.

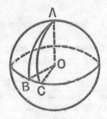

SPHERICAL DISTANCE, between two points on a SPHERE, the length of the minor ARC of the GREAT CIRCLE passing through the two points.

SPHERICAL EXCESS, E, of a SPHERICAL TRIANGLE, $E = (A + B + C) - 180°$. The number of degrees by which a given spherical triangle exceeds the number of degrees (180°) in the angles of any plane triangle.

SPHERICAL SECTOR, the figure formed by rotating a SECTOR OF A CIRCLE about a diameter. (See figure.) The volume of the spherical sector is given by $V = \frac{2}{3}\pi r^2 h = \frac{1}{6}D^2 h$.

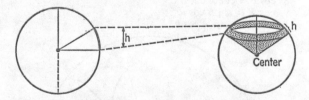

SPHERICAL TRIANGLE, the triangle formed on the surface of the sphere by the arcs of three GREAT CIRCLES. The vertices of the three spherical angles are the vertices of the triangle and are designated by A, B, and C. The arcs of the great circles are the sides of the triangle and are designated by a, b, and c. Any side of a spherical triangle is a minor arc of a great circle.

The sum of any two sides of the triangle is greater than the third side. The sum of the three sides is less than 360°. The sum of the three angles is greater than 180° and less than 540°.

In spherical triangle ABC, shown in Fig. 1, sides a, b, and c are equal in degrees to face angles BOC, AOC, and AOB respectively. SPHERICAL ANGLE CAB is equal in degrees to DIHEDRAL ANGLE C-AO-B.

The area of a spherical triangle is obtained by the formula:

$K = \dfrac{\pi r^2 E}{180}$, where E is the SPHERICAL EXCESS equal to $(A + B + C) - 180°$. If the spherical excess is in RADIANS, the formula is $K = r^2 E$.

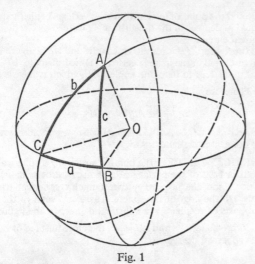

Fig. 1

Since a quadrant contains 90°, angles and arcs less than 90° are said to be in the first quadrant and angles and arcs between 90° and 180° are in the second quadrant.

The following are the laws of quadrants for right spherical triangles:

1. An angle and its opposite side are in the same quadrant.

2. If any two sides of the triangle are in the same quadrant, the third side is in the first quadrant.

3. If two sides are in different quadrants, the third side is in the second quadrant.

Right spherical triangles may be solved by using the ten fundamental theorems for spherical triangle ABC with right angle C:

1. $\sin a = \sin A \sin c.$
2. $\cos c = \cos b \cos a.$
3. $\sin b = \sin B \sin c.$
4. $\tan b = \cos A \tan c.$
5. $\tan a = \cos B \tan c.$
6. $\tan a = \tan A \sin b.$
7. $\tan b = \tan B \sin a.$
8. $\cos c = \cot A \cot B.$
9. $\cos A = \sin B \cos a.$
10. $\cos B = \sin A \cos b.$

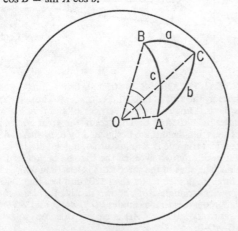

Fig. 2

In Fig. 2, ABC is a right spherical triangle with right angle C.

$$\angle AOB \doteq C,$$
$$\angle AOC \doteq b, \text{ and}$$
$$\angle BOC \doteq a.$$

To solve an isosceles triangle, ABC with $a = b$, as in Fig. 3, pass a great circle through C and perpendicular to AB at D.

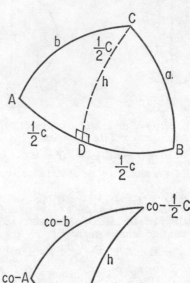

Fig. 3

Then ACD and BCD are right spherical triangles. Use NAPIER'S RULES for solving triangle ACD.

Ex.: Solve $\triangle ABC$, given $a = b = 68°20'$, and $C = 110°40'$

Sol.: Solving for A: $\sin(\text{co} - b) = \tan(\text{co} - \tfrac{1}{2}C)\tan(\text{co} - A).$
$$\cos b = \cot \tfrac{1}{2}C \cot A, \text{ or}$$
$$\cot A = \cos b \tan \tfrac{1}{2}C.$$
$$\cot A = \cos 68°20' \tan 55°20'.$$
$$\log \cos 68°20' = 9.5673 - 10$$
$$\log \tan 55°20' = \underline{\quad .1602\quad}$$
$$\log \cot A = 9.7275 - 10$$
$$A = 61°54', \text{ approx.}$$
$$B = 61°54', \text{ approx.}$$

Sol.: Solve for c: Use Napier's Rules.
$$\sin \tfrac{1}{2}c = \cos(\text{co} - b)\cos(\text{co} - \tfrac{1}{2}C).$$
$$\sin \tfrac{1}{2}c = \sin b \sin \tfrac{1}{2}C.$$
$$\sin \tfrac{1}{2}c = \sin 68°20' \sin 55°20'$$
$$\log \sin 68°20' = 9.9682 - 10$$
$$\log \sin 55°20' = \underline{9.9151 - 10}$$
$$\log \sin \tfrac{1}{2}c = 19.8833 - 20$$
$$\tfrac{1}{2}c = 49°51'.$$
$$c = 99°42'.$$

See also COSINES, LAW OF; SINES, LAW OF.

SPIRAL, the graph, in polar coordinates (*see* COORDINATES, POLAR), of the function $r = k\theta$, where k is a constant and θ is the independent VARIABLE. The word is often used to designate only that part of the graph in which θ is positive. Either is called an *Archimedian spiral*. There is also a HYPERBOLIC SPIRAL, and a logarithmic spiral, given by the equation $r = e^{a\theta}.$

Ex. 1: Let $f(\theta) = \dfrac{1}{\pi}\theta.$ Plot $f\left(\dfrac{\pi}{4}\right), f\left(\dfrac{\pi}{2}\right), f(\pi), f\left(\dfrac{3\pi}{2}\right), f(2\pi),$

$f\left(\dfrac{9\pi}{4}\right) \cdot f,$ on polar coordinates, and sketch the spiral through

them, if θ ranges through all positive values.

Sol.: See Fig. 1a.

Ex. 2: Let $f(x) = \dfrac{\theta}{\pi}$. Plot the graph of $f(\theta)$ when θ ranges over all negative values, using the fact that in this case r will be negative for each θ.

Sol.: See Fig. 1b.

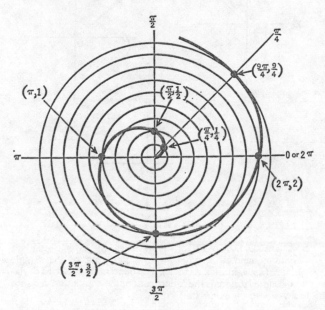

a·

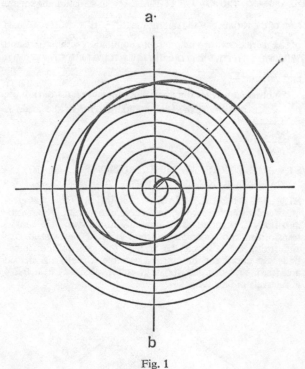

b

Fig. 1

SQUARE, in geometry, a RECTANGLE with two adjacent sides equal. It may also be defined as an equiangular and equilateral PARALLELOGRAM. Since a square is a parallelogram and a special kind of rectangle and RHOMBUS, it has all of the properties of a parallelogram, of a rhombus, and of a rectangle.

SQUARE ROOT, one of two equal FACTORS of a number. Since $16 = 4 \times 4$, a square root of 16 is 4; $(-4)(-4)$ also equals 16; therefore, -4 is also a square root of 16. The square root of an algebraic term is the square root of the NUMERICAL COEFFICIENT multiplied by the literal COEFFICIENTS, the EXPONENTS of which are one half of the exponents in the original term. The two square roots of $25x^6y^4$ are $+5x^3y^2$ and $-5x^3y^2$. The square root symbol $\sqrt{\ }$ with a VINCULUM over the number indicates the principal square root of that number, as $\sqrt{36} = 6$. Most numbers do not have exact square roots, as 12, x^3, and $24x^6y^9$. See RADICAL. See Table NO. 18.

The square root of zero is zero, but negative numbers do not have square roots in the REAL NUMBER system. Thus the graph of $y = \sqrt{x}$ shown in the figure, is limited to the right half of the plane. The process for finding the square root of a number is as follows.

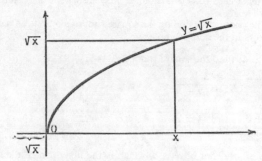

Ex. 1: Find the positive square root of 3136.

Sol.: Separate the number into pairs of DIGITS from right to left, as 31 36. If we think of 3136 as 31 hundreds + 36, we know its square root will be greater than fifty and less than 60, since 3136 is between the PERFECT SQUARES 2500 and 3600.

$$
\begin{array}{r}
5\ \ 6 \\
\sqrt{31\ 36} \\
25 \\
\hline
6\ 36 \\
6 \\
\hline
6\ 36
\end{array}
$$

$20 \times 5 = 100$

$106 \times 6 =$

When the partial root 5 is squared and placed under the first pair of digits there is a remainder of 6. Bring down the next pair of digits. Multiply the partial root 5 by 20 for the partial DIVISOR. Divide 636 by 100. Notice that the QUOTIENT 6 must be added to 100 to complete the divisor and it is also placed in the root. Multiply 6 by 106. There is no remainder. Therefore, 56 is the positive square root of 3136.

Check: $56 \times 56 = 3136$.

To find the positive square root of a number that contains a decimal, as 985.96, separate the number into pairs of digits from the decimal point: 9 85. 96. If there is an odd number of decimals add a zero to make the pair.

Ex. 2: Find the square root of 985.96.

Sol.:

$$
\begin{array}{r}
3\ 1\ .4 \\
\sqrt{9\ 85.\ 96} \\
9 \\
\hline
85 \\
61 \\
\hline
2496 \\
2496 \\
\hline
\end{array}
$$

$20 \times 3 = 60$

$61 \times 1 =$

$20 \times 31 = 620$

$624 \times 4 =$

Check: $\quad 31.4 \times 31.4 = 985.96$.

Thus, 9 is a perfect square with a square root of three. There is no remainder. Bring down the next pair. Follow the same pattern as in Example 1. Place the decimal in the root.

The square root of a number may be found by logarithms as in the following example.

Ex. 3: Find the positive square root of 635 to the nearest tenth.

$$\text{Log } N = \tfrac{1}{2} \log 635 = \tfrac{1}{2}\ 2.8028.$$

Sol.: $N = \sqrt{635} = (635)^{1/2}$.
$$\text{Log } N = 1.4014$$
$$N = 25.2.$$

Check: $25.2 \times 25.2 = 635.04.$

The square root of a number may also be found using the SLIDE RULE.

The process for finding the square root of a POLYNOMIAL is as follows in the next example.

Ex. 4: Find the square root of $a^2 + 6a + 9$.

Sol.:
$$\begin{array}{r} a\ +3 \\ \sqrt{a^2 + 6a + 9} \\ a^2 \end{array}$$

$$\begin{array}{r} 2a + 3 \\ (2a + 3)3 = \end{array} \bigg| \begin{array}{l} 6a + 9 \\ 6a + 9 \end{array}$$

The square root of a^2 is a, which is the first term of the root. Bring down $6a + 9$. Multiply the partial root a by 2 and place the $2a$ as shown. Divide $6a$ by $2a$ .Place the quotient 3 with its plus sign in the root and also add it to $2a$ for the complete divisor $2a + 3$. Multiply $2a + 3$ by 3 and place the product under $6a + 9$. There is no remainder. The square root of $a^2 + 6a + 9$ is $a + 3$.

Ex. 5: Find square root of $x^4 - 12x + 4 - 6x^3 + 13x^2$.

Sol.: Arrange in descending powers of x.

$$\begin{array}{r} x^2 - 3x\ +\ 2 \\ \sqrt{x^4 - 6x^3 + 13x^2 - 12x + 4} \\ x^4 \end{array}$$

$$\begin{array}{r} 2x^2 - 3x \\ (2x^2 - 3x)(-3x) = \end{array} \bigg| \begin{array}{l} -6x^3 + 13x^2 \\ -6x^3 + 9x^2 \end{array}$$

$$\begin{array}{r} 2x^2 - 6x + 2 \\ (2x^2 - 6x + 2)(2) = \end{array} \bigg| \begin{array}{l} +4x^2 - 12x + 4 \\ +4x^2 - 12x + 4 \end{array}$$

Check: Multiply $x^2 - 3x + 2$ by $x^2 - 3x + 2$.
$$\begin{array}{r} x^2 - 3x + 2 \\ x^2 - 3x + 2 \\ \hline x^4 - 3x^3 +\ 2x^2 \\ -3x^3 +\ 9x^2 - 6x \\ +\ 2x^2 - 6x + 4 \\ \hline x^4 - 6x^3 + 13x^2 - 12x + 4. \end{array}$$

See also TABLE NO. 18.

SQUARING THE CIRCLE, one of the three classical problems of antiquity, the problem of constructing a SQUARE with the same area as that of a given CIRCLE by using an unmarked straight edge and compass. The problem cannot be solved, since the area of the circle (if it is of radius 1) is π, and the side of the square of equal area is $\sqrt{\pi}$; the solution requires constructing $\sqrt{\pi}$ which is impossible with a straight edge and compass.

STANDARD ANGLE POSITION, the position of an angle with reference to a pair of coordinate axes, when the vertex of the angle is the ORIGIN and its initial side coincides with the positive side of the x-axis. (See figure.)

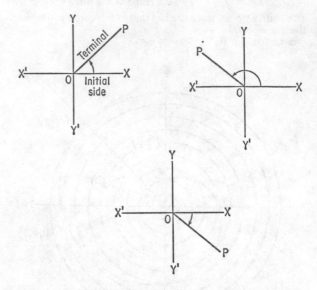

STANDARD DEVIATION, in statistics, the sample standard deviation, denoted s, equals the square root of the sample variance (*see* VARIANCE, SAMPLE). The population standard deviation, denoted σ, equals the square root of the population variance (*see* VARIANCE, POPULATION).

STANDARD ERROR OF THE MEAN, in statistics, the square root of the variance of the sample mean, $\frac{\sigma}{\sqrt{n}}$, if RANDOM SAMPLES of size n are drawn from an infinite population with mean μ and variance σ^2, where the population of sample means has mean μ and variance $\frac{\sigma^2}{n}$.

If n observations are drawn without replacement from a finite population of size N, then the standard error of the mean is

$$\sqrt{\frac{N - n}{N - 1}} \cdot \frac{\sigma}{\sqrt{n}}.$$

STANDARD NORMAL DISTRIBUTION, in statistics, the NORMAL DISTRIBUTION that has mean 0 and variance 1.

STANDARD NORMAL TABLE, in statistics, a table that gives areas under the standard normal curve, the graph of the STANDARD NORMAL DISTRIBUTION. Since any normal variable can be transformed into a standard normal variable (*see* NORMAL DISTRIBUTION), the table can be used to find probabilities (areas under the curve) for any normal variable. Usually the shaded area (see figure), denoted $A(z)$, is given for values of z from 0 to 4 at intervals of 0.01 unit.

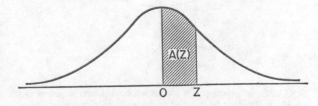

Ex.: Let x be a normal random variable with mean 53 and variance 100. Find the probability that x lies between 41 and 56.

Sol.: Since $z = \dfrac{x - \mu}{\sigma} = \dfrac{x - 53}{10}$, then

$$P(41 < x < 56) = P\left(\frac{41 - 53}{10} < z < \frac{56 - 53}{10}\right)$$
$$= P(-1.20 < z < .3) = .5028.$$

STATIONARY POINT, a point on a curve at which the TANGENT LINE is horizontal. Thus, for a function $y = f(x)$, the point at which the derivative (*see* DERIVATIVE OF A FUNCTION) $f'(x) = 0$.

STATISTIC, in statistics, a numerical quantity that is calculated from sample observations. Some common statistics are the sample mean (*see* MEAN, SAMPLE) median, proportion, range, and variance (*see* VARIANCE, SAMPLE).

STATISTICAL INFERENCE, the process of arriving at conclusions or decisions concerning the PARAMETERS of populations on the basis of information contained in the samples. Traditionally, problems of statistical inference have been classified into problems of estimation and problems of testing hypotheses.

A problem of estimation may be one in which the inference is that the "true" average life of a tube is estimated to be 5,000 hours. Such problems require that values be found for unknown parameters of distributions. Thus, the lifetimes of the tubes are considered to be values assumed by random variables having exponential distributions with the parameter θ, and the "true" average life that is estimated is the parameter θ.

A problem of testing hypotheses may be one in which the inference is the decision that one kind of corn has a higher yield than another. Such problems deal with reaching conclusions about assumed values of the parameters. Thus, if the yields of two varieties of corn are considered as random samples from populations with means μ_1 and μ_2 the decision which must be made is whether $\mu_1 > \mu_2$, $\mu_1 = \mu_2$ or $\mu_1 < \mu_2$.

STATISTICS, in applied mathematics, a body of knowledge used to analyze quantitive data with its own symbolism, terminology, content, theorems, and techniques.

The use of statistical techniques is very widespread. They are used in government, to study economic data, taxation, spending of public funds, and to evaluate the performance of military equipment, e.g., pistol bullets and huge missiles.

Industrial uses of statistics include evaluation of new products before they are marketed, quality control of products being manufactured, marketing, and the analysis of the effectiveness of advertising. Insurance companies make use of statistics in establishing their rates at a realistic level. Statistics is also used in geology, biology, psychology, educational research, sociology —in any area in which decisions must be made on the basis of incomplete information.

That part of statistics that deals primarily with the description of sample data is known as descriptive statistics. Some of the techniques of this part of statistics are the classification of data; the drawing of HISTOGRAMS that correspond to the frequency distributions that result after the data are classified; the representation of data by other sorts of graphs; the computation of sample means (*see* MEAN, SAMPLE, MEDIANS, or MODES; the computation of sample variances (*see* VARIANCE, SAMPLE), MEAN ABSOLUTE DEVIATIONS, and RANGES.

A second important kind of statistics is known as inferential statistics or as statistical inference. Statistics has been described as the science of making decisions in the face of uncertainty—that is, making the best decision on the basis of incomplete information. In order to reach a decision about a population, a sample (usually rather small in comparison with the population) of that population is selected from it. The selection is usually made by a random process, and yields a sample known as a RANDOM SAMPLE. On the basis of the random sample, the experimenter infers properties of the population. Such an inference about populations on the basis of samples is known as statistical inference.

Thus, statistical inference is the use of samples to reach conclusions about the populations from which those samples have been drawn.

STOCHASTIC VARIABLE (stoh-kas'-tik), in statistics, another name for RANDOM VARIABLE or *chance variable*.

STRAIGHT ANGLE, an ANGLE whose sides extend in opposite directions from the vertex and form a straight line. A straight angle contains 180°.

In the figure, AOB is a straight angle, since sides AO and OB form a straight line.

An axiom of geometry states that all straight angles are equal.

STRATIFIED SAMPLE, in statistics, a sample found by division of the population into compartments, called strata, so that the sample contains preassigned proportions from each of the strata. Within each stratum, the individuals are selected at random.

In a sample of male students from a university, for example, it might be desirable for the sample to contain approximately the same proportions from each of the four classes and the graduate school as the population (the university) itself does.

STROPHOID (strahf'-oid). If AQ is a variable line through fixed point $A(-a,0)$ and the y-axis at Q, with points P and P' on AQ such that $PQ = P'Q = OQ$, the LOCUS of points P and P' as AQ rotates through A is called a strophoid (see figure). The equation of the strophoid in rectangular coordinates (*see* COORDINATES, RECTANGULAR) is given by $y^2 = x^2\left(\dfrac{a + x}{a - x}\right)$. If angle $OAP = \theta$, the equation in polar coordinates (*see* COORDINATES, POLAR) is given by $r = a(\sec\theta = \tan\theta)$. The PARAMETRIC EQUATIONS are given by $x = a\sin\theta$, $y = a\tan\theta(1 + \sin\theta)$.

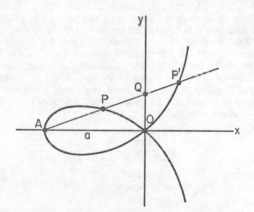

SUBSET, in mathematics, *see* SET.

SUBSTITUTION, of one quantity for another, replacing a VARIABLE by a number or another variable or expression. The variable is replaced by a number when checking the ROOT of an EQUATION or when evaluating an ALGEBRAIC EXPRESSION or FORMULA.

Ex. 1: Check the root $x = 3$ in the equation $5x + 3 = 21 - x$.

Sol.: Replace x with 3 in the equation:

$$5(3) + 3 = 21 - 3.$$

Find the numerical value of both members of the equation:

$$15 + 3 = 18; \qquad 21 - 3 = 18.$$

Thus $18 = 18$ is an identity, and the root checks.

Ex. 2: Evaluate the expression $a^2 - 2ab^2$ when $a = 3$ and $b = 4$.

Sol.: Replace a with 3 and b with 4:

$$3^2 - 2(3)(4)^2.$$

Perform the indicated operations and combine:

$$9 - 2(3)(16) = 9 - (6)(16) = 9 - 96 = -87.$$

The value of $a^2 - 2ab^2$, when $a = 3$ and $b = 4$ is -87.
See also SOLUTION OF AN EQUATION.

SUBTEND, measure off. An ANGLE of a CIRCLE is said to subtend an ARC of the circle. The subtended arc is the arc on the circumference of the circle between the sides of the angle. In the figure, angle CAB subtends arc BC.

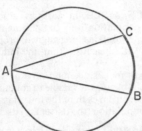

SUBTRACTION, the process of finding one of two numbers when their sum and one of the numbers are given. What number added to 5 equals 8, or $5 + ? = 8$. Then, $8 - 5 = 3$. Subtraction, therefore, is the inverse operation of ADDITION, the sum becoming the MINUEND and the given number the SUBTRAHEND in the subtraction process. From this it can be seen that the statement "from 8 subtract 5" may be written $8 - 5$. In like manner, if we subtract -5 from 8, it may be written $8 - (-5)$ which, by the NUMBER LINES, becomes the sum of their ABSOLUTE VALUES or $8 + 5$. Therefore, the simplified rule for algebraic subtraction is: *Change the sign of the subtrahend and proceed as in algebraic addition.* The subtraction process may be stated in several ways, as: from 8 subtract 5, take 5 from 8, 8 minus 5, 8 less 5, the difference of 8 and 5, 8 diminished by 5, or 5 less than 8. It must be noted that in each case 8 is the minuend and 5 the subtrahend.

If the DIGITS of the minuend are each larger than the corresponding digits of the subtrahend, use the additive method, or simply take the smaller number from the larger. Place digits in their proper columns.

Ex. 1:   749   7 hundreds + 4 tens + 9 units
          -526 5 hundreds + 2 tens + 6 units
             223   2 hundreds + 2 tens + 3 units

Check: 223   Difference
        $+526$ Subtrahend
         749   Minuend

If some of the digits of the minuend are smaller than the corresponding digits of the subtrahend, it will be necessary to use the *exchange method.*

Ex. 2:   4534   4 thousands + 5 hundreds + 3 tens + 4 units
       -1965 1 thousand + 9 hundreds + 6 tens + 5 units

Exchange 1 ten for 10 units, then subtract 5 from 14. The 3 in the ten's column is now 2, from which 6 may not be subtracted, therefore, 1 hundred may be exchanged for 10 tens, which are added to the 2 tens now in that column. Subtract 6 tens from 12 tens. Exchange one thousand for 10 hundreds and add to the 4 in the hundreds column, then subtract 9 hundreds from 14 hundreds. The operation now becomes

3 thousands + 14 hundreds + 12 tens + 14 units
1 thousand + 9 hundreds + 6 tens + 5 units
―――――――――――――――――――――――――――――――
2 thousands + 5 hundreds + 6 tens + 9 units

The difference is 2569. If the exchange is made mentally, the process is simplified.

       14 14
    3 12
     4534   Think 5 units from 14 units; 6 tens from 12 tens; 9
   -1965 hundreds from 14 hundreds; and 1 thousand from 3
     2569   thousands.

Check: 2569   Difference
        $+1965$ Subtrahend
        4534   Minuend

Ex. 3: Subtract 2387 from 6004.

   6004   Because there are no hundreds nor tens in the minu-
-2387 end, 1 thousand must be exchanged for ten hundreds, then the minuend becomes 5 thousands + 10 hundreds + 0 tens + 4 units. It is necessary to exchange 1 hundred for 10 tens, and finally 1 ten for 10 units. The example becomes

5 thousands + 9 hundreds + 9 tens + 14 units
2 thousands + 3 hundreds + 8 tens + 7 units
―――――――――――――――――――――――――――――――
3 thousands + 6 hundreds + 1 ten + 7 units

The difference is 3617.

   5 9 9 14
   6004   The small numbers above the minuend will not be
-2387 necessary after practice.
   3617

Always check by adding the difference to the subtrahend to obtain the minuend.

Check: $3617 + 2387 = 6004.$

To subtract algebraic terms, find the difference of their NUMERICAL COEFFICIENTS multiplied by their common literal FACTORS. Only terms with identical literal factors may be subtracted. To subtract POLYNOMIALS, place the terms of the subtrahend under like terms of the minuend. Mentally change all signs of the subtrahend and combine as in algebraic addition.

Ex. 4: Subtract $5x$ from $12x$.

     $12x$ Minuend
      $5x$ Subtrahend
      $7x$ *Check:* $7x + 5x = 12x.$

Ex. 5: Subtract $-3ab$ from 0.

      0
   $-3ab$
    $3ab$ *Check:* $3ab - 3ab = 0.$

Ex. 6: Subtract the sum of $4x + 2y$ and $3x - 5y$ from the sum of $5x - 3y$ and $7x + 2y$. Add:

     $4x + 2y$ $5x - 3y$
     $3x - 5y$ $7x + 2y$
     $7x - 3y$ $12x - y$

Then subtract $7x - 3y$ from $12x - y$.

   $12x - y$
   $7x - 3y$
   $5x + 2y$ *Check:* $(5x + 2y) + (7x - 3y) = 12x - y.$

To subtract COMPLEX NUMBERS, the real and the imaginary parts are subtracted separately. For example, subtract $3a - 2i$ from $6a + 5i$.

   $6a + 5i$ minuend
   $3a - 2i$ change signs of subtrahend and combine.
   $3a + 7i$

Check: $(3a + 7i) + (3a - 2i) = 6a + 5i.$

See also IMAGINARY NUMBER; REAL NUMBERS.

To subtract fractions, the NUMERATOR of the subtrahend is subtracted from the numerator of the minuend and their difference placed over the common denominator (*see* LOWEST COMMON DENOMINATOR). For example,

$$\frac{3a}{4} - \frac{a}{4} = \frac{2a}{4} \text{ or } \frac{a}{2}.$$

If the numerator of the subtrahend is a polynomial all of its signs are changed.

$$\frac{2x+5}{8} - \frac{x-3}{8} = \frac{(2x+5)-(x-3)}{8}$$
$$= \frac{2x+5-x+3}{8} = \frac{x+8}{8}.$$

Note that the x in the numerator $x - 3$ is plus, the minus in front of the fraction is a sign of operation to indicate subtraction. When the signs of the numerator are changed it becomes $-x + 3$.

SUBTRACTION AXIOM. An AXIOM OF EQUALITY (or INEQUALITY): If equal quantities are subtracted from the same or equal quantities, the differences are equal. E.g., if $a = b$ then $a - 5 = b - 5$. The axiom may be expressed symbolically as follows: If $a = b$ and $c = d$, then $a - c = b - d$.

SUBTRAHEND (sub'-trah-hend), the number that is subtracted from another number called the MINUEND. In a SUBTRACTION example such as, subtract 16 from 84, the subtrahend is 16, and is written $(+84) - (+16)$. When the sign of the subtrahend is changed, it becomes simply $84 - 16$. If the example is to subtract -16 from 84, it is written $(+84) - (-16)$ or $84 + 16$. The plus signs are used here to avoid confusing the subtraction process with the addition of signed numbers. The subtrahend may also be a POLYNOMIAL. For example,

$$(4a^2 - 6a + 3) - (3a^2 + 5a - 2).$$

$(3a^2 + 5a - 2)$ is the subtrahend and when its signs are changed, the example becomes $4a^2 - 6a + 3 - 3a^2 - 5a + 2$, and LIKE TERMS are then combined algebraically.

SUM, the result of an ADDITION operation when the ADDENDS have been combined.

SUM, LOGICAL, *see* DISJUNCTION.

SUMMATION NOTATION, in statistics, a shorthand notation for indicating sums. For example, $1 + 2 + \cdots + n$ can be written $\sum_{k=1}^{n} k$. The letter k is replaced successively by $1, 2, \ldots$, n and is called the index of summation. The first and last integers which the index is allowed to equal are called the limits of summation. In the example above, 1 is the lower limit of summation, and n is the upper limit.

SUM OF ANGLES, of any POLYGON of n sides, equals $(n - 2)$ straight angles or $(n - 2)180°$. The sum of the angles of a quadrilateral equals $(4 - 2)180°$ equals 360°. The sum of the angles of a hexagon equals $(6 - 2)180°$ equals 720°.

SUM OF TWO CUBES, a special case of FACTORING in which one factor is a BINOMIAL and the other a TRINOMIAL. The binomial factor is the sum of the CUBE ROOTS of the two cubes. The trinomial is obtained from the binomial factor. It is the square of the first term minus the product of the two terms plus the square of the second term.

Exs.: $x^3 + y^3 = (x + y)(x^2 - xy + y^2)$
$8x^3 + 27y^3 = (2x + 3y)(4x^2 - 6xy + 9y^2).$

See also DIFFERENCE OF TWO CUBES.

SUPPLEMENTARY ANGLES, two angles whose sum is 180° or a STRAIGHT ANGLE. In Fig. 1, a and b are supplementary.

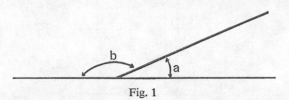

Fig. 1

Two angles are supplementary if: (1) they are adjacent angles whose exterior sides lie in a straight line (see Fig. 1); (2) they are two consecutive angles of a PARALLELOGRAM (see Fig. 2.); or (3) they are interior angles on the same side of a transversal, when the transversal cuts two PARALLEL LINES (see Fig. 3.).

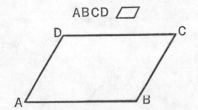

Fig. 2 ∠A is a supplement of ∠D
∠B is a supplement of ∠C

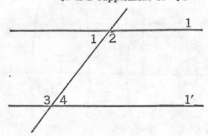

Fig. 3 ∠1 is a supplement of ∠3
∠2 is a supplement of ∠4

SURD, an IRRATIONAL NUMBER, such as $\sqrt{2}$ and $\sqrt[3]{7}$.

SURFACE, the graph in three dimensions of an equation in three variables. The surface described by the equation $x^2 + y^2 + z^2 = 1$ is a SPHERE of radius 1, center $(0,0)$.

The surface of a geometric figure is the set of points which satisfy an equation in two or more variables. A surface may be planar, such as the surface of a TRIANGLE; curved, as of a sphere; or both, as of a CONE.

SURFACE OF REVOLUTION, the surface that is generated by revolving a plane curve about a line in its plane. A SPHERE is an example of a surface of revolution.

To write the equation of a surface of revolution generated by revolving a plane curve about one of the coordinate axes in the plane of the curve, substitute the SQUARE ROOT of the sum of the squares of the two variables that are not measured along the axis of revolution, for that one of the variables that appears in the given equation. Thus, if the generating curve is given by the equation $F(x,y) = 0$, the surface generated about the x-axis is given by the equation $F(x, \sqrt{y^2 + z^2}) = 0$.

Ex. 1: Write the equation of the surface generated by revolving the parabola given by $y^2 = 4x$ about the x-axis.

Sol.: The two variables that are not measured along the x-axis (axis of revolution) are y and z. y appears in the equation, so substitute $\sqrt{y^2 + z^2}$ for y. This gives $(\sqrt{y^2 + z^2})^2 = 4x$, or $y^2 + z^2 = 4x$ for the equation of the surface of revolution.

Ex. 2: Find the equation of the surface generated by the curve $y = 1 - x$ when the plane is revolved around the x-axis.

Sol.: $\sqrt{y^2 + z^2} = 1 - x$ or $\sqrt{y^2 + z^2} + x - 1 = 0$. See Fig. 1.

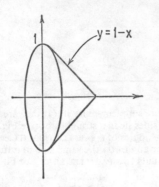

Fig. 1

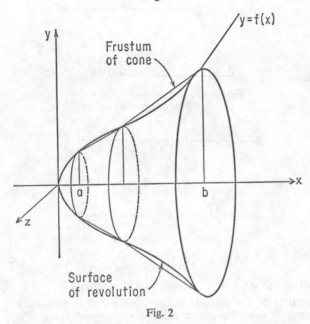

Fig. 2

If the curve $y = f(x)$ is revolved about the x-axis, the area of the surface generated may be found by integration. To find the surface area S between $x = a$ and $x = b$, use the following formula:

$$S = \int_a^b 2\pi y \sqrt{1 + (dy/dx)^2}\, dx.$$

This formula is derived by using approximations to the surface which are frustums of cones (see Fig. 2).

Ex.: Find the area S of the figure generated by the line $y = x^3$ between $x = 0$ and $x = 1$, when revolved about the x-axis.

$$\begin{aligned}
\textit{Sol.: } S &= \int_0^1 2\pi\, x^3 \sqrt{1 + (3x^2)^2}\, dx \\
&= \int_0^1 2\pi\, x^3 \sqrt{1 + 9x^4}\, dx \\
&= 2\pi(\tfrac{1}{36}) \int_0^1 36x^3 \sqrt{1 + 9x^4}\, dx \\
&= \left[2\pi\left(\frac{1}{36}\right)(1 + 9x^4)^{3/2} \cdot \frac{2}{3} \right]_0^1 = \frac{\pi}{27}(10^{3/2} - 1).
\end{aligned}$$

See also PAPPUS' THEOREM.

SURJECTION (sur-jek′-shun), in mathematics, from SET A to set B, a one-to-one MAPPING of A onto B, a function whose DOMAIN is A and whose RANGE is B.

SYLLOGISM (sil′-u-jiz-um), in LOGIC, a set of three propositions constituting an argument, these are: a *major premise*, a *minor premise*, and a *conclusion*. The propositions take the forms: (A) All a's are b; (E) No a's are b; (I) Some a's are b; or (O) Some a's are not b. (The letters A, E, I, and O are the standard letters for referring to propositions of these forms.) Aristotle classified the various syllogisms and formulated principles for identifying the valid ones (those in which the conclusion is necessarily true if the premises are true). For example:

All healthy people are happy.   (Major premise)
No lazy people are healthy.   (Minor premise)
Therefore, no lazy people are happy.   (Conclusion)

In this example "healthy" is called the middle term, and in any valid syllogism it must appear twice in the premises.

SYMBOLIC LOGIC, also known as **mathematical logic,** developed during the 19th cent. by such men as BOOLE, De Morgan, and FREGE, and in the 20th cent. by RUSSELL, WHITEHEAD, and Gödel. The systematic use of symbols in modern symbolic logic is an extension of earlier practices of letting letters stand for propositions, subject terms, and predicates. The advantage derived from a symbolic representation of arguments and the statements appearing therein is that the formal structure of such statements can more easily be revealed and the formal relationships between such statements (e.g., validity, inconsistency) more easily investigated. Such symbols are given explicit and unambiguous definitions; uniform rules are laid down for their manipulation; and, hence, methods (some of them more or less mechanical) can be evolved for testing arguments and setting out proofs of their validity.

That branch of symbolic logic which deals with arguments whose validity depends on the manner in which propositions are joined together to make more complex propositions is called the propositional (or sentential) calculus (*see* ALGEBRA OF PROPOSITIONS). Various propositional connectives are rigorously defined by truth tables which specify what the truth value of the complex proposition is under any assignment of truth values (i.e., "true" or "false") to its constituent propositions. The standard symbols for these connectives are: v (disjunction), · (conjunction), ∼ (negation), ⊃ (implication), ≡ (equivalence); these symbols are used to translate (symbolize) the ordinary English connectives: "or," "and," "not," "if . . . then," and "if and only if" respectively, although the meanings of these ordinary words is not fully captured by the symbols whose meaning is rigorously tied to the truth tables which define their use. A sample argument and its symbolization are:
Harry can vote if and only if he is a citizen and is 21 years of age. If Harry is a member of this club, he cannot be 21 years of age. Therefore, if Harry is a member of this club, he cannot vote.
(symbolization)
H ≡ (C A)
M ⊃ ∼A
Therefore, M ⊃ ∼H
The letters H, A, etc. stand for the propositions "Harry can vote," "Harry is 21 years of age," etc. The validity of this argument can now be checked by various techniques, including the construction of a more elaborate truth table analogous to the ones defining the various symbols appearing in this argument.

Arguments whose validity depends on the internal structure of the propositions themselves require more powerful techniques: namely, the quantificational calculus. In this branch of symbolic logic several new symbols are introduced, most notably the universal and existential quantifier. Many of the same rules and procedures used in the propositional calculus are absorbed into the quantificational calculus; additional rules are imposed to manipulate the quantifiers. To illustrate the method of symbolization: "All ravens are black" would be symbolized as: (x)(Rx ⊃ Bx)—read as "For all x, if x is a raven then x is black; "Some ravens are not black" would be rendered as: (∃x)(Rx · B∼x). Once again, rules are made available for proving the validity of various arguments (truth tables are no longer generally applicable as a technique for testing arguments in the quantificational calculus). Such systems of rules may be codified into an AXIOM system. The symbolic apparatus may be made much more complex (e.g., the higher predicate calculus which involves quantifying over predicate letters—the "R" and the "B" in the above symbolization of "All ravens are black"), but the area is too vast for summarization in this brief article.

Biblio.: Copi, Irving M., *Symbolic Logic* (3rd ed., 1967).

SYMMETRIC PROPERTY (sim-meh-'trik), *see* AXIOM; EQUALITY; EQUIVALENCE RELATION.

SYMMETRY (sim'-me-tree), in mathematics, the balance of a geometric figure with respect to a POINT, a LINE, or a PLANE. A geometric figure is symmetric with respect to a point if the point bisects all the segments passing through and terminated by the figure.

In Fig. 1, the figures are symmetric with respect to point O and are said to have central symmetry.

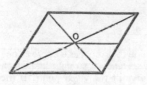

Fig. 1

A geometric figure is symmetric with respect to a line if the line bisects all the segments perpendicular to the line and terminated by the figure.

In Fig. 2, the figures are symmetrical with respect to line l and are said to have axial symmetry.

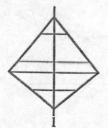
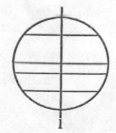

Fig. 2

A solid geometric figure is symmetric with respect to a plane, if the plane bisects all the segments PERPENDICULAR to the plane and terminated by the figure.

A graph is symmetric about a line if the graph to one side of the line is the mirror image of the graph to the other. It is symmetric about a point if for every point on the graph the corresponding point on the line through the fixed point on the other side at the same distance is also on the graph. See Fig. 3.

The equation of the AXIS OF SYMMETRY can be investigated by the following:

1. If a graph is specified by an equation, it is symmetric about

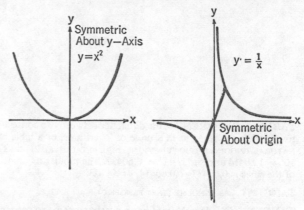

Fig. 3

the x-axis whenever replacing y by $-y$ leaves the equation unchanged.

2. A graph is symmetric around the y-axis if replacing x by $-x$ leaves the equation unchanged.

3. A graph is symmetric about the line $y = x$ if interchanging x and y leaves the equation unchanged.

4. A graph is symmetric about the origin if replacing x by $-x$ and y by $-y$ leaves the equation unchanged.

Ex.: Investigate the symmetry of the line $y = x^2$.

Sol.: We use the above tests. Transpose one side to get the equation $x^2 - y = 0$. If y is now replaced by $-y$, the value of the left hand side will change. Therefore the graph is not symmetric about the x-axis. However, if we replace x by $-x$, the value will not change, since x is squared and $(-x)^2 = x^2$. So the graph is symmetric about the y-axis. Interchanging x and y, and replacing each by its negative, changes the value of the left hand side, so the graph is not symmetric about the line $y = x$ or about the origin.

SYNTHESIS (sin'-thu-sis), in mathematics, or synthetic proof of a THEOREM, the orderly and logical sequence of deductions in a proof proceeding from the HYPOTHESIS to the CONCLUSION as in classical Euclidean geometry.

SYNTHETIC DIVISION, *see* DIVISION, SYNTHETIC.

SYSTEMATIC SAMPLE, in statistics, a sample for which the first member is chosen by chance (at random) and all the other members are determined by a pattern. For example, if a sample of 100 is desired from a population of 1000, arranged alphabetically, a number between 1 and 10 could be determined randomly. The member of the population with that number would be selected for the sample, and every tenth member after that would be automatically selected.

SYSTEMS OF EQUATIONS, two or more EQUATIONS in two or more unknowns that have solutions in common. E.g., (1) a linear system, as $\begin{cases} 3x - y = 8; \\ x + y = 4 \end{cases}$ (2) a quadratic system, $\begin{cases} x^2 + y^2 = 25 \\ 2x^2 - y^2 = 2 \end{cases}$; (3) a system consisting of a linear equation and a QUADRATIC EQUATION, as $\begin{cases} x + y = 5 \\ x^2 + y^2 = 13 \end{cases}$. Systems of equations may be solved graphically as well as algebraically. *See also* EQUATION, LINEAR.

T

TABULAR DIFFERENCE, the difference between two consecutive entries in a table, as in a table of logarithms, or a table of NATURAL TRIGONOMETRIC FUNCTIONS. E.g., in TABLE NO. 21, sin 37 10′ = 1.60414 and sin 37 11′ = 0.60437. The tabular difference of the sines is 0.60437 − 0.60414, or .00023.

TANGENT, *see* TANGENT LINE; TANGENT OF AN ANGLE.

TANGENT, COMMON (tan′-jent), a TANGENT LINE to one circle that is also a tangent to another circle. If a line is tangent to both circles and intersects the line of centers, it is called a common internal tangent. (See Fig. 1.) If a line is tangent to both circles and does not intersect the line of centers, it is called a common external tangent. (See Fig. 2.) Two circles may have one, two, three, or four common tangents.

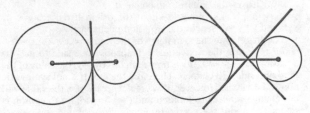

Fig. 1   Common Internal Tangents

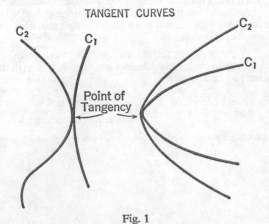

Fig. 2   Common External Tangents

TANGENT, CURVES (tan′-jent), curves that meet at a single point but do not intersect. (See Fig. 1.)

TANGENT CURVES

Fig. 1

Tangent circles are two circles that are tangent to the same line at the same point. If they are on opposite sides of the line,

the circles are tangent externally. If the circles are on the same side of the line, they are tangent internally. In Fig. 2, circles O and O' are tangent externally. Circles A and A' are tangent internally.

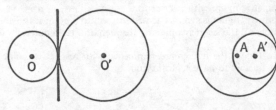

Fig. 2

TANGENT LINE, intuitively, a line that touches a curve at one point but does not cross the curve. Hence, a straight line which has the same direction as the curve at the given point. If the curve is cusped at the point, it has two directions and therefore two tangent lines. The tangent line to a curve at a point P is the limiting position of the SECANT LINE PQ, as Q approaches P along the curve, if this limiting position exists. By the limiting position of the secant, we mean that line which the secant approximates more and more closely as Q moves closer to P. (See Fig. 1.) *See also* DIRECTION OF CURVE AT A POINT.

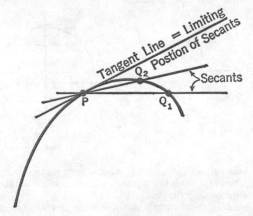

Fig. 1

The tangent to a CIRCLE is PERPENDICULAR to a RADIUS drawn to the point of tangency. See Fig. 2.

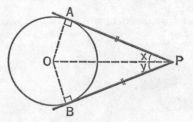

Fig. 2

Tangents to a circle from the same point are equal and make equal angles with the line drawn from the point to the center of the circle. In Fig. 2, lines PA and PB are tangents; therefore, $AP \perp OA, BP \perp OB, AP = BP$, and $\angle x = \angle y$.

To construct a tangent to circle O at a given point A on the circle, draw radius OA (see Fig. 3). Construct a perpendicular to OA at point A. AB is tangent to circle O at A since if a line is perpendicular to a radius at its point on the circle, it is tangent to the circle.

To construct a tangent to circle O from point A outside the circle, draw OA (see Fig. 4) and construct the midpoint of OA. With P as a center and PO as the radius, draw a circle intersecting circle O at B and C. Draw AB and AC. Radii OC and OB are perpendicular to AC and AB, since an angle inscribed in a semicircle is a right angle. Thus, AB and AC are tangents to circle O from A, because if a line is perpendicular to the radius at its point on the circle, it is tangent to the circle.

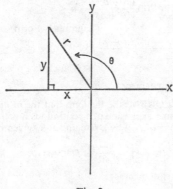

Fig. 3   Fig. 4

TANGENT OF AN ANGLE, in geometry, the RATIO of the side opposite the acute angle to the side adjacent (see Fig. 1). The tangent of an angle is the reciprocal of the COTANGENT OF AN ANGLE, i.e., tangent $\angle A = 1/\text{cotangent } \angle A$. The tangent of an acute angle is equal to the cotangent of its complementary angle. The tangent of $\angle A$ is abbreviated tan $\angle A$.

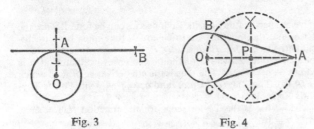

$$\tan A = \frac{a}{b}$$
$$\tan B = \frac{b}{a}$$

Fig. 1

The tangent of any angle is the ratio of the ORDINATE to the ABSCISSA when the angle is in STANDARD ANGLE POSITION. $\tan \theta =$ ordinate/abscissa $= y/x$. (See Fig. 2.)

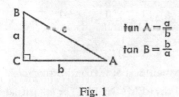

Fig. 2

The tangent is positive in quadrants I and II and negative in the quadrants II and IV.

If x is the radian measure of any angle a, then tan x is defined as shown in Fig. 3.

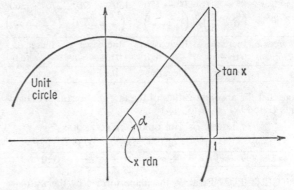

Fig. 3

The graph of $y = \tan x$ as x varies from $-\pi$ to 2π is shown in Fig. 4. The tables show the changes in the tangent as the angle is rotated through 360°.

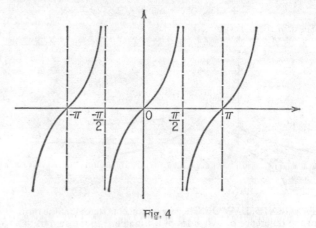

Fig. 4

Since $\tan x = \dfrac{\sin x}{\cos x}$, the derivative (*see* DERIVATIVE OF A FUNCTION), $\dfrac{d}{dx} (\tan x)$, is found by the rule for differentiating quotients:

$$\frac{d}{dx} (\tan x) = \frac{d}{dx} \frac{\sin x}{\cos x} =$$

$$\frac{\left[\dfrac{d}{dx} (\sin x)\right] \cos x - \sin x \left[\dfrac{d}{dx} (\cos x)\right]}{\cos^2 x}.$$

$\dfrac{d}{dx} (\sin x) = \cos x$ and $\dfrac{d}{dx} (\cos x) = -\sin x$.

Thus, $\dfrac{d}{dx} (\tan x) = \dfrac{\cos^2 x + \sin^2 x}{\cos^2 x} = \dfrac{1}{\cos^2 x} = \sec^2 x$.

Ex.: What is the equation of the tangent line to the curve $y = \tan x$ at $x = \pi/4$ radians?

Sol.: The slope of the tangent line is

$$\sec^2 (\pi/4) = \frac{1}{\cos^2 (\pi/4)} = \frac{1}{(\frac{1}{2})^2} = 2.$$

The line passes through the point $(\pi/4, 1)$. Its equation is therefore $y = 1 + 2(x - \pi/4)$. *See also* COSINE OF AN ANGLE; SINE OF AN ANGLE.

CHANGES IN THE TANGENT

Quadrant	I	II	III	IV
Increases in Angle	$0° - 90°$ $\left(0 - \dfrac{\pi}{2}\right)$	$90° - 180°$ $\left(\dfrac{\pi}{2} - \pi\right)$	$180° - 270°$ $\left(\pi - \dfrac{3\pi}{2}\right)$	$270° - 360°$ $\left(\dfrac{3\pi}{2} - 2\pi\right)$
Changes in Tangent	Increases 0 to $+\infty$	Increases $-\infty$ to 0	Increases 0 to $+\infty$	Increases $-\infty$ to 0
Sign	Positive	Negative	Positive	Negative

Note that the absolute values of the tangent decrease in Quadrants II and IV.

TANGENT OF THE QUADRANTAL ANGLES

Angle	0°	90°	180°	270°	360°
Tangent	0	$\pm\infty$	0	$\pm\infty$	0

TANGENT PLANE, at P, the plane formed by the TANGENT LINES at P to all curves of the surface $z = f(x,y)$, where $P = (x_0, y_0, z_0)$. A surface that fails to have a tangent plane at a point P is shown in the figure. A sufficient condition that a tangent plane exist at P is that the PARTIAL DERIVATIVES f_x and f_y be continuous in some area around P. When the tangent plane exists, the formula for it is

$$z = z_0 + f_x(x_0,y_0)(x - x_0) + f_y(x_0,y_0)(y - y_0).$$

See also TOTAL DIFFERENTIAL.

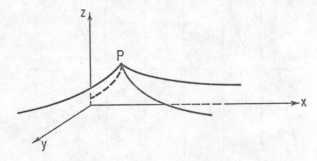

TANGENTS, LAW OF. The law of tangents states that the ratio of the difference of two sides of a triangle is to the sum of the sides as the tangent of one half the difference of the opposite angles is to the tangent of half the sum of the opposite angles. In formula form:

$$\frac{a - b}{a + b} = \frac{\tan \frac{1}{2}(A - B)}{\tan \frac{1}{2}(A + B)}, \text{ when } a > b.$$

The law is used for solving triangles when given: (1) two sides and the included angle, or (2) two angles and a side. (It is preferable to use the Law of Sines (*see* SINES, LAW OF) when two angles and a side are given.)

TANGENT VECTOR, to a curve, at a point P on the curve is given by $\mathbf{T} = \mathbf{i} \cos \phi + \mathbf{j} \sin \phi$, where ϕ is the slope of the TANGENT LINE at P. $\mathbf{T}$ is the unit tangent vector at point P.

$\mathbf{T}$ may also be defined in terms of the POSITION VECTOR from O to P, by $\mathbf{R} = \mathbf{i}x + \mathbf{j}y$. The position of P on the curve can be determined by the length of an arc, s, from some reference point, P. The vector from O to P is a functon of s, and $\mathbf{T}$ may be defined as $d\mathbf{R}/ds$. Thus, $\mathbf{T} = d\mathbf{R}/ds = \mathbf{i}\, dx/ds + \mathbf{j}\, dy/ds$.

TANH x, the hyperbolic tangent of x, defined by:

$$\tanh x = \frac{\sinh x}{\cosh x} = \frac{e^x - e^{-x}}{e^x + e^{-x}}.$$

Its derivative $\dfrac{d}{dx}(\tan x) = \mathrm{sech}^2\, x$. *See also* HYPERBOLIC FUNCTION.

TAN^{-1} x, arc tan x. *See* ARC TANGENT.

TAUTOLOGY (taw-tah'-luh-jee), a compound statement which has the truth value "true" for all possible truth values of its components. Tautologies represent valid forms of arguments. Three classical valid arguments which are used frequently are:

$$
\begin{array}{lll}
1.\ \ p \to q & 2.\ \ p \to q & 3.\ \ p \to q \\
\ \ \ \ p & \ \ \ \ \sim q & \ \ \ \ q \to r \\
\hline
\therefore\ q & \therefore \sim p & \therefore p \to r
\end{array}
$$

These three forms are called *modus ponens*, *modus tollens*, and *hypothetical syllogism*, respectively.

TAYLOR SERIES, for a given function $f(x)$, a power series expansion of $f(x)$ at $x = a$:

$$\sum_{n=0}^{\infty} a_n(x - a)^n = a_0 + a_1(x - a) + a_2(x - a)^2 + a_3(x - a)^3 \cdots$$

Given a specific function, its Taylor series can be found. Since the series and the function are to be equal, they must have identical derivatives $f'(a), f''(a), \ldots, f^{(n)}(a), \ldots$, for any value a of x. The nth derivative of the power series evaluated at a is $n! a_n(x - a)^0 = n! a_n$. This equals the nth derivative of $f(x)$, which is $f^{(n)}(a)$. Thus, $f^{(n)}(a) = n! a_n$, and $a_n = f^{(n)}(a)/n!$. This is Taylor's Formula.

Ex.: What is the Taylor series for the function $f(x) = \sin x$ with $a = 0$?

Sol.: We find successive derivatives of $\sin x$ at 0, then use the formula for a_n.

$$
\begin{aligned}
f'(0) &= \cos 0 = 1 \\
f''(0) &= -\sin 0 = 0 \\
f'''(0) &= -\cos 0 = -1 \\
f^{(4)}(0) &= \sin 0 = 0, \text{ etc.}
\end{aligned}
$$

The series is, therefore,

$$\sin x = \frac{0}{0!}(x)^0 + \frac{1}{1!}x + \frac{0}{2!}x^2 + \frac{-1}{3!}x^3 + \frac{0}{4!}x^4 + \cdots$$

$$= 0 + x + 0 - \frac{1}{3!}x^3 + 0 + \cdots.$$

See also MACLAURIN SERIES; TAYLOR'S THEOREM.

TAYLOR SERIES, REMAINDER. The nth partial sum of the TAYLOR SERIES of a function differs from the value of the function by a remainder R_n given by any of the following formulas:

$$R_n = \int_x^x \frac{(x - t)^n}{n!} f^{(n+1)}(t)\, dt.$$

$$R_n = f^{(n+1)}(c)\frac{(x - a)^{n+1}}{(n + 1)!}, a \le c \le x$$
$$\text{(Lagrange's Form).}$$

$$R_n = \frac{(x - c')^n(x - a)}{n!} f^{(n+1)}(c'), a \le c' \le x$$
$$\text{(Cauchy's Form).}$$

See also TAYLOR'S THEOREM.

TAYLOR'S THEOREM, the theorem that the nth partial sum of the TAYLOR SERIES expansion of a continuous function $f(x)$ differs from the value of $f(x)$ by a remainder R_n given by:

$$R_n = \int_a^x \frac{(x - t)^n}{n!} f^{(n+1)}(t)\, dt.$$

In symbols, this statement is:

$$f(x) = f(a) + f'(a)(x - a) + \frac{f''(a)}{2!}(x - a)^2 + \cdots + \frac{f^{(n)}(a)}{n!}(x - a)^n + R_n.$$

To prove that Taylor's series converges to a function, it is enough to show that $R_n \to 0$ as $n \to \infty$.

TERM, the part of an ALGEBRAIC EXPRESSION between a plus or minus sign. E.g., in the expression $3x^2y - 4x + 3y^2$, $3x^2y$ is a term, as is $4x$ or $3y^2$.

TERMINAL RAY, *see* COORDINATES, POLAR.

TERMINAL SIDE, *see* SIDE OF AN ANGLE.

TERMINATING DECIMAL, *see* DECIMAL, TERMINATING.

TERMS, SIMILAR, terms having identical literal COEFFICIENTS. E.g., $3x$, $2x$ and $-6x$; or $4x^2y^3$, $\frac{2}{3}x^2y^3$, and $-5x^2y^3$.

TERRESTRIAL TRIANGLE (ter-res'-tree-al), a SPHERICAL TRIANGLE on the earth's surface whose vertex is the north pole.

TESTS FOR CONVERGENCE, *see* COMPARISON TEST; INTEGRAL TEST FOR CONVERGENCE; RATIO TEST.

TESTS OF HYPOTHESES ABOUT A MEAN, in statistics to test $H_0: \mu = \mu_0$, using a random sample of size n from (1) a normal population with known variance σ^2, calculate

$$z = \frac{\bar{x} - \mu_0}{\sigma/\sqrt{n}}$$

and refer to STANDARD NORMAL TABLE (this is an exact test); (2) a normal population with unknown variance, see T-TEST; (3) any population, with known or unknown variance, calculate

$$z = \frac{\bar{x} - \mu_0}{\sigma/\sqrt{u}}$$

and refer to standard normal tables. The size of the sample must be at least 25. If σ^2 is unknown, replace it by s^2 in the preceding formula. (This is an approximate test.)

TESTS OF HYPOTHESES ABOUT A MEDIAN, *see* SIGN TEST; SIGNED-RANK TEST; and RANK-SUM TEST.

TESTS OF HYPOTHESES ABOUT A PROPORTION, in statistics, to test $H_0: \pi = \pi_0$, using a random sample of size n from a binomial population, calculate the quantity $z = \dfrac{p - \pi_0}{\sqrt{\dfrac{p(1-p)}{n}}}$,

and refer it to STANDARD NORMAL TABLES. The test is approximate. An exact test can be constructed if a table of the binomial distribution that contains the n-value is available.

TESTS OF HYPOTHESES ABOUT A VARIANCE, in statistics, to test $H_0: \sigma^2 = \sigma_0^2$, the quantity $\chi^2 = \dfrac{(n-1)s^2}{\sigma_0^2}$ is calculated and referred to chi-squared tables with $n - 1$ degrees of freedom. The test is based on a random sample of size n from a normal population.

TESTS OF HYPOTHESES ABOUT THE DIFFERENCE OF TWO MEANS, in statistics, to test $H_0: \mu_1 - \mu_2 = \Delta_0$, using two independent random samples of size n_1 and n_2 from (1) two normal populations with known variances σ_1^2 and σ_2^2, calculate

$$z = \frac{(\bar{x}_1 - \bar{x}_2) - \Delta_0}{\sqrt{\dfrac{\sigma_1^2}{n_1} + \dfrac{\sigma_2^2}{n_2}}}$$

and refer to STANDARD NORMAL TABLES (this is an exact text); (2) two normal populations with unknown but equal variances, see T-TEST; (3) two populations with known or unknown variances, calculate

$$z = \frac{(\bar{x}_1 - \bar{x}_2) - \Delta_0}{\sqrt{\dfrac{\sigma_1^2}{n_1} + \dfrac{\sigma_2^2}{n_2}}}$$

and refer to standard normal tables. The samples must each contain at least 25 observations. If σ_1^2 and σ_2^2 are unknown, replace them in the preceding formula by s_1^2 and s_2^2. (This is an approximate test.)

TESTS OF HYPOTHESES ABOUT THE DIFFERENCE OF TWO PROPORTIONS, in statistics, to test $H_0: \pi_1 - \pi_2 = 0$, using two independent random samples of size n_1 and n_2 from two binomial populations, calculate

$$z = \frac{p_1 - p_2}{\sqrt{\dfrac{p(1-p)}{n_1} + \dfrac{p(1-p)}{n_2}}}$$

and refer z to STANDARD NORMAL TABLES (p_1 denotes the proportion of successes in the first sample; p_2, the proportion of successes in the second sample; and $p = \dfrac{n_1 p_1 + n_2 p_2}{n_1 + n_2}$, which is a POOLED ESTIMATE.

To test $H_0: \pi_1 - \pi_2 = \Delta_0$, where Δ_0 is any specified number except 0, using two independent random samples of size n_1 and n_2 from two binomial populations, calculate

$$z = \frac{(p_1 - p_2) - \Delta_0}{\sqrt{\dfrac{p_1(1-p_1)}{n_1} + \dfrac{p_2(1-p_2)}{n_2}}}$$

where p_1 and p_2 are defined as above.

TESTS OF HYPOTHESES ABOUT THE EQUALITY OF TWO VARIANCES, in statistics, to test $H_0: \sigma_1^2 = \sigma_2^2$, using two independent random samples of size n_1 and n_2 from two normal populations, calculate $F = s_1^2/s_2^2$, and refer to F-tables with $n_1 - 1$ and $n_2 - 1$ degrees of freedom (s_1^2 is the variance of Sample 1 and s_2^2 is the variance of Sample 2).

TESTS OF HYPOTHESES ABOUT THE INDEPENDENCE OF TWO CRITERIA OF CLASSIFICATION, *see* CONTINGENCY TABLE.

TETRAHEDRON (tet-rah-hee'-drun), a POLYHEDRON having four faces.

THEOREM (thee'-u-rum), a mathematical statement that has been proved to be true. If a theorem is in the "if-then" form, the if-clause is the HYPOTHESIS and the then-clause is the CONCLUSION. If the statement of the theorem is a simple sentence, the complete subject is the hypothesis and the complete predicate is the conclusion. After a theorem has been proved it may be used as a reason in other proofs. (*See* FORMAL PROOF.) The following are typical theorems for which formal proof is required of students in Elementary Geometry courses.

Theorem I: If two straight lines intersect, the vertical angles are equal.

Given straight lines AB and CD intersecting in E, prove $\angle 1 = \angle 2$. (See Fig. 1.) Proof: (1) AB is a straight line. [Hypothesis.] (2) $\angle 1$ is supplementary to $\angle 3$. [If two adjacent angles have their exterior sides in a straight line, they are supplementary.] (3) CD is a straight line. [Hypothesis.] (4) $\angle 2$ is supplementary to $\angle 3$. [Same as 2.] (5) $\angle 1 = \angle 2$. [Supplements of the same angles are equal.]

Theorem II: If two sides of a triangle are equal, the angles opposite these sides are equal.

Given triangle ABC with $AC = BC$, prove $\angle A = \angle B$. (See Fig. 2.) Proof: (1) Draw auxiliary line CD bisecting $\angle C$ and meeting AB at D. [Authority for construction: An angle may have only one bisector.] (2) $\angle x = \angle y$. [A bisector divides an angle into two equal parts. (3) $AC = BC$. [Hypotheiss.] (4) $CD = CD$. [Identity Axiom.] (5) Triangle $ACD \cong$ triangle DCB. [S.A.S.] (6) $\angle A = \angle B$. [Corresponding parts of congruent triangles are equal.]

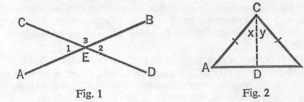

Fig. 1   Fig. 2

Theorem III: If two lines form equal alternate interior angles with a TRANSVERSAL, the lines are parallel.

Given lines l and l' cut by transversal t so that $\angle 1 = \angle 2$, prove $l \parallel l'$. (See Fig. 3.) This theorem is proved indirectly by assuming l and l' are not parallel. If they are not parallel, they will meet in some point and form a triangle with the transversal. Proof: (1) Assume l and l' intersect. [Assume the contradictory of the conclusion. Two lines in the same plane are either parallel or they intersect.] (2) Let l and l' meet in point P. They form a triangle with transversal t. [A triangle is a polygon with three sides.] (3) $\angle 1 > \angle 2$. [An exterior angle of a triangle is greater than either non-adjacent interior angle.] (4) But $\angle 1 = \angle 2$. [Hypothesis.] (5) Step 3 is false. [It contradicts a known hypothesis.] (6) Therefore, l is parallel to l'. [The contradictory of a false assumption is true.] From the theorem the following corollaries can easily be proved:

1. If two lines form equal corresponding angles with a transversal, the lines are parallel.

2. If two lines form supplementary interior angles on the same side of the transversal, the lines are parallel.

3. Two lines perpendicular to the same line are parallel. The converse of this theorem and its corollaries are true. *See also* INDIRECT PROOF.

Theorem IV: The sum of the angles of a triangle equals a STRAIGHT ANGLE.

Given triangle ABC, prove $\angle A + \angle B + \angle ACB =$ one straight angle. (See Fig. 4.) Proof: (1) Through C draw DE parallel to AB. [PARALLEL POSTULATE: Through a given point there is only one line parallel to a given line.] (2) $\angle 1 = \angle A$ and $\angle 2 = \angle B$. [If two parallel lines are cut by a transversal, the alternate interior angles are equal.] (3) $\angle 1 + \angle 2 + \angle ACB =$ one straight angle. [The sum of the angles around a point on one side of a straight line equals a straight angle.] (4) $\angle A + \angle B + \angle ACB =$ one straight angle. [A quantity may be substituted for its equal in an equation.]

Theorem V: If two sides of a QUADRILATERAL are equal and parallel, the figure is a PARALLELOGRAM.

Given quadrilateral $ABCD$, with $AB = CD$, and AB parallel to CD, prove $ABCD$ is a parallelogram. (See Fig. 5.) Proof: (1) Draw AC. [Two points determine a line.] (2) $AB \parallel CD$. [Hypothesis.] (3) $\angle x = \angle y$. [If two parallel lines are cut by a transversal the alternate interior angles are equal.] (4) $AB = CD$. [Hypothesis.] (5) $\triangle ABC \cong \triangle CDA$. [S.A.S.] (6) $AD = BC$. [Corresponding parts of congruent triangles are equal.] (7) $ABCD$ is a parallelogram. [If the opposite sides of a quadrilateral are equal it is a parallelogram.]

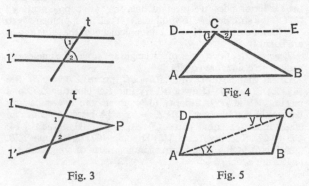

Fig. 3   Fig. 4

Fig. 5

THEOREM, BINOMIAL, *see* BINOMIAL THEOREM.

THEOREM, FACTOR, *see* FACTOR THEOREM.

THEOREM OF PYTHAGORAS, *see* PYTHAGOREAN THEOREM.

THEOREM, REMAINDER, *see* REMAINDER THEOREM.

THETA (thay'-tuh), the Greek letter symbolized by θ. θ is commonly used to designate the angle between the positive x-axis and a RAY from the ORIGIN (see figure). *See* TABLE NO. 1.

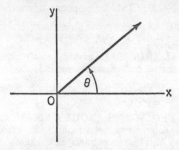

THIRD DEGREE EQUATION, *see* CUBIC EQUATION.

THIRD PROPORTIONAL, the last term of a MEAN PROPORTION. In the proportion $a:b = b:x$, the third proportional to a and b is x. To find a third proportional to two numbers, such as 3 and 9, make a mean proportion in which 3 is the first term and 9 is the second and third terms; $3:9 = 9:x$. Then $3x = 81$, and $x = 27$, the third proportional.

THIRTY-SIXTY RIGHT TRIANGLE, a RIGHT TRIANGLE whose acute angles are 30° and 60°. The sides of the triangle have the RATIO $1:2:\sqrt{3}$, where the side opposite the 30° angle is $\frac{1}{2}$ the HYPOTENUSE and the side opposite the 60° angle is $\frac{1}{2}$ the hypotenuse times $\sqrt{3}$. (See figure.)

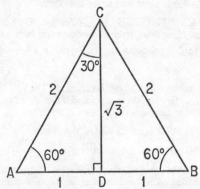

TIME, a measure of the duration between events. A scale of time is usually set up in reference to some naturally occurring, periodic phenomenon. For example, a year is the time that it takes for the earth to rotate once about the sun, and a day is the time that it takes for the earth to revolve once about its own axis. Smaller time intervals, such as the hour, minute, and second, are defined as appropriate subdivisions of the year or the day. For example, one hour can be defined as 1/24th of a day. Recently, the fundamental unit of time has been defined as the time it takes for a certain molecule to complete a certain number of vibrations.

During the 20th cent., the concept of time has undergone sweeping revisions. Previously, time was thought to be a universal quantity to which all physical phenomena could be referred. The time interval between two events was thought to be independent of the state of motion of the observer who measured it. With the publication of the special theory of relativity in 1905, A. EINSTEIN showed that this was not so and that measurements of time could not be wholly separated from measurements of spatial distances. In a purely formal sense time may be thought of as a fourth dimension in that it takes four numbers to specify the exact occurrence of an event: three to specify where it took place, and one more to specify when. Einstein showed that measurements of space and time are inextricably intertwined. In ordinary three dimensional space, height, width, and depth are interchangeable, and one can be converted to another simply by changing the orientation of an object. Einstein showed that time can also be seen as one of the length dimensions and that the degree to which it mixes in with them depends on the motion of the observer.

TIME SERIES, in statistics, a sequence of observations that are taken over a period of time, usually at regular intervals. The techniques of analyzing time series are especially valuable for the study of economic data of various kinds.

TOPOLOGY (tah-pahl'-uh-jee), a branch of geometry that deals with place and position and not quantity and measure; i.e., with those properties of a figure which remain when the figure is transformed by a one-to-one correspondence that is continuous in both directions. A correspondence is continuous in both directions if for two points, P and Q corresponding to P' and Q', as the distance between P and Q becomes zero, the distance between P' and Q' becomes zero, and vice versa. Such properties are called topological properties. E.g., compactness and connectedness. Topology is called "rubber sheet geometry" since it is concerned with properties that do not change when the figure is bent, stretched, or distorted. If a triangle is drawn on the surface of a balloon, when the balloon is blown up the triangle has a different shape. (See figure.) However, some properties

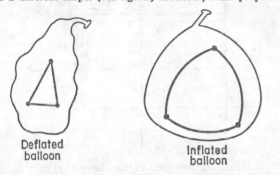

Deflated balloon   Inflated balloon

remain. What was originally inside the triangle is still inside, and what was outside is still outside. The three sides still intersect in three points. This kind of topological transformation is known as a deformation. *See also* MOEBIUS STRIP.

TORUS (toh'-rus), a doughnut-shaped surface, generated by rotating a circle about an axis in the plane of the circle. In Fig. 1,

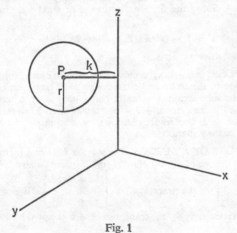

Fig. 1

circle P, of radius r, at distance k from the z-axis, has as its equation $(y - k)^2 + z = r^2$. The torus that is generated by rotating circle P about the z-axis, (Fig. 2) has as its equation, $(\sqrt{x^2 + y^2} - k)^2 + z^2 = r^2$. The volume of this torus is $2\pi^2 k r^2$. Its surface area is $4\pi^2 k r$.

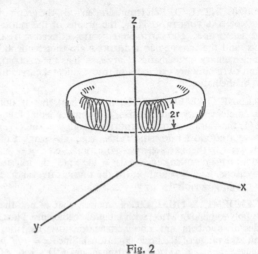

Fig. 2

TOTAL DIFFERENTIAL, for a surface $z = f(x,y)$:

$$dz = \frac{\partial z}{\partial x} \cdot dx + \frac{\partial z}{\partial y} \cdot dy.$$

See also DIFFERENTIAL; PARTIAL DERIVATIVE.

TOTIENT (to'-shent), of an integer, the number of totitives of the integer. *See* TOTATIVE OF AN INTEGER.

TOTITIVE OF AN INTEGER (tot'-i-tiv in'-ter-jer), a positive INTEGER, less than the given integer, such that the integer and the given integer have no common factors other than 1, (i.e., they are relatively prime). 1, 3, 7, and 9 are the totitives of 10.

TRACE (trays), of a line, the point of intersection of the line with a COORDINATE plane; of a plane, the lines of intersection of the given plane with the coordinate planes; of a surface, the sections of intersection (curves) of the surface with the coordinate planes.

TRACTRIX (trak'-triks), given line PT, of length a, with point T a variable point on the x-axis, the LOCUS of point P as T moves on the x-axis from $-\infty$ to $+\infty$, and PT is always tangent to the curve described by P. (See figure.) The equation of the tractrix in rectangular coordinates (*see* COORDINATES, RECTANGULAR) is given by

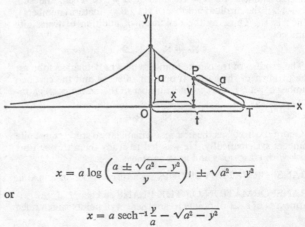

$$x = a \log \left(\frac{a \pm \sqrt{a^2 - y^2}}{y} \right) \pm \sqrt{a^2 - y^2}$$

or

$$x = a \operatorname{sech}^{-1} \frac{y}{a} - \sqrt{a^2 - y^2}$$

Its PARAMETRIC EQUATIONS are given by $x = t - 2 \tanh \dfrac{t}{a}$, $y = a \operatorname{sech} \dfrac{t}{a}$, where the parameter t is the distance from the ORIGIN to point T. The tractrix is the INVOLUTE of a CATENARY.

TRANSCENDENTAL CURVE (tran-sen-den'-tal), the graph of a TRANSCENDENTAL FUNCTION. Thus, the graphs of the TRIGONOMETRIC FUNCTIONS, LOGARITHMIC FUNCTIONS, EXPONENTIAL FUNCTIONS, and the HYPERBOLIC FUNCTIONS are transcendental curves in elementary mathematics. Curves such as the CYCLOID, SPIRAL, and CATENARY are examples of transcendental curves in advanced mathematics.

TRANSCENDENTAL FUNCTION, a FUNCTION that is not algebraic. In elementary mathematics, the transcendental functions are (1) the TRIGONOMETRIC FUNCTIONS, e.g., $y = \sin x$; (2) the INVERSE TRIGONOMETRIC FUNCTIONS, e.g., $y = \sin^{-1} x$ or $y = \arcsin x$; (3) the EXPONENTIAL FUNCTIONS, e.g., $y = 3^x$; (4) the LOGARITHMIC FUNCTIONS, e.g., $y = \log x$; (5) the HYPERBOLIC FUNCTIONS, e.g., $y = \sinh x$; (6) the INVERSE HYPERBOLIC FUNCTIONS, e.g., $y = \sinh^{-1} x$ or $y = \operatorname{arcsinh} x$.

TRANSCENDENTAL NUMBER, a NUMBER that is not the ROOT of a polynomial EQUATION with integral coefficients. Thus, transcendental numbers are not ALGEBRAIC NUMBERS (they "transcend" the range of algebraic equations). Since $x = p/q$, p and q integers, defines a RATIONAL NUMBER, and x is a root of $qx - p = 0$ (a polynomial equation with integral coefficients), a rational number cannot be transcendental. Therefore, all transcendental numbers must be irrational. However, the converse is not true. An IRRATIONAL NUMBER is not necessarily transcendental: $\sqrt{2}$ is a root of the polynomial equation with integral coefficients: $x^2 - 2 = 0$.

The two most famous transcendental numbers are E and π (see PI). Most trigonometric values are transcendental as are most common LOGARITHMS. In general, if a is algebraic and b is an irrational algebraic number, a^b is transcendental. $2^{\sqrt{3}}$, $3^{\sqrt{2}}$ are transcendental numbers.

TRANSFINITE NUMBER (trans-fahy'-nahyt), the CARDINAL NUMBER of an infinite SET. The cardinal number of a set that is equivalent to the set of NATURAL NUMBERS is denoted by $\aleph_0$ read "aleph-null". The cardinal number of the set of points on a line segment is denoted by $\aleph$ (read "aleph"). It can be shown that $\aleph_0$ is not the same as $\aleph$.

An arithmetic of transfinite numbers can be constructed. E.g., the "sum" of the transfinite numbers may be defined as follows: If the cardinal number of set X is x and of set Y is y and x and y are disjoint, the sum of the cardinal numbers, $x + y$ of the sets is the cardinal number of the UNION of X and Y. If set $A = \{$odd natural numbers$\}$ and set $B = \{$even natural numbers$\}$, the cardinal number of $A = \aleph_0$ and of $B = \aleph_0$. Then, the sum $\aleph_0 + \aleph_0$ is the cardinal number of $A \cup B = \{$natural numbers$\}$, which is $\aleph_0$. Thus, by the definition of addition of transfinite numbers,

$$\aleph_0 + \aleph_0 = \aleph_0.$$

The product of transfinite numbers may be defined as follows: The product of the cardinal number of set A and the cardinal number of set B is the cardinal number of their CARTESIAN PRODUCT, $A \times B$.

Hence, $$\aleph_0 \cdot \aleph_0 = \aleph_0.$$

Georg CANTOR was the first mathematician to study transfinite numbers systematically. He was led to study them through his work with FUNCTIONS and REAL NUMBERS.

TRANSFORMATION GROUP, see RIGID MOTIONS OF A PLANE.

TRANSFORMATION OF THE PLANE, a change in the COORDINATES of a set of points to another set of points which refer to a different set of coordinates. Transformations of the plane may be by ROTATION OF AXES, TRANSLATION OF AXES, or RIGID MOTIONS OF A PLANE.

TRANSIT INSTRUMENTS, instruments used in surveying, navigation, and astronomy to find the bearing, or azimuth, of a direction, that is, the horizontal angle between the given direction and a chosen reference direction. The instrument is equipped with an adjustable horizontal circle that may be either clamped or free to rotate about a vertical axis with the upper part of the instrument. There is also a vertical circle for determining elevation or depression. Both circles may be read through a single eyepiece through a series of prisms inside the instrument and are usually fitted with slow-motion tangent screws and verniers for precise readings. One type of transit incorporates a camera for taking a series of overlapping photographs of the region being studied.

TRANSITIVE PROPERTY, see AXIOM; EQUALITY; EQUIVALENCE RELATION.

TRANSLATION OF AXES, a TRANSFORMATION OF THE PLANE in which the new x-axis is parallel to the old x-axis and the new y-axis is parallel to the old y-axis. If the origin of the new COORDINATE SYSTEM is at the point (h,k) relative to the old coordinates, then the new coordinates of any point whose old coordinates were (x,y) are:

$$x' = x - h$$
$$y' = y - k. \quad \text{(See figure.)}$$

Ex. 1: If axes are translated so that the new origin is at the point $(-1,3)$, find the new coordinates of the point $(1,2)$.

Sol.: Since $x' = x - (-1) = x + 1$, the new x-coordinate is $1 + 1 = 2$. Similarly, the new y-coordinate is $2 - 3 = -1$.

Ex. 2: If axes are translated one unit to the right and one unit vertically, find the equation of the parabola $y = x^2$ relative to the new axes.

Sol.: Since $y' = y - 1$ and $x' = x - 1$, $y = y' + 1$ and $x = x' + 1$. Substitute for x and y in the original equation to find:

$$y' + 1 = (x' + 1)^2 = x'^2 + 2x' + 1.$$

See also ROTATION OF AXES.

TRANSPOSE, in algebra, to move a term from one member of an equation to the other and change its sign. The operation of addition or subtraction is actually being used when a term is "transposed". E.g., in $x + 3 = 5$, transposing 3 gives $x = 5 - 3$ or $x = 2$, the result obtained by adding -3 to both members of the equation.

TRANSPOSE OF A MATRIX, the MATRIX obtained by interchanging the rows and columns of a given matrix. E.g.,

$\begin{bmatrix} 1 & 0 & 3 \\ 2 & 1 & 0 \\ -4 & 0 & 1 \end{bmatrix}$ is the transpose of $\begin{bmatrix} 1 & 2 & -4 \\ 0 & 1 & 0 \\ 3 & 0 & 1 \end{bmatrix}$. If a given matrix is denoted by A, the transpose of A is denoted by A^T.

TRANSVERSAL (trans-vur'-suhl), a line that intersects two or more lines at different points. E.g., in the figure, AB is a transversal of lines l_1 and l_2; l_1 is a transversal of lines l_2 and AB; l_2 is a transversal of lines l_1 and AB. Three kinds of angle-pairs are formed when a transversal intersects two lines: ALTERNATE INTERIOR ANGLES; CORRESPONDING ANGLES; and consecutive interior angles on the same side of the transversal. In the figure, for transversal AB, the alternate interior angles are 3 and 6, 4 and 5; the corresponding angles are 1 and 5, 3 and 7, 2 and 6, 4 and 8; the consecutive interior angles on the same side of the transversal are 3 and 5, 4 and 6. See also PARALLEL LINES.

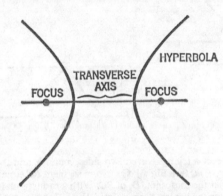

TRANSVERSE AXIS OF A HYPERBOLA (hahy-pur'-boh-lab), the segment of the line through the foci of a HYPERBOLA which lies between the two branches. (See figure.)

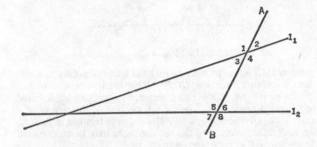

TRAPEZOID, a QUADRILATERAL with one pair of parallel sides. (See figure.) The parallel sides of a trapezoid are called the bases. If the nonparallel sides are equal, it is called an isosceles trapezoid. The base angles of an isosceles trapezoid are equal.

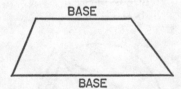

TRAPEZOIDAL RULE (trap-u-zoid'-uhl), a method of approximating the area under a curve. To approximate $\int_a^b f(x)\,dx$ divide the interval (a,b) into equal parts by a partition consisting of the points $x_0, x_1, x_2, \ldots, x_n$. Each interval (x_i, x_{i+1}), is the base of an approximating trapezoid and has length $\dfrac{b-a}{n}$ (see figure). The left side of each trapezoid has height $f(x_i)$, while the right side has height $f(x_{i+1})$.

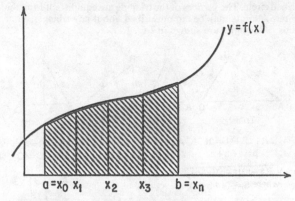

The total area of all the trapezoids is:

$$A = \frac{1}{2}\frac{b-a}{n}\left(f(x_0)+f(x_1)\right) + \frac{1}{2}\frac{b-a}{n}\left(f(x_1)+f(x_2)\right) + \cdots$$
$$+ \frac{1}{2}\frac{b-a}{n}\left(f(x_{n-1})+f(x_n)\right)$$
$$= \frac{1}{2}\frac{b-a}{n}\left(f(x_0)+f(x_1)+f(x_1)+f(x_2)+f(x_2)+\cdots\right.$$
$$\left.+f(x_n)+f(x_n)\right)$$
$$= \frac{b-a}{2n}f(x_0) + \frac{b-a}{n}\left(f(x_1)+\cdots+f(x_{n-1})\right) + \frac{b-a}{2n}f(x_n).$$

The last line in the derivation is called the trapezoidal rule.

Ex.: Approximate the area under the curve $y = x^2$ between $a = 0$, $b = 2$ by means of the trapezoidal rule with $n = 3$. Compare with the exact area computed by integration.

Sol.: Since $(b-a)/3 = 2/3$, $x_0 = 0$, $x_1 = 2/3$, $x_2 = 4/3$, and $x_3 = 2$,

$$A \approx \frac{2}{6}f(0) + \frac{2}{3}\left(f\left(\frac{2}{3}\right)+f\left(\frac{4}{3}\right)\right) + \frac{2}{6}f(2)$$
$$= 0 + \frac{2}{3}\left(\frac{4}{9}+\frac{16}{9}\right) + \frac{4}{3} = \frac{76}{27} \approx 2.81.$$

The exact area is $\displaystyle\int_0^2 x^2\,dx = \frac{x^3}{3}\bigg]_0^2 = \frac{8}{3} \approx 2.67.$

See also AREA UNDER A CURVE; SIMPSON'S RULE.

TRIANGLE, a POLYGON with three sides. The three sides intersect in three points, each of which is called a VERTEX of the triangle. The sum of the angles of a triangle equals a STRAIGHT ANGLE, or 180°. An exterior angle of a triangle is an angle formed by one side of the triangle and the adjacent side extended.

Triangles are classified according to their angles, as right, acute, or obtuse. A right triangle is a triangle with a right angle. An acute triangle is a triangle with three acute triangles. An obtuse triangle is a triangle with one obtuse angle. A triangle that does not have a right angle is called an oblique triangle.

Triangles may be classified by their sides as scalene, isosceles, or, equilateral. A scalene triangle is a triangle in which no two sides are equal. An isosceles triangle is a triangle with two equal sides. An equilateral triangle is a triangle with three equal sides.

The point of concurrency of the altitudes of the triangle is called the orthocenter of the triangle. An altitude of a triangle is the line from any vertex perpendicular to the opposite side.

The median of a triangle is the line segment from a vertex to the midpoint of the opposite sides. The point of concurrency of the medians of a triangle is called the centroid of the triangle.

The point of concurrency of the angle bisectors of a triangle is called the incenter of a triangle. A circle whose center is the incenter of the triangle and that is tangent (see TANGENT CURVES) to the three sides of the triangle is said to be inscribed in the triangle. The point of concurrency of the perpendicular bisectors of the sides of the triangle, is called the circumcenter of a triangle. A circle whose center is the circumcenter of the triangle, and that passes through the three vertices, is called a circumscribed circle. The vertices of the triangle are equidistant from the center. A circle may be circumscribed about any triangle. Four kinds of triangles are shown in Fig. 1.

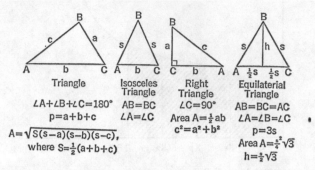

Triangle	Isosceles Triangle	Right Triangle	Equilaterial Triangle

$\angle A + \angle B + \angle C = 180°$ $AB = BC$ $\angle C = 90°$ $AB = BC = AC$

$p = a + b + c$ $\angle A = \angle C$ Area $A = \frac{1}{2}ab$ $\angle A = \angle B = \angle C$

$A = \sqrt{S(s-a)(s-b)(s-c)}$, $c^2 = a^2 + b^2$ $p = 3s$

where $S = \frac{1}{2}(a+b+c)$ Area $A = \frac{s^2}{4}\sqrt{3}$

$h = \frac{s}{2}\sqrt{3}$

Fig. 1

The sum of the lengths of the sides of a triangle is its PERIMETER p. The area A of any triangle is equal to $\frac{1}{2}$ the product of any base b and the altitude h drawn to that base, or $A = \frac{1}{2}bh$. Special formulas for the area and for the altitude of an equilateral triangle are given in Fig. 1. *See also* PYTHAGOREAN THEOREM.

To construct a triangle given the lengths, a, b, and c, of three sides (see Fig. 2): On line l, from a point A, mark off segment AB equal to c. With A as a center and a radius of length b, and with B as center and radius of length a, construct two arcs intersecting at C. Draw AC and BC. The required triangle is $\triangle ABC$.

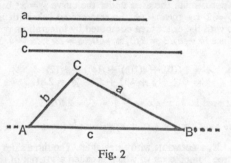

Fig. 2

To construct a triangle given two sides, b and c, and the angle included between them, $\angle A$ (see Fig. 3): On line l, construct AB equal to c. At A construct an angle equal to given angle A. On the side of the angle, mark off segment AC equal to b. Draw BC. $\triangle ABC$ is the required triangle.

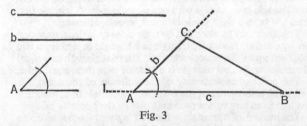

Fig. 3

To construct a triangle given two angles, A and B, and the side included between them, AB (see Fig. 4): On line l, mark off a segment equal to AB. At A construct an angle equal to $\angle A$, and at B construct an angle equal to $\angle B$. Let the intersection of the sides of $\angle A$ and $\angle B$ be point C. The required triangle is $\triangle ABC$.

To construct a triangle given a side, c, an angle, A, at the endpoint of side c, and the altitude to c, h_c (see Fig. 5): The locus of the vertex, C, is the intersection of the side of $\angle A$ and the line parallel to the side c at a distance h from that side. On line l,

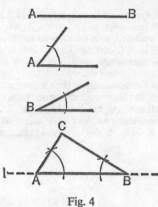

Fig. 4

construct AB equal to c. Construct the locus of points at a distance equal to h from line AB. This locus is a line parallel to AB, h units above AB. With A as a vertex, construct an angle equal to the given angle. Let C be the intersection of the side of $\angle A$ and the parallel line. Draw BC. The required triangle is $\triangle ABC$. Another triangle meeting the requirements may be constructed below side AB at a distance h from AB.

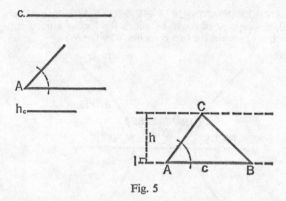

Fig. 5

To construct a triangle given two sides, a and b, and the median to side, a, m_a (see Fig. 6): Construct segment BC equal to a, and construct the midpoint, D, of BC. With a radius equal to m, and with D as the center, draw a circle. With C as a center and a radius equal to b, construct arcs intersecting the circle at A and A'. Draw AB, $A'B$, AC and $A'C$. The required triangle is $\triangle ABC$ or $\triangle A'BC$.

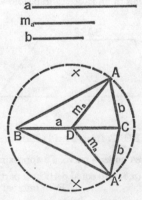

Fig. 6

To construct a triangle given a side, a, the angle opposite that side, $\angle A$, and the altitude to a, h_a (see Fig. 7): On line l, construct BC equal to a. At B construct an angle $\angle CBM$, equal to $\angle A$, and a line perpendicular to BM. Construct the perpendicular bisector of BC. Let O be the intersection of the two perpendicular lines. With O as the center and OB the radius, construct a circle. Construct a line parallel to BC at a distance equal

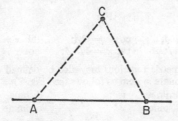

Fig. 7

to h from it. Any angle inscribed in the major arc of BC is equal to $\angle CBM$. The vertex of the required triangle may be A or A'. The required triangle is $\triangle ABC$ or $\triangle A'BC$.

TRIANGULATION, the method for finding the distance between two points by using them as vertices of a TRIANGLE (or a series of triangles) which has one side of known, or of measurable length (called the base line). When, by measurement, other sides or angles of the triangle so constructed are determined, the triangle can be solved by trigonometry. E.g., if points A and B in the figure are known, and point C is visible from both A and B, triangle ABC is constructed. By measuring angles A and B, and line AB, the distance from A to C and B to C can be determined by the Law of Sines (*see* SINES, LAW OF).

The method of triangulation is used in navigation and surveying.

TRICHOTOMY LAW (tri-kot'-uh-mee), the property that for two quantities, x and y, exactly one of the following relations is true: $x = y$, $x > y$, or $x < y$.

TRIGONOMETRIC CURVES, the graphs of the TRIGONOMETRIC FUNCTIONS (see figures). The maximim and minimum height (the AMPLITUDE) is $+1$ and -1 respectively for both sine and cosine curves. Thus, the amplitude of these curves is 1. Both the sine and the cosine curves complete a full cycle, or wave length (called the PERIOD) in 360°. Thus, the period of these curves is 360°. Since $\sin (180/2 + x) = \cos x$, the graph of the

cosine function may be obtained from that of the sine function by moving the sine curve 90° to the left (or by moving the Y-AXIS one unit to the right when each unit is 90°). The cosine curve is said to *differ in phase* by 90° from the sine curve.

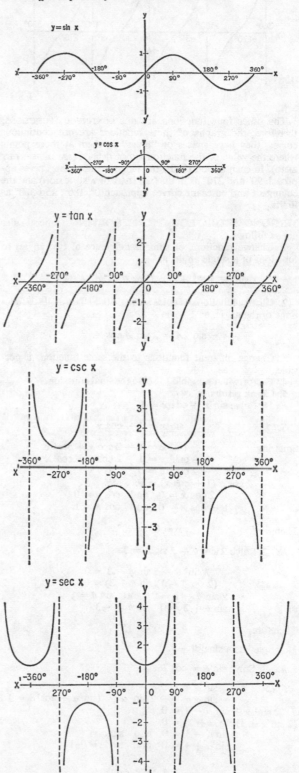

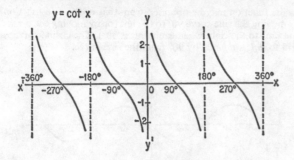

$y = \cot x$

The other four functions are not CONTINUOUS FUNCTIONS; therefore, the graphs of these functions are not continuous curves, they have spaces or "holes" in them at those points where the value of the function is not defined (*see* DIVISION BY ZERO). In each period (360°) the tangent and secant curves approach 90° and 270° as limits (*see* LIMIT OF A FUNCTION) and the cotangent and cosecant curves approach 0°, 180°, and 360° as limits.

TRIGONOMETRIC EQUATIONS, SOLVING. General rules are as follows:

1. Change functions of sum or difference of two angles to functions of a single angle, as

$$\sin (A + B) = \sin A \cos B + \cos A \sin B.$$

2. Change functions of twice an angle or half an angle to functions of the angle, as

$$\sin 2A = 2 \sin A \cos A.$$

3. Change different functions to the same function, if possible.
4. Factor when possible to solve the final equation.
5. Check results.

Ex. 1: Solve $\sin x + \cos x = 1$.

Sol.: $\qquad\qquad \sin x = 1 - \cos x$

Squaring, $\qquad \sin^2 x = 1 - 2 \cos x + \cos^2 x$
$$1 - \cos^2 x = 1 - 2 \cos x + \cos^2 x$$
$$2 \cos x - 2 \cos^2 x = 0$$
$$2 \cos x (1 - \cos x) = 0.$$
$$2 \cos x = 0 \quad \text{and} \quad \cos x = 0$$
or $\qquad 1 - \cos x = 0 \quad \text{and} \quad \cos x = 1.$

Therefore, $\qquad\qquad x = 0° \text{ or } 90°.$

Ex. 2: Solve $2 \sin^2 \theta + 5 \sin \theta = 3$.

Sol.: $\qquad 2 \sin^2 \theta + 5 \sin \theta - 3 = 0$
$$(2 \sin \theta - 1)(\sin \theta + 3) = 0.$$
$$2 \sin \theta - 1 = 0 \quad \text{and} \quad \sin \theta = \tfrac{1}{2}$$
or $\qquad \sin \theta + 3 = 0 \quad \sin \theta = -3.$

Therefore, $\qquad\qquad \theta = 30° \text{ or } 150°.$

No angle has a sine of -3.

Ex. 3: Solve $\sin \alpha = \cos 2\alpha$.

Sol.: $\qquad \sin \alpha = \cos^2 \alpha - \sin^2 \alpha$
$$\sin \alpha = 1 - 2 \sin^2 \alpha \quad (\sin^2 \alpha + \cos^2 \alpha = 1.)$$
$$2 \sin^2 \alpha + \sin \alpha - 1 = 0$$
$$(2 \sin \alpha - 1)(\sin \alpha + 1) = 0.$$
$$2 \sin \alpha - 1 = 0 \quad \text{and} \quad \sin \alpha = \tfrac{1}{2}$$
or $\qquad \sin \alpha + 1 = 0 \quad \text{and} \quad \sin \alpha = -1.$

Therefore, $\qquad \alpha = 30°, 150°, \text{ or } 270°.$

Ex. 4: Solve $\tan \beta \sec \beta = \sqrt{2}$.

Sol.: $\qquad \dfrac{\sin \beta}{\cos \beta} \cdot \dfrac{1}{\cos \beta} = \sqrt{2}$

$$\sin \beta = \sqrt{2} \cos^2 \beta$$
$$\sin \beta = \sqrt{2}(1 - \sin^2 \beta)$$
Squaring, $\qquad \sin^2 \beta = 2(1 - 2 \sin^2 \beta + \sin^4 \beta)$
$$2 \sin \beta - 5 \sin^2 \beta + 2 = 0$$
$$(2 \sin^2 \beta - 1)(\sin^2 \beta - 2) = 0.$$

$$2 \sin^2 \beta - 1 = 0 \quad \text{and} \quad \sin \beta = \sqrt{\tfrac{1}{2}} = \frac{\sqrt{2}}{2}$$
or $\qquad \sin^2 \beta - 2 = 0 \quad \text{and} \quad \sin \beta = \sqrt{2}.$
Therefore, $\qquad\qquad \beta = 45° \text{ or } 135°.$

No angle has a sine of $\sqrt{2}$.

TRIGONOMETRIC FUNCTIONS, the TRANSCENDENTAL FUNCTIONS, sine x ($\sin x$), cosine x ($\cos x$), tangent x ($\tan x$), secant x ($\sec x$), and cosecant x ($\csc x$). In geometry, the functions are defined for an acute angle of a right triangle as follows:

$$\sin x = \frac{\text{side opposite } \angle x}{\text{hypotenuse}}; \quad \cos x = \frac{\text{side adjacent } \angle x}{\text{hypotenuse}};$$

$$\tan x = \frac{\text{side opposite } \angle x}{\text{side adjacent } \angle x};$$

$$\sec x = \frac{1}{\cos x}; \quad \csc x = \frac{1}{\sin x}; \quad \cot x = \frac{1}{\tan x}$$

The trigonometric functions may be defined using a unit circle as follows (see Fig. 1):

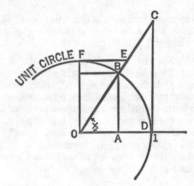

Fig. 1

$\sin x = BA;$ $\cos x = OA;$ $\text{tab } x = CD;$
$\sec x = 1/OA$ $\csc x = 1/BA;$ $\cot x = FE.$

The trigonometric functions may also be defined on the rectangular coordinate system as follows (see Fig. 2):

$$\sin \theta = \frac{\text{ordinate}}{\text{distance}} = \frac{y}{r}; \qquad \csc \theta = \frac{\text{distance}}{\text{ordinate}} = \frac{r}{y};$$

$$\cos \theta = \frac{\text{abscissa}}{\text{distance}} = \frac{x}{r}; \qquad \sec \theta = \frac{\text{distance}}{\text{abscissa}} = \frac{r}{x};$$

$$\tan \theta = \frac{\text{ordinate}}{\text{abscissa}} = \frac{y}{x}; \qquad \cot \theta = \frac{\text{abscissa}}{\text{ordinate}} = \frac{x}{y}.$$

The signs of the functions are determined by the signs of the ABSCISSA and the ORDINATE. The distance is always positive. *See* TABLE NO. 3.

The sine and cosecant are positive in the 1st and 2nd quadrants and negative in the 3rd and 4th. The cosine and secant are positive in the first and fourth quadrants and negative in the second and third. The tangent and cotangent are positive in the first and third quadrants and negative in the second and fourth.

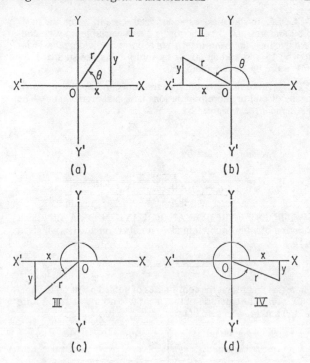

(a)   (b)

(c)   (d)

Fig. 2

The trigonometric functions were derived for positive acute angles. The functions of any angle between 90° and 360°, (except 180° and 270°) may be found by expressing it as (180° ± θ) or (360° − θ). The numerical value of the function will be the same as the function of θ; the sign of the function is determined by the quadrant. Angles of 150°, 210°, and 330° have functions of the same ABSOLUTE VALUE as the functions of 30°. Angles of 135°, 225°, and 315° have functions with the same absolute value as 45°. And the functions of angles of 120°, 240°, and 300° have the same absolute value as those of 60.

Exs.:

1. sin 140° = sin (180° − 40°) = sin 40°.
2. cos 120° = cos (180° − 60°) = −cos 60°.
3. tan 230° = tan (180° + 50°) = tan 50°.
4. tan 310° = tan (360° − 50°) = −tan 50°.
5. sec 200° = sec (180° + 20°) = −sec 20°.
6. csc 160° = csc (180° − 20°) = csc 20°.

The derivative of each CO-FUNCTION is the negative of the derivative of its corresponding trigonometric function, with each function replaced by its co-function. For example $\frac{d}{dx}(\tan x) = \sec^2 x$, while $\frac{d}{dx}(\cot x) = -\csc^2 x$.

TRIGONOMETRIC INTEGRAL SUBSTITUTIONS, changing integrals to simple form by the use of trigonometric identities. Integrals involving $a^2 - x^2$, $a^2 + x^2$, $\sqrt{a^2 - x^2}$, $\sqrt{a^2 + x^2}$, $\sqrt{x^2 - a^2}$ may often be put into simple form by using one of the trigonometric identities:

$$1 - \sin^2\theta = \cos^2\theta.$$
$$1 + \tan^2\theta = \sec^2\theta.$$
$$\sec^2\theta - 1 = \tan^2\theta.$$

Ex.: Find $\int \frac{1}{\sqrt{a^2 - x^2}}\,dx,\ a > 0.$

Sol.: Let $x = a \sin\theta$. Then $dx/d\theta = a \cos\theta$, and

$$\int \frac{dx}{\sqrt{a^2 - x^2}} = \int \frac{a\cos\theta\,d\theta}{\sqrt{a^2 - a^2\sin^2\theta}} = \int \frac{a\cos\theta\,d\theta}{a\sqrt{1 - \sin^2\theta}} = \int \frac{\cos\theta\,d\theta}{\sqrt{\cos^2\theta}}$$

$$= \int \frac{\cos\theta\,d\theta}{\pm\cos\theta}\ (\pm \text{ depends upon the sign of } \cos\theta.)$$

$$= \int \pm d\theta = \pm(\theta + C); \text{ since } \theta = \sin^{-1}(x/a), \text{ this equals } \pm(\sin^{-1}(x/a) + C).$$

Using only the principal value of $\sin^{-1}(x/a)$ means that θ will lie between $-\pi/2$ and $\pi/2$, hence $\cos\theta \geq 0$ and the ambiguous sign is plus. That is,

$$\int \frac{dx}{\sqrt{a^2 - x^2}} = \sin^{-1}(x/a) + C,$$

In general, $x = a\sin\theta$ replaces $a^2 - x^2$ by $a^2\cos^2\theta$;
               $x = a\tan\theta$ replaces $a^2 + x^2$ by $a^2\sec^2\theta$;
and $x = a\sec\theta$ replaces $x^2 - a^2$ by $a^2\tan^2\theta$.

TRIGONOMETRY (trig-uh-nom′-i-tree), the branch of mathematics that deals with the properties and applications of the ratios and functions of a triangle. The word means "triangle measurement." Trigonometry had its origins in ancient times and grew out of the attempts to study and describe the sun, moon, planets, and stars. Ancient Greek astronomers made the first important advances and PITISCUS published the first textbook in trigonometry in 1595. Plane trigonometry is the study of triangles on a plane surface and spherical trigonometry is the study of triangles on the surface of a sphere.

TRIHEDRAL ANGLE (trahy-hee′-dral), a POLYHEDRAL ANGLE with three faces. (See figure.) If two of the face angles are equal, it is an isosceles trihedral angle.

TRINOMIAL (trahy-noh′-mee-al), an ALGEBRAIC EXPRESSION having three terms, as $a^2 + 2ab + b^2$.

TRINOMIAL, PERFECT SQUARE, a TRINOMIAL whose two binomial factors (*see* FACTORING) are equal. To recognize a perfect square trinomial:

1. The first and third terms are SQUARES and their signs are plus.

2. The sign of the middle term may be plus or minus.

3. The middle term is twice the PRODUCT of the SQUARE ROOTS of the first and third terms.

The following examples are perfect square trinomials: $x^2 + 10x + 25$; $4x^2 + 12xy + 9y^2$; and $16x^2 - 56x + 49$.

TRINOMIALS, FACTORING, *see* FACTORING.

TRIRECTANGULAR SPHERICAL TRIANGLE, one of the eight spherical triangles formed when three planes pass through the center of a SPHERE, each PERPENDICULAR to the other two (See figure.)

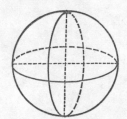 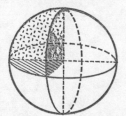

TRISECTION OF A LINE SEGMENT, to divide a LINE SEGMENT into three equal parts.

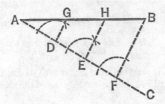

Ex.: Given segment *AB*, divide *AB* into three equal parts, (see figure.)

Sol.: At any convenient angle draw *AC*. On *AC* mark off three equal segments *AD*, *DE*, and *EF*. Draw *BF*. At *E* construct *EH* parallel to *BF* and at *D* construct *DG* parallel to *BF*. See PARALLEL LINES. *AG = GH = HB*, because if three or more parallel lines intercept equal segments on one transversal, they intercept equal segments on any transversal. (Note: This construction may be used for dividing a line into any number of equal parts.)

TRISECTION OF AN ANGLE (trahy'-sek-shun), one of the three famous construction problems that have interested mathematicians since ancient times. It has been proven impossible to trisect an angle with only COMPASSES and straight edge; however, it can be done with various mechanical devices. The other two problems are SQUARING THE CIRCLE and DUPLICATION OF THE CUBE.

TROPICAL YEAR, the length of the YEAR as measured between successive vernal EQUINOXES; also called the astronomical, equinoctial, natural or solar year. Its length is ab. 365 days, 5 hours, 48 min., 46 sec. TABLE NO. 5.

TRUTH TABLE, a tabular arrangement of the truth value (true or false) of a logical PROPOSITION. The following tables display the truth value for CONJUNCTION, $\land$, DISJUNCTION, $\lor$, and negation, $\sim$ (see NEGATION, LOGICAL).

P	Q	$P \land Q$
T	T	T
T	F	F
F	T	F
F	F	F

P	Q	$P \lor Q$
T	T	T
T	F	T
F	T	T
F	F	F

P	$\sim P$
T	F
F	T

T-SCORE, in statistics, a standardized score in which the MEAN is 50 and STANDARD DEVIATION is 10. A variable may be converted to measurements in terms of *t*-scores by dividing the deviation by 10 and adding 50, or by multiplying the standard deviate score by 10 and adding 50.

T-TEST, in statistics, a sample test concerning the mean or means of one or more populations (*see* EXPECTED VALUE). The one sample *t*-test is given by

$$T = \frac{(\bar{x} - \mu_0)\sqrt{n}}{s}$$

and the two sample *t*-test by

$$T = \frac{\bar{x}_1 - \bar{x}_2 - \delta}{\sqrt{\frac{(n_1 - 1)s_1^2 + (n_2 - 1)s_2^2}{n_1 + n_2 - 2}}\sqrt{\frac{1}{n_1} + \frac{1}{n_2}}}$$

TWO-POINT FORM OF AN EQUATION OF A LINE, an equation of a line, containing two points (x,y) and (x_2,y_2), given by:

$$\frac{y_2 - y_1}{x_2 - x_1} = \frac{y - y_2}{x - x_2},$$

where (x,y) represent the coordinates of a third point on the line.

Ex.: Find the equation of the line if two points on the line are $(-4,3)$ and $(4,-1)$. (See figure.)

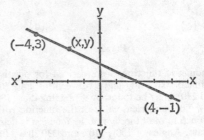

Sol.:

$$\frac{y_2 - y_1}{x_2 - x_1} = \frac{y - y_2}{x - x_2}.$$

$$\frac{-1 - 3}{4 + 4} = \frac{y + 1}{x - 4}$$

$$-\tfrac{1}{2} = \frac{y + 1}{x - 4}$$

$$x - 4 = -2y - 2$$

$$x + 2y = 2$$

See also GEOMETRY, ANALYTIC.

TYPE I ERROR, *see* ALPHA ERROR.

U

UNBIASED ESTIMATOR (un-bahy'-asd), in statistics, an ESTI-MATOR whose EXPECTED VALUE is equal to the PARAMETER for which it furnishes estimates.

A *biased estimator* is one whose expected value is not equal to the parameter for which it furnishes estimates.

UNBOUNDED FUNCTION, a FUNCTION, $f(x)$, defined on an interval, such that for any number, b, $|f(x)| > b$. E.g., the function $f(x) = 1/x$ defined on the open interval $0 < x < 1$ is not bounded; the function defined by $f(x) = \begin{cases} 1/x \text{ if } 0 < x \leq 1 \\ 0 \text{ if } x = 0. \end{cases}$ is not bounded on the closed interval $0 \leq x \leq 1$.

UNDEFINED TERM, in mathematics, those elements whose meanings are agreed upon without a formal definition (*see* DEFINITION, CHARACTERISTICS OF). The undefined terms, together with AXIOMS form the basis or foundation of a POSTULATIONAL SYSTEM. Undefined terms are necessary because attempting to give a definition of all the elements of a body of knowledge ultimately leads to CIRCULAR REASONING. Thus, the undefined terms provide the starting point for any logical system. In EUCLIDEAN GEOMETRY, undefined terms are POINT, LINE, and PLANE. In algebra, the iteral symbols x, y, a, b may be considered undefined terms.

UNIMODULAR MATRIX (yoo-ni-moj'-yuh-luhr may'-triks), a square MATRIX whose determinant is equal to 1. E.g., $\begin{bmatrix} 1 & 0 \\ 1 & 1 \end{bmatrix}$ is a unimodular matrix.

UNION, in mathematics, for any two sets, A and B, the SET of all elements which are in either set, denoted $A \cup B$. (See figure.)

Ex. 1: $A = \{1, 3, 5, 7\}$, $B = \{2, 4, 6, 8\}$. What is the union of A and B?

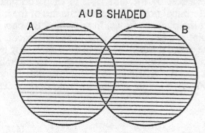

AUB SHADED

A   B

Sol.: $A \cup B = \{1, 2, 3, 4, 5, 6, 7, 8\}$.

Ex. 2: Let A be the point set which is the locus of $y = \sqrt{1 - x^2}$, and B be the locus of $y = -\sqrt{1 - x^2}$. What is the union of A and B?

Sol.: Both A and B are semicircles. Their union is the circle given by $x^2 + y^2 = 1$.

The operation of union satisfies the following algebraic laws: $A \cup A = A$; $A \cup (B \cup C) = (A \cup B) \cup C$.

UNIQUE (yoo-neek'), the only one. A solution to an EQUATION may be said to be unique; in $2x = 4$, $x = 2$, 2 is a unique solution since no other number will SATISFY the equation. The additive IDENTITY of the set of REAL NUMBERS, 0, is said to be unique, since 0 is the only element of the set for which it is true that $a + 0 = a$.

UNIT, a standard of measure, such as an inch, a DEGREE, or a RADIAN; the unit REAL NUMBER is 1, the unit IMAGINARY NUMBER is i. The UNIT CIRCLE is a circle of radius of 1 unit of distance. A unit square is a square the length of whose side is 1 unit.

UNIT CIRCLE, a CIRCLE of radius one. If the center of the circle is not otherwise specified, it may be assumed to be at the ORIGIN of the coordinate system.

UNIT DISTANCE, the distance from the ORIGIN to the point arbitrarily designated with the COORDINATE of 1 on a NUMBER LINE. The term is not applied in coordinate systems using more than one number axis unless the unit distances for each axis are the same.

UNITY ELEMENT, for any operation called "MULTIPLICATION", an element U, such that, for any element X in the set on which the operation is defined, $U \cdot X = X \cdot U = X$. E.g., in arithmetic, the unity element is 1, since any number multiplied by 1 remains unchanged. *See also* ZERO ELEMENT.

UNIVERSAL SET, *see* SET.

UNIVERSAL TIME (UT) or **Greenwich Mean Time (GMT)**, solar time measured from the PRIME MERIDIAN at Greenwich. It is the system of time usually used by astronomers and navigators. *See also* CIVIL TIME; TABLE NO.5.

UNKNOWN, of an equation, the value of a VARIABLE that satisfies the equation.

V

VALUE, of an expression, the result obtained when the indicated operations are performed. E.g., the value of $(3x)^2$ is $9x^2$; of a FUNCTION, an element of the RANGE of the function for a particular value of the DOMAIN. E.g., if $y = f(x) = 3x + 2$, the value of y at $x = 2$ is $3(2) + 2 = 8$.

VARIABLE, a quantity the value of which may change in a given discussion. A variable whose value depends on that of another variable is called a dependent variable. In the formula $C = 2\pi r$, C is the dependent variable, since its value depends on the value of r.

A variable that causes the value of another variable to change when its own value is changed is called an independent variable. Thus, in $C = 2\pi r$, the independent variable is r.

Independent variables are also known as PARAMETERS. Sometimes more than one occurs in a single equation, e.g., the volume of a CYLINDER (such as a tin can) depends on the radius, r, of the CIRCLE which forms the base, and on the height, h: $V = \pi r^2 h$.

VARIANCE, POPULATION, in statistics, $E[(x - u)^2]$, which is equivalent to $E(x^2) - u^2$. *See also* EXPECTED VALUE.

VARIANCE, SAMPLE, in statistics, a measure of dispersion (*see* DISPERSION, MEASURES OF), denoted s^2, that gives the average squared distance of the sample observations from the sample MEAN. It is usually defined by the formula

$$s^2 = \frac{\sum_{i=1}^{n} (x_i - \overline{x})^2}{n - 1};$$

It is sometimes defined as

$$s^2 = \frac{\sum_{i=1}^{n} (x_i - \overline{x})^2}{n}.$$

The variance is also known as the *mean squared deviation*. It is an estimate of the population variance σ^2. If $n - 1$ is used as the divisor in the formula for s^2, the ESTIMATOR is unbiased; if n is used as the divisor, the estimator is biased.

If the observations have been classified, the sample variance is

$$s^2 = \frac{\sum_{i=1}^{k} (x'_i - \overline{x})^2 f_i}{n - 1},$$

where x'_i denotes the midpoint of the ith class; f_i, the frequency of the ith class; $\overline{x}$, the sample mean; k, the number of classes; and n, the total number of observations.

VARIATION, the relationship between two quantities in which a change in one results in a definite change in the other.

A quantity which never changes in value is called a *constant of variation*. In the formula $C = 2\pi r$, 2 and π are constants.

The relation of two variables, which vary so that their quotient equals a constant (or the ratio remains fixed) is called *direct variation*.

Ex. 1: The circumference of a circle varies directly as the diameter. $C/d = \pi$. The constant is π.

Ex. 2: If $x/y = \frac{2}{3}$, then x varies directly as y. The ratio of any of the values of x and y in the table below is always $\frac{2}{3}$.

x	4	6	8	10	12	14	16
y	6	9	12	15	18	21	24

The change in two variables in which their product remains constant is called *inverse variation*. As one variable increases, the other decreases. In a table of values for $xy = 12$,

x	1	2	3	4	6	12
y	12	6	4	3	2	1

x varies inversely as y, and y varies inversely as x.

The direct variation of one variable with two or more other variables is called joint variation. If x varies jointly as y and z, then x varies directly as the product of y and z, or $x = kyz$, when k is the constant of variation. The distance traveled in 5 hours at 35 miles per hour is greater than the distance traveled in 4 hours at 35 miles per hour. But the distance covered in 4 hours is greater if the rate is increased to 45 miles per hour. Therefore the distance varies jointly as the rate and time. The formula may be expressed in two ways:

$$\frac{d}{rt} = k \text{ or } d = krt; \; k = 1.$$

The area A of a triangle varies jointly as the base b and the altitude h, or

$$A = kbh \text{ and } k = \tfrac{1}{2}.$$

VECTOR, a directed line segment. It may be used to represent a quantity such as a force, that has both magnitude and direction.

Vectors are usually symbolized by arrows (see figure). A vector may be described by the difference in each coordinate of the initial and terminal points. If the coordinates of the initial point are (x,y) in the plane or (x,y,z) in space and the coordinates of the end point are (x',y') or (x',y',z') the differences, x-x', y-y', and z-z', are called the coordinates of the vector. Any two vectors with the same coordinates are identical. The number of coordinates associated with a given vector is its dimension. *See also* PARALLELOGRAM, LAW OF FORCES; VECTOR, COORDINATES OF.

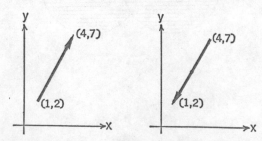

VECTOR ADDITION. Given the coordinates of two VECTORS, (a,b) and (a',b'), their resultant (vector sum) is defined as follows:

$$(a,b) + (a',b') = (a + a', b + b').$$

This definition of vector addition can be extended to any number of vectors; to find the coordinates of their vector sum, add corresponding coordinates. The same definition also applies to three-dimensional vectors.

Ex. 1: Add the following sets of vectors:

    a. $(1,2)$, $(-1,3)$.

    b. $(1,2)$, $(2,1)$, $(-3,-3)$.

    c. $(3,1,2)$, $(5,-1,-3)$.

Sol.: a. $(0,5)$ b. $(0,0)$ c. $(8,0,-1)$

Ex. 2: What is the additive inverse of the vector $(2,3)$ i.e., what vector can be added so that their sum is the zero-vector, $(0,0)$?

Sol.: Each of the components of the zero-vector is zero; the additive inverse of the given vector will therefore have in each component the additive inverse, or negative, of the component of the given vector. Thus the additive inverse in this case is $(-2, -3)$.

Check: $(2,3) + (-2,-3) = (2 + -2, 3 + -3) = (0,0)$. *See also* VECTOR, COORDINATES OF.

VECTOR, COORDINATES OF, for a VECTOR whose initial point is (x_1, y_1) and whose end point is (x_2, y_2), the ordered pair $(x_2 - x_1, y_2 - y_1)$. The x-coordinate of the vector is $x_2 - x_1$ and the y-coordinate is $y_2 - y_1$. In three dimensions, the x- and y-coordinates are the same, and the z-coordinate is $z_2 - z_1$. Parallel vectors have proportional coordinates. (See figure.) *See also* VECTOR ADDITION.

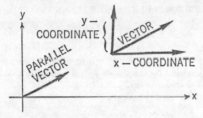

Ex. 1: What are the coordinates of: a. the vector with initial point $(1,2)$ and terminal point $(5,7)$? b. the vector with initial point $(0,0)$ and terminal point $(-3,-2)$?

Sol.: a. The x-coordinate of this vector is $5 - 1 = 4$, while the y-coordinate is $7 - 2 = 5$.

b. Its coordinates are -3 and -2. The coordinates are the same as those of the end point whenever the initial point is the origin.

VECTOR MULTIPLICATION, *see* VECTOR PRODUCT.

VECTOR PRODUCT or Cross Product, of TWO VECTORS, A and B, a third vector, whose length is $|A||B| \sin \theta$, (where θ is the angle between A and B) and which is perpendicular to the plane determined by A and B and its direction is that in which a right-threaded screw advances when its head is rotated from A to B through the angle θ. The vector product of A and B is written $A \times B$. Vector multiplication is *not* commutative (*see* COMMUTATIVE PROPERTY). The vector $A \times B$ has the same length as the vector $B \times A$, but they point in the opposite directions. (See figure.) Thus, $B \times A = -A \times B$.

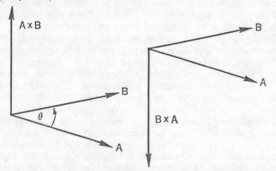

Ex. 1: Find the cross product of the two vectors $(0,1)$ and $(2,2)$.

Sol.: Since $\theta = 45°$, $A \times B = |A||B| \sin 45° = (1)(2\sqrt{2})(1/\sqrt{2}) = 2$.

The magnitude of the cross product of two vectors A and B is equal to the area of the parallelogram with two sides equal to A and two equal to B. Thus areas can be found by using the cross product.

Ex. 2: Find the area of the triangle with the vertices $a = (1,1)$, $b = (3,3)$, and $c = (4,1)$.

Sol.: Let the vector from a to b be A, and the vector from a to c be B. The area of the triangle is then half of $|A \times B|$.

$$
\begin{aligned}
\text{Area} &= \tfrac{1}{2}|A \times B| = \tfrac{1}{2}|(|A||B| \sin \theta)| \\
&= \tfrac{1}{2}|(2\sqrt{2})(3) \sin 45°| \\
&= \tfrac{1}{2}\left|(6\sqrt{2})\left(\frac{1}{\sqrt{2}}\right)\right| = \tfrac{1}{2} \cdot 6 = 3.
\end{aligned}
$$

VELOCITY, in mathematics, the derivative (*see* DERIVATIVE OF A FUNCTION) or rate of change, of the position, s, of a moving body with respect to time. If the position is given by $s = f(t)$, then velocity, v, is given by $v = ds/dt$.

Ex. 1: A body moves according to the law of motion $s = t^2 - 4t + 3$. Find its velocity in 3 seconds.

Sol.: $v = ds/dt$

    $v = 2t - 4$. In 3 seconds, $t = 3$, and $v = 2(3) - 4$, or $v = 2$ feet per second.

Ex. 2: A body moves according to $s = 3 + 4t - t^2$. When will its velocity be zero?

Sol.: $v = ds/dt$

    $v = 4 - 2t$. Let $v = 0$:

    $0 = 4 - 2t$

    $2t = 4$

    $t = 2$.

The velocity is zero when the body is in motion 2 seconds.

VELOCITY VECTOR, the derivative (*see* DERIVATIVE OF A FUNCTION) of the POSITION VECTOR with respect to time. The velocity vector is given by $v = d\mathbf{R}/dt = \mathbf{i}\, dx/dt + \mathbf{j}\, dy/dt$. By using the CHAIN RULE, v may also be expressed in terms of the TANGENT VECTOR, $\mathbf{T}$: $v = d\mathbf{R}/dt$ and $d\mathbf{R}/dt = \dfrac{d\mathbf{R}}{ds} \cdot \dfrac{ds}{dt}$. Then $v = \mathbf{T}\, ds/dt$, where $\mathbf{T} = d\mathbf{R}/ds$.

VERSED SINE (vurst sahyn), of α, the function, $1 - \cos \alpha$. Versed sine α is abbreviated as versin α.

VERTEX, (pl. vertices), of an angle, the point where the sides of the angle meet. A vertex of a POLYGON is a vertex of the angle formed by the intersection of two sides of the polygon. There are as many vertices of a polygon as there are sides. Thus, a triangle has three vertices. (See figure.)

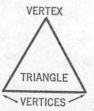

The vertex of a PARABOLA is the midpoint on the perpendicular line of a parabola from the FOCUS to the directrix (*see* CONIC SECTIONS.) It is the point on the parabola closest to the directrix.

Ex. 1: Locate the vertex of the parabolas $y = 3x^2$ and $x = -2y^2$.

Sol.: The origin is the vertex in both cases.

If the vertex of a parabola is not at the origin, but at the point (h,k), these coordinates occur in the equation of the parabola which is $(y - k) = 4p(x - h)^2$.

Ex. 2: Determine the vertex of each of the following parabolas by inspecting their equations:

a. $(y - 2) = 7(x - 1)^2$.

b. $(x - 1) = 2(y + 3)^2$ (opens to right).

c. $y = 2x^2 + 4x$ (Hint: Complete squares).

   Sol.: a. (1,2)   b. (−3,1)   c. After completing squares the equation is $y = 2(x + 1)^2 - 2$, or $y + 2 = 2(x + 1)^2$. The vertex is at (−2,−1).

VERTICAL ANGLES, two nonadjacent angles formed by two intersecting straight lines.

   In the figure, $\angle a$ and $\angle b$ are vertical angles; $\angle c$ and $\angle d$ are vertical angles.

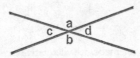

   If two straight lines intersect, the vertical angles are equal. Hence, in the figure, $\angle a = \angle b$ and $\angle c = \angle d$.

VERTICAL LINE, a line PERPENDICULAR to the horizontal AXIS in a plane, or perpendicular to the horizontal plane in SPACE.

VIÈTE or Vieta, FRANÇOIS (vee-yet′), 1540–1603, French mathematician whose chief contribution in this field was the application of algebra to geometry. He anticipated aspects of DESCARTES' invention of analytic methods in geometry, and made important contributions to trigonometry. The Law of Tangents (*see* TANGENTS, LAW OF) first appears in his works.

VINCULUM (vin′-kyoo-lum), a bar used over two or more terms to show that the terms are to be treated as a unit. The vinculum is usually used with the RADICAL SIGN $\sqrt{\ }$, as $\sqrt{16 + 9} = \sqrt{25} = 5$. *See also* GROUPING SYMBOLS.

VOLUME, the number of unit cubes contained in a solid figure. *See* TABLE NO. 4.

   A unit of volume is a cube each of whose edges is one unit in length, as 1 ft. or 1 in. (See figure.)

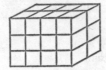

VOLUME BY INTEGRATION, for a solid of cross sectional area $A(x)$ in the plane perpendicular to the x-axis from $x = a$ on the left to $x = b$ on the right, the DEFINITE INTEGRAL:

$$V = \int_a^b A(x)\, dx.$$

$(3,2)$

$y = (2/3)x$

$A = \pi \left(\dfrac{2x}{3}\right)2$

The cross sectional area can usually be found from the solid's geometry, but sometimes integration is necessary (*see* AREA).

   Ex.: Find the volume of a right circular cone of height 3 and basal radius 2. (See figure.)

   Sol.: Consider the cone's axis to be the x-axis, the cone's vertex being the origin. The cone extends from $x = 0$ to $x = 3$. The cross section at any point is a circle whose radius is the distance from the x-axis to the line $y = \dfrac{2x}{3}$. Thus the area at any point x is $A(x) = \pi \left(\dfrac{2x}{3}\right)^2$. The volume is

$$V = \int_0^3 \pi \left(\frac{2x}{3}\right)^2 dx = \frac{4\pi}{9} \int_0^3 x^2\, dx$$

$$= \frac{4\pi}{9}\left(\left[\frac{x^3}{3}\right]_0^3\right) = \frac{4\pi}{9}(9) = 4\pi.$$

See also DEFINITE INTEGRAL.

VOLUME OF ANY GEOMETRIC SOLID, the number of times the solid contains a unit of volume.

VOLUME UNDER A SURFACE, for a surface $= F(x,y)$ defined over a region between the curves $y = g(x)$ and $y = h(x)$ extending from $x = a$ to $x = b$, the iterated integral:

$$\int_a^b dx \int_{g(x)}^{h(x)} F(x,y)\, dy.$$

   Ex.: Let $z = x^2 y$. What is the volume under this surface over the region bounded by the curve $y = 2x$ and the x-axis $(y = 0)$ between $x = 0$ and $x = \pi/2$?

$$Sol.: V = \int_0^{\pi/2} dx \int_0^{2x} x^2 y\, dy$$

$$= \int_0^{\pi/2} \left[\frac{x^2 y^2}{2}\right]_0^{2x} dx$$

$$= \int_0^{\pi/2} 2x^4\, dx = \left[\frac{2x^5}{5}\right]_0^{\pi/2} = \frac{2\left(\frac{\pi}{2}\right)^5}{5} = \frac{2 \cdot \pi^5}{2^5 \cdot 5} = \frac{\pi^5}{2^4 \cdot 5}$$

$$= \frac{\pi^5}{80}.$$

See also DOUBLE INTEGRAL.

VON NEUMANN, JOHN, 1903–1957, born Johann von Neumann; Hungarian-American mathematician, who made a number of contributions to both pure and applied mathematics and to mathematical physics. He was educated at the Univ. of Berlin, the Technische Hochschule in Zurich, and the Univ. of Budapest, where he received his doctorate in 1926. After further studies at the Univ. of Göttingen, he taught at the universities of Berlin and Hamburg. In 1930 he came to the U.S. and became a citizen in 1937. He was professor of mathematical physics at Princeton Univ. from 1931 and from 1933 was also associated with the Institute for Advanced Study at Princeton.

   During the early 1930's, Von Neumann made important contributions to the Quantum Theory. From 1945 he headed efforts at Princeton to develop an electronic COMPUTER. Among the results of his work was MANIAC (*m*athematical *a*nalyzer, *n*umerical *i*ntegrator *a*nd *c*omputer), which performed mathematical tasks that could not have been done by humans in any reasonable amount of time and thus enabled the hydrogen bomb to be built and tested. Von Neumann was a member of the General Advisory Committee of the Atomic Energy Commission from 1952 and a member of the Commission itself from 1954. He is also well known as one of the founders of the theory of games and published with Oskar Morgenstern the important *Theory of Games and Economic Behavior* in 1944, a work which opened up whole new areas of research not only in economics but also in military strategy and other fields.

W X Y Z

WALLIS, JOHN (wahl-lis), 1616–1703, English mathematician and logician, who wrote many works on mathematics. He introduced the word "mantissa" in connection with LOGARITHMS (1963) and was the first to use the symbol ∞ to designate infinity. *See also* LOGARITHM, CHARACTERISTIC OF A.

WASHER METHOD, a method of finding the volume of a solid of revolution. If the curve $y = f(x)$ is revolved around the x-axis, the cross section of the resulting solid at $x = a$ is a circular disk of radius $f(a)$. The cross-sectional area at a is thus $\pi(f(a))^2$. If the solid extends from $x = p$ to $x = r$, then the volume is:

$$V = \int_p^r \pi(f(x))^2 \, dx. \text{ (See figure)}.$$

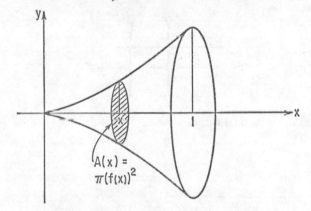

$$A(x) = \pi(f(x))^2$$

Ex.: What is the volume of the solid generated by revolving the area under the curve $y = x^2$ between $x = 0$ and $x = 2$ around the x-axis?

$$\text{Sol.: } V = \int_0^2 \pi(x^2)^2 \, dx = \pi \int_0^2 x^4 \, dx$$

$$= \pi \left(\left[\frac{x^5}{5} \right]_0^2 \right) = \frac{32\pi}{5} \text{ cubic units.}$$

See also SHELL METHOD; VOLUME BY INTEGRATION.

WEIGHTED AVERAGE, in statistics, the average obtained when each observation is multiplied by a factor, called a weight, that is an indication of that observation's relative importance. Two examples of weighted means are POOLED ESTIMATES of proportions or variances (*see* VARIANCE, POPULATION; VARIANCE, SAMPLE).

Ex.: If 3 test scores are 72, 81, and 84, the arithmetic average is $\bar{x} = 79$. But, if the instructor decides to weight the scores by .2, .35, and .45, respectively, then the average is $\bar{x} = (.2)(72) + (.35)(81) + (.45)(84) = 80.55$.

WEIGHTS AND MEASURES, *see* TABLE NOS. 4; 5; ENGLISH SYSTEM; METRIC SYSTEM.

WHITEHEAD, ALFRED NORTH, 1861–1947, b. Ramsgate, Kent, British philosopher, studied mathematics at Cambridge University. Whitehead later became professor of philosophy at Harvard Univ. His first published works, including the *Principia Mathematica* ("Mathematical Principles"), in collaboration with RUSSELL, showed his interest in the relationship between mathematics and logic. Later Whitehead was more concerned to express his interest in logic, epistemology, and metaphysics, in which he evolved a "philosophy of organism" which took its cue from the Theory of Relativity in science, arguing that the world was not composed of static substances and properties but rather a vast network of events all of which were intimately related to all others. Two of his important works in this connection are *Process and Reality* (1929) and *The Concept of Nature* (1920).

WHOLE NUMBER, an element of the set of NATURAL NUMBERS, their negatives, and ZERO. A whole number is an INTEGER.

WIDTH, the distance across a plane figure. In the figure, AD is the width of rectangle $ABCD$.

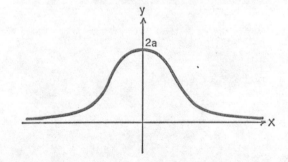

WILCOXON SIGNED-RANK TEST, *see* SIGNED-RANK TEST.

WITCH OF AGNESI, the curve that graphs the equation, $y = \dfrac{8a^3}{x^2 + 4a^2}$, in which a is a constant. Note that a curve of the same general form is given by $y = \dfrac{1}{x^2 + 1}$. (See figure.)

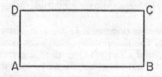

x-AXIS, the horizontal AXIS in a system of CARTESIAN COORDINATES.

x-INTERCEPT (in′-tur-sept), the point at which a line crosses the x-AXIS in a graph when y equals zero in the equation of a line.

y-AXIS, the vertical AXIS in a system of CARTESIAN COORDINATES. It is PERPENDICULAR to the x-AXIS.

y-INTERCEPT, the point at which a line crosses the y-axis in a graph when x equals zero in the equation of the line.

ZENO OF ELEA (zee′-noh ee′-lee-uh), ab. 450 B.C., an important member of a group called Eleans, who revolted against the philosophy of the PYTHAGOREANS. The Eleans were chiefly interested in trisection of an ANGLE, squaring a CIRCLE, and duplicating a CUBE. Zeno is remembered for his paradoxes, particularly those involving motion, which posed the problem of the conditions for convergence of an infinite series. Thus, he argued that motion is impossible since in order to arrive at its destination, a moving body must reach the middle of its path; before reaching that point, however, it must reach half that distance; etc. Therefore, in order to move from one place to another, a moving body must pass through an infinite number of spaces, which is impossible.

ZERO. As a place holder, the word for the symbol "0" to indicate the absence of DIGITS in a number. A number, such as 276, means 2 hundreds, 7 tens, and 6 units. The number two hundred seventy, written 270, has no units, therefore zero is used to represent the absence of the unit's digit. In the number eight hundred seven, 807, zero is written in the ten's place.

In arithmetic, 0 is the additive identity or ZERO ELEMENT; i.e., the SUM of any number and zero equals that number. The PRODUCT of any number and zero equals zero.

Division by zero cannot be defined in a manner consistent with the other basic definitions of mathematics. Therefore, expressions like cot 0° and csc 0° have no assignable limit (*see* LIMIT OF A FUNCTION). They are sometimes represented by the infinity symbol, ∞, since the COTANGENT OF AN ANGLE and the COSECANT OF AN ANGLE become larger and larger without limit as the angle approaches zero.

The origin of zero is uncertain. It has been found to exist in Mayan arithmetic. The Babylonians used a character for the absence of number, and although they used a primitive kind of place value, they did not create a system of numeration in which zero was as important as it is in our DECIMAL NUMBER SYSTEM. It is believed that the Greeks had a notion of place value, and Diophantus seemed to have used it. The Greek "lacuna" (nothing) symbolized by omicron (*o*) or the Hindu small circle (°) could be the origin of the form of zero that we now use. It is agreed that zero appeared in India in the 9th century, and probably before that, and that it is most likely a Hindu invention.

ZERO ELEMENT, for any operation called "addition," an element Z such that, for any element X in the SET on which the operation is defined, $Z + X = X + Z = X$. E.g., in ordinary arithmetic the zero element is 0, since 0 added to any number gives the same number as the sum: $5 + 0 = 0 + 5 = 5$, etc. *See also* UNITY ELEMENT.

ZERO EXPONENT, the EXPONENT of the BASE when a number is divided by itself. By the laws of exponents to divide when the bases are the same, keep the base and subtract exponents. Thus, $3^2/3^2 = 3^{2-2}$ or 3^0. But $3^2/3^2 = 9/9 = 1$. Therefore, $3^0 = 1$. In general, any base raised to the zero power is defined to be 1. E.g., $x^0 = 1$; $(6x^2y^3)^0 = 1$; $183^0 = 1$; $5x^4y^0 = 5x^4 \cdot 1 = 5x^4$.

ZERO SLOPE, the SLOPE OF A LINE that is parallel to the X-AXIS. If a line is parallel to the Y-AXIS it has no slope. In the figure, slope $m = \dfrac{\Delta y}{\Delta x}$. In line l, $\Delta y = 0$, therefore the slope of l is zero. In line l', $\Delta x = 0$ and division by zero is impossible; therefore, l' has no slope.

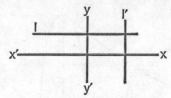

ZONE OF A SPHERE, *see* SPHERE.

Special Reference Section

NO. 1 THE GREEK ALPHABET

CAPITAL LETTER	LOWER CASE LETTER	NAME	PRONUNCIATION	CAPITAL LETTER	LOWER CASE LETTER	NAME	PRONUNCIATION
A	α	alpha	a (as in *father*)	Ξ	ξ	xi	x (as in *fix*)
B	β	beta	b (as in *boy*)	O	o	omicron	o (as in *got*)
Γ	γ	gamma	g (as in *goal*)	Π	π	pi	p (as in *play*)
Δ	δ	delta	d (as in *dawn*)	P	ρ	rho	r (as in race) or rh (as in Greek *rhododendron*)
E	ϵ	epsilon	e (as in *get*)				
Z	ζ	zeta	dz (as in Greek *Zeus*)	Σ	σ (final)	sigma	s (as in *see, lass*)
H	η	eta	e (as in *melee*) or (as in French *méchant*)	T	τ	tau	t (as in *tan*)
Θ	θ	theta	th (as in think) originally pronounced *th* as in *lighthouse*	Υ	υ	upsilon	u (as in French *tu*) or (as in German *für*)
I	ι	iota	i (as in French *lit*) or (as in *meet*)	Φ	ϕ	phi	ph, f (as in *phase, face*) (originally pronounced *ph* as in *uphill*)
K	κ	kappa	k (as in *king*)	X	χ	chi	ch (as in Scottish *loch*) (originally pronounced *ch* as in *Lockhart*)
Λ	λ	lambda	l (as in *live*)				
M	μ	mu	m (as in *may*)	Ψ	ψ	psi	ps (as in *tipsy*)
N	ν	nu	n (as in *name*)	Ω	ω	omega	o (as in *order, officer*)

NO. 2 MATHEMATICAL ABBREVIATIONS AND SYMBOLS

$A \times B$	A Cross B
$\vert\ \vert$	absolute value
adj.	adjacent
$\aleph_0$	aleph null
α	alpha error, or type I error (statistics)
alt.	alternate
H_A; H_1	alternative hypothesis (statistics)
h	altitude of a geometric figure
$\wedge$	and
$\cdots$	and so on
$\angle$; $\angle$	angle; angles
A	angle of a lune (in degrees)
antilog	antilogarithm
a	apothem of a polygon
$\lim_{x \to a}$	approaches *a* as a limit
$\overset{\frown}{AB}$	arc AB
K	area
S	area of a lateral or curved surface
B	area of base of a solid
M	area of a midsection
$\sin^{-1}$	arcsin
$\sinh^{-1}$	arcsinh
b	base of a geometric figure
e	base of the system of natural logarithms 2.718
β	beta error, or type II error (statistics)
{ }	braces
[ ]	brackets
$\aleph_0$	cardinal number of a countable, infinite set
$A \times B$	cartesian product
χ^2	chi-squared (statistics)
$\bigcirc$; $\circledS$	circle; circles
cis θ	cos θ + isin θ
colog	cologarithm
$C\begin{Bmatrix}n\\n\ r\end{Bmatrix}$; $\begin{pmatrix}n\\r\end{pmatrix}$	Combination of n things r at a time; $\dfrac{n!}{r!(n-r)!}$
$\bar{A}$	complement of set A
a + bi	complex number
P(A/B)	conditional probability of A, given B (statistics)
$\cong$	congruent
corr	corresponding
r	correlation coefficient (statistics)
csc θ	cosecant θ
cos θ	cosine θ
cot θ	cotangent θ
cvs θ	coversed sine θ
κ	curvature of a curve
$\circ$	degree
Δx	delta x
$\dfrac{d}{dx}$; f'; y'	derivative
d	diameter of a circle or sphere
cos α / cos β / cos γ	direction cosines
$\div$	divided by
$''$	double prime
$\in$	element of
$\varnothing$; $\{\ \}$	empty set
=	equal
$\equiv$	equivalent
E(x)	expected value of x (statistics)
ext	exterior
!	factorial
f(x)	function of x
>	greater than
$\geq$	greater than or equal to
gcd	greatest common denominator
glb	greatest lower bound
grad	gradient
hav θ	haversine θ
h	height of a geometric figure
cosh θ	hyperbolic cosine θ
coth θ; ctnh θ	hyperbolic cotangent θ
HL	hypotenuse-leg
sinh θ	hyperbolic sine θ
tnh θ	hyperbolic tangent θ
hyp.	hypothesis
iff; $\leftrightarrow$	if and only if
$\rightarrow$	if . . . then
i	imaginary unit; $\sqrt{1}$
$\rightarrow$	implies
Δ	increment
∞	infinity
$\int$	Integral
$\cap$	intersection

int	interior
A^{-1}	inverse of matrix A
arc sin θ	inverse sine θ
isos	isosceles
:	is to
e	lateral edge or element
lcd	least common denominator
lub	least upper bound
l	length
<; $\leq$	less than; less than or equal to
log	logarithm
$\log_b x$	logarithm of x to the base b
$\overset{m}{=}$	measured by
$\overset{\circ}{=}$	measured in degrees
—	minus
/	minute
I	moment of inertia
ln	natural logarithm
~	not
$\not\subset$	not an element of
$\neq$	not equal
$\not\equiv$	not equivalent
$\not>$	not greater than
$\not<$	not less than
H_0	null hypothesis (statistics)
$\varnothing$; { }	null set
$\vee$	or
opp	opposite
o	origin in a coordinate system
‖	parallel
$\square$	parallelogram
( )	parentheses
$\dfrac{\partial}{\partial x}$	partial derivative
%	percent
p	perimeter
$_nP_r$; $P(n,r)$	permutation of n things r at a time: $\dfrac{n!}{(n-r)!}$
$\perp$	perpendicular
π	pi 3.1416 or 22/7
+	plus
$\pm$	plus or minus
(r, θ)	polar coordinates
μ	population mean (statistics)
$'$	prime
P(A)	probability of A
$\overset{n}{\underset{i=1}{\Pi}}$	product to n terms
::	proportion
quad	quadrilateral

r	radius of circle or sphere
ρ	radius of curvature
κ	radius of gyration
r	radius vector
$\sqrt{}$	radical sign
:	ratio
x	random variable (statistics)
rect	rectangle
(x, y)	rectangular coordinates of a point in the plane
(x, y, z)	rectangular coordinates of a point in space
$\llcorner$	right angle
rt	right
cor(x,y)	sample covariance (statistics)
$\bar{x}$	sample mean (statistics)
s	sample standard deviation (statistics)
sec	secant
$''$	second
$\dfrac{d^2}{dy^2}$; f''; y''	second derivative
$\triangledown$	sector of a circle
SAA	side, angle, angle
SAS	side, angle, side
SSS	side, side, side
$\overline{AB}$	segment AB
S	semiperimeter of a triangle
~	similar to
sin θ	sine θ
l	slant height
m	slope
E	spherical excess
st	straight
$\subset$	subset
|; :; $\ni$	such that
$\overset{n}{\underset{i=1}{\Sigma}}$	sum to n terms
supp	supplementary
tan	tangent
$\exists$	there exists
$\therefore$	therefore
.; $\times$	times
T	total area
τ	torsion of a curve
A^T	transpose of matrix A
$\triangle$; $\triangle\!\!\!\triangle$	triangle; triangles
$\cup$	union
s^2	variance (statistics)
α	varies directly
vers θ	versed sine θ
V	volume
w	width

NO. 3 A REVIEW OF MATHEMATICAL FORMULAS, LAWS AND TERMS

Common Fractions

I TERMS

1. Numerator: the top number in a fraction. In a/b a is the numerator.
2. Denominator: the bottom number in a fraction. In a/b, b is the denominator.
3. Proper fraction: a fraction in which the numerator is less than the denominator.
4. Improper fraction: a fraction in which the numerator is equal to or greater than the denominator.
5. Mixed number: a number made up of a whole number and a fraction.

II OPERATIONS WITH COMMON FRACTIONS

1. To change an improper fraction to a mixed number: divide the denominator into the numerator.
2. To change a mixed number to an improper fraction: multiply the whole number by the denominator of the fraction and add the numerator, and use the result as the new numerator, keeping the original denominator.
3. Addition or subtraction of fractions with the same denominator: keep the denominator and add or subtract the numerators. $a/b + c/b = \dfrac{a+c}{b}$; $a/b - c/b = \dfrac{a-c}{b}$.

4. Addition or subtraction of fractions with different denominators: express each fraction in terms of a common denominator, then keep the denominator and add or subtract the numerators.

5. To reduce fractions to lower terms: divide the numerator and denominator by the same amount. $a/b = \dfrac{a \div c}{b \div c}$.

6. To raise fractions to higher terms: multiply the numerator and denominator by the same amount. $a/b = \dfrac{a \times c}{b \times c}$.

7. To multiply fractions: multiply the numerators and multiply the denominators. $\dfrac{a}{b} \times \dfrac{c}{d} = \dfrac{ac}{bd}$.

8. To divide fractions: invert the divisor and multiply the resulting fractions. $a/b \div c/d = a/b \times d/c = ad/bc$.

Decimal Fractions

I PLACE VALUE

tenths
hundredths
thousandths
ten-thousandths
hundred-thousandths
millionths
ten-millionths
hundred-millionths
billionths
ten-billionths
hundred-billionths

II OPERATIONS WITH DECIMALS

1. To add or subtract decimals: align the decimal points, keep the decimal and add or subtract the numbers.
2. To multiply decimals: multiply the factors and give the product as many decimal places as there are in the sum of the decimal places in the factors, counting from right to left; add as many zeroes as are needed on the left.
3. To divide decimals: move the decimal point in the divisor as many places as needed to make it a whole number, and move the decimal point in the dividend the same number of places adding zeroes as needed. Place the decimal point in the quotient above the new position of the decimal point in the dividend, and divide the numbers.
4. To change a common fraction to a decimal fraction: divide the numerator of the fraction by its denominator.
5. To change a decimal fraction to a common fraction: write the decimal fraction as a common fraction whose denominator is 10, 100, etc. according to the place value chart, and reduce the fraction to lowest terms.

III OPERATIONS WITH PERCENTS

1. The percent symbol, %, indicates a denominator of 100.
2. To write a percent as a decimal fraction: move the decimal point 2 places to the left and drop the percent symbol.
3. To write a decimal fraction as a percent: move the decimal point 2 places to the right and add the percent symbol.
4. To find a percent of a number: change the percent to a decimal fraction and multiply.

Properties of Real Numbers (a, b, c are real numbers)

1. Closure for addition and subtraction: $a + b$ is a real number; $a - b$ is a real number.
2. Closure for multiplication and division: ab is a real number; $a \div b$ is a real number.
3. Commutative property for addition: $a + b = b + a$.
4. Commutative property for multiplication: $ab = ba$.
5. Associative property of addition: $(a + b) + c = a + (b + c)$.
6. Associative property of multiplication: $(ab)c = a(bc)$.

7. Distributative property of multiplication over addition: $a(b + c) = ab + ac$.

Equality Properties

8. Reflexive property of equality: $a = a$
9. Symmetric property of equality: if $a = b$, $b = a$.
10. Transitive property of equality: if $a = b$ and $b = c$, $a = c$.
11. Addition and subtraction property of equality: if $a = b$ and $c = d$, $a \pm c = b \pm d$.
12. Multiplication and division property of equality: if $a = b$ and $c = d$, $ac = bd$ and $a \div c = b \div d$.
13. Substitution property of equality: an expression may be substituted for its equivalent in an equation.

Order Properties

14. Trichotomy property: *exactly one* of the following is true: $a < b, a > b, a = b$.
15. Addition property of inequality:
    if $a < b$ and $c \leq d$, $(a + c) < (b + d)$;
    if $a > b$ and $c \geq d$, $(a + c) > (b + d)$.
16. Subtraction property of inequality:
    if $a < b$, $(a - c) < (b - c)$;
    if $a > b$, $(c - a) > (c - b)$.
17. Multiplication property of inequality:
    if $a < b$ and $c > 0$, $ac < bc$;
    if $a > b$ and $c > 0$, $ac > bc$;
    if $a < b$ and $c < 0$, $ac > bc$;
    if $a > b$ and $c < 0$, $ac < bc$.
18. Division property of inequality:
    if $a < b$ and $c > 0$, $a/c < b/c$ and $c/a > c/b$;
    if $a < b$ and $c < 0$, $a/c > b/c$ and $c/a < c/b$;
    if $a > b$ and $c > 0$, $a/c > b/c$ and $c/a < c/b$;
    if $a > b$ and $c < 0$, $a/c < b/c$ and $c/a > c/b$.
19. Transitive property of inequality:
    if $a < b$ and $b < c$, $a < c$;
    if $a > b$ and $b > c$, $a > c$.
20. Substitution property of inequality: any expression may be substituted for its equivalent expression in an inequality.
21. Partition property: if $c = a + b$ and $b > 0$, $c > a$;
    if $c = a + b$ and $b < 0$, $c < a$.

Laws of Signs

1. Addition: when the signs are the same, keep the sign and add the absolute values of the numbers; when the signs are different, keep the sign of the number with the larger absolute value and find the difference between the absolute values of the numbers.
2. Subtraction: change the sign of the subtrahend (bottom number) and with the new sign, apply the addition laws.
3. Multiplication: $(+)(+) = +; (+)(-) = -; (-)(+) = -; (-)(-) = +$.
4. Division: $(+) \div (+) = +; (+) \div (-) = -; (-) \div (+) = -; (-) \div (-) = +$.

Laws of Exponents

1. Multiplication: if the bases are the same, keep the base and add the exponents; $a^m a^n = a^{m+n}$.
2. Division: if the bases are the same, keep the base and subtract the exponents; $a^m \div a^n = a^{m-n}$.
3. $(ab)^m = a^m b^m$.
4. $(a^m)^n = a^{mn}$.
5. $a^{m/n} = \sqrt[n]{a^m}$.
6. $a^0 = 1$.
7. $a^{-m} = 1/a^m$

Laws of Logarithms

1. If $b^p = N$, $\log_b N = p$.
2. $\log(ab) = \log a + \log b$.

3. $\log (a \div b) = \log a - \log b$.
4. $\log (a^b) = b \log a$.
5. $\log \sqrt[b]{a} = 1/b \log a$.

Algebraic Formulas

I SOLUTION OF LINEAR EQUATIONS

1. If $x + a = b$,
   $x = b - a$.
2. If $x - a = b$,
   $x = b + a$.
3. If $ax = b$,
   $x = b/a, a \neq 0$.
4. If $x/a = b$,
   $x = ba$.

II QUADRATIC EQUATION

1. If $ax^2 + bx + c = 0, x = \dfrac{-b \pm \sqrt{b^2 - 4ac}}{2a}$.

2. Discriminant of quadratic equation: $b^2 - 4ac$.
   (a) if $b^2 - 4ac = 0$, roots are real, equal, rational;
   (b) if $b^2 - 4ac < 0$, roots are imaginary;
   (c) if $b^2 - 4ac > 0$, roots are real, unequal;
   (d) if $b^2 - 4ac$ is a perfect square, roots are rational;
   (e) if $b^2 - 4ac$ is not a perfect square, and $\neq 0$, roots are irrational.

3. The sum of the roots of a quadratic equation, $r_1 + r_2 = \dfrac{-b}{a}$.

4. The product of the roots of a quadratic equation, $r_1 \cdot r_2 = \dfrac{c}{a}$.

5. The graph of the quadratic equation, $y = ax^2 + bx + c$ is a parabola, whose axis of symmetry is given by $x = \dfrac{-b}{2a}$.

III ARITHMETIC PROGRESSION

1. General form: $a, a + d, a + 2d, \ldots , a + (n - 1)d$.
2. Last term: $l = a + (n - 1)d$.
3. Sum of n terms: $S = \dfrac{n}{2}(a + l)$;

$$S = \dfrac{n}{2}2a + (n - 1)d.$$

IV GEOMETRIC PROGRESSION

1. General Form: $a, ar, ar^2, ar^3, \ldots , ar^{n-1}$.
2. Last term: $l = ar^{n-1}$.
3. Sum of n terms: $S = \dfrac{ar^n - a}{r - 1}$; $S = \dfrac{a - ar^n}{1 - r}$.

4. Sum of an infinite progression $(r < 1)$: $S = \dfrac{a}{1 - r}$.

V PERMUTATIONS

1. Permutation of n things taken r at a time: $_nP_r = \dfrac{n!}{(n - r)!}$

2. Permutation of n things r at a time, in a circle: $_nP_r = \dfrac{n!}{n}$
   $= (n - 1)!$

3. Permutation of n things r at a time when s things are of one kind, t of another, q of another, etc.: $\dfrac{n!}{s!t!q! \ldots}$.

4. Permutation of n things taken n at a time: $_nP_n = n!$

VI COMBINATIONS

1. Combination of n things taken r at a time: $_nC_r = \dfrac{_nP_r}{r!}$.

2. Combination of n things r at a time is the same as a combination of n things $n - r$ at a time: $_nC_r = {_nC_{n-r}}$.

3. Combination of n things n at a time: $_nC_n = 1$.
4. Combination of n things taken 1 at a time: $_nC_1 = n$.

GEOMETRY

Plane Geometry

I TRIANGLE FORMULAS (sides a, b, c; angles A, B, C)

1. Perimeter: $P = a + b + c$.
2. Semiperimeter: $s = \frac{1}{2}(a + b + c)$.
3. Area: $A = \frac{1}{2}bh$
   $A = \frac{1}{2}ab \sin c$
   $A = \sqrt{s(s - a)(s - b)(s - c)}$
   $A = \dfrac{a^2 \sin B \sin C}{2 \sin A}$

4. Area of right triangle: $A = \frac{1}{2} \text{leg}_1 \times \text{leg}_2$.

5. Area of equilateral triangle: $A = \dfrac{a^2 \sqrt{3}}{4}$

6. Pythagorean Theorem: In a right triangle $\text{leg}^2 + \text{leg}^2 = \text{hypotenuse}^2$

7. Altitude of equilateral triangle: $a = \dfrac{a^2 \sqrt{3}}{2}$.

8. Sum of the angles of a triangle: $\angle A + \angle B + \angle C = 180°$

9. Exterior $\angle 1$, at A of a triangle: $\angle 1 = \angle B + \angle C$.
10. If $AB = BC$ in triangle ABC, $\angle A = \angle C$.
11. If $\angle A = \angle C$ in triangle ABC, $AB = BC$.
12. In a $30° - 60°$-Right triangle:
    a. The side opposite the 30° angle equals $\frac{1}{2}$ hypotenuse;
    b. The side opposite the 60° angle equals $\frac{1}{2}$ hypotenuse $\times \sqrt{3}$;
13. In a $45° - 45°$-right triangle:
    a. A leg equals $\frac{1}{2}$ hypotenuse $\times \sqrt{2}$.
    b. The hypotenuse equals a leg $\times \sqrt{2}$.
14. When an altitude, h, is drawn to hypotenuse C, dividing it into segments p and s
    a. The altitude is the mean proportional between the segments of the hypotenuse: $\dfrac{p}{h} = \dfrac{h}{s}$.

    b. Either leg is the mean proportional between the whole hypotenuse and the segment of the hypotenuse adjacent to segment: $\dfrac{c}{a} = \dfrac{a}{p}$ and $\dfrac{c}{b} = \dfrac{b}{s}$.

II POLYGON FORMULAS

1. Perimeter of a parallelogram, opposite sides a and b: $P = 2a + 2b$.
2. Perimeter of a rectangle: $P = 2l + 2w$.
3. Perimeter of a square, side s: $P = 4s$.
4. Diagonal of a rectangle: $d = \sqrt{l^2 + w^2}$
5. Diagonal of a square, side s: $d = s\sqrt{2}$.
6. Area of a rectangle: $A = lw$.
7. Area of a parallelogram: $A = bh$.
8. Area of a square side s: $A = s^2$.
9. Area of a rhombus: $A = \frac{1}{2}d_1 \cdot d_2$
10. Area of a trapezoid: $A = \frac{1}{2}h(b_1 + b_2)$.
11. Median of a trapezoid: Median $= \frac{1}{2}(b_1 + b_2)$.
12. Area of a regular polygon: $A = \frac{1}{2}ap$.
13. The sum of the interior angles of a polygon of n sides: Sum $= 180(n - 2)$.
14. The sum of the exterior angles of a regular polygon of n sides: Sum $= 360°$
15. Each interior angle of a regular polygon of n sides: interior angle $= \dfrac{180(n - 2)°}{n}$.

16. Each exterior angle of a regular polygon of n sides: exterior angle $= \dfrac{360°}{n}$.

III CIRCLE FORMULAS

1. Circumference: $C = 2\pi r$; $C = \pi D$.

2. Area: $A = \pi r^2$; $A = \dfrac{\pi D^2}{4}$.

3. Area of a sector of a circle

   a. central angle $n°$: $A = \dfrac{n}{360}\pi r^2$

   b. central angle θ radians: $A = \frac{1}{2}r^2\theta$.

4. Length of an arc of a circle.

   a. arc $= n°$: $L = \dfrac{n}{360}2\pi r$;

   b. arc $= \theta$ radians: $L = r\theta$.

5. Area of segment of a circle

   a. central angle $n°$: $A = \dfrac{n}{360}\pi r^2 - \frac{1}{2}r^2\sin n°$

   b. central angle θ radians: $A = \frac{1}{2}r^2(\theta - \sin\theta)$

6. When chords AB and CD intersect at E the product of the segments of the chord equals the product of the segments of the other chord: $AE \times EB = CE \times ED$.

7. When a tangent line PA and secant line PBC are drawn to a circle from the same point, P, the tangent is the mean proportional between the whole secant and its external segment: $\dfrac{PC}{AP} = \dfrac{AP}{PB}$.

8. A central angle is measured by its intercepted arc.

9. An inscribed angle is measured by $\frac{1}{2}$ its intercepted arc.

10. An angle formed by a tangent and a chord drawn to the point of contact is measured by $\frac{1}{2}$ its intercepted arc.

11. An angle formed by 2 chords intersecting inside the circle is measured by $\frac{1}{2}$ the sum of its opposite intercepted arcs.

12. An angle formed by 2 tangents, a tangent and a secant, or 2 secants drawn from the same external point is measured by $\frac{1}{2}$ the difference between its intercepted major and minor arcs.

IV PROPERTIES OF SPECIAL QUADRILATERALS

1. *Parallelogram:*
   a. opposite sides are parallel;
   b. opposite sides are equal;
   c. opposite angles are equal;
   d. consecutive angles are supplementary;
   e. diagonals bisect each other;
   f. each diagonal divides the parallelogram into 2 congruent triangles.

2. *Rhombus:*
   a. opposite sides are parallel;
   b. all sides are equal;
   c. opposite angles are equal;
   d. consecutive angles are supplementary;
   e. diagonals bisect each other;
   f. diagonals are perpendicular to each other;
   g. diagonals bisect the angles of the rhombus;
   h. each diagonal divides the rhombus into 2 congruent triangles.

3. *Rectangle:*
   a. opposite sides are parallel;
   b. opposite sides are equal;
   c. all angles are right angles;
   d. diagonals bisect each other;
   e. diagonals are equal.
   f. each diagonal divides the rectangle into 2 congruent triangles.

4. *Square:*
   a. opposite sides are parallel;
   b. all sides are equal;
   c. all angles are right angles;
   d. diagonals bisect each other;
   e. diagonals bisect the angles of the square;
   f. diagonals are perpendicular to each other;
   g. each diagonal divides the square into 2 congruent triangles.

5. *Trapezoid:*
   a. Bases of a trapezoid are parallel;
   b. Base angles of an isosceles trapezoid are equal;
   c. Diagonals of an isosceles trapezoid are equal.

Solid Geometry

I PRISM
1. Area of lateral surface: $S = ep$ ($p =$ perimeter of right section).
2. Volume: $V = Bh$.

II RIGHT PRISM
1. Area of lateral surface: $S = ep$ ($p =$ perimeter of base).
2. Volume: $V = Bh$.

III PARALLELEPIPED
1. Volume: $V =$ product of the 3 dimensions.

IV RECTANGULAR PARALLELEPIPED
1. Volume: $V = Bh$.

V REGULAR PYRAMID
1. Area of lateral surface: $S = \frac{1}{2}lp$.
2. Area of lateral surface of frustum: $S = \frac{1}{2}l(p + p')$.

VI PYRAMID
1. Volume: $\frac{1}{3}Bh$
2. Volume of frustum: $V = \dfrac{h}{3}(B + B' + \sqrt{BB'})$.

VII CIRCULAR CYLINDER
1. Area of curved surface: $S = ep$ ($p =$ perimeter of right section).
2. Volume: $V = Bh = \pi r^2 h$.

VIII RIGHT CIRCULAR CYLINDER OR CYLINDER OF REVOLUTION
1. Area of curved Surface: $S = 2\pi rh$
2. Total area: $T = 2\pi rh + 2\pi r^2 = 2\pi r(h + r)$.
3. Volume: $V = \pi r^2 h$.

IX CIRCULAR CONE
1. Volume: $V = \frac{1}{3}Bh = \frac{1}{3}\pi r^2 h$.
2. Volume of frustum of cone: $V = \frac{1}{3}h(B + B' + \sqrt{BB'})$.

X RIGHT CIRCULAR CONE OR CONE OF REVOLUTION
1. Area of curved surface: $S = \pi rl$
2. Total area: $T = \pi rl + \pi r^2 = \pi r(l + r)$.
3. Volume: $V = \frac{1}{3}\pi r^2 h$.
4. Area of curved surface of frustum: $S = \pi l(r_1 + r_2)$.
5. Volume of frustum: $V = \frac{1}{3}\pi h(r_1^2 + r_2^2 + r_1 r_2)$.

XI PRISMATOID
1. Volume $= \frac{1}{6}h(B + B' + 4\text{m})$.

XII LUNE
1. Area of curved surface: $S = \dfrac{A}{90°}\pi r^2$

XIII SPHERICAL TRIANGLE
1. Area of curved surface: $S = \dfrac{E}{180°}\pi r^2$

XIV SPHERICAL POLYGON
1. Area of curved surface: $S = \dfrac{E}{180°}\pi r^2$.

XV ZONE
1. Area of curved surface: $S = 2\pi rh$

XVI SPHERE
1. Area of curved surface: $S = 4\pi r^2 = \pi d^2$

2. Volume: $V = \frac{1}{3}rS$
$$V = \frac{4}{3}\pi r^3$$
$$V = \frac{\pi d^3}{6}$$

XVII SPHERICAL PYRAMID
1. Volume: $V = \frac{1}{3}Br$

XVIII SPHERICAL SECTOR
1. Volume: $V = \frac{1}{3}rS$ ($S =$ area of zone)
$$V = \frac{2}{3}\pi r^2 h$$

XIX SPHERICAL SEGMENT OF ONE BASE
1. Volume: $V = \frac{\pi h}{2}r^2 + \frac{\pi h^3}{6}$

XX SPHERICAL SEGMENT
1. Volume: $V = \frac{\pi h}{2}(r_1^2 + r_2^2) + \frac{\pi h^2}{6}$
$$V = \frac{h}{2}\pi r_1^2 + \frac{h}{2}r_2^2 + \frac{\pi h^2}{6}$$

XXI SPHERICAL WEDGE
1. Volume: $V = \frac{r}{3} \times$ Area of its lune.

Analytic Geometry

I DISTANCE FORMULAS
1. Distance between 2 points $(x_1\ y_1)$ and (x_2, y_1) on a line parallel to the y-axis: $d = |x_2 - x_1|$.
2. Distance between 2 points (x_1, y_1) and (x_1, y_2) on a line parallel to the x-axis: $d = |y_2 - y_1|$.
3. Distance between any 2 places (x_1, y_1) and (x_2, y_2):
$$d = \sqrt{x_2 - x_1)^2 + (y_2 - y_1)^2}.$$

II LINE FORMULAS
1. Midpoint of a line joining 2 points (x_1, y_1) and (x_2, y_2):
$$m = \left(\frac{x_1 + x_2}{2}, \frac{y_1 + y_2}{2}\right).$$
2. Slope of a line through 2 points (x_1, y_1) and (x_2, y_2): $m = \frac{y_2 - y_1}{x_2 - x_1}$.
3. Angle, θ, between 2 lines, slopes m_1 and m_2: $\tan \theta = \frac{m_2 - m_1}{1 + m_1 m_2}$.
4. For 2 parallel lines, slopes m_1 and m_2: $m_1 = m_2$.
5. For 2 perpendicular lines, slopes m_1 and m_2: $m_1 = \frac{-1}{m_2}$.

III EQUATIONS OF A STRAIGHT LINE
1. Slope-intercept form, $m =$ slope, $b = y$-intercept: $y = mx + b$.
2. Slope-point form, $m =$ slope, point $= (x_2, y_1)$: $y - y_1 = m(x - x_1)$
3. 2 point form, line passing through points (x_1, y_1) and (x_2, y_2): $\frac{y - y_1}{y_2 - y_1} = \frac{x - x_1}{x_2 - x_1}$.
4. Intercept form, x-intercept $= a$, y-intercept $= b$: $\frac{x}{a} + \frac{y}{b} = 1$.
5. Equation of a circle, center $(0, 0)$ radius r: $x^2 + y^2 = r^2$.
6. Equation of a circle center (h, k) radius r: $(x - h)^2 + (y - k)^2 = r^2$.
7. Equation of an ellipse, center $(0, 0)$ semi-axes a and b: $\frac{x^2}{a^2} + \frac{y^2}{b^2} = 1$.
8. Equation of hyperbola: $\frac{x^2}{a^2} - \frac{y^2}{b^2} = 1$.

IV RELATION BETWEEN RECTANGULAR AND POLAR COORDINATES
1. $a + bi = r(\cos \theta + i \sin \theta)$:
2. $a = r \cos \theta = x$
3. $b = r \sin \theta = y$
4. $r = \sqrt{x^2 + y^2}$
5. $\theta = \arctan \frac{y}{x}$
6. $\sin \theta = \frac{y}{\sqrt{x^2 + y^2}} = \frac{y}{r}$
7. $\cos \theta = \frac{x}{\sqrt{x^2 + y^2}} = \frac{x}{r}$

V RELATION BETWEEN RECTANGULAR AND CYLINDRICAL COORDINATES
1. $x = r \cos \theta$
2. $y = r \sin \theta$
3. $z = z$
4. $r = \pm\sqrt{x^2 + y^2}$
5. $\theta = \arctan \frac{y}{x}$

VI RELATION BETWEEN RECTANGULAR AND SPHERICAL COORDINATES
1. $x = r \sin \theta \cos \phi$.
2. $y = r \sin \theta \sin \phi$.
3. $z = r \cos \theta$
4. $r = \pm\sqrt{x^2 + y^2 + z^2}$
5. $\phi = \arctan \frac{y}{x}$
6. $\theta = \arctan \frac{\sqrt{x^2 + y^2}}{z}$

Trigonometry

I FUNCTIONS OF AN ACUTE ANGLE, A RIGHT TRIANGLE, LEGS a, b, HYPOTENUSE c.
1. $\sin A = \frac{\text{opposite side}}{\text{hypotenuse}} = \frac{a}{c}$
2. $\cos A = \frac{\text{adjacent side}}{\text{hypotenuse}} = \frac{b}{c}$
3. $\tan A = \frac{\text{opposite side}}{\text{adjacent side}} = \frac{a}{b}$
4. $\csc A = \frac{\text{hypotenuse}}{\text{opposite side}} = \frac{c}{a}$
5. $\sec A = \frac{\text{hypotenuse}}{\text{adjacent side}} = \frac{c}{b}$
6. $\cot A = \frac{\text{adjacent side}}{\text{opposite side}} = \frac{b}{a}$

II FUNCTIONS OF COMPLEMENTARY ANGLES, LEGS, a, b, HYPOTENUSE c.
1. $\frac{a}{c} = \sin A = \cos B = \cos(90° - A)$.

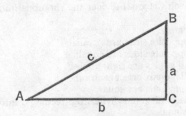

2. $\frac{b}{c} = \cos A = \sin B = \sin(90° - A)$.
3. $\frac{a}{b} = \tan A = \cot B = \cot(90° - A)$.

4. $\dfrac{b}{a} = \cot \angle = \tan B = \tan(90° - A)$.

5. $\dfrac{c}{b} = \sec A = \csc B = \csc(90° - A)$.

6. $\dfrac{c}{a} = \csc A = \sec B = \sec(90° - A)$.

III RELATIONS BETWEEN FUNCTIONS (Trigonometric Identities):

1. $\sec A = \dfrac{1}{\cos A}$

2. $\csc A = \dfrac{1}{\sin A}$

3. $\cot A = \dfrac{1}{\tan A}$

4. $\sin A \cdot \sec A = 1$

5. $\cos A \cdot \sec A = 1$

6. $\tan A \cdot \cot A = 1$

7. $\sin^2 A + \cos^2 A = 1$

8. $1 + \tan^2 A = \sec^2 A$

9. $1 + \cot^2 A = \csc^2 A$

10. $\tan A = \dfrac{\sin A}{\cos A}$

11. $\cot A = \dfrac{\cos A}{\sin A}$

IV SINE FORMULAS

1. Law of Sines: $\dfrac{a}{\sin A} = \dfrac{b}{\sin B} = \dfrac{c}{\sin C}$.

2. $\sin (A + B) = \sin A \cos B + \cos A \sin B$

3. $\sin (A - B) = \sin A \cos B - \cos A \sin B$

4. $\sin A + \sin B = 2 \sin \frac{1}{2}(A + B) \cos \frac{1}{2}(A - B)$

5. $\sin A - \sin B = 2 \cos \frac{1}{2}(A + B) \sin \frac{1}{2}(A - B)$

6. $\sin 2A = 2 \sin A \cos A$

7. $\sin \frac{1}{2} A = \pm \sqrt{\dfrac{1 - \cos A}{2}}$

8. $\sin (A + B) + \sin (A - B) = 2 \sin A \cos B$

9. $\sin (A + B) - \sin (A - B) = 2 \cos A \sin B$

V COSINE FORMULAS

1. LAW OF COSINES: $\cos A = \dfrac{b^2 + c^2 - a^2}{2bc}$

2. $\cos (A + B) = \cos A \cos B - \sin A \sin B$.

3. $\cos (A - B) = \cos A \cos B + \sin A \sin B$.

4. $\cos A + \cos B = 2 \cos \frac{1}{2}(A + B) \cos \frac{1}{2}(A - B)$.

5. $\cos A - \cos B = -2 \sin \frac{1}{2}(A + B) \sin \frac{1}{2}(A - B)$.

6. $\cos 2A = \cos^2 A - \sin^2 A$.

7. $\cos 2 A = 2 \cos^2 A - 1$.

8. $\cos 2 A = 1 - 2 \sin^2 A$.

9. $\cos \frac{1}{2} A = \pm \sqrt{\dfrac{1 + \cos A}{2}}$

10. $\cos (A + B) + \cos (A - B) = 2 \cos A \cos B$

11. $\cos (A + B) - \cos (A - B) = -2 \sin A \sin B$.

VI TANGENT FORMULAS

1. Law of Tangents: $\dfrac{\tan \frac{1}{2}(A - B)}{\tan \frac{1}{2}(A + B)} = \dfrac{a - b}{a + b}$

2. $\tan (A + B) = \dfrac{\tan A + \tan B}{1 - \tan A \tan B}$

3. $\tan (A - B) = \dfrac{\tan A - \tan B}{1 + \tan A \tan B}$

4. $\tan 2 A = \dfrac{2 \tan A}{1 - \tan^2 A}$

5. $\tan \frac{1}{2} A = \pm \sqrt{\dfrac{1 - \cos A}{1 + \cos A}}$

6. $\tan \frac{1}{2} A = \dfrac{\sin A}{1 + \cos A}$

7. $\tan \frac{1}{2} A = \dfrac{1 - \cos A}{\sin A}$

VII SUM FORMULAS

1. $\sin (A + B) = \sin A \cos B + \cos A \sin B$

2. $\cos (A + B) = \cos A \cos B - \sin A \sin B$

3. $\sin (A + B) + \sin (A - B) = 2 \sin A \cos B$

4. $\sin A + \sin B = 2 \sin \frac{1}{2}(A + B) \cos \frac{1}{2}(A - B)$

5. $\cos A + \cos B = 2 \cos \frac{1}{2}(A + B) \cos \frac{1}{2}(A - B)$

6. $\tan (A + B) = \dfrac{\tan A + \tan B}{1 - \tan A \tan B}$

7. $\cot (A + B) = \dfrac{\cot A \cot B - 1}{\cot B + \cot A}$

VIII DIFFERENCE FORMULAS

1. $\sin (A - B) = \sin A \cos B - \cos A \sin B$

2. $\cos (A - B) = \cos A \cos B + \sin A \sin B$

3. $\sin (A + B) - \sin (A - B) = 2 \cos A \sin B$

4. $\sin A - \sin B = 2 \cos \frac{1}{2}(A + B) \sin \frac{1}{2}(A - B)$

5. $\cos A - \cos B = -2 \sin \frac{1}{2}(A + B) \sin \frac{1}{2}(A - B)$

6. $\tan (A - B) = \dfrac{\tan A - \tan B}{1 + \tan A \tan B}$

7. $\cot (A - B) = \dfrac{\cot A \cot B + 1}{\cot B - \cot A}$

IX PRODUCT FORMULAS

1. $\sin A \cos B = \frac{1}{2}[\sin (A + B) + \sin (A - B)]$

2. $\cos A \sin B = \frac{1}{2}[\sin (A + B) - \sin (A - B)]$

3. $\cos A \cos B = \frac{1}{2}[\cos (A + B) + \cos (A - B)]$

4. $\sin A \sin B = -\frac{1}{2}[\cos (A + B) - \cos (A - B)]$

X DOUBLE ANGLE FORMULAS

1. $\sin 2 A = 2 \sin A \cos A$

2. $\cos 2 A = \cos^2 A - \sin^2 A$

3. $\tan 2 A = \dfrac{2 \tan A}{1 - \tan^2 A}$

4. $\cot 2 A = \dfrac{\cot^2 A - 1}{2 \cot A}$

XI HALF-ANGLE FORMULAS

1. $\sin \frac{1}{2}A = \pm \sqrt{\dfrac{1 - \cos A}{2}}$.

2. $\cos \frac{1}{2}A = \pm \sqrt{\dfrac{1 + \cos A}{2}}$.

3. $\tan \frac{1}{2}A = \pm \sqrt{\dfrac{1 - \cos A}{1 + \cos A}}$.

4. $\cot \frac{1}{2}A = \pm \sqrt{\dfrac{1 + \cos A}{1 - \cos A}}$.

5. In $\triangle ABC$, where $s = \frac{1}{2}(a + b + c)$ and

$$r = \sqrt{\dfrac{(s - a)(s - b)(s - c)}{s}},$$

$$\tan \frac{1}{2}A = \dfrac{r}{s - a}$$

XII REDUCTION FORMULAS, QUADRANT I (θ is an acute angle)

1. $\sin (90° - \theta) = \cos \theta$

2. $\cos (90° - \theta) = \sin \theta$

3. $\tan (90° - \theta) = \cot \theta$

4. $\cot (90° - \theta) = \tan \theta$

XIII REDUCTION FORMULAS, QUADRANT II (θ is an acute angle)

1. $\sin (180° - \theta) = \sin \theta$

2. $\cos (180° - \theta) = -\cos \theta$

3. $\tan (180° - \theta) = -\tan \theta$

4. $\cot (180° - \theta) = -\cot \theta$

5. $\sin (90° + \theta) = \cos \theta$

6. $\cos (90° + \theta) = -\sin \theta$

7. $\tan (90° + \theta) = -\cot \theta$

8. $\cot (90° + \theta) = -\tan \theta$

XIV REDUCTION FORMULAS, QUADRANT III (θ is an acute angle)

1. $\sin (180° + \theta) = -\sin \theta$

2. $\cos (180° + \theta) = -\cos \theta$

3. $\tan (180° + \theta) = \tan \theta$

4. $\cot (180° + \theta) = \cot \theta$

5. $\sin (270° - \theta) = -\cos \theta$

6. $\cos(270° - \theta) = -\sin\theta$
7. $\tan(270° - \theta) = \cot\theta$
8. $\cot(270° - \theta) = \tan\theta$

XV REDUCTION FORMULAS, QUADRANT IV (θ is an acute angle)

1. $\sin(360° - \theta) = -\sin\theta$
2. $\cos(360° - \theta) = \cos\theta$
3. $\tan(360° - \theta) = -\tan\theta$
4. $\cot(360° - \theta) = -\cot\theta$
5. $\sin(270° + \theta) = -\cos\theta$
6. $\cos(270° + \theta) = \sin\theta$
7. $\tan(270° + \theta) = -\cot\theta$
8. $\cot(270° + \theta) = -\tan\theta$

XVI FUNCTIONS OF A NEGATIVE ANGLE

1. $\sin(-\theta) = -\sin\theta$
2. $\cos(-\theta) = \cos\theta$
3. $\tan(-\theta) = -\tan\theta$
4. $\cot(-\theta) = -\cot\theta$
5. $\sec(-\theta) = \sec\theta$
6. $\csc(-\theta) = -\csc\theta$

XVII MOLLWEIDE'S FORMULAS

1. $\dfrac{a - b}{c} = \dfrac{\sin\frac{1}{2}(A - B)}{\cos\frac{1}{2}C}$, when $a > b$.

2. $\dfrac{a + b}{c} = \dfrac{\cos\frac{1}{2}(A - B)}{\sin\frac{1}{2}C}$.

XVIII TRIGONOMETIC FUNCTIONS OF QUADRANTAL ANGLES

Function	0°	90°	180°	270°	360°
Sine	0	1	0	−1	0
Cosine	1	0	−1	0	1
Tangent	0	Undefined	0	Undefined	0
Cotangent	Undefined	0	Undefined	0	Undefined
Secant	1	Undefined	−1	Undefined	1
Cosecant	Undefined	1	$\pm\infty$	−1	Undefined

XIX TRIGONOMETRIC FUNCTIONS OF 30°, 45°, AND 60°

Angle	Sin	Cos	Tan	Cot	Sec	Csc
30°	$\frac{1}{2}$	$\frac{1}{2}\sqrt{3}$	$\frac{1}{3}\sqrt{3}$	$\sqrt{3}$	$\frac{2}{3}\sqrt{3}$	2
45°	$\frac{1}{2}\sqrt{2}$	$\frac{1}{2}\sqrt{2}$	1	1	$\sqrt{2}$	$\sqrt{2}$
60°	$\frac{1}{2}\sqrt{3}$	$\frac{1}{2}$	$\sqrt{3}$	$\frac{1}{3}\sqrt{3}$	2	$\frac{2}{3}\sqrt{3}$

XX SIGNS OF THE TRIGONOMETRIC FUNCTIONS

Quadrant	Sin & Csc	Cos & Sec	Tan & Cot
I	+	+	+
II	+	−	−
III	−	−	+
IV	−	+	−

CALCULUS

1. Slope of secant to a curve at $P(x, y)$: $\Delta y/\Delta x = \dfrac{f(x + \Delta x) - f(x)}{\Delta x}$

2. Slope of tangent to a curve at $P(x, y)$: $dy/dx = \lim_{\Delta x \to 0} \Delta y/\Delta x$.

3. Slope of normal to a curve at $P(x, y)$: $\dfrac{-1}{dy/dx}$.

4. Length of secant to a curve: $\sqrt{(\Delta x)^2 + (\Delta y)^2}$.

5. Length of tangent to a curve: $\left|\dfrac{y\sqrt{1 + (dy/dx)^2}}{dy/dx}\right|$.

6. Length of normal to a curve: $|y\sqrt{1 + (dy/dx)^2}|$.

7. Velocity: if $s = f(t)$, $v = ds/dt$.

8. Acceleration: if $s = f(t)$, $a = d^2s/dt^2$.

9. Maximum point: if $y = f(x)$, at maximum $dy/dx = 0$ and $d^2y/dx^2 < 0$.

10. Minimum point: if $y = f(x)$, at minimum $dy/dx = 0$ and $d^2y/dx^2 > 0$.

11. Inflection point: if $y = f(x)$, at inflection point a, $d^2y/dx^2 = 0$ and d^2y/dx^2 changes sign as x increases through a.

Limits

12. $\lim\limits_{x\to a} [f(x) \pm g(x)] = \lim\limits_{x\to a} f(x) \pm \lim\limits_{x\to a} g(x)$.

13. $\lim\limits_{x\to a} f(x) \cdot g(x) = \lim\limits_{x\to a} f(x) \cdot \lim\limits_{x\to a} g(x)$.

14. $\lim\limits_{x\to a} [f(x) \div g(x)] = \lim\limits_{x\to a} f(x) \div \lim\limits_{x\to a} g(x)$ if $\lim\limits_{x\to a} g(x) \neq 0$.

15. L'Hôpital's Rule: If $f(x)$ and $g(x)$ are continuous in an interval containing $x = a$, and $f'(x)$ and $g'(x)$ exist in the interval near $x = a$, then when $f(a) = g(a) = 0$ $\lim\limits_{x\to a} \dfrac{f(x)}{g(x)} = \lim\limits_{x\to a} \dfrac{f'(x)}{g'(x)}$ provided $\lim\limits_{x\to a} \dfrac{f'(x)}{g'(x)}$ exists.

INDETERMINATE FORMS

16. $0/0$
17. ∞/∞.
18. $\infty - 0$.
19. $0 \cdot \infty$.
20. 0^0.
21. ∞^0.
22. 1^∞.
23. $\infty - \infty$.

Circular Motion for P moving along a curve given by $\theta = f(t)$, where θ is the central angle in radians.

24. Angular velocity of P at time t: $w = d\theta/dt$.

25. Angular acceleration of P at time t: $a = d^2\theta/dt^2$.

26. Differential of arc length, s, of $y = f(x)$: $s = ds = \sqrt{(dx)^2 + (dy)^2}$.

27. Arc length, s, of $f(x, y) = 0$ from $A(a, c)$ to $B(b, d)$: $s = \int_a^b ds = \int_a^b \sqrt{1 + (dy/dx)^2}\,dx$; $s = \int_c^b ds = \int_c^d \sqrt{1 + (dx/dy)^2}\,dy$.

28. Curvature at point P of $y = f(x)$: $K = \dfrac{|d^2y/dx^2|}{[1 + (dy/dx)^2]^{3/2}}$

29. Radius of curvature, R, for point P: $R = 1/|K|$, $K \neq 0$.

30. Center of curvature for $P(x, y)$ on $y = f(x)$ is $C(a, b)$ where $a = x - \dfrac{(dy/dx)[1 + (dy/dx)^2]}{d^2y/dx^2}$, $b = y + \dfrac{1 + (dy/dx)^2}{d^2y/dx^2}$

31. Mean Value Theorem: if $f(x)$ is continuous in the closed interval $a \leq x \leq b$, and dy/dx exists in the open interval $a < x < b$, then there exists one value $x = x_1$ such that $\dfrac{f(b) - f(a)}{b - a} = f'(x)$, $a < x_1 < b$.

32. Definite integral for a continuous function $f(x)$ on the closed interval $[a, b]$: $\int_a^b f(x)\,dx = \left[\int f(x)\,dx\right]_a^b = \left[F(x)\right]_a^b = F(b) - F(a)$ where $F(x)$ is an integral of $f(x)$.

33. Area, A, under a continuous curve, $y = f(x)$, bounded by the x-axis, $x = a$ and $x = b$: $A = \int_a^b f(x)\,dx$.

34. Area A, between 2 curves, $y = f(x)$, $y = g(x)$: $A = \int_a^b f(x)\,dx - \int_a^b g(x)\,dx = \int_a^b [f(x) - g(x)]\,dx$.

35. Volume of solid $A(x)$ between $x = a$ and $x = b$: $V = \int_a^b A(x)\,dx$.

36. Volume of solid of revolution
   a. generated by revolving $y = f(x)$ about the x-axis, $x = a$ and $x = b$: $V = \pi\int_a^b y^2\,dx$ (Disk method).

   b. generated by revolving the region bounded by $y_1 = f(x)$, $y_2 = g(x)$, $x = a$ and $x = b$ about the x-axis: $V = \pi\int_a^b (y_1^2 - y_2^2)\,dx$ (Washer method).

   c. generated by revolving the region bounded by $y = (x)$, the x-axis and $x = b$ about the y-axis: $V =$

$$2\pi \int_a^b xy\,dx \text{ (Shell method).}$$

37. Area of a surface of revolution, s, generated by revolving curve $f(x,y) = 0$ between $A(a, c)$ and $B(b,d)$ about the x-axis: $s = 2\pi \int_c^d x\,ds = 2\pi \int_c^d x\sqrt{1 + (dx/dy)^2}\,dy.$

38. Moment of inertia for a plane curve, s, about the
    a. x-axis: $I_x = y^2\,ds$;   b. y-axis: $I_y = x^2\,ds$;
    c. origin: $I_0 = (x^2 + y^2)\,ds.$

39. Moment of inertia for plane area, A, about the
    a. x-axis: $I_x = y^2\,dA$;   b. y-axis: $I_y = x^2\,dA$;
    c. origin: $I_0 = (x^2 + y^2)\,dA.$

40. Moment of inertia for solid of mass m about the
    a. xy-plane: $I_{xy} = z^2\,dm$;   d. x-axis: $I_x = I_{zz} + I_{xy}$;
    b. yz-plane: $I_{yz} = x^2\,dm$;   e. y-axis: $I_y = I_{xy} + I_{yz}$;
    c. xz-plane: $I_{zz} = y^2\,dm$;   f. z-axis: $I_z = I_{zz} + I_{yz}.$

41. Partial derivative for $g = f(x,y)$: $\dfrac{\partial g}{\partial x} = \lim_{\Delta x \to 0} \dfrac{\partial g}{\partial x} =$

    $\lim_{\Delta x \to 0} \dfrac{f(x + \Delta x, y) - f(x,y)}{\Delta x}$ and $\dfrac{\partial g}{\partial y} = \lim_{\Delta y \to 0} \dfrac{\partial g}{\partial x} =$

    $\lim_{\Delta y \to 0} \dfrac{f(x, y + \Delta y) - f(x,y)}{\Delta y}.$

42. Tangent plane to surface $F(x, y, z) = 0$ at $P(x, y, z)$:
    $(x - x_1)(\partial F/\partial x)_1 + (y - y_1)(\partial F/\partial y)_1 + (z - z_1)$
    $(\partial F/\partial z)_1 = 0.$

43. Normal line to surface $F(x, y, z) = 0$ at $P(x, y, z)$:
    $\dfrac{x - x_1}{(\partial F/\partial x)_1} = \dfrac{y - y_1}{(\partial F/\partial y)_1} = \dfrac{z - z_1}{(\partial F/\partial y)_1}.$

STATISTICS

Formula Review

1. Bayes' Theorem $P(B_i, A) = \dfrac{P(B_i)P(A, B_i)}{\sum\limits_{i=1}^{n} P(B_i)P(A, B_i)}$

2. Chi-squared Distribution $f(X^2) = \dfrac{(X^2)^{(n-2)/2}e^{-(x^2/2)}}{2^{n/2}(\Gamma n/2)}$

3. Chi-squared Goodness-to-fit Test
    $X^2 = \dfrac{\sum\limits_{i=1}^{k}(n_i - e_i)^2}{e_i}$

4. Correlation Coefficient $r = \dfrac{\sum\limits_{i=1}^{n}(x_i - x)(y_i - y)}{\sqrt{\sum\limits_{i=1}^{n}(x_i - x)^2 \sum\limits_{i=1}^{n}(y_i - y)^2}}$

5. Expected Value $E(x) = \overline{x} = \int_{-\infty}^{+\infty} xf(x)\,dx$

6. F-Distribution $F = \dfrac{s_1^2}{s_2^2} = \dfrac{n_2 x_1^2}{n_1 x_2^2}$

7. Fishers' z transformation $z = \tfrac{1}{2}\log_e \dfrac{1 + r}{1 - r}$

8. Mean Absolute Deviation $\int_{-\infty}^{+\infty} |x - E(x)|f(x)\,dx$

    or $\dfrac{\sum\limits_{i=1}^{n} |x_1 - E(x_i)|}{n}$

9. Moment Generating Function $\varphi(t) = \int_{-\infty}^{+\infty} e^{tx}f(x)\,dx$

10. Moment of a Frequency Distribution $\mu_r = \int_{-\infty}^{+\infty}(x - a)^r f(x)\,dx$

11. Multinomial Distribution $(x_1 + x_2 + \cdots + x_m)^n =$
    $\dfrac{n!}{a_1!a_2!\cdots u_m!} x_1^{a_1} x_2^{a_2} \cdots x_m^{a_n}$

12. Normal Distribution $\varphi(x) = \dfrac{1}{\sigma\sqrt{2\pi}}e^{-(x-A)^2/(2\sigma^2)}$

13. Poisson Distribution $f(x) = \dfrac{m^x e^{-m}}{x!}$

14. Rank Correlation Coefficient $r = 1 - \dfrac{6\sum\limits^{n} d^2}{n^3 - n}$

15. Standard Deviation $\sigma = \sqrt{\dfrac{\sum\limits_{i=1}^{n}(x_i - \overline{x})^2}{n - 1}}$

16. t $t = \dfrac{(\overline{x} - u)\sqrt{n}}{s}$

17. t Distribution $F(t_0) = \dfrac{\Gamma(n/2)}{\sqrt{\pi(n-1)}\Gamma\dfrac{(n-1)}{2}}$

    $\int_{-\infty}^{t_0} \dfrac{(1 + t^2)^{-n/2}}{n - 1}\,dt$

18. Variance σ^2

NO. 4   WEIGHTS AND MEASURES

Table of Units in Alphabetical Order

(See Table No. 5 for table of units arranged by quantity in ascending order of size).

UNIT	ABBREVIATION	QUANTITY	VALUE
abampere	abamp	current	10 amp
abcoulomb	abcoul	charge	10 coul
abfarad	abf	capacitance	10^9 farad
abhenry	abh	inductance	10^{-9} henry
abohm	abohm	resistance	10^{-9} ohm
abvolt	abvolt	potential	10^{-8} volt
acre	acre	area	160 rod²; 4840 yd²
agate	agate	length (printer's measure)	1/14 inch (appr.)
ampere	amp	current	1 coul/sec
ampere-hour	amp-hr	charge	3600 coul
ampere-turn	amp-turn	magnetomotive force	magnetomotive force of an electromagnet of 1 coil of wire carrying a current of 1 amp; 1.26 gilberts
angstrom	A	length	10^{-10} m

UNIT	ABBREVIATION	QUANTITY	VALUE
are	are, a	area	100 m²
astronomical unit	a.u.	length	92.9×10^6 mi; mean distance from earth to sun
atmosphere	atm	pressure	1.013×10^5 n/m²; 14.7 lb/in²; pressure of atmosphere at sealevel
atomic mass unit	amu	mass	1/12 mass of carbon-12; 1.6603×10^{-27} kg
bar	bar	pressure	10^6 dynes/cm²; 0.987 atm
barn	barn	area (cross section)	10^{-28} m²
barrel	bbl	dry capac.	105 dry quarts; 7056 in³
board foot	fbm	volume	1/12 ft³; 144 in³
British thermal unit	Btu	heat energy	252 calories; 1055 joules
bushel	bu	dry capac.	2150.42 in³
calorie	cal	heat energy	4.186 joules
candle	c	luminous intensity	fundamental unit of luminous intensity, defined as 1/60 the intensity of 1 cm² of an ideal black-body radiator at the melting point of platinum (2046°K); 1 lumen/steradian
carat, metric	c	weight	0.2 g; 200 milligrams
centare	ca	area	1 m²
centigram	cg	mass	0.01 gram
centiliter	cl	capacity	0.01 liter
centimeter	cm	length	0.01 meter
century	cent.	time	100 years
chain	ch	length	4 rods; 22 yd; 100 links
cord	cd	volume	128 ft³
coulomb	coul or Cb	charge	fundamental unit of charge, defined by international standard
cubic centimeter	cm³	volume	0.000001 m³; 0.001 dm³
cubic decimeter	dm³	volume	0.001 m³
cubic dekameter	dkm³	volume	1000 m³
cubic foot	ft³	volume	1/27 yd³
cubic inch	in³	volume	1/1728 ft³; 1/46,656 yd³
cubic meter	m³	volume	unit of volume equal to cube 1 m on each side
cubic millimeter	mm³	volume	10^{-9} m³; 0.001 cm³
cubic yard	yd³	volume	unit of volume equal to cube 1 yd on each side
cubit	cubit	length	1/2 yd; 18 in
cup (U.S.)	cup	liq. capacity	1/2 pint (U.S.); 8 oz.; 16 tbsp.
cup (Eng.)	cup	liq. capacity	1/2 pint (Eng.); 10 oz.; 20 tbsp.
curie	curie, c	radioactivity	a quantity of radioactive material that undergoes 3.7×10^{10} disintegrations per second
day	day, d	time	24 hours; 1440 minutes; 86,400 sec
decibel	db	loudness of sound	smallest difference in loudness detectable by human ear; normal range of ear is 130 db
decigram	dg	mass	0.1 gram
deciliter	dl	capacity	0.1 liter
decimeter	dm	length	0.1 meter
decistere	ds	volume	0.1 m³
degree	deg, °	angle	1/360 circle
degree Celsius	deg C, °C	temperature	1/100 difference between ice point and boiling point of water
degree Fahrenheit	deg F, °F	temperature	1/180 difference between ice point and boiling point of water; 5/9 deg C
degree Kelvin or absolute	deg K, °K	temperature	equal to Celsius degree; 0°C = 273°K
dekagram	dkg	mass	10 grams
dekaliter	dkl	capacity	10 liters
dekameter	dkm	length	10 meters
dekastere	dks	volume	10 steres; 10 m³
dozen	doz	counting meas.	12
dram, avoirdupois	dr	mass; weight	1/256 pound; 1/16 ounce
dram, apothecaries	dr ap	mass; weight	1/96 apothecaries pound; 1/8 apothecaries ounce; 60 grains
dram, fluid	dr fl	liq. capac.	1/8 fluid ounce; 1/128 liquid pint
drop	drop	liq. capac.	1/60 teaspoon; 1/360 fluid ounce
dyne	dyne	force	10^{-5} newton; force required to give 1-gram mass acceleration of 1 cm/sec²
electron-volt	ev	energy; mass	energy acquired by singly charged particle accelerated across 1 volt; 1.60×10^{-19} joule; 1/931 amu
erg	erg	energy; work	10^{-7} joule; work done by a force of 1 dyne acting through 1 cm

UNIT	ABBREVIATION	QUANTITY	VALUE
farad	f	capacitance	capacitance between a pair of plates when a potential difference of 1 volt will transfer 1 coulomb of charge
faraday	faraday	charge	9.65×10^4 coulombs
fathom	fath	length (depth)	6 ft; 8 spans
firkin	fir	liq. capac.	9 gal
foot	ft	length	1/3 yard; 12 in.
foot-pound	ft-lb	energy; work	work done by a force of 1 lb acting through 1 ft
fortnight	fortnight	time	2 weeks
furlong	fur	length	1/8 mi; 40 rods; 220 yd; 660 ft
gallon (U.S.)	gal	liq. capac.	231 in³; 4 qt; 8 pt; 128 fl oz
gallon (Eng.) (Imperial gallon)	gal	liq. capac.	277 in³; 4 qt; 8 pt; 160 fl oz (The Imperial gallon, used in Britain and Canada, is 25% larger than the U.S. gallon and the quart, pint, cup, and gill are correspondingly larger. The fluid ounce is the same for both.)
gauss	gauss	magnetic induetim, magnetic fluxdensity	10^{-4} weber/m²; 1 maxwell/cm²
gilbert	gilbert	magnetomotive force	0.7958 ampere-turn
gill	gi	liq. capac.	1/32 gal; 1/4 pt; 4 fl oz (U.S.); 5 fl oz (Eng.)
grain	grain, gr	mass; weight	1/7000 pound; 1/20 scruple
gram	g	mass; weight	0.001 kilogram; originally defined as mass of 1 cm³ of water at 4°C
gross	gr	counting meas.	144; 12 dozen
hand	hand	length	4 inches
hectare	ha	area	100 ares; 10^4 m²; 1 square hectometer
hectogram	hg	mass; weight	100 grams
hectoliter	hl	capacity	100 liters
hectometer	hm	length	100 meters
henry	h	inductance	inductance of a coil in which a potential of 1 volt is induced when the current changes at a rate of 1 amp/sec
hertz	hz	frequency	1 cycle or vibration per second
hogshead	hhd	liq. capac.	63 gal; 8.4 ft³ (U.S.); 10.1 ft³ (Eng.)
horsepower	hp	power	550 ft-lb/sec; 746 watts
hour	hr, h	time	60 min; 3600 sec
hundredweight, long	long cwt	weight	112 lb
hundredweight, short	cwt	weight	100 lb
inch	in	length	1/36 yd; 1/12 ft
joule	j	energy; work	10^7 ergs; work done by a force of 1 newton acting through 1 meter
kilocalorie (kilogram calorie)	kcal, C	heat energy	1000 cal; 4186 joules (the kilocalorie or large calorie is used in measuring food values)
kilogram	kg	mass; weight	fundamental unit of mass, defined by international standard; 1000 grams
kiloliter	kl	capacity	1000 liters
kilometer	km	length	1000 meters
kilowatt	kw	power	1000 watts
kilowatt-hour	kwh	energy; work	3.6×10^6 joules
knot	knot	speed	1 nautical mile per hour; 1.15 miles per hour
lambert	lambert	surface brightness	1 lumen emitted per cm² of a perfectly diffusing surface; $1/\pi$, or 0.3183 candle per cm²
league	league	length	3 miles
light-year	l-y	length	5.9×10^{12} mi; distance traveled by light in a vacuum in 1 year
link	li	length	1/100 chain; 7.92 in
liter	liter, 1	capacity	unit of capacity defined as the volume of 1 kg of water at its maximum density (4°C), intended to be equal to 1000 cm³ but actually equal to 1000.028 cm³
lumen	lumen	luminous flux	flux per steradian emitted by 1 candle; a surface of 1 cm² subtending 1 steradian and receiving 1 lumen has a brightness of π lamberts
lux	lux	surface illumination	1 lumen per m²; 10^{-4} phot
maxwell	maxwell	magnetic flux	1 line of magnetic flux; 10^{-8} weber; 10^{-8} volt-second
meter	m	length	fundamental unit of length, defined as 1,650,-763.73 wavelengths of the red-orange line in the spectrum of krypton-86; 39.37 in

UNIT	ABBREVIATION	QUANTITY	VALUE
mho	mho	conductance	conductance through a conductor when the potential is 1 volt and the current is 1 amp; the reciprocal of resistance;
microfarad	μf	capacitance	10^{-6} farad
microgram	μg	mass; weight	10^{-6} gram
microliter	μl	capacity	10^{-6} liter
micron	μ	length	10^{-6} meter
mil	mil	length	0.001 inch
mile (statute mile)	mile, mi	length	5280 ft; 1760 yd; 320 rods
mile, nautical	naut mi	length	6076.1 ft; 1852 meters; 1.15 mi
millenium	millenium	time	1000 years
millibar	millibar	pressure	10^3 dyne/cm²; 9.87×10^{-4} atm
milligram	mg	mass; weight	0.001 gram
milliliter	ml	capacity	0.001 liter
millimeter	mm	length	0.001 meter
millimicron	mμ	length	0.001 micron; 10^{-9} meter
minim	min, ♏	liq. capacity	1/60 fluid dram; 1/480 fl oz
minute	min, m	time	60 seconds; 1/60 hour
minute	min, '	angle	1/60 degree; 60 seconds
mole	mole	mass	quantity of mass of a substance numerically equal to its molecular weight, usually expressed in grams (gram-molecular weight)
month	mo	time	1/12 year (approx.); 30.42 days (mean calendar month); 29 days, 12 hr, 44 min (lunar month)
newton	n, nt	force	force required to give 1-kg mass acceleration of 1 m/sec²; 10^5 dynes
oersted	oersted	magnetic intensity	79.6 ampere-turns/meter; 1 dyne/unit magnetic pole
ohm	ohm, Ω	resistance	resistance of a conductor that allows a current of 1 amp when the potential is 1 volt
ounce, avoirdupois	oz avdp	weight, mass	1/16 pound; 437.5 grains
ounce, troy or apothecaries	oz t, oz ap	weight; mass	1/12 troy pound; 480 grains
ounce, fluid	fl oz.	liq. capac.	1/16 pt; 1/32 qt; 1/128 gal
parsec*	pc	length	1.9×10^{18} mi; 3.6 light-years
peck	pk	dry capac.	1/4 bushel; 8 dry quarts; 537.6 in³
pennyweight	dwt	weight	1/20 troy ounce; 24 grains
phot	phot	surface illumination	1 lumen per cm²; 10^4 lux
pica	pi	length (printer's meas.)	12 points; 1/6 inch (approx.)
picofarad	pf	capacitance	10^{-12} farad
pint, dry	dry pt	dry capac.	1/64 bushel; 1/2 dry quart; 33.6 in³
pint, liquid (U.S.)	liq pt	liq. capac.	8 fl oz; 1/2 liq qt; 1/8 gal; 28.9 in³
pint, liquid (Eng.)	liq pt	liq. capac.	10 fl oz; 1/2 liq qt (Eng.); 1/8 Imperial gallon; 1.2 U.S. liq pt
point	pt	length (printer's meas.)	0.013837 in; 1/72 in (approx.)
pound, avoirdupois	lb, lb avdp	weight; force; mass	fundamental unit whose mass is defined as 0.45359237 kilogram
pound, troy or apothecaries	lb t, lb ap	weight; mass	5760/7000 lb avdp; 5760 grains; 12 troy or apothecaries ounces
poundal	poundal	force	force required to give a 1-pound mass an acceleration of 1 ft/sec²; 1/32.2 pound weight
quart, dry	dry qt	dry capac.	1/32 bushel; 1/8 peck; 67.2 in³
quart, liquid (U.S.)	liq qt	liq. capac.	1/4 gal; 2 liq pt; 32 fl oz; 57.7 in³
quart, liquid (Eng.)	liq qt	liq. capac.	1/4 Imperial gal; 2 liq pt; 40 fl oz
quire	qr	paper measure	24 or 25 sheets
radian*	radian	angle	$1/2\pi$ circle; 57.3 degrees
ream	rm	paper measure	20 quires; 480 or 500 sheets; printer's perfect ream is 516 sheets
rod	rd	length	5.5 yds; 16.5 ft; 1/4 chain; 198 in
roentgen	roentgen, r	radiation	radiation through 1 cm³ of air at standard conditions sufficient to produce 1 statcoulomb of ions
score	score	counting meas.	20
scruple, apothecaries	s ap	weight; mass	20 grains; 1/3 apothecaries dram
second	sec, s	time	fundamental unit of time, defined as the duration of 9,192,631,770 periods of the radiation given off at a particular wavelength by an atom of cesium-133; 1/60 minute
second	sec, "	angle	1/60 minute; 1/3600 degree

UNIT	ABBREVIATION	QUANTITY	VALUE
slug	slug	mass	mass that attains an acceleration of 1 ft/sec² when acted on by a force of 1 pound
span	span	length	1/8 fathom; 9 inches
square centimeter	cm²	area	10^{-4} square meter
square chain	ch²	area	16 square rods; 484 yd²
square decimeter	dm²	area	0.01 m²
square dekameter	dkm²	area	1 are; 100 m²
square foot	ft²	area	1/9 yd²; 144 in²
square hectometer	hm²	area	1 hectare; 10^4 m²; 100 ares
square inch	in²	area	1/1296 yd²; 1/144 ft²
square kilometer	km²	area	10^6 m²; 100 hectares
square link	li²	area	10^{-4} square chain; 62.7 in²
square meter	m²	area	unit of area equal to square 1 meter on each side
square mile	mi²	area	640 acres; 3,097,600 yd²
square millimeter	mm²	area	10^{-6} m²; 0.01 cm²
square rod	rd²	area	30.25 yd²; 272.27 ft²; 625 square links
square yard	yd²	area	unit of area equal to square 1 yard on each side
statampere	statamp	current	3.34×10^{-10} amp
statcoulomb	statcoul	charge	3.34×10^{-10} coul
statfarad	statfarad, statf	capacitance	1.11×10^{-12} farad
stathenry	stathenry, stath	inductance	8.99×10^{11} henries
statohm	statohm	resistance	8.99×10^{11} ohms
statvolt	statvolt	potential	299.8 volts
steradian	steradian	solid angle	1/4 sphere
stere	s	volume	1 m³
stone	stone	weight	14 lb
tablespoon	tbsp	liq. capac.	3 teaspoons; 1/2 fl oz
teaspoon	tsp	liq. capac.	60 drops; 1/3 tablespoon; 1/6 fl oz
ton, short	short t, ton	weight	2000 lb
ton, long	long t	weight	2240 lb
ton, metric	t	weight	1000 kg
torr	torr	pressure	1/760 atmosphere; 1 mm of mercury
volt	volt, V	potential	potential difference between two points when 1 joule of work is done in moving 1 coulomb of charge from one point to the other
watt	watt, W	power	1 joule/sec; 1.34×10^3 hp
weber	weber	magnetic flux	1 volt-second; 10^9 maxwells
week	wk	time	7 days
yard	yd	length	fundamental unit of length in the English system, defined as 0.9144 meter; 3 ft; 36 in
year	yr, y	time	365 days, 5 hr, 48 min, 46 sec

*separate articles on these units

NO. 5 WEIGHTS AND MEASURES

Table of Units Arranged by Quantity and in Ascending Order of Size

LENGTH

The basic unit of length is the **meter**, officially defined as 1,650,-763.73 wavelengths of the red-orange light of krypton-86 under specified conditions. The **yard** is the basic unit of the English system and is defined as 3600/3937 meter.

Metric

angstrom	0.1 millimicron
millimicron	0.001 micron
micron	0.001 millimeter
millimeter	0.1 centimeter
centimeter	0.1 decimeter
decimeter	0.1 meter
meter	basic unit
dekameter	10 meters
hectometer	10 dekameters
kilometer	10 hectometers

English

mil	0.001 inch
inch	$\frac{1}{12}$ foot
hand	$\frac{1}{3}$ foot; 4 inches
link	0.01 chain; 7.9 inches
span	$\frac{3}{4}$ foot; 9 inches
foot	$\frac{1}{3}$ yard
cubit	$\frac{1}{2}$ yard; 18 inches
yard	basic unit; 3600/3937 meter
fathom	2 yards; 6 feet
rod	5.5 yards; 25 links
chain	22 yards; 100 links

Astronomical

astronomical unit	92.9×10^6 miles
LIGHT-YEAR	5.9×10^{12} miles
parsec	1.9×10^{13} miles; 3.6 light-years

furlong	40 rods; 220 yards; $\frac{1}{8}$ miles
mile	320 rods; 1760 yards; 5280 feet
nautical mile	1852 meters; 6076.1 feet (approx.)
league	3 miles

Printing

point	0.013837 inch; $\frac{1}{72}$ inch (approx.)
pica	12 points; $\frac{1}{6}$ inch (approx.)
agate	$\frac{1}{14}$ inch (approx.)

AREA

The basic units of area are the **square meter** (centare) and the **square yard**, being squares with sides equal to 1 meter and 1 yard, respectively.

Metric

| square millimeter | 0.01 square centimeter |
| square centimeter | 0.01 square decimeter |

square decimeter	0.01 square meter
square meter, centare	basic unit
square dekameter, are	100 square meters
square hectometer, hectare	100 square dekameters; 100 ares
square kilometer	100 square hectometers; 100 hectares

English

square inch	$\frac{1}{144}$ square foot
square link	0.4356 square foot; 62.7 square inches
square foot	$\frac{1}{9}$ square yard
square yard	basic unit
square rod	30.25 square yards
square chain	484 square yards; 16 square rods
acre	10 square chains; 160 square rods
square mile	640 acres

Effective cross section for nuclear reactions

barn	10^{-28} square meter (the approximate cross section of the atomic nucleus)

VOLUME

The basic units of volume are the **cubic meter** and the **cubic yard,** being cubes with sides equal to 1 meter and 1 yard, respectively.

Metric

cubic millimeter	0.001 cubic centimeter
cubic centimeter	0.001 cubic decimeter
cubic decimeter	0.001 cubic meter; 0.01 decistere
decistere	0.1 cubic meter; 0.1 stere
cubic meter, stere	basic unit
cubic dekameter	1000 cubic meters
cubic hectometer	1000 cubic dekameters
cubic kilometer	1000 cubic hectometers

English

cubic inch	$\frac{1}{1728}$ cubic foot
board foot	$\frac{1}{12}$ cubic foot
cubic foot	$\frac{1}{27}$ cubic yard
cubic yard	basic unit
cord	128 cubic feet

CAPACITY

The basic unit of capacity for both dry and liquid measure in the metric system is the **liter,** which is defined as the volume of 1 kilogram of pure water at its temperature of maximum density (approx. 4°C) and standard atmospheric pressure. The liter is equal to 1.000028 cubic decimeters. In the English system, separate units exist for dry and liquid measure. The basic unit of dry measure is the **bushel,** equal to 2150.42 cubic inches. The basic units of liquid measure are the **gallon,** equal to 231 cubic inches, used in the U.S., and the **Imperial gallon,** equal to approximately 277 cubic inches, used in Great Britain, Northern Ireland, and Canada.

Metric

microliter	0.001 milliliter
milliliter	0.1 centiliter
centiliter	0.1 deciliter
deciliter	0.1 liter
liter	basic unit
dekaliter	10 liters
hectoliter	10 dekaliters
kiloliter	10 hectoliters

English dry measure

dry pint	$\frac{1}{2}$ dry quart
dry quart	$\frac{1}{8}$ peck
peck	$\frac{1}{4}$ bushel
bushel	basic unit
cranberry barrel	5826 cubic inches
barrel	3.28 bushels; 105 dry quarts; 7056 cubic inches

U.S. liquid measure

minim	$\frac{1}{60}$ fluid dram
fluid dram	$\frac{1}{8}$ fluid ounce

British liquid measure

minim	$\frac{1}{60}$ fluid drachm
fluid drachm	$\frac{1}{8}$ fluid ounce; 1 fluid dram (U.S.)

fluid ounce	$\frac{1}{4}$ gill; 16 liq. pint	fluid ounce	$\frac{1}{5}$ gill; $\frac{1}{20}$ liquid pint
gill (U.S.)	$\frac{1}{2}$ liquid pint (U.S.)	gill (Brit.)	$\frac{1}{2}$ liquid pint (Brit.)
liquid pint (U.S.)	$\frac{1}{2}$ liquid quart (U.S.)	liquid pint (Br.)	$\frac{1}{2}$ liquid quart (Brit.)
liquid quart (U.S.)	$\frac{1}{4}$ gallon (U.S.)	liquid quart (Brit.)	$\frac{1}{4}$ Imperial gallon
gallon (U.S.)	basic unit; 128 fl oz	Imperial gallon	basic unit; 160 fl oz
firkin (U.S.)	9 gallons (U.S.)	firkin (Brit.)	9 Imperial gallons
hogshead (U.S.)	63 gallons (U.S.)	hogshead (Brit.)	63 Imperial gallons

Cooking measures (U.S.)		*Cooking measures* (British)	
drop	$\frac{1}{60}$ teaspoon (U.S.)		
teaspoon (U.S.)	$\frac{1}{3}$ tablespoon (U.S.)	teaspoon (Brit.)	$\frac{1}{3}$ tablespoon (Brit.)
tablespoon (U.S.)	$\frac{1}{16}$ cup; $\frac{1}{2}$ fluid ounce	tablespoon (Brit.)	$\frac{1}{16}$ cup; $\frac{5}{8}$ fluid ounce
cup (U.S.)	$\frac{1}{2}$ liq. pint; 8 fl oz	cup (Brit.)	$\frac{1}{2}$ liq. pint; 10 fl oz

MASS

The basic unit of mass is the **kilogram,** defined as the mass of the International Prototype Kilogram, a platinum-iridium cylinder kept at Sevres, France. The English unit of mass is the **pound,** defined as 0.45359237 kilogram. The pound is also used as a unit of weight or force and is related to the pound mass by the factor $g = 32.174$ ft/sec², the acceleration of gravity.

Metric		*English avoirdupois*	
atomic mass unit	1.657×10^{-27} kilogram	grain	$\frac{1}{7000}$ pound
microgram	0.001 milligram	dram	$\frac{1}{16}$ ounce
milligram	0.1 centigram	ounce	$\frac{1}{16}$ pound
centigram	0.1 decigram	pound	basic unit
decigram	0.1 gram	stone	14 pounds
gram	0.1 dekagram; 0.001 kilogram	short hundred-weight	100 pounds
dekagram	0.1 hectogram	long hundred-weight	112 pounds
hectogram	0.1 kilogram	short ton	2000 pounds
kilogram	basic unit	long ton	2240 pounds
metric ton	1000 kilograms		

English apothecaries		*English troy*	
grain	$\frac{1}{7000}$ pound (avoirdupois)	grain	$\frac{1}{7000}$ pound (avoirdupois)
scruple	$\frac{1}{3}$ dram; 20 grains	pennyweight	$\frac{1}{20}$ troy ounce; 24 grains
apothec. dram	$\frac{1}{8}$ ounce; 60 grains	troy dram	$\frac{1}{8}$ troy ounce; 1 apoth. dram
apothec. ounce	$\frac{1}{12}$ apothec. pound	troy ounce	$\frac{1}{12}$ troy pound; 1 apoth. oz
apothec. pound	5760 grains; 5760/7000 avoirdupois pound	troy pound	5760 grains; 5760/7000 avoirdupois pound; 1 apothec. pound

TIME

The basic unit of time is the **second,** defined as the duration of 9,192,631,770 periods of the radiation emitted at a particular wavelength by an atom of cesium-133.

nanosecond	10^{-9} second
microsecond	10^{-6} second
second	basic unit
minute	60 seconds
hour	60 minutes
day	24 hours
week	7 days

fortnight	2 weeks; 14 days
month	approximately 30 days
year	approximately 365.25 days
century	100 years
millennium	1000 years

ENERGY AND WORK

Work is done or energy used by a force acting through a distance. The basic unit of work or energy is the **joule**, equal to 1 newton-meter. Units of heat energy are based on the specific heat capacity of water.

electron-volt	1.60×10^{-19} joule
erg	10^{-7} joule; 1 dyne-cm
joule	basic unit
foot-pound	1.356 joules
calorie (heat)	4.186 joules
British thermal unit (heat)	252 calories; 1055 joules
kilocalorie (heat)	1000 calories; 4186 joules
kilowatt-hour	3.6×10 joules

FORCE

Force units are defined by Newton's Second Law, $F = ma$, relating force, mass, and acceleration. The basic unit of force is the **newton**, equal to 1 kilogram-meter per square second. The English unit of pound force is equal to 32.174 pound mass-feet per square second.

dyne	10^{-5} newton
poundal	0.138 newton; 0.031 pound force 1 pound mass-foot/square sec
newton	basic unit
pound force	4.4482 newtons; 32.174 poundals

PRESSURE

Pressure units are force units divided by area units. Thus, the basic unit is the **newton per square meter.** However, more common units are based on normal atmospheric pressure at sea level and 0°C or its equivalent barometric reading in terms of centimeters, millimeters, or inches of mercury.

atmosphere	1.013×10^{6} newtons/meter²; 14.7 pounds/inch²; 1.013 bars; 76 centimeters of mercury; 760 millimeters of mercury; 29.9 inches of mercury
bar	10^{5} newtons/meter²; 10^{6} dynes/centimeter²
dyne per square centimeter	0.1 newton/meter²; 10^{-6} bar
inch of mercury	0.003 atmosphere; 3.39×10^{3} newtons/meter²
millibar	0.001 bar; 100 newtons/meter²
millimeter of mercury	$\frac{1}{760}$ atmosphere; 1 torr; 133.3 newtons/meter²
newton per square meter	basic unit
pound per square inch	0.068 atmosphere; 47.88 newtons per square meter
torr	1 millimeter of mercury; $\frac{1}{760}$ atmosphere

POWER

Power is the rate of doing work or using energy. The basic unit of power is the **watt**, equal to 1 joule per second.

watt	basic unit
foot-pound per second	1.356 watts
horsepower	746 watts
kilowatt	1000 watts

ANGLE

second	$\frac{1}{60}$ minute
minute	$\frac{1}{60}$ degree
degree	$\frac{1}{360}$ circle

radian	$\frac{1}{2}\pi$ circle; 57.3 degrees
right angle	90 degrees; $\frac{1}{4}$ circle
straight angle	180 degrees; $\frac{1}{2}$ circle

COUNTING UNITS

pair	two
dozen	twelve
baker's dozen	thirteen
score	twenty
gross	12 dozen; 144

PAPER MEASURE

| quire | 24 or 25 sheets |
| ream | 20 quires; 480 or 500 sheets; printer's perfect ream is 516 sheets |

MISCELLANEOUS UNITS

curie	radioactivity unit equal to 3.7×10^{10} disintegrations per second
decibel	sound loudness unit equal to about $\frac{1}{130}$ greatest difference detectable by the human ear
hertz	frequency unit; 1 cycle, vibration, or revolution per second
knot	speed unit equal to 1 nautical mile per hour
mole	mass unit equal to number of grams (or other mass unit) of a substance numerically equal to the molecular weight of the substance
roentgen	radiation unit equal to the radiation through a cubic centimeter of air sufficient to produce 1 statcoulomb of ions
slug	mass unit defined by Newton's Second Law and equal to 1 pound force times 1 square second per foot; 32.174 pounds mass
steradian	solid angle unit equal to $\frac{1}{4}$ sphere; 3282.8 square degrees

TEMPERATURE SCALES

The basic unit of temperature measurement is the **degree**. Two different degrees are in common use, the Celsius degree, defined as $\frac{1}{100}$ of the temperature difference between the melting point and boiling point of water, and the Fahrenheit degree, defined as $\frac{1}{180}$ of the temperature difference between these same two reference points. The Celsius scale marks the melting point of water as 0°C, while the Fahrenheit scale marks this temperature as 32°F. Thus, to convert Fahrenheit temperatures to Celsius temperatures, one must first subtract 32, then multiply the result by $\frac{100}{180}$, or $\frac{5}{9}$. To convert Celsius temperatures to Fahrenheit, first multiply the Celsius temperature by $\frac{9}{5}$, then add 32. Two other temperature scales are used that are based on the thermodynamic properties of an ideal gas. Both of these absolute scales start at absolute zero, the lowest possible theoretical temperature. One of these scales, the Kelvin scale, is based on the Celsius scale and has the same size degree. The other scale, the Rankine scale, is based on the Fahrenheit scale. The following table compares six reference temperatures on each of these four scales:

	Fahrenheit	Celsius	Kelvin	Rankine
Absolute zero	−459.69°F	−273.15°C	0°K	0°R
Melting point of water	32°F	0°C	273.15°K	491.69°R
Triple point of water	32.01°F	0.01°C	273.16°K	491.7°R
Boiling point of water	212°F	100°C	373.15°K	671.69°R
Boiling point of sulfur	832.28°F	444.60°C	717.75°K	1291.97°R
Melting point of gold	1945.40°F	1063.00°C	1336.15°K	2405.09°R

PHOTOMETRIC UNITS

The basic unit of photometric measurements is the **candle**, defined as $\frac{1}{60}$ of the luminous intensity of 1 square centimeter of an ideal blackbody radiator at the melting point of platinum (2046°K). The visible radiation given off by a source is called luminous flux. The unit of luminous flux is the lumen, equal to $\frac{1}{4}\pi$ of the total luminous flux given off by 1 candle. The lumen is the flux per steradian, or unit solid angle, emitted by a unit candle. For a diffuse source of light, the surface brightness of the source is measured in lamberts, equal to $1/\pi$ candle per square centimeter, or 1 lumen emitted per square centimeter. The relationships between these units and those for the illumination of a surface, or illuminance, may be summarized as follows:

Luminous intensity of source

candle   basic unit

Surface illumination; illuminance

lux   1 lumen incident per square meter; 0.1 milliphot; 10^{-4} phot

Luminous flux

lumen $\frac{1}{4}\pi$ total flux emitted by 1 candle   milliphot   0.001 phot

                       foot-candle   1 lumen per square foot; 1.076 milliphots

Surface brightness or intensity

lambert $1/\pi$ candle per square centimeter; 1 lumen emitted per square centimeter of a perfectly diffusing surface   phot   1 lumen per square centimeter; 10,000 lux; 929 foot-candles

ELECTRIC UNITS

Three systems of electric units exist, the MKS-practical system, the CGS electrostatic system, and the CGS electromagnetic system. The MKS system, based on the meter and the kilogram, has superseded the other two systems in most applications. The basic unit of charge in this system is the coulomb. Current is measured in amperes, 1 ampere being equal to coulomb per second. The coulomb is defined by means of the ampere, with 1 ampere being equal to the current in the same direction in each of two coaxial loops that produces in a vacuum an attractive force between the loops equal to $6\pi^3 a^4/r^4 + 10^{-7}$ newtons, where a is the separation between the axes of the coils and r is the radius of either coil (a is much larger than r). The three systems of units and the quantities they measure are summarized in the following table:

Quantity	MKS-practical	CGS electrostatic	CGS electromagnetic
Charge	coulomb (basic unit)	statcoulomb; 3.34×10^{-10} coulomb	abcoulomb; 10 coulombs
Current (charge per second)	ampere—1 coulomb per second	statampere; 3.34×10^{-10} ampere	abampere; 10 amperes
Potential difference (energy per unit charge to move the charge from one point to another)	volt—1 joule per coulomb	statvolt; 299.8 volts	abvolt; 10^{-8} volt
Resistance (potential required per unit of current to pass current through a conductor)	ohm—1 volt per ampere	statohm; 8.99×10^{11} ohms	abohm; 10^{-9} ohm
Conductance (current in a conductor per unit of potential; inverse of resistance	mho—1 ampere per volt		
Capacitance (change in charge on a conductor corresponding to a potential change of one unit)	farad—1 coulomb per volt	statfarad; 1.11×10^{-12} farad	abfarad; 10^9 farads
Inductance (potential difference induced in a conductor by a change of one unit of current per second)	henry—1 volt-second per ampere	stathenry; 8.99×10^{11} henries	abhenry; 10^{-9} henry
Magnetic flux density or electromagnetic induction (magnetic field that exerts a force of one unit on a conductor of unit length and carrying one unit of current)	weber per square meter—1 newton per ampere-meter		gauss; 10^{-4} weber per square meter; 1 maxwell per square centimeter
Magnetic flux (total flux through a region; related to line of magnetic force)	weber—1 newton-meter per ampere; 1 volt-second		maxwell; 10^{-8} weber; 1 line
Magnetic intensity or field strength (strength of a magnetic field induced by a coil of wire of N turns and of unit length and carrying a unit of current)	ampere-turn per meter		oersted; 79.6 ampere-turns per meter
Magnetomotive force (force of a coil of wire of N turns and carrying a unit of current)	ampere-turn		gilbert; 0.7958 ampere-turn

Other electric units

ampere-hour	unit of charge equal to 3600 coulombs	microfarad	unit of capacitance equal to 10^{-6} farad
faraday	unit of charge equal to 96,500 coulombs	millihenry	unit of inductance equal to 0.001 henry
picofarad	unit of capacitance equal to 10^{-12}		

To convert weights and measures from the English system to the metric system or from the metric system to the English system, multiply by the given factor. E.g., to convert 6 in. to centimeters, look in the columns which convert inches to centimeters and multiply by the factor in the third column which is 2.54.

6 in. × 2.54 — 16.24 centimeters.

From English System	To Metric System	Factor to Multiply by
LENGTH		
feet	meters	0.3048
inches	centimeters	2.54
inches	millimeters	25.4
miles, naut.	kilometers	1.852
miles, statute	kilometers	1.609
rods	meters	5.029
yards	meters	0.9144
AREA		
acres	hectares	0.4047
square feet	sq. centimeters	929.0
square feet	sq. meters	0.0929
square inches	sq. centimeters	6.452
square miles	hectares	259.0
square miles	sq. kilometers	2.59
square rods	square meters	25.29
square yards	square meters	0.8361
VOLUME		
cubic inches	cu. centimeters	16.38
cubic feet	cubic meters	0.0283
cubic yards	cubic meters	0.765
CAPACITY – LIQUID MEASURE		
fluid drams	milliliters	3.697
fluid ounces	liters	0.0296
fluid ounces	milliliters	29.57
gallons (British)	liters	4.546
gallons (U.S.)	liters	3.785
pints (British)	liters	0.5683
pints (U.S.)	liters	0.4732
quarts (British)	liters	1.137
quarts (U.S.)	liters	0.9463
CAPACITY – DRY MEASURE		
bushels (British)	liters	36.37
bushels (U.S.)	liters	35.24
pecks (British)	liters	9.092
pecks (U.S.)	liters	8.810
pints (British)	liters	0.5682
pints (U.S.)	liters	0.5506
quarts (British)	liters	1.1364
quarts (U.S.)	liters	1.1012
MASS		
drams, avoirdupois	grams	1.772
grains	grams	0.0648
grains	milligrams	64.80
hundredweights, long	kilograms	50.80
hundredweights, short	kilograms	45.36
ounces, apothecaries and troy	grams	31.10
ounces, avoirdupois	grams	28.35
pounds, avoirdupois	kilograms	0.4536
tons, long	metric tons	1.016
tons, short	metric tons	0.907

From Metric System	To English System	Factor to Multiply by
LENGTH		
centimeters	inches	0.3937
kilometers	nautical miles	0.5396
kilometers	statute miles	0.6214
meters	feet	3.281
meters	inches	39.37
meters	yards	1.094
AREA		
square centimeters	square inches	0.155
ares	acres	0.0247
ares	square rods	3.954
hectares	acres	2.471
square kilometers	acres	247.1
square kilometers	square miles	0.3861
square meters	square feet	10.76
square meters	square yards	1.956
square millimeters	square inches	0.0016
VOLUME		
cubic centimeters	cubic inches	0.061
cubic meters	cubic feet	35.31
cubic meters	cubic yards	1.308
cubic millimeters	cubic inches	0.0001
CAPACITY – LIQUID MEASURE		
centiliters	fluid ounces	0.3382
deciliters	fluid ounces	3.382
liters	gallons (British)	0.22
liters	gallons (U.S.)	0.2642
liters	quarts (U.S.)	1.057
milliliters	fluid ounces	0.0338
CAPACITY – DRY MEASURE		
centiliters	pints (British)	0.0024
centiliters	pints (U.S.)	0.0182
liters	quarts (British)	0.9372
liters	quarts (U.S.)	0.9081
milliliters	pints (U.S.)	0.0018
MASS		
centigrams	grains	0.1543
grams	ounces, apothecaries and troy	0.0322
grams	ounces, avoirdupois	0.0353
kilograms	pounds, apothecaries and troy	2.679
kilograms	pounds, avoirdupois	2.205
metric tons	long tons	0.9842
metric tons	short tons	1.102
milligrams	grains	0.0154

NO. 7 FUNDAMENTAL CONSTANTS

CONSTANT	SYMBOL	VALUE	CONSTANT	SYMBOL	VALUE
Acceleration of gravity at earth's surface (mean)	g	9.81 m/sec^2 or 32.2 ft/sec^2	Mass of neutron	m_n	1.67×10^{-27}kg
			Mass of proton	m_p	1.67×10^{-27}kg
			Mass of sun	M_s	1.99×10^{30}kg
Atmospheric pressure at sea level	(none)	1.013×10^5 n/m^2 or 14.7 lb/in	Permeability of free space	μ_0	4×10^{-7} weber/amp-m
			Pi	π	3.1416
Avogadro's number	N_0	6.025×10^{23} (per mole)	Planck's constant	h	6.625×10^{-34} joule-sec
Boltzmann's constant	k	1.380×10^{-23} joule/deg		$\bar{h} = h/2\pi$	1.05×10^{-34} joule-sec
Charge of electron	e	1.602×10^{-19} coulomb	Radius of first Bohr orbit of hydrogen atom	r_1	5.3×10^{-11}m
Charge-to-mass ratio of electron	e/m	1.76 coul/kg			
			Radius of earth (mean)	r_e	6.371×10^3m
Dielectric constant of free space	ϵ_0	8.85 coul^2/n-m^2	Radius of sun (mean)	r_s	6.965×10^8m
			Rydberg constant for hydrogen	R_H	109678 cm^{-1}
e (base of natural logarithms)	e	2.7183	Speed of light in free space	c	2.998×10^8 m/sec
Electrostatic constant	K	9.00×10^9 n-m^2/coul^2	Speed of sound at sea level and 0°C (STP)	v	331 m/sec
Gravitational constant	G	6.670×10^{-11} n-m^2/kg^2			
Mass of earth	M_e	5.98×10^{24}kg	Universal gas constant	R	$.314 \times 10^3$ joule/mole-deg
Mass of electron	m	9.11×10^{-31}kg			
Mass of hydrogen atom	m_H	1.6×10^{-27}kg			

NO. 8 ROMAN NUMERALS

NUMBER	ROMAN NUMERAL	NUMBER	ROMAN NUMERAL
1	I	70	LXX
2	II	76	LXXVI
3	III	80	LXXX
4	IV	87	LXXXVII
5	V	90	XC
6	VI	98	XCVIII
7	VII	100	C
8	VIII	101	CI
9	IX	115	CXV
10	X	150	CL
11	XI	200	CC
12	XII	300	CCC
13	XIII	400	CD
14	XIV	500	D
15	XV	600	DC
16	XVI	700	DCC
17	XVII	800	DCCC
18	XVIII	900	CM
19	XIX	1,000	M
20	XX	1,970	MCMLXX
21	XXI	2,000	MM
30	XXX	5,000	$\bar{\text{V}}$
32	XXXII	10,000	$\bar{\text{X}}$
40	XL	50,000	$\bar{\text{L}}$
43	XLIII	100,000	$\bar{\text{C}}$
50	L	150,000	$\overline{\text{CL}}$
54	LIV	500,000	$\bar{\text{D}}$
60	LX	560,000	$\overline{\text{DLX}}$
65	LXV	1,000,000	$\bar{\text{M}}$

+	1	2	3	4	5	6	7	8	9	10	11	12
1	2	3	4	5	6	7	8	9	10	11	12	13
2	3	4	5	6	7	8	9	10	11	12	13	14
3	4	5	6	7	8	9	10	11	12	13	14	15
4	5	6	7	8	9	10	11	12	13	14	15	16
5	6	7	8	9	10	11	12	13	14	15	16	17
6	7	8	9	10	11	12	13	14	15	16	17	18
7	8	9	10	11	12	13	14	15	16	17	18	19
8	9	10	11	12	13	14	15	16	17	18	19	20
9	10	11	12	13	14	15	16	17	18	19	20	21
10	11	12	13	14	15	16	17	18	19	20	21	22
11	12	13	14	15	16	17	18	19	20	21	22	23
12	13	14	15	16	17	18	19	20	21	22	23	24

×	1	2	3	4	5	6	7	8	9	10	11	12
1	1	2	3	4	5	6	7	8	9	10	11	12
2	2	4	6	8	10	12	14	16	18	20	22	24
3	3	6	9	12	15	18	21	24	27	30	33	36
4	4	8	12	16	20	24	28	32	36	40	44	48
5	5	10	15	20	25	30	35	40	45	50	55	60
6	6	12	18	24	30	36	42	48	54	60	66	72
7	7	14	21	28	35	42	49	56	63	70	77	84
8	8	16	24	32	40	48	56	64	72	80	88	96
9	9	18	27	36	45	54	63	72	81	90	99	108
10	10	20	30	40	50	60	70	80	90	100	110	120
11	11	22	33	44	55	66	77	88	99	110	121	132
12	12	24	36	48	60	72	84	96	108	120	132	144

NO. 11 NUMBERS TABLE

NAME	U.S. & FRENCH SYSTEMS	NO. OF ZEROS	NAME	BRITISH & GERMAN SYSTEMS	NO. OF ZEROS
million	1,000 thousands (1,000,000)	6	million	1,000 thousands (1,000,000)	6
			milliard	1,000 millions (1,000,000,000)	9
milliard} billion }	1,000 millions (1,000,000,000)	9	billion	1,000,000 millions	12
trillion	1,000 billions	12	trillion	1,000,000 billions	18
quadrillion	1,000 trillions	15	quadrillion	1,000,000 trillions	24
quintillion	1,000 quadrillions	18	quintillion	1,000,000 quadrillions	30
sextillion	1,000 quintillions	21	sextillion	1,000,000 quintillions	36
septillion	1,000 sextillions	24	septillion	1,000,000 sextillions	42
octillion	1,000 septillions	27	octillion	1,000,000 septillions	48
nonillion	1,000 octillions	30	nonillion	1,000,000 octillions	54
decillion	1,000 nonillions	33	decillion	1,000,000 nonillions	60
undecillion	1,000 decillions	36	undecillion	1,000,000 decillions	66
duodecillion	1,000 undecillions	39	duodecillion	1,000,000 undecillions	72
tredecillion	1,000 duodecillions	42	tradecillion	1,000,000 duodecillions	78
quattuordecillion	1,000 tredecillions	45	quattuordecillion	1,000,000 tredecillions	84
quindecillion	1,000 quattordecillions	48	quindecillion	1,000,000 quattuordecillions	90
sexdecillion	1,000 quindecillions	51	sexdecillion	1,000,000 quindecillions	96
septendecillion	1,000 sexdecillions	54	septendecillion	1,000,000 sexdecillions	102
octodecillion	1,000 septendecillions	57	octodecillion	1,000,000 septendecillions	108
novemdecillion	1,000 octodecillions	60	novemdecillion	1,000,000 octodecillions	114
vignitillion	1,000 novemdecillions	63	vigintillion	1,000,000 novemdecillions	120

NO. 12 DECIMAL AND PERCENT EQUIVALENTS OF COMMON FRACTIONS

FRACTION	DECIMAL EQUIVALENT	PERCENT EQUIVALENT	FRACTION	DECIMAL EQUIVALENT	PERCENT EQUIVALENT
1/2	.5	50%			
1/3	.33...	33 1/3%	4/6	.66...	66 2/3%
2/3	.66...	66 2/3%	5/6	.833...	83 1/3%
1/4	.25	25%	1/7	.1429 (nearest ten-thousandth)	14 2/7%
2/4	.5	50%	2/7	.2857 "	28 4/7%
3/4	.75	75%	3/7	.4286 "	42 6/7%
1/5	.2	20%	4/7	.5714 "	57 1/7%
2/5	.4	40%	5/7	.7143 "	71 3/7%
3/5	.6	60%	6/7	.8571 "	85 5/7%
4/5	.8	80%	1/8	.125	12 1/2%

FRACTION	DECIMAL EQUIVALENT	PERCENT EQUIVALENT	FRACTION	DECIMAL EQUIVALENT	PERCENT EQUIVALENT
1/6	.166. . .	16 2/3%	2/8	.25	25%
2/6	.33. . .	33 1/3%	3/8	.375	37 1/2%
3/6	.5	50%	4/8	.5	50%
5/8	.625	62 1/2%	6/10	.6	60%
6/8	.75	75%	7/10	.7	70%
7/8	.875	87 1/2%	8/10	.8	80%
1/9	.11. . .	11 1/9%	9/10	.9	90%
2/9	.22. . .	22 2/9%	1/11	.0909. . .	9 10/11%
3/9	.33. . .	33 1/3%	1/12	.0833. . .	8 1/3%
4/9	.44. . .	44 4/9%	1/13	.0769 (nearest ten-thousandth)	7 9/13%
5/9	.55. . .	55 5/9%	1/14	.0714 "	7 1/7%
6/9	.66. . .	66 2/3%	1/15	.066. . .	6 2/3%
7/9	.77. . .	77 7/9%	1/16	.0625	6 1/4%
8/9	.88. . .	88 8/9%	1/17	.0588 (nearest ten-thousandth)	5 15/17%
1/10	.1	10%	1/18	.055. . .	5 1/2%
2/10	.2	20%	1/19	.0526 (nearest ten-thousandth)	5 2/19%
3/10	.3	30%	1/20	.05	5%
4/10	.4	40%	1/32	.03125	3 1/8%
5/10	.5	50%	1/64	.015625	1 9/16%

NO. 13   DERIVATIVES

In the following formulas, u, v and y are differentiable functions, a, c, and n are constants, and $\ln u = \log_e u$.

1. $\dfrac{dc}{dx} = 0.$

2. $\dfrac{d}{dx} x = 1.$

3. $\dfrac{d}{dx}(cv) = c\dfrac{dv}{dx}.$

4. $\dfrac{d}{dx}x^n = nx^{n-1}, n > 1$ if $x = 0.$

5. $\dfrac{dy}{dx} = \dfrac{dy}{du} \cdot \dfrac{du}{dx}.$

6. $\dfrac{d}{dx}(u + v) = \dfrac{du}{dx} + \dfrac{dv}{dx}.$

7. $\dfrac{d}{dx}(uv) = u\dfrac{dv}{dx} + v\dfrac{du}{dx}.$

8. $\dfrac{d}{dx}\left(\dfrac{u}{v}\right) = \dfrac{v\dfrac{du}{dx} - u\dfrac{dv}{dx}}{v^2}$

9. $\dfrac{du^n}{dx} = nu^{n-1}\dfrac{du}{dx}, n > 1$ if $u = 0.$

10. $\dfrac{d}{dx}(\sin u) = \cos u \cdot \dfrac{du}{dx}.$

11. $\dfrac{d}{dx}(\cos u) = -\sin u \dfrac{du}{dx}.$

12. $\dfrac{d}{dx}(\tan u) = \sec^2 u \dfrac{du}{dx}.$

13. $\dfrac{d}{dx}(\cot u) = -\csc^2 u \dfrac{du}{dx}.$

14. $\dfrac{d}{dx}(\sec u) = \sec u \tan u \dfrac{du}{dx}.$

15. $\dfrac{d}{dx}(\csc u) = -\csc u \cot u \dfrac{du}{dx}.$

16. $\dfrac{d}{dx}(\sinh x) = \cosh x.$

17. $\dfrac{d}{dx}(\cosh x) = \sinh x.$

18. $\dfrac{d}{dx}(\tanh x) = \operatorname{sech}^2 x.$

19. $\dfrac{d}{dx}(\operatorname{ctnh} x) = -\operatorname{csch}^2 x.$

20. $\dfrac{d}{dx}(\operatorname{sech} x) = -\operatorname{sech} x \tanh x.$

21. $\dfrac{d}{dx}(\operatorname{csch} x) = -\operatorname{csch} x \operatorname{ctnh} x.$

22. $\dfrac{d}{dx}(\ln u) = \dfrac{\dfrac{du}{dx}}{u}.$

23. $\dfrac{d}{dx}(\log_a u) = \log_a e \cdot \dfrac{\dfrac{du}{dx}}{u}, a > 0$ and $a \neq 1.$

24. $\dfrac{d}{dx}(e^u) = e^u \cdot \dfrac{du}{dx}.$

25. $\dfrac{d}{dx}(a^u) = \ln a \cdot a^u \cdot \dfrac{du}{dx}, a > 0.$

26. $\dfrac{d}{dx}(\arcsin u) = \dfrac{\dfrac{du}{dx}}{\sqrt{1 - u^2}}, |u| < 1.$

27. $\dfrac{d}{dx}(\arccos u) = -\dfrac{\dfrac{du}{dx}}{\sqrt{1 - u^2}}, |u| < 1.$

28. $\dfrac{d}{dx}(\arctan u) = \dfrac{\dfrac{du}{dx}}{1 + u^2}.$

29. $\dfrac{d}{dx}(\operatorname{arc cot} u) = -\dfrac{\dfrac{du}{dx}}{1 + u^2}.$

30. $\dfrac{d}{dx}(\operatorname{arc sec} u) = \dfrac{\dfrac{du}{dx}}{u\sqrt{u^2 - 1}}, -\pi < \sec^{-1} u < -\dfrac{\pi}{2}, 0 < \sec^{-1} u < \dfrac{\pi}{2},$

31. $\dfrac{d}{dx}(\operatorname{arc csc} u) = -\dfrac{\dfrac{du}{dx}}{u\sqrt{u^2 - 1}}, -\pi < \csc^{-1} u < \dfrac{\pi}{2}, 0 < \csc^{-1} u < \dfrac{\pi}{2}.$

32. $\dfrac{d}{dx}(\sinh^{-1} x) = \dfrac{1}{\sqrt{x^2 + 1}}.$

33. $\dfrac{d}{dx}(\cosh^{-1} x) = \dfrac{1}{\sqrt{x^2 - 1}}, |x| > 1.$

34. $\dfrac{d}{dx}(\tanh^{-1} x) = \dfrac{1}{1 - x^2}, |x| < 1.$

35. $\dfrac{d}{dx}(\operatorname{ctnh}^{-1} x) = \dfrac{1}{1 - x^2}, |x| > 1.$

36. $\dfrac{d}{dx}(\operatorname{sech}^{-1} x) = \dfrac{-1}{x\sqrt{1 - x^2}}, 0 < x < 1.$

37. $\dfrac{d}{dx}(\operatorname{csch}^{-1} x) = \dfrac{-1}{|x|\sqrt{1 + x^2}}, x \neq 0.$

1. $\int df(x) = f(x).$

2. $d\int f(x)dx = f(x)dx.$

3. $\int 0 \cdot dx = C.$

4. $\int aj(x)dx = a\int f(x)dx.$

5. $\int (u = v)dx = \int u\,dx = \int v\,dx.$

6. $\int u\,dv = uv - \int v\,du.$

7. $\int \frac{u\,dv}{dx}dx = dx. uv - \int v\frac{du}{dx}$

8. $\int f(y)dx = \int \frac{f(y)dy}{\frac{dy}{dx}};$

9. $\int u^n\,du = \frac{u^{n+1}}{n+1}, n \neq -1.$

10. $\int \frac{du}{u} = \log u.$

11. $\int e^u\,du = e^u.$

12. $\int b^u\,du = \frac{b^u}{\log b}.$

13. $\int \sin u\,du = -\cos u.$

14. $\int \cos u\,du = \sin u.$

In the following tables, the constant of integration, C, is omitted but should be added to the result of every integration. The letter x represents any variable; u represents any function of x; the remaining letters represent arbitrary constants, unless otherwise indicated; all angles are in radians. Unless otherwise mentioned $\log_e u = \log u$.

15. $\int \tan u\,du = \log \sec u = -\log \cos u.$

16. $\int \operatorname{ctn} u\,du = \log \sin u = -\log \csc u.$

17. $\int \sec u\,du = \log(\sec u + \tan u) = \log\tan\left(\frac{u}{2} + \frac{\pi}{4}\right).$

18. $\int \csc u\,du = \log(\csc u - \operatorname{ctn} u) = \log\tan\frac{u}{2}.$

19. $\int \sin^2 u\,du = \frac{1}{2}u - \frac{1}{2}\sin u \cos u.$

20. $\int \cos^2 u\,du = \frac{1}{2}u + \frac{1}{2}\sin u \cos u.$

21. $\int \sec^3 u\,du = \tan u.$

22. $\int \csc^2 u\,du = -\operatorname{ctn} u.$

23. $\int \tan^2 u\,du = \tan u - u.$

24. $\int \operatorname{ctn}^2 u\,du = -\operatorname{ctn} u - u.$

25. $\int \frac{du}{u^2 + a^2} = \frac{1}{a}\tan^{-1}\frac{u}{a}.$

26. $\int \frac{du}{u^2 - a^2} = \frac{1}{2a}\log\left(\frac{u-a}{u+a}\right) = -\frac{1}{a}\operatorname{ctnh}^{-1}\left(\frac{u}{a}\right),$ if $u^2 > a^2, = \frac{1}{2a}\log\left(\frac{a-u}{a+u}\right) = -\frac{1}{a}\tanh^{-1}\left(\frac{u}{a}\right),$ if $u^2 > a^2.$

27. $\int \frac{dn}{\sqrt{a^2 - u}} = \sin^{-1}\left(\frac{u}{a}\right).$

28. $\int \frac{du}{\sqrt{u^2 \pm u^2}} = \log(u + \sqrt{u^2 \pm a^2}).$

29. $\int \frac{du}{\sqrt{2au - u^2}} = \cos^{-1}\left(\frac{a-u}{a}\right).$

30. $\int \frac{du}{u\sqrt{u^2 - a^2}} = \frac{1}{a}\sec^{-1}\left(\frac{u}{a}\right).$

31. $\int \frac{du}{u\sqrt{a^2 \pm u^2}} = -\frac{1}{a}\log_a\left(\frac{a + \sqrt{a^2 \pm u^2}}{u}\right).$

32. $\int \sqrt{a^2 - u^2} \cdot du = \frac{1}{2}(u\sqrt{a^2 - u^2} + a^2 \sin^{-1}\frac{u}{a}).$

33. $\int \sqrt{u^2 \pm a^2}\,du = \frac{1}{2}[u\sqrt{u^2 \pm a^2} \pm a^2 \log(u + \sqrt{u^2 \pm a^2})].$

34. $\int \sinh u\,du = \cosh u.$

35. $\int \cosh u\,du = \sinh u.$

36. $\int \tanh u\,du = \log(\cosh u).$

37. $\int \operatorname{ctnh} u\,du = \log(\sinh u).$

38. $\int \operatorname{sech} u\,du = \sin^{-1}(\tanh u).$

39. $\int \operatorname{csch} u\,du = \log\left(\tanh\frac{u}{2}\right).$

40. $\int \operatorname{sech} u \cdot \tanh u \cdot du = -\operatorname{sech} u.$

41. $\int \operatorname{csch} u \cdot \operatorname{ctnh} u \cdot du = -\operatorname{csch} u.$

NO. 15   SIMPLE INTEREST TABLE

Simple interest is calculated by multiplying the principal by the rate by the time: I = Prn. The amount (after the interest is added to the principal) is given by A = P + Prn or A = P(1 + rn). The table gives the interest, I, on $1.00 at simple interest from ½% to 8% per year for a period of from 1 to 90 days. Eg. to find the interest on $1.00 invested at a rate of 6% per year for a period of 60 days, read down the column marked number of days to 60, then across to the column marked 6%.

This gives .0100, which means that $1.00 will yield $0.01 (one cent) in interest. The amount that the principal yields is A = P + Prn, so A = $1.01.

The table may be used for any amount by multiplying the number found in the table by the principal. Thus, if $500.000 is invested at 6% per year for 60 days, multiply .01 that is found in the table for $1.00 by the actual principal, $500.000. The interest is ($500.00) × (.01) = $5.00. The amount = $505.00.

Number of days	½%	1%	1½%	2%	2½%	3%	3½%	4%	4½%	5%	5½%	6%	7%	8%
1	.00001	.00003	.00004	.00006	.00007	.00008	.00010	.00011	.00013	.00014	.00015	.00017	.00019	.00022
2	.00003	.00006	.00008	.00011	.00014	.00017	.00019	.00022	.00025	.00028	.00031	.00033	.00039	.00044
3	.00004	.00008	.00013	.00017	.00021	.00025	.00029	.00033	.00038	.00042	.00046	.00050	.00058	.00067
4	.00006	.00011	.00017	.00022	.00028	.00033	.00039	.00044	.00050	.00056	.00061	.00067	.00078	.00089
5	.00007	.00014	.00021	.00028	.00035	.00042	.00049	.00056	.00063	.00069	.00076	.00083	.00097	.00111
6	.00008	.00017	.00025	.00033	.00042	.00050	.00058	.00067	.00075	.00083	.00092	.00100	.00117	.00133
7	.00010	.00019	.00029	.00039	.00049	.00058	.00068	.00078	.00088	.00097	.00107	.00117	.00136	.00156
8	.00011	.00022	.00033	.00044	.00056	.00067	.00078	.00089	.00100	.00111	.00122	.00133	.00156	.00178
9	.00013	.00025	.00038	.00050	.00063	.00075	.00088	.00100	.00113	.00125	.00138	.00150	.00175	.00200

238

Table No. 15 continued

Number of days	½%	1%	1½%	2%	2½%	3%	3½%	4%	4½%	5%	5½%	6%	7%	8%
10	.00014	.00028	.00042	.00056	.00069	.00083	.00097	.00111	.00125	.00139	.00153	.00167	.00194	.00222
11	.00015	.00031	.00046	.00061	.00076	.00092	.00107	.00122	.00138	.00153	.00168	.00183	.00214	.00244
12	.00017	.00033	.00050	.00067	.00083	.00100	.00117	.00133	.00150	.00167	.00183	.00200	.00233	.00267
13	.00018	.00036	.00054	.00072	.00090	.00108	.00126	.00144	.00163	.00181	.00199	.00217	.00253	.00289
14	.00019	.00039	.00058	.00078	.00097	.00117	.00136	.00156	.00175	.00194	.00214	.00233	.00272	.00311
15	.00021	.00042	.00063	.00083	.00104	.00125	.00146	.00167	.00188	.00208	.00229	.00250	.00292	.00333
16	.00022	.00044	.00067	.00089	.00111	.00133	.00156	.00178	.00200	.00222	.00244	.00267	.00311	.00356
17	.00024	.00047	.00071	.00094	.00118	.00142	.00165	.00189	.00213	.00236	.00260	.00283	.00331	.00378
18	.00025	.00050	.00075	.00100	.00125	.00150	.00175	.00200	.00225	.00250	.00275	.00300	.00350	.00400
19	.00026	.00053	.00079	.00105	.00132	.00158	.00185	.00211	.00238	.00264	.00290	.00317	.00369	.00422
20	.00028	.00056	.00083	.00111	.00139	.00167	.00194	.00222	.00250	.00278	.00306	.00333	.00389	.00444
21	.00029	.00058	.00088	.00117	.00146	.00175	.00204	.00233	.00263	.00292	.00321	.00350	.00408	.00467
22	.00031	.00061	.00092	.00122	.00153	.00183	.00214	.00244	.00275	.00306	.00336	.00367	.00428	.00489
23	.00032	.00064	.00096	.00128	.00160	.00192	.00224	.00256	.00288	.00319	.00351	.00383	.00447	.00511
24	.00033	.00067	.00100	.00133	.00167	.00200	.00233	.00267	.00300	.00333	.00367	.00400	.00467	.00533
25	.00035	.00069	.00104	.00139	.00174	.00208	.00243	.00278	.00313	.00347	.00382	.00412	.00486	.00556
26	.00036	.00072	.00108	.00144	.00181	.00217	.00253	.00289	.00325	.00361	.00397	.00433	.00506	.00578
27	.00038	.00075	.00113	.00150	.00188	.00225	.00263	.00300	.00338	.00375	.00413	.00450	.00525	.00600
28	.00039	.00078	.00117	.00156	.00194	.00233	.00272	.00311	.00350	.00389	.00428	.00467	.00544	.00622
29	.00040	.00081	.00121	.00161	.00210	.00242	.00282	.00322	.00363	.00403	.00443	.00483	.00564	.00644
30	.00042	.00083	.00125	.00167	.00208	.00250	.00292	.00333	.00375	.00417	.00458	.00500	.00583	.00667
31	.00043	.00086	.00129	.00172	.00215	.00258	.00301	.00344	.00388	.00431	.00474	.00517	.00603	.00689
32	.00044	.00089	.00133	.00178	.00222	.00267	.00311	.00356	.00400	.00444	.00489	.00533	.00622	.00711
33	.00046	.00092	.00138	.00183	.00229	.00275	.00321	.00367	.00413	.00458	.00504	.00550	.00642	.00733
34	.00047	.00094	.00142	.00189	.00236	.00283	.00331	.00378	.00425	.00465	.00519	.00567	.00661	.00756
35	.00049	.00097	.00146	.00194	.00243	.00292	.00340	.00389	.00438	.00479	.00535	.00583	.00681	.00778
36	.00050	.00100	.00150	.00200	.00250	.00300	.00450	.00400	.00450	.00493	.00550	.00600	.00700	.00800
37	.00051	.00103	.00154	.00206	.00257	.00308	.00360	.00411	.00463	.00507	.00565	.00617	.00719	.00822
38	.00053	.00106	.00158	.00211	.00264	.00317	.00369	.00422	.00475	.00521	.00581	.00633	.00739	.00844
39	.00054	.00108	.00163	.00217	.00271	.00325	.00379	.00433	.00488	.00534	.00596	.00650	.00758	.00867
40	.00056	.00111	.00167	.00222	.00278	.00333	.00389	.00444	.00500	.00548	.00611	.00667	.00778	.00889
41	.00057	.00114	.00171	.00228	.00285	.00342	.00399	.00456	.00513	.00562	.00626	.00683	.00797	.00911
42	.00058	.00117	.00175	.00233	.00292	.00350	.00408	.00467	.00525	.00575	.00642	.00700	.00817	.00933
43	.00060	.00119	.00179	.00239	.00299	.00358	.00418	.00478	.00538	.00589	.00657	.00717	.00836	.00956
44	.00061	.00122	.00183	.00244	.00306	.00367	.00428	.00489	.00550	.00603	.00672	.00733	.00856	.00978
45	.00063	.00125	.00188	.00250	.00313	.00375	.00438	.00500	.00563	.00616	.00688	.00750	.00875	.01000
46	.00064	.00128	.00192	.00256	.00319	.00383	.00437	.00511	.00575	.00630	.00703	.00767	.00894	.01022
47	.00065	.00131	.00196	.00261	.00326	.00392	.00457	.00522	.00588	.00644	.00718	.00783	.00914	.01044
48	.00067	.00133	.00200	.00267	.00333	.00400	.00467	.00533	.00600	.00657	.00733	.00800	.00933	.01067
49	.00068	.00136	.00204	.00272	.00340	.00408	.00476	.00544	.00613	.00671	.00749	.00817	.00953	.01089
50	.00069	.00139	.00208	.00278	.00347	.00417	.00486	.00556	.00625	.00684	.00764	.00833	.00972	.01111
51	.00071	.00142	.00213	.00283	.00354	.00425	.00496	.00567	.00638	.00698	.00779	.00850	.00992	.01133
52	.00072	.00144	.00210	.00289	.00361	.00433	.00506	.00578	.00650	.00712	.00794	.00867	.01011	.01156
53	.00074	.00147	.00221	.00294	.00368	.00442	.00515	.00589	.00663	.00726	.00810	.00883	.01031	.01178
54	.00075	.00150	.00225	.00300	.00375	.00450	.00525	.00600	.00675	.00740	.00825	.00900	.01050	.01200
55	.00076	.00153	.00229	.00306	.00382	.00458	.00535	.00611	.00688	.00753	.00840	.00917	.01069	.01222
56	.00078	.00156	.00233	.00311	.00389	.00467	.00544	.00622	.00700	.00767	.00856	.00933	.01089	.01244
57	.00079	.00158	.00238	.00317	.00386	.00475	.00554	.00633	.00713	.00780	.00871	.00950	.01108	.01267
58	.00081	.00161	.00242	.00322	.00403	.00483	.00564	.00644	.00725	.00794	.00886	.00967	.01128	.01289
59	.00082	.00164	.00246	.00328	.00410	.00492	.00574	.00656	.00738	.00808	.00901	.00983	.01147	.01311
60	.00083	.00167	.00250	.00333	.00417	.00500	.00583	.00667	.00750	.00822	.00917	.01000	.01167	.01333
61	.00085	.00169	.00254	.00339	.00424	.00508	.00593	.00678	.00763	.00836	.00932	.01017	.01186	.01356
62	.00086	.00172	.00258	.00344	.00431	.00517	.00603	.00689	.00775	.00849	.00947	.01033	.01206	.01378
63	.00088	.00175	.00263	.00350	.00438	.00525	.00613	.00700	.00788	.00863	.00963	.01050	.01225	.01400
64	.00089	.00178	.00267	.00356	.00444	.00533	.00622	.00711	.00800	.00877	.00978	.01067	.01244	.01422
65	.00090	.00181	.00270	.00361	.00451	.00542	.00632	.00722	.00813	.00890	.00993	.01083	.01264	.01444
66	.00092	.00183	.00275	.00367	.00458	.00550	.00642	.00733	.00825	.00904	.01008	.01100	.01283	.01467
67	.00093	.00186	.00279	.00372	.00465	.00558	.00651	.00744	.00838	.00917	.01024	.01117	.01303	.01489
68	.00094	.00189	.00283	.00378	.00472	.00567	.00661	.00756	.00850	.00931	.01039	.01133	.01322	.01511
69	.00096	.00192	.00288	.00383	.00479	.00575	.00671	.00767	.00863	.00945	.01054	.01150	.01342	.01533

Number of days	½%	1%	1½%	2%	2½%	3%	3½%	4%	4½%	5%	5½%	6%	7%	8%
70	.00097	.00194	.00292	.00389	.00486	.00583	.00681	.00778	.00875	.00959	.01069	.01167	.01361	.01556
71	.00099	.00197	.00296	.00394	.00493	.00592	.00690	.00789	.00888	.00973	.01085	.01183	.01381	.01578
72	.00100	.00200	.00300	.00400	.00500	.00600	.00700	.00800	.00900	.00986	.01100	.01200	.01400	.01600
73	.00101	.00203	.00304	.00406	.00507	.00608	.00710	.00811	.00913	.01000	.01115	.01217	.01419	.01622
74	.00103	.00206	.00308	.00411	.00514	.00617	.00719	.00822	.00925	.01014	.01131	.01233	.01439	.01644
75	.00104	.00208	.00313	.00417	.00521	.00625	.00729	.00833	.00938	.01027	.01146	.01250	.01458	.01667
76	.00106	.00211	.00317	.00422	.00528	.00633	.00739	.00844	.00950	.01041	.01161	.01267	.01478	.01689
77	.00107	.00214	.00321	.00428	.00535	.00642	.00749	.00856	.00963	.01055	.01176	.01283	.01497	.01711
78	.00108	.00217	.00325	.00433	.00542	.00650	.00758	.00867	.00975	.01068	.01192	.01300	.01517	.01733
79	.00110	.00219	.00329	.00439	.00549	.00658	.00768	.00878	.00988	.01082	.01207	.01317	.01536	.01756
80	.00111	.00222	.00333	.00444	.00556	.00667	.00778	.00889	.01000	.01096	.01222	.01333	.01556	.01778
81	.00113	.00225	.00338	.00450	.00563	.00675	.00788	.00900	.01013	.01110	.01238	.01350	.01575	.01800
82	.00114	.00228	.00342	.00456	.00569	.00683	.00797	.00911	.01025	.01123	.01253	.01367	.01594	.01822
83	.00115	.00231	.00346	.00461	.00576	.00692	.00807	.00922	.01038	.01137	.01268	.01383	.01614	.01844
84	.00117	.00233	.00350	.00467	.00583	.00700	.00817	.00933	.01050	.01151	.01283	.01400	.01633	.01867
85	.00118	.00236	.00354	.00472	.00590	.00708	.00826	.00944	.01063	.01164	.01299	.01417	.01653	.01889
86	.00119	.00239	.00358	.00478	.00597	.00717	.00836	.00956	.01075	.01178	.01314	.01433	.01672	.01911
87	.00121	.00242	.00363	.00483	.00604	.00725	.00846	.00967	.01088	.01192	.01329	.01450	.01692	.01933
88	.00122	.00244	.00367	.00489	.00611	.00733	.00856	.00978	.01100	.01205	.01344	.01467	.01711	.01956
89	.00124	.00247	.00371	.00494	.00618	.00742	.00865	.00989	.01113	.01219	.01360	.01483	.01731	.01978
90	.00125	.00250	.00375	.00500	.00625	.00750	.00875	.01000	.01125	.01233	.01375	.01500	.01750	.02000
91	.00126	.00253	.00379	.00506	.00632	.00758	.00885	.01011	.01138	.01247	.01390	.01517	.01769	.02022
92	.00128	.00256	.00383	.00511	.00639	.00767	.00894	.01022	.01150	.01260	.01406	.01533	.01789	.02044
93	.00129	.00258	.00388	.00517	.00646	.00775	.00904	.01033	.01163	.01274	.01421	.01550	.01808	.02067
94	.00131	.00261	.00392	.00522	.00653	.00783	.00914	.01044	.01175	.01288	.01436	.01567	.01828	.02089
95	.00132	.00264	.00396	.00528	.00660	.00792	.00924	.01056	.01188	.01301	.01451	.01583	.01847	.02111
96	.00133	.00267	.00400	.00533	.00667	.00800	.00933	.01067	.01200	.01315	.01467	.01600	.01867	.02133
97	.00135	.00269	.00404	.00539	.00674	.00808	.00943	.01078	.01213	.01329	.01482	.01617	.01886	.02156
98	.00136	.00272	.00408	.00544	.00681	.00817	.00953	.01089	.01225	.01342	.01497	.01633	.01906	.02178
99	.00138	.00275	.00413	.00550	.00688	.00825	.00963	.01100	.01238	.01356	.01513	.01650	.01925	.02200
100	.00139	.00278	.00417	.00556	.00694	.00833	.00972	.01111	.01250	.01370	.01528	.01667	.01944	.02222

NO. 16   COMPOUND INTEREST TABLE

Compound interest means that the interest is added to the principal at the end of a period so that the new interest is calculated on the new amount for the next period. Compound interest may be calculated by the formula $A = P(1 + r)^n$ when interest is compounded annually. When interest is compounded q times per year the formula becomes $A = P\left(1 + \dfrac{r}{q}\right)^{nq}$.

The table gives the amount, A, for $1.00 invested at rates of interest from ½% to 8% compounded annually, for a period of from one year to 50 years. E.g., to find the amount $1.00 would be worth if invested for 20 years at 5% compounded annually, read down the column marked n to 20, then across to the column marked 5%. This gives 2.65329 which means that the original $1.00 will grow to $2.65 in twenty years.

The table can be used for any principal by multiplying the principal by the amount found in the table. Eg. to find the amount if $500.00 is invested for 20 years at 5% compounded annually, multiply $500.00 × 2.65329 (the amount for $1.00) giving $1326.65.

To find the amount if $500.00 is invested for 10 years at 4% compounded quarterly, use the formula $A = P\left(1 + \dfrac{r}{q}\right)^{nq}$ where q is 4 (quarterly means 4 times a year). Then use $A = \$500.00\left(1 + \dfrac{.04}{4}\right)^{10 \times 4}$ or $A = \$500.00\,(1 + .01)^{40}$. Read down the column marked n to 40 then across to the column marked .01 which gives 1.48886. Multiplying by $500.00 gives $A = \$744.43$.

n	½%	1%	1½%	2%	2½%	3%	3½%	4%	4½%	5%	5½%	6%	7%	8%
1	1.00500	1.01000	1.01500	1.02000	1.02500	1.03000	1.03500	1.04000	1.04500	1.05000	1.05500	1.06000	1.07000	1.08000
2	1.01002	1.02010	1.03022	1.04040	1.05062	1.06090	1.07122	1.08160	1.09202	1.10250	1.11302	1.12360	1.14490	1.16640
3	1.01507	1.03030	1.04567	1.06120	1.07689	1.09272	1.10871	1.12486	1.14116	1.15762	1.17424	1.19101	1.22504	1.25971
4	1.02015	1.04060	1.06136	1.08243	1.10381	1.12550	1.14752	1.16985	1.19251	1.21550	1.23882	1.26247	1.31079	1.36048
5	1.02525	1.05101	1.07728	1.10408	1.13140	1.15927	1.18768	1.21665	1.24618	1.27628	1.30696	1.33822	1.40255	1.46932
6	1.03037	1.06152	1.09344	1.12616	1.15969	1.19405	1.22925	1.26531	1.30226	1.34009	1.37884	1.41851	1.50073	1.58687
7	1.03552	1.07213	1.10984	1.14868	1.18868	1.22987	1.27227	1.31593	1.36086	1.40710	1.45467	1.50363	1.60578	1.71382
8	1.04070	1.08285	1.12649	1.17165	1.21840	1.26677	1.31680	1.36856	1.42210	1.47745	1.53468	1.59384	1.71818	1.85093
9	1.04591	1.09368	1.14338	1.19509	1.24886	1.30477	1.36289	1.42331	1.48609	1.55132	1.61909	1.68947	1.83845	1.99900
10	1.05114	1.10462	1.16054	1.21899	1.28008	1.34391	1.41059	1.48024	1.55296	1.62889	1.70814	1.79084	1.96715	2.15892

n	½%	1%	1½%	2%	2½%	3%	3½%	4%	4½%	5%	5½%	6%	7%	8%
11	1.05639	1.11566	1.17794	1.24337	1.31208	1.38423	1.45996	1.53945	1.62285	1.71033	1.80209	1.89829	2.10485	2.33163
12	1.06167	1.12682	1.19561	1.26824	1.34488	1.42576	1.51106	1.60103	1.69588	1.79585	1.90120	2.01219	2.25219	2.51817
13	1.06698	1.13809	1.21355	1.29360	1.37851	1.46853	1.56395	1.66507	1.77219	1.88564	2.00577	2.13292	2.40984	2.71962
14	1.07232	1.14947	1.23175	1.31947	1.41297	1.51258	1.61869	1.73167	1.85194	1.97993	2.11609	2.26090	2.57853	2.93719
15	1.07768	1.16096	1.25023	1.34586	1.44829	1.55796	1.67534	1.80094	1.93528	2.07892	2.23247	2.39655	2.75903	3.17216
16	1.08307	1.17257	1.26898	1.37278	1.48450	1.60470	1.73398	1.87298	2.02237	2.18287	2.35526	2.54035	2.95216	3.42594
17	1.08848	1.18430	1.28802	1.40024	1.52161	1.65284	1.79467	1.94790	2.11337	2.29201	2.48480	2.69277	3.15881	3.70001
18	1.09392	1.19614	1.30734	1.42824	1.55965	1.70243	1.85748	2.02581	2.20847	2.40661	2.62146	2.85433	3.37993	3.99601
19	1.09939	1.20810	1.32695	1.45681	1.59865	1.75350	1.92250	2.10684	2.30786	2.52695	2.76564	3.02559	3.61652	4.31570
20	1.10489	1.22019	1.34685	1.48594	1.63861	1.80611	1.98978	2.19112	2.41171	2.65329	2.91775	3.20713	3.86968	4.66095
21	1.11042	1.23239	1.36705	1.51566	1.67958	1.86029	2.05943	2.27876	2.52024	2.78596	3.07823	3.39956	4.14056	5.03383
22	1.11597	1.24471	1.38756	1.54597	1.72157	1.91610	2.13151	2.36991	2.63365	2.92526	3.24753	3.60353	4.43040	5.43654
23	1.12155	1.25716	1.40837	1.57689	1.76461	1.97358	2.20611	2.46471	2.75216	3.07152	3.42615	3.81974	4.74052	5.87146
24	1.12715	1.26973	1.42950	1.60843	1.80872	2.03279	2.28332	2.56330	2.87601	3.22509	3.61458	4.04893	5.07236	6.34118
25	1.13279	1.28243	1.45094	1.64060	1.85394	2.09377	2.36324	2.66583	3.00543	3.38635	3.81339	4.29187	5.42743	6.84847
26	1.13845	1.29525	1.47270	1.67341	1.90029	2.15659	2.44595	2.77246	3.14067	3.55567	4.02312	4.54938	5.80735	7.39635
27	1.14415	1.30820	1.49480	1.70688	1.94780	2.22128	2.53156	2.88336	3.28200	3.73345	4.24440	4.82234	6.21386	7.98806
28	1.14987	1.32129	1.51722	1.74102	1.99649	2.28792	2.62017	2.99870	3.42969	3.92012	4.47784	5.11168	6.64883	8.62710
29	1.15562	1.33450	1.53998	1.77584	2.04640	2.35656	2.71187	3.11865	3.58403	4.11613	4.72412	5.41838	7.11425	9.31727
30	1.16140	1.34784	1.56308	1.81136	2.09756	2.42726	2.80679	3.24339	3.74531	4.32194	4.98395	5.74349	7.61225	10.06265
31	1.16720	1.36132	1.58652	1.84758	2.15000	2.50008	2.90503	3.37313	3.91385	4.53803	5.25806	6.08810	8.14511	10.86766
32	1.17304	1.37494	1.61032	1.88454	2.20375	2.57508	3.00670	3.50805	4.08998	4.76494	5.54726	6.45338	8.71527	11.73708
33	1.17890	1.38869	1.63447	1.92223	2.25885	2.65233	3.11194	3.64838	4.27403	5.00318	5.85236	6.84058	9.32533	12.67604
34	1.18480	1.40257	1.65899	1.96067	2.31532	2.73190	2.22086	3.79431	4.46636	5.25334	6.17424	7.25102	9.97811	13.69013
35	1.19072	1.41660	1.68388	1.99988	2.37320	2.81386	3.33359	3.94608	4.66734	5.51601	6.51382	7.68608	10.67658	14.78534
36	1.19668	1.43076	1.70913	2.03988	2.43253	2.89827	3.45026	4.10393	4.87737	5.79181	6.87208	8.14725	11.42394	15.96817
37	1.20266	1.44507	1.73477	2.08068	2.49334	2.98522	3.57102	4.26808	5.09686	6.08140	7.25005	8.63608	12.22361	17.24562
38	1.20867	1.45952	1.76079	2.12229	2.55568	3.07478	3.69601	4.43881	5.32621	6.38547	7.64880	9.15425	13.07927	18.62527
39	1.21472	1.47412	1.78721	2.16474	2.61957	3.16702	3.82537	4.61636	5.56589	6.70475	8.06948	9.70350	13.99482	20.11529
40	1.22079	1.48886	1.81401	2.20803	2.68506	3.26203	3.95925	4.80102	5.81636	7.03998	8.51330	10.28571	14.97445	21.72452
41	1.22689	1.50375	1.84122	2.25220	2.75219	3.35989	4.09783	4.99306	6.07810	7.39198	8.98154	10.90286	16.02266	23.46248
42	1.23303	1.51878	1.86884	2.29724	2.82099	3.46069	4.24125	5.19278	6.35161	7.76158	9.47552	11.55703	17.14425	25.33948
43	1.23919	1.53397	1.89687	2.34318	2.89152	3.56451	4.38970	5.40049	6.63743	8.14966	9.99667	12.25045	18.34435	27.36664
44	1.24539	1.54931	1.92533	2.39005	2.96380	3.67145	4.54334	5.61651	6.93612	8.55715	10.54649	12.98548	19.62845	29.55597
45	1.25162	1.56481	1.95421	2.43785	3.03790	3.78159	4.70235	5.84117	7.24824	8.98500	11.12655	13.76461	21.00245	31.92044
46	1.25787	1.58045	1.98352	2.48661	3.11385	3.89504	4.86694	6.07482	7.57441	9.43425	11.73851	14.59048	22.47262	34.47408
47	1.26416	1.59626	2.01327	2.53634	3.19169	4.01189	5.03728	6.31781	7.91526	9.90597	12.38413	15.46591	24.04570	37.23201
48	1.27048	1.61222	2.04347	2.58707	3.27148	4.13225	5.21358	6.57052	8.27145	10.40126	13.06526	16.39387	25.72890	40.21057
49	1.27684	1.62834	2.07413	2.63881	3.35327	4.25621	5.39606	6.83334	8.64367	10.92133	13.78384	17.37750	27.52992	43.42741
50	1.28322	1.64463	2.10524	2.69158	3.43710	4.38390	5.58492	7.10668	9.03263	11.46739	14.54196	18.42015	29.45702	46.90161

A sample of random numbers containing 2,500 digits, taken from a sample set of 1,000,000 digits. For an explanation and examples of the use of random number tables, see RANDOM NUMBERS; RANDOM NUMBER TABLES in the text division.

53479	81115	98036	12217	59526	40238	40577	39351	43211	69255
97344	70328	58116	91964	26240	44643	83287	97391	92823	77578
66023	38277	74523	71118	84892	13956	98899	92315	65783	59640
99776	75723	03172	43112	83086	81982	14538	26162	24899	20551
30176	48979	92153	38416	42436	26636	83903	44722	69210	69117
81874	83339	14988	99937	13213	30177	47967	93793	86693	98854
19839	90630	71863	95053	55532	60908	84108	55342	48479	63799
09337	33435	53869	52769	18801	25820	96198	66518	78314	97013
31151	58295	40823	41330	21093	93882	49192	44876	47185	81425
67619	52515	03037	81699	17106	64982	60834	85319	47814	08075
61946	48790	11602	83043	22257	11832	04344	95541	20366	55937
04811	64892	96346	79065	26999	43967	63485	93572	80753	96582
05763	39601	56140	25513	86151	78657	02184	29715	04334	15678
73260	56877	40794	13948	96289	90185	47111	66807	61849	44686
54909	09976	76580	02645	35795	44537	64428	35441	28318	99001
42583	36335	60068	04044	29678	16342	48592	25547	63177	75225
27266	27403	97520	23334	36453	33699	23672	45884	41515	04756
49843	11442	66682	36055	32002	78600	36924	59962	68191	62580
29316	40460	27076	69232	51423	58515	49920	03901	26597	33068
30463	27856	67798	16837	74273	05793	02900	63498	00782	35097
28708	84088	65535	44258	33869	82530	98399	26387	02836	36838
13183	50652	94872	28257	78547	55286	33591	61965	51723	14211
60796	76639	30157	40295	99476	28334	15368	42481	60312	42770
13486	46918	64683	07411	77842	01908	47796	65796	44230	77230
34914	94502	39374	34185	57500	22514	04060	94511	44612	10485
28105	04814	85170	86490	35695	03483	57315	63174	71902	71182
59231	45028	01173	08848	81925	71494	95401	34049	04851	65914
87437	82758	71093	36833	53582	25986	46005	42840	81683	21459
29046	01301	55343	65732	78714	43644	46248	53205	94868	48711
62035	71886	94506	15263	61435	10369	42054	68257	14385	79436
38856	80048	59973	73368	52876	47673	41020	82295	26430	87377
40666	43328	87379	86418	95841	25590	54137	94182	42308	07361
40588	90087	37729	08667	37256	20317	53316	50982	32900	32097
78237	86556	50276	20431	00243	02303	71029	49932	23254	00862
98247	67474	71455	69540	01169	03320	67017	92543	97977	52728
69977	78558	65430	32627	28312	61815	14598	79728	55699	91348
39843	23074	40814	03713	21891	96353	96806	24595	26203	26009
62880	87277	99895	99965	34374	42556	11679	99605	98011	48867
56138	64927	29454	52967	86624	62422	30163	76181	95317	39264
90804	56026	48994	64569	67465	60180	12972	03848	62582	93855
09665	44672	74762	33357	67301	80546	97659	11348	78771	45011
34756	50403	76634	12767	32220	34545	18100	53513	14521	72120
12157	73327	74196	26668	78087	53636	52304	00007	05708	63538
69384	07734	94451	76428	16121	09300	67417	68587	87932	38840
93358	64565	43766	45041	44930	69970	16964	08277	67752	60292
38879	35544	99563	85404	04913	62547	78406	01017	86187	22072
58314	60298	72394	69668	12474	93059	02053	29807	63645	12792
83568	10227	99471	74729	22075	10233	21575	20325	21317	57124
28067	91152	40568	33705	64510	07067	64374	26336	79652	31140
05730	75557	93161	80921	55873	54103	34801	83157	04534	81368

From *A Million Random Digits with 100,000 Normal Deviates* (The Free Press, Glencoe, Ill., 1955), courtesy of The Rand Corporation.

Square and cube roots of numbers that are not found in the table may be determined by using the following relationships: $\sqrt{100n} = 10\sqrt{n}$ (e.g., $\sqrt{4500}$ cannot be found from the table. But $\sqrt{4500} = \sqrt{100 \cdot 45}$. Therefore, $n = 45$ and $\sqrt{100 \cdot 45} = 10\sqrt{45}$. $\sqrt{45}$ is given in the table as 6.7082. Thus, $\sqrt{4500} = $ 10·6.7082, or 67.82.); $\sqrt{1000n} = 10\sqrt{10n}$; $\sqrt{0.1n} = 0.1\sqrt{10n}$; $\sqrt{0.01n} = 0.1\sqrt{n}$; $\sqrt{0.001n} = 0.01\sqrt{10n}$; $\sqrt[3]{1000n} = 10\sqrt[3]{n}$; $\sqrt[3]{10,000n} = 10\sqrt[3]{10n}$; $\sqrt[3]{100,000n} = 10\sqrt[3]{100n}$; $\sqrt[3]{0.1n} = 0.1\sqrt[3]{100n}$; $\sqrt[3]{0.01n} = 0.1\sqrt[3]{10n}$; $\sqrt[3]{0.001n} = 0.1\sqrt[3]{n}$.

n	n^2	n^3	$\sqrt{n}$	$\sqrt{10n}$	$\sqrt[3]{n}$	$\sqrt[3]{10n}$	$1/n$
1	1	1	1.0000	3.1623	1.0000	2.1544	1.00000
2	4	8	1.4142	4.4721	1.2599	2.7144	.50000
3	9	27	1.7321	5.4772	1.4423	3.1072	.33333
4	16	64	2.0000	6.3246	1.5874	3.4200	.25000
5	25	125	2.2361	7.0711	1.7110	3.6840	.20000
6	36	216	2.4495	7.7460	1.8171	3.9149	.16667
7	49	343	2.6458	8.3666	1.9129	4.1213	.14286
8	64	512	2.8284	8.9443	2.0000	4.3089	.12500
9	81	729	3.0000	9.4868	2.0801	4.4814	.11111
10	100	1 000	3.1623	10.0000	2.1544	4.6416	.10000
11	121	1 331	3.3166	10.4881	2.2240	4.7914	.09091
12	144	1 728	3.4641	10.9545	2.2894	4.9324	.08333
13	169	2 197	3.6056	11.4018	2.3513	5.0658	.07692
14	196	2 744	3.7417	11.8322	2.4101	5.1925	.07143
15	225	3 375	3.8730	12.2475	2.4662	5.3133	.06667
16	256	4 096	4.0000	12.6491	2.5198	5.4288	.06250
17	289	4 913	4.1232	13.0384	2.5713	5.5397	.05882
18	324	5 832	4.2426	13.4164	2.6207	5.6462	.05556
19	361	6 859	4.3589	13.7841	2.6684	5.7489	.05263
20	400	8 000	4.4721	14.1421	2.7144	5.8480	.05000
21	441	9 261	4.5826	14.4914	2.7589	5.9439	.04762
22	484	10 648	4.6904	14.8324	2.8020	6.0368	.04545
23	529	12 167	4.7958	15.1658	2.8439	6.1269	.04348
24	576	13 824	4.8990	15.4919	2.8845	6.2145	.04167
25	625	15 625	5.0000	15.8114	2.9242	6.2996	.04000
26	676	17 576	5.0990	16.1245	2.9625	6.3825	.03846
27	729	19 683	5.1962	16.4317	3.0000	6.4633	.03704
28	784	21 952	5.2915	16.7332	3.0366	6.5421	.03571
29	841	24 389	5.3852	17.0294	3.0723	6.6191	.03448
30	900	27 000	5.4772	17.3205	3.1072	6.6943	.03333
31	961	29 791	5.5678	17.6068	3.1414	6.7679	.03258
32	1 024	32 768	5.6569	17.8885	3.1748	6.8399	.03125
33	1 089	35 937	5.7446	18.1659	3.2075	6.9104	.03030
34	1 156	39 304	5.8400	18.4391	3.2396	6.9795	.02941
35	1 225	42 875	5.9161	18.7083	3.2711	7.0473	.02857
36	1 296	46 656	6.0000	18.9737	3.3019	7.1138	.02778
37	1 369	50 653	6.0828	19.2354	3.3322	7.1791	.02703
38	1 444	54 872	6.1644	19.4936	3.3620	7.2432	.02632
39	1 521	59 319	6.2450	19.7484	3.3912	7.3061	.02564
40	1 600	64 000	6.3246	20.0000	3.4200	7.3681	.02500
41	1 681	68 921	6.4031	20.2485	3.4482	7.4290	.02439
42	1 764	74 088	6.4807	20.4939	3.4760	7.4889	.02381
43	1 849	79 507	6.5574	20.7364	3.5034	7.5478	.02326
44	1 936	85 184	6.6333	20.9762	3.5303	7.6059	.02273
45	2 025	91 125	6.7082	21.2132	3.5569	7.6631	.02222
46	2 116	97 336	6.7823	21.4476	3.5830	7.7194	.02174
47	2 209	103 823	6.8557	21.6795	3.6088	7.7750	.02128
48	2 304	110 592	6.9282	21.9089	3.6342	7.8297	.02083
49	2 401	117 649	7.0000	22.1359	3.6593	7.8837	.02041
50	2 500	125 000	7.0711	22.3606	3.6840	7.9370	.02000
51	2 601	132 651	7.1414	22.5832	3.7084	7.9896	.01961
52	2 704	140 608	7.2111	22.8035	3.7325	8.0415	.01923
53	2 809	148 877	7.2801	23.0217	3.7563	8.0927	.01887
54	2 916	157 464	7.3485	23.2379	3.7798	8.1433	.01852
55	3 025	166 375	7.4162	23.4521	3.8030	8.1932	.01818
56	3 136	175 616	7.4833	23.6643	3.8259	8.2426	.01786
57	3 249	185 193	7.5498	23.8747	3.8485	8.2913	.01754

n	n^2	n^3	$\sqrt{n}$	$\sqrt{10n}$	$\sqrt[3]{n}$	$\sqrt[3]{10n}$	$1/n$
58	3 364	195 112	7.6158	24.0832	3.8709	8.3396	.01724
59	3 481	205 379	7.6811	24.2899	3.8930	8.3872	.01695
60	3 600	216 000	7.7460	24.4949	3.9149	8.4343	.01667
61	3 721	226 981	7.8103	24.6982	3.9365	8.4809	.01639
62	3 844	238 328	7.8740	24.8998	3.9579	8.5270	.01613
63	3 969	250 047	7.9373	25.0998	3.9791	8.5726	.01587
64	4 096	262 144	8.0000	25.2982	4.0000	8.6177	.01563
65	4 225	274 625	8.0623	25.4951	4.0207	8.6624	.01538
66	4 356	287 496	8.1240	25.6905	4.0412	8.7066	.01515
67	4 489	300 763	8.1854	25.8844	4.0615	8.7503	.01493
68	4 624	314 432	8.2462	26.0768	4.0817	8.7937	.01471
69	4 761	328 509	8.3066	26.2679	4.1016	8.8366	.01449
70	4 900	343 000	8.3666	26.4575	4.1213	8.8790	.01429
71	5 041	357 911	8.4262	26.6458	4.1408	8.9211	.01408
72	5 184	373 248	8.4853	26.8328	4.1602	8.9628	.01389
73	5 329	389 017	8.5440	27.0185	4.1793	9.0041	.01370
74	5 476	405 224	8.6023	27.2029	4.1983	9.0450	.01351
75	5 625	421 875	8.6603	27.3861	4.2172	9.0856	.01333
76	5 776	438 976	8.7178	27.5681	4.2358	9.1258	.01316
77	5 929	456 533	8.7750	27.7489	4.2543	9.1657	.01299
78	6 084	474 552	8.8318	27.9285	4.2727	9.2052	.01282
79	6 241	493 039	8.8882	28.1069	4.2908	9.2443	.01269
80	6 400	512 000	8.9443	28.2843	4.3089	9.2832	.01250
81	6 561	531 441	9.0000	28.4605	4.3267	9.3217	.01235
82	6 724	551 368	9.0554	28.6356	4.3445	9.3599	.01220
83	6 889	571 787	9.1104	28.8097	4.3621	9.3978	.01205
84	7 056	592 704	9.1652	28.9828	4.3795	9.4354	.01190
85	7 225	614 125	9.2195	29.1548	4.3968	9.4727	.01176
86	7 396	636 056	9.2736	29.3258	4.4140	9.5097	.01163
87	7 569	658 503	9.3274	29.4958	4.4310	9.5464	.00149
88	7 744	681 472	9.3808	29.6648	4.4480	9.5828	.01136
89	7 921	704 969	9.4340	29.8329	4.4647	9.6190	.01124
90	8 100	729 000	9.4868	30.0000	4.4814	9.6549	.01111
91	8 281	753 571	9.5394	30.1662	4.4979	9.6905	.01099
92	8 464	778 688	9.5917	30.3315	4.5144	9.7259	.01087
93	8 649	804 357	9.6437	30.4959	4.5307	9.7610	.01075
94	8 836	830 584	9.6954	30.6594	4.5468	9.7959	.01064
95	9 025	857 375	9.7468	30.8221	4.5629	9.8305	.01053
96	9 216	884 736	9.7980	30.9838	4.5789	9.8648	.01042
97	9 409	912 673	9.8489	31.1448	4.5947	9.8990	.01031
98	9 604	941 192	9.8995	31.3050	4.6104	9.9329	.01020
99	9 801	970 299	9.9499	31.4643	4.6261	9.9666	.01010
100	10 000	1 000 000	10.0000	31.6228	4.6416	10.0000	.01000
101	10 201	1 030 301	10.0499	31.7805	4.6570	10.0332	.00990
102	10 404	1 061 208	10.0995	31.9374	4.6723	10.0662	.00980
103	10 609	1 092 727	10.1489	32.0936	4.6875	10.0990	.00971
104	10 816	1 124 864	10.1980	32.2490	4.7027	10.1316	.00962
105	11 025	1 157 625	10.2470	32.4037	4.7177	10.1640	.00952
106	11 236	1 191 016	10.2956	32.5576	4.7326	10.1961	.00943
107	11 449	1 225 043	10.3449	32.7109	4.7475	10.2281	.00935
108	11 664	1 259 712	10.3923	32.8634	4.7622	10.2599	.00926
109	11 881	1 295 029	10.4403	33.0152	4.7769	10.2914	.00917
110	12 100	1 331 000	10.4881	33.1663	4.7914	10.3228	.00909
111	12 321	1 367 631	10.5357	33.3167	4.8059	10.3540	.00901
112	12 544	1 404 928	10.5830	33.4664	4.8203	10.3850	.00893
113	12 769	1 442 897	10.6302	33.6155	4.8346	10.4158	.00850
114	12 996	1 481 544	10.6771	33.7639	4.8488	10.4464	.00877
115	13 225	1 520 875	10.7238	33.9117	4.8629	10.4769	.00870
116	13 456	1 560 896	10.7703	34.0588	4.8770	10.5072	.00862
117	13 689	1 601 613	10.8167	34.2053	4.8910	10.5373	.00855
118	13 924	1 643 032	10.8628	34.3511	4.9049	10.5672	.00847
119	14 161	1 685 159	10.9087	34.4964	4.9187	10.5970	.00840

n	n^2	n^3	$\sqrt{n}$	$\sqrt{10n}$	$\sqrt[3]{n}$	$\sqrt[3]{10n}$	$1/n$
120	14 400	1 728 000	10.9545	34.6410	4.9324	10.6266	.00833
121	14 641	1 771 561	11.0000	34.7851	4.9461	10.6560	.00826
122	14 884	1 815 848	11.0454	34.9285	4.9597	10.6853	.00820
123	15 129	1 860 867	11.0905	35.0714	4.9732	10.7144	.00813
124	15 376	1 906 624	11.1355	35.2136	4.9866	10.7434	.00806
125	15 625	1 953 125	11.1803	35.3553	5.0000	10.7722	.00800
126	15 876	2 000 376	11.2250	35.4965	5.0133	10.8008	.00794
127	16 129	2 048 383	11.2694	35.6371	5.0265	10.8293	.00787
128	16 384	2 097 152	11.3137	35.7771	5.0397	10.8577	.00781
129	16 641	2 146 689	11.3578	35.9166	5.0528	10.8859	.00775
130	16 900	2 197 000	11.4018	36.0555	5.0658	10.9139	.00769
131	17 161	2 248 091	11.4455	36.1939	5.0788	10.9418	.00763
132	17 424	2 299 968	11.4891	36.3318	5.0916	10.9696	.00758
133	17 689	2 352 637	11.5326	36.4692	5.1045	10.9972	.00752
134	17 956	2 406 104	11.5758	36.6060	5.1172	11.0247	.00746
135	18 225	2 460 375	11.6190	36.7424	5.1299	11.0521	.00741
136	18 496	2 515 456	11.6619	36.8782	5.1426	11.0793	.00735
137	18 769	2 571 353	11.7047	37.0135	5.1551	11.1064	.00730
138	19 044	2 628 072	11.7473	37.1484	5.1676	11.1334	.00725
139	19 321	2 685 619	11.7898	37.2827	5.1801	11.1602	.00719
140	19 600	2 744 000	11.8322	37.4166	5.1925	11.1869	.00714
141	19 881	2 803 221	11.8743	37.5500	5.2048	11.2135	.00709
142	20 164	2 863 288	11.9164	37.6829	5.2171	11.2399	.00704
143	20 449	2 924 207	11.9583	37.8153	5.2293	11.2662	.00699
144	20 736	2 985 984	12.0000	37.9473	5.2415	11.2924	.00694
145	21 025	3 048 625	12.0416	38.0789	5.2536	11.3185	.00690
146	21 316	3 112 136	12.0831	38.2110	5.2656	11.3445	.00685
147	21 609	3 176 523	12.1244	38.3406	5.2776	11.3703	.00680
148	21 904	3 241 792	12.1655	38.4708	5.2896	11.3960	.00676
149	22 201	3 307 949	12.2066	38.6005	5.3015	11.4217	.00671
150	22 500	3 375 000	12.2475	38.7298	5.1333	11.4471	.00667
151	22 801	3 442 951	12.2882	38.8587	5.3251	11.4725	.00662
152	23 104	3 511 808	12.3288	38.9872	5.3368	11.4978	.00658
153	23 409	3 581 577	12.3693	39.1152	5.3485	11.5230	.00654
154	23 716	3 652 264	12.4097	39.2428	5.3601	11.5480	.00649
155	24 025	3 723 875	12.4499	39.3700	5.3717	11.5730	.00645
156	24 336	3 796 416	12.4900	39.4968	5.3832	11.5978	.00641
157	24 649	3 869 893	12.5300	39.6232	5.3947	11.6225	.00637
158	24 964	3 944 312	12.5698	39.7492	5.4061	11.6471	.00633
159	25 281	4 019 679	12.6095	39.8748	5.4175	11.6717	.00629
160	25 600	4 096 000	12.6491	40.0000	5.4288	11.6961	.00625
161	25 921	4 173 281	12.6886	40.1248	5.4401	11.7204	.00621
162	26 244	4 251 528	12.7279	40.2492	5.4514	11.7446	.00617
163	26 569	4 330 747	12.7672	40.3733	5.4626	11.7687	.00613
164	26 896	4 410 944	12.8063	40.4969	5.4737	11.7927	.00610
165	27 225	4 492 125	12.8452	40.6202	5.4848	11.8167	.00606
166	27 556	4 574 296	12.8841	40.7431	5.4959	11.8405	.00602
167	27 889	4 657 463	12.9229	40.8656	5.5069	11.8642	.00599
168	28 224	4 741 632	12.9615	40.9878	5.5178	11.8878	.00595
169	28 561	4 826 809	13.0000	41.1096	5.5288	11.9114	.00592
170	28 900	4 913 000	13.0384	41.2311	5.5397	11.9348	.00588
171	29 241	5 000 211	13.0767	41.3522	5.5505	11.9582	.00585
172	29 584	5 088 448	13.1149	41.4729	5.5613	11.9815	.00581
173	29 929	5 177 717	13.1530	41.5933	5.5721	12.0046	.00578
174	30 276	5 268 024	13.1909	41.7133	5.5828	12.0277	.00575
175	30 625	5 359 375	13.2288	41.8330	5.5934	12.0507	.00571
176	30 976	5 451 776	13.2665	41.9524	5.6041	12.0736	.00568
177	31 329	5 545 233	13.3041	42.0714	5.6147	12.0965	.00564
178	31 684	5 639 752	13.3417	42.1901	5.6252	12.1192	.00562
179	32 041	5 735 339	13.3791	42.3084	5.6357	12.1418	.00559
180	32 400	5 832 000	13.4164	42.4264	5.6462	12.1644	.00556
181	32 761	5 929 741	13.4536	42.5441	5.6567	12.1869	.00552

n	n^2	n^3	$\sqrt{n}$	$\sqrt{10n}$	$\sqrt[3]{n}$	$\sqrt[3]{10n}$	$1/n$
182	33 124	6 028 568	13.4907	42.6615	5.6671	12.2093	.00549
183	33 489	6 128 487	13.5278	42.7785	5.6774	12.2316	.00546
184	33 856	6 229 504	13.5647	42.8952	5.6877	12.2539	.00543
185	34 225	6 331 625	13.6015	43.0116	5.6980	12.2760	.00541
186	34 596	6 434 856	13.6382	43.1277	5.7083	12.2981	.00538
187	34 969	6 539 203	13.6748	43.2435	5.7185	12.3201	.00535
188	35 344	6 644 672	13.7113	43.3590	5.7287	12.3420	.00532
189	35 721	6 751 269	13.7477	43.4741	5.7388	12.3639	.00529
190	36 100	6 859 000	13.7841	43.5890	5.7489	12.3856	.00526
191	36 481	6 967 871	13.8203	43.7036	5.7590	12.4073	.00524
192	36 864	7 077 888	13.8564	43.8178	5.7690	12.4289	.00521
193	37 249	7 189 057	13.8924	43.9318	5.7790	12.4505	.00518
194	37 636	7 301 384	13.9284	44.0454	5.7890	12.4719	.00515
195	38 025	7 414 875	13.9642	44.1588	5.7890	12.4933	.00513
196	38 416	7 529 536	14.0000	44.2719	5.8088	12.5147	.00510
197	38 809	7 645 373	14.0357	44.3847	5.8186	12.5359	.00508
198	39 204	7 762 392	14.0713	44.4972	5.8285	12.5571	.00505
199	39 601	7 880 599	14.1067	44.6094	5.8383	12.5782	.00503
200	40 000	8 000 000	14.1421	44.7214	5.8480	12.5992	.00500
201	40 401	8 120 601	14.1775	44.8330	5.8578	12.6202	.00498
202	40 804	8 242 408	14.2127	44.9444	5.8675	12.6411	.00495
203	41 209	8 365 427	14.2478	45.0555	5.8771	12.6619	.00493
204	41 616	8 489 664	14.2829	45.1664	5.8868	12.6827	.00490
205	42 025	8 615 125	14.3178	45.2769	5.8964	12.7033	.00488
206	42 436	8 741 816	14.3527	45.3872	5.9059	12.7240	.00485
207	42 849	8 869 743	14.3875	45.4973	5.9155	12.7445	.00483
208	43 264	8 998 912	14.4222	45.6070	5.9250	12.7650	.00481
209	43 681	9 129 329	14.4568	45.7165	5.9344	12.7854	.00478
210	44 100	9 261 000	14.4914	45.8258	5.9439	12.8058	.00476
211	44 521	9 393 931	14.5258	45.9347	5.9533	12.8261	.00474
212	44 944	9 528 128	14.5602	46.0435	5.9627	12.8463	.00472
213	45 369	9 663 597	14.5945	46.1519	5.9721	12.8665	.00469
214	45 796	9 800 344	14.6287	46.2601	5.9814	12.8866	.00467
215	46 225	9 938 375	14.6629	46.3681	5.9007	12.9066	.00465
216	46 656	10 077 696	14.6969	46.4758	6.0000	12.9266	.00463
217	47 089	10 218 313	14.7309	46.5833	6.0092	12.9465	.00461
218	47 524	10 360 232	14.7648	46.6905	6.0185	12.9664	.00459
219	47 961	10 503 459	14.7987	46.7974	6.0277	12.9862	.00457
220	48 400	10 648 000	14.8324	46.9042	6.0368	13.0059	.00455
221	48 841	10 793 861	14.8661	47.0106	6.0459	13.0256	.00452
222	49 284	10 941 048	14.8997	47.1169	6.0550	13.0452	.00450
223	49 729	11 089 567	14.9332	47.2229	6.0641	13.0648	.00448
224	50 176	11 239 424	14.9666	47.3286	6.0732	13.0843	.00446
225	50 625	11 390 625	15.0000	47.4342	6.0822	13.1037	.00444
226	51 076	11 543 176	15.0333	47.5395	6.0912	13.1231	.00442
227	51 529	11 697 083	15.0665	47.6445	6.1002	13.1424	.00441
228	51 984	11 852 352	15.0997	47.7494	6.1091	13.1617	.00439
229	52 441	12 008 989	15.1328	47.8539	6.1180	13.1809	.00437
230	52 900	12 167 000	15.1658	47.9583	6.1269	13.2001	.00435
231	53 361	12 326 391	15.1987	48.0625	6.1358	13.2192	.00433
232	53 824	12 487 168	15.2316	48.1664	6.1446	13.2382	.00431
233	54 289	12 649 337	15.2643	48.2701	6.1534	13.2572	.00429
234	54 756	12 812 904	15.2971	48.3736	6.1622	13.2761	.00427
235	55 225	12 977 875	15.3297	48.4768	6.1710	13.2950	.00426
236	55 696	13 144 256	15.3623	48.5798	6.1797	13.3139	.00424
237	56 169	13 312 053	15.3948	48.6827	6.1885	13.3326	.00422
238	56 644	13 481 272	15.4273	48.7852	6.1972	13.3514	.00420
239	57 121	13 651 919	15.4596	48.8876	6.2058	13.3700	.00418
240	57 600	13 824 000	15.4919	48.9898	6.2145	13.3887	.00417
241	58 081	13 997 521	15.5242	49.0918	6.2231	13.4072	.00415
242	58 564	14 172 488	15.5564	49.1935	6.2317	13.4258	.00413
243	59 049	14 348 907	15.5885	49.2950	6.2403	13.4442	.00412
244	59 536	14 526 784	15.6205	49.3964	6.2488	13.4626	.00410

n	n^2	n^3	$\sqrt{n}$	$\sqrt{10n}$	$\sqrt[3]{n}$	$\sqrt[3]{10n}$	$1/n$
245	60 025	14 706 125	15.6525	49.4975	6.2573	13.4810	.00408
246	60 516	14 886 936	15.6844	49.5984	6.2658	13.4993	.00407
247	61 009	15 069 223	15.7162	49.6991	6.2743	13.5176	.00405
248	61 504	15 252 992	15.7480	49.7896	6.2828	13.5358	.00403
249	62 001	15 438 249	15.7797	49.8999	6.2912	13.5540	.00402
250	62 500	15 625 000	15.8114	50.0000	6.2996	13.5721	.00400
251	63 001	15 813 251	15.8430	50.0999	6.3080	13.5902	.00398
252	63 504	16 003 008	15.8745	50.1996	6.3164	13.6082	.00397
253	64 009	16 194 277	15.9060	50.2991	6.3247	13.6262	.00395
254	64 516	16 387 064	15.9374	50.3984	6.3330	13.6441	.00394
255	65 025	16 581 375	15.9687	50.4975	6.3413	13.6620	.00392
256	65 536	16 777 216	16.0000	50.5964	6.3496	13.6798	.00391
257	66 049	16 974 593	16.0312	50.6952	6.3579	13.6976	.00389
258	66 564	17 173 512	16.0624	50.9737	6.3661	13.7153	.00388
259	67 081	17 373 979	16.0935	50.8920	5.3743	13.7330	.00386
260	67 600	17 576 000	16.1245	50.9902	6.3825	13.7507	.00385
261	68 121	17 779 581	16.1555	51.0882	6.3907	13.7683	.00383
262	68 644	17 984 728	16.1864	51.1860	6.3988	13.7859	.00382
263	69 169	18 191 447	16.2173	51.2835	6.4070	13.8034	.00380
264	69 696	18 399 744	16.2481	51.3809	6.4151	13.8209	.00379
265	70 225	18 609 625	16.2788	51.4782	6.4232	13.8383	.00377
266	70 756	18 821 096	16.3095	51.5752	6.4312	13.8557	.00376
267	71 289	19 034 163	16.3401	51.6720	6.4393	13.8730	.00375
268	71 824	19 248 832	16.3707	51.7687	6.4473	13.8903	.00373
269	72 361	19 465 109	16.4012	51.8652	6.4553	13.9076	.00372
270	72 900	19 683 000	16.4317	51.9615	6.4633	13.9248	.00370
271	73 441	19 902 511	16.4621	52.0577	6.4713	13.9420	.00369
272	73 984	20 123 648	16.4924	52.1536	6.4702	13.9591	.00368
273	74 529	20 346 417	16.5227	52.2494	6.4872	13.9762	.00366
274	75 076	20 570 824	16.5530	52.3450	6.4951	13.9932	.00365
275	75 625	20 796 875	16.5831	52.4404	6.5030	14.0102	.00364
276	76 176	21 024 576	16.6133	52.5357	6.5108	14.0272	.00362
277	76 729	21 253 933	16.6433	52.6308	6.5187	14.0441	.00361
278	77 284	21 484 952	16.6733	52.7257	6.5265	14.0610	.00360
279	77 841	21 717 639	16.7033	52.8205	6.5343	14.0778	.00358
280	78 400	21 952 000	16.7332	52.9150	6.5421	14.0946	.00357
281	78 961	22 188 041	16.7631	53.0094	6.5499	14.1114	.00356
282	79 524	22 425 768	16.7929	53.1037	6.5577	14.1281	.00355
283	80 089	22 665 187	16.8226	53.1977	6.5654	14.1448	.00353
284	80 656	22 906 304	16.8523	53.2917	6.5731	14.1614	.00352
285	81 225	23 149 125	16.8819	53.3854	6.5808	14.1780	.00351
286	81 796	23 393 656	16.9115	53.4790	6.5885	14.1946	.00350
287	82 369	23 639 903	16.9411	53.5724	6.5962	14.2111	.00348
288	82 944	23 887 872	16.9706	53.6656	6.6039	14.2276	.00347
289	83 521	24 137 569	17.0000	53.7587	6.6115	14.2440	.00346
290	84 100	24 389 000	17.0294	53.8517	6.6191	14.2604	.00345
291	84 681	24 642 171	17.0587	53.9444	6.6267	14.2768	.00344
292	85 264	24 897 088	17.0880	54.0370	6.6343	14.2931	.00342
293	85 849	25 153 757	17.1172	54.1295	6.6419	14.3094	.00341
294	86 436	25 412 184	17.1464	54.2218	6.6494	14.3257	.00340
295	87 025	25 672 375	17.1756	54.3139	6.6569	14.3419	.00339
296	87 616	25 934 336	17.2047	54.4059	6.6644	14.3581	.00338
297	88 209	26 198 073	17.2337	54.4977	6.6719	14.3743	.00337
298	88 804	26 463 592	17.2627	54.5894	6.6794	14.3904	.00336
299	89 401	26 730 899	17.2916	54.6809	6.6869	14.4065	.00334
300	90 000	27 000 000	17.3205	54.7723	6.6943	14.4225	.00333
301	90 601	27 270 901	17.3494	54.8635	6.7018	14.4385	.00332
302	91 204	27 543 608	17.3782	54.9545	6.7092	14.4545	.00331
303	91 809	27 818 127	17.4069	55.0454	6.7166	14.4704	.00330
304	92 416	28 094 464	17.4356	55.1362	6.7240	14.4863	.00329
305	93 025	28 372 625	17.4643	55.2268	6.7313	14.5022	.00328
306	93 636	28 652 616	17.4929	55.3173	6.7387	14.5180	.00327
307	94 249	28 934 443	17.5214	55.4076	6.7460	14.5338	.00326

n	n^2	n^3	$\sqrt{n}$	$\sqrt{10n}$	$\sqrt[3]{n}$	$\sqrt[3]{10n}$	$1/n$
308	94 864	29 218 112	17.5499	55.4978	6.7533	14.5496	.00325
309	95 481	29 503 629	17.5784	55.5878	6.7606	14.5653	.00324
310	96 100	29 791 000	17.6068	55.6776	6.7679	14.5810	.00323
311	96 721	30 080 231	17.6352	55.7674	6.7752	14.5967	.00322
312	97 344	30 371 328	17.6635	55.8570	6.7824	14.6123	.00321
313	97 969	30 664 297	17.6918	55.9464	6.7897	14.6279	.00319
314	98 596	30 959 144	17.7201	56.0357	6.7969	14.6434	.00318
315	99 225	31 255 875	17.7482	56.1249	6.8041	14.6590	.00317
316	99 856	31 554 496	17.7764	56.2139	6.8113	14.6745	.00316
317	100 489	31 855 013	17.8045	56.3028	6.8185	14.6899	.00315
318	101 124	32 157 432	17.8326	56.3915	6.8256	14.7054	.00314
319	101 761	32 461 759	17.8606	56.4801	6.8328	14.7208	.00313
320	102 400	32 768 000	17.8885	56.5085	6.8399	14.7361	.00313
321	103 041	33 076 161	17.9165	56.6569	6.8470	14.7515	.00312
322	103 684	33 386 248	17.9444	56.7450	6.8541	14.7668	.00311
323	104 329	33 698 267	17.9722	56.8331	6.8612	14.7820	.00310
324	104 976	34 012 224	18.0000	56.9210	6.8683	14.7973	.00309
325	105 625	34 328 125	18.0278	57.0088	6.8753	14.8125	.00308
326	106 276	34 645 976	18.0555	57.0964	6.8824	14.8277	.00307
327	106 929	34 965 783	18.0831	57.1839	6.8894	14.8428	.00306
328	107 584	35 287 552	18.1108	57.2713	6.8964	14.8579	.00305
329	108 241	35 611 289	18.1384	57.3585	6.9034	14.8730	.00304
330	108 900	35 937 000	18.1659	57.4456	6.9104	14.8881	.00303
331	109 561	36 264 691	18.1934	57.5326	6.9174	14.9031	.00302
332	110 224	36 594 368	18.2209	57.6194	6.9244	14.9181	.00301
333	110 889	36 926 037	18.2483	57.7062	6.9313	14.9330	.00300
334	111 556	37 259 704	18.2757	57.7927	6.9382	14.9480	.00299
335	112 225	37 595 375	18.3030	57.8792	6.9452	14.9629	.00299
336	112 896	37 933 056	18.3303	57.9655	6.9521	14.9777	.00298
337	113 569	38 272 753	18.3576	58.0517	6.9589	14.9926	.00297
338	114 244	38 614 472	18.3848	58.1378	6.9658	15.0074	.00296
339	114 921	38 958 219	18.4120	58.2237	6.9727	15.0222	.00295
340	115 600	39 304 000	18.4391	58.3095	6.9795	15.0370	.00294
341	116 281	39 651 821	18.4662	58.3952	6.9864	15.0517	.00293
342	116 964	40 001 688	18.4932	58.4808	6.9932	15.0664	.00292
343	117 649	40 353 607	18.5203	58.5662	7.0000	15.0810	.00292
344	118 336	40 707 584	18.5472	58.6515	7.0068	15.0957	.00291
345	119 025	41 063 625	18.5742	58.7367	7.0136	15.1103	.00290
346	119 716	41 421 736	18.6011	58.8218	7.0203	15.1249	.00289
347	120 409	41 781 923	18.6279	58.9067	7.0271	15.1394	.00288
348	121 104	42 144 192	18.6548	58.9915	7.0339	15.1540	.00287
349	121 801	42 508 549	18.6815	59.0762	7.0406	15.1685	.00287
350	122 500	42 875 000	18.7083	59.1608	7.0473	15.1830	.00286
351	123 201	43 243 551	18.7350	59.2453	7.0540	15.1974	.00285
352	123 904	43 614 208	18.7617	59.3296	7.0607	15.2118	.00284
353	124 609	43 986 977	18.7883	59.4138	7.0674	15.2262	.00283
354	125 316	44 361 864	18.8149	59.4979	7.0740	15.2406	.00282
355	126 025	44 738 875	18.8414	59.5819	7.0807	15.2549	.00282
356	126 736	45 118 016	18.8680	59.6657	7.0873	15.2692	.00281
357	127 449	45 499 293	18.8944	59.7495	7.0940	15.2835	.00280
358	128 164	45 882 712	18.9209	59.8331	7.1006	15.2978	.00279
359	128 881	46 268 279	18.9473	59.9166	7.1072	15.3120	.00279
360	120 600	46 656 000	18.9737	60.0000	7.1138	15.3262	.00278
361	130 321	47 045 881	19.0000	60.0833	7.1204	15.3404	.00277
362	131 044	47 437 928	19.0263	60.1664	7.1269	15.3545	.00276
363	131 769	47 832 147	19.0526	60.2495	7.1335	15.3686	.00275
364	132 496	48 228 544	19.0788	60.3324	7.1400	15.3827	.00275
365	133 225	48 627 125	19.1050	60.4152	7.1466	15.3968	.00274
366	133 956	49 027 896	19.1311	60.4979	7.1531	15.4109	.00273
367	134 689	49 430 863	19.1572	60.5805	7.1596	15.4249	.00272
368	135 424	49 836 032	19.1833	60.6630	7.1661	15.4389	.00272
369	136 161	50 243 409	19.2094	60.7454	7.1726	15.4529	.00271

n	n^2	n^3	$\sqrt{n}$	$\sqrt{10n}$	$\sqrt[3]{n}$	$\sqrt[3]{10n}$	$1/n$
370	136 900	50 653 000	19.2354	60.8276	7.1791	15.4668	.00270
371	137 641	51 064 811	19.2614	60.9098	7.1855	15.4807	.00270
372	138 384	51 478 848	19.2873	60.9918	7.1920	15.4946	.00269
373	139 129	51 895 117	19.3132	61.0737	7.1984	15.5085	.00268
374	139 876	52 313 624	19.3391	61.1555	7.2048	15.5223	.00267
375	140 625	52 734 375	19.3649	61.2372	7.2112	15.5362	.00267
376	141 376	53 157 376	19.3907	61.3188	7.2177	15.5500	.00266
377	142 129	53 582 633	19.4165	61.4003	7.2240	15.5637	.00265
378	142 884	54 010 152	19.4422	61.4817	7.2304	15.5775	.00265
379	143 641	54 439 939	19.4679	61.5630	7.2368	15.5912	.00264
380	144 400	54 872 000	19.4936	61.6441	7.2432	15.6049	.00263
381	145 161	55 306 341	19.5192	61.7252	7.2495	15.6186	.00262
382	145 924	55 742 968	19.5448	61.8062	7.2558	15.6322	.00262
383	146 689	56 181 887	19.5704	61.8870	7.2622	15.6459	.00261
384	147 456	56 623 104	19.5959	61.9677	7.2685	15.6595	.00260
385	148 225	57 066 625	19.6214	62.0484	7.2748	15.6731	.00260
386	148 996	57 512 456	19.6469	62.1289	7.2811	15.6866	.00259
387	149 769	57 960 603	19.6723	62.2093	7.2874	15.7001	.00258
388	150 544	58 411 072	19.6977	62.2897	7.2936	15.7137	.00258
389	151 321	58 863 869	19.7231	62.3699	7.2999	15.7271	.00257
390	152 100	59 319 000	19.7484	62.4500	7.3061	15.7406	.00256
391	152 881	59 776 471	19.7737	62.5300	7.3124	15.7541	.00256
392	153 664	60 236 288	19.7990	62.6099	7.3186	15.7675	.00255
393	154 449	60 698 457	19.8242	62.6897	7.3248	15.7809	.00254
394	155 236	61 162 984	19.8494	62.7694	7.3310	15.7942	.00254
395	156 025	61 629 875	19.8746	62.8490	7.3372	15.8076	.00253
396	156 816	62 099 136	19.8998	62.9285	7.3434	15.8209	.00253
397	157 609	62 570 773	19.9249	63.0079	7.3496	15.8342	.00252
398	158 404	63 044 792	19.9499	63.0872	7.3558	15.8475	.00251
399	159 201	63 521 199	19.9750	63.1665	7.3619	15.8608	.00251
400	160 000	64 000 000	20.0000	63.2456	7.3681	15.8740	.00250
401	160 801	64 481 201	20.0250	63.3246	7.3742	15.8872	.00249
402	161 604	64 964 808	20.0499	63.4035	7.3803	15.9004	.00249
403	162 409	65 450 827	20.0749	63.4823	7.3864	15.9136	.00248
404	163 216	65 939 264	20.0998	63.5610	7.3925	15.9268	.00248
405	164 025	66 430 125	20.1246	63.6396	7.3987	15.9399	.00247
406	164 836	66 923 416	20.1494	63.7181	7.4047	15.9530	.00246
407	165 649	67 419 143	20.1742	63.7966	7.4108	15.9661	.00246
408	166 464	67 917 312	20.1990	63.8749	7.4169	15.9791	.00245
409	167 281	68 417 929	20.2238	63.9531	7.4229	15.9922	.00244
410	168 100	68 921 000	20.2485	64.0312	7.4290	16.0052	.00244
411	168 921	69 426 531	20.2731	64.1093	7.4350	16.0182	.00243
412	169 744	69 934 528	20.2978	64.1872	7.4410	16.0312	.00243
413	170 569	70 444 997	30.3224	64.2651	7.4470	16.0442	.00242
414	171 396	70 957 944	20.3470	64.3428	7.4530	16.0571	.00242
415	172 225	71 473 375	20.3716	64.4205	7.4590	16.0700	.00241
416	173 056	71 991 296	20.3961	64.4981	7.4650	16.0829	.00240
417	173 889	72 511 713	20.4206	64.5755	7.4710	16.0958	.00240
418	174 724	73 034 632	20.4451	64.6529	7.4770	16.1086	.00239
419	175 561	73 560 059	20.4695	64.7302	7.4829	16.1215	.00239
420	176 400	74 088 000	20.4939	64.8074	7.4889	16.1343	.00238
421	177 241	74 618 461	20.5183	64.8845	7.4948	16.1471	.00238
422	178 084	75 151 448	20.5426	64.9615	7.5007	16.1599	.00237
423	178 929	75 686 967	20.5670	65.0385	7.5067	16.1726	.00236
424	179 776	76 225 024	20.5913	65.1153	7.5126	16.1853	.00236
425	180 625	76 765 625	20.6155	65.1920	7.5185	16.1981	.00235
426	181 476	77 308 776	20.6398	65.2687	7.5244	16.2108	.00235
427	182 329	77 854 483	20.6640	65.3452	7.5302	16.2234	.00234
428	183 184	78 402 752	20.6882	65.4217	7.5361	16.2361	.00234
429	184 041	78 953 589	20.7123	65.4981	7.5420	16.2487	.00233
430	184 900	79 507 000	20.7364	65.5744	7.5478	16.2613	.00233
431	185 761	80 062 991	20.7605	65.6506	7.5537	16.2739	.00232
432	186 624	80 621 568	20.7846	65.7267	7.5595	16.2865	.00231

n	n^2	n^3	$\sqrt{n}$	$\sqrt{10n}$	$\sqrt[3]{n}$	$\sqrt[3]{10n}$	$1/n$
433	187 489	81 182 737	20.8087	65.8027	7.5654	16.2991	.00231
434	188 356	81 746 504	20.8327	65.8787	7.5712	16.3116	.00230
435	189 225	82 312 875	20.8567	65.9545	7.5770	16.3241	.00230
436	190 096	82 881 856	20.8806	66.0303	7.5828	16.3366	.00229
437	190 969	83 453 453	20.9045	66.1060	7.5886	16.3491	.00229
438	191 844	84 027 672	20.9285	66.1816	7.5944	16.3616	.00228
439	192 721	84 604 519	20.9523	66.2571	7.6001	16.3740	.00228
440	193 600	85 184 000	20.9762	66.3325	7.6059	16.3864	.00227
441	194 481	85 766 121	21.0000	66.4078	7.6117	16.3988	.00227
442	195 364	86 350 888	21.0238	66.4831	7.6174	16.4112	.00226
443	196 249	86 938 307	21.0476	66.5583	7.6232	16.4236	.00226
444	197 136	87 528 384	21.0713	66.6333	7.6289	16.4359	.00225
445	198 025	88 121 125	21.0950	66.7083	7.6346	16.4483	.00225
446	198 916	88 716 536	21.1187	66.7832	7.6403	16.4606	.00224
447	199 809	89 314 623	21.1424	66.8581	7.6460	16.4729	.00224
448	200 704	89 915 392	21.1660	66.9328	7.6517	16.4851	.00223
449	201 601	90 518 849	21.1896	67.0075	7.6574	16.4974	.00223
450	202 500	91 125 000	21.2132	67.0820	7.6631	16.5096	.00222
451	203 401	91 733 851	21.2368	67.1565	7.6688	16.5219	.00222
452	204 304	92 345 408	21.2603	67.2310	7.6744	16.5341	.00221
453	205 209	92 959 677	21.2838	67.3053	7.6801	16.5462	.00221
454	206 116	93 576 664	21.3073	67.3795	7.6857	16.5584	.00220
455	207 025	94 196 375	21.3307	67.4537	7.6914	16.5705	.00220
456	207 936	94 818 816	21.3542	67.5278	7.6970	16.5827	.00219
457	208 849	95 443 993	21.3776	67.6018	7.7026	16.5948	.00219
458	209 764	96 071 912	21.4009	67.6757	7.7082	16.6069	.00218
459	210 681	96 702 579	21.4243	67.7495	7.7138	16.6190	.00218
460	211 600	97 336 000	21.4476	67.8233	7.7194	16.6310	.00217
461	212 521	97 972 181	21.4709	67.8970	7.7250	16.6431	.00217
462	213 444	98 611 128	21.4942	67.9706	7.7306	16.6551	.00216
463	214 369	99 252 847	21.5174	68.0441	7.7362	16.6671	.00216
464	215 296	99 897 344	21.5407	68.1176	7.7418	16.6791	.00216
465	216 225	100 544 625	21.5639	68.1909	7.7473	16.6911	.00215
466	217 156	101 194 696	21.5870	68.2642	7.7529	16.7030	.00215
467	218 089	101 847 563	21.6102	68.3374	7.7584	16.7150	.00214
468	219 024	102 503 232	21.6333	68.4105	7.7639	16.7269	.00214
469	219 961	103 161 709	21.6564	68.4836	7.7695	16.7388	.00213
470	220 900	103 823 000	21.6795	68.5566	7.7750	16.7507	.00213
471	221 841	104 487 111	21.7025	68.6294	7.7805	16.7626	.00212
472	222 784	105 154 048	21.7256	68.7023	7.7860	16.7744	.00212
473	223 729	105 823 817	21.7486	68.7750	7.7915	16.7863	.00211
474	224 676	106 496 424	21.7715	68.8477	7.7970	16.7981	.00211
475	225 625	107 171 875	21.7945	68.9202	7.8025	16.8099	.00211
476	226 576	107 850 176	21.8174	68.9928	7.8079	16.8217	.00210
477	227 529	108 531 333	21.8403	69.0652	7.8134	16.8334	.00210
478	228 484	109 215 352	21.8632	69.1375	7.8188	16.8452	.00209
479	229 441	109 902 239	21.8861	69.2098	7.8243	16.8569	.00209
480	230 400	110 592 000	21.9089	69.2820	7.8297	16.8687	.00208
481	231 361	111 284 641	21.9317	69.3542	7.8352	16.8804	.00208
482	232 324	111 980 168	21.9545	69.4262	7.8406	16.8921	.00207
483	233 289	112 678 587	21.9773	69.4982	7.8460	16.9037	.00207
484	234 256	113 379 904	22.0000	69.5701	7.8514	16.9154	.00207
485	235 225	114 084 125	22.0227	69.6419	7.8568	16.9270	.00206
486	236 196	114 791 256	22.0454	69.7137	7.8622	16.9387	.00206
487	237 169	115 501 303	22.0681	69.7854	7.8676	16.9503	.00205
488	238 144	116 214 272	22.0907	69.8570	7.8730	16.9619	.00205
489	239 121	116 930 169	22.1133	69.9285	7.8784	16.9734	.00204
490	240 100	117 649 000	22.1359	70.0000	7.8837	16.9850	.00204
491	241 081	118 370 771	22.1585	70.0714	7.8891	16.9965	.00204
492	242 064	119 095 488	22.1811	70.1427	7.8944	17.0081	.00203
493	243 049	119 823 157	22.2036	70.2140	7.8998	17.0196	.00203
494	244 036	120 553 784	22.2261	70.2851	7.9051	17.0311	.00202

n	n^2	n^3	$\sqrt{n}$	$\sqrt{10n}$	$\sqrt[3]{n}$	$\sqrt[3]{10n}$	$1/n$
495	245 025	121 287 375	22.2486	70.3562	7.9105	17.0426	.00202
496	246 016	122 023 936	22.2711	70.4273	7.9158	17.0540	.00202
497	247 009	122 763 473	22.2935	70.4982	7.9211	17.0655	.00201
498	248 004	123 505 992	22.3159	70.5691	7.9264	17.0769	.00201
499	249 001	124 251 499	22.3383	70.6399	7.9317	17.0884	.00200
500	250 000	125 000 000	22.3607	70.7107	7.9370	17.0998	.00200

NO. 19   COMMON LOGARITHM TABLE

EXPLANATION

The logarithm of a number is composed of a characteristic and mantissa. The table of common logarithms gives the mantissa of logarithms whose characteristic is 0. When using the table, therefore, it is understood that the numbers found in the first column, N, have a decimal point between the first two digits. E.g., 100 in column 1 should be read 1.00; 151 read 1.51; etc. The decimal point is not shown in the mantissa but is understood to be before the first digit. E.g., in the second column, 0, adjacent to 150 in the first column, N, the mantissa 17609 should be read .17609, and an appropriate characteristic included.

The table gives 5 digit mantissas. The logarithm of a number up to four digits may be determined directly from the table. The first three digits of the number are located in the first column, N, and the mantissa found in the column corresponding to the last digit of the number. E.g., to read the mantissa of 2.357, locate 235 in the N column. Move along the row corresponding to 235 until reaching the 7 column. The number 236 appears. For convenience, the first two digits of the 5 place mantissas are omitted. The first two digits are found in the *first* 5 digit mantissa that appears in a preceding 0 column. Thus, for the number 2.357 the mantissa is 37236. The last three digits of the mantissa of 1.164, found in the 4 column in the row corresponding to 116, are 595; the first two digits are found in the 0 column corresponding to N = 115: 06. The mantissa for log 1164 is .06595. The mantissa of log 1446 is found by locating 144 in the N column and reading across to the 6 column: *017. The asterisk, *, indicates that the first two digits are to be read from the *next* 0 column, the one corresponding to 1450. Thus, the mantissa of the log of 1446 is 16017; the mantissa of the log of 1.412 is .14983 and the mantissa of the log of 1.413 is .15014.

When the logarithm of a number greater than four digits is required it may be found by interpolation. The interpolation may be facilitated by using the table of proportional parts, found in the last column, headed PP. In the PP table the numbers at the top of the table represent the differences between mantissas; the numbers at the left side of the table represent the differences between the numbers whose log is required and the next smaller number that appears in the table. The number to the right of this difference in the PP table is the amount to be added to the last digits of the mantissa of the smaller number. To find the log of 1.9217 using the PP table, determine the numbers greater and less than 1.9217 that are in the table. They are 1.9220 (1.922) and 1.9210 (1.921). The mantissa for 19220 is 28375; for 19210 it is 28353. The difference between these mantissas is 22. The difference between 19217 (the number whose log is required) and 19210 (the next smaller number that appears in the table) is 7. In the PP table headed 22, read down the left side to 7; 15.4 is to the right of 7 in the table; add 15.4 to the last digits of 28353 (the mantissa of the number less than the required number). The result, 28368.4 or approximately 28368, is the mantissa of 19217.

COMMON LOGARITHMS
100–110

N	0	1	2	3	4	5	6	7	8	9	PP		
100	00 000	043	087	130	173	217	260	303	346	389			
101	432	475	518	561	604	647	689	732	775	817	44	43	42
102	860	903	945	988	*030	*072	*115	*157	*199	*242	1 4.4	4.3	4.2
103	01 284	326	368	410	452	494	536	578	620	662	2 8.8	8.6	8.4
104	703	745	787	828	870	912	953	995	*036	*078	3 13.2	12.9	12.6
105	02 119	160	202	243	284	325	366	407	449	490	4 17.6	17.2	16.8
											5 22.0	21.5	21.0
106	531	572	612	653	694	735	776	816	857	898	6 26.4	25.8	25.2
107	938	979	*019	*060	*100	*141	*181	*222	*262	*302	7 30.8	30.1	29.4
108	03 342	383	423	463	503	543	583	623	663	703	8 35.2	34.4	33.6
109	743	782	822	862	902	941	981	*021	*060	*100	9 39.6	38.7	37.8
110	04 139	179	218	258	297	336	376	415	454	493			
N	0	1	2	3	4	5	6	7	8	9	PP		

COMMON LOGARITHMS
111–160

N	0	1	2	3	4	5	6	7	8	9
111	532	571	610	650	689	727	766	805	844	883
112	922	961	999	*038	*077	*155	*154	*192	*231	*269
113	05 308	346	385	423	461	500	538	576	614	652
114	690	729	767	805	843	881	918	956	994	*032
115	06 070	108	145	183	221	258	296	333	371	408
116	446	483	521	558	595	633	670	707	744	781
117	819	856	893	930	967	*004	*041	*078	*115	*151
118	07 188	225	262	298	335	372	408	445	482	518
119	555	591	628	664	700	737	773	809	846	882
120	918	954	990	*027	*063	*099	*135	*171	*207	*243
121	08 279	314	350	386	422	458	493	529	565	600
122	636	672	707	743	778	814	849	884	920	955
123	991	*026	*061	*096	*132	*167	*202	*237	*272	*307
124	09 342	377	412	447	482	517	552	587	621	656
125	691	726	760	795	830	864	899	934	968	*003
126	10 037	072	106	140	175	209	243	278	312	346
127	380	415	449	483	517	551	585	619	653	687
128	721	755	789	823	857	890	924	958	992	*025
129	11 059	093	126	160	193	227	261	294	327	361
130	394	428	461	494	528	561	594	628	661	694
131	11 727	760	793	826	860	893	926	959	992	*025
132	12 057	090	123	156	189	222	254	287	320	352
133	385	418	450	483	516	548	581	613	646	678
134	710	743	775	808	840	872	905	937	969	*001
135	13 033	066	098	130	162	194	226	258	290	322
136	354	386	418	450	481	513	545	577	609	640
137	672	704	735	767	799	830	862	893	925	956
138	988	*019	*051	*082	*144	*145	*176	*208	*239	*270
139	14 301	333	364	395	426	457	489	520	551	582
140	613	644	675	706	737	768	799	829	860	891
141	922	953	983	*014	*045	*076	*106	*137	*168	*198
142	15 229	259	290	320	351	381	412	442	473	503
143	534	564	594	625	655	685	715	746	776	806
144	836	866	897	927	957	987	*017	*047	*077	*107
145	16 137	167	197	227	256	286	316	346	376	406
146	435	465	495	524	554	584	613	643	673	702
147	732	761	791	820	850	879	909	938	967	997
148	17 026	056	085	114	143	173	202	231	260	289
149	319	348	377	406	435	464	493	522	551	580
150	17 609	638	667	696	725	754	782	811	840	869
151	898	926	955	984	*013	*041	*070	*099	*127	*156
152	18 184	213	241	270	298	327	355	384	412	441
153	469	498	526	554	583	611	639	667	696	724
154	752	780	808	837	865	893	921	949	977	*005
155	19 033	061	089	117	145	173	201	229	257	285
156	312	340	368	396	424	451	479	507	535	562
157	590	618	645	673	700	728	756	783	811	838
158	866	893	921	948	976	*003	*030	*058	*085	*112
159	20 140	167	194	222	249	276	303	330	358	385
160	412	439	466	493	520	548	575	602	629	656

N	0	1	2	3	4	5	6	7	8	9

PP

	41	40	39	38
1	4.1	4.0	3.9	3.8
2	8.2	8.0	7.8	7.6
3	12.3	12.0	11.7	11.4
4	16.4	16.0	15.6	15.2
5	20.5	20.0	19.5	19.0
6	24.6	24.0	23.4	22.8
7	28.7	28.0	27.3	26.6
8	32.8	32.0	31.2	30.4
9	36.9	36.0	35.1	34.2

	37	36	35	34
1	3.7	3.9	3.5	3.4
2	7.4	7.2	7.0	6.8
3	11.1	10.8	10.5	10.2
4	14.8	14.4	14.0	13.6
5	18.5	18.0	17.5	17.0
6	22.2	21.6	21.0	20.4
7	25.9	25.2	24.5	23.8
8	29.6	28.8	28.0	27.2
9	33.3	32.4	31.5	30.6

	35	34	33
1	3.5	3.4	3.3
2	7.0	6.8	6.6
3	10.5	10.2	9.9
4	14.0	13.6	13.2
5	17.5	17.0	16.5
6	21.0	20.4	19.8
7	24.5	23.8	23.1
8	28.0	27.2	26.4
9	31.5	30.6	29.7

	32	31	30
1	3.2	3.1	3.0
2	6.4	6.2	6.0
3	9.6	9.3	9.0
4	12.8	12.4	12.0
5	16.0	15.5	15.0
6	19.2	18.6	18.0
7	22.4	21.7	21.0
8	25.6	24.8	24.0
9	28.8	27.9	27.0

	29	28
1	2.9	2.8
2	5.8	5.6
3	8.7	8.4
4	11.6	11.2
5	14.5	14.0
6	17.4	16.8
7	20.3	19.6
8	23.2	22.4
9	26.1	25.2

Table No. 19 continued

COMMON LOGARITHMS
161–210

N	0	1	2	3	4	5	6	7	8	9
161	683	710	737	763	790	817	844	871	898	925
162	952	978	*005	*032	*059	*085	*112	*139	*165	*192
163	21 219	245	272	299	325	352	378	405	431	458
164	484	511	537	564	590	617	643	669	696	722
165	748	775	801	827	854	880	906	932	958	985
166	22 011	037	063	089	115	141	167	194	220	246
167	272	298	324	350	376	401	427	453	479	505
168	531	557	583	608	634	660	686	712	737	763
169	789	814	840	866	891	917	943	968	994	*019
170	23 045	070	096	121	147	172	198	223	249	274
171	300	325	350	376	401	426	452	477	502	528
172	553	578	603	629	654	679	704	729	754	779
173	805	830	855	880	905	930	955	980	*005	*030
174	24 055	080	105	130	155	180	204	229	254	279
175	304	329	353	378	403	428	452	477	502	527
176	551	576	601	625	650	674	699	724	748	773
177	797	822	846	871	895	920	944	969	993	*018
178	25 042	066	091	115	139	164	188	212	237	261
179	285	310	334	358	382	406	431	455	479	503
180	527	551	575	600	624	648	672	696	720	744
181	768	792	816	840	864	888	912	935	959	983
182	26 007	031	055	079	102	126	150	174	198	221
183	245	269	293	316	340	364	387	411	435	458
184	482	505	529	553	576	600	623	647	670	694
185	717	741	764	788	811	834	858	881	905	928
186	951	975	998	*021	*045	*068	*091	*114	*138	*161
187	27 184	207	231	254	277	300	323	346	370	393
188	416	439	462	485	508	531	554	577	600	623
189	646	669	692	715	738	761	784	807	830	852
190	875	898	921	944	967	989	*012	*035	*058	*081
191	28 103	126	149	171	194	217	240	262	285	307
192	330	353	375	398	421	443	466	488	511	533
193	556	578	601	623	646	668	691	713	735	758
194	780	803	825	847	870	892	914	937	959	981
195	29 003	026	048	070	092	115	137	159	181	203
196	226	248	270	292	314	336	358	380	403	425
197	447	469	491	513	535	557	579	601	623	645
198	667	688	710	732	754	776	798	820	842	863
199	885	907	929	951	973	994	*016	*038	*060	*081
200	30 103	125	146	168	190	211	233	255	276	298
201	320	341	363	384	406	428	449	471	492	514
202	535	557	578	600	621	643	664	685	707	728
203	750	771	792	814	835	856	878	899	920	942
204	963	984	*006	*027	*048	*069	*091	*112	*133	*154
205	31 175	197	218	239	260	281	302	323	345	366
206	387	408	429	450	471	492	513	534	555	576
207	597	618	639	660	681	702	723	744	765	785
208	806	827	848	869	890	911	931	952	973	994
209	32 015	035	056	077	098	118	139	160	181	201
210	222	243	263	284	305	325	346	366	387	408

N	0	1	2	3	4	5	6	7	8	9

PP

	27	26
1	2.7	2.6
2	5.4	5.2
3	8.1	7.8
4	10.8	10.4
5	13.5	13.0
6	16.2	15.6
7	18.9	18.2
8	21.6	20.8
9	24.3	23.4

	25
1	2.5
2	5.0
3	7.5
4	10.0
5	12.5
6	15.0
7	17.5
8	20.0
9	22.5

	24	23
1	2.4	2.3
2	4.8	4.6
3	7.2	6.9
4	9.6	9.2
5	12.0	11.5
6	14.4	13.8
7	16.8	16.1
8	19.2	18.4
9	21.6	20.7

	24	23
1	2.4	2.3
2	4.8	4.6
3	7.2	6.9
4	9.6	9.2
5	12.0	11.5
6	14.4	13.8
7	16.8	16.1
8	19.2	18.4
9	21.6	20.7

	22
1	2.2
2	4.4
3	6.6
4	8.8
5	11.0
6	13.2
7	15.4
8	17.6
9	19.8

COMMON LOGARITHMS
211–260

N	0	1	2	3	4	5	6	7	8	9
211	428	449	469	490	510	531	552	572	593	613
212	634	654	675	695	715	736	756	777	797	818
213	838	858	879	899	919	940	960	980	*001	*021
214	33 041	062	082	102	122	143	163	183	203	224
215	244	264	284	304	325	345	365	385	405	425
216	445	465	486	506	526	546	566	586	606	626
217	646	666	686	706	726	746	766	786	806	826
218	846	866	885	905	925	945	965	985	*005	*025
219	34 044	064	084	104	124	143	163	183	203	223
220	242	262	282	301	321	341	361	380	400	420
221	439	459	479	498	518	537	557	577	596	616
222	635	655	674	694	713	733	753	772	792	811
223	830	850	869	889	908	928	947	967	986	*005
224	35 025	044	064	083	102	122	141	160	180	199
225	218	238	257	276	295	315	334	353	372	392
226	411	430	449	468	488	507	526	545	564	583
227	603	622	641	660	679	698	717	736	755	774
228	793	813	832	851	870	889	908	927	946	965
229	984	*003	*021	*040	*059	*078	*097	*116	*135	*154
230	36 173	192	211	229	248	267	286	305	324	342
231	361	380	399	418	436	455	474	493	511	530
232	549	568	586	605	624	642	661	680	698	717
233	736	754	773	791	810	829	847	866	884	903
234	922	940	959	977	996	*014	*033	*051	*070	*088
235	37 107	125	144	162	181	199	218	236	254	273
236	291	310	328	346	365	383	401	420	438	457
237	475	493	511	530	548	566	585	603	621	639
238	658	676	694	712	731	749	767	785	803	822
239	840	858	876	894	912	931	949	967	985	*003
240	38 021	039	057	075	093	112	130	148	166	184
241	202	220	238	256	274	292	310	328	346	364
242	382	399	417	435	453	471	489	507	525	543
243	561	578	596	614	632	650	668	686	703	721
244	739	757	775	792	810	828	846	863	881	899
245	917	934	952	970	987	*005	*023	*041	*058	*076
246	39 094	111	129	146	164	182	199	217	235	252
247	270	287	305	322	340	358	375	393	410	428
248	445	463	480	498	515	533	550	568	585	602
249	620	637	655	672	690	707	724	742	759	777
250	794	811	829	846	863	881	898	915	933	950
251	39 967	985	*002	*019	*037	*054	*071	*088	*106	*123
252	40 140	157	175	192	209	226	243	261	278	295
253	312	329	346	364	381	398	415	432	449	466
254	483	500	518	535	552	569	586	603	620	637
255	654	671	688	705	722	739	756	773	790	807
256	824	841	858	875	892	909	926	943	960	976
257	993	*010	*027	*044	*061	*078	*095	*111	*128	*145
258	41 162	179	196	212	229	246	263	280	296	313
259	330	347	363	380	397	414	430	447	464	481
260	497	514	531	547	564	581	597	614	631	647

N	0	1	2	3	4	5	6	7	8	9

PP

	21
1	2.1
2	4.2
3	6.3
4	8.4
5	10.5
6	12.6
7	14.7
8	16.8
9	18.9

	20	19
1	2.0	1.9
2	4.0	3.8
3	6.0	5.7
4	8.0	7.6
5	10.0	9.5
6	12.0	11.4
7	14.0	13.3
8	16.0	15.2
9	18.0	17.1

	18	17
1	1.8	1.7
2	3.6	3.4
3	5.4	5.1
4	7.2	6.8
5	9.0	8.5
6	10.8	10.2
7	12.6	11.9
8	14.4	13.6
9	16.2	15.3

	18
1	1.8
2	3.6
3	5.4
4	7.2
5	9.0
6	10.8
7	12.6
8	14.4
9	16.2

Table No. 19 continued

COMMON LOGARITHMS
261–310

N	0	1	2	3	4	5	6	7	8	9
261	664	681	697	714	731	747	764	780	797	814
262	830	847	863	880	896	913	929	946	963	979
263	996	*012	*029	*045	*062	*078	*095	*111	*127	*144
264	42 160	177	193	210	226	243	259	275	292	308
265	325	341	357	374	390	406	423	439	455	472
266	488	504	521	537	553	570	586	602	619	635
267	651	667	684	700	716	732	749	765	781	797
268	813	830	846	862	878	894	911	927	943	959
269	975	991	*008	*024	*040	*056	*072	*088	*104	*120
270	43 136	152	169	185	201	217	233	249	265	281
271	297	313	329	345	361	377	393	409	425	441
272	457	473	489	505	521	537	553	569	584	600
273	616	632	648	664	680	696	712	721	743	759
274	775	791	807	823	838	854	870	886	902	917
275	933	949	965	981	996	*012	*028	*044	*059	*075
276	44 091	107	122	138	154	170	185	201	217	232
277	248	264	279	295	311	326	342	358	373	389
278	404	420	436	451	467	483	498	514	529	545
279	560	576	592	607	623	638	654	669	685	700
280	716	731	747	762	778	793	809	824	840	855
281	871	886	902	917	932	948	963	979	994	*010
282	45 025	040	056	071	086	102	117	133	148	163
283	179	194	209	225	240	255	271	286	301	317
284	332	347	362	378	393	408	423	439	454	469
285	484	500	515	530	545	561	576	591	606	621
286	637	652	667	682	697	712	728	743	758	773
287	788	803	818	834	849	864	879	894	909	924
288	939	954	969	984	*000	*015	*030	*045	*060	*075
289	46 090	105	120	135	150	165	180	195	210	225
290	240	255	270	285	300	315	330	345	359	374
291	389	404	419	434	449	464	479	494	509	523
292	538	553	568	583	598	613	627	642	657	672
293	687	702	716	731	746	761	776	790	805	820
294	835	850	864	879	894	909	923	938	953	967
295	982	997	*012	*026	*041	*056	*070	*085	*100	*114
296	47 129	144	159	173	188	202	217	232	246	261
297	276	290	305	319	334	349	363	378	392	407
298	422	436	451	465	480	494	509	524	538	553
299	567	582	596	611	625	640	654	669	683	698
300	47 712	727	741	756	770	784	799	813	828	842
301	857	871	885	900	914	929	943	958	972	986
302	48 001	015	029	044	058	073	087	101	116	130
303	144	159	173	187	202	216	230	244	259	273
304	287	302	316	330	344	359	373	387	401	416
305	430	444	458	473	487	501	515	530	544	558
306	572	586	601	615	629	643	657	671	686	700
307	714	728	742	756	770	785	799	813	827	841
308	855	869	883	897	911	926	940	954	968	982
309	996	*010	*024	*038	*052	*066	*080	*094	*108	*122
310	49 136	150	164	178	192	206	220	234	248	262

PP

	17		16		15		14
1	1.7	1	1.6	1	1.5	1	1.4
2	3.4	2	3.2	2	3.0	2	2.8
3	5.1	3	4.8	3	4.5	3	4.2
4	6.8	4	6.4	4	6.0	4	5.6
5	8.5	5	8.0	5	7.5	5	7.0
6	10.2	6	9.6	6	9.0	6	8.4
7	11.9	7	11.2	7	10.5	7	9.8
8	13.6	8	12.8	8	12.0	8	11.2
9	15.3	9	14.4	9	13.5	9	12.6

COMMON LOGARITHMS
311–360

N	0	1	2	3	4	5	6	7	8	9		PP
311	49 276	290	304	318	332	346	360	374	388	402		
312	415	429	443	457	471	485	499	513	527	541		**14**
313	554	568	582	596	610	624	638	651	665	679		
314	693	707	721	734	748	762	776	790	803	817	1	1.4
315	831	845	859	872	886	900	914	927	941	955	2	2.8
											3	4.2
316	969	982	996	*010	*024	*037	*051	*065	*079	*092	4	5.6
317	50 106	120	133	147	161	174	188	202	215	229	5	7.0
318	243	256	270	284	297	311	325	338	352	365	6	8.4
319	379	393	406	420	433	447	461	474	488	501	7	9.8
320	515	529	542	556	569	583	596	610	623	637	8	11.2
											9	12.6
321	651	664	678	691	705	718	732	745	759	772		
322	786	799	813	826	840	853	866	880	893	907		
323	920	934	947	961	974	987	*001	*014	*028	*041		
324	51 055	068	081	095	108	121	135	148	162	175		
325	188	202	215	228	242	255	268	282	295	308		
326	322	335	348	362	375	388	402	415	428	441		
327	455	468	481	495	508	521	534	548	561	574		
328	587	601	614	627	640	654	667	680	693	706		
329	720	733	746	759	772	786	799	812	825	838		
330	851	865	878	891	904	917	930	943	957	970		
331	983	996	*009	*022	*035	*048	*061	*075	*088	*101		
332	52 114	127	140	153	166	179	192	205	218	231		**13**
333	244	257	270	284	297	310	323	336	349	362		
334	375	388	401	414	427	440	453	466	479	492	1	1.3
335	504	517	530	543	556	569	582	595	608	621	2	2.6
											3	3.9
336	634	647	660	673	686	699	711	724	737	750	4	5.2
337	763	776	789	802	815	827	840	853	866	879	5	6.5
338	892	905	917	930	943	956	969	982	994	*007	6	7.8
339	53 020	033	046	058	071	084	097	110	122	135	7	9.1
340	148	161	173	186	199	212	224	237	250	263	8	10.4
											9	11.7
341	275	288	301	314	326	339	352	364	377	390		
342	403	415	428	441	453	466	479	491	504	517		
343	529	542	555	567	580	593	605	618	631	643		
344	656	668	681	694	706	719	732	744	757	769		
345	782	794	807	820	832	845	857	870	882	895		
346	908	920	933	945	958	970	983	995	*008	*020		
347	54 033	045	058	070	083	095	108	120	133	145		
348	158	170	183	195	208	220	233	245	258	270		
349	283	295	307	320	332	345	357	370	382	394		
350	54 407	419	432	444	456	469	481	494	506	518		
351	531	543	555	568	580	593	605	617	630	642		
352	654	667	679	691	704	716	728	741	753	765		
353	777	790	802	814	827	839	851	864	876	888		**12**
354	900	913	925	937	949	962	974	986	998	*011		
355	55 023	035	047	060	072	084	096	108	121	133	1	1.2
											2	2.4
356	145	157	169	182	194	206	218	230	242	255	3	3.6
357	267	279	291	303	315	328	340	352	364	376	4	4.8
358	388	400	413	425	437	449	461	473	485	497	5	6.0
359	509	522	534	546	558	570	582	594	606	618	6	7.2
360	630	642	654	666	678	691	703	715	727	739	7	8.4
											8	9.6
											9	10.8

N	0	1	2	3	4	5	6	7	8	9		PP

Table No. 19 continued

COMMON LOGARITHMS
361–410

N	0	1	2	3	4	5	6	7	8	9	PP
361	751	763	775	787	799	811	823	835	847	859	
362	871	883	895	907	919	931	943	955	967	979	
363	991	*003	*015	*027	*038	*050	*062	*074	*086	*098	
364	56 110	122	134	146	158	170	182	194	205	217	
365	229	241	253	265	277	289	301	312	324	336	
366	348	360	372	384	396	407	419	431	443	455	
367	467	478	490	502	514	526	538	549	561	573	
368	585	597	608	620	632	644	656	667	679	691	
369	703	714	726	738	750	761	773	785	797	808	
370	820	832	844	855	867	879	891	902	914	926	
371	56 937	949	961	972	984	996	*008	*019	*031	*043	
372	57 054	066	078	089	101	113	124	136	148	159	
373	171	183	194	206	217	229	241	252	264	276	
374	287	299	310	322	334	345	357	368	380	392	
375	403	415	426	438	449	461	473	484	496	507	
376	519	530	542	553	565	576	588	600	611	623	
377	634	646	657	669	680	692	703	715	726	738	
378	749	761	772	784	795	807	818	830	841	852	
379	864	875	887	898	910	921	933	944	955	967	
380	978	990	*001	*013	*024	*035	*047	*058	*070	*081	
381	58 092	104	115	127	138	149	161	172	184	195	
382	206	218	229	240	252	263	274	286	297	309	
383	320	331	343	354	365	377	388	399	410	422	
384	433	444	456	467	478	490	501	512	524	535	
385	546	557	569	580	591	602	614	625	636	647	
386	659	670	681	692	704	715	726	737	749	760	
387	771	782	794	805	816	827	838	850	861	872	
388	883	894	906	917	928	939	950	961	973	984	
389	995	*006	*017	*028	*040	*051	*062	*073	*084	*095	
390	59 106	118	129	140	151	162	173	184	195	207	
391	218	229	240	251	262	273	284	295	306	318	
392	329	340	351	362	373	384	395	406	417	428	
393	439	450	461	472	483	494	506	517	528	539	
394	550	561	572	583	594	605	616	627	638	649	
395	660	671	682	693	704	715	726	737	748	759	
396	770	780	791	802	813	824	835	846	857	868	
397	879	890	901	912	923	934	945	956	966	977	
398	988	999	*010	*021	*032	*043	*054	*065	*076	*086	
399	60 097	108	119	130	141	152	163	173	184	195	
400	60 206	217	228	239	249	260	271	282	293	304	
401	314	325	336	347	358	369	379	390	401	412	
402	423	433	444	455	466	477	487	498	509	520	
403	531	541	552	563	574	584	595	606	617	627	
404	638	649	660	670	681	692	703	713	724	735	
405	746	756	767	778	788	799	810	821	831	842	
406	853	863	874	885	895	906	917	927	938	949	
407	959	970	981	991	*002	*013	*023	*034	*045	*055	
408	61 066	077	087	098	109	119	130	140	151	162	
409	172	183	194	204	215	225	236	247	257	268	
410	278	289	300	310	321	331	342	352	363	374	
N	0	1	2	3	4	5	6	7	8	9	PP

PP side tables:

	12
1	1.2
2	2.4
3	3.6
4	4.8
5	6.0
6	7.2
7	8.4
8	9.6
9	10.8

	11
1	1.1
2	2.2
3	3.3
4	4.4
5	5.5
6	6.6
7	7.7
8	8.8
9	9.9

COMMON LOGARITHMS
411–455

N	0	1	2	3	4	5	6	7	8	9		PP
411	384	395	405	416	426	437	448	458	469	479		
412	490	500	511	521	532	542	553	563	574	584		
413	595	606	616	627	637	648	658	669	679	690		
414	700	711	721	731	742	752	763	773	784	794		**10**
415	805	815	826	836	847	857	868	878	888	899		
											1	1.0
416	909	920	930	941	951	962	972	982	993	*003	2	2.0
417	62 014	024	034	045	055	066	076	086	097	107	3	3.0
418	118	128	138	149	159	170	180	190	201	211	4	4.0
419	221	232	242	252	263	273	284	294	304	315	5	5.0
420	325	335	346	356	366	377	387	397	408	418	6	6.0
											7	7.0
421	428	439	449	459	469	480	490	500	511	521	8	8.0
422	531	542	552	562	572	583	593	603	613	624	9	9.0
423	634	644	655	665	675	685	696	706	716	726		
424	737	747	757	767	778	788	798	808	818	829		
425	839	849	859	870	880	890	900	910	921	931		
426	941	951	961	972	982	992	*002	*012	*022	*033		
427	63 043	053	063	073	083	094	104	114	124	134		
428	144	155	165	175	185	195	205	215	225	236		
429	246	256	266	276	286	296	306	317	327	337		
430	347	357	367	377	387	397	407	417	428	438		
431	63 448	458	468	478	488	498	508	518	528	538		
432	548	558	568	579	589	599	609	619	629	639		
433	649	659	669	679	689	699	709	719	729	739		
434	749	759	769	779	789	799	809	819	829	839		
435	849	859	869	879	889	899	909	919	929	939		
												10
436	949	959	969	979	988	998	*008	*018	*028	*038	1	1.0
437	64 048	058	068	078	088	098	108	118	128	137	2	2.0
438	147	157	167	177	187	197	207	217	227	237	3	3.0
439	246	256	266	276	286	296	306	316	326	335	4	4.0
440	345	355	365	375	385	395	404	414	424	434	5	5.0
											6	6.0
441	444	454	464	473	483	493	503	513	523	532	7	7.0
442	542	552	562	572	582	591	601	611	621	631	8	8.0
443	640	650	660	670	680	689	699	709	719	729	9	9.0
444	738	748	758	768	777	787	797	807	816	826		
445	836	846	856	865	875	885	895	904	914	924		
446	933	943	953	963	972	982	992	*002	*011	*021		
447	65 031	040	050	060	070	079	089	099	108	118		
448	128	137	147	157	167	176	186	196	205	215		
449	225	234	244	254	263	273	283	292	302	312		
450	65 321	331	341	350	360	369	379	389	398	408		
451	418	427	437	447	456	466	475	485	495	504		
452	514	523	533	543	552	562	571	581	591	600		
453	610	619	629	639	648	658	667	677	686	696		
454	706	715	725	734	744	753	763	772	782	792		
455	801	811	820	830	839	849	858	868	877	887		
N	0	1	2	3	4	5	6	7	8	9		PP

COMMON LOGARITHMS
456–505

N	0	1	2	3	4	5	6	7	8	9
456	896	906	916	925	935	944	954	963	973	982
457	992	*001	*011	*020	*030	*039	*049	*058	*068	*077
458	66 087	096	106	115	124	134	143	153	162	172
459	181	191	200	210	219	229	238	247	257	266
460	276	285	295	304	314	323	332	342	351	361
461	370	380	389	398	408	417	427	436	445	455
462	464	474	483	492	502	511	521	530	539	549
463	558	567	577	586	596	605	614	624	633	642
464	652	661	671	680	689	699	708	717	727	736
465	745	755	764	773	783	792	801	811	820	829
466	839	848	857	867	876	885	894	904	913	922
467	932	941	950	960	969	978	987	997	*006	*015
468	67 025	034	043	052	062	071	080	089	099	108
469	117	127	136	145	154	164	173	182	191	201
470	210	219	228	237	247	256	265	274	284	293
471	302	311	321	330	339	348	357	367	376	385
472	394	403	413	422	431	440	449	459	468	477
473	486	495	504	514	523	532	541	550	560	569
474	578	587	596	605	614	624	633	642	651	660
475	669	679	688	697	706	715	724	733	742	752
476	761	770	779	788	797	806	815	825	834	843
477	852	861	870	879	888	897	906	916	925	934
478	943	952	961	970	979	988	997	*006	*015	*024
479	68 034	043	052	061	070	079	088	097	106	115
480	124	133	142	151	160	169	178	187	196	205
481	215	224	233	242	251	260	269	278	287	296
482	305	314	323	332	341	350	359	368	377	386
483	395	404	413	422	431	440	449	458	467	476
484	485	494	502	511	520	529	538	547	556	565
485	574	583	592	601	610	619	628	637	646	655
486	664	673	681	690	699	708	717	726	735	744
487	753	762	771	780	789	797	806	815	824	833
488	842	851	860	869	878	886	895	904	913	922
489	931	940	949	958	966	975	984	993	*002	*011
490	69 020	028	037	046	055	064	073	082	090	099
491	69 108	117	126	135	144	152	161	170	179	188
492	197	205	214	223	232	241	249	258	267	276
493	285	294	302	311	320	329	338	346	355	364
494	373	381	390	399	408	417	425	434	443	452
495	461	469	478	487	496	504	513	522	531	539
496	548	557	566	574	583	592	601	609	618	627
497	636	644	653	662	671	679	688	697	705	714
498	723	732	740	749	758	767	775	784	793	801
499	810	819	827	836	845	854	862	871	880	888
500	897	906	914	923	932	940	949	958	966	975
501	984	992	*001	*010	*018	*027	*036	*044	*053	*062
502	70 070	079	088	096	105	114	122	131	140	148
503	157	165	174	183	191	200	209	217	226	234
504	243	252	260	269	278	286	295	303	312	321
505	329	338	346	355	364	372	381	389	398	406

N	0	1	2	3	4	5	6	7	8	9	PP

PP

	9
1	0.9
2	1.8
3	2.7
4	3.6
5	4.5
6	5.4
7	6.3
8	7.2
9	8.1

	8
1	0.8
2	1.6
3	2.4
4	3.2
5	4.0
6	4.8
7	5.0
8	6.4
9	7.2

	9
1	0.9
2	1.8
3	2.7
4	3.6
5	4.5
6	5.4
7	6.3
8	7.2
9	8.1

COMMON LOGARITHMS
506–555

N	0	1	2	3	4	5	6	7	8	9	PP
506	415	424	432	441	449	458	467	475	484	492	
507	501	509	518	526	535	544	552	561	569	578	
508	586	595	603	612	621	629	638	646	655	663	
509	672	680	689	697	706	714	723	731	740	749	
510	757	766	774	783	791	800	808	817	825	834	
511	842	851	859	868	876	885	893	902	910	919	
512	927	935	944	952	961	969	978	986	995	*003	
513	71 012	020	029	037	046	054	063	071	079	088	
514	096	105	113	122	130	139	147	155	164	172	
515	181	189	198	206	214	223	231	240	248	257	
516	265	273	282	290	299	307	315	324	332	341	
517	349	357	366	374	383	391	399	408	416	425	
518	433	441	450	458	466	475	483	492	500	508	
519	517	525	533	542	550	559	567	575	584	592	
520	600	609	617	625	634	642	650	659	667	675	
521	684	692	700	709	717	725	734	742	750	759	
522	767	775	784	792	800	809	817	825	834	842	
523	850	858	867	875	883	892	900	908	917	925	
524	933	941	950	958	966	975	983	991	999	*008	
525	72 016	024	032	041	049	057	066	074	082	090	
526	099	107	115	123	132	140	148	156	165	173	
527	181	189	198	206	214	222	230	239	247	255	
528	263	272	280	288	296	304	313	321	329	337	
529	346	354	362	370	378	387	395	403	411	419	
530	428	436	444	452	460	469	477	485	493	501	
531	509	518	526	534	542	550	558	567	575	583	
532	591	599	607	616	624	632	640	648	656	665	
533	673	681	689	697	705	713	722	730	738	746	
534	754	762	770	779	787	795	803	811	819	827	
535	835	843	852	860	868	876	884	892	900	908	
536	916	925	933	941	949	957	965	973	981	989	
537	997	*006	*014	*022	*030	*038	*046	*054	*062	*070	
538	73 078	086	094	102	111	119	127	135	143	151	
539	159	167	175	183	191	199	207	215	223	231	
540	239	247	255	263	272	280	288	296	304	312	
541	320	328	336	344	352	360	368	376	384	392	
542	400	408	416	424	432	440	448	456	464	472	
543	480	488	496	504	512	520	528	536	544	552	
544	560	568	576	584	592	600	608	616	624	632	
545	640	648	656	664	672	679	687	695	703	711	
546	719	727	735	743	751	759	767	775	783	791	
547	799	807	815	823	830	838	846	854	862	870	
548	878	886	894	902	910	918	926	933	941	949	
549	957	965	973	981	989	997	*005	*013	*020	*028	
550	74 036	044	052	060	068	076	084	092	099	107	
551	74 115	123	131	139	147	155	162	170	178	186	
552	194	202	210	218	225	233	241	249	257	265	
553	273	280	288	296	304	312	320	327	335	343	
554	351	359	367	374	382	390	398	406	414	421	
555	429	437	445	453	461	468	476	484	492	500	
N	0	1	2	3	4	5	6	7	8	9	PP

	8
1	0.8
2	1.6
3	2.4
4	3.2
5	4.0
6	4.8
7	5.6
8	6.4
9	7.2

Table No. 19 continued

COMMON LOGARITHMS
556–605

N	0	1	2	3	4	5	6	7	8	9
556	507	515	523	531	539	547	554	562	570	578
557	586	593	601	609	617	624	632	640	648	656
558	663	671	679	687	695	702	710	718	726	733
559	741	749	757	764	772	780	788	796	803	811
560	819	827	834	842	850	858	865	873	881	889
561	896	904	912	920	927	935	943	950	958	966
562	974	981	989	997	*005	*012	*020	*028	*035	*043
563	75 051	059	066	074	082	089	097	105	113	120
564	128	136	143	151	159	166	174	182	189	197
565	205	213	220	228	236	243	251	259	266	274
566	282	289	297	305	312	320	328	335	343	351
567	358	366	374	381	389	397	404	412	420	427
568	435	442	450	458	465	473	481	488	496	504
569	511	519	526	534	542	549	557	565	572	580
570	587	595	603	610	618	626	633	641	648	656
571	664	671	679	686	694	702	709	717	724	732
572	740	747	755	762	770	778	785	793	800	808
573	815	823	831	838	846	853	861	868	876	884
574	891	899	906	914	921	929	937	944	952	959
575	967	974	982	989	997	*005	*012	*020	*027	*035
576	76 042	050	057	065	072	080	087	095	103	110
577	118	125	133	140	148	155	163	170	178	185
578	193	200	208	215	223	230	238	245	253	260
579	268	275	283	290	298	305	313	320	328	335
580	343	350	358	365	373	380	388	395	403	410
581	418	425	433	440	448	455	462	470	477	485
582	492	500	507	515	522	530	537	545	552	559
583	567	574	582	589	597	604	612	619	626	634
584	641	649	656	664	671	678	686	693	701	708
585	716	723	730	738	745	753	760	768	775	782
586	790	797	805	812	819	827	834	842	849	856
587	864	871	879	886	893	901	908	916	923	930
588	938	945	953	960	967	975	982	989	997	*004
589	77 012	019	026	034	041	048	056	063	070	078
590	085	093	100	107	115	122	129	137	144	151
591	159	166	173	181	188	195	203	210	217	225
592	232	240	247	254	262	269	276	283	291	298
593	305	313	320	327	335	342	349	357	364	371
594	379	386	393	401	408	415	422	430	437	444
595	452	459	466	474	481	488	495	503	510	517
596	525	532	539	546	554	561	568	576	583	590
597	597	605	612	619	627	634	641	648	656	663
598	670	677	685	692	699	706	714	721	728	735
599	743	750	757	764	772	779	786	793	801	808
600	815	822	830	837	844	851	859	866	873	880
601	887	895	902	909	916	924	931	938	945	952
602	960	967	974	981	988	996	*003	*010	*017	*025
603	78 032	039	046	053	061	068	075	082	089	097
604	104	111	118	125	132	140	147	154	161	168
605	176	183	190	197	204	211	219	226	233	240
N	0	1	2	3	4	5	6	7	8	9

8
1 0.8
2 1.6
3 2.4
4 3.2
5 4.0
6 4.8
7 5.6
8 6.4
9 7.2

7
1 0.7
2 1.4
3 2.1
4 2.8
5 3.5
6 4.2
7 4.9
8 5.0
9 6.3

PP

COMMON LOGARITHMS
606–655

N	0	1	2	3	4	5	6	7	8	9	PP	
606	247	254	262	269	276	283	290	297	305	312		
607	319	326	333	340	347	355	362	369	376	383		
608	390	398	405	412	419	426	433	440	447	455		
609	462	469	476	483	490	497	504	512	519	526		
610	533	540	547	554	561	569	576	583	590	597		
611	78 604	611	618	625	633	640	647	654	661	668		
612	675	682	689	696	704	711	718	725	732	739		
613	746	753	760	767	774	781	789	796	803	810		
614	817	824	831	838	845	852	859	866	873	880		
615	888	895	902	909	916	923	930	937	944	951		
616	958	965	972	979	986	993	*000	*007	*014	*021		
617	79 029	036	043	050	057	064	071	078	085	092		
618	099	106	113	120	127	134	141	148	155	162		
619	169	176	183	190	197	204	211	218	225	232		
620	239	246	253	260	267	274	281	288	295	302		
621	309	316	323	330	337	344	351	358	365	372		7
622	379	386	393	400	407	414	421	428	435	442		
623	449	456	463	470	477	484	491	498	505	511	1	0.7
624	518	525	532	539	546	553	560	567	574	581	2	1.4
625	588	595	602	609	616	623	630	637	644	650	3	2.1
											4	2.8
626	657	664	671	678	685	692	699	706	713	720	5	3.5
627	727	734	741	748	754	761	768	775	782	789	6	4.2
628	796	803	810	817	824	831	837	844	851	858	7	4.9
629	865	872	879	886	893	900	906	913	920	927	8	5.6
630	934	941	948	955	962	969	975	982	989	996	9	6.3
631	80 003	101	017	024	030	037	044	051	058	065		
632	072	079	085	092	099	106	113	120	127	134		
633	140	147	154	161	168	175	182	188	195	202		
634	209	216	223	229	236	243	250	257	264	271		
635	277	284	291	298	305	312	318	325	332	339		
636	346	353	359	366	373	380	387	393	400	407		
637	414	421	428	434	441	448	455	462	468	475		
638	482	489	496	502	509	516	523	530	536	543		
639	550	557	564	570	577	584	591	598	604	611		
640	618	625	632	638	645	652	659	665	672	679		
641	686	693	699	706	713	720	726	733	740	747		
642	754	760	767	774	781	787	794	801	808	814		
643	821	828	835	841	848	855	862	868	875	882		
644	889	895	902	909	916	922	929	936	943	949		
645	956	963	969	976	983	990	996	*003	*010	*017		
646	81 023	030	037	043	050	057	064	070	077	084		6
647	090	097	104	111	117	124	131	137	144	151	1	0.6
648	158	164	171	178	184	191	198	201	211	218	2	1.2
649	224	231	238	245	251	258	265	271	278	285	3	1.8
650	81 291	298	305	311	318	325	331	338	345	351	4	2.4
											5	3.0
651	358	365	371	378	385	391	398	405	411	418	6	3.6
652	425	431	438	445	451	458	465	471	478	485	7	4.2
653	491	498	505	511	518	525	531	538	544	551	8	4.8
654	558	564	571	578	584	591	598	604	611	617	9	5.4
655	624	631	637	644	651	657	664	671	677	684		

N	0	1	2	3	4	5	6	7	8	9	PP

COMMON LOGARITHMS
656–705

N	0	1	2	3	4	5	6	7	8	9	PP
656	690	697	704	710	717	723	730	737	743	750	
657	757	763	770	776	783	790	796	803	809	816	
658	823	829	836	842	849	856	862	869	875	882	
659	889	895	902	908	915	921	928	935	941	948	
660	954	961	968	974	981	987	994	*000	*007	*014	
661	82 020	027	033	040	046	053	060	066	073	079	
662	086	092	099	105	112	119	125	132	138	145	
663	151	158	164	171	178	184	191	197	204	210	
664	217	223	230	236	243	249	256	263	269	276	
665	282	289	295	302	308	315	321	328	334	341	
666	347	354	360	367	373	380	387	393	400	406	
667	413	419	426	432	439	445	452	458	465	471	
668	478	484	491	497	504	510	517	523	530	536	
669	543	549	556	562	569	575	582	588	595	601	
670	607	614	620	627	633	640	646	653	659	666	
671	82 672	679	685	692	698	705	711	718	724	730	
672	737	743	750	756	763	769	776	782	789	795	
673	802	808	814	821	827	834	840	847	853	860	
674	866	872	879	885	892	898	905	911	918	924	
675	930	937	943	950	956	963	969	975	982	988	
676	995	*001	*008	*014	*020	*027	*033	*040	*046	*052	
677	83 059	065	072	078	085	091	097	104	110	117	
678	123	129	136	142	149	155	161	168	174	181	
679	187	193	200	206	213	219	225	232	238	245	
680	251	257	264	270	276	283	289	296	302	308	
681	315	321	327	334	340	347	353	359	366	372	
682	378	385	391	398	404	410	417	423	429	436	
683	442	448	455	461	467	474	480	487	493	499	
684	506	512	518	525	531	537	544	550	556	563	
685	569	575	582	588	594	601	607	613	620	626	
686	632	639	645	651	658	664	670	677	683	689	
687	696	702	708	715	721	727	734	740	746	753	
688	759	765	771	778	784	790	797	803	809	816	
689	822	828	835	841	847	853	860	866	872	879	
690	885	891	897	904	910	916	923	929	935	942	
691	948	954	960	967	973	979	985	992	998	*004	
692	84 011	017	023	029	036	042	048	055	061	067	
693	073	080	086	092	098	105	111	117	123	130	
694	136	142	148	155	161	167	173	180	186	192	
695	198	205	211	217	223	230	236	242	248	255	
696	261	267	273	280	286	292	298	305	311	317	
697	323	330	336	342	348	354	361	367	373	379	
698	386	392	398	404	410	417	423	429	435	442	
699	448	454	460	466	473	479	485	491	497	504	
700	84 510	516	522	528	535	541	547	553	559	566	
701	572	578	584	590	597	603	609	615	621	628	
702	634	640	646	652	658	665	671	677	683	689	
703	696	702	708	714	720	726	733	739	745	751	
704	757	763	770	776	782	788	794	800	807	813	
705	819	825	831	837	844	850	856	862	868	874	
N	0	1	2	3	4	5	6	7	8	9	PP

	7
1	0.7
2	1.4
3	2.1
4	2.8
5	3.5
6	4.2
7	4.9
8	5.6
9	6.3

COMMON LOGARITHMS
706–755

N	0	1	2	3	4	5	6	7	8	9	PP
706	880	887	893	899	905	911	917	924	930	936	
707	942	948	954	960	967	973	979	985	991	997	
708	85 003	009	016	022	028	034	040	046	052	058	6
709	065	071	077	083	089	095	101	107	114	120	1 0.6
710	126	132	138	144	150	156	163	169	175	181	2 1.2
711	187	193	199	205	211	217	224	230	236	242	3 1.8
712	248	254	260	266	272	278	285	291	297	303	4 2.4
713	309	315	321	327	333	339	345	352	358	364	5 3.0
714	370	376	382	388	394	400	406	412	418	425	6 3.6
715	431	437	443	449	455	461	467	473	479	485	7 4.2
716	491	497	503	509	516	522	528	534	540	546	8 4.8
717	552	558	564	570	576	582	588	594	600	606	9 5.4
718	612	618	625	631	637	643	649	655	661	667	
719	673	679	685	691	697	703	709	715	721	727	
720	733	739	745	751	757	763	769	775	781	788	
721	794	800	806	812	818	824	830	836	842	848	
722	854	860	866	872	878	884	890	896	902	908	
723	914	920	926	932	938	944	950	956	962	968	
724	974	980	986	992	998	*004	*010	*016	*022	*028	
725	86 034	040	046	052	058	064	070	076	082	088	
726	094	100	106	112	118	124	130	136	141	147	
727	153	159	165	171	177	183	189	195	201	207	
728	213	219	225	231	237	243	249	255	261	267	
729	273	279	285	291	297	303	308	314	320	326	
730	332	338	344	350	356	362	368	374	380	386	
731	86 392	398	404	410	415	421	427	433	439	445	
732	451	457	463	469	475	481	487	493	499	504	
733	510	516	522	528	534	540	546	552	558	564	
734	570	576	581	587	593	599	605	611	617	623	
735	629	635	641	646	652	658	664	670	676	682	
736	688	694	700	705	711	717	723	729	735	741	
737	747	753	759	764	770	776	782	788	794	800	
738	806	812	817	823	829	835	841	847	853	859	
739	864	870	876	882	888	894	900	906	911	917	
740	923	929	935	941	947	953	958	964	970	976	
741	982	988	994	999	*005	*011	*017	*023	*029	*035	6
742	87 040	046	052	058	064	070	075	081	087	093	1 0.6
743	099	105	111	116	122	128	134	140	146	151	2 1.2
744	157	163	169	175	181	186	192	198	204	210	3 1.8
745	216	221	227	233	239	245	251	256	262	268	4 2.4
746	274	280	286	291	297	303	309	315	320	326	5 3.0
747	332	338	344	349	355	361	367	373	379	384	6 3.6
748	390	396	402	408	413	419	425	431	437	442	7 4.2
749	448	454	460	466	471	477	483	489	495	500	8 4.8
750	506	512	518	523	529	535	541	547	552	558	9 5.4
751	564	570	576	581	587	593	599	604	610	616	
752	622	628	633	639	645	651	656	662	668	674	
753	679	685	691	697	703	708	714	720	726	731	
754	737	743	749	754	760	766	772	777	783	789	
755	795	800	806	812	818	823	829	835	841	846	

Table No. 19 continued

COMMON LOGARITHMS
756–805

N	0	1	2	3	4	5	6	7	8	9	PP	
756	852	858	864	869	875	881	887	892	898	904		
757	910	915	921	927	933	938	944	950	955	961		
758	967	973	978	984	990	996	*001	*007	*013	*018		
759	88 024	030	036	041	047	053	058	064	070	076		
760	081	087	093	098	104	110	116	121	127	133		
761	138	144	150	156	161	167	173	178	184	190		
762	195	201	207	213	218	224	230	235	241	247		
763	252	258	264	270	275	281	287	292	298	304		
764	309	315	321	326	332	338	343	349	355	360		
765	366	372	377	383	389	395	400	406	412	417		
766	423	429	434	440	446	451	457	463	468	474		
767	480	485	491	497	502	508	513	519	525	530		
768	536	542	547	553	559	564	570	576	581	587		5
769	593	598	604	610	615	621	627	632	638	643		
770	649	655	660	666	672	677	683	689	694	700	1	0.5
771	705	711	717	722	728	734	739	745	750	756	2	1.0
772	762	767	773	779	784	790	795	801	807	812	3	1.5
773	818	824	829	835	840	846	852	857	863	868	4	2.0
774	874	880	885	891	897	902	908	913	919	925	5	2.5
775	930	936	941	947	953	958	964	969	975	981	6	3.0
776	986	992	997	*003	*009	*014	*020	*025	*031	*037	7	3.5
777	89 042	048	053	059	064	070	076	081	087	092	8	4.0
778	098	104	109	115	120	126	131	137	143	148	9	4.5
779	154	159	165	170	176	182	187	193	198	204		
780	209	215	221	226	232	237	243	248	254	260		
781	265	271	276	282	287	293	298	304	310	315		
782	321	326	332	337	343	348	354	360	365	371		
783	376	382	387	393	398	404	409	415	421	426		
784	432	437	443	448	454	459	465	470	476	481		
785	487	492	498	504	509	515	520	526	531	537		
786	542	548	553	559	564	570	575	581	586	592		
787	597	603	609	614	620	625	631	636	642	647		
788	653	658	664	669	675	680	686	691	697	702		
789	708	713	719	724	730	735	741	746	752	757		
790	763	768	774	779	785	790	796	801	807	812		
791	89 818	823	829	834	840	845	851	856	862	867		
792	873	878	883	889	894	900	905	911	916	922		
793	927	933	938	944	949	955	960	966	971	977		
794	982	988	993	998	*004	*009	*015	*020	*026	*031		
795	90 037	042	048	053	059	064	069	075	080	086		
796	091	097	102	108	113	119	124	129	135	140		
797	146	151	157	162	168	173	179	184	189	195		
798	200	206	211	217	222	227	233	238	244	249		
799	255	260	266	271	276	282	287	293	298	304		
800	90 309	314	320	325	331	336	342	347	352	358		
801	363	369	374	380	385	390	396	401	407	412		
802	417	423	428	434	439	445	450	455	461	466		
803	472	477	482	488	493	499	504	509	515	520		
804	526	53_	536	542	547	553	558	563	569	574		
805	580	585	590	596	601	607	612	617	623	628		
N	0	1	2	3	4	5	6	7	8	9	PP	

COMMON LOGARITHMS
806–850

N	0	1	2	3	4	5	6	7	8	9	PP	
												6
806	634	639	644	650	655	660	666	671	677	682		
807	687	693	698	703	709	714	720	725	730	736	1	0.6
808	741	747	752	757	763	768	773	779	784	789	2	1.2
809	795	800	806	811	816	822	827	832	838	843	3	1.8
810	849	854	859	865	870	875	881	886	891	897	4	2 4
											5	3.0
811	902	907	913	918	924	929	934	940	945	950	6	3.6
812	956	961	966	972	977	982	988	993	998	*004	7	4.2
813	91 009	014	020	025	030	036	041	046	052	0⌒7	8	4.8
814	062	068	073	078	084	089	094	100	105	110	9	4.5
815	116	121	126	132	137	142	148	153	158	164		
816	169	174	180	185	190	196	201	206	212	217		
817	222	228	233	238	243	249	254	259	265	270		
818	275	281	286	291	297	302	307	312	318	323		
819	328	334	339	344	350	355	360	365	371	376		
820	381	387	392	397	403	408	413	418	424	429		
821	434	440	445	450	455	461	466	471	477	482		
822	487	492	498	503	508	514	519	524	529	535		
823	540	545	551	556	561	566	572	577	582	587		
824	593	598	603	609	614	619	624	630	635	640		
825	645	651	656	661	666	672	677	682	687	693		
826	698	703	709	714	719	724	730	735	740	745		
827	751	756	761	766	772	777	782	787	793	798		
828	803	808	814	819	824	829	834	840	845	850		
829	855	861	866	871	876	882	887	892	897	903		
830	908	913	918	924	929	934	939	944	950	955		5
											1	0.5
831	960	965	971	976	981	986	991	997	*002	*007	2	1.0
832	92 012	018	023	028	033	038	044	049	054	059	3	1.5
833	065	070	075	080	085	091	096	101	106	111	4	2.0
834	117	122	127	132	137	143	148	153	158	163	5	2.5
835	169	174	179	184	189	195	200	205	210	215	6	3.0
											7	3.5
											8	4.0
836	221	226	231	236	241	247	252	257	262	267	9	4.5
837	273	278	283	288	293	298	304	309	314	319		
838	324	330	335	340	345	350	355	361	366	371		
839	376	381	387	392	397	402	407	412	418	423		
840	428	433	438	443	449	454	459	464	469	474		
841	480	485	490	495	500	505	511	516	521	526		
842	531	536	542	547	552	557	562	567	572	578		
843	583	588	593	598	603	609	614	619	624	629		
844	634	639	645	650	655	660	665	670	675	681		
845	686	691	696	701	706	711	716	722	727	732		
846	737	742	747	752	758	763	768	773	778	783		
847	788	793	799	804	809	814	819	824	829	834		
848	840	845	850	855	860	865	870	875	881	886		
849	891	896	901	906	911	916	921	927	932	937		
850	942	947	952	957	962	967	973	978	983	988		

N	0	1	2	3	4	5	6	7	8	9	PP

COMMON LOGARITHMS
851–895

N	0	1	2	3	4	5	6	7	8	9	PP
851	92 993	998	*003	*008	*013	*018	*024	*029	*034	*039	
852	93 044	049	054	059	064	069	075	080	085	090	
853	095	100	105	110	115	120	125	131	136	141	
854	146	151	156	161	166	171	176	181	186	192	6
855	197	202	207	212	217	222	227	232	237	242	
											1 0.6
856	247	252	258	263	268	273	278	283	288	293	2 1.2
857	298	303	308	313	318	323	328	334	339	344	3 1.8
858	349	354	359	364	369	374	379	384	389	394	4 2.4
859	399	404	409	414	420	425	430	435	440	445	5 3.0
860	450	455	460	465	470	475	480	485	490	495	6 3.6
											7 4.2
861	500	505	510	515	520	526	531	536	541	546	8 4.8
862	551	556	561	566	571	576	581	586	591	596	9 4.5
863	601	606	611	616	621	626	631	636	641	646	
864	651	656	661	666	671	676	682	687	692	697	
865	702	707	712	717	722	727	732	737	742	747	
866	752	757	762	767	772	777	782	787	792	797	
867	802	807	812	817	822	827	832	837	842	847	
868	852	857	862	867	872	877	882	887	892	897	
869	902	907	912	917	922	927	932	937	942	947	
870	952	957	962	967	972	977	982	987	992	997	
871	94 002	007	012	017	022	027	032	037	042	047	
872	052	057	062	067	072	077	082	086	091	096	
873	101	106	111	116	121	126	131	136	141	146	
874	151	156	161	166	171	176	181	186	191	196	
875	201	206	211	216	221	226	231	236	240	245	
876	250	255	260	265	270	275	280	285	290	295	5
877	300	305	310	315	320	325	330	335	340	345	1 0.5
878	349	354	359	364	369	374	379	384	389	394	2 1.0
879	399	404	409	414	419	424	429	433	438	443	3 1.5
880	448	453	458	463	468	473	478	483	488	493	4 2.0
											5 2.5
881	498	503	507	512	517	522	527	532	537	542	6 3.0
882	547	552	557	562	567	571	576	581	586	591	7 3.5
883	596	601	606	611	616	621	626	630	635	640	8 4.0
884	645	650	655	660	665	670	675	680	685	689	9 4.5
885	694	699	704	709	714	719	724	729	734	738	
886	743	748	753	758	763	768	773	778	783	787	
887	792	797	802	807	812	817	822	827	832	836	
888	841	846	851	856	861	866	871	876	880	885	
889	890	895	900	905	910	915	919	924	929	934	
890	939	944	949	954	959	963	968	973	978	983	
891	988	993	998	*002	*007	*012	*017	*022	*027	*032	
892	95 036	041	046	051	056	061	066	071	075	080	
893	085	090	095	100	105	109	114	119	124	129	
894	134	139	143	148	153	158	163	168	173	177	
895	182	187	192	197	202	207	211	216	221	226	
N	0	1	2	3	4	5	6	7	8	9	PP

COMMON LOGARITHMS
896–945

N	0	1	2	3	4	5	6	7	8	9		PP
896	231	236	240	245	250	255	260	265	270	274		
897	279	284	289	294	299	303	308	313	318	323		
898	328	332	337	342	347	352	357	361	366	371		4
899	376	381	386	390	395	400	405	410	415	419	1	0.4
900	424	429	434	439	444	448	453	458	463	468	2	0.8
											3	1.2
901	472	477	482	487	492	497	501	506	511	516	4	1.6
902	521	525	530	535	540	545	550	554	559	564	5	2.0
903	569	574	578	583	588	593	598	602	607	612	6	2.4
904	617	622	626	631	636	641	646	650	655	660	7	2.8
905	665	670	674	679	684	689	694	698	703	708	8	3.2
											9	3.6
906	713	718	722	727	732	737	742	746	751	756		
907	761	766	770	775	780	785	789	794	799	804		
908	809	813	818	823	828	832	837	842	847	852		
909	856	861	866	871	875	880	885	890	895	899		
910	904	909	914	918	923	928	933	938	942	947		
911	95 952	957	961	966	971	976	980	985	990	995		
912	999	*004	*009	*014	*019	*023	*028	*033	*038	*042		
913	96 047	052	057	061	066	071	076	080	085	090		
914	095	099	104	109	114	118	123	128	133	137		
915	142	147	152	156	161	166	171	175	180	185		
916	190	194	199	204	209	213	218	223	227	232		
917	237	242	246	251	256	261	265	270	275	280		
918	284	289	294	298	303	308	313	317	322	327		
919	332	336	341	346	350	355	360	365	369	374		
920	379	384	388	393	398	402	407	412	417	421		
921	426	431	435	440	445	450	454	459	464	468		
922	473	478	483	487	492	497	501	506	511	515		
923	520	525	530	534	539	544	548	553	558	562		
924	567	572	577	581	586	591	595	600	605	609		
925	614	619	624	628	633	638	642	647	652	656		5
926	661	666	670	675	680	685	689	694	699	703	1	0.5
927	708	713	717	722	727	731	736	741	745	750	2	1.0
928	755	759	764	769	774	778	783	788	792	797	3	1.5
929	802	806	811	816	820	825	830	834	839	844	4	2.0
930	848	853	858	862	867	872	876	881	886	890	5	2.5
											6	3.0
931	895	900	904	909	914	918	923	928	932	937	7	3.5
932	942	946	951	956	960	965	970	974	979	984	8	4.0
933	988	993	997	*002	*007	*011	*016	*021	*025	*030	9	4.5
934	97 035	039	044	049	053	058	063	067	072	077		
935	081	086	090	095	100	104	109	114	118	123		
936	128	132	137	142	146	151	155	160	165	169		
937	174	179	183	188	192	197	202	206	211	216		
938	220	225	230	234	239	243	248	253	257	262		
939	267	271	276	280	285	290	294	299	304	308		
940	313	317	322	327	331	336	340	345	350	354		
941	359	364	368	373	377	382	387	391	396	400		
942	405	410	414	419	424	428	433	437	442	447		
943	451	456	460	465	470	474	479	483	488	493		
944	497	502	506	511	516	520	525	529	534	539		
945	543	548	552	557	562	566	571	575	580	585		
N	0	1	2	3	4	5	6	7	8	9		PP

Table No. 19 continued

COMMON LOGARITHMS
946–995

N	0	1	2	3	4	5	6	7	8	9		PP
946	589	594	598	603	607	612	617	621	626	630		
947	635	640	644	649	653	658	663	667	672	676		
948	681	685	690	695	699	704	708	713	717	722		4
949	727	731	736	740	745	749	754	759	763	768		
950	772	777	782	786	791	795	800	804	809	813	1	0.4
											2	0.8
951	818	823	827	832	836	841	845	850	855	859	3	1.2
952	864	868	873	877	882	886	891	896	900	905	4	1.6
953	909	914	918	923	928	932	937	941	946	950	5	2.0
954	955	959	964	968	973	978	982	987	991	996	6	2.4
955	98 000	005	009	014	019	023	028	032	037	041	7	2.8
											8	3.2
956	046	050	055	059	064	068	073	078	082	087	9	3.6
957	091	096	100	105	109	114	118	123	127	132		
958	137	141	146	150	155	159	164	168	173	177		
959	182	186	191	195	200	204	209	214	218	223		
960	227	232	236	241	245	250	254	259	263	268		
961	272	277	281	286	290	295	299	304	308	313		
962	318	322	327	331	336	340	345	349	354	358		
963	363	367	372	376	381	385	390	394	399	403		
964	408	412	417	421	426	430	435	439	444	448		
965	453	457	462	466	471	475	480	484	489	493		
966	498	502	507	511	516	520	525	529	534	538		
967	543	547	552	556	561	565	570	574	579	583		
968	588	592	597	601	605	610	614	619	623	628		
969	632	637	641	646	650	655	659	664	668	673		
970	677	682	686	691	695	700	704	709	713	717		
971	98 722	726	731	735	740	744	749	753	758	762		5
972	767	771	776	780	784	789	793	798	802	807		
973	811	816	820	825	829	834	838	843	847	851	1	0.5
974	856	860	865	869	874	878	883	887	892	896	2	1.0
975	900	905	909	914	918	923	927	932	936	941	3	1.5
											4	2.0
976	945	949	954	958	963	967	972	976	981	985	5	2.5
977	989	994	998	*003	*007	*012	*016	*021	*025	*029	6	3.0
978	99 034	038	043	047	052	056	061	065	069	074	7	3.5
979	078	083	087	092	096	100	105	109	114	118	8	4.0
980	123	127	131	136	140	145	149	154	158	162	9	4.5
981	167	171	176	180	185	189	193	198	202	207		
982	211	216	220	224	229	233	238	242	247	251		
983	255	260	264	269	273	277	282	286	291	295		
984	300	304	308	313	317	322	326	330	335	339		
985	344	348	352	357	361	366	370	374	379	383		
986	388	392	396	401	405	410	414	419	423	427		
987	432	436	441	445	449	454	458	463	467	471		4
988	476	480	484	489	493	498	502	506	511	515		
989	520	524	528	533	537	542	546	550	555	559	1	0.4
990	564	568	572	577	581	585	590	594	599	603	2	0.8
											3	1.2
991	607	612	616	621	625	629	634	638	642	647	4	1.6
992	651	656	660	664	669	673	677	682	686	691	5	2.0
993	695	699	704	708	712	717	721	726	730	734	6	2.4
994	739	743	747	752	756	760	765	769	774	778	7	2.8
995	782	787	791	795	800	804	808	813	817	822	8	3.2
											9	3.6
N	0	1	2	3	4	5	6	7	8	9		PP

COMMON LOGARITHMS
996–1000

N	0	1	2	3	4	5	6	7	8	9	PP
996	826	830	835	839	843	848	852	856	861	865	
997	870	874	878	883	887	891	896	900	904	909	
998	913	917	922	926	930	935	939	944	948	952	
999	957	961	965	970	974	978	983	987	991	996	
1000	00 000	004	009	013	017	022	026	030	035	039	
N	0	1	2	3	4	5	6	7	8	9	PP

NO. 20   NATURAL LOGARITHMS

EXPLANATION

The table of natural logarithms gives the characteristic and mantissa of the natural logarithm of the number. From N = 1.0 to N = 10.0, and from N = 10 to N = 100, the characteristic and the first digit of the mantissa are not included for all numbers. The appropriate characteristic and first digit from the logarithm in the preceeding "0" column should be used unless an asterisk (*) appears. When an asterisk appears, the characteristic and first digit from the logarithm in the succeeding "0" column should be used. E.g., to find log 1.72, read down column 1 to N = 1.7, then across to the column headed "2". The number 4232 appears. The "0" column preceeding this gives the logarithm 0.53063. Thus, 0.5 should be included in the logarithm of 1.72. Thus, log 1.72 is .54232. To find log 2.22 use 9751 from the table and 0.7 from log 2.10 giving log 2.22 = 0.79751. However, log 2.23 appears as *0200. Thus, uses 0.8 from log 2.30 giving log 2.23 = 0.80200

0.00–2.99

N	0	1	2	3	4	5	6	7	8	9

Subtract 10 from each entry (0.00–0.99)

N	0	1	2	3	4	5	6	7	8	9
0.0		5.395	6.088	6.493	6.781	7.004	7.187	7.341	7.474	7.592
0.1	7.697	7.793	7.880	7.960	8.034	8.103	8.167	8.228	8.285	8.339
0.2	8.391	8.439	8.486	8.530	8.573	8.614	8.653	8.691	8.727	8.762
0.3	8.796	8.829	8.861	8.891	8.921	8.950	8.978	9.006	9.032	9.058
0.4	9.084	9.108	9.132	9.156	9.179	9.201	9.223	9.245	9.266	9.287
0.5	9.307	9.327	9.346	9.365	9.384	9.402	9.420	9.438	9.455	9.472
0.6	9.489	9.506	9.522	9.538	9.554	9.569	9.584	9.600	9.614	9.629
0.7	9.643	9.658	9.671	9.685	9.699	9.712	9.726	9.739	9.752	9.764
0.8	9.777	9.789	9.802	9.814	9.826	9.837	9.849	9.861	9.872	9.883
0.9	9.895	9.906	9.917	9.927	9.938	9.949	9.959	9.970	9.980	9.990
1.0	0.0 0000	0995	1980	2956	3922	4879	5827	6766	7696	8618
1.1	9531	*0436	*1333	*2222	*3130	*3976	*4842	*5700	*6551	*7395
1.2	0.1 8232	9062	9885	*0701	*1511	*2314	*3111	*3902	*4686	*5464
1.3	0.2 6236	7003	7763	8518	9267	*0010	*0748	*1481	*2208	*2930
1.4	0.3 3647	4359	5066	5767	6464	7156	7844	8526	9204	9878
1.5	0.4 0547	1211	1871	2527	3178	3825	4469	5108	5742	6373
1.6	7000	7623	8243	8858	9470	*0078	*0682	*1282	*1879	*2473
1.7	0.5 3063	3649	4232	4812	5389	5962	6531	7098	7661	8222
1.8	8779	9333	9884	*0432	*0977	*1519	*2058	*2594	*3127	*3658
1.9	0.6 4185	4710	5233	5752	6269	6783	7294	7803	8310	8813
2.0	9315	9813	*0310	*0804	*1295	*1784	*2271	*2755	*3237	*3716
2.1	0.7 4194	4669	5142	5612	6081	6547	7011	7473	7932	8390
2.2	8846	9299	9751	*0200	*0648	*1093	*1536	*1978	*2418	*2855
2.3	0.8 3291	3725	4157	4587	5015	5442	5866	6289	6710	7129
2.4	7547	7963	8377	8789	9200	9609	*0016	*0422	*0826	*1228
2.5	0.9 1629	2028	2426	2822	3216	3609	4001	4391	4779	5166
2.6	5551	5935	6317	6698	7078	7456	7833	8208	8582	8954
2.7	9325	9695	*0063	*0430	*0796	*1160	*1523	*1885	*2245	*2604
2.8	1.0 2962	3318	3674	4028	4380	4732	5082	5431	5779	6126
2.9	6471	6815	7185	7500	7841	8181	8519	8856	9192	9527
N	0	1	2	3	4	5	6	7	8	9

Table No. 20 continued

3.00–8.99

N	0	1	2	3	4	5	6	7	8	9
3.0	9861	*0194	*0526	*0856	*1186	*1514	*1841	*2168	*2493	*2817
3.1	1.1 3140	3462	3783	4103	4422	4740	5057	5373	5688	6002
3.2	6315	6627	6938	7248	7557	7865	8173	8479	8784	9089
3.3	9392	9695	9996	*0297	*0597	*0896	*1194	*1491	*1788	*2083
3.4	1.2 2378	2671	2964	3256	3547	3837	4127	4415	4703	4990
3.5	5276	5562	5846	6130	6413	6695	6976	7257	7536	7815
3.6	8093	8371	8647	8923	9198	9473	9746	*0019	*0291	*0563
3.7	1.3 0833	1103	1372	1641	1909	2176	2442	2708	2972	3237
3.8	3500	3763	4025	4286	4547	4807	5067	5325	5584	5841
3.9	6098	6354	6609	6864	7118	7372	7624	7877	8128	8379
4.0	8629	8879	9128	9377	9624	9872	*0118	*0364	*0610	*0854
4.1	1.4 1099	1342	1585	1828	2070	2311	2552	2792	3031	3270
4.2	3508	3746	3984	4220	4456	4692	4927	5161	5395	5629
4.3	5862	6094	6326	6557	6787	7018	7247	7476	7705	7933
4.4	8160	8387	8614	8840	9065	9290	9515	9739	9962	*0185
4.5	1.5 0408	0630	0851	1072	1293	1513	1732	1951	2170	2388
4.6	2606	2823	3039	3256	3471	3687	3902	4116	4330	4543
4.7	4756	4969	5181	5393	5604	5814	6025	6235	6444	6653
4.8	6862	7070	7277	7485	7691	7898	8104	8309	8515	8719
4.9	8924	9127	9331	9534	9737	9939	*0141	*0342	*0543	*0744
5.0	1.6 0944	1144	1343	1542	1741	1939	2137	2334	2531	2728
5.1	2924	3120	3315	3511	3705	3900	4094	4287	4481	4673
5.2	4866	5058	5250	5441	5632	5823	6013	6203	6393	6582
5.3	6771	6959	7147	7335	7523	7710	7896	8083	8269	8455
5.4	8640	8825	9010	9194	9378	9562	9745	9928	*0111	*0293
5.5	1.7 0475	0656	0838	1019	1199	1380	1560	1740	1919	2098
5.6	2277	2455	2633	2811	2988	3166	3342	3519	3695	3871
5.7	4047	4222	4397	4572	4746	4920	5094	5267	5440	5613
5.8	5786	5958	6130	6302	6473	6644	6815	6985	7156	7326
5.9	7495	7665	7834	8002	8171	8339	8507	8675	8842	9009
6.0	1.7 9176	9342	9509	9675	9840	*0006	*0171	*0336	*0500	*0665
6.1	1.8 0829	0993	1156	1319	1482	1645	1808	1970	2131	2294
6.2	2455	2616	2777	2938	3098	3258	3418	3578	3737	3896
6.3	4055	4214	4372	4530	4688	4845	5003	5160	5317	5473
6.4	5630	5786	5942	6097	6253	6408	6563	6718	6872	7026
6.5	7180	7334	7487	7641	7794	7947	8099	8251	8403	8555
6.6	8707	8858	9010	9160	9311	9462	9612	9762	9912	*0061
6.7	1.9 0211	0360	0509	0658	0806	0954	1102	1250	1398	1545
6.8	1692	1839	1986	2132	2279	2425	2571	2716	2862	3007
6.9	3152	3297	3442	3586	3730	3874	4018	4162	4305	4448
7.0	4591	4734	4876	5019	5161	5303	5445	5586	5727	5869
7.1	6009	6150	6291	6431	6571	6711	6851	6991	7130	7269
7.2	7408	7547	7685	7824	7962	8100	8238	8376	8513	8650
7.3	8787	8924	9061	9198	9334	9470	9606	9742	9877	*0013
7.4	2.0 0148	0283	0418	0553	0687	0821	0956	1089	1223	1357
7.5	1490	1624	1757	1890	2022	2155	2287	2419	2551	2683
7.6	2815	2946	3078	3209	3340	3471	3601	3732	3862	3992
7.7	4122	4252	4381	4511	4640	4769	4898	5027	5156	5284
7.8	5412	5540	5668	5796	5924	6051	6179	6306	6433	6560
7.9	6686	6813	6939	7065	7191	7317	7443	7568	7694	7819
8.0	7944	8069	8194	8318	8443	8567	8691	8815	8939	9063
8.1	9186	9310	9433	9556	9679	9802	9924	*0047	*0169	*0291
8.2	2.1 0413	0535	0657	0779	0900	1021	1142	1263	1384	1505
8.3	1626	1746	1866	1986	2106	2226	2346	2465	2585	2704
8.4	2823	2942	3061	3180	3298	3417	3535	3653	3771	3889
8.5	4007	4124	4242	4359	4476	4593	4710	4827	4943	5060
8.6	5176	5292	5409	5524	5640	5756	5871	5987	6102	6217
8.7	6332	6447	6562	6677	6791	6905	7020	7134	7248	7361
8.8	7475	7589	7702	7816	7929	8042	8155	8267	8380	8493
8.9	8605	8717	8830	8942	9054	9165	9277	9389	9500	9611
N	0	1	2	3	4	5	6	7	8	9

9.00–10.09

N	0	1	2	3	4	5	6	7	8	9
9.0	9722	9834	9944	*0055	*0166	*0276	*0387	*0497	*0607	*0717
9.1	2.2 0827	0937	1047	1157	1266	1375	1485	1594	1703	1812
9.2	1920	2029	2138	2246	2354	2462	2570	2678	2786	2894
9.3	3001	3109	3216	3324	3431	3538	3645	3751	3858	3965
9.4	4071	4177	4284	4390	4496	4601	4707	4813	4918	5024
9.5	5129	5234	5339	5444	5549	5654	5759	5863	5968	6072
9.6	6176	6280	6384	6488	6592	6696	6799	6903	7006	7109
9.7	7213	7316	7419	7521	7624	7727	7829	7932	8034	8136
9.8	8238	8340	8442	8544	8646	8747	8849	8950	9051	9152
9.9	9253	9354	9455	9556	9657	9757	9858	9958	*0058	*0158
10.0	2.3 0259	0358	0458	0558	0658	0757	0857	0956	1055	1154

10–99

N	0	1	2	3	4	5	6	7	8	9
1	2.30259	39790	48491	56495	63906	70805	77259	83321	89037	94444
2	99573	*04452	*09104	*13549	*17805	*21888	*25810	*29584	*33220	*36730
3	3.40120	43309	46579	49651	52636	55535	58352	61092	63759	66356
4	68888	71357	73767	76120	78419	80666	82864	85015	87120	89182
5	91202	93183	95124	97029	98898	*00733	*02535	*04305	*06044	*07754
6	4.09434	11087	12713	14313	15888	17439	18965	20469	21951	23411
7	24850	26268	27667	29046	30407	31749	33073	34381	35671	36945
8	38203	39445	40672	41884	43082	44265	45435	46591	47734	48864
9	49981	51086	52179	53260	54329	55388	56435	57471	58497	59512

100–149

N	0	1	2	3	4	5	6	7	8	9
10	4.6 0517	1512	2497	3473	4439	5396	6344	7283	8213	9135
11	4.7 0048	0953	1850	2739	3620	4493	5359	6217	7068	7912
12	8749	9579	*0402	*1218	*2028	*2831	*3628	*4419	*5203	*5981
13	4.8 6753	7520	8280	9035	9784	*0572	*1265	*1998	*2725	*3447
14	4.9 4164	4876	5583	6284	6981	7673	8361	9043	9721	*0395

150–349

N	0	1	2	3	4	5	6	7	8	9
15	5.0 1064	1728	2388	3044	3695	4343	4986	5625	6260	6890
16	7517	8140	8760	9375	9987	*0595	*1199	*1799	*2396	*2990
17	5.1 3580	4166	4749	5329	5906	6479	7048	7615	8178	8739
18	9296	9850	*0401	*0949	*1494	*2036	*2575	*3111	*3644	*4175
19	5.2 4702	5227	5750	6269	6786	7300	7811	8320	8827	9330
20	9832	*0330	*0827	*1321	*1812	*2301	*2788	*3272	*3754	*4233
21	5.3 4711	5186	5659	6129	6598	7064	7528	7990	8450	8907
22	9363	9816	*0268	*0717	*1165	*1610	*2053	*2495	*2935	*3372
23	5.4 3808	4242	4674	5104	5532	5959	6383	6806	7227	7646
24	8064	8480	8894	9306	9717	*0126	*0533	*0939	*1343	*1745
25	5.5 2146	2545	2943	3339	3733	4126	4518	4908	5296	5683
26	6068	6452	6834	7215	7595	7973	8350	8725	9099	9471
27	9842	*0212	*0580	*0947	*1313	*1677	*2040	*2402	*2762	*3121
28	5.6 3479	3835	4191	4545	4897	5249	5599	5948	6296	6643
29	6988	7332	7675	8017	8358	8698	9036	9373	9709	*0044
30	5.7 0378	0711	1043	1373	1703	2031	2359	2685	3010	3334
31	3657	3979	4300	4620	4939	5257	5574	5890	6205	6519
32	6832	7144	7455	7765	8074	8383	8690	8996	9301	9606
33	9909	*0212	*0513	*0814	*1114	*1413	*1711	*2008	*2305	*2600
34	5.8 2895	3188	3481	3773	4064	4354	4644	4932	5220	5507

N	0	1	2	3	4	5	6	7	8	9

Table No. 20 continued

350–949

N	0	1	2	3	4	5	6	7	8	9
35	5793	6079	6363	6647	6930	7212	7493	7774	8053	8332
36	8610	8888	9164	9440	9715	9990	*0263	*0536	*0808	*1080
37	5.9 1350	1620	1889	2158	2426	2693	2959	3225	3489	3754
38	4017	4280	4542	4803	5064	5324	5584	5842	6101	6358
39	6615	6871	7126	7381	7635	7889	8141	8394	8645	8896
40	9146	9396	9645	9894	*0141	*0389	*0635	*0881	*1127	*1372
41	6.0 1616	1859	2102	2345	2587	2828	3069	3309	3548	3787
42	4025	4263	4501	4737	4973	5209	5444	5678	5912	6146
43	6379	6611	6843	7074	7304	7535	7764	7993	8222	8450
44	8677	8904	9131	9357	9582	9807	*0032	*0256	*0479	*0702
45	6.1 0925	1147	1368	1589	1810	2030	2249	2468	2687	2905
46	3123	3340	3556	3773	3988	4204	4419	4633	4847	5060
47	5273	5486	5698	5910	6121	6331	6542	6752	6961	7170
48	7379	7587	7794	8002	8208	8415	8621	8826	9032	9236
49	9441	9644	9848	*0051	*0254	*0456	*0658	*0859	*1060	*1261
50	6.2 1461	1661	1860	2059	2258	2456	2654	2851	3048	3245
51	3441	3637	3832	4028	4222	4417	4611	4804	4998	5190
52	5383	5575	5767	5958	6149	6340	6530	6720	6910	7099
53	7288	7476	7664	7852	8040	8227	8413	8600	8786	8972
54	9157	9342	9527	9711	9895	*0079	*0262	*0445	*0628	*0810
55	6.3 0992	1173	1355	1536	1716	1897	2077	2257	2436	2615
56	2794	2972	3150	3328	3505	3683	3859	4036	4212	4388
57	4564	4739	4914	5089	5263	5437	5611	5784	5957	6130
58	6303	6475	6647	6819	6990	7161	7332	7502	7673	7843
59	8012	8182	8351	8519	8688	8856	9024	9192	9359	9526
60	6.3 9693	9859	*0026	*0192	*0357	*0523	*0688	*0853	*1017	*1182
61	6.4 1346	1510	1673	1836	1999	2162	2325	2487	2649	2811
62	2972	3133	3294	3455	3615	3775	3935	4095	4254	4413
63	4572	4731	4889	5047	5205	5362	5520	5677	5834	5990
64	6147	6303	6459	6614	6770	6925	7080	7235	7389	7543
65	7697	7851	8004	8158	8311	8464	8616	8768	8920	9072
66	9224	9375	9427	9677	9828	9979	*0129	*0279	*0429	*0578
67	6.5 0728	0877	1026	1175	1323	1471	1619	1767	1915	2062
68	2209	2356	2503	2649	2796	2942	3088	3233	3379	3524
69	3669	3814	3959	4103	4247	4391	4535	4679	4822	4965
70	5108	5251	5393	5536	5678	5820	5962	6103	6244	6386
71	6526	6667	6808	6948	7088	7228	7368	7508	7647	7786
72	7925	8064	8203	8341	8479	8617	8755	8893	9030	9167
73	9304	9441	9578	9715	9851	9987	*0123	*0259	*0394	*0530
74	6.6 0665	0800	0935	1070	1204	1338	1473	1607	1740	1874
75	2007	2141	2274	2407	2539	2672	2804	2936	3068	3200
76	3332	3463	3595	3726	3857	3988	4118	4249	4379	4509
77	4639	4769	4898	5028	5157	5286	5415	5544	5673	5801
78	5929	6058	6185	6313	6441	6568	6696	6823	6950	7077
79	7203	7330	7456	7582	7708	7834	7960	8085	8211	8336
80	8461	8586	8711	8835	8960	9084	9208	9332	9456	9580
81	9703	9827	9950	*0073	*0196	*0319	*0441	*0564	*0686	*0808
82	6.7 0930	1052	1174	1296	1417	1538	1659	1780	1901	2022
83	2143	2263	2383	2503	2623	2743	2863	2982	3102	3221
84	3340	3459	3578	3697	3815	3934	4052	4170	4288	4406
85	4524	4641	4759	4876	4993	5110	5227	5344	5460	5577
86	5693	5809	5926	6041	6157	6273	6388	6504	6619	6734
87	6849	6964	7079	7194	7308	7422	7537	7651	7765	7878
88	7992	8106	8219	8333	8446	8559	8672	8784	8897	9010
89	9122	9234	9347	9459	9571	9682	9794	9906	*0017	*0128
90	6.8 0239	0351	0461	0572	0683	0793	0904	1014	1124	1235
91	1344	1454	1564	1674	1783	1892	2002	2111	2220	2329
92	2437	2546	2655	2763	2871	2979	3087	3195	3303	3411
93	3518	3626	3733	3841	3948	4055	4162	4268	4375	4482
94	4588	4694	4801	4907	5013	5118	5224	5330	5435	5541
N	0	1	2	3	4	5	6	7	8	9

950–1099

N	0	1	2	3	4	5	6	7	8	9
95	5646	5751	5857	5961	6066	6171	6276	6380	6485	6589
96	6693	6797	6901	7005	7109	7213	7316	7420	7523	7626
97	7730	7833	7936	8038	8141	8244	8346	8449	8551	8653
98	8755	8857	8959	9061	9163	9264	9366	9467	9568	9669
99	9770	9871	9972	*0073	*0174	*0274	*0375	*0475	*0575	*0675
100	6.9 0776	0875	0975	1075	1175	1274	1374	1473	1572	1672
101	1771	1870	1968	2067	2166	2264	2363	2461	2560	2658
102	2756	2854	2952	3049	3147	3245	3342	3440	3537	3634
103	3731	3828	3925	4022	4119	4216	4312	4409	4505	4601
104	4698	4794	4890	4986	5081	5177	5273	5368	5464	5559
105	5655	5750	5845	5940	6035	6130	6224	6319	6414	6508
106	6602	6697	6791	6885	6979	7073	7167	7261	7354	7448
107	7541	7635	7728	7821	7915	8008	8101	8193	8286	8379
108	8472	8564	8657	8749	8841	8934	9026	9118	9210	9302
109	9393	9485	9577	9668	9760	9851	9942	*0033	*0125	*0216
N	0	1	2	3	4	5	6	7	8	9

NO. 21 VALUES AND COMMON LOGARITHMS OF EXPONENTIAL AND HYPERBOLIC FUNCTIONS

0.00–0.34

x	e^x	e^{-x}	$\log(e^x)$	sinh x	cosh x	tanh x	coth x	log sinh x	log cosh x	log tanh x	log coth x
0.00	1.0000	1.00000	.00000	0.00000	1.00000	0.00000	∞	− ∞	.00000	− ∞	∞
0.01	1.0101	0.99005	.00434	.01000	1.00005	.01000	100.003	.00001	.00002	.99999	.00001
0.02	1.0202	.98020	.00869	.02000	1.00020	.02000	50.007	.30106	.00009	.30097	.69903
0.03	1.0305	.97045	.01303	.03000	1.00045	.02999	33.343	.47719	.00020	.47699	.52301
0.04	1.0408	.96079	.01737	.04001	1.00080	.03998	25.013	.60218	.00035	.60183	.39817
0.05	1.0513	0.95123	.02171	0.05002	1.00125	0.04996	20.017	.69915	.00054	.69861	.30139
0.06	1.0618	.94177	.02606	.06004	1.00180	.05993	16.687	.77841	.00078	.77763	.22237
0.07	1.0725	.93239	.03040	.07006	1.00245	.06989	14.309	.84545	.00106	.84439	.15561
0.08	1.0833	.92312	.03474	.08009	1.00320	.07983	12.527	.90355	.00139	.90216	.09784
0.09	1.0942	.91393	.03909	.09012	1.00405	.08976	11.141	.95483	.00176	.95307	.04693
0.10	1.1052	0.90484	.04343	0.10017	1.00500	0.09967	10.0333	.00072	.00217	.99856	.00144
0.11	1.1163	.89583	04777	.11022	1.00606	.10956	9.1275	.04227	.00262	.03965	.96035
0.12	1.1275	.88692	.05212	.12029	1.00721	.11943	8.3733	.08022	.00312	.07710	.92290
0.13	1.1388	.87810	.05646	.13037	1.00846	.12927	7.7356	.11517	.00366	.11151	.88849
0.14	1.1503	.86936	.06080	.14046	1.00982	.13909	7.1895	.14755	.00424	.14330	.85670
0.15	1.1618	0.86071	.06514	0.15056	1.01127	0.14889	6.7166	.17772	.00487	.17285	.82715
0.16	1.1735	.85214	.06949	.16068	1.01283	.15865	6.3032	.20597	.00554	.20044	.79956
0.17	1.1853	.84367	.07383	.17082	1.01448	.16838	5.9389	.23254	.00625	.22629	.77371
0.18	1.1972	.83527	.07817	.18097	1.01624	.17808	5.6154	.25762	.00700	.25062	.74938
0.19	1.2092	.82696	.08252	.19115	1.01810	.18775	5.3263	.28136	.00779	.27357	.72643
0.20	1.2214	0.81873	.08686	0.20134	1.02007	0.19738	5.0665	.30392	.00863	.29529	.70471
0.21	1.2337	.81058	.09120	.21155	1.02213	.20697	4.8317	.32541	.00951	.31590	.68410
0.22	1.2461	.80252	.09554	.22178	1.02430	.21652	4.6186	.34592	.01043	.33549	.66451
0.23	1.2586	.79453	.09989	.23203	1.02657	.22603	4.4242	.36555	.01139	.35416	.64584
0.24	1.2712	.78663	.10423	.24231	1.02894	.23550	4.2464	.38437	.01239	.37198	.62802
0.25	1.2840	0.77880	.10857	0.25261	1.03141	0.24492	4.0830	.40245	.01343	.38902	.61098
0.26	1.2969	.77105	.11292	.26294	1.03399	.25430	3.9324	.41986	.01452	.40534	.59466
0.27	1.3100	.76338	.11726	.27329	1.03667	.26362	3.7933	.43663	.01564	.42099	.57901
0.28	1.3231	.75578	.12160	.28367	1.03946	.27291	3.6643	.45282	.01681	.43601	.56399
0.29	1.3364	.74826	.12595	.29408	1.04235	.28213	3.5444	.46847	.01801	.45046	.54954
0.30	1.3499	0.74082	.13029	0.30452	1.04534	0.29131	3.4327	.48362	.01926	.46436	.53564
0.31	1.3634	.73345	.13463	.31499	1.04844	.30044	3.3285	.49830	.02054	.47775	.52225
0.32	1.3771	.72615	.13897	.32549	1.05164	.30951	3.2309	.51254	.02187	.49067	.50933
0.33	1.3910	.71892	.14332	.33602	1.05495	.31852	3.1395	.52637	.02323	.50314	.49686
0.34	1.4049	.71177	.14766	.34659	1.05836	.32748	3.0536	.53981	.02463	.51518	.48482

Table No. 21 continued

0.35–0.94

x	e^x	e^{-x}	$\log(e^x)$	$\sinh x$	$\cosh x$	$\tanh x$	$\coth x$	log $\sinh x$	log $\cosh x$	log $\tanh x$	log $\coth x$
0.35	1.4191	0.70469	.15200	0.35719	1.06188	0.33638	2.9729	.55290	.02607	.52682	.47318
0.36	1.4333	.69767	.15635	.36783	1.06550	.34521	2.8968	.56564	.02755	.53809	.46191
0.37	1.4477	.69073	.16069	.37850	1.06923	.35399	2.8249	.57807	.02907	.54899	.45101
0.38	1.4523	.68386	.16503	.38921	1.07307	.36271	2.7570	.59019	.03063	.55956	.44044
0.39	1.4770	.67706	.16937	.39996	1.07702	.37136	2.6928	.60202	.03222	.56980	.43020
0.40	1.4918	0.67032	.17372	0.41075	1.08107	0.37995	2.6319	.61358	.03385	.57973	.42027
0.41	1.5068	.66365	.17806	.42158	1.08523	.38847	2.5742	.62488	.03552	.58936	.41064
0.42	1.5220	.65705	.18240	.43246	1.08950	.39693	2.5193	.63594	.03723	.59871	.40120
0.43	1.5373	.65051	.18675	.44337	1.09388	.40532	2.4672	.64677	.03897	.60780	.39229
0.44	1.5527	.64404	.19109	.45434	1.09837	.41364	2.4175	.65738	.04075	.61663	.38337
0.45	1.5683	0.63763	.19543	0.46534	1.10297	0.42190	2.3702	.66777	.04256	.62521	.37479
0.46	1.5841	.63128	.19978	.47640	1.10768	.43008	2.3251	.67797	.04441	.63355	.36645
0.47	1.6000	.62500	.20412	.48750	1.11250	.43820	2.2821	.68797	.04630	.64167	.35833
0.48	1.6161	.61878	.20846	.49865	1.11743	.44624	2.2409	.69779	.04822	.64957	.35043
0.49	1.6323	.61263	.21280	.50984	1.12247	.45422	2.2016	.70744	.05018	.65726	.34274
0.50	1.6487	0.60653	.21715	0.52110	1.12763	0.46212	2.1640	.71692	.05217	.66475	.33525
0.51	1.6653	.60050	.22149	.53240	1.13289	.46995	2.1279	.72624	.05419	.67205	.32795
0.52	1.6820	.59452	.22583	.54375	1.13827	.47770	2.0934	.73540	.05625	.67916	.32084
0.53	1.6989	.58861	.23018	.55516	1.14377	.48538	2.0602	.74442	.05834	.68608	.31392
0.54	1.7160	.58275	.23452	.56663	1.14938	.49299	2.0284	.75330	.06046	.69284	.30716
0.55	1.7333	0.57695	.23886	0.57815	1.15510	0.50052	1.9979	.76204	.06262	.69942	.30058
0.56	1.7507	.57121	.24320	.58973	1.16094	.50798	1.9686	.77065	.06481	.70584	.29416
0.57	1.7683	.56553	.24755	.60137	1.16690	.51536	1.9404	.77914	.06703	.71211	.28789
0.58	1.7860	.55990	.25189	.61307	1.17297	.52267	1.9133	.78751	.06929	.71822	.28178
0.59	1.8040	.55433	.25623	.62483	1.17916	.52990	1.8872	.79576	.07157	.72419	.27581
0.60	1.8221	0.54881	.26058	0.63665	1.18547	0.53705	1.8620	.80390	.07389	.73001	.26999
0.61	1.8404	.54335	.26492	.64854	1.19189	.54413	1.8378	.81194	.07624	.73570	.26430
0.62	1.8589	.53794	.26926	.66049	1.19844	.55113	1.8145	.81987	.07861	.74125	.25875
0.63	1.8776	.53259	.27361	.67251	1.20510	.55805	1.7919	.82770	.08102	.74667	.25333
0.64	1.8965	.52729	.27795	.68459	1.21189	.56490	1.7702	.83543	.08346	.75197	.24803
0.65	1.9155	0.52205	.28229	0.69675	1.21879	0.57167	1.7493	.84308	.08593	.75715	.24285
0.66	1.9348	.51685	.28663	.70897	1.22582	.57836	1.7290	.85063	.08843	.76220	.23780
0.67	1.9542	.51171	.29098	.72126	1.23297	.58498	1.7095	.85809	.09095	.76714	.23286
0.68	1.9739	.50662	.29532	.73363	1.24025	.59152	1.6906	.86548	.09351	.77197	.22803
0.69	1.9937	.50158	.29966	.74607	1.24765	.59798	1.6723	.87278	.09609	.77669	.22331
0.70	2.0138	0.49659	.30401	0.75858	1.25517	0.60437	1.6546	.88000	.09870	.78130	.21870
0.71	2.0340	.49164	.30835	.77117	1.26282	.61068	1.6375	.88715	.10134	.78581	.21419
0.72	2.0544	.48675	.31269	.78384	1.27059	.61691	1.6210	.89423	.10401	.79022	.20978
0.73	2.0751	.48191	.31703	.79659	1.27849	.62307	1.6050	.90123	.10670	.79453	.20547
0.74	2.0959	.47711	.32138	.80941	1.28652	.62915	1.5895	.90817	.10942	.79875	.20125
0.75	2.1170	0.47237	.32572	0.82232	1.29468	0.63515	1.5744	.91504	.11216	.80288	.19712
0.76	2.2383	.46767	.33006	.83530	1.30297	.64108	1.5599	.92185	.11493	.80691	.19309
0.77	2.1598	.46301	.33441	.84838	1.31139	.64693	1.5458	.92859	.11773	.81086	.18914
0.78	2.1815	.45841	.33875	.86153	1.31994	.65271	1.5321	.93527	.12055	.81472	.18528
0.79	2.2034	.45385	.34309	.87478	1.32862	.65841	1.5188	.94190	.12340	.81850	.18150
0.80	2.2255	0.44933	.34744	0.88811	1.33743	0.66404	1.5059	.94846	.12627	.82219	.17781
0.81	2.2479	.44486	.35178	.90152	1.34638	.66959	1.4935	.95498	.12917	.82581	.17419
0.82	2.2705	.44043	.35612	.91503	1.35547	.67507	1.4813	.96144	.13209	.82935	.17065
0.83	2.2933	.43605	.36046	.92863	1.36468	.68048	1.4696	.96784	.13503	.83281	.16719
0.84	2.3164	.43171	.36481	.94233	1.37404	.68581	1.4581	.97420	.13800	.83620	.16380
0.85	2.3396	0.42742	.36915	0.95612	1.38353	0.69107	1.4470	.98051	.14099	.83952	.16048
0.86	2.3632	.42316	.37349	.97000	1.39316	.69626	1.4362	.98677	.14400	.84277	.15723
0.87	2.3869	.41895	.37784	.98398	1.40293	.70137	1.4258	.99299	.14704	.84595	.15405
0.88	2.4109	.41478	.38218	.99806	1.41284	.70642	1.4156	.99916	.15009	.84906	.15094
0.89	2.4351	.41066	.38652	1.01224	1.42289	.71139	1.4057	.00528	.15317	.85211	.14789
0.90	2.4596	0.40657	.39087	1.02652	1.43309	0.71630	1.3961	.01137	.15627	.85509	.14491
0.91	2.4843	.40252	.39521	1.04090	1.44342	.72113	1.3867	.01741	.15939	.85801	.14199
0.92	2.5093	.39852	.39955	1.05539	1.45390	.72590	1.3776	.02341	.16254	.86088	.13912
0.93	2.5345	.39455	.40389	1.06998	1.46453	.73059	1.3687	.02937	.16570	.86368	.13632
0.94	2.5600	.39063	.40824	1.08468	1.47530	.73522	1.3601	.03530	.16888	.86642	.13358
x	e^x	e^{-x}	$\log(e^x)$	$\sinh x$	$\cosh x$	$\tanh x$	$\coth x$	log $\sinh x$	log $\cosh x$	log $\tanh x$	log $\coth x$

0.95–1.54

x	e^x	e^{-x}	$\log(e^x)$	sinh x	cosh x	tanh x	coth x	log sinh x	log cosh x	log tanh x	log coth x
0.95	2.5857	0.38674	.41258	1.09948	1.48623	0.73978	1.3517	.04119	.17208	.86910	.13090
0.96	2.6117	.38289	.41692	1.11440	1.49729	.74428	1.3436	.04704	.17531	.87173	.12827
0.97	2.6379	.37908	.42127	1.12943	1.50851	.74870	1.3356	.05286	.17855	.87431	.12569
0.98	2.6645	.37531	.42561	1.14457	1.51988	.75307	1.3279	.05864	.18181	.87683	.12317
0.99	2.6912	.37158	.42995	1.15983	1.53141	.75736	1.3204	.06439	.18509	.87930	.12070
1.00	2.7183	0.36788	.43429	1.17520	1.54308	0.76159	1.3130	.07011	.18889	.88172	.11828
1.01	2.7456	.36422	.43864	1.19069	1.55491	.76576	1.3056	.07580	.19171	.88409	.11591
1.02	2.7732	.36060	.44298	1.20630	1.56689	.76987	1.2989	.08146	.19504	.88642	.11358
1.03	2.8011	.35701	.44732	1.22203	1.57904	.77391	1.2921	.08708	.19839	.88869	.11131
1.04	2.8292	.35346	.45167	1.23788	1.59134	.77789	1.2855	.09268	.20176	.89092	.10908
1.05	2.8577	0.34994	.45601	1.25386	1.60379	0.78181	1.2791	.09825	.20515	.89310	.10690
1.06	2.8864	.34646	.46035	1.26996	1.61641	.78566	1.2728	.10379	.20855	.89524	.10476
1.07	2.9154	.34301	.46470	1.28619	1.62919	.78946	1.2667	.10930	.21197	.89733	.10267
1.08	2.9447	.33960	.46904	1.30254	1.64214	.79320	1.2607	.11479	.21541	.89938	.10062
1.09	2.9743	.33622	.47338	1.31903	1.65525	.79688	1.2549	.12025	.21886	.90139	.09861
1.10	3.0042	0.33287	.47772	1.33565	1.66852	0.80050	1.2492	.12569	.22233	.90336	.09664
1.11	3.0344	.32956	.48207	1.35240	1.68196	.80406	1.2437	.13111	.22582	.90529	.09471
1.12	3.0649	.32628	.48641	1.36929	1.69557	.80757	1.2383	.13649	.22931	.90718	.09282
1.13	3.0957	.32303	.49075	1.38631	1.70934	.81102	1.2330	.14186	.23283	.90903	.09097
1.14	3.1268	.31982	.49510	1.40347	1.72329	.81441	1.2279	.14720	.23636	.91085	.08915
1.15	3.1582	0.31664	.49944	1.42078	1.73741	0.81775	1.2229	.15253	.23990	.91262	.08738
1.16	3.1899	.31349	.50378	1.43822	1.75171	.82104	1.2180	.15783	.24346	.91436	.08564
1.17	3.2220	.31037	.50812	1.45581	1.76618	.82427	1.2132	.16311	.24703	.91607	.08393
1.18	3.2544	.30728	.51247	1.47355	1.78083	.82745	1.2085	.16836	.25062	.91774	.08226
1.19	3.2871	.30422	.51681	1.49143	1.79565	.83058	1.2040	.17360	.25422	.91938	.08062
1.20	3.3201	0.30119	.52115	1.50946	1.81066	0.83365	1.1995	.17882	.25784	.92099	.07901
1.21	3.3535	.29820	.52550	1.52764	1.82584	.83668	1.1952	.18402	.26146	.92256	.07744
1.22	3.3872	.29523	.52984	1.54598	1.84121	.83965	1.1910	.18920	.26510	.92410	.07590
1.23	3.4212	.29229	.53418	1.56447	1.85676	.84258	1.1868	.19437	.26876	.92561	.07439
1.24	3.4556	.28938	.53853	1.58311	1.87250	.84546	1.1828	.19951	.27242	.92709	.07291
1.25	3.4903	0.28651	.54287	1.60192	1.88842	0.84828	1.1789	.20464	.27610	.92854	.07146
1.26	3.5254	.28365	.54721	1.62088	1.90454	.85106	1.1750	.20975	.27979	.92996	.07004
1.27	3.5609	.28083	.55155	1.64001	1.92084	.85380	1.1712	.21485	.28349	.93135	.06865
1.28	3.5966	.27804	.55590	1.65930	1.93734	.85648	1.1676	.21993	.28721	.93272	.06728
1.29	3.6328	.27527	.56024	1.67876	1.95403	.85913	1.1640	.22499	.29093	.93406	.06594
1.30	3.6693	0.27253	.56458	1.69838	1.97091	0.86172	1.1605	.23004	.29467	.93537	.06463
1.31	3.7062	.26982	.56893	1.71818	1.98800	.86428	1.1570	.23507	.29842	.93665	.06335
1.32	3.7434	.26714	.57327	1.73814	2.00528	.86678	1.1537	.24009	.30217	.93791	.06209
1.33	3.7810	.26448	.57761	1.75828	2.02276	.86925	1.1504	.24509	.30594	.93914	.06086
1.34	3.8190	.26185	.58195	1.77860	2.04044	.87167	1.1472	.25008	.30972	.94035	.05965
1.35	3.8574	0.25924	.58630	1.79909	2.05833	0.87405	1.1441	.25505	.31352	.94154	.05846
1.36	3.8962	.25666	.59064	1.81977	2.07643	.87639	1.1410	.26002	.31732	.94270	.05730
1.37	3.9354	.25411	.59498	1.84062	2.09473	.87869	1.1381	.26496	.32113	.94384	.05616
1.38	3.9749	.25158	.59933	1.86166	2.11324	.88095	1.1351	.26990	.32495	.94495	.05505
1.39	4.0149	.24908	.60367	1.88289	2.13196	.88317	1.1323	.27482	.32878	.94604	.05396
1.40	4.0552	0.24660	.60801	1.90430	2.15090	0.88535	1.1295	.27974	.33262	.94712	.05288
1.41	4.0960	.24414	.61236	1.92591	2.17005	.88749	1.1268	.28464	.33647	.94817	.05183
1.42	4.1371	.24171	.61670	1.94770	2.18942	.88960	1.1241	.28952	.34033	.94919	.05081
1.43	4.1787	.23931	.62104	1.96970	2.20900	.89167	1.1215	.29440	.34420	.95020	.04980
1.44	4.2207	.23693	.62538	1.99188	2.22881	.89370	1.1189	.29926	.34807	.95119	.04881
1.45	4.2631	0.23457	.62973	2.01427	2.24884	0.89569	1.1165	.30412	.35196	.95216	.04784
1.46	4.3060	.23224	.63407	2.03686	2.26910	.89765	1.1140	.30896	.35585	.95311	.04689
1.47	4.3492	.22993	.63841	2.05965	2.28058	.89958	1.1116	.31379	.35976	.95404	.04596
1.48	4.3929	.22764	.64276	2.08265	2.31029	.90147	1.1093	.31862	.36367	.95495	.04505
1.49	4.4371	.22537	.64710	2.10586	2.33123	.90332	1.1070	.32343	.36759	.95584	.04416
1.50	4.4817	0.22313	.65144	2.12928	2.35241	0.90515	1.1048	.32823	.37151	.95672	.04328
1.51	4.5267	.22091	.65578	2.15291	2.37382	.90694	1.1026	.33303	.37545	.95758	.04242
1.52	4.5722	.21871	.66013	2.17676	2.39547	.90870	1.1005	.33781	.37939	.95842	.04158
1.53	4.6182	.21654	.66447	2.20082	2.41736	.91042	1.0984	.34258	.38334	.95924	.04076
1.54	4.6646	.21438	.66881	2.22510	2.43949	.91212	1.0963	.34735	.38730	.96005	.03995
x	e^x	e^{-x}	$\log(e^x)$	sinh x	cosh x	tanh x	coth x	log sinh x	log cosh x	log tanh x	log coth x

Table No. 21 continued

1.55–2.14

x	e^x	e^{-x}	$\log(e^x)$	$\sinh x$	$\cosh x$	$\tanh x$	$\coth x$	log $\sinh x$	log $\cosh x$	log $\tanh x$	log $\coth x$
1.55	4.7115	0.21225	.67316	2.24961	2.46186	0.91379	1.0943	.35211	.39126	.96084	.03916
1.56	4.7588	.21014	.67750	2.27434	2.48448	.91542	1.0924	.35686	.39524	.96162	.03838
1.57	4.8066	.20805	.68184	2.29930	2.50735	.91703	1.0905	.36160	.39921	.96238	.03762
1.58	4.8550	.20598	.68619	2.32449	2.53047	.91860	1.0886	.36633	.40320	.96313	.03687
1.59	4.9037	.20393	.69053	2.34991	2.55384	.92015	1.0868	.37105	.40719	.96386	.03614
1.60	4.9530	0.20190	.69487	2.37557	2.57746	0.92167	1.0850	.37577	.41119	.96457	.03543
1.61	5.0028	.19989	.69921	2.40146	2.60135	.92316	1.0832	.38048	.41520	.96528	.03472
1.62	5.0531	.19790	.70356	2.42760	2.62549	.92462	1.0815	.38518	.41921	.96597	.03403
1.63	5.1039	.19593	.70790	2.45397	2.64990	.92606	1.0798	.38987	.42323	.96664	.03336
1.64	5.1552	.19398	.71224	2.48059	2.67457	.92747	1.0782	.39456	.42725	.96730	.03270
1.65	5.2070	0.19205	.71659	2.50746	2.69951	0.92886	1.0766	.39923	.43129	.96795	.03205
1.66	5.2593	.19014	.72093	2.53459	2.72472	.93022	1.0750	.40391	.43532	.96858	.03142
1.67	5.3122	.18825	.72527	2.56196	2.75021	.93155	1.0735	.40857	.43937	.96921	.03079
1.68	5.3656	.18637	.72961	2.58959	2.77596	.93286	1.0720	.41323	.44341	.96982	.03018
1.69	5.4195	.18452	.73396	2.61748	2.80200	.93415	1.0705	.41788	.44747	.97042	.02958
1.70	5.4739	0.18268	.73830	2.64563	2.82832	0.93541	1.0691	.42253	.45153	.97100	.02900
1.71	5.5290	.18087	.74264	2.67405	2.85491	.93665	1.0676	.42717	.45559	.97158	.02842
1.72	5.5845	.17907	.74699	2.70273	2.88180	.93786	1.0663	.43180	.45966	.97214	.02786
1.73	5.6407	.17728	.75133	2.73168	2.90897	.93906	1.0649	.43643	.46374	.97269	.02731
1.74	5.6973	.17552	.75567	2.76091	2.93643	.94023	1.0636	.44105	.46782	.97323	.02677
1.75	5.7546	0.17377	.76002	2.79041	2.96419	0.94138	1.0623	.44567	.47191	.97376	.02624
1.76	5.8124	.17205	.76436	2.82020	2.99224	.94250	1.0610	.45028	.47600	.97428	.02572
1.77	5.8709	.17033	.76870	2.85026	3.02059	.94361	1.0598	.45488	.48009	.97479	.02521
1.78	5.9299	.16864	.77304	2.88061	3.04925	.94470	1.0585	.45948	.48419	.97529	.02471
1.79	5.9895	.16696	.77739	2.91125	3.07821	.94576	1.0574	.46408	.48830	.97578	.02422
1.80	6.0496	0.16530	.78173	2.94217	3.10747	0.94681	1.0562	.46867	.49241	.97626	.02374
1.81	6.1104	.16365	.78607	2.97340	3.13705	.94783	1.0550	.47325	.49652	.97673	.02327
1.82	6.1719	.16203	.79042	3.00492	3.16694	.94884	1.0539	.47783	.50064	.97719	.02281
1.83	6.2339	.16041	.79476	3.03674	3.19715	.94983	1.0528	.48241	.50476	.97764	.02236
1.84	6.2965	.15882	.79910	3.06886	3.22768	.95080	1.0518	.48698	.50889	.97809	.02191
1.85	6.3598	0.15724	.80344	3.10129	3.25853	0.95175	1.0507	.49154	.51302	.97852	.02148
1.86	6.4237	.15567	.80779	3.13403	3.28970	.95268	1.0497	.49610	.51716	.97895	.02105
1.87	6.4883	.15412	.81213	3.16709	3.32121	.95359	1.0487	.50066	.52130	.97936	.02064
1.88	6.5535	.15259	.81647	3.20046	3.35305	.95449	1.0477	.50521	.52544	.97977	.02023
1.89	6.6194	.15107	.82082	3.23415	3.38522	.95537	1.0467	.50976	.52959	.98017	.01983
1.90	6.6859	0.14957	.82516	3.26816	3.41773	0.95624	1.0458	.51430	.53374	.98057	.01943
1.91	6.7531	.14808	.82950	3.30250	3.45058	.95709	1.0448	.51884	.53789	.98095	.01905
1.92	6.8210	.14661	.83385	3.33718	3.48378	.95792	1.0439	.52338	.54205	.98133	.01867
1.93	6.8895	.14515	.83819	3.37218	3.51733	.95873	1.0430	.52791	.54621	.98170	.01830
1.94	6.9588	.14370	.84253	3.40752	3.55123	.95953	1.0422	.53244	.55038	.98206	.01794
1.95	7.0287	0.14227	.84687	3.44321	3.58548	0.96032	1.0413	.53696	.55455	.98242	.01758
1.96	7.0993	.14086	.85122	3.47923	3.62009	.96109	1.0405	.54148	.55872	.98276	.01724
1.97	7.1707	.13946	.85556	3.51561	3.65507	.96185	1.0397	.54600	.56290	.98311	.01689
1.98	7.2427	.13807	.85990	3.55234	3.69041	.96259	1.0389	.55051	.56707	.98344	.01656
1.99	7.3155	.13670	.86425	3.58942	3.72611	.96331	1.0381	.55502	.57126	.98377	.01623
2.00	7.3891	0.13534	.86859	3.62686	3.76220	0.96403	1.0373	.55953	.57544	.98409	.01591
2.01	7.4633	.13399	.87293	3.66466	3.79865	.96473	1.0366	.56403	.57963	.98440	.01560
2.02	7.5383	.13266	.87727	3.70283	3.83549	.96541	1.0358	.56853	.58382	.98471	.01529
2.03	7.6141	.13134	.88162	3.74138	3.87271	.96609	1.0351	.57303	.58802	.98502	.01498
2.04	7.6906	.13003	.88596	3.78029	3.91032	.96675	1.0344	.57753	.59221	.98531	.01469
2.05	7.7679	0.12874	.89030	3.81958	3.94832	0.96740	1.0337	.58202	.59641	.89560	.01440
2.06	7.8460	.12745	.89465	3.85926	3.98671	.96803	1.0330	.58650	.60061	.98589	.01411
2.07	7.9248	.12619	.89899	3.89932	4.02550	.96865	1.0324	.59099	.60482	.98617	.01383
2.08	8.0045	.12493	.90333	3.93977	4.06570	.96926	1.0317	.59547	.60903	.98644	.01356
2.09	8.0849	.12369	.90768	3.98061	4.10430	.96986	1.0311	.59995	.61324	.98671	.01329
2.10	8.1662	0.12246	.91202	4.02186	4.14431	0.97045	1.0304	.60443	.61745	.98697	.01303
2.11	8.2482	.12124	.91636	4.06350	4.18474	.97103	1.0298	.60890	.62167	.98723	.01277
2.12	8.3311	.12003	.92070	4.10555	4.22558	.97159	1.0292	.61337	.62589	.98748	.01252
2.13	8.4149	.11884	.92505	4.14801	4.26685	.97215	1.0286	.61784	.63011	.98773	.01227
2.14	8.4994	.11766	.92939	4.19089	4.30855	.97269	1.0281	.62231	.63433	.98798	.01202
x	e^x	e^{-x}	$\log(e^x)$	$\sinh x$	$\cosh x$	$\tanh x$	$\coth x$	log $\sinh x$	log $\cosh x$	log $\tanh x$	log $\coth x$

2.15–2.74

x	e^x	e^{-x}	$\log(e^x)$	$\sinh x$	$\cosh x$	$\tanh x$	$\coth x$	log $\sinh x$	log $\cosh x$	log $\tanh x$	log $\coth x$
2.15	8.5849	0.11648	.93373	4.23419	4.35067	0.97323	1.0275	.62677	.63856	.98821	.01179
2.16	8.6711	.11533	.93808	4.27791	4.39323	.97375	1.0270	.63123	.64278	.98845	.01155
2.17	8.7583	.11418	.94242	4.32205	4.43623	.97426	1.0264	.63569	.64701	.98868	.01132
2.18	8.8463	.11304	.94676	4.36663	4.47967	.97477	1.0259	.64015	.65125	.98890	.01110
2.19	8.9352	.11192	.95110	4.41165	4.52356	.97526	1.0254	.64460	.65548	.98912	.01088
2.20	9.0250	0.11080	.95545	4.45711	4.56791	0.97574	1.0249	.64905	.65972	.98934	.01066
2.21	9.1157	.10970	.95979	4.50301	4.61271	.97622	1.0244	.65350	.66396	.98955	.01045
2.22	9.2073	.10861	.96413	4.54936	4.65797	.97668	1.0239	.65795	.66820	.98975	.01025
2.23	9.2999	.10753	.96848	4.59617	4.70370	.97714	1.0234	.66240	.67244	.98996	.01004
2.24	9.3933	.10646	.97282	4.64344	4.74989	.97759	1.0229	.66684	.67668	.99016	.00984
2.25	9.4877	0.10540	.97716	4.69117	4.79657	0.97803	1.0225	.67128	.68093	.99035	.00965
2.26	9.5831	.10435	.98151	4.73937	4.84372	.97846	1.0220	.67572	.68518	.99054	.00946
2.27	9.6794	.10331	.98585	4.78804	4.89136	.97888	1.0216	.68016	.68943	.99073	.00927
2.28	9.7767	.10228	.99019	4.83720	4.93948	.97929	1.0211	.68459	.69368	.99091	.00909
2.29	9.8749	.10127	.99453	4.88684	4.98810	.97970	1.0207	.68903	.69794	.99109	.00891
2.30	9.9742	0.10026	.99888	4.93696	5.03722	0.98010	1.0203	.69346	.70219	.99127	.00873
2.31	10.074	.09926	1.00322	4.98758	5.08684	.98049	1.0199	.69789	.70645	.99144	.00856
2.32	10.176	.09827	1.00756	5.03870	5.13697	.98087	1.0195	.70232	.71071	.99161	.00839
2.33	10.278	.09730	1.01191	5.09032	5.18762	.98124	1.0191	.70675	.71497	.99178	.00822
2.34	10.381	.09633	1.01625	5.14245	5.23878	.98161	1.0187	.71117	.71923	.99194	.00806
2.35	10.486	0.09537	1.02059	5.19510	5.29047	0.98197	1.0184	.71559	.72349	.99210	.00790
2.36	10.591	.09442	1.02493	5.24827	5.34269	.98233	1.0180	.72002	.72776	.99226	.00774
2.37	10.697	.09348	1.02928	5.30196	5.39544	.98267	1.0176	.72444	.73203	.99241	.00759
2.38	10.805	.09255	1.03362	5.35618	5.44873	.98301	1.0173	.72885	.73630	.99256	.00744
2.39	10.913	.09163	1.03796	5.41093	5.50256	.98335	1.0169	.73327	.74056	.99271	.00729
2.40	11.023	0.09072	1.04231	5.46623	5.55695	0.98367	1.0166	.73769	.74484	.99285	.00715
2.41	11.134	.08982	1.04665	5.52207	5.61189	.98400	1.0163	.74210	.74911	.99299	.00701
2.42	11.246	.08892	1.05099	5.57847	5.66739	.98431	1.0159	.74652	.75338	.99313	.00687
2.43	11.359	.08804	1.05534	5.63542	5.72346	.98462	1.0156	.75093	.75766	.99327	.00673
2.44	11.473	.08716	1.05968	5.69294	5.78010	.98492	1.0153	.75534	.76194	.99340	.00660
2.45	11.588	0.08629	1.06402	5.75103	5.83732	0.98522	1.0150	.75975	.76621	.99353	.00647
2.46	11.705	.08544	1.06836	5.80969	5.89512	.98551	1.0147	.76415	.77049	.99366	.00634
2.47	11.822	.08459	1.07271	5.86893	5.95352	.98579	1.0144	.76856	.77477	.99379	.00621
2.48	11.941	.08374	1.07705	5.92876	6.01250	.98607	1.0141	.77296	.77906	.99391	.00609
2.49	12.061	.08291	1.08139	5.98918	6.07209	.98635	1.0138	.77737	.78334	.99403	.00597
2.50	12.182	0.08209	1.08574	6.05020	6.13229	0.98661	1.0136	.78177	.78762	.99415	.00585
2.51	12.305	.08127	1.09008	6.11183	6.19310	.98688	1.0133	.78617	.79191	.99426	.00574
2.52	12.429	.08046	1.09442	6.17407	6.25453	.98714	1.0130	.79057	.79619	.99438	.00562
2.53	12.554	.07966	1.09877	6.23692	6.31658	.98739	1.0128	.79497	.80048	.99449	.00551
2.54	12.680	.07887	1.10311	6.30040	6.37927	.98764	1.0125	.79937	.80477	.99460	.00540
2.55	12.807	0.07808	1.10745	6.36451	6.44259	0.98788	1.0123	.80377	.80906	.99470	.00530
2.56	12.936	.07731	1.11179	6.42926	6.50656	.98812	1.0120	.80816	.81335	.99481	.00519
2.57	13.066	.07654	1.11614	6.49464	6.57118	.98835	1.0118	.81256	.81764	.99491	.00509
2.58	13.197	.07577	1.12048	6.56068	6.63646	.98858	1.0115	.81695	.82194	.99501	.00499
2.59	13.330	.07502	1.12482	6.62738	6.70240	.98881	1.0113	.82134	.82623	.99511	.00489
2.60	13.464	0.07427	1.12917	6.69473	6.76901	0.98903	1.0111	.82573	.83052	.99521	.00479
2.61	13.599	.07354	1.13351	6.76276	6.83629	.98924	1.0109	.83012	.83482	.99530	.00470
2.62	13.736	.07280	1.13785	6.83146	6.90426	.98946	1.0107	.83451	.83912	.99540	.00460
2.63	13.874	.07208	1.14219	6.90085	6.97292	.98966	1.0104	.83890	.84341	.99549	.00451
2.64	14.013	.07136	1.14654	6.97092	7.04228	.98987	1.0102	.84329	.84771	.99558	.00442
2.65	14.154	0.07065	1.15088	7.04169	7.11234	0.99007	1.0100	.84768	.85201	.99566	.00434
2.66	14.296	.06995	1.15522	7.11317	7.18312	.99026	1.0098	.85206	.85631	.99575	.00425
2.67	14.440	.06925	1.15957	7.18536	7.25461	.99045	1.0096	.85645	.86061	.99583	.00417
2.68	14.585	.06856	1.16391	7.25827	7.32683	.99064	1.0094	.86083	.86492	.99592	.00408
2.69	14.732	.06788	1.16825	7.33190	7.39978	.99083	1.0093	.86522	.86922	.99600	.00400
2.70	14.880	0.06721	1.17260	7.40626	7.47347	0.99101	1.0091	.86960	.87352	.99608	.00392
2.71	15.029	.06654	1.17694	7.48137	7.54791	.99118	1.0089	.87398	.87783	.99615	.00385
2.72	15.180	.06588	1.18128	7.55722	7.62310	.99136	1.0087	.87836	.88213	.99623	.00377
2.73	15.333	.06522	1.18562	7.63383	7.69905	.99153	1.0085	.88274	.88644	.99631	.00369
2.74	15.487	.06457	1.18997	7.71121	7.77578	.99170	1.0084	.88712	.89074	.99638	.00362
x	e^x	e^{-x}	$\log(e^x)$	$\sinh x$	$\cosh x$	$\tanh x$	$\coth x$	log $\sinh x$	log $\cosh x$	log $\tanh x$	log $\coth x$

Table No. 21 continued

2.75–5.40

x	e^x	e^{-x}	$\log(e^x)$	$\sinh x$	$\cosh x$	$\tanh x$	$\coth x$	log sinh x	log cosh x	log tanh x	log coth x
2.75	15.643	0.06393	1.19431	7.78935	7.85328	0.99186	1.0082	.89150	.89505	.99645	.00355
2.76	15.800	.06329	1.19865	7.86828	7.93157	.99202	1.0080	.89588	.89936	.99652	.00348
2.77	15.959	.06266	1.20300	7.94799	8.01065	.99218	1.0079	.90026	.90367	.99659	.00341
2.78	16.119	.06204	1.20734	8.02849	8.09053	.99233	1.0077	.90463	.90798	.99666	.00334
2.79	16.281	.06142	1.21168	8.10980	8.17122	.99248	1.0076	.90901	.91229	.99672	.00328
2.80	16.445	0.06081	1.21602	8.19192	8.25273	0.99263	1.0074	.91339	.91660	.99679	.00321
2.81	16.610	.06021	1.22037	8.27486	8.33506	.99278	1.0073	.91776	.92091	.99685	.00315
2.82	16.777	.05961	1.22471	8.35862	8.41823	.99292	1.0071	.92213	.92522	.99691	.00309
2.83	16.945	.05901	1.22905	8.44322	8.50224	.99306	1.0070	.92651	.92953	.99698	.00302
2.84	17.116	.05843	1.23340	8.52867	8.58710	.99320	1.0069	.93088	.93385	.99704	.00296
2.85	17.288	0.05784	1.23774	8.61497	8.67281	0.99333	1.0067	.93525	.93816	.99709	.00291
2.86	17.462	.05727	1.24208	8.70213	8.75940	.99346	1.0066	.93963	.94247	.99715	.00285
2.87	17.637	.05670	1.24643	8.79016	8.84686	.99359	1.0065	.94400	.94679	.99721	.00279
2.88	17.814	.05614	1.25077	8.87907	8.93520	.99372	1.0063	.94837	.95110	.99726	.00274
2.89	17.993	.05558	1.25511	8.96887	9.02444	.99384	1.0062	.95274	.95542	.99732	.00268
2.90	18.147	0.05502	1.25945	9.05956	9.11458	0.99396	1.0061	.95711	.95974	.99737	.00263
2.91	18.357	.05448	1.26380	9.15116	9.20564	.99408	1.0060	.96148	.96405	.99742	.00258
2.92	18.541	.05393	1.26814	9.24368	9.29761	.99420	1.0058	.96584	.96837	.99747	.00253
2.93	18.728	.05340	1.27248	9.33712	9.39051	.99431	1.0057	.97021	.97269	.99752	.00248
2.94	18.916	.05287	1.27683	9.43149	9.48436	.99443	1.0056	.97458	.97701	.99757	.00243
2.95	19.106	0.05234	1.28117	9.52681	9.57915	0.99454	1.0055	.97895	.98133	.99762	.00238
2.96	19.298	.05182	1.28551	9.62308	9.67490	.99464	1.0054	.98331	.98565	.99767	.00233
2.97	19.492	.05130	1.28985	9.72031	9.77161	.99475	1.0053	.98768	.98997	.99771	.00229
2.98	19.688	.05079	1.29420	9.81851	9.86930	.99485	1.0052	.99205	.99429	.99776	.00224
2.99	19.886	.05029	1.29854	9.91770	9.96798	.99496	1.0051	.99641	.99861	.99780	.00220
3.00	20.086	.04979	1.30288	10.018	10.068	.99505	1.0050	.00078	.00293	.99785	.00215
3.05	21.115	.04736	1.32460	10.534	10.581	.99552	1.0045	.02259	.02454	.99805	.00195
3.10	22.198	.04505	1.34631	11.076	11.122	.99595	1.0041	.04440	.04616	.99824	.00176
3.15	23.336	.04285	1.36803	11.647	11.690	.99633	1.0037	.06620	.06779	.99841	.00159
3.20	24.533	.04076	1.38974	12.246	12.287	.99668	1.0033	.08799	.08943	.99856	.00144
3.25	25.790	.03877	1.41146	12.876	12.915	.99700	1.0030	.10977	.11108	.99869	.00131
3.30	27.113	.03688	1.43317	13.538	13.575	.99728	1.0027	.13155	.13273	.99882	.00118
3.35	28.503	.03508	1.45489	14.234	14.269	.99754	1.0025	.15332	.15439	.99893	.00107
3.40	29.964	.03337	1.47660	14.965	14.999	.99777	1.0022	.17509	.17605	.99903	.00097
3.45	31.500	.03175	1.49832	15.734	15.766	.99799	1.0020	.19685	.19772	.99912	.00088
3.50	33.115	.03020	1.52003	16.543	16.573	.99818	1.0018	.21860	.21940	.99921	.00079
3.55	34.813	.02872	1.54175	17.392	17.421	.99835	1.0017	.24036	.24107	.99928	.00072
3.60	36.598	.02732	1.56346	18.286	18.313	.99851	1.0015	.26211	.26275	.99935	.00065
3.65	38.475	.02599	1.58517	19.224	19.250	.99865	1.0014	.28385	.28444	.99941	.00059
3.70	40.447	.02472	1.60689	20.211	20.236	.99878	1.0012	.30559	.30612	.99947	.00053
3.75	42.521	.02352	1.62860	21.249	21.272	.99889	1.0011	.32733	.32781	.99952	.00048
3.80	44.701	.02237	1.65032	22.339	22.362	.99900	1.0010	.34907	.34951	.99957	.00043
3.85	46.993	.02128	1.67203	23.486	23.507	.99909	1.0009	.37081	.37120	.99961	.00039
3.90	49.402	.02024	1.69375	24.691	24.711	.99918	1.0008	.39254	.39290	.99964	.00036
3.95	51.935	.01925	1.71546	25.958	25.977	.99926	1.0007	.41427	.41459	.99968	.00032
4.00	54.598	.01832	1.73718	27.290	27.308	.99933	1.0007	.43600	.43629	.99971	.00029
4.10	60.340	.01657	1.78061	30.162	30.178	.99945	1.0005	.47946	.47970	.99976	.00024
4.20	66.686	.01500	1.82404	33.336	33.351	.99955	1.0004	.52291	.52310	.99980	.00020
4.30	73.700	.01357	1.86747	36.843	36.857	.99963	1.0004	.56636	.56652	.99984	.00016
4.40	81.451	.01227	1.91090	40.719	40.732	.99970	1.0003	.60980	.60993	.99987	.00013
4.50	90.017	.01111	1.95433	45.003	45.014	.99975	1.0002	.65324	.65335	.99989	.00011
4.60	99.484	.01005	1.99775	49.737	49.747	.99980	1.0002	.69668	.69677	.99991	.00009
4.70	109.95	.00910	2.04118	54.969	54.978	.99983	1.0002	.74012	.74019	.99993	.00007
4.80	121.51	.00823	2.08461	60.751	60.759	.99986	1.0001	.78355	.78361	.99994	.00006
4.90	134.29	.00745	2.12804	67.141	67.149	.99989	1.0001	.82699	.82704	.99995	.00005
5.00	148.41	.00674	2.17147	74.203	74.210	.99991	1.0001	.87042	.87046	.99996	.00004
5.10	164.02	.00610	2.21490	82.008	82.014	.99993	1.0001	.91389	.91389	.99997	.00003
5.20	181.27	.00552	2.25833	90.633	90.639	.99994	1.0001	.95729	.95731	.99997	.00003
5.30	200.34	.00499	2.30176	100.17	100.17	.99995	1.0000	.00074	.00074	.99998	.00002
5.40	221.41	.00452	2.34519	110.70	110.71	.99996	1.0000	.04415	.04417	.99998	.00002
x	e^x	e^{-x}	$\log(e^x)$	$\sinh x$	$\cosh x$	$\tanh x$	$\coth x$	log sinh x	log cosh x	log tanh x	log coth x

5.50–10.00

x	e^x	e^{-x}	$\log(e^x)$	$\sin x$	$\cosh x$	$\tanh x$	$\coth x$	log $\sin x$	log $\cosh x$	log $\tanh x$	log $\coth x$
5.50	244.69	.00409	2.38862	122.34	122.35	.99997	1.0000	.08758	.08760	.99999	.00001
5.60	270.43	.00370	2.43205	135.21	135.22	.99997	1.0000	.13101	.13103	.99999	.00001
5.70	298.87	.00335	2.47548	149.43	149.44	.99998	1.0000	.17444	.17445	.99999	.00001
5.80	330.30	.00303	2.51891	165.15	165.15	.99998	1.0000	.21787	.21788	.99999	.00001
5.90	365.04	.00274	2.56234	182.52	182.52	.99998	1.0000	.26130	.26131	.99999	.00001
6.00	403.43	.00248	2.60577	201.71	201.72	.99999	1.0000	.30473	.30475	.00000	.00000
6.10	445.86	.00224	2.64920	222.93	222.93	.99999	1.0000	.34817	.34817	.00000	.00000
6.20	492.75	.00203	2.69263	246.37	246.38	.99999	1.0000	.39159	.39161	.00000	.00000
6.30	544.57	.00184	2.73606	272.29	272.29	.99999	1.0000	.43503	.43503	.00000	.00000
6.40	601.85	.00166	2.77948	300.92	300.92	.99999	1.0000	.47845	.47845	.00000	.00000
6.50	665.14	.00150	2.82291	332.57	332.57	1.0000	1.0000	.52188	.52188	.00000	.00000
6.60	735.10	.00136	2.86634	367.55	367.55	1.0000	1.0000	.56532	.56532	.00000	.00000
6.70	812.41	.00123	2.90977	406.20	406.20	1.0000	1.0000	.60874	.60874	.00000	.00000
6.80	897.85	.00111	2.95320	448.92	448.92	1.0000	1.0000	.65217	.65217	.00000	.00000
6.90	992.27	.00101	2.99663	496.14	496.14	1.0000	1.0000	.69560	.69560	.00000	.00000
7.00	1096.6	.00091	3.04006	548.32	548.32	1.0000	1.0000	.73903	.73903	.00000	.00000
7.10	1212.0	.00083	3.08349	605.98	605.98	1.0000	1.0000	.78246	.78246	.00000	.00000
7.20	1339.4	.00075	3.12692	669.72	669.72	1.0000	1.0000	.82589	.82589	.00000	.00000
7.30	1480.3	.00068	3.17035	740.15	740.15	1.0000	1.0000	.96932	.86932	.00000	.00000
7.40	1636.0	.00061	3.21378	817.99	817.99	1.0000	1.0000	.91275	.91275	.00000	.00000
7.50	1808.0	.00055	3.25721	904.02	904.02	1.0000	1.0000	.95618	.95618	.00000	.00000
7.60	1998.2	.00050	3.30064	999.10	999.10	1.0000	1.0000	.99961	.99961	.00000	.00000
7.70	2208.3	.00045	3.34407	1104.2	1104.2	1.0000	1.0000	.04305	.04305	.00000	.00000
7.80	2440.6	.00041	3.38750	1220.3	1220.3	1.0000	1.0000	.08647	.08647	.00000	.00000
7.90	2697.3	.00037	3.43093	1348.6	1348.6	1.0000	1.0000	.12988	.12988	.00000	.00000
8.00	2981.0	.00034	3.47436	1490.5	1490.5	1.0000	1.0000	.17333	.17333	.00000	.00000
8.10	3294.5	.00030	3.51779	1647.2	1647.2	1.0000	1.0000	.21675	.21675	.00000	.00000
8.20	3641.0	.00027	3.56121	1820.5	1820.5	1.0000	1.0000	.26019	.26019	.00000	.00000
8.30	4023.9	.00025	3.60464	2011.9	2011.9	1.0000	1.0000	.30360	.30360	.00000	.00000
8.40	4447.1	.00022	3.64807	2223.5	2223.5	1.0000	1.0000	.34704	.34704	.00000	.00000
8.50	4914.8	.00020	3.69150	2457.4	2457.4	1.0000	1.0000	.39048	.39048	.00000	.00000
8.60	5431.7	.00018	3.73493	2715.8	2715.8	1.0000	1.0000	.43390	.43390	.00000	.00000
8.70	6002.9	.00017	3.77836	3001.5	3001.5	1.0000	1.0000	.47734	.47734	.00000	.00000
8.80	6634.2	.00015	3.82179	3317.1	3317.1	1.0000	1.0000	.52076	.52076	.00000	.00000
8.90	7332.0	.00014	3.86522	3666.0	3666.0	1.0000	1.0000	.56419	.56419	.00000	.00000
9.00	8103.1	.00012	3.90865	4051.5	4051.5	1.0000	1.0000	.60762	.60762	.00000	.00000
9.10	8955.3	.00011	3.95208	4477.6	4477.6	1.0000	1.0000	.65105	.65105	.00000	.00000
9.20	9897.1	.00010	3.99551	4948.6	4948.6	1.0000	1.0000	.69448	.69448	.00000	.00000
9.30	10938	.00009	4.03894	5469.0	5469.0	1.0000	1.0000	.73791	.73791	.00000	.00000
9.40	12088	.00008	4.10408	6044.2	6044.2	1.0000	1.0000	.78134	.78134	.00000	.00000
9.50	13360	.00007	4.12580	6679.9	6679.9	1.0000	1.0000	.82477	.82477	.00000	.00000
9.60	14765	.00007	4.14751	7382.4	7382.4	1.0000	1.0000	.86820	.86820	.00000	.00000
9.70	16318	.00006	4.21266	8158.8	8158.8	1.0000	1.0000	.91163	.91163	.00000	.00000
9.80	18034	.00006	4.25609	9016.9	9016.9	1.0000	1.0000	.95506	.95506	.00000	.00000
9.90	19930	.00005	4.29952	9965.2	9965.2	1.0000	1.0000	.99849	.99849	.00000	.00000
10.00	22026	.00005	4.34294	11013.2	11013.2	1.0000	1.0000	.04191	.04191	.00000	.00000
x	e^x	e^{-x}	$\log(e^x)$	$\sin x$	$\cosh x$	$\tanh x$	$\coth x$	log $\sin x$	log $\cosh x$	log $\tanh x$	log $\coth x$

NO. 22 NATURAL TRIGONOMETRIC FUNCTIONS
EXPLANATION

The table of Natural Trigonometric Functions gives the values of the functions of angles from 0° to 90° at 10 minute intervals. The name of the function appears at the top and bottom of each column; the angles appear in the first and last column. The angles from 0°–45° appear (from *top* to *bottom*) in the first column. The angles from 45°–90° appear in the last column (from *bottom* to *top*). To locate a trigonometric function for an angle between 0° and 45° use the headings at the *top* of the columns. To locate a function for angles between 45° and 90° use the

headings at the *bottom* of the columns. E.g. to locate tan 9°40′, read *down* the first column to 9°40′, and read to the right to the column headed, *at the top*, "Tan". The number .1703 is tan 9°40′. To find cot 80°20′, read *up* the last column to 80°20′, and read to the left to the column headed, *at the bottom*, "Cot". The number .1703 is cot 80°20′. Note that for complementary angles (9°40′ and 80°20′) the function of one (tan 9°40′) equals the cofunction of the other (cot 80°20′).

0°–8° 50′   90°–81° 10′

Angle	Sin	Cos	Tan	Csc	Sec	Cot	Angle
0° 0′	.0000	1.0000	.0000		1.0000		90° 0′
10′	.0029	1.0000	.0029	343.78	1.0000	343.77	89° 50′
20′	.0058	1.0000	.0058	171.89	1.0000	171.89	40′
30′	.0087	1.0000	.0087	114.59	1.0000	114.59	30′
40′	.0116	.9999	.0166	85.946	1.0001	85.940	20′
50′	.0145	.9999	.0145	68.757	1.0001	68.750	10′
1° 0′	.0175	.9998	.0175	57.299	1.0002	57.290	89° 0′
10′	.0204	.9998	.0204	49.114	1.0002	49.104	88° 50′
20′	.0233	.9997	.0233	42.976	1.0003	42.964	40′
30′	.0262	.9997	.0262	38.202	1.0003	38.188	30′
40′	.0291	.9996	.0291	34.382	1.0004	34.368	20′
50′	.0320	.9995	.0320	31.258	1.0005	31.242	10′
2° 0′	.0349	.9994	.0349	28.654	1.0006	28.636	88° 0′
10′	.0378	.9993	.0378	26.451	1.0007	26.432	87° 50′
20′	.0407	.9992	.0407	24.562	1.0008	24.542	40′
30′	.0436	.9990	.0437	22.926	1.0010	22.904	30′
40′	.0465	.9989	.0466	21.494	1.0011	21.470	20′
50′	.0494	.9988	.0495	20.230	1.0012	20.206	10′
3° 0′	.0523	.9986	.0524	19.107	1.0014	19.081	87° 0′
10′	.0552	.9985	.0553	18.103	1.0015	18.075	86° 50′
20′	0581	.9983	.0582	17.198	1.0017	17.169	40′
30′	.0610	.9981	.0612	16.380	1.0019	16.350	30′
40′	.0640	.9980	.0641	15.637	1.0021	15.605	20′
50′	.0669	.9978	.0670	14.958	1.0022	14.924	10′
4° 0′	.0698	.9976	.0699	14.336	1.0024	14.301	86° 0′
10′	.0727	.9974	.0729	13.763	1.0027	13.727	85° 50′
20′	.0756	.9971	.0758	13.235	1.0029	13.197	40′
30′	.0785	.9969	.0787	12.745	1.0031	12.706	30′
40′	.0814	.9967	.0816	12.291	1.0033	12.251	20′
50′	.0843	.9964	.0846	11.868	1.0036	11.826	10′
5° 0′	.0872	.9962	.0875	11.474	1.0038	11.430	85° 0′
10′	.0901	.9959	.0904	11.105	1.0041	11.059	84° 50′
20′	.0929	.9957	.0934	10.758	1.0043	10.712	40′
30′	.0958	.9954	.0963	10.433	1.0046	10.385	30′
40′	.0987	.9951	.0992	10.128	1.0049	10.078	20′
50′	.1016	.9948	.1022	9.8391	1.0052	9.7882	10′
6° 0′	.1045	.9945	.1051	9.5668	1.0055	9.5144	84° 0′
10′	.1074	.9942	.1080	9.3092	1.0058	9.2553	83° 50′
20′	.1103	.9939	.1110	9.0652	1.0061	9.0098	40′
30′	.1132	.9936	.1139	8.8337	1.0065	8.7769	30′
40′	.1161	.9932	.1169	8.6138	1.0068	8.5555	20′
50′	.1190	.9929	.1198	8.4047	1.0072	8.3450	10′
7° 0′	.1219	.9925	.1228	8.2055	1.0075	8.1442	83° 0′
10′	.1248	.9922	.1257	7.0396	1.0079	7.9530	82° 50′
20′	.1276	.9918	.1287	6.8998	1.0082	7.7704	40′
30′	.1305	.9914	.1317	6.7655	1.0086	7.5958	30′
40′	.1334	.9911	.1346	6.6363	1.0090	7.4287	20′
50′	.1363	.9907	.1376	6.5121	1.0094	7.2687	10′
8° 0′	.1392	.9903	.1405	7.1853	1.0098	7.1154	82° 0′
10′	.1421	.9899	.1435	7.0396	1.0102	6.9682	81° 50′
20′	.1449	.9894	.1465	6.8998	1.0107	6.8269	40′
30′	.1478	.9890	.1495	6.7655	1.0111	6.6921	30′
40′	.1507	.9886	.1524	6.6363	1.0116	6.5606	20′
50′	.1536	.9881	.1554	6.5121	1.0120	6.4348	81° 10′
Angle	Cos	Sin	Cot	Sec	Csc	Tan	Angle

ANGLE	SIN	COS	TAN	CSC	SEC	COT	ANGLE
9° 0'	.1564	.9877	.1584	6.3925	1.0125	6.3138	81° 0'
10'	.1593	.9872	.1614	6.2772	1.0129	6.1970	80° 50'
20'	.1622	.9868	.1644	6.1661	1.0134	6.0844	40'
30'	.1650	.9863	.1673	6.0589	1.0139	6.9758	30'
40'	.1679	.9858	.1703	5.9554	1.0144	5.8708	20'
50'	.1708	.9853	.1733	5.8554	1.0149	5.7694	10'
10° 0'	.1736	.9848	.1763	5.7588	1.0154	5.5713	80° 0'
10'	.1765	.9843	.1793	5.6653	1.0160	5.5764	79° 50'
20'	.1794	.9838	.1823	5.5749	1.0165	5.4845	40'
30'	.1822	.9833	.1853	5.4874	1.0170	5.3955	30'
40'	.1851	.9827	.1883	5.4026	1.0176	5.3093	20'
50'	.1880	.9822	.1914	5.3205	1.0181	5.2257	10'
11° 0'	.1908	.9816	.1944	5.2408	1.0187	5.1446	79° 0'
10'	.1937	.9811	.1974	5.1636	1.0193	5.0568	78° 50'
20'	.1965	.9805	.2004	5.0886	1.0199	4.9894	40'
30'	.1994	.9799	.2035	5.0159	1.0205	4.9152	30'
40'	.2022	.9793	.2065	4.9452	1.0211	4.8430	20'
50'	.2051	.9787	.2095	4.8765	1.0217	4.7729	10'
12° 0'	.2079	.9781	.2126	4.8097	1.0223	4.7046	78° 0'
10'	.2108	.9775	.2156	4.7448	1.0230	4.6382	77° 50'
20'	.2136	.9769	.2186	4.6817	1.0236	4.5736	40'
30'	.2164	.9763	.2217	4.6202	1.0243	4.5107	30'
40'	.2193	.9757	.2247	4.5604	1.0249	4.4494	20'
50'	.2221	.9750	.2278	4.5022	1.0256	4.3897	10'
13° 0'	.2250	.9744	.2309	4.4454	1.0263	4.3315	77° 0'
10'	.2278	.9737	.2339	4.3901	1.0270	4.2747	76° 50'
20'	.2306	.9730	.2370	4.3362	1.0277	4.2193	40'
30'	.2334	.9724	.2401	4.2837	1.0284	4.1653	30'
40'	.2363	.9717	.2432	4.2324	1.0291	4.1126	20'
50'	.2391	.9710	.2462	4.1824	1.0299	4.0611	10'
14° 0'	.2419	.9703	.2493	4.1336	1.0306	4.0108	76° 0'
10'	.2447	.9696	.2524	4.0859	1.0314	3.9617	75° 50'
20'	.2476	.9689	.2555	4.0394	1.0321	3.9136	40'
30'	.2504	.9681	.2586	3.9939	1.0329	3.8667	30'
40'	.2532	.9674	.2617	3.9495	1.0337	3.8208	20'
50'	.2560	.9667	.2648	3.9061	1.0345	3.7760	10'
15° 0'	.2588	.9659	.2679	3.8637	1.0353	3.7321	75° 0'
10'	.2616	.9652	.2711	3.8222	1.0361	3.6891	74° 50'
20'	.2644	.9644	.2742	3.7817	1.0369	3.6470	40'
30'	.2672	.9636	.2773	3.7420	1.0377	3.6059	30'
40'	.2700	.9628	.2805	3.7032	1.0386	3.5656	20'
50'	.2728	.9621	.2836	3.6652	1.0394	3.5261	10'
16° 0'	.2756	.9613	.2867	3.6280	1.0403	3.4874	74° 0'
10'	.2784	.9605	.2899	3.5915	1.0412	3.4495	73° 50'
20'	.2812	.9596	.2931	3.5559	1.0421	3.4124	40'
30'	.2840	.9588	.2962	3.5209	1.0429	3.3759	30'
40'	.2868	.9580	.2994	3.4867	1.0439	3.3402	20'
50'	.2896	.9572	.3026	3.4532	1.0448	3.3052	10'
17° 0'	.2924	.9563	.3057	3.4203	1.0457	3.2709	73° 0'
10'	.2952	.9555	.3089	3.3881	1.0466	3.2371	72° 50'
20'	.2979	.9546	.3121	3.3565	1.0476	3.2041	40'
30'	.3007	.9537	.3153	3.3255	1.0485	3.1716	30'
40'	.3035	.9528	.3185	3.2951	1.0495	3.1397	20'
50'	.3062	.9520	.3217	3.2653	1.0505	3.1084	10'
18° 0'	.3090	.9511	.3249	3.2361	1.0515	3.0777	72° 0'
10'	.3118	.9502	.3281	3.2074	1.0525	3.0475	71° 50'
20'	.3145	.9492	.3314	3.1792	1.0535	3.0178	40'
30'	.3173	.9483	.3346	3.1515	1.0545	2.9887	30'
40'	.3201	.9474	.3378	3.1244	1.0555	2.9600	20'
50'	.3228	.9465	.3411	3.0977	1.0566	2.9319	71° 10'
ANGLE	COS	SIN	COT	SEC	CSC	TAN	ANGLE

ANGLE	SIN	COS	TAN	CSC	SEC	COT	ANGLE
19° 0′	.3256	.9455	.3443	3.0716	1.0576	2.9042	71° 0′
10′	.3283	.9446	.3476	3.0458	1.0587	2.8770	70° 50′
20′	.3311	.9436	.3508	3.0206	1.0598	2.8502	40′
30′	.3338	.9426	.3541	2.9957	1.0608	2.8239	30′
40′	.3365	.9417	.3574	2.9713	1.0619	2.7980	20′
50′	.3393	.9407	.3607	2.9474	1.0631	2.7725	10′
20° 0′	.3420	.9307	.3640	2.9238	1.0642	2.7475	70° 0′
10′	.3448	.9387	.3673	2.9006	1.0653	2.7228	69° 50′
20′	.3475	.9377	.3706	2.8779	1.0665	2.6985	40′
30′	.3502	.9367	.3739	2.8555	1.0676	2.6746	30′
40′	.3529	.9356	.3772	2.8334	1.0688	2.6511	20′
50′	.3557	.9346	.3805	2.8117	1.0700	2.6279	10′
21° 0′	.3584	.9336	.3839	2.7904	1.0711	2.6051	69° 0′
10′	.3611	.9325	.3872	2.7695	1.0723	2.5826	68° 50′
20′	.3638	.9315	.3906	2.7488	1.0736	2.5605	40′
30′	.3665	.9304	.3939	2.7285	1.0738	2.5386	30′
40′	.3692	.9293	.3973	2.7085	1.0760	2.5172	20′
50′	.3719	.9283	.4006	2.6888	1.0773	2.4960	10′
22° 0′	.3746	.9272	.4040	2.6695	1.0785	2.4751	68° 0′
10′	.3773	.9261	.4074	2.6504	1.0798	2.4545	67° 50′
20′	.3800	.9250	.4108	2.6316	1.0811	2.4342	40′
30′	.3827	.9239	.4142	2.6131	1.0824	2.4142	30′
40′	.3854	.9228	.4176	2.5949	1.0837	2.3945	20′
50′	.3881	.9216	.4210	2.5770	1.0850	2.3750	10′
23° 0′	.3907	.9205	.4245	2.5593	1.0864	2.3559	67° 0′
10′	.3934	.9194	.4279	2.5419	1.0877	2.3369	66° 50′
20′	.3961	.9182	.4314	2.5247	1.0891	2.3183	40′
30′	.3987	.9171	.4348	2.5078	1.0904	2.2998	30′
40′	.4014	.9159	.4383	2.4912	1.0918	2.2817	20′
50′	.4041	.9147	.4417	2.4748	1.0939	2.2637	10′
24° 0′	.4067	.9135	.4452	2.4586	1.0946	2.2400	66° 0′
10′	.4094	.9124	.4487	2.4426	1.0961	2.2286	65° 50′
20′	.4120	.9112	.4522	2.4269	1.0975	2.2113	40′
30′	.4147	.9100	.4557	2.4114	1.0989	2.1943	30′
40′	.4173	.9088	.4592	2.3961	1.1004	2.1775	20′
50′	.4200	.9075	.4628	2.3811	1.1019	2.1609	10′
25° 0′	.4226	.9063	.4663	2.3662	1.1034	2.1445	65° 0′
10′	.4253	.9051	.4699	2.3515	1.1049	2.1283	64° 50′
20′	.4279	.9038	.4734	2.3371	1.1064	2.1123	40′
30′	.4305	.9026	.4770	2.3228	1.1079	2.0965	30′
40′	.4331	.9013	.4806	2.3088	1.1095	2.0809	20′
50′	.4358	.9001	.4841	2.2949	1.1110	2.0655	10′
26° 0′	.4384	.8988	.4877	2.2812	1.1126	2.0503	64° 0′
10′	.4410	.8975	.4913	2.2677	1.1142	2.0353	63° 50′
20′	.4436	.8962	.4950	2.2543	1.1158	2.0204	40′
30′	.4462	.8949	.4986	2.2412	1.1174	2.0057	30′
40′	.4488	.8936	.5022	2.2282	1.1190	1.9912	20′
50′	.4514	.8923	.5059	2.2153	1.1207	1.9768	10′
27° 0′	.4540	.8910	.5095	2.2027	1.1223	1.9626	63° 0′
10′	.4566	.8897	.5132	2.1902	1.1240	1.9486	62° 50′
20′	.4592	.8884	.5169	2.1779	1.1257	1.9347	40′
30′	.4617	.8870	.5206	2.1657	1.1274	1.9210	30′
40′	.4643	.8857	.5243	2.1537	1.1291	1.9074	20′
50′	.4669	.8843	.5280	2.1418	1.1308	1.8940	10′
28° 0′	.4695	.8829	.5317	2.1301	1.1326	1.8807	62° 0′
10′	.4720	.8816	.5354	2.1185	1.1343	1.8676	61° 50′
20′	.4746	.8802	.5392	2.1070	1.1361	1.8546	40′
30′	.4772	.8788	.5430	2.0957	1.1379	1.8418	30′
40′	.4797	.8774	.5467	2.0846	1.1397	1.8291	20′
50′	.4823	.8760	.5505	2.0736	1.1415	1.8165	61° 10′
ANGLE	COS	SIN	COT	SEC	CSC	TAN	ANGLE

Angle	Sin	Cos	Tan	Csc	Sec	Cot	Angle
29° 0'	.4848	.8746	.5543	2.0627	1.1434	1.8040	61° 0'
10'	.4874	.8732	.5581	2.0519	1.1452	1.7917	60° 50'
20'	.4899	.8718	.5619	2.0413	1.1471	1.7796	40'
30'	.4924	.8704	.5658	2.0308	1.1490	1.7675	30'
40'	.4950	.8689	.5696	2.0204	1.1509	1.7556	20'
50'	.4975	.8675	.5735	2.0101	1.1528	1.7437	10'
30° 0'	.5000	.8660	.5774	2.0000	1.1547	1.7321	60° 0'
10'	.5025	.8646	.5812	1.9900	1.1566	1.7205	59° 50'
20'	.5050	.8631	.5851	1.9801	1.1586	1.7090	40'
30'	.5075	.8616	.5890	1.9703	1.1606	1.6977	30,
40'	.5100	.8601	.5930	1.9606	1.1626	1.6864	20,
50'	.5125	.8587	.5969	1.9511	1.1646	1.6753	10,
31° 0'	.5150	.8572	.6009	1.9416	1.1666	1.6643	59° 0'
10'	.5175	.8557	.6048	1.9323	1.1687	1.6534	58° 50'
20'	.5200	.8542	.6088	1.9230	1.1707	1.6426	40'
30'	.5225	.8526	.6128	1.9139	1.1728	1.6319	30,
40'	.5250	.8511	.6168	1.9048	1.1749	1.6212	20,
50'	.5275	.8496	.6208	1.8959	1.1770	1.6107	10,
32° 0'	.5299	.8480	.6249	1.8871	1.1792	1.6003	58° 0'
10'	.5324	.8465	.6289	1.8783	1.1813	1.5900	57° 50'
20'	.5348	.8450	.6330	1.8697	1.1835	1.5798	40'
30'	.5373	.8434	.6371	1.8612	1.1857	1.5697	30'
40'	.5398	.8418	.6412	1.8527	1.1879	1.5597	20'
50'	.5422	.8403	.6453	1.8443	1.1901	1.5497	10'
33° 0'	.5446	.8387	.6494	1.8361	1.1924	1.5399	57° 0'
10'	.5471	.8371	.6536	1.8279	1.1946	1.5301	56° 50'
20'	.5495	.8355	.6577	1.8198	1.1969	1.5204	40'
30'	.5519	.8339	.6619	1.8118	1.1992	1.5108	30'
40'	.5544	.8323	.6661	1.8039	1.2015	1.5013	20'
50'	.5568	.8307	.6703	1.7960	1.2039	1.4919	10'
34° 0'	.5592	.8290	.6745	1.7883	1.2062	1.4826	56° 0'
10'	.5616	.8274	.6787	1.7806	1.2086	1.4733	55° 50'
20'	.5640	.8258	.6830	1.7730	1.2110	1.4641	40'
30'	.5664	.8241	.6873	1.7655	1.2134	1.4550	30'
40'	.5688	.8225	.6616	1.7581	1.2158	1.4460	20'
50'	.5712	.8208	.6959	1.7507	1.2183	1.4370	10'
35° 0'	.5736	.8192	.7002	1.7434	1.2208	1.4281	55° 0,
10'	.5760	.8175	.7046	1.7362	1.2233	1.4193	54° 50,
20'	.5783	.8158	.7089	1.7291	1.2258	1.4106	40,
30'	.5807	.8141	.7133	1.7221	1.2283	1.4019	30,
40'	.5831	.8124	.7177	1.7151	1.2309	1.3934	20,
50'	.5854	.8107	.7221	1.7081	1.2335	1.3848	10,
36° 0'	.5878	.8090	.7265	1.7013	1.2361	1.3764	54° 0'
10'	.5901	.8073	.7310	1.6945	1.2387	1.3680	53° 50'
20'	.5925	.8056	.7355	1.6878	1.2413	1.3597	40'
30'	.5948	.8039	.7400	1.6812	1.2440	1.3514	30'
40'	.5972	.8021	.7445	1.6746	1.2467	1.3432	20'
50'	.5995	.8004	.7490	1.6681	1.2494	1.3351	10'
37° 0'	.6018	.7986	.7536	1.6616	1.2521	1.3270	53° 0'
10'	.6041	.7969	.7581	1.6553	1.2549	1.3190	52° 50'
20'	.6065	.7951	.7627	1.6489	1.2577	1.3111	40'
30'	.6088	.7934	.7673	1.6427	1.2605	1.3032	30'
40'	.6111	.7916	.7720	1.6365	1.2633	1.2954	20'
50'	.6134	.7898	.7766	1.6303	1.2661	1.2876	10'
38° 0'	.6157	.7880	.7813	1.6243	1.2690	1.2799	52° 0'
10'	.6180	.7862	.7860	1.6183	1.2719	1.2723	51° 50'
20'	.6202	.7844	.7907	1.6123	1.2748	1.2647	40'
30'	.6225	.7826	.7954	1.6064	1.2778	1.2572	30'
40'	.6248	.7808	.8002	1.6005	1.2807	1.2497	20'
50'	.6271	.7790	.8050	1.5948	1.2837	1.2423	51° 10'
Angle	Cos	Sin	Cot	Sec	Csc	Tan	Angle

Table No. 22 continued

Angle	Sin	Cos	Tan	Csc	Sec	Cot	Angle
39° 0′	.6293	.7771	.8098	1.5890	1.2868	1.2349	51° 0′
10′	.6316	.7753	.8146	1.5833	1.2898	1.2276	50° 50′
20′	.6338	.7735	.8195	1.5777	1.2929	1.2203	40′
30′	.6361	.7716	.8243	1.5721	1.2960	1.2131	30′
40′	.6383	.7698	.8292	1.5666	1.2991	1.2059	20′
50′	.6406	.7679	.8342	1.5611	1.3022	1.1988	10′
40° 0′	.6428	.7660	.8391	1.5557	1.3054	1.1918	50° 0′
10′	.6450	.7642	.8441	1.5504	1.3086	1.1847	49° 50′
20′	.6472	.7623	.8491	1.5450	1.3118	1.1778	40′
30′	.6494	.7604	.8541	1.5398	1.3151	1.1708	30′
40′	.6517	.7585	.8591	1.5345	1.3184	1.1640	20′
50′	.6539	.7566	.8642	1.5294	1.3217	1.1571	10′
41° 0′	.6561	.7547	.8693	1.5283	1.3250	1.1504	49° 0′
10′	.6583	.7528	.8744	1.5192	1.3284	1.1436	48° 50′
20′	.6604	.7509	.8796	1.5141	1.3318	1.1369	40′
30′	.6626	.7490	.8847	1.5092	1.3352	1.1303	30′
40′	.6648	.7470	.8899	1.5042	1.3386	1.1237	20′
50′	.6670	.7451	.8952	1.4993	1.3421	1.1171	10′
42° 0′	.6691	.7431	.9004	1.4945	1.3456	1.1106	48° 0′
10′	.6713	.7412	.9057	1.4897	1.3492	1.1041	47° 50′
20′	.6734	.7392	.9110	1.4849	1.3527	1.0977	40′
30′	.6756	.7373	.9163	1.4802	1.3563	1.0913	30′
40′	.6777	.7353	.9217	1.4755	1.3600	1.0850	20′
50′	.6799	.7333	.9271	1.4709	1.3636	1.0786	10′
43° 0′	.6820	.7314	.9325	1.4663	1.3673	1.0724	47° 0′
10′	.6841	.7294	.9380	1.4617	1.3711	1.0661	46° 50′
20′	.6862	.7274	.9435	1.4572	1.3748	1.0599	40′
30′	.6884	.7254	.9490	1.4527	1.3786	1.0538	30′
40′	.6905	.7234	.9545	1.4483	1.3824	1.0477	20′
50′	.6926	.7214	.9601	1.4439	1.3863	1.0416	10′
44° 0′	.6947	.7193	.9657	1.4396	1.3902	1.0355	46° 0′
10′	.6967	.7173	.9713	1.4352	1.3941	1.0295	45° 50′
20′	.6988	.7153	.9770	1.4310	1.3980	1.0235	40′
30′	.7009	.7133	.9827	1.4267	1.4020	1.0176	30′
40′	.7030	.7112	.9884	1.4225	1.4061	1.0117	20′
50′	.7050	.7092	.9942	1.4183	1.4101	1.0058	45° 10′
45° 0′	.7071	.7071	1.0000	1.4142	1.4142	1.0000	45° 0′
Angle	Cos	Sin	Cot	Sec	Csc	Tan	Angle

The table of Logarithms of Trigonometric Functions gives the logs of the functions for angles from 0°–90° at 10 minute intervals. The name of the function appears at the top and bottom of each column and the angles appear in the first and last columns. The angles from 0°–45° appear (from *top* to *bottom*) in the first column. The angles from 45°–90° appear in the last column (from *bottom* to *top*). To locate a log of a trigonometric function between 0° and 45° use the headings at the *top* of the columns. To locate the log of a function between 45° and 90° use the headings at the *bottom* of the columns. E.g., to locate log cos 21° 10′, read *down* the first column to 21°10′, and to the right to the column

headed, *at the top* "Log Cos." The number .96966 appears. The characteristic is found by using the integral part of the logarithm of 21°0′, 9, and subtracting 10. Thus, log cos 21°10′ is 9.96966–10. To find log sin 68°50′ read *up* the last column to 68°50′ and to the left to the column headed, *at the bottom*, "Log sin." The number .96966 appears. The characteristic is found by using the integral part of log sin 68°0′ and subtracting 10. Thus, log sin 68°50′ is 9.96966–10. Note that for complementary angles the log of a function of one angle equals the log of the cofunction of the complement of the angle.

0°–7° 50′   Subtract 10 from the logarithm shown   90°–82° 10′

Angle	Log sin	Log cos	Log tan	Log csc	Log sec	Log cot	Angle
0° 0′	——	——	——	——	——	——	90° 0′
10′	7.46373	10.00000	7.46363	12.53627	10.00000	12.53627	89° 50′
20′	.76475	9.99999	.76476	.23525	.00001	.23524	40′
30′	.94084	.99998	.94086	.05916	.00002	.05914	30′
40′	8.06578	.99997	8.06581	11.93420	.00003	11.93419	20′
50′	.16268	.99995	.16273	.83732	.00005	.83727	10′
1° 0′	8.24186	9.99993	8.24192	11.75814	10.00007	11.75808	89° 0′
10′	.30879	.99991	.30888	.69121	.00009	.69112	88° 50′
20′	.36678	.99988	.36689	.63322	.00012	.63311	40′
30′	.41792	.99985	.41807	.58208	.00015	.58193	30′
40′	.46366	.99982	.46385	.53634	.00018	.53615	20′
50′	.50504	.99978	.50527	.49496	.00022	.49473	10′
2° 0′	8.54282	9.99974	8.54308	11.45718	10.00026	11.45692	88° 0′
10′	.57757	.99969	.57788	.42243	.00031	.42212	87° 50′
20′	.60973	.99964	.61009	.39027	.00036	.38991	40′
30′	.63968	.99959	.64009	.36032	.00041	.35991	30′
40′	.66769	.99953	.66816	.33231	.00047	.33184	20′
50′	.69400	.99947	.69453	.30600	.00053	.30547	10′
3° 0′	8.71880	9.99940	8.71940	11.28120	10.00060	11.28060	87° 0′
10′	.74226	.99934	.74292	.25774	.00066	.25708	86° 50′
20′	.76451	.99926	.76525	.23549	.00074	.23475	40′
30′	.78568	.99919	.78649	.21432	.00081	.21351	30′
40′	.80585	.99911	.80674	.19415	.00089	.19326	20′
50′	.82513	.99903	.82610	.17487	.00097	.17390	10′
4° 0′	8.84358	9.99894	8.84464	11.15642	10.00106	11.15536	86° 0′
10′	.86128	.99885	.86243	.13872	.00115	.13757	85° 50′
20′	.87829	.99876	.87953	.12171	.00124	.12047	40′
30′	.89464	.99866	.89598	.10536	.00134	.10402	30′
40′	.91040	.99856	.91185	.08960	.00144	.08815	20′
50′	.92561	.99845	.92716	.07439	.00155	.07284	10′
5° 0′	8.94030	9.99834	8.94195	11.05970	10.00166	11.05805	85° 0′
10′	.95450	.99823	.95027	.04550	.00177	.04373	84° 50′
20′	.96825	.99812	.97013	.03175	.00188	.02987	40′
30′	.98157	.99800	.98358	.01843	.00200	.01642	30′
40′	.99450	.99787	.99662	.00550	.00213	.00338	20′
50′	9.00704	.99775	9.00930	10.99296	.00225	10.99070	10′
6° 0′	.901923	9.99761	9.02162	10.98037	10.00239	10.97838	84° 0′
10′	.03109	.99748	.03361	.96891	.00252	.96639	83° 50′
20′	.04262	.99734	.04528	.95738	.00266	.95472	40′
30′	.05386	.99720	.05666	.94614	.00280	.94334	30′
40′	.06481	.99705	.06775	.93519	.00295	.93225	20′
50′	.07548	.99690	.07858	.92452	.00310	.92142	10′
7° 0′	9.08589	9.99675	9.08914	10.91411	10.00325	10.91086	83° 0′
10′	.09606	.99659	.09947	.90394	.00341	.90053	82° 50′
20′	.10599	.99643	.10956	.89401	.00357	.89044	40′
30′	.11570	.99627	.11943	.88430	.00373	.88057	30′
40′	.12519	.99610	.12909	.87481	.00390	.87091	20′
50′	.13447	.99593	.13854	.86553	.00407	.86146	82° 10′
Angle	Log cos	Log sin	Log cot	Log sec	Log csc	Log tan	Angle

8°–17° 50' Subtract 10 from the logarithm shown 82°–72° 10'

Angle	Log sin	Log cos	Log tan	Log csc	Log sec	Log cot	Angle
8° 0'	9.14356	9.99575	9.14780	10.85644	10.00425	10.85220	82° 0'
10'	.15245	.99557	.15688	.84755	.00443	.84312	81° 50'
20'	.16116	.99539	.16577	.83884	.00461	.83423	40'
30'	.16970	.99520	.17450	.83030	.00480	.82550	30'
40'	.17807	.99501	.18306	.82193	.00499	.81694	20'
50'	.18628	.99482	.19146	.81372	.00518	.80854	10'
9° 0'	9.19433	9.99462	9.19971	10.80567	10.00538	10.80029	81° 0'
10'	.20223	.99442	.20782	.79777	.00558	.79218	80° 50'
20'	.20999	.99421	.21578	.79001	.00579	.78422	40'
30'	.21761	.99400	.22361	.78239	.00600	.77639	30'
40'	.22509	.99379	.23130	.77491	.00621	.76870	20'
50'	.23244	.99357	.23887	.76756	.00643	.76113	10'
10° 0'	9.23967	9.99335	9.24632	10.76033	10.00665	10.75368	80° 0'
10'	.24677	.99313	.25365	.75323	.00687	.74635	79° 50'
20'	.25376	.99290	.26086	.74624	.00710	.73914	40'
30'	.26063	.99267	.26797	.73937	.00733	.73203	30'
40'	.26739	.99243	.27496	.73261	.00757	.72504	20'
50'	.27405	.99219	.28186	.72595	.00781	.71814	10'
11° 0'	9.28060	9.99197	9.28865	10.71940	10.00803	10.71135	79° 0'
10'	.28705	.99176	.29535	.71295	.00830	.70465	78° 50'
20'	.29340	.99145	.30195	.70660	.00855	.69805	40'
30'	.29966	.99119	.30846	.70034	.00881	.69154	30'
40'	.30582	.99093	.31489	.69498	.00907	.68511	20'
50'	.31189	.99067	.32122	.68811	.00937	.67878	10'
12° 0'	9.31788	9.99040	9.32747	10.68212	10.00960	10.67253	78° 0'
10'	.32378	.99013	.33365	.67622	.00987	.66635	77° 50'
20'	.32960	.98986	.33974	.67040	.01014	.66026	40'
30'	.33534	.98958	.34576	.66466	.01042	.65424	30'
40'	.34100	.98930	.35170	.65900	.01070	.64830	20'
50'	.34658	.98901	.35757	.65342	.01099	.64243	10'
13° 0'	9.35209	9.98872	9.36336	10.64791	10.01129	10.63664	77° 0'
10'	.35752	.98843	.36909	.64248	.01157	.63091	76° 50'
20'	.36289	.98813	.37476	.63711	.01187	.62524	40'
30'	.36819	.98783	.38035	.63181	.01217	.61965	30'
40'	.37341	.98753	.38589	.62659	.01247	.61411	20'
50'	.37858	.98722	.39136	.62142	.01278	.60864	10'
14° 0'	9.38368	9.98690	9.39677	10.61632	10.01310	10.60323	76° 0'
10'	.38871	.98659	.40212	.61129	.01341	.59788	75° 50'
20'	.39369	.98627	.40742	.60431	.01373	.59258	40'
30'	.39860	.98594	.41266	.60140	.01406	.58734	30'
40'	.40346	.98561	.41784	.59654	.01439	.58216	20'
50'	.40825	.98528	.42297	.59175	.01472	.57703	10'
15° 0'	9.41300	9.98494	9.42805	10.58700	10.01506	10.57195	75° 0'
10'	.41768	.98460	.43308	.58232	.01540	.56692	74° 50'
20'	.42232	.98426	.43806	.57768	.01574	.56194	40'
30'	.42690	.98391	.44299	.57310	.01609	.55701	30'
40'	.43143	.98356	.44787	.56857	.01644	.55213	20'
50'	.43591	.98320	.45271	.56409	.01680	.54729	10'
16° 0'	9.44034	9.98284	9.45750	10.55966	10.01716	10.54250	74° 0'
10'	.44472	.98248	.46224	.55528	.01752	.53776	73° 50'
20'	.44905	.98211	.46694	.55095	.01789	.53306	40'
30'	.45334	.98174	.47160	.54666	.01826	.52840	30'
40'	.45758	.98136	.47622	.54242	.01864	.52378	20'
50'	.46178	.98098	.48080	.53822	.01902	.51920	10'
17° 0'	9.46594	9.98060	9.48534	10.53406	10.01940	10.51466	73° 0'
10'	.47005	.98021	.48984	.52995	.01979	.51016	72° 50'
20'	.47411	.97982	.49430	.52589	.02018	.50570	40'
30'	.47814	.97942	.49872	.52186	.02058	.50128	30'
40'	.48213	.97902	.50311	.51787	.02098	.49689	20'
50'	.48607	.97861	.50746	.51393	.02139	.49254	72° 10'

Angle	Log cos	Log sin	Log cot	Log sec	Log csc	Log tan	Angle

Subtract 10 from the logarithm shown

ANGLE	LOG SIN	LOG COS	LOG TAN	LOG CSC	LOG SEC	LOG COT	ANGLE
18° 0′	9.48998	9.97821	9.51178	10.51002	10.02179	10.48822	72° 0′
10′	.49385	.97779	.51606	.50615	.02221	.48394	71° 50′
20′	.49768	.97738	.52031	.50232	.02262	.47969	40′
30′	.50148	.97696	.52452	.49852	.02304	.47548	30′
40′	.50523	.97653	.52870	.49477	.02347	.47130	20′
50′	.50896	.97610	.53285	.49104	.02390	.46715	10′
19° 0′	9.51264	9.97567	9.53697	10.48736	10.02433	10.46303	71° 0′
10′	.51629	.97523	.54106	.48371	.02477	.45894	70° 50′
20′	.51991	.97479	.54512	.48009	.02521	.45488	40′
30′	.52350	.97435	.54915	.47640	.02565	.45085	30′
40′	.52705	.97390	.55315	.47295	.02610	.44685	20′
50′	.53056	.97344	.55712	.46944	.02656	.44288	10′
20° 0′	9.53405	9.97299	9.56107	10.46595	10.02701	10.43893	70° 0′
10′	.53751	.97252	.56498	.46249	.02748	.43502	69° 50′
20′	.54093	.97206	.56887	.45907	.02794	.43113	40′
30′	.54433	.97159	.57274	.45567	.02841	.42726	30′
40′	.54769	.97111	.57658	.45231	.02889	.42342	20′
50′	.55102	.97063	.58039	.44898	.02937	.41961	10′
21° 0′	9.55433	9.97015	9.58418	10.44567	10.02985	10.41582	69° 0′
10′	.55761	.96966	.58794	.44239	.03034	.41206	68° 50′
20′	.56085	.96917	.59168	.43915	.03083	.40832	40′
30′	.56408	.96868	.59540	.43592	.03132	.40460	30′
40′	.56727	.96818	.59909	.43273	.03182	.40091	20′
50′	.57044	.96767	.60276	.42956	.03233	.39724	10′
22° 0′	9.57358	9.96717	9.60641	10.42642	10.03283	10.39359	68° 0′
10′	.57669	.96665	.61004	.42331	.03335	.38996	67° 50′
20′	.57978	.96614	.61364	.42022	.03386	.38636	40′
30′	.58284	.96562	.61722	.41716	.03438	.38278	30′
40′	.58588	.96509	.62079	.41412	.03491	.37921	20′
50′	.58889	.96456	.62433	.41111	.03544	.37567	10′
23° 0′	9.59188	9.96403	9.62785	10.40812	10.03697	10.37215	67° 0′
10′	.59484	.96349	.63135	.40516	.03651	.36865	66° 50′
20′	.59778	.96294	.63484	.40222	.03706	.36516	40′
30′	.60070	.96240	.63830	.39930	.03760	.36170	30′
40′	.60359	.96185	.64175	.39641	.03815	.35825	20′
50′	.60646	.96129	.64517	.39354	.03871	.35483	10′
24° 0′	9.60931	9.96073	9.64858	10.39069	10.03927	10.35142	66° 0′
10′	.61214	.96017	.65197	.38726	.03983	.34803	65° 50′
20′	.61494	.95960	.65535	.38506	.04040	.34465	40′
30′	.61773	.95902	.65870	.38227	.04098	.34130	30′
40′	.62049	.95844	.66204	.37951	.04156	.33796	20′
50′	.62323	.95786	.66537	.37677	.04214	.33463	10′
25° 0′	9.62595	9.95728	9.66867	10.37405	10.04272	10.33133	65° 0′
10′	.62865	.95668	.67196	.37135	.04332	.32804	64° 50′
20′	.63133	.95609	.67524	.36867	.04391	.32476	40′
30′	.63398	.95549	.67850	.36602	.04451	.32150	30′
40′	.63662	.95488	.68174	.36338	.04512	.31826	20′
50′	.63924	.95427	.68497	.36076	.04573	.31503	10′
26° 0′	9.64184	9.95366	9.68818	10.35816	10.04634	10.31182	64° 0′
10′	.64442	.95304	.69138	.35558	.04696	.30862	63° 50′
20′	.64698	.95242	.69457	.35302	.04758	.30543	40′
30′	.64953	.95179	.69774	.35047	.04821	.30226	30′
40′	.65205	.95116	.70089	.34795	.04884	.29911	20′
50′	.65456	.95052	.70404	.34544	.04948	.29596	10′
27° 0′	9.65705	9.94988	9.70717	10.34395	10.05012	10.29283	63° 0′
10′	.65952	.94923	.71028	.34048	.05077	.28972	62° 50′
20′	.66197	.94858	.71339	.33803	.05142	.28661	40′
30′	.66441	.94793	.71648	.33559	.05207	.28352	30′
40′	.66682	.94727	.71955	.33318	.05273	.28045	20′
50′	.66922	.94660	.72262	.33078	.05340	.27738	62° 10′
ANGLE	LOG COS	LOG SIN	LOG COT	LOG SEC	LOG CSC	LOG TAN	ANGLE

Angle	Log sin	Log cos	Log tan	Log csc	Log sec	Log cot	Angle
28° 0′	9.67161	9.94593	9.72567	10.32839	10.05407	10.27433	62° 0′
10′	.67398	.94526	.72872	.32602	.05474	.27128	61° 50′
20′	.67633	.94458	.73175	.32367	.05542	.26825	40′
30′	.67866	.94390	.73476	.32134	.05610	.26524	30′
40′	.68098	.94321	.73777	.31902	.05679	.26223	20′
50′	.68328	.94252	.74077	.31672	.05748	.25923	10′
29° 0′	9.68557	9.94182	9.74375	10.31443	10.05818	10.25625	61° 0′
10′	.68784	.94112	.74673	.31216	.05888	.25327	60° 50′
20′	.69010	.94041	.74969	.30990	.05959	.25031	40′
30′	.69234	.93970	.75264	.30766	.06030	.24736	30′
40′	.69456	.93898	.75558	.30564	.06102	.24442	20′
50′	.69677	.93826	.75852	.30323	.06174	.24148	10′
30° 0′	9.69897	9.93753	9.76144	10.30103	10.06247	10.23856	60° 0′
10′	.70115	.93680	.76435	.29885	.06320	.23565	59° 50′
20′	.70332	.93606	.76725	.29668	.06394	.23275	40′
30′	.70547	.93532	.77015	.29453	.06468	.22985	30′
40′	.70761	.93457	.77303	.29239	.06543	.22697	20′
50′	.70973	.93382	.77591	.29027	.06618	.22409	10′
31° 0′	9.71184	9.93307	9.77877	10.28816	10.06693	10.22123	59° 0′
10′	.71393	.93230	.78163	.28607	.06770	.21837	58° 50′
20′	.71602	.93154	.78448	.28398	.06846	.21552	40′
30′	.71809	.93077	.78732	.28191	.06923	.21268	30′
40′	.72014	.92999	.79015	.27986	.07001	.20985	20′
50′	.72218	.92921	.79797	.27782	.07079	.20703	10′
32° 0′	9.72421	9.92842	9.79579	10.27579	10.07158	10.20421	58° 0′
10′	.72622	.92763	.79860	.27378	.07237	.20140	57° 50′
20′	.72823	.92683	.80140	.27177	.07317	.19860	40′
30′	.73022	.92603	.80419	.26978	.07397	.19581	30′
40′	.73219	.92522	.80697	.26781	.07478	.19303	20′
50′	.73416	.92441	.80975	.26584	.07559	.19025	10′
33° 0′	9.73611	9.92359	9.81252	10.26389	10.07641	10.18748	57° 0′
10′	.73805	.92277	.81528	.26195	.07723	.18472	56° 50′
20′	.73997	.92194	.81803	.26003	.07806	.18197	40′
30′	.74189	.92111	.82078	.25811	.07889	.17922	30′
40′	.74379	.92027	.82352	.25621	.07973	.17648	20′
50′	.74568	.91942	.82626	.25432	.08058	.17374	10′
34° 0′	9.74756	9.91857	9.82899	10.25244	10.08143	10.17101	56° 0′
10′	.74943	.91772	.83171	.25057	.08228	.16829	55° 50′
20′	.75128	.91686	.83442	.24872	.08314	.16558	40′
30′	.75313	.91599	.83713	.24687	.08401	.16287	30′
40′	9.75496	9.91512	9.83984	10.24504	10.08488	10.16016	20′
50′	.75678	.91425	.84254	.24322	.08575	.15746	10′
35° 0′	9.75859	9.91336	9.84523	10.24141	10.08664	10.15477	55° 0′
10′	.76039	.91248	.84791	.23961	.08752	.15209	54° 50′
40′	.76218	.91158	.85059	.23782	.08842	.14941	40′
30′	.76395	.91069	.85327	.23605	.08931	.14673	30′
40′	.76572	.90978	.85594	.23428	.09022	.14406	20′
50′	.76747	.90889	.85860	.23253	.09111	.14140	10′
36° 0′	9.76922	9.90796	9.86126	10.23078	10.09204	10.13874	54° 0′
10′	.77095	.90704	.86392	.22905	.09296	.13608	53° 50′
20′	.77268	.90611	.86656	.22732	.09389	.13344	40′
30′	.77439	.90518	.86921	.22561	.09482	.13079	30′
40′	.77609	.90424	.87185	.22391	.09576	.12815	20′
50′	.77778	.90330	.87448	.22222	.09670	.12552	10′
37° 0′	9.77946	9.90235	9.87711	10.22054	10.09765	10.12289	53° 0′
10′	.78113	.90139	.87974	.21887	.09861	.12026	52° 50′
20′	.78280	.90043	.88236	.21720	.09957	.11764	40′
30′	.78445	.89947	.88498	.21555	.10053	.11502	30′
40′	.78609	.89849	.88759	.21391	.10151	.11241	20′
50′	.78772	.89752	.89020	.21228	.10248	.10980	52° 10′
Angle	Log cos	Log sin	Log cot	Log sec	Log csc	Log tan	Angle

38°–45° Subtract 10 from the logarithm shown 52°–45°

Angle	Log sin	Log cos	Log tan	Log csc	Log sec	Log cot	Angle
38° 0'	9.78934	9.89653	9.89281	10.21066	10.10347	10.10719	52° 0'
10'	.79095	.89554	.89541	.20905	.10446	.10459	51° 50'
20'	.79256	.89455	.89801	.20744	.10545	.10199	40'
30'	.79415	.89354	.90061	.20585	.10646	.09939	30'
40'	.79573	.89254	.90320	.20427	.10746	.09680	20'
50'	.79731	.89152	.90578	.20279	.10848	.09422	10'
39° 0'	9.79887	9.89050	9.90837	10.20113	10.10950	10.09163	51° 0'
10'	.80043	.88948	.91095	.19957	.11052	.08905	50° 50'
20'	.80197	.88844	.91353	.19803	.11156	.08647	40'
30'	.80351	.88741	.91610	.19649	.11259	.08390	30'
40'	.80504	.88636	.91868	.19496	.11364	.08132	20'
50'	.80656	.88531	.92125	.19344	.11469	.07875	10'
40° 0'	9.80807	9.88425	9.92381	10.19193	10.11575	10.07619	50° 0'
10'	.80957	.88319	.92638	.19043	.11681	.07362	49° 50'
20'	.81106	.88212	.92894	.18894	.11788	.07106	40'
30'	.81254	.88105	.93150	.18746	.11895	.06850	30'
40'	.81402	.87996	.93406	.18598	.12004	.06594	20'
50'	.81549	.87887	.93661	.18451	.12113	.06339	10'
41° 0'	9.81694	9.87778	9.93916	10.18306	10.12222	10.06084	49° 0'
10'	.81839	.87668	.94171	.18161	.12332	.05829	48° 50'
20'	.81983	.87557	.94426	.18017	.12443	.05574	40'
30'	.82126	.87446	.94681	.17874	.12554	.05319	30'
40'	.82269	.87334	.94935	.17731	.12666	.05065	20'
50'	.82410	.87221	.95190	.17590	.12779	.04810	10'
42° 0'	9.82551	9.87107	9.95444	10.17449	10.12893	10.04556	48° 0'
10'	8.2691	.86993	.95698	.17309	.13007	.04302	47° 50'
20'	.82830	.86879	.95952	.17170	.13121	.04048	40'
30'	.82968	.86763	.96205	.17032	.13231	.03795	30'
40'	.83106	.86647	.96459	.16894	.13353	.03541	20'
50'	.83242	.86530	.96712	.16758	.13470	.03288	10'
43° 0'	9.83378	9.86413	9.96960	10.16622	10.13587	10.03034	47° 0'
10'	.83513	.86295	.97219	.16487	.13705	.02781	46° 50'
20'	.83648	.86176	.97472	.16352	.13824	.02528	40'
30'	.83781	.86056	.97725	.16219	.13944	.02275	30'
40'	.83914	.85936	.97978	.16086	.14064	.02022	20'
50'	.84046	.85815	.98231	.15954	.14185	.01769	10'
44° 0'	9.84177	9.85693	9.98484	10.15823	10.14307	10.01516	46° 0'
10'	.84318	.85571	.98737	.15692	.14429	.01263	45° 50'
20'	.84437	.85448	.98989	.15563	.14552	.01011	40'
30'	.84566	.85324	.99242	.15434	.14676	.00758	30'
40'	.84694	.85200	.99495	.15306	.14800	.00505	20'
50'	.84822	.85074	.99747	.15178	.14926	.00253	10'
45° 0'	9.84949	9.84949	10.00000	10.15051	10.15051	10.00000	45° 0'
Angle	Log cos	Log sin	Log cot	Log sec	Log csc	Log tan	Angle